DATE DUE

DEMCO, INC. 38-2971

American Pop

American Pop

c. 1

Popular Culture Decade by Decade

VOLUME 3
1960–1989

Edited by Bob Batchelor

GREENWOOD PRESS
Westport, Connecticut • London

Library of Congress Cataloging-in-Publication Data

American pop : popular culture decade by decade / Bob Batchelor, set editor.
p. cm.
Includes bibliographical references and index.
ISBN 978-0-313-34410-7 (set : alk. paper)—ISBN 978-0-313-36412-9 (v. 1 : alk. paper)—
ISBN 978-0-313-36414-3 (v. 2 : alk. paper)—ISBN 978-0-313-36416-7 (v. 3 : alk. paper)—
ISBN 978-0-313-36418-1 (v. 4 : alk. paper)   1. Popular culture—United States.
2. United States—Civilization.   3. National characteristics, American.   I. Batchelor, Bob.
E169.1.A4475   2009
973—dc22   2008036699

British Library Cataloguing in Publication Data is available.

Copyright © 2009 by Greenwood Publishing Group, Inc.

Library of Congress Catalog Card Number: 2008036699
ISBN: 978-0-313-34410-7 (set)
        978-0-313-36412-9 (vol 1)
        978-0-313-36414-3 (vol 2)
        978-0-313-36416-7 (vol 3)
        978-0-313-36418-1 (vol 4)

First published in 2009

Greenwood Press, 88 Post Road West, Westport, CT 06881
An imprint of Greenwood Publishing Group, Inc.
www.greenwood.com

Printed in the United States of America

The paper used in this book complies with the
Permanent Paper Standard issued by the National
Information Standards Organization (Z39.48–1984).

10 9 8 7 6 5 4 3 2 1

The publisher has done its best to make sure the instructions and/or recipes in this book are correct.
However, users should apply judgment and experience when preparing recipes, especially parents
and teachers working with young people. The publisher accepts no responsibility for the outcome
of any recipe included in this volume.

Contents

VOLUME THREE, 1960–1989

Foreword: Popular Culture's Roots Run Deep *by Ray B. Browne*	vii
Preface	xiii
Introduction	xvii

1960s

Timeline of Popular Culture Events, 1960s	2
Overview of the 1960s	6
Advertising of the 1960s	18
Architecture of the 1960s	25
Books, Newspapers, Magazines, and Comics of the 1960s	35
Entertainment of the 1960s	48
Fashion of the 1960s	66
Food of the 1960s	75
Music of the 1960s	83
Sports and Leisure of the 1960s	96
Travel of the 1960s	108
Visual Arts of the 1960s	117
Endnotes for the 1960s	123

1970s

Timeline of Popular Culture Events, 1970s   126

Overview of the 1970s   130

Advertising of the 1970s   150

Architecture of the 1970s   156

Books, Newspapers, Magazines, and Comics of the 1970s   163

Entertainment of the 1970s   174

Fashion of the 1970s   188

Food of the 1970s   194

Music of the 1970s   199

Sports and Leisure of the 1970s   208

Travel of the 1970s   217

Visual Arts of the 1970s   225

Endnotes for the 1970s   229

1980s

Timeline of Popular Culture Events, 1980s   232

Overview of the 1980s   237

Advertising of the 1980s   251

Architecture of the 1980s   257

Books, Newspapers, Magazines, and Comics of the 1980s   263

Entertainment of the 1980s   273

Fashion of the 1980s   288

Food of the 1980s   296

Music of the 1980s   302

Sports and Leisure of the 1980s   314

Travel of the 1980s   321

Visual Arts of the 1980s   326

Endnotes for the 1980s   331

Resource Guide   333

Index   341

Foreword: Popular Culture's Roots Run Deep

Ray B. Browne

Ray and Pat Browne Popular Culture Library
Bowling Green State University, Bowling Green, Ohio

Although *American Pop* focuses on popular culture as it developed in the twentieth century, it is critical that readers understand that most of these topics did not spring to life without roots running deep into the nation's past. In today's fast-paced, computer-dominated society, it is easy to forget history and innovation because so much of American idealism is based on looking toward the bright future. We are a nation obsessed with the idea that better days are on the horizon.

What one discovers when examining the development of culture over the course of the twentieth century is that each innovation builds off a predecessor. America has always had a popular culture, although what that means might change with each new technological breakthrough, national craze, or demographic shift. And, while defining culture is not an easy task, it can be seen as a kind of living entity. Similar to a growing garden, culture is the gatherings of community beliefs and behaviors, which depends on its roots for sustenance. As the plants grow both individually and collectively, they develop and influence the surrounding societies.

People in Colonial America, for example, had their cultural roots deeply implanted from the cultures of the lands from which they emigrated, but every people or group of individuals must harmonize the old with the new in order to justify one's culture. The unifying themes that emerged from the development of a new national culture enabled people to make sense of the world and their relationship to it. American colonists, therefore, adjusted to the old-world cultures of the people who were already settling the nation, while at the same time creating a new popular culture based on their lives as members of the new country.

The harmonization of the new with the old might be called *folk-pop* or *pop-folk* because the result led to a new everyday culture. This evolution is a neverending process in which the new is blended with the old and a new is born. Human nature demands cultural and individual cooperation for safety and advancement, which it achieves in various ways. Inventions and discoveries, for example, are not as helpful in shaping cultures as are innovation and dissemination of those inventions and discoveries. Culture must speak to its constituencies in their vernacular before it can be understood and fully appreciated. Cultures both lead and follow cultural politics, policies, and social movements.

The fields of entertainment from which the colonists could draw were rich: traveling acrobats, jugglers, circuses of various kinds, animal shows, "magic lantern" shows, group or individual singers, Black "Olios" (one-act specialities), drinking houses, card games, and other group activities.

In the conventional forms of culture development certain figures stand tall. Benjamin Franklin, after his move to Philadelphia, contributed in various ways through his writings in *Poor Richard's Almanac* (1732–1757) and others. He stated that his highest admiration was for "the people of this province…chiefly industrious farmers, artificers [skilled craftsmen] or men in trade [who] are fond of freedom." Inventor of the lightning rod and the Franklin Stove, and many more technological and cultural innovations, no one did more to advance popular culture in these early days than Franklin. In the twenty-first century, one finds similar figures who are much revered for their ability to create. Steve Jobs, Apple founder and executive, is a modern day Franklin in many respects, inventing products that transform popular culture, while at the same time, cementing his place in that history.

Less comprehensive but far more inflammatory were the political contributions of Thomas Paine (1737–1809). On January 10, 1776, he published *Common Sense* and sold it for a few cents so that everybody could own a copy. In a few months no fewer than 500,000 copies had been sold. Another of his great contributions was *The American Crisis,* which opens with the fiery words, "These are the times that try men's souls." Paine intuited and valued the power of the popular culture and wrote his works as if by a common citizen for other common citizens. Today's Thomas Paines may be the countless citizen journalists, primarily Internet-based, blogging, posting, and carrying out the kind of agenda Paine advocated. The writer turned to pamphlets as a method of keeping down price, just as today's bloggers use inexpensive tools to reach audiences nationwide.

Another powerful voice in popular culture was Harriet Beecher Stowe. Through *Uncle Tom's Cabin* (1852) Stowe alerted the public to the evils of slavery (with the help of the Almighty, in her words). After the enormous success of the work, the author claimed that God had dictated the book, with her merely writing down His words. Regardless of these claims, for the next 50 years the work was performed on stages worldwide more frequently than any other play in English (with the possible exception of Shakespeare's collected works).

A little more than a century later, racism still plagued the nation, but instead of being represented by a novel, two charismatic leaders took center stage. Dr. Martin Luther King Jr. and Malcolm X stood at opposite poles in the fight for equality, King preaching nonviolence, while Malcolm advocated "by any means necessary." As powerful as these leaders were, however, they became icons after their assassinations. As a result, their images transcend who they were as leaders, attaining a kind of immortality as popular culture figures.

Colonists loved professional plays. The first such presentation in America was "Ye Beare and Ye Cubbin Accomac County" staged in Virginia in 1665. The first theater in the Colonies was built in Williamsburg, Virginia, sometime between 1716 and 1718.

Romeo and Juliet may have been presented in New York City in 1730 and *Richard III* in 1750, in addition to Williamsburg a year later. In 1752 the Charleston, South Carolina, theater presented 58 different offerings, including Shakespeare. Fourteen of Shakespeare's plays were staged 150 times in pre-Revolutionary Virginia, and from the 1850s to the Civil War Shakespeare was performed in all the major cities and several small ones.

For the second half of the nineteenth century one of the distributors of popular culture was widespread black-faced minstrelsy—thousands of such dramatics were presented on stage by whites with faces blackened by charcoal. No one can identify exactly when and why the first Negro minstrel show became so popular. Some authorities suggest that African Americans seem to be natural-born entertainers. Others are firm in their belief that the minstrel show flourished because blacks saw it as a means of social equality with whites who otherwise held them in slavery.

Minstrelsy was in its heyday from 1830 to 1870. So-called songsters, cheap songbooks running from 20 to some 50 pages and selling for 10–50 cents, were the main distributors of minstrel pieces, as well as songs from other sources. During the popularity of the minstrel show there were more than 100 shows running and some 2,000 songsters distributing at least 20,000 songs. Not all minstrel shows were black-on-white. Some were black-on-black, after black actors realized that white shows were exploiting them and they could in fact create their own shows. Minstrel shows were later eclipsed by vaudeville.

From these beginnings, one can trace the origins of Tin Pan Alley, which helped launch ragtime and jazz. In addition, the songsters and minstrel shows initiated a kind of crossover success that became the gold standard in the music business. "Crossing over," or scoring hit records in different genres, would come to define many of the industry's biggest stars from Elvis Presley and Johnny Cash to Chuck Berry and Little Richard.

The most enduring form of popular culture is the printed page, even though some observers feel that books, magazines, and newspapers are doomed in the Internet age. Books in particular, though, carry a special place in peoples' hearts, not only as tools for learning but as objects of affection. Many readers simply like to hold a book in their hands and feel the pages glide through their fingers. Even the most ardent techie does not get the same emotional lift from reading text on a screen, whether a laptop or handheld device.

The most influential literary form breaching the gap between the nineteenth and twentieth centuries has been the detective story. This form of literature has from its beginning satisfied deep interests of large groups. From the earliest times, people have wanted answers to the mysteries of life that keeps us continually looking back at history. Our fascination with the archaeological and anthropological past, for example, leads many to believe in monsters such as Big-Foot (Sasquatch) and the Loch Ness Monster. Many small towns and local villages have similar folktales of creatures frequenting dark mountains, forests, and deep lakes. Today, this love affair with fear and the unknown drives much of the current film and television industries. From the low budget sensation *The Blair Witch Project* to big budget movies filled with blood and gore, people thrive on their imaginations resulting from a collective indoctrination to fear.

These prehistoric beings supposedly living among us also help keep alive the mysteries and manifestations of the past, delivering some kind of answer in the form of explanations and comforting conclusions. Histories and mysteries need what scholar Russel Nye called a "hook" to keep readers on the edge of their curiosity. But mysteries search more deeply into human existence and help explain us to ourselves. Einstein was certainly right when he said, "The most beautiful thing we can experience is the mysterious. It is the source of all true art and science." The enticement of the mysterious is a never fading light in the darkness of life's many anxieties.

Literary interest in horror developed in Europe in Mary Shelley's *Frankenstein* (1818) and pushed ahead vigorously in the *Memoirs* of Francois Eugene Vidocq, a reformed French thief who joined the police force and electrified Europe with publication of his underground activities in 1829. Edgar Allan Poe (1809–1849) caught the imagination of Americans beginning with *Murders in the Rue Morgue* (1841). Film scholars see Poe's writing inspiring the American film noir movement in the 1940s, 1950s, and 1960s.

The coals ignited by the interest in mystery and drama glowed especially in the publication of the adventures of Sherlock Holmes and Dr. Watson in 1887. Many Americans tried their pens at the art. Mark Twain published several works in the type, for instance, but found little success. But the door into the riches of mysteries had been opened to authors and readers of the twenty-first century. Mystery, having metamorphosed through the broadened titles of "Crime Fiction" and lately "Novels of Suspense," is the most popular form of fiction today, and is being used by historians for the true human emotions and actions contained in them. Historians a century or more from now may find themselves doing the same with the novels of Stephen King or James Patterson, novelists who sell millions of books, yet are taken less seriously by the cultural elite because they do so well.

One of the results of popular culture's interest in the make-believe and distortion of the minstrel show was the literary hoax, which flourished in such works as Poe's "Balloon Hoax," published in the *New York Sun* on April 13, 1844, an account of eight men crossing the Atlantic in a large balloon held up by coal gas. Others include Mark Twain's "The Petrified Man" (one of several by him), in which a character is discovered with his thumb on his nose in the timeless insulting gesture—the credulous public does not recognize the joke.

Other real-life hoaxes cropped up on every street corner. P. T. Barnum (1810–1891), famous for working under the philosophy that there's a sucker born every minute, opened his American Museum of Freaks in New York City, exhibiting all kinds of freaks and captivating the public especially with his Cardiff Giant, a plaster duplicate of the discovery on a farm outside Cardiff, New York. It was 10 feet long and weighed 3,000 pounds and had been proven a hoax, but still fascinated the public. The hoax, literary or physical, fed the American dreams of freedom and expansion and was an example of the American dream of personal fulfillment.

Another stalk growing from the same root included the works of the so-called Southwest humorists, who carried on in their stories and language the literature of the hoax. David Ross Locke (Petroleum V. Nasby), Henry Wheeler Show (Josh Billings), and George Washington and his Sut Lovingood stories created exaggerated physical and linguistic caricatures of their fellow citizens in a world they expected and hoped would be recognized as hoaxes. Instead of laughable hoaxes, however, they created a world of reality that is carried over in American popular culture today. The stereotype of the illiterate Southerner has a central role in the twenty-first century, particularly in television sit-coms and movies. The standup routines of Jeff Foxworthy and Larry the Cable Guy are built around the premise of the South being strangely (although often lovingly) different than the rest of the nation.

Another popular form of literature developed out of the idea of the hoax—graphic caricature and literature. Although the caricature had been common from the earliest days of America, the so-called common caricature known as the comic strip narrative, developed by the Swiss cartoonist Rodolphe Topfer in 1846, was probably introduced into America in the *San Francisco Examiner* on February 16, 1896, as "The Yellow Kid." Since then most newspapers have run their series of comic pages in the United States and abroad—especially in Japan, where they are read by all members of a family under the name *anime*. They are likewise pervasive in American (and world) culture, especially in animation, movies, and advertising, particularly when used to pitch products to children and young people.

Because of our growing knowledge of and interest in archaeology and anthropology, our interest in the 6,000 or so languages spoken worldwide, and the suspicion that humanity may be doomed to future space travel and colonization, more works are developing in comics and movies of the extreme past and the imaginative future. Such comic strips and books, now called graphic novels, to a certain extent feed on the hoax works of the nineteenth century and intellectually are not rocket science, as we freely admit.

Many of the ideas and artwork in today's comic books are useful in understanding modern popular culture and its influence. For example, graphic novels have been published for both political parties in the 2008 presidential campaigns. Furthermore, many of the ideas and artwork are highly suggestive to the genuine rocket scientist, and the art work is highly prized for its newness of ideas and execution of detail by comic book aficionados. One original picture of Mickey Mouse, for example, recently sold for $700,000. Many comic book fans live in a world of their own making, but to a certain extent in America's broad, rich, and complicated popular culture, each area is something of an island of culture all its own, justifying its existence.

Just as English poet William Wordsworth said that the child is father to the man, so a culture in one form and one power or another is always a product and variant of its predecessors. It grows and alters or breaks down the restrictions of its sometimes elite, sometimes popular predecessors as the force of the new development becomes overwhelming and suggestive. Sometimes the popular culture grows and sometimes fades, but, although it may diminish in use and memory, it seldom disappears. Popular culture is like animated wall murals and graffiti that permanently etches a record of the lifeblood of a culture of the moment.

The cornucopia of twentieth century present and developing American popular culture has resulted from the free flow of opportunity provided by its predecessors. So it was up to the last century. The garden of popular culture seemed to the culture traditionalist a patch of weeds overwhelming the flowers. But a new culture in the process of finding and developing itself was not crowded. The new cultures were driven by the changing dynamic of a new people in a new land with opportunities for all men and women to live by and in the cultures they both desired and found satisfactory. Suggestions and opportunities will continue to be found and developed.

The power of the twentieth century continues to develop in the twenty-first as the richest and most energetic culture so far produced continues to flourish—sometimes to the bewilderment and consternation of the citizenry, but always irresistibly, Americans and non-Americans—as long as human nature insists that it wants or needs something new, improved, or just different and finds it in America. Popular culture is the voice of a worldwide, but especially American, growing insistence on democracy in all aspects of life, and the voices of the people—especially in America—will continue to flourish, be creative, and heard.

From the beginning, American popular culture, given a virgin land in which to grow, has developed fully and rapidly. Its influence has been especially forceful domestically and globally in the twentieth century as a result of its growth in the preceding century in the arts and extended cultures. American popular culture impacts the cultures of the world everyday, creating and resolving tensions that are labeled "Created and Made in America." In the popular cultural world in all its manifestations the most influential label on world life at the present is and in the future will be "Lived in America."

Preface

American Pop: Popular Culture Decade by Decade provides a survey of popular culture across America from 1900 to the present and presents the heart and soul of America, acting as a unifying bridge across time and bringing together generations of diverse backgrounds. Whether looking at the bright lights of the Jazz Age in the 1920s, the rock 'n' roll and lifestyle revolutions of the 1960s and 1970s, or the thriving social networking Web sites of today, each period in America's cultural history develops its own unique take on the qualities that define our lives. *American Pop* is a four-volume set that examines the trends and events across decades and eras by shedding light on the experiences of Americans young and old, rich and poor, along with the influences of arts, entertainment, sports, and other cultural forces.

Based partly on Greenwood's "American Popular Culture through History" series, this four-volume set is designed to give students and general readers a broad and interdisciplinary overview of the numerous aspects of popular culture. Each of the topical chapters stands alone as a testament to the individual decade, yet taken together, they offer an integrated history and allow readers to make connections among each of the decades. Of course, this organization also encourages readers to compare the sometimes striking differences among decades.

WHAT'S INCLUDED IN *AMERICAN POP*

The volumes in this set cover the following chronological periods.

- Volume 1, 1900–1929
- Volume 2, 1930–1959
- Volume 3, 1960–1989
- Volume 4, 1990–Present

Each volume, in turn, covers the popular culture of the decades through chapters focused on specific areas of popular culture, including:

An Overview of the Decade	Fashion
Advertising	Food
Architecture	Music
Books, Newspapers, Magazines, and Comics	Sports and Leisure
	Travel
Entertainment	Visual Arts

In addition, each group of chapters is preceded by a timeline of events for the decade, which gives extra oversight and context to the study of the period.

Sidebars and Other Features

Within many of the chapters, the text is supplemented by sidebars that feature the significant, fascinating, troubling, or just plain weird people, trends, books, movies, radio and television programs, advertisements, places, and events of the decade. In addition sidebars provide lists of new words and phrases for the decade; new foods introduced during the decade; and "How Others See Us," information on how people outside of the United States adopted, reacted to, or disdained American popular culture. The chapters are enhanced with photos and illustrations from the period. Each volume closes with a Resource Guide, providing selected books, articles, Web sites, and videos for further research.

The appendices feature "The Cost of Products"—which spans from 1900 to the present and shows the prices of selected items from food to clothing to furniture—and a list of potential classroom resources of activities and assignments for teachers to use in a school setting. A carefully selected general bibliography for the set, covering popular culture resources of a general or sizeable nature, rounds out the final volume. A comprehensive index offers access to the entire set.

ACKNOWLEDGMENTS

American Pop is an audacious project that pulls together more than one million words about popular culture in the twentieth and twenty-first centuries. A series like this one owes a large debt to many wonderful authors, researchers, writers, and editors. First and foremost, my deepest gratitude goes out to Ray B. Browne, the series editor of the original "American Popular Culture through History" books. Like so many other popular culture scholars over the past several decades, I owe Ray more than I could ever hope to repay.

I would also like to thank all of the authors who poured their collective hearts into the series: David Blanke, Kathleen Drowne, Patrick Huber, William H. Young, Nancy K. Young, Robert Sickels, Edward J. Rielly, Kelly Boyer Sagert, Scott Stoddart, and Marc Oxoby. Their work provides the backbone of this collection. Several excellent writers contributed to the more than 300 sidebars that appear throughout this set: Mary Kay Linge, Ken Zachmann, Martha Whitt, Micah L. Issitt, Josef Benson, Cindy Williams, Joy Austin, Angelica Benjamin, Peter Lazazzaro, Jillian Mann, Vanessa Martinez, Jessica Schultz, Jessica Seriano, and Brie Tomaszewski.

Not even Superman could edit a collection like *American Pop* without a superstar team of editors. I have been lucky to benefit from the wisdom and leadership skills of

Kristi Ward and Anne Thompson throughout the project. *American Pop* would not exist without their enthusiasm, hard work, and dedication. Thanks also to Cindy Williams for her original editing of the project. She is wonderful.

My great honor in editing *American Pop* has been picking up where Ray left off. I have had the pleasure of writing three books in the series, so all told, I have spent more than five years of my life with this series. My sincere thanks go to my parents, Jon and Linda Bowen, and my brother Bill Coyle for their support. As always, my wife, Kathy, has lived this collection with me. I appreciate her sense of humor, sound advice, and thoughtfulness. My whole heart belongs to our daughter Kassie. Her smile, hugs, and kisses were always awesome diversions from writing and editing.

Bob Batchelor
University of South Florida
Tampa, Florida

Introduction

The greatest compliment that can be paid to the 1960–1989 period is that its lasting popular culture images still have resonance in the twenty-first century, ranging from the glamour of President John F. Kennedy (JFK) and his "Camelot" administration to the harsh images captured in the jungles of Vietnam and the deaths of African Americans fighting for civil rights. Terms popularized during this time help people better understand today's world, such as ending any type of scandal with "-gate" after the Watergate crisis that brought down the Nixon Administration. Any overseas war is likened to Vietnam.

Perhaps the current national fascination with the 1960s, 1970s, and 1980s is based solely on the fact that the people currently controlling mass communications came of age or grew up in those eras. There isn't a night that goes by that a viewer could not find programming focused on these decades on TV, from CBS's summer 2008 hit *Swingtown* to VH1's *I Love the 70s* and *I Love the 80s*. One suspects, however, that the fascination and appeal of these decades runs deeper.

The decades under consideration were times of great change in America, which were reflected in the nation's culture. Transformation and evolution seemed palpable, as if one could simply feel the winds of change by sticking a finger in the air. Some commentators have attributed this to JFK, who served up a breath of fresh air after the considerably older Dwight Eisenhower. Interestingly, Ronald Reagan did not have youth on his side in the 1980s, but his charisma more or less willed Americans into believing a better day stood at the horizon. These leaders do not deserve all the credit for a timeframe that encompassed such dynamic change, but their leadership cleared the canvas a bit.

The challenge in analyzing American popular culture in the second half of the twentieth century is finding a way to both capture the broadness of the field and at the same time keep the survey manageable. By examining popular culture within the following categories—leaders, money, innovation, and culture—an overview of the 1960–1989 period will emerge that discusses the major issues driving everyday America during the era. From a broad perspective, these forces transform society almost the same way wind changes local or regional weather—most of the time invisibly, yet powerfully, but in other instances with force and intensity. Therefore, while popular culture is ever-shifting, the often undetected forces of technology, economics, political systems, and culture are working their magic on the system. All the roots of popular culture trace back to these forces.

Many instances of pop culture transformation blur the lines between these topics. For example, 1980s filmmakers used the Vietnam War and the cultural rifts it incited as central storylines in movies that implicitly questioned Ronald Reagan's foreign policy. Like many pundits and critics, these filmmakers saw a similarity between the earlier conflict and America taking on the role as the world's police force. The real-life war in Southeast Asia took on an additional role, providing authors, artists, and commentators with a method for questioning current diplomacy. Vietnam remains a focus of television programs, movies, novels, and nonfiction works.

At its core, popular culture is about context. It may be difficult, if not impossible, to statistically measure the impact of John F. Kennedy on the cultural development of the 1960s, but understanding the nuances of his role provides a framework for grasping the broader meaning of culture both during and after his tenure as an iconic political leader.

The ability to examine the actions of the government or a particular leader or group of leaders is arguably the most positive aspect of popular culture. Rooted in free speech, the rise of mass media enabled Americans to criticize their leaders and institutions, thus opening new opportunities for collective education and information. In the 1960s this meant that 250,000 protestors could gather on the mall in the nation's capital to protest the ongoing war in Vietnam.

As millions of Americans interacted with mass media, whether by watching the same movies or listening to radio programs, a common language developed that opened lines of communication between disparate groups. The downside to this unintended focus on mass communications, some argued, was that a growing fascination with pop culture actually diverted attention from important challenges the nation faced, ultimately serving as a kind of placebo. Therefore, popular culture enabled people to feel good about the world around them without really forcing them to directly confront critical issues.

LEADERS

Some eras in American history have been defined by the events that unfolded during that timeframe, while others have been closely linked to the president who presided over the time. The 1960–1989 timeframe featured a series of presidents that dominated the scene both politically and culturally.

Certainly, Ronald Wilson Reagan served as the most pervasive icon of American life in the 1980s. Reagan's election initiated a conservative political movement that swept the country and his powerful rhetoric ushered in a renewed sense of patriotism. Named *Time* magazine's "Man of the Year" after the 1980 presidential election, the 72-year-old Reagan seemed a curious hero for America; his Hollywood charm blended with his blunt criticism of the Jimmy Carter administration helped him win the election by a 10-point margin.

The public clearly had enough of Carter, who was blamed for the Iran hostage crisis, gas shortages, and the economic woes brought on by soaring interest rates. In contrast, Reagan offered a markedly different, more positive and patriotic view. His simple message, delivered with a grandfatherly air, captured the public's imagination and gave them a renewed sense of hope.

Scholars debate the role Reagan played in formulating policies carried out during his administration, particularly regarding the economy and foreign affairs. Critics charge that "The Great Manipulator" (one of Reagan's unflattering nicknames) played the public role of president, while strong leaders in his Cabinet actually ran the country. Others view Reagan as the ultimate activist president, setting the nation on a transformational course that now defines the modern age.

Under Reagan's watch, the administration began a series of reforms that marked some of the most significant economic and social policy changes in half a century. According to Richard Thornburgh, Attorney General in the Reagan administration, "The status of the individual in society, fiscal integrity, the idea of true federalism, the idea of Government closer to the people, the idea of the toughness of the American fiber, which means a firm line with criminals at home and with our adversaries abroad, the principles which put together the real genesis of the Reagan victory. Those principles are now a majority view."[1]

Reagan earned the nickname "The Great Communicator" for his uncanny knack of understanding the public's concerns and responding in an optimistic, believable manner. His carefully crafted speeches and his effective presentation method made him appear grandfatherly and appealed to the masses that bought into his family values campaign. Reagan's conservatism gave the public a sense of calm after decades of strife, from the lingering pain of Vietnam and Watergate to the psychological scars of the Iran hostage crisis and faltering economy of the 1970s, symbolized by a nationwide gas shortage and soaring interest rates.

The president's campaign commercial "Morning in America" encapsulated his philosophy—American values connecting patriotism, family, and moral conviction were the things that separated America from the rest of the world, and particularly the Soviet Union's "Evil Empire."

However, Reagan's Republican party did not do so well in the 1984 election, which returned a Democratic majority to Congress that subsequently blocked one of his more ambitious plans: the Strategic Defense Initiative—dubbed "Star Wars" by the media—an arsenal of satellites to render useless any nuclear attacks waged by the Soviets.

In hindsight, however, Reagan's legacy consisted of an enormous debt, a booming economy that collapsed as soon as he left office, and a reputation for not really being in control. Despite this, he remains one of America's most popular presidents.

MONEY

Thomas J. Watson Jr. took over his father's company, International Business Machines (IBM), in 1952 and ran it until 1971. During that time he transformed an already strong business into a global monolith. The younger Watson realized the potential of the computer and, against his father's wishes, redirected IBM's efforts toward the new technology. The gamble paid off and IBM became synonymous with computers worldwide. By 1983 the personal computer (PC) was so pervasive that *Time* magazine named the PC its "Man of the Year."

After World War II, Watson Jr. had returned to IBM a new, more confident man. He did not automatically defer to his father. Now more strategic and analytical in his thinking, Watson realized that new computer technology would make IBM's tabulating products obsolete. His iron-willed father, however, thought only a handful of computers would be needed in the entire country.

The battle between father and son about the future of computers signified a changing of the guard. After years of being hounded about electronics by his son, Watson Sr. finally relented. Watson Jr. quickly doubled the research and development budget and hired hundreds of engineers to build IBM's first computers. The two Watsons spent a decade working together. The father passed along his sales secrets while the son took on more leadership tasks. Both men shared a quick, explosive temper. The legendary shouting matches between the two became part of company folklore.

Watson Jr. became president of IBM in 1952 and CEO in 1956, just six weeks before Watson Sr. passed away. Becoming more like his father, who ran IBM with an iron fist that critics labeled cult-like, the son instituted a highly competitive corporate culture among the highest-ranking executives. Watson pushed his managers and scientists to constantly be at the cutting-edge of technological innovation.

Watson Jr. was an instinctive leader and demanded quick decisions. His leadership style set the tone for the relentless innovation required in the computer industry. He drove his employees to be decisive and to take risks. Watson purposely hired and promoted outspoken, competitive managers, against the grain of corporate "yes men" that many executives surrounded themselves with.

By the early 1960s IBM clearly dominated the burgeoning computer industry. But this lead did not satisfy Watson. Rather than resting on his laurels, Watson authorized that $5 billion be spent developing a new line of computers that would make all others obsolete—including IBM's own. The staggering sum was almost three times IBM's revenues and an audacious gamble.[2]

Watson directed company researchers to work on a family of small computers rather than large, outmoded machines. Since the computers would be designed to solve a company's every need, it was dubbed the System/360, after the circumference of a circle.

The risk Watson took with the System/360 turned IBM into a pressure cooker. When the project, run by Watson's younger brother Dick, slid off schedule, Watson demoted his brother, which essentially ended Dick's career. The move shamed Watson, but he was determined that IBM would thrive.

Ultimately, the System/360 was a hit around the globe—the gamble paid off for IBM. The company ruled the computer industry, controlling about 70 percent of the world's computers. IBM had 35,000 installed computers in 1970, a significant increase from the 11,000 it had in 1964. Financially, the System/360 doubled revenues, reaching $7.5 billion in 1970, while the company's market value jumped from $14 billion to $36 billion.[3]

IBM's early domination of the computer market enabled the company to develop other systems that would soon define the computer age. In 1981 IBM introduced the first PC, which enabled the technology industry to thrive. IBM's new PC required a software operating system so that users could experience the full power of the computer. Microsoft, led by Bill Gates and Paul Allen, developed the programming language and the operating system, thus beginning the next phase of the technology revolution.

Under Watson's reign, IBM stood as the greatest corporate success story of the post–World War II era. The company created incredible wealth for shareholders, among the best in business history. As a result of Watson's decision to push IBM into computers and the resulting achievement, *Fortune* magazine called Watson (arguably) the greatest capitalist who ever lived.[4] By concentrating on computers, IBM paved the way for the information age. At the end of the 1980s, more than 45 million homes owned and operated some form of personal computer and they were considered an essential for business success.[5]

INNOVATION

During the three decades from 1960 to 1989 television changed considerably, not only the box itself but also the programming that appeared on the airwaves. It is difficult to weigh which aspect had a more dramatic transformation, but TV content more closely reflected American popular culture. In this respect, innovation represents the way programming evolved during this timespan. During the 1960s television became the dominant form of mass communications, with about 60 million households having at least one box, despite Kennedy administration FCC chairman Newton Minow labeling the medium a "vast wasteland." In the 1980s much of the national cultural discussion centered on television shows, from the latest antics between Sam and Diane on *Cheers* to who killed J. R. Ewing on *Dallas.*

Between 1960 and 1989 the most important change in programming may have been in the portrayal of African Americans. In contrast to the great strides African Americans made in film roles in previous decades, they had less success in television. Most of the top shows of the 1960s had no black lead actors.

The 1970s saw a significant increase in shows either addressing race or featuring blacks in strong roles. Two of the initial efforts were *Sanford and Son* and *The Flip Wilson Show,* the first variety show hosted by an African American. The success of *All in the Family* in confronting race and bigotry through comedy led to the spin-off *The Jeffersons,* which eventually became the longest running comedy in TV history (11 seasons) with lead black characters.

Despite the pervasiveness of Reagan conservatism in the 1980s and television's few positive portrayals of the black experience, *The Cosby Show* debuted on NBC in 1984. Few expected it to become the dominant show on television, ultimately running through 1992. Inspired by comedian and actor Bill Cosby, the program did not rely on traditional one-liner jokes and racial stereotypes. Instead, *The Cosby Show* enabled viewers to see a strong, upper middle class black family dealing with day-to-day life.

The criticism of earlier shows such as *The Jeffersons* and *Good Times* was that they relied too heavily on the buffoonery of the central African American lead male character, thus playing into common racist stereotypes. In contrast, Cosby and his television family cared for one another in a loving family system. Bill Cosby's groundbreaking role as Cliff Huxtable single handedly changed the way many Americans felt about blacks. In its first season *The Cosby Show* placed third in the Nielsen ratings. Then, for the next five years, the show topped the ratings to tie with *All in the Family* as the only two shows to do so for that amount of time.

The evolution of lily-white television in the 1960s to the positive African American experience on *The Cosby Show* reveals the strides America made in lessening racism between 1960 and 1989. No one would argue that having a sitcom about blacks as the top show on TV for five straight seasons means that racism disappeared. However, at least in popular culture terms the depiction provided by the Huxtables pushed the discussion in a positive direction.

CULTURE

For 13 seconds on May 4, 1970, Ohio National Guardsmen opened fire on students protesting the Vietnam War at Kent State University in Kent, Ohio, killing four and wounding nine others. What had started as a small campus demonstration—one of thousands nationwide—instantly transformed into a symbol of the Vietnam era worldwide. A Pulitzer Prize winning photograph taken at the shooting—an anguished young woman kneeling over the body of a dead student with her arms raised in despair—ended the Woodstock era. Any lingering idyllic "free love" notions of the 1960s disappeared with the Kent State massacre.

On April 30, 1970, President Nixon appeared on national television to announce that United States troops were invading Cambodia to strike suspected guerrilla strongholds. The new policy contradicted his previous plan that pledged a "Vietnamization" of the war to gradually reduce America's involvement in the conflict.

Reaction to the escalation of the war effort was immediate and intense, especially on the nation's college campuses where over 1.5 million students protested the announcement. Nixon fueled the outrage by labeling the student protesters "bums" who were "blowing up the campuses."

After the shootings, officials shut down Kent State, which remained closed for the rest of the school year. As news about the tragedy spread, campus unrest escalated nationwide. Nearly 500 colleges were closed or disrupted. Ten days later, another campus shooting occurred at Jackson State University in Mississippi, when police and state patrolmen fired into a dormitory at the all-black school, killing two students and wounding nine others. The lack of attention given to the massacre at Jackson State embittered many in the African American community.

The Kent State Massacre bookends a generation that began with the assassination of President John F. Kennedy in 1963 and included the murder of his brother Robert F. Kennedy and civil rights activist Martin Luther King Jr. in 1968. Kent State immediately transformed from a sleepy Midwestern college into the symbolic epicenter of student protest in the Vietnam era. Kent State will always be a symbol of antiwar protest and government repression. The incident has been immortalized in countless books and even a television movie, but nothing was more stinging than the Crosby, Stills, Nash, and Young song "Ohio" written by Neil Young with its haunting refrain, "Four dead in Ohio!"

It is impossible to overstate the cultural importance of John F. Kennedy, the Civil Rights struggle, Vietnam, and Watergate. The short 14-year span between Kennedy's inauguration and Nixon's resignation may have been the most tumultuous era in modern American history outside the two World Wars and the Great Depression. Seismic changes took place. Unlike the crises of earlier times, a primed and ready mass communications industry stood poised to deliver it all to an eager public. Therefore, one must underscore the burgeoning mass media that helped define popular culture at the time while also preserving it for future generations. Is it possible to imagine a world without the grainy black-and-white images of Kennedy and Nixon debating on the election trail, the Kennedy assassination film, or Nixon's robotic arm wave as he boarded the helicopter leaving the White House in 1974?

One could argue that the period of time between 1960 and 1989 retains its significance because the expanding media was there to record it all. Furthermore, as the era progressed, the way people interacted with mass communications increased geometrically. Looking back, the transition from Walter Cronkite and the CBS Evening News to a 24-hour a day, always on news cycle seemed linear.

However, more outlets meant additional time to fill and advertising dollars to be made, which resulted in more stuff, fluff, and filler deemed newsworthy. As news programming stuffed itself full of soft stories, popular culture leapt in as well. The news cycle needed to be fed, particularly as cable television spread across the nation and the number of channels multiplied. The increased attention and time spent discussing popular culture naturally led to greater interest, which in turn, led to more coverage—a vicious cycle built on the consumer's demand for more.

The 1960–1989 timeframe also set the stage for the end of the century and the beginning of the next by preparing people to dive even deeper into the pop culture bubble. In the 1960s and 1970s, one might be able to escape the constant need for greater access and information. However, the introduction of personal computers and home video games in the 1980s opened Pandora's Box, guaranteeing the triumph of the wired and wireless future.

NOTES

1. Roger Rosenblatt, "Ronald Reagan, Person of the Year," *Time,* January 2, 1980, 4.
2. John Greenwald, "The *Time* 100: Thomas J. Watson, Jr.," *Time,* December 7, 1998, 172–73.
3. Greenwald, "The *Time* 100."
4. Steve Lohr, "I.B.M.'s Computing Pioneer, Thomas Watson Jr., Dies at 79," *The New York Times,* January 1, 1994, http://query.nytimes.com/gst/fullpage.html?res=980DEED8153EF932A35752 C0A962958260.
5. Greenwald, "The *Time* 100," 173.

1960s

Timeline

of Popular Culture Events, 1960s

1960

February 18–28: The Winter Olympics are held in Squaw Valley, California. A major highlight of the games occurs when the American hockey team upsets the heavily favored Russian team and wins the gold medal.

March 5: Elvis Presley is discharged from the U.S. Army.

May: Joan Baez and Pete Seeger play at the Newport Folk Festival.

August 26–September 11: The Summer Olympics take place in Rome, Italy. Cassius Clay, the future Muhammad Ali, wins the gold medal in light heavyweight boxing; other major U.S. winners are Wilma Rudolph, Rafer Johnson, and the basketball team.

September 26: John Kennedy and Richard Nixon engage in the first of their televised presidential debates.

Martin Milner and George Maharis take their first ride in their Corvette on the television series *Route 66*.

John Fitzgerald Kennedy is elected president, the first Roman Catholic and the youngest man (43) to hold the office.

1961

May 9: Newton Minow labels television a "vast wasteland" before a gathering of the National Association of Broadcasters.

June 16: Russian ballet star Rudolf Nureyev defects to the United States.

July 2: Ernest Hemingway kills himself with a shotgun in his Ketchum, Idaho, home.

October 1: Roger Maris of the New York Yankees breaks Babe Ruth's single-season home-run record by hitting his 61st.

Bob Dylan begins to perform in Greenwich Village clubs.

Jacqueline Kennedy wears a pillbox hat to the presidential Inauguration, setting off a pillbox craze among American women.

The first Hardee's fast-food restaurant opens, specializing in charcoal-broiled hamburgers and cheeseburgers.

Wilma Rudolph is named Female Athlete of the Year by the Associated Press.

1962

February 20: John Glenn becomes the first American to orbit Earth.

July 19: Ray Charles's album *Modern Sounds in Country & Western Music* goes gold.

July 22: Actress Marilyn Monroe dies of an apparent drug overdose.

September 25: Sonny Liston becomes heavyweight boxing champion by knocking out Floyd Patterson.

October: Federal legislation is approved declaring LSD a hallucinogenic drug that must be regulated by law.

October 14: James Brown records *The James Brown Show Live at the Apollo,* one of the most famous live albums of all time.

Wilt Chamberlain scores 100 points in a game, a National Basketball Association (NBA) record.

Jack Paar concludes his run as host of *The Tonight Show* (actually called *The Jack Paar Show* during his tenure); substitute hosts preside until Johnny Carson takes over on October 1.

Students for a Democratic Society (SDS) releases its Port Huron Statement.

The Beverly Hillbillies strike oil on television as one of the most popular television series ever.

1963

February 11: Sylvia Plath, author of *The Bell Jar,* commits suicide.

August 24: Little Stevie Wonder becomes the first performer to simultaneously top the American pop singles, pop albums, and rhythm and blues singles charts.

August 28: Dr. Martin Luther King Jr. delivers his "I Have a Dream" speech at the Lincoln Memorial in Washington, D.C.

November 22–26: Millions of people remain in front of their television sets to watch events relating to the assassination and funeral of President John F. Kennedy, with regular programming returning on November 26.

November 22: Vice-President Lyndon B. Johnson assumes the presidency.

Schlitz sells beer in new tab-opening aluminum cans.

Julia Child demonstrates on television how to prepare *bœuf bourguignon,* the first of a series of cooking lessons on educational television stations.

Joan Baez, Pete Seeger, and other artists perform at the first nonprofit Newport Folk Festival.

1964

February 9: The Beatles perform on *The Ed Sullivan Show.*

February 25: Cassius Clay (later Muhammad Ali) becomes heavyweight boxing champion by knocking out Sonny Liston.

March 13: Kitty Genovese is murdered outside her apartment building in New York City while neighbors ignore her pleas for help.

April: Twelve Beatles records are on the top 100 list.

June 5: Jim Ryun, a high school student, runs the mile in less than four minutes.

July 23: The first Arby's fast-food restaurant, specializing in roast beef sandwiches, opens.

December 20: ABC, CBS, and NBC simultaneously broadcast in color for the first time.

Los Angeles Dodger pitcher Sandy Koufax is named athlete of the year.

A San Francisco bar features topless go-go girls.

Students initiate the Free Speech Movement in October at the University of California, Berkeley.

At the Summer Olympics in Tokyo, the United States wins 90 medals, the Soviet Union 96.

The 1964 Civil Rights Act is signed. The Act denies federal funds to schools that refuse to desegregate.

1965

March 2: A teach-in to oppose the Vietnam War occurs at the University of Michigan, beginning a new antiwar tactic.

March: The restaurant T.G.I. Friday's, which caters to young singles, opens in New York City.

April 9: The Astrodome, an indoor domed sports facility, opens in Houston.

May 25: In a rematch, Muhammad Ali knocks out Sonny Liston in the first round with the famous "phantom punch."

July 25: Bob Dylan switches to an electric guitar at the Newport Folk Festival, sending a shock wave through his traditional folk audience.

October 22: The Highway Beautification Act is enacted to improve the appearance of the nation's highways.

Vatican II ends in Rome; church officials later issue new guidelines that modernize Catholic ritual and church architecture.

Head Start, a U.S. program to provide free preschool to economically disadvantaged children, is established.

1966

January 1: Cigarette packages start carrying a warning that "Cigarette smoking may be hazardous to your health."

January 1: Simon and Garfunkel's "The Sounds of Silence" is number one in *Billboard* for the week.

January 17: Truman Capote's novel *In Cold Blood* is published.

March 6: Barry Sadler's "Ballad of the Green Berets" begins a 13-week reign atop the charts.

June 13: The U.S. Supreme Court rules that Ernesto Miranda's rights were violated during questioning after his arrest, leading to promulgation of the Miranda rights in law and on countless television crime shows.

July 31: Radio station WOR-FM in New York City switches its programming to rock as FM stations begin their association with the counterculture.

October 29: Betty Friedan and other advocates for women's rights create the National Organization for Women (NOW).

Physician Sam Sheppard, model for the lead character on the television series *The Fugitive*, is found not guilty of murdering his wife.

The Starship *USS Enterprise* makes its first flight as *Star Trek* launches on NBC.

Medicare and Medicaid programs go into effect (after approval by Congress and President Johnson in 1965 as amendments to the Social Security Act of 1935).

1967

January 15: The Green Bay Packers defeat the Kansas City Chiefs 35–21 in the first Super Bowl.

April 13: Random House publishes the supernatural thriller *Rosemary's Baby* by Ira Levin.

April 28: Muhammad Ali refuses induction into the Armed Services and is subsequently stripped of his championship and convicted of violating Selective Service laws.

June 2: The Beatles' album *Sgt. Pepper's Lonely Hearts Club Band* is available for sale in the United States.

June 16–18: The Monterey International Pop Festival occurs in Monterey, California, beginning "The Summer of Love."

September 9: William Styron's *The Confessions of Nat Turner* is published by Random House and engenders controversy over its depiction of Turner.

The Rolling Stones perform the song "Let's Spend the Night Together" on *The Ed Sullivan Show,* but Sullivan requires them to change the lyric to "Let's Spend Some Time Together."

Johnny Carson wears a Nehru jacket on *The Tonight Show* in February, creating an instant fashion craze.

The Smothers Brothers Comedy Hour premieres on CBS.

The rock-musical *Hair* opens on Broadway in December.

1968

January 16: Abbie Hoffman and Jerry Rubin found the Youth International Party, a radical group better known as the Yippies.

March 31: President Johnson announces that he will not run for re-election.

March 4: The *New York Times* runs an article entitled "An Arrangement: Living Together for Convenience, Security, Sex," which publicizes the growing practice of college students living together outside marriage.

April: Students for a Democratic Society (SDS) members occupy buildings at Columbia University to protest the Vietnam War.

May 20–June 14: Dr. Benjamin Spock, author of *Baby and Child Care,* and four other antiwar protestors are tried for conspiring to aid draft resisters; Spock and three others are convicted, but the verdict is later overturned.

June 3: Valerie Solanas shoots and seriously wounds pop artist Andy Warhol.

July 29: The encyclical *Humanae Vitae* by Pope Paul VI is published, reaffirming opposition by the Catholic Church to artificial means of birth control.

August 26–29: Television viewers watch massive antiwar demonstrations at the Democratic National Convention in Chicago.

October 16: Tommie Smith and John Carlos protest U.S. racial injustice and South African apartheid with a black-glove salute after winning medals at the Olympic Games in Mexico City.

November: Richard M. Nixon is elected president.

December 3: Elvis Presley returns from films to concert performances with a televised performance popularly known as "The 68 Comeback."

The science-fiction film *2001: A Space Odyssey* opens in New York City.

The documentary *Hunger in America* airs on CBS.

Tom Wolfe's *The Electric Kool-Aid Acid Test* appears, describing the 1964 LSD trip across the country by Ken Kesey and his Merry Pranksters.

Jeannie C. Riley achieves a gold record with her single "Harper Valley PTA."

Jacqueline Kennedy marries Greek shipping tycoon Aristotle Onassis.

1969

January 12: The New York Jets deliver on quarterback Joe Namath's promise of victory by defeating the favored Baltimore Colts, 16–7, in Super Bowl III.

February 8: The first commercial Boeing 747 flight lands successfully.

March 2: The *Concorde* supersonic airliner makes its first flight.

April 29: Bandleader Duke Ellington celebrates his 70th birthday at a White House party hosted by President Richard Nixon.

May 25: The film *Midnight Cowboy* opens.

June 17: The play *Oh, Calcutta!,* featuring total nudity, opens Off-Broadway.

June 27: Police raid the Stonewall Inn, a gay bar in Greenwich Village, precipitating the "Stonewall Riots" and the beginning of the gay liberation movement.

July 11: Harper Lee's novel of southern racism, *To Kill a Mockingbird,* is published.

July: The film *Easy Rider,* starring Peter Fonda and Dennis Hopper, opens.

August: Members of Charles Manson's "family" commit multiple murders, including the murder of actress Sharon Tate.

August 15–17: Almost half a million people watch many of the country's most famous singers and musicians perform at a festival in Woodstock, New York.

October 16: The "Amazin' Mets" complete their World Series triumph over the heavily favored Baltimore Orioles.

October 21: Jack Kerouac, author of *On the Road,* dies of alcoholism.

December 6: The Rolling Stones perform at the Altamont Music Festival in California; one person dies in a confrontation with members of the Hell's Angels motorcycle gang.

The Doors' Jim Morrison is arrested and charged with obscene actions while performing in Miami.

Delacorte Press publishes Kurt Vonnegut's novel *Slaughterhouse-Five.*

Neil Armstrong walks on the moon on July 20. Millions watch the event on television.

The film based on Arlo Guthrie's popular song by the same name, *Alice's Restaurant,* opens.

Overview

of the 1960s

The 1960s brought both increased comfort and growing social challenges. The increasingly urban economy proved healthy, improving quality of life for the majority of Americans. Salaries, corporate profits, increased use of credit and installment buying, and a strong stock market characterized the economic life of the decade.

Developments in health care held out the promise of a longer life, while Medicare and Medicaid made health care more accessible to millions of Americans. The 1960s initially seemed to most Americans like a new world, younger and more energetic. President John F. Kennedy and his family brought glamour, charm, and enthusiasm to the political scene. That spirit soon dissolved, however, as the president, his brother, and prominent civil rights leaders were assassinated.

Although democratic ideals spread through the Civil Rights and feminist movements, changes were often accompanied by social upheaval, including demonstrations and riots. More people viewed crime as a deeply ingrained threat to everyday peace and security. The Vietnam War, generally supported by Americans early in the decade, became a catalyst for powerful social protest. As the news media intensified its scrutiny of America's role in Vietnam, gruesome images of death and carnage filled the television airwaves, introducing many directly to the horrors of modern warfare.

THE ECONOMY AND HEALTH CARE

During the 1960s, Americans continued to move from farms and small towns into cities or suburbs, while many others already in cities opted to move out into the surrounding suburban communities. Most Americans benefited from the continuing economic expansion as the country shifted from an industrial economy to a postindustrial business and service economy less reliant on heavy industrial manufacturing.[1] Salaries tended to rise, with per capita income close to $4,000 by 1970, almost double what it had been 10 years before. Three-fourths of Americans in this robust economy owned their homes. Both household installment buying and car loans more than doubled during the decade, and the credit card became a common means of purchasing large and small items for most families.

Discount stores that purchased directly from manufacturers and featured high-volume sales, self-service, and low prices began to push aside traditional department stores. In 1962 alone, four major discount chains—Wal-Mart, Kmart, Target, and Woolco—opened.

As the decade approached its end, prices and interest rates began to rise, depressing the housing market, real earnings, and business profits. Unemployment increased. The economic despair felt by many average Americans increased the social anxiety raging across the nation.

Health care became more available to Americans in 1966, when Medicare and Medicaid programs went into effect. Approved by Congress and President Johnson in 1965 as an amendment to the Social Security Act of 1935, provided compulsory health insurance for all U.S. citizens 65 years old or older who were eligible for Social Security or Railroad Retirement benefits. Medicare also made available hospital insurance and, for a monthly premium, an optional medical insurance plan to cover physician and outpatient services. Medicaid provided medical assistance to low-income Americans.

The combination of prosperity and expanded social programs for the poor created advances in medical care. William Chardack developed the pacemaker in 1960. Eye surgery proved easier and safer with laser surgery, first used by Dr. Charles Campbell in 1962. In the same year, Valium became available as a muscle relaxant, helping to ease both physical and emotional pain. Soft contact lenses were invented in 1965. In 1963, Dr. Michael De Bakey invented an artificial heart to keep pumping blood while a patient underwent heart surgery. Four years later South African Christiaan Barnard performed the first successful heart transplant. By 1969, a Houston surgeon, Denton A. Cooley, was able to implanted an artificial heart in a patient.

The dangers of cigarette smoking became more evident during the 1960s, and many Americans tried to stop smoking. In 1964, the Surgeon

Dr. Benjamin Spock (center, foreground) leading march to the United Nations to demand a cease-fire in Vietnam, 1965. Prints & Photographs Division, Library of Congress.

DR. BENJAMIN SPOCK (1903–1998)

As the oldest of six children born into a middle-class Connecticut family, Benjamin Spock found himself immersed in childcare at an early age. He later attended medical school and eventually specialized in pediatrics, drawing on his own childhood experience. Moved by the common difficulties he saw among young parents, Dr. Spock decided to write a baby care manual. His theory was simple; he believed that parents should use their "common judgment" and support their children's development on their own terms instead of relying on discipline. Spock's manual, published in 1946, was first titled *The Common Sense Book of Baby and Child Care*. The title was changed in subsequent editions to *Baby and Child Care* and by 2004 was in its eighth edition (2004) as *Dr. Spock's Baby and Child Care*, co-authored by Dr. Robert Needlman. Dr. Spock's obituary in the *New York Times* on March 17, 1998, noted that Spock's first wife, Jane, played an active role in writing the book. He dedicated the fourth edition in 1976 was dedicated to her. Spock's baby care manual became the second best-selling non-fiction book after the Bible, and for 50 years Spock was among the leading voices in baby care. Some critics, however, blamed Spock for creating a generation of young adults who eschewed social order to pursue self-indulgent goals. Former Vice President Spiro Agnew led the criticism against Spock, saying that he helped to create an "undue permissiveness" in the new generation. Dr. Spock allied himself with the liberal, anti-war movement of the 1960s and took part in protests and demonstrations against the war in Vietnam, which furthered backlash against him. Spock couldn't see the benefit of protecting children who might later be killed in war. Until his death in 1998, Dr. Spock continued to write about child psychology, but his views became more conservative over time. He focused on what he saw as the decay of American morals. Spock's motivation, however, stemmed not so much from pursuing social conservatism as from concern for children's welfare, perhaps the constant strain that guided his life.

General's Report linked smoking to lung cancer and a number of other illnesses, including heart attacks. In 1965, national legislation required that a warning label be placed on tobacco products: "Caution: Cigarette smoking may be hazardous to your health."

Parents continued to look to the "baby doctor," Benjamin Spock, for assistance, as they had been doing since *The Common Sense Book of Baby and Child Care* first appeared in 1946. Renamed *Baby and Child Care*, the book still provided information about infant nutrition and illnesses while reassuring parents who were fearful of their new parental responsibilities. During the 1960s, some Americans accused Dr. Spock, who became a prominent activist against the war in Vietnam, of fostering rebellion by encouraging permissive child-rearing practices.

POLITICS AND POLITICAL LEADERS

John F. Kennedy was elected president in 1960 by a razor-thin margin over Richard Nixon. Kennedy, at 43, was the youngest man ever elected president and the first president born in the twentieth century. His stylish wife Jacqueline (almost universally referred to as Jackie) and their young children, John and Caroline, brought vigor and exuberance to the White House.

President Kennedy, aided by his brother Robert, who served as Attorney General, promised that the United States would put a man on the moon before the end of the decade, encouraged physical fitness, and embraced the Civil Rights Movement. The president's audacious goals for revitalizing America led to his presidency being labeled "Camelot," after the mythical land of King Arthur and his Knights of the Round Table.

As television use increased during the 1960s, the telegenic Kennedys used the new medium to their advantage. In 1960, Kennedy performed calmly and confidently during the first-ever televised presidential debates to establish himself as a legitimate presidential candidate against the better known Richard Nixon. Later, Americans followed the First Lady on a televised tour of the White House. She also appeared regularly at cultural events and set fashion trends with her bouffant hairstyle and pillbox hat. Meanwhile, millions of Americans were charmed by photographs of the president taking his family boating or playing with his children. President Kennedy understood the power of images and used the visual tactics at his disposal to set the tone for his administration.

On November 22, 1963, President Kennedy was assassinated while riding in an open limousine in Dallas, Texas. The event was traumatic for Americans because the First Family had become so much a part of their lives through television and the print media. Television stations covered Kennedy's funeral live, which ushered in a period of national mourning. Many Americans felt that a special time of youth, excitement, and promise had been snuffed out almost before it began.

Police officers soon apprehended President Kennedy's apparent assassin, Lee Harvey Oswald. Two days after his arrest, however, Dallas nightclub owner Jack Ruby burst through a crowd of re-

porters and television crews while Oswald faced transfer to another facility, shooting him at point-blank range. Oswald died in the attack, ironically caught on live television. Oswald's death, and the subsequent death of Ruby from cancer in 1967, left open many still debated conspiracy theories regarding the president's death—including that others, including Cuban dictator Fidel Castro, organized crime figures, and perhaps even government agents, might have been involved in the assassination.

Lyndon Baines Johnson succeeded Kennedy as president and inaugurated a series of Great Society programs meant to spread American prosperity to a wider number of people. The War on Poverty, for example, modeled after the Franklin Delano Roosevelt's New Deal. Johnson sought to extend economic opportunity and justice. Johnson's efforts included the Food Stamp Act to help low-income families afford nutritious food; the

The caisson bearing the body of President Kennedy moves into National Cemetery, November 25, 1963. Prints & Photographs Division, Library of Congress.

TIME MAGAZINE "MAN OF THE YEAR"

1960 U.S. Scientists

1961 John F. Kennedy (35th U.S. President)

1962 Pope John XXIII

1963 Martin Luther King Jr. (Civil Rights leader)

1964 Lyndon B. Johnson (36th U.S. President)

1965 General William C. Westmoreland (Army Chief of Staff)

1966 Twenty-Five and Under

1967 Lyndon B. Johnson (36th U.S. President)

1968 William Anders, Frank Borman, and James Lovell (astronauts)

1969 The Middle Americans

Economic Opportunity Act, which established the Job Corps and VISTA (a domestic version of the Peace Corps created under President Kennedy to assist underdeveloped nations); the Housing and Urban Development Acts to provide additional public housing and assistance in affording adequate housing; and the previously mentioned Medicare and Medicaid programs.

Few presidential campaigns have divided the public as much as the 1968 race for the White House, ultimately won by Nixon. The campaign was marked by a strong showing in the Democratic primaries by Senator Eugene McCarthy, who attracted vehement support from young voters who stood opposed to the Vietnam War; the assassination of Robert F. Kennedy, at the time a U.S. Senator from New York; widespread antiwar demonstrations at the Democratic Convention in Chicago; and a strong showing by segregationist George Wallace, Governor of Alabama, who carried five southern states in the general election. Americans split not only along party affiliation, but by age, race, views on women's rights, and the United States' foreign policy issues. For the rest of the decade, the generation gap and other manifestations of national divisiveness would haunt the nation.

CIVIL RIGHTS

Americans saw both African Americans and women differently in the 1960s, as both groups struggled to achieve equal opportunity in basic areas of daily life. While the modern Civil Rights Movement began in the 1950s, it accelerated in the 1960s.

Although many men and women were deeply involved in the movement, the most widely recognized leader was Dr. Martin Luther King Jr., He was a Baptist minister and head of the Southern Christian Leadership Conference. He preached nonviolent resistance patterned after the Indian leader Mahatma Gandhi. King and his followers employed a wide range of nonviolent strategies, including boycotts, sit-ins, and marches. King's efforts included demonstrations in Birmingham, Alabama, in 1963 that were met by brutal police repression and were widely reported on television news, leading to expanded popular support for the Civil Rights Movement. During the March on Washington in the same year, Dr. King gave his famous "I Have a Dream Speech" in front of the Lincoln Memorial, which presented his vision of a society in which all people would be judged by their character rather than their skin color. The speech quickly became one of the most famous moments in American history, taking its place with President Kennedy's Inaugural Speech as two 1960s speeches that countless Americans would revere, and schoolchildren would study and memorize.

On April 3, 1968, King gave his final speech, "I've Been to the Mountaintop," in which he described both his vision of the future and his belief that he would not live to see it. That prophecy came true the following day when he was shot and killed in Memphis, Tennessee.

The assassination of Dr. King by James Earl Ray, who was arrested and convicted of the murder, sparked riots in several cities and further divided the nation. Earlier race riots had occurred in Harlem in New York in 1964 and 1967, in the Watts section of Los Angeles in 1965, and in Detroit during the summer of 1967.

Many groups violently opposed the struggle for equal rights during the decade, including organizations such as the Ku Klux Klan. Many other politicians, individuals, and state government officials fought against civil rights activists, sometimes violently. Segregationists understood that the church was often the center of life in African American communities and was the center of civil

Dr. Martin Luther King Jr. addressing a crowd on a street in Lakeview, New York, May 12, 1965. Prints & Photographs Division, Library of Congress.

rights planning. Consequently, there was a wave of church bombings, especially in Arkansas and Alabama. The most deadly attack was directed against the Sixteenth Street Baptist Church in Birmingham, Alabama, on September 15, 1963. Four girls, aged 10 to 14, died in their Sunday School classrooms. In 1964, three civil rights workers—Michael Schwerner and Andrew Goodman, both white, and James Chaney, an African American working with the National Association of Colored People (NAACP)—were murdered in Mississippi by Ku Klux Klan members. Medgar Evers, a prominent NAACP activist, was gunned down outside his home in Jackson, Mississippi, in 1963. These and other deaths contributed to both a clearer understanding of the dangers involved in the Civil Rights Movement and wider support for ending racial injustice.

Malcolm X (born Malcolm Little), a charismatic speaker who in 1964 left the black separatist organization the Nation of Islam, was murdered in 1965 by three African Americans who had ties to the Nation of Islam, although it was never proved that they were acting on behalf of the organization. Increasingly during the 1960s, segments of the African American community became more militant, often carrying out their struggle for justice under the Black Power slogan. A broad concept with an assortment of economic, educational, political, and social associations, Black Power often included a militant commitment to black nationalism, that is, African American advancement without reliance on white assistance and without much interest in integration.

The Black Panthers, inspired by Malcolm X, rejected the nonviolent, integrationist approach of Dr. King. In 1966, Huey Newton and Bobby Seale founded the Black Panthers in North Oakland, California, naming the organization after an animal that combined blackness with a reputation for fierceness. The Black Panthers adopted a paramilitary style of clothing and demeanor. They focused on community service through social programs such as free breakfasts for school children. Committed to black nationalism, the organization grew more confrontational. In 1967 the Black Panthers were involved in a shootout with Oakland police that attracted a great deal of media attention. An officer was killed, and Newton, who was wounded, was convicted of manslaughter. His conviction was later overturned.

Despite the skepticism many African Americans felt toward government action, the federal government did take many strong stands in favor of equal rights during the 1960s. Important legislation included the Civil Rights Act of 1964, which outlawed racial segregation in public facilities and banned gender discrimination; ratification of the Twenty-Fourth Amendment to the U.S. Constitution in 1964, prohibiting poll and other voting taxes; the Voting Rights Act of 1965, making literacy tests for voting illegal and authorizing federal examiners to register voters in federal and state elections; and the Civil Rights Act of 1968, which included several provisions to ensure fair housing practices.

African Americans were not alone, though, in seeking redress of conditions they considered illegal and unjust. The American Indian Movement (AIM) tried to focus the nation's attention on treaty violations. Founded in 1968 in Minneapolis, Minnesota, the organization pushed for stronger self-governing on Indian lands and for the U.S. government to uphold treaty agreements. To dramatize their demands, members of the organization and supporters temporarily occupied Alcatraz Island, site of the famous former prison, in 1969. A Sioux treaty, they claimed, required that unused federal land revert to Indian ownership.

On the whole, the American Indian civil rights efforts were much smaller in scope than efforts waged by African Americans. The federal government, however, did enact the American Indian Civil Rights Act of 1968 in an attempt to ensure that Native Americans living under tribal governments possessed the same civil right protections enjoyed by other Americans.

THE FEMINIST MOVEMENT

Gender joined race as a focus of civil rights struggle as women increasingly concluded that a variety of forces had kept them from realizing their potential. The resulting growth in the feminist movement brought about major changes in American society.

Betty Friedan, a graduate of Smith College and a middle-class housewife, felt in the 1950s that despite her marriage, children, and comfortable home, she missed something in life. Wondering whether other women had similar feelings, she mailed a questionnaire to other Smith graduates. The results of her survey and additional research convinced her that the root of the problem was in the feminine mystique, that is, the generally accepted view of the ideal woman as a person defined by marriage and motherhood. The result was her book *The Feminine Mystique* (1963), which argued that women lose their self-identity within such a definition and stop growing intellectually and emotionally.

Friedan's book propelled her into the forefront of the feminist movement. In 1966, she and other women formed the National Organization for Women (NOW). Friedan served as its initial president. Chapters rapidly formed throughout the country and advocated for changes in a number of common practices, such as help-wanted ads that stipulated hiring men only and airlines firing stewardesses (later called flight attendants) if they married or reached the age of 32. NOW published a bill of rights for women, argued for a woman's right to decide whether to have an abortion, and pushed the concept of equal pay for equal work regardless of gender.

Many significant changes occurred during the 1960s, at least partly in response to the feminist movement. Title VII of the 1964 Civil Rights Act outlawed sex discrimination in businesses that employed 25 or more people, the Equal Employment Opportunity Commission (EEOC) banned males-only (and females-only) advertisements in newspapers, women were permitted to rise in the military beyond the rank of colonel, laws against abortion began to ease, and the word "sexism" moved permanently into the English lexicon to denote a pattern of ingrained discrimination against women.

During the 1960s, women's career paths became more varied, with expanding opportunities in business and the military, although pay disparities on the basis of gender remained. The federal government attempted to address the problem by passing the Equal Pay Act in 1963.

The popular media continued to portray women in traditional roles, as in television series such as *The Adventures of Ozzie and Harriet* and *Leave It to Beaver*. Readers of such popular women's magazines as *McCall's* and *Ladies' Home Journal* would have seen little evidence of a feminist movement. Nonetheless, changes took place, and not only in the workplace. Women furthered their education in greater numbers, with bachelor's degrees conferred on women increasing between 1960 and 1970 from about 136,000 to 343,000, and master's degrees rising from approximately 26,000 to 83,000, laying the groundwork for subsequent gains by women.[2]

CRIME

Despite general prosperity and improvement in the quality of life, not all was well in the United States during the 1960s. In addition to conflict over civil rights and feminism, crime and war negatively impacted society at home and abroad.

The Kitty Genovese case symbolized a growing impersonality of modern urban society to many Americans. In the early morning of March 13, 1964, Kitty Genovese was attacked and murdered outside her New York City apartment building. Her calls for help lasted for 35 minutes and were ignored by other residents. The incident struck Americans as indicative of a society that had turned away from the concept of neighbors helping neighbors to a world in which individuals lived in fear and isolation, neither responding to others' troubles nor able to expect assistance for their own.

Increasingly, Americans, especially the elderly and those living alone in large cities, had come to view their apartments or houses as something akin to forts. Multiple door locks, window locks, and drawn window shades replaced open windows and evenings spent sitting on the front porch. The Genovese murder alerted Americans to the isolation in which many people lived and prompted a greater commitment to interacting with neighbors.

The decade also witnessed a number of horrific serial and mass killings that engendered widespread fear throughout the country. Albert DeSalvo, known as the "Boston Strangler," raped and killed 13 women from 1962 to 1964 in eastern Massachusetts. The crimes received national media coverage; DeSalvo was convicted only of robbery and rape, not of murder, and it remains questionable whether he committed the murders. In 1966, Charles Whitman murdered his mother and wife and then climbed to the top of a clock tower at the University of Texas in Austin. From his perch there he killed 13 more and wounded 31 before being shot to death by police.

In 1969, Americans were shocked by the brutal and bizarre murders carried out by Charles Manson and his followers in California, the victims including actress Sharon Tate, the pregnant wife of film director Roman Polanski. Fortunately, the murderers were apprehended and sentenced to prison terms before they could continue their attacks. The horrific nature of these crimes, the fact that they occurred across the United States, and the massive media attention given them ended for millions of Americans the feeling that "it couldn't happen here."

Amid the public perception that criminal violence threatened the safety of average Americans, the Supreme Court issued a controversial decision affirming the rights of the accused, specifically the right against self-incrimination. Their decision stemmed from the case of Ernesto Miranda, a 23-three-year-old man arrested on suspicion of kidnapping and rape. After two hours of questioning by police, Miranda confessed and ultimately was convicted. He appealed the verdict all the way to the Supreme Court, which ruled that the rights to remain silent and have an attorney present during questioning were fundamental to preserving the Fifth Amendment protection against self-incrimination. The decision was by a five-to-four majority vote of the Court. Henceforth, police were obliged to "Mirandize" a suspect before questioning. That is, they had to inform the individual of his or her basic rights to remain silent, have an attorney present, and be provided with an attorney if he or she could not afford one, along with the caution that anything the suspect said may be used against him or her in court. This Miranda warning became well known to most Americans through police shows on television. Meanwhile, many Americans felt that the warnings went too far in protecting criminals rather than victims of crimes.

Statistics seemed to support the impression that Americans were more in danger of criminal violence during the 1960s than they had been in the past. The rate of violent crimes, in fact, grew sharply. From 1960 to 1970, rates of aggravated assault, rape, and murder or manslaughter nearly doubled to 163, 19, and 8 per 100,000 people. In addition, the rate for robberies increased from 60 to 171.[3]

Crime was increasingly perceived by Americans not only as actions by individuals or small groups of people against isolated victims and businesses, but as an evil embedded in the fabric of society. The extent to which organized crime had become rooted in the United States became visible to Americans when Joe Valachi, a member of the Genovese crime family, testified before a Senate committee. He described how the Mafia, also known as the Cosa Nostra, was organized in crime families throughout the country and carried out its gambling, extortion, and other illegal activities through legitimate companies and with the assistance of corrupt politicians and government figures.

Americans, though, felt much more frightened of street crime and random violence than of organized crime, which remained largely hidden to most Americans. The rise in crime and random violence in many ways mirrored what they witnessed on the nightly news, increasingly in films, and on television.

WAR IN SOUTHEAST ASIA

At the beginning of the 1960s, fewer than 800 U.S. military personnel operated in Vietnam.[4] Military advisors, most famously the Special Forces (popularly known as the Green Berets), counseled the Vietnamese in a variety of areas, from military strategy to methods of improving the country's agriculture, health care, and finances. Americans also trained Vietnamese military and instructed them in communications, intelligence gathering, and use of weapons. They believed that these efforts would enable South Vietnam to develop the ability to retain its independence from communist North Vietnam. The other countries in the former Indochina, Laos, and Cambodia, also faced communist threats.

At the time of President Kennedy's assassination, the number of American military in Vietnam jumped to 16,000. However, civil unrest in South Vietnam began to make the evening news back home in the United States. Although Americans were horrified by some of the scenes they viewed on television, most still largely supported the war effort, which they believed would contain the spread of communism. Supporting their president and nation in time of war was

During the Vietnam War, an Army chemical warfare specialist emerges from checking a Viet Cong tunnel, 1966. Prints & Photographs Division, Library of Congress.

the traditionally patriotic approach, and that remained the case through the middle of the decade. Thus, there was little opposition to President Lyndon Johnson's appeal for congressional support in early August of 1964 when two American destroyers apparently came under attack by North Vietnamese torpedo boats in the Gulf of Tonkin. The U.S. Congress, with just two senators in opposition, passed the Tonkin Gulf Resolution on August 7. The resolution granted President Johnson the authority to "take all necessary measures to repel an armed attack against the forces of the United States and to prevent further aggression." The open-ended wording permitted Johnson to carry out an undeclared war largely as he saw fit.

Between 1964 and 1968, the United States moved from an advisory role to spearheading the military action against North Vietnam and the guerrilla forces in the South known as the Viet Cong. As 1968 began, close to half a million U.S. military personnel were in Vietnam, and over 16,000 Americans had been killed in the conflict. The Viet Cong proclaimed a cease-fire in conjunction with the annual three-day Vietnamese holiday known as Tet, scheduled to begin on January 30; however, they instead infiltrated cities and towns across South Vietnam and launched waves of attacks. North Vietnamese units joined the Tet Offensive in selected cities. Viet Cong even entered the U.S. Embassy compound in Saigon.

The communist assaults were repelled, in some cases with great loss of American lives, and the Viet Cong as a coherent military force was largely destroyed. Although a military defeat for the communist forces, the Tet Offensive proved a psychological and public relations victory for them. Millions of Americans concluded that American forces were unable to secure even the largest cities of South Vietnam. Images like the one by AP photographer Eddie Adams of General Nguyen Ngoc Loan executing a Viet Cong suspect with a pistol shot point-blank at his head further aroused opposition to the war. Many people questioned whether the Vietnamese government deserved the American support.

President Richard Nixon responded to the growing loss of public support for American involvement by beginning a process of demilitarization, gradually turning over primary responsibility for carrying out combat actions to the South Vietnamese. This policy increased scrutiny on the administration's policies and actually led to greater protest by antiwar demonstrators, particularly on America's college campuses.

In 1969, Americans at home learned that U.S. soldiers had massacred large numbers of Vietnamese civilians at a village called My Lai the previous year. Estimates of the number of victims ranged from 200 to 500. While large numbers of Americans were angered by the incident at My Lai, they also were greatly disturbed by rising death tolls. In the spring of 1969, the number of U.S. military personnel in Vietnam peaked at close to 550,000. Nixon's Vietnamization plan reduced that total to about 475,000 by the end of the year, at which point over 40,000 Americans had been killed in the conflict.

Attitudes toward patriotism and supporting the nation in wartime changed. The demand to end the war grew as a more critical attitude spread among Americans of all ages. Many felt that they should not blindly support American foreign policy. The soldier, traditionally a hero, fell in stature. Many Americans blamed all soldiers for what some had done, while others associated soldiers with drugs. For the first time in American history, returning veterans were often

The peace symbol. Courtesy of Shutterstock.

THE PEACE SYMBOL

The "peace symbol," as it is known in the United States, is one of the most widely recognized symbols in the world. The design is credited to British artist Gerald Holtom, a member of the Campaign for Nuclear Disarmament (CND), who combined graphic representations of the semaphore signals for the letters "N" and "D," to stand for nuclear disarmament. The symbol emerged in 1958 and was used by the CND in marches and demonstrations. The person often credited with making the CND logo part of the U.S. anti-war movement is Bayard Rustin, a friend and associate of Martin Luther King Jr. Rustin brought the symbol to the United States, where he took part in civil rights demonstrations. The "peace symbol," as it soon came to be known, was co-opted by the American counterculture in the late 1960s, and was co-opted as a symbol for the anti-violence and anti-war movements. Some soon came to hate the symbol for its association with 60s youth culture and dissent. Members of the American armed forces sometimes called it the "footprint of the great American chicken." Because the symbol was never copyrighted, it has often been used by designers and commercial artists for commercial gain. While the idea of turning a symbol of political action into a simple designer pattern may have angered some in the anti-war movement, it is symbolic of a pervasive phenomenon in American consumer culture—that any idea, even "peace," may be used to turn a profit.

treated poorly by the civilian population. Many Vietnam veterans found it difficult to find a job because employers were concerned about drug use, worried about veterans' emotional stability, or simply transferred feelings about the war to the returning soldiers.

THE CUBAN MISSILE CRISIS

Shortly after taking office in 1961, President Kennedy was faced with a plan developed by the Eisenhower administration for overthrowing Cuban dictator Fidel Castro. Kennedy approved the plan and on April 17, 1961, an invasion force of Cuban exiles went ashore at the Bay of Pigs. Quickly defeated, the invasion marked an embarrassing beginning in foreign affairs for the new president.

In the aftermath of the Bay of Pigs incident, President Kennedy urged Americans to take steps to protect themselves in case of attack, and encouraged them to construct fallout shelters. Many companies offered underground shelters ranging from simple concrete block constructions to elaborate facilities that could comfortably house a whole family behind termite-proof walls and twelve-gauge corrugated metal doors. Top-of-the-line shelters included not only furniture and appliances but pool tables, wine cellars, and other conveniences of home. While waiting to put

their shelters into official use during an atomic war, many families used the rooms as recreation rooms or children's playhouses.

By October 1962, Cuba was even more on the minds of Americans as a nuclear war with the Soviet Union seemed a distinct possibility. Premier Nikita Khrushchev of the Soviet Union deployed two dozen nuclear-armed ballistic missiles in Cuba. On October 22, 1962, President Kennedy announced a quarantine of the island, with American ships ready to confront any vessels carrying offensive weapons.

With Soviet ships en route to Cuba and a confrontation looming, Americans feared nuclear war. Many individuals prayed, churches held prayer services, and families stockpiled food and supplies. While the Kennedy Administration sought a solution during the agonizing six-day period, citizens prepared for war. Finally, Khrushchev agreed to dismantle the missiles. The United States gave a collective sigh of relief, having perhaps come closer to a nuclear war than at any other time in its history.

THE FAMILY, RELIGION, AND VALUES

The 1960s witnessed intense upheaval in many areas that had been stable for most of the nation's history. The various issues involving the Vietnam

War and the rights of women and minorities, the political turmoil of the 1968 presidential election, changing sexual standards, increased drug use, and radically different styles in clothes, put great strain not only on the country as a whole but also on individual families.

Moral and religious issues, played out in a variety of behavioral patterns, were often at the heart of family conflicts. Sexual freedom, including pre-marital sex, multiple sexual relationships, and unmarried couples living together, proved difficult for many parents to tolerate, let alone accept. Drug use also caused a great deal of family dissension.

Established religion lost much of its hold on young people in the 1960s. Those who did search for spiritual insights often traveled unconventional paths, such as into drugs and religious cults. In addition, church institutions and worshippers sought to bring about fundamental changes in organized religions. Religions began to view themselves as more closely linked to this life, and sharp divisions between clergy and laity weakened.

Roman Catholics watched the deliberations of the Second Vatican Council called by Pope John XXIII in 1962. By the time the council concluded its deliberations in 1965, there was a new pope, Paul VI, and the Catholic Church would never be the same. Lay people began to play a greater role in the church, the traditional practice of going to confession declined, the altar was turned around so that the priest faced parishioners, and Catholics were able to eat meat on non-Lenten Fridays. One of the most difficult issues for Catholics in the 1960s involved birth control. Although the Catholic Church continued to prohibit artificial means of birth control, including condoms and the pill, many Catholic women of childbearing age chose to practice birth control during at least part of their married lives.

Many Protestant groups also modernized. They were less inclined to interpret the Bible literally, more inclined to engage in ecumenical functions with Catholics, and grew interested in the Social Gospel, focusing on the poor and those deprived of basic human rights. African American churches particularly stood at the forefront of the Civil Rights Movement, with some of the most famous clergymen of the decade, such as Martin Luther King Jr., coming from the Southern Baptist tradition. Many churches in the Catholic and Protestant traditions began to offer social services to the poor in their communities, providing food and clothes for those in need.

Jewish Americans also became more involved in modern movements, especially Civil Rights. The Six-Day War between Israel and some of its primarily Moslem neighbors boosted Jewish Americans' sense of Jewish identity.

Social consciousness kept some young people involved in the established religions, but many older Americans sharply disagreed with the modernizing trends and what they saw as a shift from spiritual to political and social concerns.

With so many changes in American society, many families found it increasingly difficult to function as they had before. Children and parents found themselves disagreeing over many areas of everyday life. Even when family members were not at odds, they were apt to go their separate ways much of the time because mothers were more likely to work outside the home, multiple cars allowed children to drive to school or play, and fathers often worked a greater distance from home.

Advertising

of the 1960s

Several social and technological changes, along with a new advertising philosophy, came together to make the 1960s a golden age in advertising, ultimately changing advertising forever. Teenagers and young adults increasingly turned away from their parents' generation in many ways, including political, moral, and sexual attitudes. They adopted new clothing styles, hairstyles, and new fashions. They prided themselves on being anti-consumer, but that attitude was more wishful thinking than reality. Advertisers built their marketing strategies on the younger generation's desire for change.

At the same time, major developments in technology made it possible to market products more effectively. In 1950, fewer than four million households in the United States had televisions. By the middle of the 1960s, the total had risen to over 50 million,[1] and by the middle of the decade, color television replaced black and white programming.

The maturation of the 35-millimeter single-lens camera permitted photographers to do location shooting more easily and cheaply than before, freeing them from studio settings. Polaroid cameras allowed photographers to run quick lighting checks. Television crews had more mobile equipment, including hand-held cameras, to permit more flexibility in selecting locations.

As the 1960s opened, most advertising agencies still retained their old in-house structural division between art directors and copywriters, but by the end of the decade, the two groups worked together as a creative team.

THE NEW MARKETS

Advertisers in the 1960s inherited a largely conservative consumer public. Most American buyers tended to consider their purchases carefully. Older buyers especially, their financial conservatism grounded in the Great Depression, required serious demonstration of need to purchase a particular object. They were likely to stay with brands and styles, although automobile manufacturers had made inroads in changing the way consumers viewed new products. Men were especially conservative in clothing and usually wore their clothes until they actually wore out. Young parents inherited children's clothes from relatives and friends and often passed the clothes on to other children. This approach to buying did not make for a dynamic world of consumers, and it tended toward conformity.

Then along came the new, young generation of the 1960s. At the beginning of the decade almost one-half of Americans were 25 or younger, and the trend toward a youthful population continued.[2]

ADVERTISING SLOGANS OF THE 1960S

"You can trust your car to the man who wears the star," Texaco, 1962*

"Fly the friendly skies," United Airlines, 1965

"How about a nice Hawaiian Punch?," Hawaiian Punch, 1962

"Ring around the collar," Wisk detergent, 1968*

"Let Hertz put you in the driver's seat," Hertz, 1961*

"Who's that behind those Foster Grants?" Foster Grant, 1965*

"We try harder," Avis car rental, 1963*

"The Pepsi generation," Pepsi-Cola, 1964*

"Please don't squeeze the Charmin," Charmin, 1964*

"Mama Mia! That's a spicy meatball!" "Plop, plop, fizz, fizz, oh, what a relief it is;" "I can't believe I ate the whole thing;" and "Try it, you'll like it," Alka-Seltzer, 1960s; 1970s*

"You've come a long way, baby," Virginia Slims cigarettes, 1968

"Nothin' says lovin' like bakin' in the oven," Pillsbury, 1965

"Things go better with Coke," Coca-Cola, 1963

"Cuckoo for Cocoa Puff," Cocoa Puffs, early 1960s

"Two Scoops of Raisins," Kellogg's Raisin Bran cereal, late 1960s

"Weiner Song," Oscar Meyer, 1963

"Betcha can't eat just one," Lay's Potato Chips, early 1960s

"You can trust your car to the man who wears the star," 1962

"Let your fingers do the walking," AT&T Yellow Pages, early 1960s

"The Great American Chocolate Bar," Hershey's, 1969

"Uh-oh, SpaghettiO's," SpaghettiOs, 1965

---

*Among *Advertising Age's* 100 Best Ads of 20th Century. http://adage.com/century/.

In addition, America's young were also changing in attitude, rejecting many social, moral, and political beliefs of their parents' generation. The younger generation felt that advertising was essentially fraudulent and manipulative. The mass conformity of society, in their view, resulted from both manipulation and intellectual stagnation. The young saw themselves as anti-consumer and anti-advertising.

Feeling a need to rebel against what they saw as a restrictive set of social norms, and determined to assert their individuality, millions of young Americans turned to new styles in clothing, eating, and entertainment. Change became good, static conformity bad. The young turned toward the new and then the newer. The advertising world dubbed the young of the 1960s "The Now Generation."

Advertisers and manufacturers recognized the Now Generation as a major consumer market. The "throwaway" world came with them, from disposable diapers to clothes discarded because they were out of style. To appeal to the young, agencies took out ads in underground newspapers and magazines. They introduced psychedelic graphics and used long-haired models in hip clothing. Rock music provided background to commercials that attempted to make consumer goods more interesting. While fostering this new consumerism, advertisers offered their products as anti-consumer, antiestablishment, and anticonformity. "New and improved" became an omnipresent slogan.

Advertisements by the J. Walter Thompson agency proclaimed 7-Up the "Uncola" and trumpeted the drink amid psychedelic butterflies and sunrises, even describing it as "Wet and Wild" to appeal to the sexual revolution. Pontiac ads imitated the film Bonnie and Clyde; young men and women dressed like the famous outlaws emerged from a bank robbery and made their escape in a 1930s Packard that they quickly exchanged for a new Pontiac Firebird convertible.

The concepts "young," "counterculture," and "creative" became virtually synonymous within advertising agencies in the 1960s. To be creative was to think young. To think young was to identify with the young counterculture. By the mid-1960s, advertisers were aiming a youthful image more at older generations than the young themselves.

After all, those who weren't young could act and think young by buying the right car, wearing the right clothing styles, cooking in the right oven, buying the right anything. Advertisers understood the reality that despite the huge population of young Americans, most of the money was still in the adults' pocketbooks.

Hip advertising appeared regularly in such mainstream magazines as *Life, Look,* and even *Ladies Home Journal.* Cars were an obvious way to appeal to people's desire to act and think young. Batten, Barton, Durstine, and Osborn (BBDO) invited drivers to catch "Dodge Fever." The Oldsmobile was billed as the "Youngmobile;" in commercials, buyers were summoned to the music of guitars and tambourines and the invitation to "escape from the ordinary." The transforming power of the Ford Mustang was much heralded; it was the car that could turn humdrum citizens into exciting men and women of the world.

Men and women were told in advertisements and commercials for almost every conceivable type of product to think young and reject the blandishments of mass consumer society. Collectors of S&H Green Stamps were assured that "with this little square you swing." Booth's House of Lords gin was the "nonconformist gin." Tareyton smokers were so determined to assert their individuality that they "would rather fight than switch." Consumers were assured that they were ignoring "the ad man" when they purchased a Fisher stereo.

Advertising to Women and Minorities

Despite the advertising agencies' infatuation with counterculture, the women's liberation movement, or "feminism" as it was commonly called in the 1960s, was not part of marketing strategy until the end of the decade. Then agencies began to target the new woman, often with decidedly traditional products in mind. For example, J. Walter Thompson had its client Pond change the color of its hand lotion from traditional white to pink, and its wearers were shown in such nontraditional feminine activities as applying a blowtorch to a sculpture or working on a motorcycle.

Another product marketed to liberated women was the Virginia Slims extra-long cigarette manufactured by Philip Morris. The long, slim cigarette was featured in Leo Burnett advertisements and commercials with trim, beautiful women stylishly attired. "You've come a long way, baby, to get where you've got to today," women were told when the Virginia Slims brand was introduced in 1968. Presumably, the long way toward liberation included smoking long cigarettes while remaining essentially sex objects.

Also in the 1960s African Americans began to be recognized as important consumers. Although idealism regarding equal rights played a role in some marketing strategies, the primary reason for targeting African Americans was expressed in the title of the book *The $30 Billion Negro,* published in 1969. The African American author, D. Parke Gibson, who ran an advertising firm, made a compelling case for bringing African Americans into the marketing equation. Gibson pointed out that during the late 1960s, African Americans, then still often referred to as Negroes, were spending over $30 billion on goods and services.[3] The African American community consisted of six million families. Approximately 40 percent of these families owned their own homes, over 50 percent owned at least one car, and 75 percent of African American households had one or more television sets. African Americans made up 11 percent of the total U.S. population and 92 percent of the nonwhite U.S. population. Further, nonwhites constituted approximately 75 percent of the global population, so a changed attitude toward attracting nonwhite consumers at home promised the possibility of even larger markets abroad.

Initially, most advertising to African American consumers occurred in black publications and on black-audience radio stations. *Ebony* magazine was the favorite with advertisers attempting to reach the best educated and most affluent members of the population. The news weekly *Jet,* a homemaker's magazine called *Tan,* and *Negro Digest* provided avenues for advertising, as did *Tuesday,* a monthly magazine supplement for largely white-oriented Sunday newspapers and other publications.

Advertisements in these African American outlets involved many of the same products and marketing themes found in ads placed in white markets. The major difference lay in use of African American models. Clairol, for example, continued

promoting hair coloring with its famous line—
"Does she…or doesn't she?" This provocative
question was quickly followed-up with, "Hair
Color so natural only her hairdresser knows for
sure!" Not surprisingly, the other famous question
in Clairol ads, "Is it true blondes have more fun?"
was dropped in black-oriented advertising.

Pepsi-Cola was losing a lot of African American consumers to Coca-Cola in the early 1960s.
The company hired Harvey C. Russell as vice
president for special markets in 1962. At that time,
Russell was the highest-ranking African American executive in a major U.S. business firm. New
marketing strategies for the African American
consumer followed. Pepsi advertisements, for example, were among the first to feature a woman
with an Afro hairstyle. Recognizing that African
Americans averaged 10 years younger than the
national population, Pepsi increased its sales by
emphasizing the theme it also used nationally:
"Now It's Pepsi—for Those Who Think Young."

Reflecting some advertising courage, Greyhound took the image of the bus, a symbol of
segregation in the South, and tried to make it an
instrument for integration. Rosa Parks had refused
to move to the back of a bus, setting in motion a
major component of the Civil Rights Movement.
(See Overview of the 1950s.) "Freedom Riders"
rode buses south to take up the cause of racial
justice. Then, in the 1960s, Greyhound Lines embarked on a minority hiring plan, bringing in African Americans including a high-ranking sales
executive, salespeople, and drivers. The former
Brooklyn Dodgers pitcher, Joe Black, one of the
first African Americans to play major league baseball, signed on as a vice president and special markets representative. By 1964, African American
drivers were operating buses in the South. Meanwhile, Greyhound was also a pioneer in integrated
advertising in both white and black publications,
with ads showing black and white passengers
being welcomed aboard by a black driver.

Some companies advertised their products in
campaigns that used African American history,
an important effort at a time when most schoolchildren, black and white, knew little if anything
about the important historical contributions of
black Americans. Among the companies and campaigns were American Oil's *American Traveler's*

Guide to Negro History, National Distillers' (maker
of Old Taylor whiskey) *Ingenious Americans,*
Pepsi-Cola's *Adventures in Negro History,* and
Scott Paper's *Distaff to History.* The Scott Paper
Company booklet featured important African
American women and proved so popular that it
was serialized in newspapers. The Pepsi materials
were adopted by more than 500 school systems.
All of these Negro History programs were widely
disseminated.

THE CREW CUT CROWD AND OTHER ADVERTISING PHENOMENA

Advertisers used hip attitudes and details of
style to market a think-and-act-young mentality
to not only the young but to more affluent older
Americans. Most advertisers tended to ignore
the large number of young people who didn't
buy into the counterculture, but there were some
exceptions.

When Young and Rubicam took on the Peace
Corps as a client in the late 1960s, the agency essentially advertised against the counterculture.
One commercial for the Peace Corps used the
song "Age of Aquarius" from the musical *Hair*
and an image of a disembodied head of a long-
haired man in the stars. The voiceover stated,
"it's one thing to predict the future; it's another to
help make it." The point was that the Peace Corps
solved real problems in the real world. A radio ad
in 1968 featured a mother urging her son to act
like everyone else and get out and demonstrate.
"Anybody that would join the Peace Corps," she
warned her son, "is a troublemaker." The ad
turned the counterculture opposition to mass
conformity on its head, and implied that the real
individual was the young man or woman who
joined the Peace Corps.

David Ogilvy ran a major, and certainly unique,
advertising agency in the 1960s. He paid close attention to market research and rejected humor
in his commercials and ads, claiming that no one
wanted to buy products from a clown. In his own
individualistic way he produced a number of creative and effective efforts. One of Ogilvy's most
famous print advertisements was for Rolls Royce.
A photograph of the automobile took up the top
half of the page, and a lot of text detailing the

many advantages of a Rolls Royce the bottom. The most memorable portion of the ad, though, was the quotation right below the picture: "At 60 miles an hour the loudest noise in this new Rolls-Royce comes from the electric clock."

Research remained important during the 1960s, although industry increasingly came to agree with Bill Bernbach that good research, while helpful, was less important than creativity. There were some new directions in research. The old determiners of potential buyers were demographics, social class, and psychological characteristics. To this mix were added lifestyle patterns relating to attitudes, feelings, work habits, and leisure activities.

Products had been marketed to children for decades, but in the 1960s researchers took a closer look at how to approach children, sometimes at the behest of advertising agencies and in other cases to warn against misleading children (and their parents) into unwise purchases. Strong protests against advertising directed toward children began in the second half of the decade.

Researchers found that the children most susceptible to advertising were below thirteen years of age; teens had learned that products in advertisements and commercials often turned out to be different in real life. Advertisers learned that effective approaches included depicting children wanting specific toys or specific brands rather than generalized products. Children responded more strongly to moving pictures than still pictures, and to action verbs rather than nouns. Making acquisition of a particular toy or other desirable product contingent on purchasing a product (which might include, for example, a required coupon) continued to be common. An image of a child enjoying a product was another successful advertising gambit.

Also during the 1960s, advertisers came under legal scrutiny for misleading advertising. One of the most prominent cases involved Colgate's Rapid Shave. A television commercial showed Rapid Shave making it easy to shave the sand from sandpaper. It turned out that instead of sandpaper, the commercial had used a sheet of Plexiglas with loose sand on it. The sand pulled easily down the sheet of Plexiglas, leaving a bare swath. The Federal Trade Commission ruled the commercial misleading and issued a cease-and-desist order on December 29, 1961. Bates and Colgate strongly contested the ruling, claiming that it would preclude all substitute materials in advertising. After several lower court rulings, the U.S. Supreme Court ruled in support of the FTC on April 6, 1965.

SUPERSTARS OF ADVERTISING: BILL BERNBACH AND MARY WELLS

William Bernbach (1911–1982) and Mary Wells (1928–)were the two most important members of the advertising world during the 1960s. Bernbach, co-founder of Doyle Dane Bernbach, may well have been the most important advertising executive in the industry's history.

Bernbach was born in 1911 in New York City and attended New York University. He was working in the mailroom of Schenley Distillers when

Working on a layout in his office, Bill Bernbach, legendary co-founder of Doyle Dane Bernbach. © Bettmann/CORBIS.

he submitted an advertisement to the company's advertising department. The ad was eventually used in *The New York Times,* although the identity of its creator wasn't known at the time. Bernbach claimed authorship and was rewarded with a salary raise and a transfer to the advertising department.

After serving in the army during World War II, Bernbach joined Grey Advertising and eventually became creative director. Grey was one of the more creative and flexible of the large advertising agencies; for example, Grey broke with most of its competitors by hiring Italians, Jews, and other religious and ethnic minorities. In this relatively open environment, Bernbach cultivated his then radical advertising philosophy, arguing that making a persuasive ad was more art than science.

In 1949, Bernbach joined with Maxwell Dane and Ned Doyle to form Doyle Dane Bernbach (DDB), with Bernbach as president. He implemented changes that soon spread throughout the industry, including the consolidation of the art and copywriting functions into one department. At Doyle Dane Bernbach, a creative team worked together to create an advertisement in which text and visuals complemented each other. Writers and artists became the powers within advertising, with corresponding increases in their salaries. The account executive was no longer chief decision-maker, and marketing research and media analysis became secondary to creativity.

Doyle Dane Bernbach hit it big with its first account, which was for a bargain department store named Ohrbach's. DDB transformed Ohrbach's image into that of a sophisticated store, significantly improving both its clientele and its revenue. Then came Volkswagen and Avis, two of DDB's most famous accounts. The resulting advertising campaigns were enormously successful and securely established the firm's reputation.

In addition, DDB created political ads on behalf of the Lyndon Johnson presidential campaign of 1964. In one of the most famous political ads in history, a young girl plucks petals from a flower while counting from one to nine. Then a male voice counts backward as the camera closes on the child's right eye, which yields to a picture of a nuclear explosion. The final voiceover warns voters to "Vote for President Johnson on

Advertisement in the very successful campaign created by Doyle Dane Bernbach, "You Don't Have to Be Jewish to Love Levy's," shows comedian Godfrey Cambridge with a sandwich made with Levy's Jewish rye bread. Others in the series included a Native American man and an Asian boy. Prints & Photographs Division, Library of Congress.

November third. The stakes are too high for you to stay home." Although it never mentioned Republican candidate Barry Goldwater by name, the ad powerfully reinforced the sense many held that Goldwater was trigger-happy and might lead the United States into a nuclear war.

One DDB copywriter in the Hall of Fame is Mary Wells, probably the second most important advertising figure of the 1960s. Wells, after serving as fashion advertising manager for Macy's department store, joined the McCann-Erickson advertising agency in 1953. In 1956, she joined Doyle Dane Bernbach, eventually becoming copy chief and a vice president. In 1964, she moved to Jack Tinker and Partners, where she teamed with artist Stewart Greene and copywriter Richard Rich to develop award-winning television commercials that made effective use of humor, a Wells trademark. Major accounts for Wells at Tinker and Partners included Alka-Seltzer and Braniff Airlines. The Alka-Seltzer commercials established another important creative relationship for Wells, with the director Howard Zieff.

Wells, Rich, and Greene formed their own agency in 1966, with Wells as president, and the new firm, Wells, Rich, Greene, Inc. (WRG), helped define advertising for the rest of the decade and beyond. As DDB had done earlier, WRG made creative use of self-putdowns for clients' products. Advertisements for Alka-Seltzer included the famous line "I Can't Believe I Ate the Whole Thing." Wells again worked with Howard Zieff, a widely acclaimed director of commercials in the 1960s. Zieff also directed WRG's memorable "Driving School" commercial for American Motors, in which the driving instructor encountered one disastrous student after another, and the "Little Italy" spot for American Motors that starred a young Robert DeNiro.

Architecture

of the 1960s

The 1960s featured enormous variety in architecture, with no single theme or set of principles dominating. As the decade opened, the major influences on architecture were older architects, and as the decade ended there were increasing attempts to incorporate classic architecture into modern buildings and to preserve the great buildings of America's past.

Three giants from earlier decades still held sway over much of architectural thought as the 1960s opened—Frank Lloyd Wright, Walter Gropius, and Le Corbusier (Charles–Édouard Jeanneret)—although Wright had died in 1959, Le Corbusier would die in 1965, and Gropius would die in 1969. Wright followed an organic approach, which reflected his belief that a building should rise out of its environment and remain part of it. Gropius helped to establish the International Style, which featured industrial designs and a focus on the building's purpose and later served on the Harvard University faculty. Le Corbusier, like Gropius, took a "modern" approach to architecture, and thought of buildings as machines that consisted of an interplay of geometric forms. Le Corbusier sought to define buildings as strictly human constructions separate from the natural world.

Mies van der Rohe and Philip Johnson continued the modern international style, the former especially influential because of his position as director of the Illinois Institute of Technology, as well as designer of several of the school's buildings. Mies's architectural style descended directly from Gropius and had considerable influence on Johnson's early career. Other important architects in the 1960s included Richard Neutra, whose efforts to integrate houses into their natural environment, especially in California, echoed Wright's philosophy, and Utzon Saarinen, whose TWA terminal at New York's Kennedy Airport seemed to many viewers to resemble a bird ready to take flight.

Much was happening in the 1960s. Urban renewal raised issues of fair housing for the poor. Changes in transportation, roads, and inner cities shifted increasing numbers of people into suburbs, and businesses followed. Shopping centers grew in numbers and diversified in form. With prosperity widespread, but hardly universal in the 1960s, additional office space was required. Renewed emphases on educational opportunity and the arts led to new schools and museums. The Second Vatican Council changed the way Catholics worshipped, and new types of churches that brought parishioners into closer contact with the celebrant were required.

LEADING FIGURES OF AMERICAN ARCHITECTURE

Louis Kahn and Robert Venturi were the two most important architects of the 1960s because of the buildings they created and how those buildings reflected their attitudes. Kahn expressed a serious social conscience and believed that architecture should speak to the people. Venturi put into practice his conviction that art should imitate life. His architectural designs embodied an array of ways in which everyday Americans lived, including strip malls, neon signs, and even trash cans.

Louis Kahn

Louis I. Kahn's (1901–1974) social consciousness, pluralism regarding architectural traditions, combination of theory and practice, and influence on younger architects reflected the spirit of the 1960s and helped shape architecture for the rest of the century. Kahn moved with his family from Estonia to the United States in 1905. He studied music and painting before earning a degree in architecture from the University of Pennsylvania, where he studied under Paul Cret, a Beaux-Arts classicist. (The Beaux-Arts, or Second Empire style, usually featured a square plan, classic detail, mansard roof, and considerable use of columns, among other characteristics.) Kahn later traveled in Europe, held a fellowship to the American Academy in Rome, and taught at Yale University and the University of Pennsylvania. Kahn's education and travels encouraged an openness to different styles and influences.

Much of Kahn's early work centered on improving public housing, and anticipated the concern in the 1960s for public housing that would more sensitively respect the occupants' individuality.

Kahn believed in spaces that followed a natural order of importance in a building. His view of a primal, or central, space ordering the surrounding spaces and offering limitless possibilities gave his architectural followers great freedom and fit the spirit of the 1960s.

Incorporating the traditional and contemporary into his work, Kahn felt that a building should reflect connections, including human connections inspired by the building. Light was a major interest for Kahn, who believed that humans gravitate toward light. Kahn also believed that architecture should come from the people and speak clearly to the people, an attitude that meshed well with the political and social "power to the people" movements of the 1960s. Kahn created one of his best known buildings, the Richards Medical Research Building, for the University of Pennsylvania. Completed in 1965, its towers seemed to recall the hill towns of Tuscany that Kahn had visited. He created a beautiful building which connections among its parts were clearly evident, but unfortunately he lost sight of the research functions to be performed there. That would not be the case with what is perhaps Kahn's masterpiece, the Salk Institute at La Jolla, California (1968).

Kahn worked with Jonas Salk, who developed an effective polio vaccine in the 1950s, to design a building complex that used structural originality and beauty to serve the research needs of scientists. The Institute recalled both Roman ruins and medieval monasteries. It included two rows of four-story towers that housed private studies for the researchers. Laboratories along the perimeter of the complex were linked by bridges and staircases to the towers. Between the rows of towers was a central canal with a small stream that flowed toward the Pacific Ocean, symbolizing humanity's infinite search for knowledge.

Robert Venturi

Robert Venturi (1925–) earned a B.A. degree and a M.F.A. at Princeton University. He studied under Jean Labatut, director of the graduate program in architecture at Princeton, who was inclined toward the Beaux-Arts style and encouraged wide study in art history and archaeology. Venturi spent the mid-1950s as a fellow at the American Academy in Rome, although unlike Kahn his interests were more in the Renaissance Mannerists than in classical Rome. Venturi later worked for Kahn as a junior designer in his firm and as a teaching assistant at the University of Pennsylvania.

Even more than Kahn, Venturi came to reject high-tech modernism and championed an inclusive, common-people focus in his architecture. He made extensive use of pop art in his designs and, more than any of his predecessors, welded mass culture to high culture. Art was for the people, so Venturi looked to see what the people were doing. What he saw included highway strips, housing subdivisions, billboards, neon signs, gas stations, fast-food restaurants, and shopping centers. All of this was the stuff of art for Venturi, and he incorporated it into his designs.

Venturi published a book entitled *Complexity and Contradiction in Architecture* in 1966, written with the assistance of Denise Scott Brown, a colleague at Pennsylvania who later became his wife. The book had an enormous impact, more even than his buildings, on the younger generation of architects and on architecture for the remainder of the century.

Espousing a wide-ranging inclusiveness, Venturi readily grasped the contradictions in modern life. No summary can equal his own words:

> Architects can no longer afford to be intimidated by the puritanically moral language of orthodox Modern architecture. I like elements which are hybrid rather than "pure," compromising rather than "clean," distorted rather than "straight-forward," ambiguous rather than "articulated," perverse as well as impersonal, boring as well as "interesting," conventional rather than "designed"....I include the non sequitur and proclaim the duality.
>
> I am for richness of meaning rather than clarity of meaning....I prefer "both-and" to "either-or"....A valid architecture evokes many levels of meaning and combinations of focus: its space and its elements become readable and workable in several ways at once.[1]

One of Venturi's best known buildings is the Guild House in Philadelphia (1963), an apartment building for elderly residents sponsored by the Society of Friends. Designed to resemble Philadelphia row houses, it borrows from several sources: a central arch from classical architecture, a large marquee sign reading "Guild House" imitative of pop art, double-hung windows borrowed from housing projects, a white-glazed brick facade on part of the front that echoes Renaissance palaces, and a fake antenna on top of the building to symbolize how the elderly spend much time watching television. The completed structure achieves a result Venturi desired in his buildings—an apparently common building at first sight, with complexities and contradictions in design continuing to appear the longer one looks.

A design for Copley Square in Boston shows Venturi's unorthodox use of space. Believing that Americans were uncomfortable with large, undefined space, Venturi defined the space by filling it. Keeping with his artistic acceptance of ordinary items from everyday life, he used not only trees, bushes, and benches, but trash cans, drains, and lampposts in his design.

STORES AND OFFICES

As Americans moved into the suburbs, urban businesses increasingly followed. Improved highways facilitated the relocation of stores, as suburbanites preferred the comfort and flexibility of cars to public transportation. The exodus of businesses from downtown areas left citizens who lacked the money to move with fewer purchasing options and therefore higher prices.

These changes translated into enormous growth in suburban shopping centers. Realtors and builders worked closely to construct both shopping centers and residential developments. As shopping centers proved profitable, architects were called on to create larger complexes to provide pleasant shopping experiences.

The strip shopping center was popular in the 1950s and 1960s, and returned to favor in the 1980s. A strip usually included a supermarket and a variety of other stores. Many strips were built along highways, with the consumer able to survey the entire range of stores. Parking was usually available in front or along the sides of the stores, and delivery trucks unloaded at the rear.

A second type of shopping center was the campus center, designed as a freestanding complex often out in the country. A true shopping center is not just a random collection of stores, but a group of stores designed and constructed together, often with shared management and marketing. A shopping center has at least one anchor, a major store that draws large numbers of consumers, along with smaller stores to encourage impulse shopping. The anchor for the strip was usually a supermarket, sometimes with a department store as a second anchor; the campus anchor more typically was a department store. The campus shopping center permitted overall planning and invited greater participation from architectural firms. It was one unit, much like a college campus, with green space and parking lots planned to add practical and aesthetic dimensions to the buildings themselves. One of the finest examples from the 1960s is Century City in Los Angeles (1964), which boasted two department stores as its anchors.

Shopping centers initially excluded stores that undermined the family atmosphere, such as liquor and secondhand establishments. Nor were recreational buildings, including movie houses and restaurants, part of these complexes. Before long, however, restaurants were added, and pizza parlors became particularly popular.

The primary problem with the campus center was that customers were subject to inclement weather as they moved from store to store. It was therefore inevitable that all of the stores within a shopping center would eventually be enclosed. Thus was born the mall.

The first enclosed shopping mall was Southdale Regional Shopping Center in Edina, outside Minneapolis, which opened in 1956. During the 1960s, the shopping mall began to assume its place as not only a place to shop, but also as a community recreational center and teen hangout. An early mall plan was the dumbbell design, with two large anchor stores at each end and smaller stores lining the aisle between them. The aisle had to be narrow enough for consumers to see window displays on both sides yet wide enough to avoid creating a sense of overcrowding.

Malls quickly grew, and more complex designs to accommodate additional anchors, more stores, two or more levels of shops, courtyards with plants and even trees, skylights, and escalators were introduced. Restaurants were added to encourage more malls to stay open longer. The Paramus Park Shopping Center in Paramus, New Jersey (1962), added a food court which featured a large seating area for an array of fast-food franchises. Theaters helped malls become day and night facilities, and the larger and more imaginative planners included other recreational opportunities, such as skating rinks.

The guru of shopping-center design was Victor Gruen, who designed Southdale. His *Shopping Towns U.S.A.: The Planning of Shopping Centers* (1960) became the bible of shopping-center planning and was followed in 1973 by his *Centers for the Urban Environment: Survival of the Cities.*

By the publication of Gruen's second book, city planners were trying to renew inner cities devastated by the exodus of businesses. A few shopping centers started to appear in city centers. San Francisco helped lead the way in restoring old buildings and transforming them into shopping centers that offered upscale fashion shops, crafts, and gourmet food. Ghirardelli Square, a block of industrial buildings along the north end waterfront in San Francisco, was redesigned (1964) into an inviting complex of shops and restaurants.

Many Americans left the cities to live and shop elsewhere, but continued to work in them. In fact, the need for office space grew dramatically during the 1960s, a need in part filled by looking upward. Skyscrapers had long been important symbols of American ambition and success; so while many new offices opened in suburban office parks, others appeared in new buildings downtown.

Technological advances, including new building materials and computer designing, permitted great variation and innovation in skyscraper design. Mies van der Rohe, the master of the glass curtain wall (which seemed to drop from the top down rather than bear structural weight) and champion of a minimalist approach, created skyscrapers such as the One Charles Center in Baltimore (1963) and Chicago's Federal Center (1964). With improvements in concrete, the curtain could convey a greater sense of solidity and make use of contrasts between light and shadow, as in New York City's Pan Am Building (1963) (later renamed MetLife).

Other architects chose to highlight the skeleton rather than the skin by bringing forward the steel structure in buildings like the John Hancock Center in Chicago, constructed during the late

RFK Stadium, built in Washington, D.C., in 1961 was typical of many sports stadiums built during the 1960s. AP Photo.

COOKIE-CUTTER STADIUMS

The so-called "cookie-cutter" stadium was a type of sports arena popularized in the 1960s and 1970s, that was designed to be used by multiple sports teams. The stadiums were circular in design, fully enclosed, and had seating and other elements that could be moved to accommodate different types of sports contests. The design trend started with Washington D.C.'s RFK Stadium, which was completed in 1961 and served both the Washington Redskins football team and the Washington Senators baseball team. Nearly identical stadiums were constructed in Saint Louis, Pittsburgh, Philadelphia, Cincinnati, and Atlanta, giving rise to the term "cookie cutter," a somewhat derisive term for the utilitarian trend. At the time of their construction, the multi-purpose stadiums were hailed for their modern, innovative design, though others objected to the trend, generally for aesthetic reasons. The main criticism was that the stadiums were unattractive and "drab" or "uninteresting." If the trend was unimaginative, it was certainly functional, as it allowed cities to maximize space. In the early 1990s, a wave of new sports complexes, outfitted with the latest innovations in television, stereo, and computer control systems, signaled the end of the cookie-cutter era. Though the cookie cutters were sometimes maligned in their heyday, a generation of Americans expressed a feeling of loss when the old stadiums were torn down. Whether from fear of the unknown or reverence for the past, the cookie cutters became symbolic of a bygone era in sports history.

1960s and completed in 1970 and designed by Fazlur Khan of the highly respected SOM team (Skidmore, Owings, Merrill). A system of diagonal braces created a kind of exoskeleton that helped reduce effect of the wind. At its completion, the 100-story Hancock Center was second in height only to the Empire State Building.

The concept of a tube within a tube became popular in tall buildings that went up in the late 1960s, including the John Hancock Center. A variety of refinements were employed, such as combining a central tube that enclosed elevator and utilities and an exterior tube that formed the outer walls, including tightly spaced columns, to distribute the structural load of the building (Brunswick Building, Chicago, SOM, 1965); bundling tubes together to gain support from common walls (Sears Tower, Chicago, SOM, 1974); and enclosing the surrounding sheer walls (the inner tube) with an outer tube of concrete columns and beams (One Shell Plaza, Houston, SOM, 1971).

HOMES

Although the ranch style home was prevalent in new developments and suburbs, many Americans continued to live in their older city homes and farm houses (or new but similar versions). These houses were constructed of traditional materials such as wood, brick, or stone, and contained familiar rooms (kitchen, bath, bedrooms) arranged in the old square or rectangular design. Many families modernized their homes by adding aluminum siding in the 1960s, eliminating the need to repaint every few years. The parlor of old-style houses, however, gave way to the living room, and in turn to the "family room," which increasingly became the center of family life. The family room typically revolved around a television set, and the living room, in houses that had both, became a formal sitting room for company.

During the 1960s, average Americans added kitchen counters to increase work space, purchased automatic washers and dryers to avoid trips to the laundromat, rested in reclining chairs, and bought carpets with strong colors or very visible designs (but preferred tile for bathroom floors). Such living was quite comfortable if not necessarily aesthetic.

One of the major demographic changes in the United States during the 1960s was people's movement to the suburbs. Most Americans in the suburbs found themselves living in homes similar in appearance to their neighbors' residences, as many people were unable to afford individually designed houses. These "little boxes" might be criticized as conformist by many observers, but others looked at the same houses and saw a strong community bond among neighbors socializing at backyard barbecues.

Those Americans who had the financial wherewithal to seek individuality in homes found plenty of architects and ideas available. Many wealthy Americans opted for second homes, a practice that mushroomed during the 1960s as a means of getting away from the pressures of daily life. Owners of second homes, which were usually set in rustic settings, often wanted buildings that meshed with the environment.

California style homes were based on the organic theory of architecture, with the climate and vegetation of large portions of the state conducive to this approach. These houses, popular in the 1960s, were typically low, with unpainted wood, gently pitched roofs, and lots of glass to view the outdoors. Interior spaces were usually quite open, with only partial, freestanding barriers separating kitchen, living room, and dining room. Large terraces or decks helped blur the distinction between outside and indoors.

Most Americans, of course, used more economical ways to stamp their individuality on their suburban homes, such as interior decorating and gardening.

Despite the trend toward suburban neighborhoods, large numbers of Americans lacked individualized living spaces. A great deal of public housing was constructed in the 1960s, some necessitated by demolition of existing housing—often rundown tenements—during urban renewal efforts in inner cities. Public housing was also built as the result of emerging social consciousness. Despite good intentions, limited public funding and many architects' desire to work on other projects were ongoing problems.

About 500,000 federally supported public housing units were created in the United States during the early years of the 1960s; by the end of the decade, that total had almost doubled.[2] These units, of course, had their positive aspects: fireproof construction, good lighting, private bathrooms, equipped kitchens, and so forth. Yet a project like the Robert Taylor Homes in Chicago (1962), with 28 identical 16-story buildings often proved dehumanizing, ultimately substituting one type of slum (better constructed, of course) for another.

Some serious efforts were made to be more sensitive to the psychological as well as the physical needs of inhabitants. President Kennedy's commissioner of urban renewal, William Slayton, was directed to encourage better planning, and some progressive projects were constructed. They included The St. Francis Square, San Francisco (1963) and Warren Gardens, Roxbury, Massachusetts (1969). Both sought to escape the project look by employing variety in building materials and design, creative landscaping, and individual touches like front and back doors and private yards. Major urban problems, including increased drug use, inadequate education and job training, and broken families, did much to undermine these advances.

VATICAN II AND CHURCH ARCHITECTURE

Churches and synagogues accounted for a significant percentage of creatively designed buildings in the post-World War II decades. Some of this growth resulted from the need for new places to worship in the growing suburbs, with an often unhappy consequence being the abandonment of inner-city places of worship.

The new and aesthetically appealing houses of worship built in the 1960s included, among others, the Central United Protestant Church, Richland, Washington (1965), with steeply pitched roof, angled ceiling, and nave and sanctuary joined as one space; the First Unitarian Church and School, Rochester, New York (1963), with open space, individual chair seats, and light filtering in from the corners; and the Trinity Episcopal Church, Concord, Massachusetts (1963), which wedded old and new in its expression of Gothic characteristics, such as arches and ribbed vaulting, while focusing worshippers' attention on the triangular stained glass window above and behind the altar.

In the 1960s The Second Vatican Council precipitated enormous changes in the Catholic Church, including its liturgy, which led to major alterations in how Catholic churches were designed. Pope Pius XII died in 1958 and was succeeded by John XXIII (Angelo Giuseppe Roncalli). John XXIII quickly endeared himself to Catholics and non-Catholics alike with his preference for the human touch and much less pomp than was customary. He soon became one of the most reform-minded popes in history. John XXIII announced the Second Vatican Council in January 1959 and formally opened the proceedings on October 11, 1962. Although he lived for only the first of four sessions, the council continued until 1965 under Pope Paul VI. Vatican II was the twenty-first ecumenical (that is, world-wide) council and only the second to be designated a Vatican Council (the first having occurred in 1870). It included more delegates than any previous ecumenical council (about 2,600 bishops in attendance), was most representative (earlier councils were European dominated), included the most non-Catholic and lay observers, and differed in its mission (to promote peace and unity rather than defend dogma or attack enemies of the church).

Vatican II produced 16 documents that redefined the Catholic Church as a community of the whole people of God rather than a primarily hierarchical organization, expanded roles for lay members, and asserted that the church function within rather than outside the world.

One document produced during the first session of Vatican II was immediately relevant to church architecture—*The Constitution on the Sacred Liturgy*. This document emphasized the importance of liturgy in the life of Catholics as the "outstanding means by which the faithful can express in their lives, and manifest to others, the mystery of Christ," and required "that all the faithful be led to that full, conscious, and active participation in liturgical celebrations which is demanded by the very nature of the liturgy." Catholics should, the document continued, "participate knowingly, devoutly, and actively" in this "mystery of faith."[3] Clearly, changes were required to achieve these goals.

These changes included permission to use vernacular language during Mass. Although continued use of Latin was permitted, the vernacular soon replaced most of the Latin, enabling the congregation to better understand and participate in the Mass.

With these new directives for the Eucharist, along with new emphasis on the collective "people of God," physical changes in Catholic churches were necessary. Priest and congregation had to be closer together to jointly participate in the liturgy. In pre–Vatican II churches, the altar was against the front wall, and the priest "said" Mass with his back to the people, with the exceptions of distributing communion and preaching the epistle and gospel. In addition, an altar railing essentially fenced off the congregation from the altar.

To accommodate the changes to the liturgy, the altar was turned around and simplified so that the priest faced the congregation and spoke across a low altar to worshippers who were able to see all of the priest's actions. In old churches, the original altars might remain, but new ones were constructed for daily use. Altar railings disappeared, eliminating a symbol of separation.

There were other areas of change as well. Older churches usually contained a wide array of statues, not just of Jesus, but also of Mary and other saints. Statues were still permitted, but *The Constitution on the Sacred Liturgy* urged limiting their number and moderating their impact. This call to greater simplicity encouraged more modern styles in the statuary, Stations of the Cross, and other artwork.

Furthermore, the document called for revision of the canons and statutes governing all of the material objects associated with liturgy, which invited greater creativity in church construction, including both interior and exterior elements, altars, tabernacles, and baptisteries.

Changes in the sacrament of penance were also mandated. Although it would take 10 years before the new *Rite of Penance* was promulgated (December 2, 1973), the revised liturgy for penance, now usually called the Rite of Reconciliation, resulted in changes in the physical structure of the church. The old confessional typically was a small room with a central section for the priest and a section on each side for penitents; priest and penitent were separated by a wall with a window that could be opened by sliding a panel across to permit communication. The penitent confessed

in anonymity, which did not encourage extensive dialogue. After Vatican II, and especially from the 1970s on, new churches featured a reconciliation room where the parishioner and priest could speak face-to-face in more of a counseling format. In old churches, many confessionals were re-modeled into reconciliation rooms.

The new vision of the role of lay Catholics and the nature of liturgical rites bore quick fruit in church architecture. Sacristy and nave came closer together, often almost merging when seats surrounded the altar on three sides, a common approach to bringing worshippers closer to the altar. Altars devoid of their previous ornate decorations moved close to the congregation, with no altar railings intervening. Tabernacles, usually in the center of old altars, now moved off the altar, often to the side. Simplicity, light, and closeness dominated, while modern, often abstract images replaced the old brightly colored larger-than-life statues of saints. The choir, rather than being located in a high loft at the back of the church, was more likely somewhere in front, and the accompaniment was often a small organ or guitars rather than the grand pipe organs of the past.

Post–Vatican II churches mushroomed during the 1960s, especially in the suburbs. Some of the new buildings achieved considerable architectural renown, among them the Church of St. Jude in San Francisco (1969), with its almost square nave virtually merging with the sanctuary area, and with seating surrounding the forward altar on three sides; St. Mary's Cathedral, San Francisco (under construction from 1963 until 1970), one of the first Catholic churches planned from inception according to Vatican Council directives, and despite its size maintaining a sense of closeness with no columns impeding the vision of the altar from the seating in front and along the sides; and St. Francis de Sales, Muskegon, Michigan (1967), which combined soaring height with natural light from cut-in skylights, the height by contrast with the length of the nave making priest and worshippers feel closer together than they actually were. Vast numbers of existing churches were remodeled to facilitate the new requirements of the liturgy and the vision of a community rather than hierarchy of participants.

PRESERVING HISTORY

The 1960s saw a strong desire to preserve some of the great buildings of the past. The groundwork for addressing this problem had been laid in earlier decades with the establishment of the Historical American Buildings Survey (HABS) in 1933 and the congressionally chartered National Trust for Historic Preservation in 1949. The former was to document the history of American buildings; the latter to preserve relevant information and coordinate preservation efforts. Nonetheless, destruction of historically important buildings continued to occur.

This decade was also a turning point in the struggle to retain buildings that were important within American history and culture. By the early 1960s, about 25 percent of buildings listed on the HABS had disappeared.[4] Consciousness, however, had been raised by Jane Jacobs, who in her book *The Death and Life of Great American Cities* (1961) argued for "The Need for Aged Buildings." Jacobs argued that a strong contingent of representative buildings must be preserved for the sake of different types of people who had lived, worked, and played in them—buildings she described as "not museum-piece old buildings, not old buildings in an excellent and expensive state of rehabilitation—although these make fine ingredients—but also a good lot of plain, ordinary, low-value old buildings, including some rundown old buildings."[5]

One old building that stirred up considerable passion in the decade was New York's Pennsylvania

Pennsylvania (Penn) Station, New York City, a beautiful Beaux-Art style building constructed in 1910 and demolished in 1963, led to the creation of better preservation of historical landmarks. Prints & Photographs Division, Library of Congress.

Station, modeled somewhat on an ancient Roman bath complex. Utilitarianism won out, and Pennsylvania Railroad demolished the station in 1963. However, its loss was one reason the New York City Landmarks Preservation Commission was established in 1965, charged with reviewing all buildings that had been standing for at least 30 years and designating those it deemed appropriate to be official landmarks. Owners who violated the commission's judgments were subject to penalties.

Other cities established similar commissions, including St. Louis, Denver, and San Francisco. The U.S. Congress approved a National Historic Preservation Act to require preservation of historic architectural works. Financial incentives, including tax credits, supported preservation efforts, and financial assistance was made available to private groups through the National Trust for Historic Preservation.

One of the preservation battlegrounds was the Grand Central Terminal in New York City, a 1913 Beaux-Arts train station. The Landmarks Preservation Commission named Grand Central an official landmark in 1967. The owner, Penn Central Transportation Company, challenged the decision, arguing economic hardship for the corporation, and later, as it carried its battle to the nation's Supreme Court, that the original decision was unconstitutional. The battle continued until June 1978, when the Supreme Court upheld the landmarks law. A very public train ride featuring prominent architects and Mrs. Jacqueline Kennedy Onassis, the former First Lady, had helped to mobilize popular opinion behind the preservation effort.

Books

Newspapers, Magazines, and Comics of the 1960s

Three giants of fiction, all of whom won a Nobel Prize for Literature in their careers, passed from the scene during the 1960s. Ernest Hemingway, who revolutionized fiction in the 1920s in both style and subject, committed suicide in 1961. William Faulkner, the chronicler of post–Civil War southern society died in 1962. John Steinbeck, who set many of his novels in his native California during the Great Depression and remains best known for *The Grapes of Wrath*, 1939 about Oklahoma sharecroppers driven from their land by 1937 Dust Bowl storms, died in 1968.

There also was a changing of the guard in American poetry during the 1960s, as a number of American poets died during the decade, including e. e. cummings (1962), Robert Frost (1963), William Carlos Williams (1963), T. S. Eliot (1965), and Carl Sandburg (1967).

Creative nonfiction joined fiction and poetry as an important literary genre during the 1960s. Creative nonfiction refers to nonfiction prose that uses language not merely to inform or to persuade, but also embraces the nuances, connotations, and complexities of fiction and poetry. New Journalism (also called the nonfiction novel) replaced the ideal of objective reporting and distancing the writer from his or her subject with the author's subjective involvement.

The 1960s also witnessed great interest in magazines and newspapers. Some of the old standards remained popular, along with new magazines that appealed to special segments of society. The decade was a time of great activity in newspaper journalism, with so-called underground newspapers sprouting throughout the country.

FICTION

New voices arose during the decade, often challenging traditional political, social, and literary norms. Many looked toward new lifestyles for their subjects, explored different ways of constructing narratives, and reexamined the very nature of what it meant to write a novel. The Beats, African American and Native American authors and proponents of what came to be known as metafiction, contributed engaging and often highly successful novels. A number of Jewish authors brought the Jewish-American experience to public consciousness.

The Beats came to prominence during the 1950s, but continued to wield great influence on the literary scene during the 1960s. Jack Kerouac achieved something of cult status with his *On the Road* (1957), which captured the wandering, nonconformist mood of many of his generation. *On the Road* remained popular throughout the 1960s, its

Books

treatment of drug and sexual experiences appealing to a new generation of young men and women.

William S. Burroughs and Ken Kesey were also important novelists of the Beat generation. Burroughs's *The Naked Lunch,* first published in Paris in 1959, appeared in the United States in 1962. The heavily scatological content and explicit treatment of drug use stirred the fires of censorship and led to a four-year legal battle in Massachusetts that ultimately failed to suppress the book. Burroughs followed *Naked Lunch* with *The Soft Machine* (1961), *The Ticket that Exploded* (1962), and *Nova Express* (1964).

Kesey drew on his experiences working in a psychiatric ward and volunteering in a government experiment with LSD and other drugs in writing *One Flew Over the Cuckoo's Nest* (1962). The novel focuses on Chief Bromden, a Native American mental patient forced to undergo multiple shock treatments; a rigidly authoritarian Nurse Ratched; and the hero of the story, Randle Patrick McMurphy, whose nonconformist but humane attitude induces the patients to gain some joy from each other. Chief Bromden escapes from the "cuckoo's nest" while McMurphy is subjected to shock treatments and a lobotomy. The novel questioned who the insane ones really were and attacked the conformist powers of institutional society. The story became a successful film in the 1970s and starred Jack Nicholson as McMurphy.

The strongest black voice in American fiction during the decade was James Baldwin. Baldwin secured an important position in fiction and social protest with his 1953 novel *Go Tell It on the Mountain.* The novel was widely read during the 1960s and was followed by *Giovanni's Room* in 1955 and *Another Country* in 1962. Baldwin's fiction explored the difficulties of being African American and homosexual. Baldwin spent much of his time in France, but despite his rightful anger over racial injustice, continued to believe in the possibilities of American society. His essays, gathered in such collections as *Nobody Knows My Name* (1961) and *The Fire Next Time* (1963), were viewed by many critics as better than his fiction. Baldwin's essays also helped gain support for enforcing civil rights on behalf of black Americans.

N. Scott Momaday sought to bring both himself and modern society to a greater understanding of Native American history and culture. Momaday, son of a Kiowa father and a Cherokee mother learned first-hand of life on reservations and was educated in Kiowa and Cherokee culture as well as the broader American society. His novel *House Made of Dawn* (1968) won a Pulitzer Prize (the first novel by a Native American to be so honored) and helped introduce what has been called the Native American Renaissance, a rich harvest of outstanding fiction, poetry, and nonfiction by Native American writers. Abel, the protagonist of *House Made of Dawn,* is a returning veteran of World War II whose life reflects the alienation, alcoholism, and difficulty finding a good job that afflict many Native Americans whose culture has been systematically destroyed by white Americans. Finally, Abel overcomes his difficulties and reunites with his grandfather as the old man dies.

The Jewish American experience also yielded an impressive body of fiction, by such writers as Bernard Malamud, Saul Bellow, and Philip Roth. Malamud's *The Fixer* (1966) helped secure his lasting reputation as both an outstanding chronicler of Jewish life in the United States and one of the country's foremost novelists. *The Fixer,* about a seemingly ordinary man accused of the ritual murder of a Christian child, won both a Pulitzer Prize for fiction and a National Book Award.

Saul Bellow, who was awarded the Nobel Prize for Literature in 1976 grew up in Quebec, but set most of his fiction in Chicago and New York City. His highly successful novel of the 1960s, *Herzog* (1964) tells the story of Moses Herzog, a sort of everyman who complains, charms, is deceived, but survives his personal crises.

Philip Roth's *Portnoy's Complaint* (1969) features Alexander Portnoy's memories, especially of childhood, with a heavy emphasis on sex. Many readers were put off by the descriptions of young Portnoy's skills at masturbation and criticized Roth for moving away from middle-class Jewish subjects to depict Jewish characters as bizarre, even grotesque.

Kurt Vonnegut achieved great success in the 1960s, especially on college campuses, for

Kurt Vonnegut, center, visiting during the filming of one of his plays, *Happy Birthday, Wanda June,* with actress Susannah York on the right. Courtesy of Photofest.

combining social criticism with highly innovative approaches to storytelling that pulled apart the traditional concept of narrative as a coherent, cause-to-effect, beginning-middle-end plot. Vonnegut gained popular acceptance with his novel *Cat's Cradle* (1963), a strong indictment of contemporary science, religion, and politics. Vonnegut's structural experimenting reached its apex, though, with *Slaughterhouse-Five or The Children's Crusade: A Duty-Dance with Death* (1969). In it, the main character, Billy Pilgrim moves among three worlds: as a prisoner of war in Dresden during the World War II firebombing of the city, as a husband and father in the present, and in a fantasy realm on the planet Tralfamadore (where he was mated with an earthling porn star). At one point, Billy Pilgrim (his name representing his time travels), watches a war movie backward, which makes everything turn out better as the flyers return safely to their bases. Billy imagines the film continuing, with the soldiers turning in their uniforms and becoming happy high school students again; even Hitler is transformed into an innocent baby. The novel was both an antiwar book and an assault on contemporary society's dehumanizing impact, summed up in the phrase

of acceptance that repeatedly appeared in the story: "So it goes."

Metafiction

Other novelists also looked closely at not only the story as artifact or product, but as a process intimately related to its author, giving rise to what critics have labeled metafiction. This approach to fiction paralleled the rejection of traditional values and expectations found throughout American society during the 1960s. The meaning of "meta" in this context is to go beyond or transcend. Metafiction goes beyond traditional views of fiction by being self-reflective, by looking closely at the act of writing and the writer. Metafiction usually is highly personal, grounded in the belief that the most important reality is personal reality. Style is often more important than plot and characterization. Heroes tend to be nontraditional types of protagonists often far removed from what readers are accustomed to viewing as heroic.

Thomas Pynchon's *V* (1963), and *The Crying of Lot 49* (1966) overturned most fictional expectations, and were centered around labyrinthine plots that tended toward the absurd, repeatedly running serious moments into comedy and imitating other writers' styles with exuberant humor rather than satiric intent.

Richard Brautigan was perhaps the most popular metafiction writers during the 1960s, especially among college students and young people living in communes. A reclusive writer seldom seen in public or photographed, Brautigan served as a role model for the 1960s dropout. His works of fiction consisted of loosely ordered prose pieces, little plot, criticism of modern society's destruction of nature, and a irreverent tone. *Trout Fishing in America* (1967), for example, included such elements as a "Kool-Aid wino," many references to the narrator and the book itself, personification of Trout Fishing in America as someone the narrator meets at the Big Wood River near Ketchum, Idaho just after Hemingway's death (ironically linking the book with the great chronicler of fishing in America, Hemingway), a surrealistic satire on destroyers of the environment in which a trout stream is cut up and sold by the foot, and a concluding chapter entitled "The Mayonnaise Chapter" because the narrator says that he "always wanted to write a book that ended with the word Mayonnaise."

Catch-22

Seldom does a title work its way into the popular lexicon. That, however, occurred with the title of Joseph Heller's World War II novel *Catch-22* (1961), a novel that became something of a commentary on what many increasingly saw as an irrational political and military system in the United States during the 1960s, even though the novel is set in a previous war. In the novel, Captain John Yossarian tries to claim insanity to escape the certain death that would result if he were to follow his squadron commanders' insane orders. His doctor, though, points out the Catch-22 principle: that a flyer must be insane to be excused from combat, but proves his sanity by the very fact that he wants to escape from the mission. Conversely, Doc Daneeka acknowledges that Yossarian's tentmate, Orr, is crazy but that Orr must request to be grounded, which he does not do precisely because he is crazy. Unable to function logically within a crazy system, namely the war-making apparatus, Yossarian deserts. Other characters take other approaches. Orr pretends to be merely a not very bright joker and utilizes cunning to thwart the efforts of Colonel Cathcart, the ultra-authoritarian villain of the novel. The symbolic and nameless

---

HOW OTHERS SEE US

Parlez-Vous Franglais?

In the postwar era as never before, English-language terms and idioms surged into everyday use among non-English speakers. As people in France made plans for "le week-end" and Norwegians discussed the latest "boksing" match, linguists and critics in these countries and many others began to push back.

A 1964 polemic by French literature professor René Etiemble, *Parlez-Vous Franglais,* brought the controversy to international attention. Etiemble's goal was to fight off the invasion of Anglicisms that, he felt, threatened the French language and France's culture. His book was a sharp criticism of American mores, values, and education (or lack thereof). To resist Anglicization in language, Etiemble argued, was to resist Americanization in general. Others in France, as well as writers and TV commentators in Spain, the Netherlands, Italy, and elsewhere, echoed Etiemble's clarion call. Language academies such as L'Académie Française and the Real Academia Española turned their attention to vetting which English loan-words might have a legitimate function and which should be rejected and replaced with home-grown alternatives. Thus French speakers were encouraged to look forward to "le fin de la semaine," an authentically French term for the end-of-the-week days of rest.

It was not, however, an entirely successful effort. As linguist David Crystal pointed out, the process of word-loaning is complex and affected by many factors, from "snob value" to commercial marketing to student exchanges to sheer practicality. As mass media grew more global, holding the line on language became increasingly difficult.

Soldier in White, bandaged mummylike and kept alive while fluids enter his body at one end and exit at the other, is a grotesque joke that stands for the impersonal manipulation of individuals by the institutions of modern society.

The novel is one of the most important and lasting antiwar writings of American literature, but it also comments on the essential irrationality of the human condition. Countless people who have never even heard of the novel use the phrase "catch-22" to express irrational but irrefutable contradictions that put people in no-win situations.

Popular Authors

John Updike and William Styron were more mainstream novelists. Updike published 10 volumes of fiction during the 1960s and also wrote poetry and book reviews. Updike's novel *The Centaur,* 1963, told the story of a high school teacher during a three-day period, and was heavy in mythological allusions. It brought Updike a National Book Award and considerable critical acclaim. *Rabbit, Run,* 1960, more rooted in social realism, introduced Harry "Rabbit" Angstrom, a former high school basketball star disenchanted with his present life and what he felt were a stultifying town, job, and family. Harry would appear in several more novels.

Styron encountered controversy for his depiction of Nat Turner in *The Confessions of Nat Turner* (1967). In real life, Turner led a slave rebellion in 1831 that resulted in the deaths of more than fifty whites in Virginia. In the novel, Turner is in jail, where he reflects on his past life. His owner, Samuel Turner, had supposedly promised Nat his freedom, but went broke and sold Nat to Reverend Mr. Eppes. Having promised to free Nat, Eppes reneged and sold him to slave traders. As the novel progresses, Nat becomes increasingly filled with hatred, has a homosexual affair that induces considerable guilt, and undergoes a religious conversion that propels him into a prophetic state in which he believes he is ordained to kill whites. *The Confessions of Nat Turner* won a Pulitzer Prize for fiction but engendered great opposition from many African American writers and critics who believed the novel inaccurate and racist.

A number of women also left their lasting marks on the American reading public, including Flannery O'Connor, Harper Lee, and Joyce Carol Oates.

O'Connor brought her Roman Catholic background and Georgia heritage to her explorations of character. Her often rural figures rose above their commonplace situations as O'Connor laid bare their eternal yearnings. Her stories are rich in religious symbolism and revelations of the humanity within characters that some critics have labeled grotesques. O'Connor is considered one of America's finest short story writers as well as an effective novelist. She died in 1964 at the age of thirty-nine after a long struggle with disseminated lupus. Her second and final novel, *The Violent Bear It Away,* appeared in 1960; a second collection of short stories, *Everything That Rises Must Converge,* was published the year after her death. Despite her early death, O'Connor's reputation continued to rise. *The Flannery O'Connor Bulletin,* dedicated to the study of her life and work, originated in the 1970s and became *The Flannery O'Connor Review* in 2001.

Harper Lee's novel *To Kill a Mockingbird* (1960) presents a story of racism and injustice set in 1930s Alabama. The narrator, Jean Louise "Scout" Finch, who ages from six to eight during the story, recounts the case of Tom Robinson, an African American on trial for allegedly raping a

Gregory Peck, left, the star of the movie adaptation of *To Kill a Mockingbird* (1962), with author Harper Lee during filming. Courtesy of Photofest.

white woman. Convinced of his innocence, Jean's father, Atticus Finch, defends Robinson. Atticus demonstrates his defendant's innocence, but the white jury finds him guilty anyway. Robinson is subsequently killed trying to escape. Another important story line involves Boo Radley, who despite being treated as an outcast and even something of a monster by his neighbors, rescues Scout and her brother Jem when the father of the woman Robinson was accused of raping tries to kill the children to exact revenge on Atticus. The novel's powerful questioning of racial and social justice and institutional hypocrisy earned Lee a Pulitzer Prize. The novel was made into a film in 1962 starring Gregory Peck, who won the Academy Award for his performance as Atticus.

One of the new fictional voices in the 1960s was Joyce Carol Oates. Her first collection of short stories, *By the North Gate,* was published in 1963 and was followed by the novels *With Shuddering Fall* (1964), *Expensive People* (1968), and *them* (1969), which won a National Book Award. Oates, a prolific writer, is known for writing about the physical and emotional violence with which seemingly ordinary people find themselves afflicted.

Set in another land but with many lessons that youthful readers of the 1960s found relevant to their own searching was the fantasy fiction of British medievalist J.R.R. Tolkien. The works that stirred readers' imagination so strongly during the decade had appeared earlier: *The Hobbit* in 1937, and the three volumes that compose *The Lord of the Rings (The Fellowship of the Ring, The Two Towers, The Return of the King)* in the 1950s. A key to the popularity of these books was their issuance in inexpensive paperback editions during the 1960s. *The Hobbit* describes a place called Middle-earth, and the trilogy picks up the story about 50 years later in the same realm. Middle-earth is a simpler place, where the struggle between good and evil is rendered in concrete terms. Tolkien, drawing on his knowledge of linguistics and the Middle Ages, created not only a new place but a language, mythology, and society to make it come alive. The major story line throughout the trilogy is the effort, finally successful, to destroy a ring that contains such power that its possessor could control the world of Middle-earth.

Many Tolkien societies and discussion groups were formed during the late 1960s, while Tolkien's stories helped to legitimize fantasy as a mode of fiction to be taken seriously by readers and literary critics alike.

Best Sellers

Early in the 1960s, readers devoured copies of the political novel *Advise and Consent* by Allen Drury; the long historical novel, *Hawaii,* by James Michener; Irving Stone's story of the artist Michelangelo, *The Agony and the Ecstasy;* and lots of sex, from Henry Miller's *Tropic of Cancer* to Harold Robbins's *The Carpetbaggers.*

By 1962, in the year of the Cuban Missile Crisis, novels of nuclear confrontation and political intrigue at the highest levels excited the general public. Two of the leading sellers of the year were *Fail-Safe,* an account of a mistaken nuclear attack on the Soviet Union by the United States, by Eugene Burdick and Harvey Wheeler; and *Seven Days in May,* about an attempt to overthrow an American president viewed by military leaders as too soft on communism, by Fletcher Knebel and Charles W. Bailey II.

Morris L. West's novel *The Shoes of the Fisherman,* 1963, about a Catholic pope, made the best seller lists in 1963, perhaps helped by public interest in the Second Vatican Council and the wide popularity enjoyed by Pope John XXIII. Spy novels such as John le Carré's *The Spy Who Came in from the Cold* and Ian Fleming's *You Only Live Twice* and *The Man with the Golden Gun* continued to be popular. Jacqueline Susann hit it big with *Valley of the Dolls,* a supposed exposé of Hollywood in the mid-1960s that appealed to readers who liked a vicarious mix of sex, drugs, and other sins.

Novels that broke through in the late 1960s included the supernatural spellbinder *Rosemary's Baby,* by Ira Levin; Arthur Hailey's *Airport,* about a plane in danger of being blown up by a mad bomber; Michael Crichton's story of the dangers of bacteriological warfare research, *The Andromeda Strain;* and Mario Puzo's account of the Mafia in *The Godfather,* which tended to portray murderers and similar types as almost sympathetic if not admirable, and was made into a series of three popular films.

NOTABLE BOOKS

Rabbit, Run, John Updike, 1960

A Separate Peace, John Knowles, U.S., 1960

To Kill a Mockingbird, Harper Lee, 1960

Catch-22, Joseph Heller, 1961

Tropic of Cancer, Henry Miller, 1961

A Clockwork Orange, Anthony Burgess, 1962

One Flew Over the Cuckoo's Nest, Ken Kesey, 1962

Ship of Fools, Katherine Anne Porter, 1962

Silent Spring, Rachel Carson, 1962

The Feminine Mystique, Betty Friedan, 1963

The Spy Who Came in from the Cold, John le Carré, 1964

Dune, Frank Herbert, 1965

Up the Down Staircase, Bel Kaufman, 1965

In Cold Blood, Truman Capote, 1966

The Valley of the Dolls, Jacqueline Susann, 1966

Rosemary's Baby, Ira Levin, 1967

Trout Fishing in America, Richard Brautigan, 1967

Airport, Arthur Hailey, 1968

The Double Helix, James Watson, 1968

2001: A Space Odyssey, Arthur C. Clarke, 1968

The Andromeda Strain, Michael Crichton, 1969

The Godfather, Mario Puzo, 1969

Portnoy's Complaint, Philip Roth, 1969

Slaughterhouse-Five, Kurt Vonnegut Jr., 1969

CREATIVE NONFICTION

Truman Capote's *In Cold Blood* (1966) was one of the most influential and controversial examples of New Journalism, also known as the nonfiction novel. Originally published in four installments in *The New Yorker* in 1965, *In Cold Blood* recounts the 1959 murders of Kansas farmer Herbert Clutter, his wife, Bonnie, and their two children by Dick Hickock and Perry Smith. Capote deepened his narrative into a sociological examination of the small-town milieu in which the Clutters lived, a psychological portrayal of the murderers, and an indirect indictment of capital

punishment. Capote became close to the murderers during his research, which may have helped lead to the double reference of the title—to the slaying of the farm family and the governmental execution of the convicted killers.

Capote viewed his book as a nonfiction novel, an apparent oxymoron that led some critics to question how much of the account originated in the author's imagination. Capote used clear literary devices, such as beginning the account in the middle of the story, well after the murders, and presenting the crimes as a flashback after Hickock and Smith were captured. He also included long passages of dialogue that he said he recalled from memory. *In Cold Blood* received the 1966 Mystery Writers of America's Edgar Allan Poe Award, usually given to a work of fiction. Despite the controversy, Capote's book stimulated other mixed-genre

Books

Truman Capote, author of *In Cold Blood* and other books 1966. Like his childhood friend Harper Lee, he published an exceedingly popular and well-reviewed book in the 1960s, and both of their books went on to successful film versions. Prints & Photographs Division, Library of Congress.

Books

works that staked out a middle ground between journalism and fiction. It also helped, along with Capote's flamboyant lifestyle and personality, to make him a major celebrity in both the literary and social scenes. *In Cold Blood* was also released as a critically acclaimed movie in 1967. It was directed by Richard Brooks and starring Robert Blake, Scott Wilson, and John Forsythe.

Norman Mailer was another important practitioner of New Journalism. Mailer originally gained fame with his first novel, *The Naked and the Dead,* in 1948. By the 1960s, he had turned increasingly to politics and creative reportage. A major celebrity who appeared regularly on late-night television talk shows, Mailer published during the decade, among other works, *Armies of the Night* and *Miami and the Siege of Chicago,* both in 1968. The former grew out of Mailer's participation in an antiwar demonstration at the Pentagon in 1967; the latter was in response to the political conventions of 1968 that nominated Richard Nixon and Hubert Humphrey in a placid event in Miami amid a massive storm of antiwar demonstrations in Chicago. The books featured the author as a major character within the narrative plots.

Another popular nonfiction novel was Tom Wolfe's *The Electric Kool-Aid Acid Test* (1968), about novelist Ken Kesey's travels, both physical and drug-induced. In 1964, Kesey set off in a 1939 Day-Glo-painted International Harvester bus with a group of friends known as the Merry Pranksters. Kesey and company interacted with the Hell's Angels motorcycle group and staged acid tests, which were multimedia happenings that included LSD, dancing, strobe lights, and rock music. Wolfe's account of Kesey's experiences was a subjective treatment that used fiction techniques, including typographic oddities to convey inner reality and selective descriptive details combined with authorial conclusions (often guesses as to what the characters were feeling and thinking). The effect was to convey not only the action but the spirit of the times.

Hunter S. Thompson, a journalist during the first half of the decade for such prestigious publications as *Time,* the *New York Herald Tribune,* the *National Observer,* and the *Nation* was another important New Journalism author. An article that Thompson wrote for the *Nation* in 1964 on

motorcycle gangs marked a turning point both in his career and in the genre. Thompson disagreed with the common perception of Hell's Angels as a bunch of thugs and spent much time with the group in the mid-1960s. The result was a book called *Hell's Angels: A Strange and Terrible Saga* (1967). Thompson became part of the story, blurring the line between source and reporter. His unorthodox treatment of subjects usually given little serious treatment in the press came to be known as "gonzo journalism."

Susan Sontag came to public attention in the middle of the decade as a social critic with essays in such magazines as *Partisan Review, The Evergreen Review,* and *Commentary.* She followed with a book collection entitled *Against Interpretation and Other Essays* (1966). Her essays covered many subjects, including science-fiction films, pornography, and art criticism. Sontag traveled to North Vietnam during the war, itself a highly controversial act, and published an account of her experiences in *Trip to Hanoi* (1968). Another collection of essays, *Styles of Radical Will,* appeared in 1969. Sontag combined her reporting and analyses with a leftist political point of view that challenged many actions and pronouncements of the government and other American institutions.

The 1960s witnessed a growing interest in protecting the environment and living in harmony with nature, an attitude increasingly evident in the creative nonfiction of the decade. Much of the best nature writing was antiestablishment, and resisted political and economic pressures to use the land for profit.

Loren Eiseley's professional training as an anthropologist at the Universities of Nebraska and Pennsylvania, combined with a personal commitment to protecting nature, led to a number of books, beginning with *The Immense Journey* (1946). Eiseley produced several books—*The Firmament of Time* (1960), *The Mind of Nature* (1962), *The Unexpected Universe* (1969)—that revealed a deep human connection to the surrounding natural world. Eiseley wrote in a manner accessible to nonscientists in which his personal values came through clearly.

Edward Abbey combined science with a strong sense of self and a commitment to appreciating the natural environment. Abbey argued for ecocentrism, the view that nature existed for itself rather than to serve humankind, and condoned ecodefense, including environmental terrorism (property destruction and other crimes) to protect the environment. *Desert Solitaire,* 1968, which reflects Abbey's interest in the American Southwest, is usually considered one of his most important books.

POETRY

Robert Frost was the most famous and beloved poet in the United States at the beginning of the decade. He read his poem "The Gift Outright," a celebration of westward expansion and the people's surrender to the land that he saw as defining the new nation, at the inauguration of President John F. Kennedy in January 1961. A traditionalist, Frost used formal conventions, but filled them with colloquial speech. A poet of nature and New England, he perpetuated the myth that real America was rural New England while comparing outer nature with the inner self.

The United States, however, had changed greatly. The country was increasingly urban, and truths were less absolute and harder to decipher. The individual self stepped forward in a more materialistic world in place of the collective we.

More reflective of the changing times were the Beats, who came to prominence during the 1950s and continued to wield great influence in poetry, fiction, and society during the 1960s. The Beats tended toward a bohemian lifestyle, rejected many of modern society's standards and values, and sought enlightenment and freedom through love (and sex), drugs, and Eastern religions, especially Zen Buddhism. They opposed the Vietnam War, and typically supported progressive social movements, such as civil rights. The Beats congregated in San Francisco, fusing the Beat movement with a San Francisco renaissance of the arts.

Allen Ginsberg may have been the most important of the Beat poets. He had considerable knowledge of earlier poetic traditions and incorporated some aspects of them into his own new directions in writing. The long line is one major example. Ginsberg adopted an unusually long poetic line in imitation of William Blake, Walt Whitman, Christopher Smart (another eighteenth-century

British poet), and the Bible. He popularized the approach in his groundbreaking long poem, "Howl," in *Howl and Other Poems* (1956).

By the 1960s, Ginsberg was widely known as a revolutionary poet, an antiwar activist, a student of Buddhism in India, and a popular reader of his poetry on college campuses throughout the United States. His important books of poetry in the decade included *Kaddish and Other Poems* (1961), *Reality Sandwiches* (1963), and *Planet News* (1968).

Another important Beat/San Francisco poet during the 1960s was Lawrence Ferlinghetti, whose *A Coney Island of the Mind* (1958) remained enormously popular throughout the decade, especially among college students. Ferlinghetti published additional books during the decade and included a record of himself reading his poetry with *Starting from San Francisco* (1961). This encouraged the idea that poetry should be heard and helped popularize the growing phenomenon of poets giving public readings of their works. He also helped publish other poets as co-founder of City Lights in San Francisco, an all-paperback store, and publisher of City Light Books, the Pocket Poets Series, and the magazine *Beatitude.* The fourth book in the Pocket series was Ginsberg's *Howl and Other Poems.*

The Beats are often credited with helping to spawn the beatniks and hippies. The columnist Herb Caen used the term "beatnik," derived from "beat," in a *San Francisco Chronicle* column on April 2, 1958. The term caught on and was usually used in a derogatory, sometimes comic way. Images of the beatnik reached a wide audience through the character Maynard G. Krebs (played by Bob Denver) on the television series *The Many Loves of Dobie Gillis* (1959–1963) and through *MAD* magazine, with its satiric mock magazine *Beatnik: The Magazine for Hipsters,* September 1960. The line of descent from Beats to hippies can be traced through such common ground as support for peace, love, drugs, and sexual freedom, and opposition to conformity and received authority.

As the Vietnam War dragged on throughout the 1960s, the large majority of America's poets, not just the Beats, turned against it, with many engaging quite actively in antiwar efforts. Robert Lowell, who came from an old Boston patrician

Books

family and had been sentenced to a year in New York's West Street jail for opposing America's war efforts during World War II, helped lead protestors against the Pentagon in 1967. Lowell became, through collections like *For the Union Dead* (1964) and *Notebook 1967–1968* (1969); revised as *Notebook* in 1970, and for his social commitment, one of the most respected poets of his time.

Robert Bly believed that poetry should be simple in diction, concrete in image, and direct in expression in order to combine the external landscape (often his native Minnesota) with the mystical or imaginative landscape of the mind. During the 1960s, living out his conviction that the poet should be society's conscience, Bly helped create American Writers against the Vietnam War and organize the series "Poets Reading Against the Vietnam War." Important collections of his 1960s poems include *The Light Around the Body* (1967), *The Morning Glory* (1969), *The Teeth-Mother Naked at Last* (1970), and *The Shadow-Mothers* (1970).

Social activism in poetry also included a growing commitment to other major movements of the decade, such as black consciousness and the Civil Rights Movement. At the beginning of the 1960s, Langston Hughes was the best known and most respected voice among African American poets. Known as "the bard of Harlem" and acclaimed for his use of jazz and African American rhythms in his poetry, Hughes remained productive until his death in 1967. He edited anthologies, including *New Negro Poets* (1964) and *The Best Short Stories by Negro Writers* (1967) by younger black writers and served as lyricist on the musicals *Black Nativity* (1961), *Jericho-Jim Crow* (1964), and *The Prodigal Son* (1965), which brought gospel music to the stage. His final volume of poetry, *The Panther and the Lash: Poems of our Times* (1967), demonstrated his growing involvement in civil rights and the black power movement.

One of the most widely read poets of the 1960s was Rod McKuen, who was derided by critics for his sentimental poetry but became a mass-marketed best seller devoured by youthful readers who responded to his sensitive persona and love-filled lyrics. Also a songwriter and singer, McKuen often performed his own works. His 1960s collections of poems included *Stanyan Street and Other Sorrows* (1966), *Listen to the Warm* (1967), and *In Someone's Shadow* (1969).

The image of the sensitive, troubled poet too fragile to cope with the pressures of everyday life was both persona and self for Sylvia Plath. As a student at Smith College, Plath suffered a nervous breakdown and attempted suicide. Her autobiographical novel *The Bell Jar* spoke for young modern women who resisted traditional self-defining roles of wife and mother. Originally published in England in 1963, the book was released in the United States in 1971 and became extremely popular with young American readers during the 1970s. During the 1960s, however, most American readers knew Plath as a poet, author of the collections *The Colossus and Other Poems* (1962) and *Ariel* (1966) as wife of the British poet Ted Hughes, and for her death by suicide in 1963. Plath composed the *Ariel* poems in London, where she lived with her two young children after her marriage broke up in 1962. Although some of the poems expressed a mother's love for her children, others conveyed their creator's anger against the major male figures in her life, her husband and father. In February 1963, she committed suicide.

MAGAZINES AND NEWSPAPERS

Americans continued to read old standbys during the 1960s in both magazines and newspapers. *Time*, *Newsweek*, and *U.S. News & World Report* brought readers national and international news. One of the publishing highlights of the year was *Time*'s "Man of the Year."

Life and *Look* were large-format weekly magazines that specialized in large photo spreads with easy-to-read stories that focused mostly on celebrities. *The Saturday Evening Post* continued its long tradition of publishing fiction and featured covers by American painter Norman Rockwell. In 1963, the magazine used the last of its Rockwell covers, its 317th, and dropped cover paintings as part of an updating designed to boost readership. The effort did not succeed, and the magazine went out of business in 1971.

Ebony was *Life* for the African American community that substituted black models in the ads and features on subjects of interest to a mainstream

NEW MAGAZINES

Tiger Beat, 1965

Southern Living, 1966

Ranger Rick, 1967

Rolling Stone, 1967

Runner's World, 1966

Surfer, 1960

WORDS AND PHRASES

a-okay

beach bunny

bowser bag (restaurant bag for leftovers)

brain drain

crash pad

crunch (crisis or showdown)

daddy-o/daddio

far out

groovy

hairy (dangerous or menacing)

jet set

kook

mind-blowing

noise pollution

nuke

out of sight

Peacenik

Pop Art

psychedelic

status symbol

swinging

teach-in

Teeny-bopper

unisex

WASP (White Anglo-Saxon Protestant)

Books

black readership. Johnson Publications, producer of *Ebony,* also brought out *Jet,* a news magazine that was more cutting-edge in its approach to social issues than *Ebony; Tan,* which was marketed to African American homemakers; and *Negro Digest,* which was similar to the more white-oriented *Reader's Digest.*

There were magazines for every member of the family. Women were the targets of many large circulation magazines. *Ladies' Home Journal, Better Homes and Gardens,* and *McCall's* were designed especially for homemakers. If a woman wanted a little vicarious adventure, she could read *True Confessions* and other romance magazines. *TV Guide* offered the family a weekly guide to what was playing on television. The man of the house could enjoy his sports on the page as well as on television, thanks to *Sport, Baseball Digest,* the venerable sports paper *The Sporting News,* and a variety of other sports publications. Teenagers could keep up with their favorite celebrities in *Tiger Beat.* The whole family could enjoy *National Geographic* and in its pages travel to exotic places without leaving the comfort of home.

Changing times were reflected in many magazines, including *Playboy, Cosmopolitan,* and *Ramparts.* Hugh Hefner's *Playboy* proposed a sexually free lifestyle minus commitment, along with centerfolds of young women devoid of clothes. *Cosmopolitan,* edited by Helen Gurley Brown, attempted to justify a similar philosophy for women, defending sexual pleasure apart from marriage and motherhood for the career woman. As *Playboy* and *Cosmopolitan* both reflected and contributed to a rejection of traditional sexual attitudes, *Ramparts* broke ground politically. A radical magazine, *Ramparts* featured articles by such activists as Eldridge Cleaver; printed exposés,

including a report that the Central Intelligence Agency had channeled funds to religious, educational, and other cultural institutions to counter left-wing political action; published the diaries of Argentinian revolutionary Che Guevara, who had helped Castro come to power in Cuba; and argued at length that the John Kennedy assassination was a conspiracy being covered up by the government.

Major newspapers, especially eastern papers, continued to exercise considerable sway over public opinion, among them *The New York Times, Washington Post,* and *Boston Globe.* In smaller

Entertainment

of the 1960s

What happened during the 1960s in film, television, dance, and drama did not occur in isolation, but as part of the larger social, political, and aesthetic changes of the decade.

Television, which was rapidly becoming the country's foremost mass medium, sought to appeal to the large majority rather than smaller slices of American opinion. Yet even here change could not be ignored, as the growing importance of television journalism brought vivid images conflicts involving race, gender, and the Vietnam War. In the 1960s the power of the media to shape culture was both growing rapidly and becoming somewhat understood. Marshall McLuhan asserted that "the medium is the message."[1] The image came to define reality rather than represent it.

Film, drama and sometimes dance began to present frank explorations of racial, sexual, gender, and political issues.

FILMS

As the 1960s progressed, changes in society began to impact films in content and production values. Counterculture patterns, including drug use, greater sexual freedom, and a general straining against traditional mores, came up against the Motion Picture Production Code, established in 1930 by the Motion Picture Producers and Distributors of America (MPPDA), which later became the Motion Picture Association of America (MPAA). Increasingly, filmmakers found themselves unable to receive approval from the Production Code Administration (PCA), which administered the Code. In 1966, Jack Valenti, the new president of the MPAA, reexamined the Code in light of Supreme Court rulings on obscenity and changing attitudes toward censorship. The result was a new, voluntary self-regulating rating system that made it easier for filmmakers to distribute their films and also enabled filmgoers to know what the films would contain in such areas as sex and violence. The ratings, which since the 1960s have undergone some revisions, included four categories: G for films suitable for a general audience; M for films suitable for a mature audience, with parental guidance suggested; R for films restricted to viewers at least 16 years of age unless accompanied by a parent or adult guardian; and X for films to which only those 16 years of age or older would be admitted. The criteria reflected in these categories were principally language, sex, and violence. Moderate profanity was allowed in R films; nudity was usually X material. Filmmakers could get away with more violence than sexual behavior and obscene language without losing an R rating.

With the new ratings system and revolutionary changes in society as context, films began to explore new frontiers in such areas as race, sex, drugs, violence, and the supernatural.

Two of the most important films to challenge racial prejudice were released in 1967 and starred Sidney Poitier: *Guess Who's Coming to Dinner* and the Oscar-winning *In the Heat of the Night*. In the former, African American Poitier comes to dinner, guest of his white fiancée, to meet her parents, played by film immortals Spencer Tracy and Katharine Hepburn. The film uses humor and accomplished acting (with Hepburn winning the Oscar for best performance by an actress in a leading role) to make tolerance more palatable.

In the Heat of the Night stars Poitier as a homicide detective from Philadelphia, who is passing through a small Mississippi town when he is arrested for murdering a prominent white man. Poitier is soon cleared but maneuvered into helping the bigoted sheriff, played by Rod Steiger

(who won an Oscar as best actor for his performance), solve the crime. Poitier's character encounters redneck and southern aristocrat types who would like him dead. Finally, the successful northern black detective and the southern white sheriff discover some glimmerings of respect for each other before Poitier's character catches his train for Philadelphia. The most dramatic moment in the film comes when Poitier's character slaps a wealthy white patrician after the man had slapped him for daring to question him.

Although both films clearly broke important ground, they came under fire from more militant sectors of the Civil Rights Movement for relying on black characters (doctor, chief homicide detective) who represented only a small portion of the African American community.

Sex and drugs made their way into mainstream films as never before. *Midnight Cowboy*, which

Easy Rider (1969). Directed by Dennis Hopper. Shown from left: Dennis Hopper, Peter Fonda, Jack Nicholson. It combined elements of a "road film" and a "buddy film" in a bleak portrayal of 1960s America. Courtesy of Photofest.

won Oscars in 1969 for best film and best director (John Schlesinger), introduced its audience to the world of male homosexuality in New York City. Joe Buck, played by Jon Voight, leaves Texas for New York to become a stud for wealthy women; instead, he turns to hustling tricks to support himself and his new friend, the dying Ratso Rizzo (Dustin Hoffman). The X rating the film received from the MPAA appeared not to hurt its standing with the public or with the Academy of Motion Picture Arts and Sciences.

Easy Rider was the creation of Peter Fonda and Dennis Hopper, who starred in the movie (as Captain America and Billy, respectively), wrote the screenplay, and served as director (Hopper) and producer (Fonda). Jack Nicholson played an alcoholic young lawyer who joins them on their motorcycle trip to find freedom and the real America, a trip financed by a cocaine deal. Nicholson's char-

acter is murdered along the way by rednecks, but Fonda's and Hopper's characters end up tripping through a psychedelic New Orleans. The two heroes get murdered on the road after leaving the Big Easy, a lesson of sorts in a film that attempted to portray just about every aspect of counterculture.

Meanwhile, more traditional sex fantasies were conjured up by sex kittens like Raquel Welch in *One Million Years B.C.,* 1966, in which she demonstrated that the first clothing ever invented was the bikini; Jane Fonda, who wore a skintight black suit in *Barbarella,* 1967; and Ursula Andress in the first James Bond film, *Dr. No,* 1962.

One of the most successful films of the decade, *The Graduate,* 1967, starred Dustin Hoffman as a college graduate who becomes involved with Mrs. Robinson, the wife of his father's business partner, and then falls in love with her daughter. Mrs. Robinson, played by Anne Bancroft,

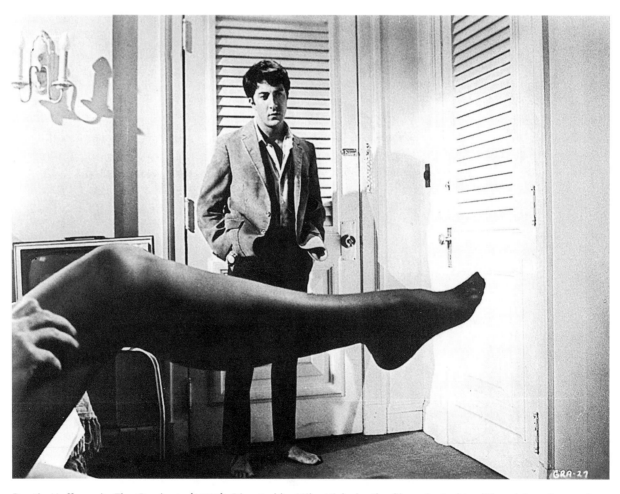

Dustin Hoffman in *The Graduate* (1967). Directed by Mike Nichols, the film rejected traditional American values and made a major star of Hoffman. Courtesy of Photofest.

became a symbol of the older generation's moral degeneration, and the film ends with the young lovers heading off for a life of love and truth. Director Mike Nichols won an Oscar for the film, which depicted the alienation of the younger generation from the old. The film also earned acclaim for its soundtrack, which won three Grammy awards for Simon and Garfunkel.

Mainstream films also became much more graphic in depicting violence and increasingly glorified the outlaw. The most striking example was *Bonnie and Clyde,* 1967, which featured Warren Beatty and Faye Dunaway as Depression-era bank robbers and murderers turned anti-establishment heroes fighting an oppressive social and legal system. In addition to romanticizing the gangsters, the film, directed by Arthur Penn, offered several especially violent scenes, including Bonnie and Clyde being riddled with bullets when law officers ambush them in the film's final scene.

A similar ending occurs in *Butch Cassidy and the Sundance Kid,* 1969, when the outlaws, played by Paul Newman and Robert Redford, are caught in a trap by Bolivian soldiers. The two die in a hail of bullets as they attempt a suicidal but heroic charge. Never have outlaws been so handsome, witty, and charming—and unrealistic. As in *Bonnie and Clyde,* the audience inevitably rooted for the bad guys to outfox the forces of law and order.

Characters such as those depicted by Beatty, Redford, and Newman reflected a growing interest in a different type of hero, the antihero. Antiheroes, rather than conveying the traditional characteristics associated with heroes, reflected values and patterns of behavior more often associated with villains, or at best with failures. The antihero tended to be portrayed not as corrupt or ineffectual, but as in some way appealing and admirable, even if ultimately defeated. As American society increasingly turned away from inherited values in politics, sex, race relations, and many other areas of life, it proved more amenable to characters who similarly defied standard notions of heroism.

Violence also came to living rooms and marital relationships in films of the 1960s. Elizabeth Taylor and Richard Burton starred as husband and wife Martha and George in the film version of Edward Albee's play *Who's Afraid of Virginia Woolf?,* 1966, directed by Mike Nichols. Costar-

ring were George Segal and Sandy Dennis as a young couple invited over to George and Martha's home after a faculty party. Martha verbally attacks George and attempts to seduce biology professor Nick. George responds by inducing the young wife, Honey, to acknowledge that George and Martha's son is dead, ending a fantasy that the childless couple had maintained to make their life more bearable. Taylor and Dennis both won Oscars for their leading and supporting roles, and although most viewers recognized the success of the film, they also found it hard to take because of its unrelenting anger and mutual abuse.

A film that led viewers into frightening supernatural terrain was *Rosemary's Baby,* 1968. The film was directed by Roman Polanski (whose wife, Sharon Tate, would become one of Charles Manson's victims in 1969) and starred Mia Farrow as a young mother who gives birth to a baby who supposedly is Satan's son, the result of an unusually graphic rape scene in which Satan assumes the form of her husband. There is no happy ending, as one of the Satanists proclaims "Here's to year one!" The forces of Satan, played, in keeping with the spirit of the times, by members of the older generation, triumph over the youthful hopes of the young mother.

In the 1960s, many antiwar films focused on the possibility of nuclear war as an outcome of the Cold War. Sometimes the enemy was Russia; at other times the enemy was closer to home, in the guise of war-hungry American military leaders and corrupt or weak American politicians. Accidental war also proved good fodder for films. The most entertaining and outrageous of these films was *Dr. Strangelove: or, How I Learned to Stop Worrying and Love the Bomb,* 1964, directed by Stanley Kubrick. In this movie, General Jack D. Ripper, played by Sterling Hayden, isolates his air force base and launches World War III. The commies, Ripper is convinced, are literally polluting America to rob men of their sex drive. General Buck Turgidson, brilliantly overplayed by George C. Scott, supports the first strike, but is opposed by the otherwise ineffective president, one of three roles played by Peter Sellers. Sellers also plays the British officer held prisoner by Ripper and the wheelchair-bound technical genius who becomes so excited by the prospect of war that he propels himself from his chair shouting "Mein Führer, I can walk!"—revealing himself as a secret Nazi born again in a new attempt to conquer, or destroy, the world. Ultimately, one bomber makes it through and drops its payload on Russia. The film, though enormously funny, also proved frightening in its satiric portrayal of what might go wrong when crazies with the technological means to destroy the world run around loose.

The major commercial film depicting the Vietnam War during the 1960s was a personal project of John Wayne's, *The Green Berets,* 1968. The movie was based on Robin Moore's novel *The Green Berets,* 1965, and capitalized on Barry Sadler's "The Ballad of the Green Berets," which became a big hit in 1966. Ultimately, however, the film was a vehicle for Wayne to convey his views of the war and his definition of patriotism. David Janssen of television's *The Fugitive* played a skeptical reporter who comes around to Wayne's way of thinking after seeing Vietcong fiendishness and the suffering of innocent Vietnamese children. The film was not one of Wayne's best efforts; even geographical details were wrong, such as having the sun set in the East, into the South China Sea.

Other popular genres included horror and gothic films at one extreme and beach films at the other. Horror films made people afraid of old houses, dark nights, and even shower stalls. *What Ever Happened to Baby Jane?,* 1962, popularized a subgenre of the horror/gothic film known as the "menopausal murder story." Such films featured elderly women, often played by longtime leading actresses, who did horrible things in the darkness of their also aging homes. In this Robert Aldrich film, a reclusive Jane (Bette Davis), a former child vaudeville star known as Baby Jane, learns that her sister, Blanche (Joan Crawford), plans to have her committed to an asylum and sell off the old mansion; Jane locks the wheelchair-bound Blanche in her room. The film used two actresses who in real life were bitter rivals, which provided an interesting touch.

The master of horror during the 1960s, though, remained the director Alfred Hitchcock. His *Psycho,* 1960, included one of the most famous horror scenes of all time: Janet Leigh being stabbed to death while taking a shower in her motel room. Anthony Perkins played the murderer, who masquerades as his dead mother while running the Bates Motel. Another memorable Hitchcock horror film during the decade was *The Birds,* 1963, in which birds wage war on humans. Hitchcock also turned out espionage films during the decade and hosted his own television series, *Alfred Hitchcock Presents.*

Viewers also had numerous beach films from which to choose. American-International Pictures produced some of the most popular beach films, several of which starred former lead Mousketeer of Walt Disney's *The Mickey Mouse Club,* Annette Funicello, and singer Frankie Avalon. These included *Beach Party,* 1963, *How to Stuff a Wild Bikini,* 1965, and *Beach Blanket Bingo,* 1965. Given Annette's image, carefully maintained by Disney, as young America's pretty and pure sweetheart, the films stayed away from the social turmoil and changing sexual mores flowing through American society. Annette, in fact, was not permitted to wear a bikini, and her relationship with love interest Frankie Avalon remained unceasingly chaste.

There was plenty of other escapist fare in the 1960s. Elvis Presley, back from the army, starred in 27 films during the decade, typically featured as a singing pilot, race car driver, and so on. His costars were among the most beautiful actresses of the times: Juliet Prowse in *G.I. Blues,* 1960, and Ann-Margret in *Viva Las Vegas,* 1964. The films did little to secure Elvis's long-term fame, but they did bring in the cash. One of the great social events of the decade was the King's marriage in 1967 to Priscilla Beaulieu, whom Elvis met when she was 14 and he was stationed in Germany, as was Priscilla's father, a career military man. The approximately 10-year difference in their ages excited considerable attention but did not seem to harm Elvis's standing with his fans.

The James Bond films fed millions of men's fantasies during the 1960s, as they imagined themselves like Agent 007: handsome, suave, owner of high-powered cars and other advanced gadgets, victorious over assorted villains, and always getting the beautiful and exotic girl. The original Bond, and for many still the ultimate, was played by Sean Connery. The first Bond film was *Dr. No,* 1962, followed by *From Russia with Love,* 1963, *Goldfinger,* 1964, *Thunderball,* 1965, and *You Only Live Twice,* 1967. The stories usually occurred in exotic locations where Bond battled

HOW OTHERS SEE US

The Spaghetti Western

Hollywood's cowboy films had always found eager foreign audiences. When the American film industry turned away from the Western genre in about 1960, European studios began to fill the gap with their own product. From 1962 to 1973, filmmakers from Italy, Spain, and Germany produced 200 to 600 Westerns. Their low-budget movies were huge moneymakers outside the United States, and would eventually win a prominent place in American pop culture, though at first they had mainly a cult following among American moviegoers. Disparaging critics, while hurling insults ("those peculiar marathons of cowboys, gore, dubbing, sadism and trompe l'oeil" was one of the more restrained descriptions), dubbed the films "spaghetti Westerns"—a label that their young creators seized with pleasure.

Then-unknown Italian director Sergio Leone created the first landmark film of the genre, *A Fistful of Dollars,* in 1964. With his $200,000 budget he hired an American television actor, Clint Eastwood, and shot on location near Almeria in Spain, a desert landscape that mimicked the American Southwest. Leone's story of the mercenary Man With No Name reveled in all the stereotypes of the cowboy movie while adding a mythic quality and an operatic sensibility.

Music was a critical element in Leone's film. The score by Ennio Morricone included theme music for each major character, in keeping with the movie's broadly dramatic, classically operatic mood. Huge, empty vistas were interlaced with tiny details—a gunfighter's shifting eyes, the sound of buzzing flies—to make the film's extreme and stylized violence seem at once hyperdramatic and hyperreal.

Cold War enemies of Great Britain and the Free World. Some of the title songs, such as Shirley Bassey's "Goldfinger" and Nancy Sinatra's "You Only Live Twice," became hits; the Bond films also helped their beautiful, foreign-born actresses achieve fame, among them Ursula Andress, Daniela Bianchi, Honor Blackman, and Shirley Eaton. The Bond women, especially in the later Connery films of the 1960s, helped to change the Western world's taste in beautiful women from busty, big-hipped sex-pots like Marilyn Monroe and Jayne Mansfield to slender, youthful types who looked as if they would be as much at home riding a bike or climbing a mountain as inviting a handsome secret agent into their boudoir.

Finally, there were the alternative and underground films. Some of the films already discussed, such as *Easy Rider,* were clearly out of the mainstream in content and mode of production even though they were distributed commercially. The so-called art film tended toward less narrative continuity than most commercial films and often shifted in unusual ways between realism and subjectivity. Individual style was especially important in the art films, and the content more explicitly represented social and sexual changes in American culture than did most commercial cinema.

Andy Warhol especially stretched the boundaries of films—and sometimes the limits of viewers' patience—as he moved from minimal, avant-garde films to commercial productions. *Sleep,* 1963, for example, is simply a film of a person sleeping. For *Empire,* Warhol trained a camera on the Empire State Building from 1963 to 1964, thereby producing probably the longest film in history.

Underground films usually emanated from New York City or San Francisco and represented subcultures and their sexual, aesthetic, drug, and political proclivities. Such films were usually little more than documentaries of these groups and proved even less commercially viable than art films.

TELEVISION

Television became the dominant communications medium in American society during the 1960s. At the beginning of the decade, over 45 million households had at least one television, and that figure would rise to almost 60 million by the end of the 1960s.[2] The three major networks, the Columbia Broadcasting System (CBS), the National Broadcasting Company (NBC), and the American Broadcasting Company (ABC) dominated programming. A small amount of alternative programming was provided by the new Public Broadcasting Service (PBS), founded in 1969, and by cable television, available in about seven percent of homes by the end of the decade.[3]

During the 1960s television transformed from a New York-based industry with single sponsors controlling shows to a Hollywood-based system with multiple sponsorship and network control over shows. Major film studios and independent companies produced the shows, which were licensed, distributed, and often owned by the networks. The A. C. Nielsen Corporation measured viewer attention, *TV Guide* magazine published television schedules, and the Federal Communications Commission (FCC) regulated the industry. The movement to color programming by the mid-1960s attracted even more viewers. The evening network news programs expanded in 1963 from 15 to 30 minutes, turning such news anchormen as Walter Cronkite on CBS and the team of Chet Huntley and David Brinkley on NBC into the primary dispensers of news to the masses.

These changes did not proceed without controversy. In 1961, FCC chairman Newton Minow blasted the television industry for its lack of quality programming, labeling the small screen a "vast wasteland."[4] In the same year, Senator Thomas Dodd of Connecticut opened his Senate hearings on violence in television. The hearings ran out of gas in 1964, but did prompt a partial shift from action adventure shows to sitcoms, as well as several research projects that explored the effects of television violence on children.

The Untouchables, 1959–1963, starring Robert Stack as Prohibition-era crime fighter Eliot Ness, came under fire by Dodd and also by Italian American groups who objected to the show's depiction of Italian Americans as gangsters. The series toned down its violence and incorporated more gangsters with non-Italian names.

Television sought to avoid controversy in order to not offend its viewers. Throughout the decade, television, much more than theater films, stayed as far removed as possible from the changes going on in American society. Series from the 1950s about all-American families, such as *Father Knows Best,* 1954–1963, starring Robert Young, and *The Adventures of Ozzie and Harriet,* 1952–1966, with Ozzie and Harriet Nelson playing themselves along with their actual sons David and future

rock star Ricky, continued their success into the 1960s. Robert Young left *Father Knows Best* after the 1959–60 season, but the show continued in reruns on prime time for the next three years.

Wisdom and comedy combined in *The Andy Griffith Show,* 1960–1968. Griffith played Sheriff Andy Taylor of Mayberry, North Carolina, who provided commonsense guidance to son Opie (Ron Howard) and bumbling Deputy Barney Fife (Don Knotts). Knotts won five Emmys from the Academy of Television Arts and Sciences for his role as best supporting actor.[5] The series featured an endearing set of town characters including Frances Bavier as Aunt Bee and Jim Nabors, whose character spun off his own series, *Gomer Pyle, U.S.M.C.*

Broad comedy characterized the families and friends on *The Dick Van Dyke Show,* 1961–1966 and *The Beverly Hillbillies,* 1962–1971, two of television's all-time popular series. A favorite with

---

NOTABLE TV SHOWS

The Andy Griffith Show

The Beverly Hillbillies

Bewitched

Candid Camera

The Dick Van Dyke Show

Doctor Who

The Ed Sullivan Show

Gilligan's Island

Gomer Pyle, U.S.M.C.

Gunsmoke

Hee-Haw

I Dream of Jeannie

The Lucy Show

Mission: Impossible

Rowan and Martin's Laugh In

Star Trek

The Tonight Show

The Twilight Zone

Wagon Train

What's My Line

both viewers and critics, the series won numerous Emmys, including four as top program in its field, three for Van Dyke, and two for Mary Tyler Moore, who played his wife. *The Beverly Hillbillies,* which starred Buddy Ebsen as Jed Clampett, patriarch of an Ozarks family that struck it rich in oil and moved to Hollywood, was even more popular with viewers, finishing number one in the Nielsen ratings for the 1962–1963 and 1963–1964 seasons.

Some families were more unusual, and were based on popular comic series, such as the mock-horror characters of *The Munsters,* 1964–1966, and *The Addams Family,* 1964–1966. *The Flintstones,* 1960–1966, were a popular animated family that featured Fred and Wilma Flintstone. *The Flintstones* parodied suburban life in the 1960s, as the characters enjoyed all the modern conveniences of life, prehistoric style, while maintaining traditional spousal stereotypes. The show introduced the nonsense phrase "Yabba Dabba Doo!" into the American lexicon.

The most consistent reflection of political issues in television entertainment occurred on crime and western series with good triumphing over bad in moral struggles. Crime-fighting took many forms, from J. Edgar Hoover's agents (led by Efrem Zimbalist Jr.) tracking down spies, counterfeiters, and other unsavory types on *The F.B.I.,* 1965–1974, to the three youthful hippie cops of *The Mod Squad,* 1968–1973, to the interracial anti-espionage team of Robert Culp and Bill Cosby in *I Spy,* 1965–1968, to the James Bond spoof *Get Smart* starring Don Adams, 1965–1970. Raymond Burr exonerated his clients while discovering the true evildoers on *Perry Mason,* 1957–1966, and later was a wounded chief of detectives confined to a wheelchair in *Ironside,* 1967–1971.

In one of the most remarkable series of the 1960s, David Janssen starred on *The Fugitive,* 1963–1967, as Dr. Richard Kimble, who searched the country for the one-armed murderer of his wife, both to gain justice for her and exonerate himself. Kimble was being taken by train to be executed for the murder when a derailment allowed him to escape from Lt. Philip Gerard. Throughout the series, Gerard pursued Kimble, and Kimble pursued the one-armed murderer. Along the way, Kimble assumed a long line of new identities and solved countless problems for others. The series

to some extent paralleled the real-life case of Dr. Sam Sheppard, who was convicted of murdering his wife but continued to claim that she had been killed by an intruder. During the years of the series, Dr. Sheppard was granted a new trial and found not guilty.

Batman, 1966–1968, was futuristic with its gadgets, including the Batmobile. Batman (Adam West) and youthful sidekick Robin (Dick Grayson) battled a host of unusual villains, such as the Penguin (Burgess Meredith) and the Riddler (Frank Gorshin), to preserve the peace and security of Gotham City.

Westerns of the 1960s reflected an increasingly complex society—for example, they emphasized strong independent women, presented a more balanced depiction of Native Americans, and de-emphasized violence when television violence became a major issue during the early 1960s. The rise of the adult western in the 1950s had introduced greater complexity into the motivation and behavior of such heroes as Matt Dillon on *Gunsmoke,* 1955–1975. Yet the genre continued to appeal to those who saw moral issues in stark good-versus-evil terms, with good triumphing. That attitude fell increasingly out of favor with the escalation of antiwar sentiment and civil strife over racial and generational issues in the second half of the 1960s, and with a growing realization that traditional ideas of right were often inadequate.

The "family" western emerged in the late 1950s and continued through the early 1960s. These films featured western families, usually minus the mother, and included *The Rifleman,* 1958–1963, starring Chuck Connors as the widowed Lucas McCain rearing his son and *The Virginian,* 1962–1971, with Lee J. Cobb and James Drury. *The Big Valley,* 1965–1969, was unusual in that the widowed mother, played by Barbara Stanwyck, headed up the family.

The most popular of the family westerns (next to *Gunsmoke,* the most popular television western of all time), though, was *Bonanza,* 1959–1973. Bonanza starred Lorne Greene as Ben Cartwright and Michael Landon, Dan Blocker, and Pernell Roberts as sons Little Joe, Hoss, and Adam. The series was the number one rated show on television for three consecutive seasons, from 1964–1967 and, resisting the overall drop in popularity of

Gunsmoke was the top-rated television show at the beginning of the 1960s and continued on the air until 1975. Its 20 years on television (1955–1975) were the most ever by a prime-time series with continuing characters. The main characters included (left to right): James Arness (as Marshal Matt Dillon); Amanda Blake (Kitty Russell); Milburn Stone (Doc Adams); and Dennis Weaver (Deputy Chester Goode). Courtesy of Photofest.

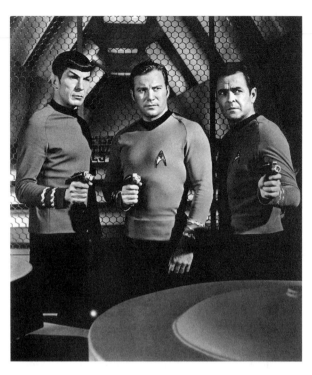

The original *Star Trek*, which was shown on television on NBC from 1966 to 1969. Shown from left: Leonard Nimoy (as Lt. Cmdr. Spock), William Shatner (as Captain James T. Kirk), and James Doohan (as Montgomery Scott "Scotty"). Courtesy of Photofest.

westerns, remained in the top 10 from 1961 to 1971. *Gunsmoke* also bucked the 1960's anti-western trend. Starring James Arness as Marshal Matt Dillon, Amanda Blake as Kitty Russell, and Milburn Stone as crusty Doc Adams, the series was set in historic Dodge City, Kansas. The show featured a supporting cast that included Burt Reynolds as part-Indian blacksmith Quint Asper (1962–1965), Dennis Weaver as Deputy Chester Goode (1955–1964), and Ken Curtis as Festus Haggen (1964–1975). *Gunsmoke* was the top-rated show from 1957 to 1961. After dropping out of the top 10 (1963–1967), it reached fourth place in the 1967–1968 season, and continued in the top 10 through 1972–1973.

The 1960s began with westerns holding the top three spots in the ratings for the 1959–1960, 1960–1961, and 1961–1962 seasons, thanks to *Gunsmoke, Wagon Train, Have Gun Will Travel,*

and *Bonanza.* By 1969–1970, *Gunsmoke* and *Bonanza* stood alone as the only westerns in the top 30. The demise of the western reflected not only the political changes in the United States but also the reality that with the western directed primarily toward adults throughout the 1960s, large numbers of children had come of age without connecting with the genre. In addition, President Kennedy had proclaimed space a "new frontier," and as Americans' attention turned skyward, television followed suit.

Among the space shows during the 1960s, *Star Trek,* 1966–1969, was the most memorable. Producer Gene Roddenberry saw his series as something of a replacement for the traditional western, characterizing the series as a "Wagon Train to the stars," a reference to the *Wagon Train* series, 1957–1965. Captain James Kirk (William Shatner), the unrelentingly logical Mr. Spock (Leonard Nimoy), Dr. McCoy (DeForest Kelley), and the rest of the crew of the starship *Enterprise* engaged various forms of alien life in battle on its interstellar jour-

STAR TREK

In 1964, screenwriter and producer Gene Roddenberry proposed a groundbreaking new series to NBC studios. Roddenberry's creation, now known around the world as the "Star Trek" universe, featured a unique blend of science fiction and moral drama and became one of the most successful franchises in history. It has evolved through five hit television series, films, and hundreds of novels into a detailed fictional universe. The original Star Trek series debuted in 1966 and remained on the air for three years. Though the special effects were laughable and the acting melodramatic, if endearing, the show developed a loyal audience often known (either derisively or affectionately) as "Trekkies." Set against the backdrop of space, Star Trek addressed serious issues, like violence and race relations, that were too sensitive for more realistic series. Star Trek is also often credited with featuring the first interracial kiss on television. Though the series was cancelled for poor ratings, fans protested to such an extent that the producers decided to convert the franchise to film. Star Trek made its big screen debut in 1979 with *Star Trek: the Motion Picture,* and was followed by a series of successful sequels. NBC eventually decided to bring the universe back to television with *Star Trek: The Next Generation,* which ran from 1987 to 1993 and led to three additional series. Over the years, the Star Trek universe has had an enormous cultural impact. From spawning one of the world's most detailed fictional languages, "Klingon," to inspiring a generation of physicists and engineers to create new innovations, Star Trek occupies a unique place in American culture.

neys. Although not particularly popular during its original run, the series attracted loyal fans known as Trekkies who faithfully followed the show in reruns and staged *Star Trek* conventions.

The 1960s offered considerable diversity. Doctor shows were in, especially series that featured young, handsome doctors like Richard Chamberlain on *Dr. Kildare,* 1961–1966, and Vince Edwards on *Ben Casey,* 1961–1966. Critics loved *The Twilight Zone,* 1959–1965, created and hosted by playwright Rod Serling. The program featured unusual, provocative stories that often ended with an ironic twist. The show earned four Emmys but never ranked in Nielsen's top 35. Conversely, critics mocked *The Lawrence Welk Show,* 1955–1982, lamented that the show appealed to an aged audience, and did not take seriously the squeaky clean cast of Welk's musical family and their "champagne music." The show ran on network television for 16 years and produced additional new episodes in syndication for more than another decade. Its popularity peaked during the second half of the 1960s as a statement of traditional values.

Ed Sullivan came across as a wooden and inarticulate host on *The Ed Sullivan Show* (originally called *Toast of the Town*). From 1948 to 1971 this Sunday night fixture introduced viewers to a world of talent including trick-performing dogs, Senor Wences and his talking box, Elvis Presley, and the Beatles. Sullivan was a favorite among comedians and impressionists, and his habits of hugging himself with crossed arms and welcoming his audience to a "really big shew" were often imitated. Sullivan changed popular culture in the United States. The performances by Elvis (shot from the waist up to hide his pelvic gyrations) in 1956 and the Beatles in 1964 introduced them to millions of American viewers for the first time and remain among the most important moments in television history. In addition, Sullivan integrated television by featuring a long list of African American performers, including Lena Horne and Pearl Bailey.

Viewers could see regular people on *Candid Camera,* 1960–1967. Allen Funt started directing a hidden camera at normal people in the late 1940s, but had his steadiest run on television during the 1960s. The point was to find the humor in everyday activities by filming people simply doing what they normally did. The show also set up gags or practical jokes and filmed people's reactions. Individuals encountered vending machines that talked back and restaurants that served miniscule portions of food. Finally, the unsuspecting victims would hear the revealing words, "Smile, you're on *Candid Camera.*"

Millions of Americans continued to retire for the night with *The Tonight Show* starring Jack

Entertainment

Paar and, from 1962 on, Johnny Carson. Carson, with his opening monologue, comedy skits, and wide range of entertaining guests, was so popular that it was said he lowered the birth rate, as viewers refused to turn their attention from his show.

Television moved into social satire during the 1960s. *Rowan and Martin's Laugh-In,* 1968–1973, emphasized humor and gentle mockery rather than serious social satire. Headed by Dan Rowan and Dick Martin and featuring a large and talented cast (Ruth Buzzi, Judy Carne, Goldie Hawn, Arte Johnson, Lily Tomlin and others), the show offered a fast-paced series of sketches, one-liners, and cameo performances by celebrities, including politicians. *Laugh-In* expressions such as "You bet your bippy" and "Sock it to me" entered the nation's lexicon. Even Richard Nixon appeared on the show, inviting the audience to "Sock it to me." The series was number one in the Nielsen ratings during its first two seasons, but declined as many of its stars moved on to other ventures.

While *Laugh-In* offended few, *The Smothers Brothers Comedy Hour,* 1967–1969, offended many people in high places within the industry. Tom and Dick Smothers started off inoffensively enough with folk songs, witty repartee, and enough mainstream guests such as George Burns, Jim Nabors, and Eva Gabor to offset their irreverent tone. The show appealed to a youthful audience and included Leigh French as Goldie O'Keefe, a "hippie chick" who boasted of her drug experiences in terminology that older viewers did not sufficiently understand to get upset about. *The Smothers Brothers* moved steadily leftward in its second and third seasons and ran into increasing trouble with CBS executives and censors. CBS pulled the plug on the series on April 3, 1969, claiming that Tom Smothers had not provided an acceptable tape of the show's next broadcast in time for appropriate review by the Program Practices Department and local stations.

Throughout the decade, social scientists, politicians, educators, parents, and others had been looking carefully at the effects of television programming on children. In 1969, *Sesame Street* began to offer preschool children both entertainment and education on PBS. An outstanding creative team and high production values made the show a welcome partner to parents and teachers.

HOW OTHERS SEE US

Can You Tell Me How to Get to *Plaza Sesamo?*

The children's television show *Sesame Street* was one American product that was never meant to be marketed outside the United States. Created by the nonprofit Children's Television Workshop and aimed squarely at American preschoolers, its early episodes were not filmed with separated (and therefore dub-able) sound tracks, unlike most American TV programs, which were heavily pushed into foreign markets.

Even so, TV networks from Jamaica, Canada, and Australia immediately clamored for the rights to air the show, and within three years of its 1969 debut *Sesame Street* was being broadcast in 48 nations, from Japan to Iran to Poland to Nigeria. Aired in its original English with occasional local-language voice-overs, the show soon had children the world over counting in English and singing the English alphabet.

While parents appreciated the show's high entertainment and educational value, many became concerned about its U.S.-centric point of view. (After watching a *Sesame Street* film about cows, an English father asked his son if he knew where milk came from. "Of course," said the boy, "America.") In 1972, a Spanish-language version of the program, *Plaza Sesamo,* began production in Mexico City with CTW participation. The new show was broadcast throughout Latin America and led to more than 30 *Sesame Street* siblings, including *Sesamstrasse* in Germany, *Ulitsa Sezam* in Russia, *Zhima Jie* in China, and *Alam Simsim* in Egypt. Still, the impact of the original English-language run continued to reverberate, one more factor in the rise of English as a global tongue.

The heart of *Sesame Street* was a group of Muppets created by Jim Henson—Ernie and Bert, Big Bird, Oscar the Grouch, Cookie Monster, and Kermit the Frog. The show was set on a city street to appeal to urban youth and included a serious commitment to ethnic diversity. Snappy tunes made learning the alphabet and many other things fun. Some observers worried that the rapid pace of the show would depress children's attention span, but teachers found that youngsters who had watched *Sesame Street* started school with much better knowledge of numbers and letters than their predecessors.

RADIO IN THE 1960s

As TV's variety, comedy, and drama shows gained viewers in the mid-1950s, similar programs disappeared from the nation's radio stations. Adults continued to tune in to radio for breaking news events and informational programs, but by 1960 radio had been eclipsed as America's primary home entertainment medium.

One demographic comprised the exception: teenagers and young adults. Many broadcasters turned to rock-and-roll music to stay afloat. Local AM stations in Kansas City and Dallas developed the "Top 40" format, whose loud disk jockeys and pop songs were ubiquitous nationwide in the early to late 1960s. A new invention, the battery-operated portable transistor radio, encouraged young people to take their favorite stations with them wherever they went. Teenagers and young adults stayed glued to the radio, listening to the latest songs at home and in the car. Especially during the mid to late 1960s, everyone was listening to singles on the radio by the Supremes and other Motown performers, the Beatles, the Rolling Stones, James Brown, Bob Dylan, the Kinks, Simon and Garfunkel, the Beach Boys, Jimi Hendrix, and others. Weekly radio programs offered countdown shows of the newly ranked top 10 singles.

By the late 1960s, however, FM radio was fast becoming the favorite of music lovers. Stereo broadcasting was authorized by the Federal Communications Commission in 1961—for FM stations only. With superior sound quality, but limited

MAJOR TOP-40 DJS

Johnny Dolan (WHB-AM, Kansas City)

"Murray the K" Kaufman (WINS-AM and WOR-FM, New York City)

Don Keyes (KLIF-AM, Dallas)

"Cousin Brucie" Morrow (WABC-AM, New York City)

"The Real" Don Steele (KHJ-AM, Los Angeles)

FREEFORM RADIO PIONEERS

Tom Donahue (KMPX-FM, San Francisco)

Dave Herman (WMMR-FM, Philadelphia)

John Leonard (KPFA-FM, Berkeley, California)

Scott Muni (WOR-FM and WNEW-FM, New York City)

Vin Scelsa (WFMU-FM, East Orange, New Jersey)

geographic reach, FM outlets experimented with long-form rock broadcasting; many stations offered progressive jazz and classical music. Album-oriented rock, or AOR, and loose "freeform" programming offered an alternative to the limited playlists of the longer-reach AM stations.

DANCE

Dances such as The Twist, The Frug, The Jerk, The Mashed Potato, The Funky Chicken, and The Swim were popular during the 1960s. Such dances, as short-lived as most of them were, showed teens' determination of to manufacture new forms of entertainment sharply different from those of their parents. The dances conveyed enthusiasm and spontaneity, a sense of individualism, and a clear preference for the unconventional. Like of the changing fashion, hair styles, and music, these dances belonged to a youth culture determined to create rather than inherit.

The dances had some fairly standard movements, but nothing as firmly established as the steps of most ballroom dances; however, the freedom conveyed by these dances fit the spirit of the 1960s—freedom of movement, freedom from the traditions of the older generation, and freedom to express oneself with spontaneous adjustments to the minimal patterns associated with the dances.

Pantomime played an important role in many of the popular dances of the decade. The Swim involved dancers extending and retracting their arms as if they were swimming. Sometimes, a dancer would hold his or her nose with one hand while slowly sinking to the floor as if submerging in a swimming pool. The Jerk usually included holding one arm aloft while slowly sinking to the floor in a series of jerky movements that brought

Entertainment

the entire body down, the arm following suit, then slowly jerking back upright with the other arm rising. The Funky Chicken usually accompanied soul music and included chicken-like movements.

The dance that most symbolized the 1960s and opened the dance floor to countless other dances, was The Twist. Unlike many popular dances of the time, The Twist had a long history. It grew out of a nineteenth century twisting dance that was popular in African American settings; in the 1930s, the Sensational Nightingales, a gospel group, invited listeners to "do the twist." The 1960s version of the dance was the work of Hank Ballard, who recorded "The Twist" in the late 1950s. The song quickly spawned an accompanying dance. By July 1960, the song was a hit, and Dick Clark wanted to feature it on his *American Bandstand* show. Clark felt that Ballard, although an important rhythm and blues artist, was too associated with songs that included sexual allusions (like "Sexy Ways") to fit his show's wholesome image. Clark therefore encouraged a young singer named Chubby Checker to record the song, which Checker tried out on *The Dick Clark Show* (an evening version of the daytime *American Bandstand*) in August 1960. Both the song and dance became hits; Checker's version climbed to the top of the charts by September. In 1962, Checker's "The Twist" became the first record since Bing Crosby's "White Christmas" to make a return trip to first place after being off the charts.

"The Twist" precipitated some two dozen "Twist" songs, such as "Let's Twist Again" (Checker,

Chubby Checker demonstrates the twist in the film *Twist around the Clock* (1961). The coats and ties worn by Checker and the band are typical attire of the early to mid-1960s pop music entertainers. Courtesy of Photofest.

1961), "Twist and Shout" (The Isley Brothers, 1961), and "Twistin' the Night Away" (Sam Cooke, 1962).

When teens were not dancing, they were often watching Dick Clark's *American Bandstand, 1956–1989*. The show was enormously influential, and helped make stars of such performers as Chubby Checker, Frankie Avalon, Fabian, and the Everly Brothers. Clark deserves credit for bringing white and black teenagers together in a social context on national television for the first time and for featuring many African American performers.

Young adults increasingly favored discotheques (so-called discos), which originated in France and featured records (disks) rather than live bands. The discotheques, such as New York's Peppermint Lounge, which featured Joey Dee and the Star-lighters and gave rise to the song "The Pepper-mint Twist," were most often found in cities. Some of the discos also highlighted attractive young women dancing on stages, in cages, or in otherwise prominent places. These "go-go dancers" typically wore skimpy attire and high boots, which came to be known as go-go boots.

A dance that went over well with the slightly older crowd was The Limbo. An individual dancer would dance up to a stick held horizontally by two people, perhaps to Chubby Checker's 1962 "Limbo Rock," and attempt to move underneath the stick, body bent back, without falling to the floor.

Ballet also won headlines in the 1960s, often for political reasons. In 1960, the American Ballet Theatre became the first U.S. company to tour Russia. On June 16, 1961, the great Russian ballet dancer Rudolf Nureyev defected to the West while performing in Paris. He subsequently performed with the Royal Ballet in London. His defection was seen in the United States as another sign of Western superiority in the Cold War competition.

In 1962, Nureyev debuted in the United States in *Don Quixote* for Ruth Page's Chicago Opera Ballet. Nureyev excited considerable attention, not only because he had made such a bold political statement, but also for his innovative and athletic dancing style and strong personality.

Throughout the 1960s, new venues for fine ballet kept opening up. William Christensen started Ballet West in Salt Lake City in 1963. In 1964, Virginia Williams, with $7 million from the Ford Foundation, created the Boston Ballet and the New York City Ballet, which opened in Lincoln Center's New York State Theater.

The most important creative force in presenting great ballet to American audiences in the 1960s was another Russian-born defector, George Balanchine. Born Georgi Balanchivadze in St. Petersburg in 1904, the ballet dancer defected while performing in Europe in 1924. Balanchine moved to the United States in 1933 to create the American Ballet Company. Viewed by many critics as the finest choreographer of the mid-twentieth century, Balanchine continued to produce exciting ballets throughout the decade for the New York City Ballet, that in 1948 he had helped to create. These ballets included *A Midsummer Night's Dream*, 1962, *Tarantella*, 1964, *Don Quixote*, 1965, and *Jewels*, 1967.

NOTABLE THEATER

Camelot, 1960 (873 perfs.)

How to Succeed in Business Without Really Trying, 1961 (1,417 perfs.)

Mary, Mary, 1961 (1,572 perfs.)

A Funny Things Happened on the Way to the Forum, 1962 (964 perfs.)

Barefoot in the Park, 1963 (1,530 perfs.)

Hello, Dolly!, 1964 (2,844 perfs.)

Funny Girl, 1964 (1,348 perfs.)

Fiddler on the Roof, 1964 (3,242 perfs.)

Cactus Flower, 1965 (1,234 perfs.)

Man of La Mancha, 1965 (2,328 perfs)

The Odd Couple, 1965 (964 perfs.)

Mame, 1966 (1,508 perfs.)

Cabaret, 1966 (1,165 perfs.)

Hair, 1968 (1,750 perfs.)

Promises, Promises, 1968 (1,281 perfs.)

1776, 1969 (1,217 perfs.)

Oh! Calcutta!, 1969 (1,314 perfs.)

Entertainment

DRAMA

The great masters of American drama at the beginning of the 1960s were Tennessee Williams and Arthur Miller. Williams had established himself with such hits as *The Glass Menagerie,* 1945, and *A Streetcar Named Desire,* 1947, and Miller with *Death of a Salesman,* 1949. In 1961, Tennessee Williams created *The Night of the Iguana* about a group of people at a seedy coastal hotel in Mexico, with the iguana symbolizing the bondage afflicting the human participants. *The Night of the Iguana* earned Williams his fourth New York Drama Critics' Circle Award.

By the 1960s, Arthur Miller was as well known to the general public for his marriage to actress Marilyn Monroe, previously married to baseball great Joe DiMaggio, as for his drama. They married in 1956, and Miller wrote the screenplay *The Misfits* for his wife. Released in 1960, *The Misfits* was the final film for both Monroe and Clark Gable. The following year, Miller and Monroe divorced, and Monroe committed suicide in 1962. Ironically, possibly Miller's best play during the 1960s was *After the Fall,* 1964, an autobiographical exploration of the playwright's life, including his wives.

Musicals, long popular with American audiences and viewed by many drama historians as a particularly American genre, continued to play well on Broadway with audiences that preferred traditional fare. The list of memorable musicals from the decade includes *The Sound of Music,* by Richard Rodgers and Oscar Hammerstein II, which won a Tony for best musical in 1960; *Oliver!,* 1963, by Lionel Bart; *Hello Dolly!,* 1964, which starred Carol Channing and set a record by winning 10 Tonys; *Funny Girl,* 1964, by Jule Styne and starring Barbara Streisand; and *Cabaret,* 1966, by John Kander and Fred Ebb.

Camelot, 1960, another of the blockbuster musicals of the 1960s, occupies a special place in American culture. The show, by Frederick Loewe and Alan Jay Lerner, starred Richard Burton as King Arthur, Julie Andrews as Queen Guenevere, and Robert Goulet as Lancelot. The story of a faraway time and place of great ideals ruled by a brave and honorable king was a favorite of President and Mrs. Kennedy. After the president's

assassination, Mrs. Kennedy compared the Kennedy presidency to Arthur's legendary city, Camelot, thereby establishing a lasting analogy between the abbreviated administration and a line from the musical: "…one brief shining moment that was known as Camelot." The association became a lasting epithet (some would say myth) that defined Kennedy's term in office and the country at that time.[6] Although musicals would continue to be produced, they would never again occupy such a powerful position on the Broadway stage.

The new star of comedy was Neil Simon, who had honed his writing skills in early television on *Your Show of Shows,* 1950–1954, starring Sid Caesar and Imogene Coca. Simon produced nine hit comedies in the decade, each examining a particular aspect of contemporary life. Finding comedy in discordant personalities, he created a spontaneous young bride and conservative husband in *Barefoot in the Park,* 1963, and most famously the mismatched roommates of *The Odd Couple,* 1965, compulsively tidy Felix Unger and slob Oscar Madison. *The Odd Couple* starred two of the great comic actors of the century, Art Carney and Walter Matthau, and translated on both the large and small screens into highly successful film in 1967 and television versions that ran from 1970 to 1975, the former teaming Jack Lemmon with Matthau, the latter substituting Tony Randall and Jack Klugman. In his later plays of the 1960s, such as *The Last of the Red-Hot Lovers,* 1969, Simon turned to the sexual revolution for comic situations. Although critics debated the quality of Simon's plays, he undeniably influenced the shape of American popular comedy.

Some of the great social issues of the day—racial justice, feminism, the antiwar movement, the continued rise of rock music, and sexual freedom—left their mark on American drama.

One of the most important African American dramatists of the decade was Lorraine Hansberry. Hansberry became the first African American woman to have a play on Broadway when *A Raisin in the Sun* opened in 1959. The play chronicled Hansberry's own family plight and highlighted a black family's difficulties trying to move from a Chicago apartment into a nice house in a white neighborhood. Critics applauded the play for its sophisticated depth and realism in tackling racial and gender issues, and for its excellent performances, especially by Sidney Poitier as Walter Lee Younger. Some African Americans, however, saw the play as championing white middle-class values and noted its use of terms such as "Negro" and "colored," which were increasingly rejected by black activists during the 1960s as white-imposed designations. *A Raisin in the Sun* was turned into a successful film in 1961, with Poitier reprising his stage role.

In 1973, a musical version, *Raisin,* appeared on Broadway. A second Hansberry play, *The Sign in Sidney Brustein's Window,* opened on Broadway in 1964. This play consisted mainly of white characters, including a homosexual, as Hansberry demonstrated her ability to explore not only racial and gender but also sexual and political issues. Unfortunately, this very talented playwright died in 1965 of cancer. The title of a compilation of her writings transformed into a 1969 off-Broadway hit that summed up her great potential and tragic loss: *To Be Young, Gifted, and Black.*

Megan Terry was a major figure in the rise of feminist drama, and supported new venues for little known but talented playwrights. Terry helped to found the New York Open Theater and was its playwright-in-residence from 1963 to 1968. A leader in experimental theater, she was largely responsible for developing the transformation play, which required actors to engage in continuous improvisation and transform a play in response to changing settings, incidents in the plot, and nuances in character development.

Terry was also an important pioneer in using drama to protest the Vietnam War. Her *Viet Rock: A Folk War Movie,* produced by the Open Theater in 1966, was the first significant play about the war. The play departed from traditional musicals in important ways, including its use of rock music and interaction between players and audience. At the end of the play, all the performers dropped to the ground amid giant explosions, with Americans and Vietnamese killed indiscriminately. A coda, however, offered hope for the future, with the actors rising and entering the audience, each actor touching a viewer's hand, face, or hair.

Opposition to the war in American society was part of a larger movement of anti-traditionalism.

Many young people rejected the status quo and authority across the board, including their parents' views on sexual morality. Changing attitudes toward sex appeared on the stage, sometimes in conjunction with rock music.

Hair: The American Tribal Love-Rock Musical premiered at Joseph Papp's off-Broadway Public Theater in December 1967. In April 1968, it opened on Broadway. The story line involves

NOTABLE ACTORS

Julie Andrews, 1935–

Richard Burton, 1925–1984

Sean Connery, 1930–

Doris Day, 1924–

Sandra Dee, 1942–2005

Clint Eastwood, 1930–

Cary Grant, 1904–1986

Audrey Hepburn, 1929–1993

Katharine Hepburn, 1907–2003

Rock Hudson, 1925–1985

Jack Lemmon, 1925–2001

Steve McQueen, 1930–1980

Paul Newman, 1925–2008

Sidney Poitier, 1927–

Elvis Presley, 1935–1977

Debbie Reynolds, 1932–

Elizabeth Taylor, 1932–

Spencer Tracy, 1900–1967

John Wayne, 1907–1979

Raquel Welch, 1940–

HIGHEST GROSSING MOVIES

1. *The Sound of Music,* 1965, $79,000,000

2. *The Graduate,* 1968, $49,078,000

3. *Doctor Zhivago,* 1965, $46,550,000

4. *Butch Cassidy,* 1969, $46,039,000

5. *Mary Poppins,* 1964, $41,000,000

Entertainment

ACADEMY AWARD WINNERS

1960 Picture: *The Apartment*

Director: Billy Wilder, *The Apartment*
Actor: Burt Lancaster, *Elmer Gantry*
Actress: Elizabeth Taylor, *Butterfield 8*

1961 Picture: *West Side Story*

Director: Jerome Robbins and Robert Wise, *West Side Story*
Actor: Maximillian Schell, *Judgment at Nuremberg*
Actress: Sophia Loren, *Two Women*

1962 Picture: *Lawrence of Arabia*

Director: David Lean, *Lawrence of Arabia*
Actor: Gregory Peck, *To Kill a Mockingbird*
Actress: Anne Bancroft, *The Miracle Worker*

1963 Picture: *Tom Jones*

Director: Tony Richardson, *Tom Jones*
Actor: Sidney Poitier, *Lilies of the Field*
Actress: Patricia Neal, *Hud*

1964 Picture: *My Fair Lady*

Director: George Cukor, *My Fair Lady*
Actor: Rex Harrison, *My Fair Lady*
Actress: Julie Andrews, *Mary Poppins*

1965 Picture: *The Sound of Music*

Director: Robert Wise, *The Sound of Music*

Actor: Lee Marvin, *Cat Ballou*
Actress: Julie Christie, *Darling*

1966 Picture: *A Man for All Seasons*

Director: Fred Zinnemann, *A Man for All Seasons*
Actor: Paul Scofield, *A Man for All Seasons*
Actress: Elizabeth Taylor, *Who's Afraid of Virginia Woolf?*

1967 Picture: *In the Heat of the Night*

Director: Mike Nichols, *The Graduate*
Actor: Rod Stieger, *In the Heat of the Night*
Actress: Katharine Hepburn, *Guess Who's Coming to Dinner*

1968 Picture: *Oliver!*

Director: Sir Carol Reed, *Oliver!*
Actor: Cliff Robertson, *Charly*
Actress: Katharine Hepburn, *The Lion in Winter,* and Barbra Streisand, *Funny Girl*

1969 Picture: *Midnight Cowboy*

Director: John Schlesinger, *Midnight Cowboy*
Actor: John Wayne, *True Grit*
Actress: Maggie Smith, *The Prime of Miss Jean Brodie*

Claude, due to be inducted into the military. He decides instead to burn his draft card, but mistakenly burns his library card. Claude's friends stage a party with drugs, leading to a hallucinogenic trip about war's futility. The next day, they encounter Claude at the induction station, his hair already cut military style, and he becomes invisible to them.

Hair was shocking at the time for its male and female nudity and references to a wide range of sexual relationships, including interracial, gay, bisexual, and non-monogamous. It also seemed to condone drug use and was the first Broadway musical to use rock music. Among the songs that earned lasting popularity were "Aquarius/Let the Sunshine In," "Good Morning Starshine," and "Hair." *Hair* proved both artistically and commer-

cially successful, running on Broadway for 1,750 performances.

The Boys in the Band, by presenting public discussion of homosexuality and a range of generally sympathetic gay characters, became part of the gay liberation movement that developed in the late 1960s. This movement was partly in response to the Stonewall Inn riot, which grew out of a police raid on a Greenwich Village gay bar, the Stonewall Inn, on Friday night, June 27, 1969. A policeman reportedly hit a patron on the head, and bystanders threw rocks and a burning garbage can into the building. Hundred of police arrived and beat gays with billy clubs, and the riot continued over the weekend. The incident is often credited with giving birth to the gay liberation movement.

NOTABLE MOVIES

Psycho (1960)

Spartacus (1960)

Where the Boys Are (1960)

Breakfast at Tiffany's (1961)

Dr. No (1962)

The Manchurian Candidate (1962)

To Kill a Mockingbird (1962)

It's a Mad Mad Mad Mad World (1963)

Dr. Strangelove or: How I Learned to Stop Worrying and Love the Bomb (1964)

The Pink Panther (1964)

Mary Poppins (1964)

Doctor Zhivago (1965)

Bonnie and Clyde (1967)

Cool Hand Luke (1967)

Guess Who's Coming to Dinner (1967)

The Graduate (1967)

The Lion in Winter (1968)

The Producers (1968)

2001: A Space Odyssey (1968)

Butch Cassidy and the Sundance Kid (1969)

Easy Rider (1969)

The Wild Bunch (1969)

So much experimentation was going on in American drama during the 1960s that new production venues were required. Off Off-Broadway was born. Plays typically by unknown playwrights pushed the envelope in both content and form and were available to audiences that wanted to see something other than traditional imitative drama that either reflected or aspired to Broadway. Off Off-Broadway was a sure sign that drama in the 1960s was a living art form at least as much concerned with the present and future as with the past.

Fashion

of the 1960s

In an era that was reacting against the establishment, fashion both followed and precipitated political action. Americans tended toward the practical and casual in clothing. The Sears mail-order catalog was more influential than Parisian haute couture, even if Sears and its competitors were not entirely free from foreign influence.

The mail-order business brought American fashion to the farms and towns of the countryside, and only those who could not afford to buy what they saw failed to follow the prevailing fashions. Changes were occurring, however, that would prepare Americans for radical alterations in clothing. World War II lured women out of their homes and into the workplace, and many even dressed in blue jeans like men as they labored in defense plants. After the war, many women refused to merely return to the home to cook and clean.

The steady migration of farmers off the land and into towns and cities continued during the decade. At the same time, there was movement into the suburbs from the cities. The U.S. population was both increasing and growing younger. By 1965, about one-half of the U.S. population was younger than 25; and for the first time in the nation's history there were more students attending college than farmers working the land.[1] The rules transmitted from the previous generations—in politics, religion, sexuality, the roles of the sexes, use of drugs, and countless other tings—were growing more fragile by the day. For many Americans, the only rule that remained was that there were no rules. Fashion was an important part of these changes.

THE INFLUENCE OF FRENCH HAUTE COUTURE

The arbiters of fashion in Paris, though less influential on American fashion than on European dress, continued to be part of the U.S. fashion world throughout the decade, although in an increasingly reduced role. The most important conduit for French style was the First Lady, Jacqueline Kennedy, who had the single greatest influence on the way American women dressed during the decade, especially in the early 1960s. Glamorous and cultured, she exhibited impeccable taste in fashion and the arts. American designer Oleg Cassini described her taste in fashion quite simply as the best.

That best in evening wear might be a Cassini gown, black on top with a gold skirt and large gold bow at the waist. The high-bodice, floor-length empire style was especially favored by the First Lady; American women imitated her by ordering their own empire evening gowns through Sears for $25.

Then there was Jackie in a Chanel suit, with bouffant hairstyle and pillbox hat. A pillbox-hat craze swept over the United States, and again inexpensive versions were available for women of modest means. Sears featured a variety of pillbox hats in its catalogs for $3–$5.

Jackie was often photographed in casual moments. This allowed the public to see her in a riding suit complete with trousers, or wearing wraparound sunglasses, which precipitated another fashion craze. Mrs. Kennedy's influence on fashion began to decline after President Kennedy was assassinated.

After the Johnsons replaced the Kennedys in the White House, the influence of haute couture on American fashion declined sharply, especially as much of the country turned increasingly antiestablishment. French designers, though, continued to have their moments, some of them through pairing fashion with painting. Yves St. Laurent borrowed Piet Mondrian's rectangular shapes for a 1965 line of straight jersey dresses. Emilio Pucci and other designers borrowed from

Op Art painters the black and white lines that created optical illusions of constant movement. Pop art, with its bright colors and bold but simple designs, also influenced fashion designers such as Mary Quant, the British popularizer of the miniskirt.

Emanuel Ungaro, born in Aix-en-Provence to an Italian tailor, opened his own design house in the mid-1960s; it was the last of the old-time haute couture enterprises. The self-contained world of high fashion could no longer dictate international fashion, and labels could not guarantee acceptance. Designers looked outward for inspiration, taking direction from what real people were wearing, and haute couture came increasingly to be viewed as old-fashioned.

MEN'S FASHIONS

Two jackets, the Nehru and the Mao, were popular among men. Pierre Cardin saw Sammy Davis Jr. in a lapel-free jacket with a turtleneck shirt and got an idea for a modification of the jacket (no lapel and a small stiff collar) worn by Indian Prime Minister Jawaharlal Nehru, who had died in 1964. In 1967 and 1968 Cardin's jacket was worn by celebrities such as talk-show host Johnny Carson, football star Joe Namath, and baseball pitcher Denny McLain. Sears included a so-called perma-press Nehru in their children's Winnie-the-Pooh collection, and even featured it on the cover of their 1969 summer catalog. The Mao jacket, named after Chinese communist leader Mao Zedong (also spelled Mao Tse-tung) was similar to the Nehru but longer. It fit a growing anti-American attitude that coincided with declining support for the Vietnam War.

At the beginning of the 1960s, the well-dressed serious man still favored a dark two-piece suit with white shirt. The more adventurous man sported the three-piece Italian look. The major changes in fashionable men's suits involved synthetic fibers and lighter weight fabrics. Short hair was the norm, although mothers might have wanted their sons to get a Prince Charles cut, named after the teen heir to the British throne. The style featured longish hair on top with a touch of a ducktail at the back and bangs that fell forward about halfway down the forehead. In reality, the cut was

FASHION TRENDS OF THE 1960s

The decade began with Jackie Kennedy's classic look, proceeded through miniskirts and the English look, and ended with hippie styles and bell bottoms. Military fashions and turtlenecks were also popular during the decade. Marketers recognized the increasing significance of clothing designed specifically for the youth market.

Women's styles included: two-piece suits; sleeveless or three-quarters sleeve dresses, A-line skirts; pillbox hats; casual slacks with chic sweaters; bouffant hairstyles; miniskirts; hip hugging pants; and pantsuits, which were common by end of decade.

Younger women's styles included: mini-skirts; crocheted dresses; granny dresses; baby doll empire waist dresses; and tops.

Men's style included: sports coats instead of suits; skinny ties; Nehru jackets; turtlenecks.

Young people's styles included: Beatle and British-influenced long hair and skinny fashions; the hippie look: jeans, T-shirts, tie-dyed clothing; day-glo colors; granny glasses; long straight hair for both males and females.

Fashion

only a modified version of the 1950s look associated with the actor Edd "Kookie" Byrnes.

The turtleneck became ubiquitous among men, worn for all occasions and with slacks, jeans, and sport coats. As the turtleneck rose in popularity, the tie declined. Even in formal settings (except for restaurants that maintained traditional dress codes), the turtleneck minus tie with sport coat became the American look. Actors Paul Newman and Steve McQueen sported turtlenecks, and millions of other men did the same.

AMERICAN INFORMALITY

The United States' democratic spirit perceived all men (if not women) as created equal; a theoretically classless society might dress similarly. Mail-order catalogs tended to homogenize fashion while making purchases easier and sometimes cheaper. Informal clothes also fit the casualness of backyards and patios in the suburbs.

Sports also played an important role in American fashion as greater numbers of Americans went outside to play rather than work. Spectator sports, such as baseball and football, were joined by a wide range of other athletic endeavors, among them skiing, hiking, boating, golf, and tennis. Participation in these sports called for functional and comfortable clothing. Before long, stretch pants and parkas had moved from ski slopes to everyday life—along with clothes from other outdoor activities.

As Jackie Kennedy gave a kind of last-gasp rejuvenation to haute couture, the young, handsome president exuded informality, especially after his grandfatherly predecessor, Dwight Eisenhower. The American public was fed a steady diet of photographs of John Kennedy sailing or playing with his children, and of the Kennedy clan playing touch football. President Kennedy, who was often hatless, minus a tie, and wearing an open-collar shirt helped to set a youthful, active, informal standard. Hat sales plummeted for men, and as the 1960s moved forward, young women also eschewed head coverings because of changing hairstyles.

Haute couture had offered full ensembles, but the sportswear industry offered separates that consumers could mix and match as they wished.

Sport coats began to replace traditional suits and came in a variety of colors and designs, including prints, plaids, stripes, and checks. Men wore them not only with dress slacks but with casual slacks and even jeans. The very nature of the suit began to change with the introduction of the leisure suit, and the seersucker suit became a popular and light alternative for the man who chose to retain some degree of formality. In the early 1960s Sears offered matching his and hers seersucker suits (for the woman, though, a skirt rather than slacks, and a double-breasted jacket with large buttons). A juvenile version was available for boys.

Synthetic fibers led to growing comfort in casual and semiformal wear. Lighter clothes that could be washed and worn without ironing or dry cleaning offered the comfort and functionality previously found only in sportswear. Suits, sport coats, and slacks were made from easy-to-care-for polyester, and double-knit polyester slacks and pant suits became enormously popular with women of all ages as the decade advanced.

Spandex clothes originally produced for sports, such as in stretch ski slacks, quickly migrated into everyday wear, including undergarments. Lycra, an Invista (formerly DuPont) trademark, yielded the Little Godiva step-in girdle in 1960. By the end of the decade, though, the girdle would virtually disappear.

The bikini, much to the delight of males, remained a favorite in swimwear, along with one-piece designs. Other popular casual items included culottes (women's trousers or long shorts cut to look like skirts) and, for an evening on the town, the simple "little nothing" black dress popularized by actress Audrey Hepburn in the film *Breakfast at Tiffany's* (1961).

THE BRITISH ARE COMING

Just as Americans seemingly threw off the last vestiges of French haute couture, they turned to the British. Much of the credit (or blame) rested with four musicians named George Harrison, John Lennon, Paul McCartney, and Ringo Starr, better known collectively as the Beatles. The Beatles arrived in the United States in 1964 and reached a national audience by appearing on *The Ed Sullivan Show,* perhaps the most influential television program of its time. Teens took to them passionately and "Beatlemania" hit.

The Beatles' "mop-top" hairstyle was often copied by young American men. The mop-top look ushered in a decade of changing hairstyles for men and women, long for men, and either super short or long and straight for women (although the Afro also became popular). Hair became a political statement. The 1960s were not the first time in American history when hair symbolized rejection of the older generation's social, political, and sexual attitudes (e.g., women's bobbed hair during the Jazz Age), but it was the period when hair reached its highest symbolic level, before antiestablishment trends in hair were adopted by the masses and became totally respectable.

The most popular British contribution to women's clothing styles (at least with men) was the miniskirt. The British designer Mary Quant deserves primary but not exclusive credit for the new style. Rather than look toward the traditional haute couture houses, she turned her attention to what young girls on British streets were wearing. She emphasized the short skirt, worn anywhere from two to nine inches above the knee, in her designs, thereby legitimizing the miniskirt in the fashion world. Many mothers and grandmothers, of course, along with a few men, were scandalized by the revealing attire.

The London look created by Quant included miniskirt, patterned stockings, a short, tight ribbed sweater, and high boots. *Seventeen* magazine featured Quant's clothes in the 1961 spring

Two images of Mary Quant, with her trademark asymmetrical bobbed hair style, created by Vidal Sassoon, working on clothing designs in London, 1967. Quant's mini-skirts and body-skimming fashions were highly popular and influential among young women in the United Kingdom, the United States, and worldwide. Prints & Photographs Division, Library of Congress.

issue, and J. C. Penney marketed her designs the next year, assuring Quant's influence on American fashion. A few years later, Quant helped popularize the woman's pantsuit.

What really set off the miniskirt was a pair of go-go boots. Go-go bars and discotheques spread rapidly in the early 1960s from Paris to U.S. cities, and usually featured young women in very short dresses and very tall boots, dancing in a readily visible location, sometimes in a hanging cage. Nancy Sinatra, Frank Sinatra's daughter, brought the go-go boots out of bars and into countless closets with the song "These Boots are Made for Walkin'" (1966). Nancy often appeared in white miniskirt and white go-go boots as her song climbed to number one on the charts.

That same year, a waiflike teen named Leslie Hornby was refining the British mod look (bobbed hair, miniskirt, long eyelashes, bright colors, and a very slim, boyish figure). Twiggy, as she was known, came from a working-class London neighborhood. She modeled for *Woman's Mirror* and was labeled the "face of 1966" by the *Daily Express.* Twiggy traveled to the United States in 1967, and Americans were enchanted by her. *Newsweek* called her hairstyle "the most radiant and evocative new image" of the year.[2] Twiggy's hair had been cut and styled by the famous hair stylist Leonard, but Vidal Sassoon was more influential overall as a hair stylist. Sassoon developed a boyish cut—short, sculpted, with sometimes asymmetrical sideburns and exposed nape of the neck—for Mary Quant's mannequins.

By 1967 Sears was advertising its women's London look designs, including hip-hugging checked pants, a "Dapper Dot" shirt with wide pointed collars and wide dotted tie, and a visor cap to match or contrast. Textured vests and paisley shirts were in for men, and ties worked only if they were wide (3½–5 inches) and similarly colorful—the idea that a man should wear a striped tie against a single-color, preferably white, shirt had been discarded. Big was the order of the day—big collars, big lapels.

THE YOUTHFUL LOOK

The designers, makers, and sellers of fashion were looking closely at what young people

wanted. Young people comprised a large segment of the fashion market, along with those who turned to clothes and hairstyles to retrieve a bit of their youth. Developments like the miniskirt, the Twiggy look, and the slim ideal (styles such as hip-hugger slacks could be worn attractively only by the slim) taught the world that young was both beautiful and sexy. In many ways, the 1960s was a young decade—with its youthful president, new frontiers in space, the Job Corps summoning men and women (primarily young) to help create a better world, the declining average age of U.S. citizens—even young lifestyles were rooted in suburbia.

At the beginning of the 1960s, the traditional view remained that young people were defined primarily within the context of their families. Sears proudly championed its "look-alike" fashions, identical dresses for all the women and girls in the family, with above-the-knee skirts, of course, only for the children. The assumption was that a child wanted to dress like her parent. For play, there were matching sportswear sets of white poplin jackets and tapered slacks for mother, teen girl, and little girl. Boys were not left out; they could have the Sears seersucker suit to match Dad's.

The look-alike approach soon shifted to look-different, especially for teens. Sears continued its practice of reflecting changes in fashion, but as always avoided extremes. Hippies, for example, did not appear in Sears catalogs, but the "urchin look" did. By 1966, Sears urchins sported scooped-neck dresses with ribbed bodices and argyle-like skirts just above the knee, or turtleneck double-knit dresses with ribbing to the hips, again cut slightly above the knee. Sears urchins remained unfailingly modest.

Not so the young vulgarians, as they were called. These vulgarians were usually street-smart kids most readily found in northern urban centers. These fashion descendants of the James Dean-era rebellious youth of the 1950s usually saw themselves as rebels with a cause, sometimes with many.

The female vulgarians took over the fashionable bouffant hairstyle of the late 1950s and early 1960s, opting for its high beehive version laboriously constructed with setting gel, big plastic rollers, hair dryer, rat-tail comb, and heavy-duty

Aqua Net hairspray. Heavy eyeliner, white lipstick, tight black miniskirt, padded bra, and large mohair cardigan or high school letter jacket completed the look.

Male vulgarians spent almost as much time as the girls getting their hair right, and usually crisscrossed their hair in overlapping sections from nape of the neck to top of the head, with a large wave curling far over the forehead. This style required a heavy application of hair grease such as Brylcreem. These boys favored tight sharkskin suits, leather raincoats, and the wraparound sunglasses that Jackie Kennedy had made famous.

Both male and female vulgarians exhibited their hairstyles and dancing techniques on Dick Clark's *American Bandstand,* dancing to the songs of their favorites—Bobby Darin, Frankie Avalon, Bobby Rydell. Vulgarians also gave high marks to a number of songs by girls' groups: The Crystals' "Then He Kissed Me" (1963), The Shangri-Las' "Leader of the Pack" (1964), and The Shirelles' "Will You Love Me Tomorrow?" (1960). The young vulgarian look faded by mid-decade, but the youthful look continued to exercise its appeal in various manifestations.

THE ANTIESTABLISHMENT EARTHQUAKE

Reactions against the establishment took many forms in the 1960s, including sexual, racial, and political. The drug culture interacted with some or all of these factors to create the hippies. The growing antiwar movement picked up steam after the Tet Offensive of 1968. Clothing and hair fashions reflected wearers' attitudes; to a great extent, how one looked reflected how one thought.

For example, see-through blouses, the ubiquitous miniskirt, and even pierced earrings (considered symbolically more erotic than clip-on or screw-type earrings) reflected sexual openness. Undergarments also changed, especially among young women, with bikini panties, panty hose, and tights in, and with girdles out.

Another fashion that followed liberalized sexual mores was the playboy bunny outfit. Hugh Hefner had started *Playboy* magazine in the 1950s, but decided to expand into playboy clubs in the early 1960s. Hefner opened the first of his

A woman examines her friend's necklace as they wait for a jazz band in San Francisco's Golden Gate Park, California, in 1967. The necklace indicates which tribe one belongs to within the hippie subculture in San Francisco. AP Photo.

clubs in Chicago on February 29, 1960. So-called Playboy Bunnies served drinks in their tightly corseted swimsuit-like costumes with white collars, black bow ties, fishnet stockings, rabbit ears, and the most distinctive detail—white bunny tails gracing their derrières.

Bunny costumes left nothing to the imagination regarding the gender of the wearer, but long hair on males, short hair on females, and high-heeled boots, hip-huggers, and ruffled shirts sometimes made it difficult to tell male from female. Prominent among the clothing similarities between the sexes was a shared obsession with blue jeans, often worn skin tight.

The reason a particular fashion became popular was usually impossible to reduce to just one factor. For example, one important reason for the mushrooming popularity of blue jeans during

HIPPIE FASHION

In 1960s America, fashion and politics collided in a way never before seen in American history. Dissent against the popular order spread throughout American culture, creating a vibrant counterculture that challenged the norms and values of society. In the fashion world, the trend started with the "mod fashions" of the early sixties, including loose fabrics with bold patterns and stunning decorative elements. This gave way to a psychedelic fashion trend, which featured brightly colored fabrics, paisley patterns, and other designs that brought psychedelic hallucination into fashion chic. This relatively short-lived trend gave rise to a fashion tradition now known simply as "hippie clothing," used in reference to the youth movement of the same name. The basic trends in hippie fashion were simplicity and comfort and the uniting thread was to defy the fashion conventions of previous generations. As the tradition developed and expanded well into the 1970s, designers borrowed elements from global fashion trends, including Indian and Asian designs, Native American beads, and African cloth patterns to create a gestalt sense of fashion. Ironically, while the youth movement sought to avoid conforming to existing standards of fashion, many dove headlong into a new kind of conformity, meeting the standards and norms of a culture derived from combating those same elements in society.

Model Dale Kole wears bell-bottom pants and a matching midriff halter top with cape-like sleeves presented by Geno at California's spring-resort wear shown in Beverly Hills, California, in November 1964. AP Photo.

the decade was the rejection of middle-class, materialistic norms. Jeans were initially working-class wear for farmers, miners, and manual laborers.

Quickly, however, jeans became associated with sexiness and turned fashionable. They came in a wide variety of styles during the decade, including hip-huggers, flared legs, bell bottoms, cuffed, patched, or cut off to make shorts. Because the tattered look was especially desirable, manufacturers began producing jeans that already looked seriously worn. New jeans also came with bright patches over imaginary holes. Mainstream America took up the fashion, and men began wearing jeans with their sport coats and turtlenecks.

Also popular, although never to the extent of jeans, were bib overalls previously worn by farmers and train engineers. The same rejection of the middle class applied to overalls, but they lent themselves less readily to improvisational alterations.

During the 1960s, African Americans started to switch from imitating white society to expressing their uniqueness. They embraced the concept of "black is beautiful" in many ways, including hairstyles. Instead of bleaching and straightening their hair, many African Americans started wearing the Afro, a natural style with unstraightened curls cut in a somewhat rounded shape. The Afro, however, had little to do with Africa. Tanzania even banned the Afro as an example of Western colonialism. Nonetheless, the style became quite popular and was worn by James Brown, Jessie Jackson, and Angela Davis, among countless others. Those like Diana Ross, who preferred to keep their options open, relied on Afro wigs.

The cornrow hairdo, with hair divided into sections and braided close to the scalp, conveyed the same pride in one's African American heritage. So did the dashiki (a loose, brightly colored African garment that resembled a tunic) and the caftan (similar to the dashiki but full-length). Some Americans, including whites, adopted these styles without much attention to the clothing's heritage, giving birth to a new radical chic. White designers started employing black models for other than African American markets. Paco Rabanne was almost expelled from the Chambre Syndicale de la Couture Parisienne after he introduced black women into haute couture modeling in 1966.

Members of the drug culture especially liked bright colors and patterns that visually paralleled their hallucinogenic experiences with LSD. Psychedelic shirts and ties were popular, along with almost anything else psychedelic, such as posters. Day-Glo colors appeared in clothing as well as on posters, guitars, and vans. Then there was the tie-dyeing craze.

Tie-dyeing could be done with any garments or fabric, but T-shirts were the most common. Tie-dyeing is an ancient process, practiced by Chinese and Nigerians many centuries ago. It involves knotting the fabric and dipping the cloth into dyes to create clothing with splotches of color. The tie-dyed T-shirt was a favorite with hippies and others who wanted to rebel against traditional values: it was cheap, homemade (in the dyeing), easy, and unique with no two garments quite identical, yet it united wearers in a sort of community.

As with anything popular, commercialism reared its head and nonhippies adopted the tie-dyeing trend. Best Foods, maker of Rit dye, sent out half a million booklets showing how to tie-dye clothes and saw its dye sales jump sharply. Department stores threw tie-dye parties. Burlington Industries started manufacturing tie-dyed clothes, and customers could wander among aisles of tie-dyed items at Macy's.

The hippie culture—which consisted of students, artists, and others who had dropped out of mainstream society, and who were also known as flower children—was in full swing by 1967, when a June 16–18 concert in Monterey, California, inaugurated the Summer of Love. Hippies had surfaced two years earlier in the Haight-Ashbury section of San Francisco. Seeking a nonmaterialistic, peace-loving society in which they could be their natural and individual selves, they adopted certain fashions in clothing as well as in lifestyle. An easy openness toward sex, rejection of nine-to-five jobs, and adoption of communal living by some were a few of the behavioral characteristics of hippies.

Long, straight hair dominated among female hippies, fashioned after the folk singers Joan Baez and Mary Travers. Many males also wore their hair long, often adding beards and mustaches. Granny dresses and granny glasses were popular, the latter among both sexes. Female hippies usually either purchased their dresses in thrift shops or made them, but in either case the dresses were long and full—the antithesis of the miniskirt and mod look. Granny glasses, also known as Ben Franklin spectacles, received a huge impetus from Roger McGuinn of the Byrds, who wore them to protect his sensitive eyes from stage lights. The glasses were usually small, sometimes square, with partial wire rims.

Fashion

DISPOSABLE DIAPERS TO THE RESCUE

Perhaps the most universal change in fashion and clothing in the 1960s was the decrease in the use of cloth diapers, which were cost effective and could be used repeatedly. Yet rinsing, washing, and drying dirty diapers was unpleasant and time consuming. Life became much simpler with disposable diapers. Procter and Gamble was first to enter the disposable diaper business in 1961 with its Pampers, which proved so popular that when other companies introduced their own versions, many consumers went right on calling all of them "pampers." By the end of the twentieth century, almost every parent made some use of disposable diapers, and most used nothing else, despite concern that disposable diapers increased diaper rash and caused other problems for babies.

Blue jeans were usually worn hip-hugging and very tight with bell bottoms. Bright colors on shirts and blouses, working-class, and ethnic clothes such as bandannas and Native-American style jackets and vests, love beads, peace jewelry, and flowers in one's hair—sung about by Scott McKenzie in his 1967 hit song "San Francisco (Wear Some Flowers in Your Hair")"—all helped to identify the hippie.

Vietnam War activists tended in some ways to be the opposite of the flower children. Rather than drop out of society, they became actively involved in opposing the Vietnam War through demonstrations, sit-ins, teach-ins, flag burnings, and other activities designed to raise America's consciousness against the war. These efforts increased after the Tet Offensive of 1968, which, although a major defeat for the communists, was perceived in the United States as proof that no place in Vietnam was secure from enemy attack and that the United States was no closer to winning the war than it had been years before.

There was little to distinguish Vietnam War protesters from hippies in appearance except for the overt symbols of the protesters' beliefs: military jackets adorned with flags and antiwar statements, antiwar buttons, the omnipresent antiwar symbol of the upside down bomber within a circle, the V for peace sign made with fingers, and perhaps an armful of posters or pamphlets.

Fashion

Food

of the 1960s

For those with sufficient money, the 1960s were a time of new favorites when eating out or dining in. International influences, especially French, became important, and increasing numbers of relatively affluent Americans turned to cookbooks and television programs to learn how to make their dinner tables *au courant* (up-do-date).

Changes in how Americans ate reflected other changes in American society. With increasing numbers of people on the move, eating habits also became more mobile, which resulted in tremendous growth in fast-food restaurants.

Many other food-related developments occurred during the 1960s. Farming continued its transition from small family farms to large agri-businesses. Technology affected farms, food processing, marketing, cooking, and consumption. At the same time, the United States was a place of considerable poverty and malnutrition. A growing social consciousness, aided by print and television exposés, led to attempts at home and abroad to address the terrible problem of hunger.

DINING IN STYLE

In the 1960s, being a good cook was not enough; that was for one's mother and grandmother. Home-style cooking, unless ethnic, was out, and nouveau cuisine was in; its influences were many, including French cuisine, instant foods, the microwave and freezer, the Kennedy administration, and Julia Child.

The new American suburban lifestyle demanded spending a lot of time on the road, and while Americans aspired to elegant dining, time was often in short supply. Instant foods and increasingly popular kitchen appliances such as the freezer and microwave helped. Freezers had been around for years, and a new compact microwave from Amana went into widespread distribution in 1967.

The makings of dinners homemakers could serve with pride could be found on the shelves of the pantry and in the freezer. Cans of condensed soup and boxes of dried soup mixes made many things possible, and so did a variety of products. With a freezer at hand, there was no need to rush off to the supermarket to buy a nice cut of meat. Suburban chefs in doubt about how to proceed could refer to the helpful 1960s cookbook, *Cooking from the Pantry Shelf. Easy Gourmet Cooking* struck culinary purists as an oxymoron, but summed up the direction that numerous new cooks took.

The more dramatic the main course, the simpler the salad might be—possibly iceberg lettuce with an occasional slice of tomato and cucumber. Roquefort, Thousand Island, and French dressings were popular. A salad's simple flavors cleansed the palate after the inevitable preliminaries of cheese, crackers, dip, and chips. Cheese balls were popular, as was Edam cheese in its red wax shell. Lipton's dried onion soup mix combined with sour cream continued its popularity as the ubiquitous California dip. Ridged potato chips, the most famous being Ruffles, proved much sturdier than traditional chips for dipping.

A trendy alternative to traditional soup was gazpacho. This Spanish dish is a cold blend of vegetables (with a dominant tomato flavor) and red wine vinegar, olive oil, and Italian or French bread crumbs.

Of all the vegetable dishes served with home-prepared meals, none equaled green beans amandine for ease and popularity. Almonds were everywhere in the 1960s and added extra flavor to green beans. The dish was easy to prepare; simply heat a few almonds in a little melted butter, add beans, and serve. If potatoes were part of a meal, they usually were baked and served alongside meat entrees.

The main course, however, might take more effort. Two favorites of the Kennedys were beef stroganoff and beef Wellington. The former, given the availability of canned gravy, canned mushrooms, canned minced onions, and even canned roast beef, could be prepared easily. The latter, though, was more difficult to prepare, but that did not deter Americans from trying. Its French and British Isles background gave beef Wellington an international cachet. For busy gourmets, frozen beef tenderloin and frozen puff pastry simplified this popular dish.

Campbell's mushroom soups were popular in the 1960s, especially after the company released its Golden Mushroom version. The suburban chef might add Campbell's Golden Mushroom soup to make skillet-cooked chicken that looked and tasted good. String bean casseroles graced many dinner tables in the 1960s, requiring only some of the most common 1960s ingredients: string beans, mushroom soup, sherry, instant minced onions, and slivered almonds. A garnish of canned French-fried onions perfected the dish.

Wine, of course, accompanied most meals. French wines were popular, but those in the know might serve a special California vintage.

Then came dessert. Grandmother's pies and cakes were decidedly too old-fashioned. The 1960s featured cheesecakes topped by fruit pie fillings, fruit cocktail cakes, and grasshopper pies, among other sweet concoctions with or without various alcoholic additives.

Fire was also big in the 1960s. Flambéing, dousing food with liquor and then setting it on fire, could be a bit dangerous, but it made quite an impression, whether the food was a steak, cherries jubilee, crêpes suzette, or anything else combustible. Fire also helped to provide one of the most popular party dishes—fondue. Fondue seemed French (the name derived from the French verb *fondre,* to melt), but actually originated in Switzerland as a means of salvaging hard cheese and stale bread. The point was to melt cheese (and other ingredients) and dip French bread into it. People would sit around the fondue dish and take turns dipping. Variants of fondue included dipping chunks of meat into boiling oil or pieces of cake or fruit into hot chocolate.

COOKBOOKS

Many people associated nouveau cuisine with French culture, which paved the way for a teacher of fine cooking made easy, Julia Child. Along with co-authors Simone Beck and Louisette Bertholle, Child published *Mastering the Art of French Cooking* in 1961. The following year, she began her televised show, *The French Chef,* on a Massachusetts public broadcasting station. Before long, channels throughout the country were carrying her program.

Like good teachers everywhere, Julia Child made the difficult seem easy. She relied on ingredients that could be found in local grocery stores, and she led her viewers through the cooking process in a clear and methodical way. Countless households began to enjoy their own creations of boeuf bourguignon and chocolate mousse, and along the way learned the importance of using fresh ingredients.

The interest in international cuisine also led to a series of international cookbooks from Time-Life Books. In 1968 alone, Time-Life produced M.F.K. Fisher's *The Cooking of Provincial France,* Waverley Root's *The Cooking of Italy,* Emily Hahn's

Julia Child gets ready to do a program on how to roast a chicken on *The French Chef,* which ran on PBS from 1962 to 1973. Courtesy of Photofest.

Food

JULIA CHILD (1912–2004)

Celebrity chef Julia Child paved the way for the phenomenon of television cooking, which has since culminated in the cable television Food Network and twenty-first century celebrity chefs such as Emeril Lagasse and Wolfgang Puck. After completing an undergraduate degree, Child worked in the Office of Strategic Services, a branch of the U.S. government's intelligence services and traveled to China where she met and married fellow OSS employee Paul Child. The couple was transferred to the American Embassy in Paris, where Child decided to enroll in the world famous Cordon Bleu cooking school to study French cuisine. After graduating in 1961, Child and two colleagues published the book *Mastering the Art of French Cooking,* which became a national success and made Child a household name. After returning to the United States, Child was asked to audition for a cooking show on Boston public television. *The French Chef* debuted in 1962 and was an enormous success. Child received an Emmy Award in 1966 and her series was syndicated on more than 90 television stations and extended through spin off programs for which Child tackled other types of global cuisine. Child took the mystery out of gourmet cuisine and encouraged a generation of home chefs to expand their palates. With her endearing demeanor and characteristic voice, simultaneously warbling and encouraging, Child became the first American chef to gain the type of celebrity usually reserved for film stars. Child died in 2003 at age 91, leaving a rich legacy as an inspiration to hundreds of chefs who now spin their spatulas in her shadow.

The Cooking of China, Jonathan Norton Leonard's *Latin American Cooking,* and Dale Brown's *American Cooking.*

ETHNIC AND HEALTH FOODS

As the decade progressed, interest in ethnic and health foods increased. Soul food became popular with large numbers of white Americans who sympathized with civil rights movements or who merely wanted to appear hip. Ham hocks, collard greens, corn bread, chitterlings (a pig's small intestines), black-eyed peas, and sweet potato pie were a few of the items that became popular. This interest gave rise to soul-food restaurants such as the famous Sylvia's in Harlem, which quickly became so popular that proprietors Sylvia and Herbert Wood had to move to a larger building and add on a new dining room.

Japanese food also grew in popularity. Diners could visit Japanese steakhouses and watch the chefs prepare and cook the food before their eyes. Meals were prepared at a large grill on one side of a spacious table around which diners sat; the preparation and cooking offered an exciting and dramatic experience for the audience. Sushi bars began to appear in certain areas of the country, especially on the west coast.

Other ethnic groups also contributed their foods to American tables, both at home and in restaurants. Dishes from India presented new tastes for palates unaccustomed to Eastern spices. In some restaurants, diners would sit on cushions on the floor, soaking up the environment. Southeast Asian restaurants, featuring Vietnamese, Cambodian, or Thai foods, started appearing during the decade as well.

Health food became especially associated with countercultural types during the 1960s. Many ingredients popular (or at least accepted) in previous eras—such as white sugar, monosodium glutamate (MSG), bleached white flour, processed cheese, and canned vegetables and fruits—were rejected along with the older generation's political and religious values. Organic food, brown rice, yogurt, whole wheat flour, sunflower seeds, and similar natural foods were championed. Many Americans became vegetarians, for political as much as health reasons, seeing in the nation's devouring of red meat another manifestation of the lust for violence and slaughter that produced the Vietnam War.

The most famous restaurant for antiestablishment figures may have been one that existed for less than a year but that inspired one of the era's most popular resistance songs. Alice Brock started (and closed) her restaurant, The Back Room, in Stockbridge, Massachusetts in 1965. The Back Room was a simple luncheonette where Brock baked her own bread and served health food. Arlo Guthrie, son of folk singer Woody Guthrie, wrote a song called "Alice's Restaurant," which he sang at the 1969 Woodstock festival. The restaurant came to stand for a world of peace, hope, harmony, and rejection of establishment values.

FAST FOOD RESTAURANTS

As Americans accepted the seemingly incongruous mixture of instant food and French cuisine, they also frequented fast-food restaurants to such an extent that these establishments mushroomed, especially along highways and in shopping malls. Hamburgers, chicken, tacos, and pizza, accompanied by French fries and soft drinks were among the favorites.

McDonald's, first created in 1940 as a San Bernadino, California drive-in owned by Dick and Mac McDonald, enjoyed tremendous growth after Ray Kroc bought out the brothers in 1961. McDonald's introduced its Big Mac sandwich in 1968; also during the decade it began to open restaurants around the world, cementing its position as number one among hamburger chains.[1]

Burger King also enjoyed considerable growth during the 1960s. Begun in 1954 in Miami, Florida, and having introduced its Whopper three years later, Burger King operated 274 restaurants by 1967. This number would increase to about 2,000 franchises by the mid 1970s. Hardee's began in 1961 in North Carolina, using a then-rare charcoal broiler, and had 200 outlets by the end of the decade. Wendy's was started in 1969 in Ohio by David R. Thomas, who had been successful running Kentucky Fried Chicken franchises and who named the new chain after his daughter.

Harland "Colonel" Sanders had started his Colonel Sanders' Kentucky Fried Chicken restaurants in 1955, selling "finger lickin' good" chicken made with his "secret blend of herbs and spices." In 1964, with over 600 franchises, Sanders sold the business but continued with Kentucky Fried Chicken as a good-will ambassador.

Varying the fast-food menu, Arby's specialized in roast beef, opening its first restaurant in Ohio in 1964 and adding its first franchise the following year. Taco Bell, named after its creator, Glenn Bell, began in California in 1962 and quickly spread eastward. Busy travelers could dine on seafood at Long John Silver's Fish 'n Chips starting in 1969 in Lexington, Kentucky. Thomas Monaghan, a former seminarian and Marine, opened his first Domino's Pizza restaurant in Detroit with his brother Jim in 1960. Domino's specialized in delivering phone orders within 30 minutes.

Family restaurants were also popular during the decade. Red Lobster, an especially popular family restaurant, began in Florida in 1968—the creation of William Darden. Howard Johnson's restaurants had been around since the mid-1930s and by the early 1960s numbered over 600, many located near highways and exit ramps.

OTHER DEVELOPMENTS

All of this eating and driving was bound to result in weight gain, so it was inevitable that a chain like Weight Watchers would arise. Jean Nidetch, a Queens, New York, housewife who had shed 70 pounds, began helping other people lose weight through group therapy and careful dieting. In 1966, she published her *Weight Watchers Cookbook*.

The growing business of food production was also visible in the steady stream of acquisitions and mergers during the 1960s. Coca-Cola bought Minute Maid, Campbell Soup bought Pepperidge Farms, Proctor and Gamble bought J. A. Folger, H. J. Heinz bought Starkist (and created Charlie the Tuna to sell its product), Pepsi-Cola bought Mountain Dew, and Borden bought Cracker Jack. H. W. Lay and Frito merged to become Frito-Lay, and Frito-Lay and Pepsi-Cola merged to become PepsiCo Incorporated.

Government and religion also were involved in what people ate. The U.S. government passed the Fair Packaging and Labeling Act in 1966 to require accurate and clear labeling of food weights, and the U.S. Federal Meat Inspection Act was passed in 1967 to improve the safety of the

---

FOOD HIGHLIGHTS OF THE 1960s

1963 *The French Chef*, starring Julia Child and aimed at demystifying French cooking for the American home cook, premiers on Boston's WGBH-TV.

1963 The Oscar Mayer "Wiener Jingle" debuts on radio and is an immediate hit among listeners.

1963 In his first television appearance, spokesclown and goodwill ambassador Ronald McDonald is portrayed by Willard Scott, later an NBC weatherman.

1964 Pop-Tarts, pastries to "cook" in the toaster, and Lucky Charms cereal are introduced to the American breakfast table.

1965 Bugles corn snacks make their first appearance.

1965 Poppin' Fresh, the energetic and giggly spokes-character for Pillsbury's refrigerated doughs, makes his television debut. Within three years, the Pillsbury Doughboy has an 87 percent recognition factor among consumers.

1965 Shake 'n Bake mix, to coat chicken and fish, is introduced.

1965 McDonald's becomes a publicly traded company. On the first day the stock was available, an investor would have paid $2,250 to buy 100 shares; by the end of December 2006, the same investor would own 74,360 shares worth about $3.3 million.

1966 The Birds Eye division of General Foods launches Cool Whip, a nondairy dessert topping and the first product of its kind.

1969 Nearly 60 percent of Americans say they believe agricultural chemicals pose a threat to their health.

1969 Long before the era of energy bars, Pillsbury markets Space Food Sticks, an energy snack developed by Pillsbury for the Apollo moon flights.

Food

meat products that reached America's tables. The fish industry worried in 1966 when the Roman Catholic Church dropped its ban on eating meat on non-Lenten Fridays, but there was no clear damage. In fact, many restaurants continued to offer Friday fish specials for decades.

DRINK

Diners needed something quick to drink with their fast food, and a number of new soft drinks entered the market in the 1960s. Coca-Cola introduced Sprite in 1967 to do battle with the old favorite 7-Up. Royal Crown's Diet-Rite became the first sugar-free nationally distributed soft drink in 1962, and appealed to the growing numbers of people concerned with dieting. Coke countered Tab in 1963, and two years later PepsiCo introduced Diet Pepsi.

Other new drinks were introduced during the 1960s as well. Consumers could drink their breakfast, courtesy of Carnation Company's Carnation Instant Breakfast (introduced in 1964); people could emulate the astronauts by drinking orange-flavored Tang (marketed nationwide in 1965), and many raised a glass to toast the 1969 moon landing, which Neil Armstrong and crew could reciprocate with the Tang they had in their galley; and athletes and would-be athletes could turn to Gatorade (1965) to replace fluids lost during physical exercise. Gatorade was named for the University of Florida Gators because a university kidney specialist, Robert Cade, developed it after testing the university's football players for fluid loss through perspiration.

Coffee was also a growth industry in the 1960s. General Foods started marketing Maxim, a freeze-dried instant coffee, in 1964. Taster's Choice freeze-dried instant, from Nestlé, arrived in 1966 and quickly became number one among instants. Coffee Rich nondairy creamer (named after its developer, Robert Edward Rich) gave coffee drinkers in 1960 a nonperishable milk or cream substitute. The following year, Coffee-Mate from Carnation entered the market.

Changes in containers also occurred in the 1960s. Consumers were buying most of their milk in stores rather than receiving home delivery, and that milk was increasingly packaged in waxed paperboard cartons rather than glass bottles. Aluminum cans meanwhile were becoming popular for beer and soft drinks. First used in 1960, their popularity was greatly enhanced by the development of easy-open tabs on the cans.

FOOD ISSUES IN THE 1960s

Agriculture Upheavals

Although the population of the United States continued to increase during the 1960s, and the amount of land devoted to agriculture remained fairly constant, fewer farmers were necessary to meet the food needs of the country.

Farmers improved their productivity with the help of advanced farm implements and greater use of fertilizers, pesticides, and herbicides to increase crop yield and reduce loss to insect and weed infestation. By the end of the decade, the number of farms decreased while the average size of farms increased. Large agribusinesses were squeezing out family farms, a process that would accelerate in future decades.

Farmers' own productivity worked against them by yielding large surpluses, which depressed prices. During the 1960s, federal agricultural policy included a combination of guaranteed price, soil conservation, land set-asides, and use of food surpluses in food-stamp and school-lunch programs. The Food and Agriculture Act of 1962 created price support payments for farmers to make up the difference between former and current world price levels for their products. Cash payments to remove cropland from production continued throughout the decade.

Still, large numbers of agricultural workers received no help. Migrant workers, many of them Mexican American, were worst off, working excruciatingly long and hard hours picking vegetables and fruit for whatever owners paid them. That began to change in the early 1960s when the CBS documentary *Harvest of Shame,* 1960, publicized the plight of migrant workers, and César Chávez founded the National Farm Workers Association (1962). By 1968, Chávez and the union were receiving strong public support for both their strike and their proposed boycott of table grapes. Chávez's efforts both dramatized

Food

César Chávez's work in the 1960s on behalf of migrant workers, who are still essential to U.S. agriculture, publicized the key role they play in the food supply system in the United States. Courtesy of Shutterstock.

Food

the boycott and brought a moral power to the effort, encouraging prominent political leaders such as Robert Kennedy, Eugene McCarthy, and Hubert Humphrey to add their support. In 1970, the boycott ended, with most table grape owners (farmers?) having agreed to recognize and negotiate with the union, now known as the United Farm Workers (UFW) after NFWA's merger with the Agricultural Workers Organizing Committee.

Poverty

Michael Harrington's *The Other America: Poverty in the United States,* 1962, was one of the most important books published in the 1960s. Writing of "a culture of poverty" within the affluent United States, Harrington brought to public consciousness the existence of a nation within a nation, one easy to overlook because few Americans were actually dying of starvation.

Subsequent books, government studies, broadcast documentaries, and demonstrations brought hunger and poverty more clearly to the attention of middle class and wealthy Americans. In 1967 President Johnson's Science Advisory Committee released a massive study entitled *The World Food Problem,* which examined the effects of growing populations and demands by the wealthy on food supplies. The 1968 CBS documentary *Hunger in America* explored hunger in the country, and focused especially on malnutrition among infants, including Native Americans. In that same year, after the assassination of its original organizer, Dr. Martin Luther King Jr., the Poor People's March on Washington protested hunger and the government's inadequate efforts to solve the problem. Further evidence of the continuing crisis came in the same year when the Citizens Board of Inquiry into Hunger and Malnutrition in the United States reported that only 18 percent of the country's poor were being helped by federal food programs.

The evidence of widespread hunger in the United States generated enough compassion and outrage to bring about changes that helped large numbers of Americans but did not completely eradicate the problem. In 1963 President Kennedy signed into law the Public Welfare Amendments to the 1935 Social Security Act. These amendments fixed federal support to states at 75 percent of the expenses for counseling, job training, and placement for individuals on public assistance.

The food stamp program, established in 1964 with the Food Stamp Act, provided a variety of food to needy families. The Agriculture Department developed eligibility criteria to attempt to ensure that those who needed the stamps received them. By the end of 1967, 2.7 million Americans were benefiting from food stamps, and food stamp funding continued to rise.[2]

Pollution

The safety of food and the welfare of the environment were increasingly, impacted by developments in manufacturing, technology, and use of chemicals during the 1960s. Rachel Carson's *Silent Spring*, 1962, did for the environment what Michael Harrington's *The Other America* accomplished regarding poverty. A book whose influence continued throughout the century, *Silent Spring* warned that pesticides such as DDT (dichloro-diphenyl-trichloroethane) were causing great damage to wildlife and, by extension, to humans. Likening the effect of heavy use of pesticides to nuclear fallout, she cautioned against a silent world in which the birds have been poisoned along with the poisoned insects they ate. In 1969, Congress passed the National Environmental Policy Act mandating that federal agencies provide environmental impact reports. By that time, Carson's warnings about DDT had been widely accepted. Studies subsequent to the publication of *Silent Spring* demonstrated that DDT accumulated in fatty tissues, increasing in concentration up the food chain, and caused cancer in test animals. Ninety percent of fish sold in the United States were discovered to be contaminated with the pesticide. Milk also began to test positive for DDT, the result of cows eating grain sprayed with it. By the end of the decade, DDT was outlawed by several states and was being phased out by the federal government. With few exceptions, it was not available for use in the United States after 1972.

Food

Music

of the 1960s

The 1960s were a time of enormous change in music, with musical performers turning both to the past and to the new for inspiration. Folk music experienced a rebirth, with folk singers making the guitar as commonplace in the 1960s, especially for the young, as the piano was for their parents and grandparents. Folk music reflected the antiestablishment trend of the times as folk singers joined the vanguard in protesting the Vietnam War and demanding equal rights for people of color.

Country music spread from southern and rural regions into all parts of the country. Classical music opened itself to African American artists and embraced popular culture. Jazz, meanwhile, became a medium for some of the decade's most innovative musical trends, and also entered the political world as a vehicle for black aspirations and a repository of black cultural traditions.

Soul music expressed the black experience in powerful songs that were often emotionally powerful. Rock, though, was the most powerful force in music during the decade. The new revolution in rock was triggered by a British group, the Beatles, and much else also happened in rock, from San Francisco to Woodstock, and everywhere in between.

FOLK MUSIC

Folk music had declined in popularity during the 1950s, in part because much of the post-Depression folk music had been antiestablishment. Senator Joseph McCarthy, the House Un-American Activities Committee (HUAC), and others attempted to hunt down musicians and other artists who seemed sympathetic to communism. To criticize the United States struck such witch-hunters as playing into the hands of the red menace.

By the late 1950s, however, folk music, especially commercial folk music, was making a comeback. The Kingston Trio led the way with a string of successful songs, including Pete Seeger's "Where Have All the Flowers Gone?" The Kingston Trio formed in 1956 when Dave Guard, Bob Shane, and Nick Reynolds came together in California.

Pete Seeger and the Weavers, a group he helped form, ran into trouble in the 1950s because of their left-wing politics. Seeger left the Weavers in 1958, and the group disbanded in 1963. Seeger himself was convicted of contempt for Congress in 1961 as a result of his refusal to answer questions before the HUAC in the mid-1950s. The conviction was overturned in 1962, but Seeger continued to be blacklisted from network television. His political difficulties, however, endeared him to the folk music crowd, and he was vitally important in the folk music revival of the 1960s. Woody Guthrie's songs remained popular, with "This Land Is Your Land" becoming a rallying cry for those who struggled for freedom and equality during the 1960s.

Bob Dylan, with guitar and harmonica, recording in 1965. Prints & Photographs Division, Library of Congress.

Woody Guthrie's son, Arlo, took his own place in folk music during the 1960s. His song, "Alice's Restaurant," was about an antiestablishment restaurant that he discovered, draft resistance, and a vision of peace and harmony. He sang the song at the Woodstock Festival in 1969, the same year the song served as the centerpiece of a film by the same title.

Leading folk musicians in the 1960s were Bob Dylan, Joan Baez, and the trio of Peter, Paul, and Mary, all of whom took folk music back into social activism, especially in support of the Civil Rights Movement and in opposition to the Vietnam War. Woody Guthrie was Dylan's hero and model. Dylan's first album, *Bob Dylan,* 1962, was primarily a collection of traditional folk songs and included the Dylan-composed homage "Song to Woody." His 1964 album *The Times They Are a-Changin'* continued to establish him as a leading protest singer. By the middle of the decade, Dylan had moved into folk rock, shocking the audience at the 1965 Newport Folk Festival by switching to an electric guitar. Folk purists objected, but the change only increased Dylan's fame. Throughout the decade, Dylan was widely revered not only as a singer and musician but also as a poet. Many of his songs were sung by such luminaries as Joan Baez and Peter, Paul, and Mary, the latter striking it big with "Blowin' in the Wind."

Joan Baez released 12 albums of folk songs and songs of protest during the 1960s, among them the anthem of the Civil Rights Movement, "We Shall Overcome." Consistently taking stands on behalf of justice and peace, Baez spoke and sang at many demonstrations in southern cities, marched with Martin Luther King Jr. in the March on Washington in 1963, established the Institute for the Study of Non-violence in California in 1965, and

AMERICA'S SONGWRITER: BOB DYLAN (1941–)

Born Robert Zimmerman in the small city of Duluth, Minnesota, the musician, writer, performer, and producer known worldwide as Bob Dylan eventually became one of the most influential figures in American music. Dylan adopted his pseudonym, a tribute to poet Dylan Thomas, while performing at small clubs in Minneapolis. In 1960, Dylan left college and moved to New York City where he became a regular at New York coffee houses and helped to establish Greenwich Village as the epicenter of the folk rock movement. In 1962, after one of his performances was reviewed in the *New York Times,* Dylan was offered a recording contract and released his first album to critical acclaim. Dylan's second album, entitled "Freewheelin' Bob Dylan," was a much larger hit and heralded his emergence as a leader of the genre. While Dylan's characteristically gravelly voice and penchant for moving lyricism made him a popular, if unusual, performer, it was as a songwriter that Dylan exerted his strongest influence. Over the years, Dylan has written dozens of the most popular songs in the history of American rock, earning him numerous honors, including being listed among *Time* magazine's 100 Most Influential Individuals of the Twentieth Century. From protest songs that mirrored the sentiments of a generation of disenfranchised youth to becoming one of the most popular songwriters of a century, Dylan is an iconic figure in American culture who has also changed with the times, remaining relevant into the twenty-first century.

withheld a portion of her income taxes to protest defense spending.

In 1961 Peter Yarrow, Paul Stookey, and Mary Travers founded the enormously popular trio Peter, Paul, and Mary. Yarrow and Stookey played acoustic guitars, and the trio excelled in lyrical renditions and pleasing harmonies. Like many other folk artists, they combined folk songs with protest themes. Their 1962 hit recording of "If I Had a Hammer," composed by Pete Seeger and Lee Hays, called for justice, freedom, and love; the following year they had another hit with Bob Dylan's "Blowin' in the Wind." Another of the trio's top recordings was Woody Guthrie's "This Land Is Your Land," and one of their most acclaimed children's songs was "Puff (the Magic Dragon)," which narrates a boy's loss of youthful imagination and capacity for fantasy as he grows into adulthood.

Two very different venues for folk music demonstrated its popularity during the 1960s—the television show *Hootenanny* and the series of Newport Folk Festivals in Newport, Rhode Island. Pete Seeger is usually credited with popularizing the hootenanny. A hootenanny features performers playing and singing seemingly more for each other than for the audience. There is considerable interaction among performers, but the audience is also often engaged in active participation. The hootenanny proved popular at festivals, clubs, and private parties. The television version was hosted by Jack Linkletter and was taped before live audiences at college campuses. Performers ranged from traditional folk singers such as the Carter Family to modern groups, among them the Chad Mitchell Trio and the Limeliters. Unfortunately, the program blacklisted some performers, among them Seeger and the Weavers, because of their left-wing views. That led many artists, including Joan Baez, the Kingston Trio, and Peter, Paul, and Mary, to boycott the program. Television's *Hootenanny,* partly because of the political controversy associated with it, lasted only from April 1963 to September 1964.

The Newport Folk Festival occurred nine times from 1959 to 1969, and featured a wide array of individuals and groups. George Wein, a Boston pianist, conceived the idea of the festival and coproduced the first one; however, Wein discontinued the festival after two years because it lost money. Pete Seeger then persuaded Wein to create a nonprofit organization, the Newport Folk Foundation, to sponsor the festival and use proceeds to support folk music research and scholarships. The nonprofit Newport Folk Festival began in 1963 and was held annually through the rest of the decade. In its first year, some 40,000 people attended the three-day concert, listening to, among others, Joan Baez, Judy Collins, and Bob Dylan. The 1965 festival was the venue at which Dylan switched from pure folk to folk rock. The switch in musical technique and lyrics (which lacked the social-activist content commonly associated with his early music) so surprised and upset his fans that they roundly booed his performance as a sellout of pure folk music and the fight for social justice.

As the decade progressed, rock music played an increasingly important role at the Newport festivals, and drugs became a serious problem. Under pressure from the Newport City Council, the Newport Folk Foundation canceled the 1970 festival, and the next year the city council withdrew the foundation's license.

Bob Dylan was one of the performers responsible for merging folk themes, including social and political protest, with big-beat music and electric sounds, to produce folk rock. Dylan's album *Bringing It All Back Home*, 1965, used a backup rock-and-roll band; combined with his performance at the 1965 Newport Folk Festival, the album placed him in the vanguard of the folk rock movement. Jim McGuinn and songwriter Gene Clark formed The Byrds and reached number one on the charts with Dylan's "Mr. Tambourine Man" (1965). *Sweetheart of the Rodeo,* 1968, was especially important among The Byrds' albums in fusing folk with rock. Paul Simon and Art Garfunkel hit it big with "Scarborough Fair," "Sounds of Silence" (their first number one hit), and a string of other popular songs that often combined folk and rock. Their successful albums included *Parsley, Sage, Rosemary, and Thyme,* 1966, *Bookends,* 1968, and *Bridge Over Troubled Water,* 1970. Simon and Garfunkel recorded the soundtrack for the film *The Graduate,* 1967). One of the songs on the soundtrack, "Sounds of Silence" reaching the top of the charts and the soundtrack winning three Grammy Awards.

Music

BRITAIN'S OWN FOLK MUSIC

Legendary American songwriter Bob Dylan rose to fame with his acoustic protest music of the early 1960s and reinvented himself (to the initial horror of folk traditionalists) when he "went electric" in 1965. Dylan toured Great Britain that spring, appealing to listeners on that side of the Atlantic and inspiring rock musicians there, including the wildly successful British Invasion bands. The new musical genre that emerged from the U.S. and Canada in the mid-1960s, a fusion of folk and rock music, formed the foundation for an eclectic style of electric folk music in Britain that was pioneered by such bands as Pentangle and the Fairport Convention.

Early members of the Fairport Convention looked to America for inspiration and material, so much so that the band was heralded as the "British Jefferson Airplane" with its 1968 debut album. Many listeners presumed the band was American, and the pollenization was not viewed as a liability; vocalist Iain Matthews has said the band did nothing to dispel that notion.

Fairport Convention's early albums combined original material with songs by American artists, including Dylan, and the group entered the British singles charts with "Si Tu Dois Partir," a French-language cover version of Dylan's "If You Gotta Go." As the band defined its own sound, it drew increasingly on traditional European and especially Anglo-Celtic roots. Calling Fairport Convention "England's seminal folk-rock band," one critic wrote that the band's vitality came from "merging the contemporary electric mode with ancient Celtic folk motifs."

Following the release of the band's classic album *Liege and Lief,* founder Ashley Hutchings left Fairport Convention to form Steeleye Span. Forty years later, Fairport Convention continues to tour Britain and the United States with its acoustic lineup, and its spin-off band The Dylan Project is a tribute to Bob Dylan's entire oeuvre.

COUNTRY MUSIC

Country music began to escape from its traditionally southern, rural, and white roots during the 1960s. There were several reasons for the spread of country music: A growing feeling of alienation by individuals in large urban centers and a desire to return to their roots; a moderation of the nasal twang associated with country singers; replacement of the fiddle and steel guitar with a wider range of instruments; and a rise of artists who transcended the hillbilly and honky-tonk image. Market studies indicated that by the middle of the decade a large majority of country music consumers were urban dwellers.

Nashville, Tennessee, was the heart of country music, and performing at the Grand Ole Opry in Nashville was a sure sign that a country music artist had arrived. By the end of the 1960s, about 300 country performers, 300 record labels, 400 publishers, and 900 songwriters were based or represented in or near Nashville.[1] The so-called Nashville West was located in Bakersfield, California, where Merle Haggard and Buck Owens moved. Also during the 1960s, a country music center emerged in Austin, Texas. Known as the center of progressive country (a mixture of country and western), Austin hosted Willie Nelson among others.

During the 1960s, radio stations, primarily AM, brought country music to listeners throughout the United States, and American soldiers in Vietnam and elsewhere helped spread country music around the globe. Strangely enough, given country music's virtually all-white history, one of the entertainers most responsible for the rapid diffusion of country music during the 1960s was an African American, the great rhythm and blues singer Ray Charles. Charles released *Modern Sounds in Country & Western* in 1962 and followed with *Modern Sounds in Country & Western, Volume 2* the next year. Among the songs on these albums were "I Can't Stop Loving You" and Hank Williams's "Your Cheating Heart." As with Bob Dylan's transformation into a folk rock performer, Charles's movement into country caused considerable controversy among his fans. It would still be several years, however, before the color barrier in country music truly fell. Charley Pride was an important pioneer, though he sang ballads in a voice that did not sound particularly country. He appeared at the Grand Ole Opry in 1967, the first African American ever to headline there.

The Queen of Country Music during the early 1960s was Patsy Cline. An individualist and versatile singer, Cline influenced future generations of country singers even after her death in a 1963 airplane crash. Her hits included "I Fall to Pieces," "Crazy," "Walkin' After Midnight," and the posthumous "Sweet Dreams (of You)" and "Faded Love."

Patsy Cline's successor as most popular female country vocalist in the 1960s was Loretta Lynn. Born in Butcher Hollow (pronounced "Holler"), Kentucky, in 1936, Lynn was a true rags-to-riches story. Married at 13, pregnant at 14, and the mother of four children by 18, she overcame her early poverty and became one of the first female country singers to have wide appeal among women as well as men. She related to real problems women encountered with such stand-up-for-your-rights songs as "Don't Come Home A-Drinkin' (With Lovin' on Your Mind)" and "You Ain't Woman Enough (To Take My Man)."

Many listeners contrasted Loretta Lynn with Tammy Wynette, whom many unfairly saw as pushing a doormat philosophy of womanhood with her most famous song, "Stand by Your Man" (1968), which she co-wrote with her producer, Billy Sherrill. Often referred to as the First Lady of Country Music, Tammy Wynette became one of the most successful female country vocalists of all time. When she married male country star George Jones in 1969, the couple became known as Mr. and Mrs. Country Music.

During the 1960s, country music remained politically conservative. Merle Haggard, a former San Quentin inmate, was inspired by a Johnny Cash concert at the prison to join the prison band. By 1960, Haggard was free and starting his singing career. "I'm a Lonesome Fugitive" (1966) hit number one on the country charts, but the song that made him nationally famous (or infamous, depending on one's political beliefs) was "Okie from Muskogee" (1969), which venerated the nation's flag while attacking hippies and draft-card burners. The song made Haggard President Nixon's favorite country singer and helped Haggard win a pardon for his earlier burglary conviction from California Governor Ronald Reagan.

Chet Atkins entertained President Kennedy in 1961 at the Press Photographers' Ball and also performed at the White House. A skilled guitarist who cut numerous records, Atkins also served as a tal-ent scout, record producer, and vice president for the RCA Corporation. Among the future country stars that he at least partly discovered were Charley Pride, Bobby Bare, and Waylon Jennings.

Johnny Cash established himself as a country giant during the 1950s and 1960s. Cash identified with the down-and-out, including prison inmates. Two of his top albums in the decade were *Ring of Fire*, 1963, and *Johnny Cash at Folsom*, 1968. Cash also recorded *Johnny Cash at San Quentin*, 1969. In 1968, he married June Carter, a member of the famous folk music family, the Carters, and the following year had his own television show from Nashville. *The Johnny Cash Show* ran until May 1971, bringing country music to a mass audience. Among the regulars were Mother Maybelle and the Carter Family, wife June, the Statler Brothers, and Carl Perkins.

Other country singers had television shows as well. Glen Campbell starred on *The Glen Campbell Goodtime Hour* from 1969 to 1972. The theme song was Campbell's hit "Gentle on My Mind," which won a Grammy in the country category in 1967, the same year that Campbell won in pop for "By the Time I Get to Phoenix." The most popular country television show was *Hee Haw*, co-hosted by Buck Owens and Roy Clark. The show, a medley of country music, corny humor, and appearances by guest stars, all done from a very fake cornfield, originated in 1969. CBS dropped the show in 1971 even though it was in the top 20, and *Hee Haw* went into first-run syndication until 1993, a hit for most of its long life.

POP

Rock had been pushing traditional pop music aside since the 1950s, but pop never died out. Audiences remained for the easy listening, often romantic and nostalgic lyrics of singers such as Frank Sinatra, known as the "Chairman of the Board" and "Ol' Blue Eyes." His hit singles in the 1960s included "It Was a Very Good Year," and "Strangers in the Night." His successful albums included *Sinatra's Sinatra*, 1963, *September of My Years*, 1965, *Strangers in the Night*, 1966, and *My Way*, 1969.

Other pop hits included Tony Bennett's "I Left My Heart in San Francisco" (1962), Connie

Music

Francis's "Everybody's Somebody's Fool" (1960) and "Where the Boys Are" (1961), and Bobby Vinton's "Roses Are Red" (1962).

Smooth crooners like Andy Williams, Perry Como, Johnny Mathis, and Nat "King" Cole remained popular. Williams had two of the top albums for 1963 with *Days of Wine and Roses* and *Moon River and Other Great Movie Themes*. Throughout most of the 1960s, Williams had a regular variety show on television and did occasional television specials. Perry Como reached gold with his 1963 and 1966 Christmas albums. Johnny Mathis registered a string of hit albums in the early 1960s, including *Heavenly,* 1960, and *Faithfully,* 1962. Nat "King" Cole's album *Unforgettable* reached gold in 1964.

The two most successful composers of pop music in the decade were Henry Mancini and Burt Bacharach. Mancini achieved his first great success with "Moon River," from the film *Breakfast at Tiffany's,* 1961. Mancini won two Academy Awards for his score for the film as well as a Grammy for "Moon River." Another Grammy Award and Oscar followed for "The Days of Wine and Roses" from the 1962 film of the same title. Burt Bacharach also created highly successful movie scores, earning Academy Award nominations for the songs "Alfie" (from *Alfie,* 1966) and "The Look of Love" (from *Casino Royale,* 1967). Bacharach won an Academy Award in 1969 for "Raindrops Keep Fallin' on My Head" (from *Butch Cassidy and the Sundance Kid*).

Bobby Darin, winner of two Grammy Awards in 1959, for Best New Artist of the Year and Best Vocal Performance, Male (for "Mack the Knife"), was a gifted songwriter and singer. He established his own music publishing and recording firm in 1963 and steadily moved away from the teenage market toward adult audiences. He focused more on albums than singles. He also turned to acting, winning an Oscar nomination for best supporting actor in *Captain Newman, M.D., 1963.*

Among women vocalists, the 1960s belonged to Barbra Streisand. Her first album, *The Barbra Streisand Album,* 1963, went gold, as did her next six albums. She starred in the 1964 Broadway musical *Funny Girl,* based on the life of singer and comedienne Fanny Brice. Starting in 1965, Streisand turned to television and appeared in a series of popular specials, including a 1967 concert

taped live in New York City's Central Park. Her first television special, *My Name Is Barbra,* 1965, won five Emmy Awards. In 1968, she won an Oscar for a film reprise of her *Funny Girl* role.

As successful as these artists were, however, they were no longer in the mainstream of modern music. The takeover by rock in the 1950s was slowed by the "payola" scandals of 1959–1960. Congressional investigations revealed widespread pay-offs by record companies and music publishers to induce disc jockeys to play their material. The scandals' fallout led to over 250 disc jockeys being convicted for accepting cash or gifts to play certain records. Elvis Presley's induction into the army also contributed to rock's problems. Elvis returned from the army in 1960 and resumed his recording career with considerable success.

The teen audience in the 1960s was heavily influenced in its choice of favorites by Dick Clark, who followed Bob Horn as host of *Bandstand* on WFIL-TV in Philadelphia in 1956. By August 1957, Clark's renamed *American Bandstand* had gone national on ABC. The approach was simple but successful. Teens danced to records as guest stars lip-synched their own records. The dance contests, spotlight dances, and rating of new songs became staples of the program. Dick Clark helped make stars, including Chubby Checker, Buddy Holly, Frankie Avalon, and the Everly Brothers. In 1963, the daily program was reduced to Saturday afternoons. Nonetheless, Dick Clark remained with *American Bandstand* until 1989, adapting endlessly to new music and becoming a music icon. One important accomplishment of the show was that it featured white and black teenagers together on a national television program for the first time and offered African American singers and musicians national exposure.

The Beach Boys appeared on *American Bandstand* in the early 1960s. Hailing from California, Brian, Dennis, and Carl Wilson formed a band in 1961 with their cousin Mike Love and friend Al Jardine. They went through several names before settling on the Beach Boys, a happy complement to some of their early hits, such as "Surfin'" (1962), "Surfin' Safari" (1962), "Surfin' USA" (1963), "Surfer Girl" (1963), and "Fun, Fun, Fun" (1964). Three later songs—"I Get Around" (1964), "Help Me, Rhonda" (1965), and "Good

HIT SONGS OF THE 1960s

"Are You Lonesome Tonight?" (Elvis Presley)—1960

"The Twist" (Chubby Checker)—1960

"Crazy" (Patsy Cline)—1961

"I Want to Hold Your Hand" (The Beatles)—1964

"(I Can't Get No) Satisfaction" (The Rolling Stones)—1965

"Good Vibrations" (Beach Boys)—1966

"Light My Fire" (The Doors)—1967

"Respect" (Aretha Franklin)—1967

"Hey Jude" (The Beatles)—1968

"Aquarius/Let the Sunshine In" (The Fifth Dimension)—1969

Vibrations" (1966)—reached number one on the charts. "California Girls" (1965), another hit, helped create the mystique of the beautiful California girl. The Beach Boys' close harmonies, coupled with dense musical layering, helped create what came to be known as the California sound. One of their greatest artistic accomplishments was *Pet Sounds,* 1966, usually credited with being the first concept album, a unified cycle of music intended to be heard from beginning to end. Artistically successful but commercially disappointing, the album was the model for the Beatles' later *Sgt. Pepper's Lonely Hearts Club Band,* 1967.

ROCK

Music and American culture were changed forever in 1964 when John Lennon, Paul McCartney, George Harrison, and Ringo Starr, better known as the Beatles, arrived in the United States. Their appearance on *The Ed Sullivan Show* launched Beatlemania. Huge crowds turned out for Beatles concerts at such places as the Coliseum in Washington, D.C. and New York's Carnegie Hall. Girls swooned, and boys grew their hair long in the Beatles' mop-top fashion. The media reported on every detail of the band members' lives. The invasion made everything British (including music, hair, and clothes) popular.

The hits followed fast and furious. "I Want to Hold Your Hand" sold more than a million copies within 10 days of being released in the United States in 1964. Twelve Beatles records were among the 100 bestselling records in April of that year. Five occupied the top five positions. In that same year, the singles "I Want to Hold Your Hand," "Can't Buy Me Love," "A Hard Day's Night," and "I Feel Fine," and the albums *Meet the Beatles!, The Beatles' Second Album, Something New, Beatles '65,* and *The Beatles' Story* all went gold.

The Beatles also turned to films, with *A Hard Day's Night,* 1964, and *Help!,* 1965. As the group showed greater complexity in their music, they withdrew from live performances. The Beatles experimented with Indian mysticism and drugs, made additional films (*The Magical Mystery Tour,* 1967, and the animated *Yellow Submarine,* 1968), and released the concept album *Sgt. Pepper's Lonely Hearts Club Band,* 1967, and the double album known officially as *The Beatles,* 1968, and unofficially as the "White Album" after its cover.

Romantic themes began to yield to social consciousness in songs such as "Eleanor Rigby" and "Paperback Writer." There was increasing intellectual subtlety in both lyrics and music in the *Sgt. Pepper's* collection and the "White Album," as well as greater attention to how songs fit together. The Beatles introduced new sounds with orchestral instruments, especially stringed instruments. Even album covers became part of the artistic effect for the Beatles. The *Sgt. Pepper's* cover, for example, combined psychedelic and pop art effects.

John Lennon married the Japanese artist Yoko Ono, and Paul McCartney married photographer Linda Eastman. With career aspirations diverging and personal and legal tensions rising among the four, they split in 1970. For years, Beatles fans longed for a reunion. That dream died with the murder of John Lennon outside his New York City apartment in 1980.

The popularity of the Beatles triggered a deluge of British groups into the United States, including Herman's Hermits, the Dave Clark Five, the Who, and the Rolling Stones. Most British groups, if not imitating the Beatles, at least tried to capitalize on their popularity. The Rolling Stones, though, were deliberately pitched as an anti-Beatles group. Featuring vocalist Mick Jagger and guitarist Keith

The Beatles performing in their second film, *Help!* (1965). Directed by Richard Lester. Left to right: Paul McCartney, George Harrison, Ringo Starr, and John Lennon. Courtesy of Photofest.

Richards, the group also included bass player Bill Wyman and drummer Charlie Watts. The Rolling Stones projected an image of sex, drugs, violence, and occultism. Their music, derived ultimately from the earthiest versions of rhythm and blues, differed from the Beatles' sound, which evolved out of the rock music of Elvis Presley, Buddy Holly, and the Everly Brothers. The Stones' hits included "(I Can't Get No) Satisfaction" (1965), "Ruby Tuesday" (1967), and "Honky Tonk Woman" (1969). They also released albums with titles like *Their Satanic Majesties Request,* 1967, and *Let It Bleed,* 1969. When the Rolling Stones performed "Let's Spend the Night Together" on *The Ed Sullivan Show* in 1967, they mumbled or altered the most objectionable lines at Sullivan's insistence.

A group named the Monkees was the brainchildren of Columbia Pictures, which decided to fashion a television show about a group of young men trying to make a go of a rock-and-roll band, in imitation of the Beatles' film *A Hard Day's Night,* 1964. Three stars were from the United

States (Mickey Dolenz, Peter Tork, Mike Nesmith); one (David Jones) was from England. Musical talent was less a requirement than the right mixture of personalities.

The television show, *The Monkees,* ran two seasons (1966–1968) on NBC and the group released a number of hit songs, including "Last Train to Clarksville" (1966), "I'm a Believer" (1966), and "Daydream Believer" (1967). They also had several gold albums. Live performances, however, revealed to audiences that the Monkees had not played their instruments on their records. After a public rebellion by the Monkees, Screen Gems let them play as well as sing on their records and, by the end of the decade, the Monkees' attempt to become a serious band came to an end.

San Francisco became the center of flower power, hippie life, and psychedelic rock during the 1960s. A Swiss chemist, Albert Hofmann, invented a drug in 1938 that he named Lysergsaure-diathylamid and abbreviated LSD-25. The drug distorted time, created a sense of the self melting into one's surroundings, and made objects appear fluid. By the 1950s, the term "psychedelic" had been applied to these phenomena. In 1965, the federal government banned the distribution of LSD, widely known as acid. Musical performers attempted to parallel the effects of LSD in their music by creating less structured performances, increasing volume, and adding other sensory stimuli such as flashing lights.

One of the most famous San Francisco groups was the Grateful Dead, led by Jerry Garcia. The Grateful Dead actually played a mix of folk and blues in addition to psychedelic rock, but became associated with drugs because of their advocacy for legalizing marijuana, the fact that they lived for a time on Ashbury Street in the Haight-Ashbury section of the city, and their performances (before adopting the "Grateful Dead" name) at Ken Kesey's acid tests (symposia sponsored by the writer at which participants took LSD). The Grateful Dead released popular albums such as *The Grateful Dead,* 1967, and *Anthem of the Sun,* 1968, but achieved more lasting fame for their enthusiastic live performances and remarkably faithful fans who called themselves Dead Heads.

The Jefferson Airplane debuted in San Francisco in 1965, and in 1966 Grace Slick joined the group as lead vocalist. The group lived together in Haight-Ashbury and tied themselves closely to the psychedelic rock-drug movement. The album *Surrealistic Pillow,* 1967, was a hit, and two of its songs, "Somebody to Love" and "White Rabbit," made the top 10. The latter, loosely based on Lewis Carroll's *Alice's Adventures in Wonderland,* was an explicit call to use drugs. Grace Slick combined considerable singing and songwriting talent with an outrageousness that varied from dressing like a nun to flashing her breasts.

Jimi Hendrix and Janis Joplin were two of the most talented and tragic figures of the San Francisco psychedelic scene. Hendrix, one of the most gifted guitarists of the decade, teamed with Noel Redding and Mitch Mitchell to form the Jimi Hendrix Experience. Hendrix was especially skilled at creating striking effects with feedback from his guitar, and his music fused blues, rock, and jazz improvisations.

Hendrix's most memorable appearances included his performances at the Monterey Inter-

Jimi Hendrix fused blues, rock, and jazz improvisations and was especially skilled at creating striking effects with feedback from his guitar. Courtesy of Photofest.

national Pop Festival in 1967 and the Woodstock Music and Art Fair in 1969. At the former, his performance included simulated masturbation and the actual burning of his guitar; the latter featured his unusual and controversial interpretation of "The Star-Spangled Banner." On September 18, 1970, Hendrix died after a drug overdose. He was not quite 28 years old. The combination of extraordinary talent, drugs, and an early and tragic death made Hendrix for many people a symbol of the promises, confusions, and excesses of the 1960s.

Influenced by Billie Holiday and Bessie Smith, Janis Joplin helped create "blue-eyed soul," blues sung by white artists. Her live performances, like Hendrix's, could be outrageous. She often drank whiskey while performing and mingled singing with running, jumping, and occasionally screaming. Heavy drinking made her voice raspy, which, along with her haggard appearance, caused her blues renditions to seem all the more genuine. Her albums included *Cheap Thrills,* 1968, and *I Got Dem Ol' Kozmic Blues Again Mama!,* 1969. After at least half a dozen overdoses, Joplin died

MUSIC FESTIVALS

The June 1967 Monterey Pop Festival ushered in the so-called Summer of Love. Festival organizers included an all-star cast, among them John Phillips of the Mamas and the Papas, Paul McCartney of the Beatles, Paul Simon, Smokey Robinson, and Brian Wilson of the Beach Boys. The three-day festival included Country Joe and the Fish, Janis Joplin, Jefferson Airplane, Otis Redding, and the Grateful Dead. Jim Hendrix introduced the Jimi Hendrix Experience to American audiences, lighting his guitar on fire and breaking it over an amplifier. The Monterey Pop Festival was enormously successful and generally trouble free, and inspired a number of other large-scale festivals, including the Woodstock festival.

The Woodstock Music and Art Fair (as it was formally called) occurred in New York State from August 15 to 17, 1969. Organizers named it after the village of Woodstock, Bob Dylan's home, hoping that the folk-rock star would participate. He didn't; however, many other stars did participate, including Jimi Hendrix, Joan Baez, the Who, Janis Joplin, the Grateful Dead, Jefferson Airplane, and Creedence Clearwater Revival. The highlight of the event was the controversial rendition of "The Star-Spangled Banner" by Jimi Hendrix. Woodstock encountered numerous problems, including overcrowding, a lot of rain and mud, inadequate restroom facilities, and demands by some performers to be paid in advance. On the whole, the festival remained peaceful despite the hardships endured by the audience of close to half a million.

The festival earned a permanent place in American culture as a defining moment of the 1960s. It represented an open, classless society of music, sex, drugs, love, and peace, all the more so because the event remained largely free of violence and the tragic consequences one might expect from so large a gathering of young people.

from a heroin overdose at age 27, three weeks after Jimi Hendrix's death. A 1979 film, *The Rose,* starring Bette Midler, was based on her life.

Many other groups and individual artists also left their mark on the 1960s. The Doors, for example, became a symbol of the decade's combination of enormous talent and tragic lack of self-discipline. Jim Morrison, a talented singer, poet, and musician, founded the group. The Doors were successful with their first album, *Doors,* in early 1967. The single "Light My Fire" reached number one in July. The Doors' music combined hard rock with broad images and psychological insights.

Things began to go downhill for the group in March 1969, when Morrison arrived late and intoxicated at a concert in Miami. He reportedly exposed himself on stage and was convicted of profanity and indecent exposure. This resulted in canceled concerts and difficulty getting airtime for their records. The group rebounded in 1970, but then Morrison left for France. In July 1971, Morrison was found dead of an apparent heart attack. Oliver Stone made a successful film about the group, *The Doors,* 1991, starring Val Kilmer as Morrison.

Another enormously successful group was the Mamas and the Papas, consisting of John Phillips, his wife Michelle, Ellen Naomi Cohen (known as Cass Elliott), and Dennis Doherty. Appreciated for their well-written lyrics, melodious harmonies, and versatility, the Mamas and the Papas released such hits as "California Dreamin'" (1966) and "Monday, Monday" (1966). They also had a string of top 10 albums, but by the end of the decade the Mamas and the Papas had decided to go their own ways. "Mama" Cass, unfortunately, had little time to pursue an individual career, as she died in a London hotel in 1974, by, according to legend, choking to death on a ham sandwich, but in reality apparently of a heart attack.

SOUL

Soul emerged out of gospel music and rhythm and blues (R&B). The term "soul" had been used in relation to gospel music long before its adoption by rhythm and blues and later by "soul" performers. Ray Charles popularized the style with his synthesis of religious and R&B. In 1960, Charles had his first number one hit, "Georgia on My Mind," a soulful rendition that fused with pop. Part of his genius was in taking a song, for example "Take These Chains From My Heart" (1963), that had essentially nothing to do with soul traditions and giving it a soul treatment. The result increased his own popularity and that of soul music with mass audiences.

Soul music fit well with the 1960's social movements, especially Civil Rights, and developments like Black Power and the Black Is Beautiful theme. In addition, growing numbers of whites who wanted to express solidarity with African Americans, or who merely wanted to be chic, sought out soul, including fashions and food.

Aretha Franklin was perhaps the finest of the female soul singers, and had such hits as "I Never Loved a Man (The Way I Love You)" (1967), "Chain of Fools" (1967), "Since You've Been Gone" (1968), and "I Say a Little Prayer" (1968). Drawing from such sources as singing with her minister father in Detroit, the sounds of Ray Charles, and personal tragedies (especially her mother's departure and death when Aretha was 6 and 10, respectively years later), she poured personal emotion into her songs.

Otis Redding also helped to spread soul music and convert white audiences. A shy young man from Georgia, Redding was signed by Jim Stewart, who, although white, emphasized soul on the STAX label that he started with his sister, Estelle Axton (the name of the company derived from the first two letters of brother and sister's last names). By 1965, Redding's songs, such as "Mr. Pitiful" and "I've Been Loving You Too Long," were being well received. He proved enormously popular while touring Europe and performed at the Monterey Pop Festival in 1967. In November 1967, he recorded the song that would become his greatest hit, "Dock of the Bay." On December 10, Redding was killed in a plane crash. Redding's "Dock of the Bay" was released in January; it sold four million records by the end of May.[2]

The ultimate soul performer, though, was James Brown, the "Godfather of Soul." Also known as the "Hardest-Working Man in Show Business," Brown worked almost every night, performing to audiences in large concert halls. The song that most forcefully called out to the social and racial struggles of the decade was "Say It Loud, I'm Black and I'm Proud" (1968). Brown, himself from a troubled background, promoted stay-in-school campaigns for youth, encouraged African American business efforts, and worked for equal rights. He

entertained the troops in Vietnam, and wherever he performed did so with extraordinary energy.

The largest black-owned company at the end of the 1960s was Motown, short for Motortown (Detroit). Berry Gordy Jr., a former Detroit autoworker, started Motown in 1959. He hired talented writers, musicians, producers, engineers, arrangers, and singers, and established a sort of assembly-line approach to music under strict controls. Gordy also made extensive use of modern recording technology, gaudy costumes, and carefully choreographed dance steps for his performers. He brought soul music closer to pop so his recordings would appeal to a wide audience, including white listeners. The Motown sound tended to be smoother than the sharp-edged soul that some other labels were producing, but still often retained such traditional soul techniques as rhythmic repetitions and call-and-response patterns of phrasing. Gordy liked to sign young performers, often complete unknowns, and mold them into Motown artists.

The list of Motown hits in the 1960s was impressive: Marvin Gaye's "How Sweet It Is (To Be Loved By You)" (1964), and "I Heard It Through the Grapevine" (1968); Barrett Strong's "Money (That's What I Want)," Motown's first national hit (1960); Smokey Robinson and the Miracles' "Shop Around," the first Motown song to reach number one (1960), and "My Girl" (1964). An ability to coin lyrics that connected deeply with listeners' fears, hopes, and anxieties was a hallmark of Motown, a direct result of the talented lyricists that Gordy employed. For example, Jimmy Ruffin's "What Becomes of the Broken-hearted" (1966) was seemingly aimed directly at each listener and to the times. The Four Tops' "I Can't Help Myself (Sugar Pie, Honey Bunch)" (1965) and "Reach Out I'll Be There" (1966) were popular as well.

Motown was known for its girls groups. The Marvelettes hit it big with "Please Mr. Postman" (1961), which reached number one on both the pop and R&B charts. Martha Reeves and the Vandellas had "(Love Is Like a) Heat Wave" (1963), "Dancing in the Street" (1964), and "Jimmy Mack" (1967). Other hits included Mary Wells's "My Guy" (1964) and Gladys Knight and the Pips' "I Heard It Through the Grapevine" (1967), which was released prior to the Marvin Gaye version.

Music

The most successful girl group was the Supremes, which later became Diana Ross and the Supremes. The original trio consisted of Detroit singers Diana Ross, Florence Ballard, and Mary Wilson, who started their career as the Primettes before signing with Berry Gordy in 1961. Their first chart-topper was "Where Did Our Love Go?" in 1964. Their most famous song was "Stop! In The Name of Love" (1965), the fourth of five consecutive number one singles. "You Can't Hurry Love" (1966) began a run of four more consecutive tunes that topped the charts. In 1967, the name of the group was changed to give top billing to Diana Ross, and Florence Ballard was replaced by Cindy Birdsong. The final hit before Ross departed to pursue a solo career was "Someday We'll Be Together" (1969).

Even children were potential Motown performers. Little Stevie Wonder, blind like the great Ray Charles, was just 12 years old when he began with Motown. In 1963, at age 13, Wonder had several successful singles and his first two albums, *The 12 Year Old Genius* and *Tribute to Uncle Ray,* the latter a homage to Ray Charles. Later 1960s hits included "Uptight (Everything's Alright)" (1965), with its effective use of hip slang ("Everything's alright. Uptight. Out of sight."), "Shoo-Be-Doo-Be-Doo-Da-Day" (1968), "For Once in My Life" (1968), and "Yester-Me, Yester-You, Yesterday" (1969).

Phil Spector was another highly successful producer during the 1960s. The Crystals recorded "Uptown," "Da Doo Ron Ron," and "Then He Kissed Me." The Ronettes' hits included "Be My Baby," "Do I Love You?" and "Walking in the Rain." Spector's other successes included hits by the Righteous Brothers (e.g., "You've Lost That Lovin' Feeling") and, in 1963, what many consider the finest Christmas album ever produced, *A Christmas Gift for You,* more commonly known as *Phil Spector's Christmas Album.*

CLASSICAL AND JAZZ

While not in the music headlines during the 1960s, classical music and jazz retained fans, and even gained new ones. Classical music accounted for between 5 and 10 percent of record sales during the 1960s.[3]

Aaron Copland and Leonard Bernstein were widely recognized as the foremost American composers of their time. Copland's 1960s compositions included *Nonet,* 1960, composed for nine stringed instruments; and *Connotations for Orchestra,* 1962. Copland also conducted the New York Philharmonic and in 1960 directed the Boston Symphony on a tour of the Far East.

Leonard Bernstein was a great showman and educator as well as composer and director. He popularized classical music through music, books, and television specials. Bernstein directed the New York Philharmonic from 1959 to 1969 (including a special television concert in 1963 in honor of the assassinated John F. Kennedy) and inaugurated the New York Lincoln Center for the Performing Arts in 1962.

The first television superstar of classical music, Bernstein conducted three nationally televised Young's People's Concerts (1964, 1965, 1966) in which he used Beatles songs to clarify aspects of classical music. He also wrote books in which he sought to make classical music more understandable and fun.

As the 1960s progressed, Bernstein became increasingly political. His concerns included civil rights (championing the Black Panthers), ending the Vietnam War, and supporting Israel.

The pianist Van Cliburn, who had won the Moscow Tchaikovsky Competition, sold albums on which he played Beethoven, Chopin, and Mozart.

African Americans won widespread acceptance in classical music in the 1960s. Leontyne Price, inspired by Marian Anderson, who had been the first African American to sing at the New York Metropolitan Opera (1955), appeared there in 1961. Her performance as Leonora in Verdi's *Il Trovatore* earned her a 40-minute standing ovation. African Americans also moved into important conducting positions: Henry Lewis was the conductor of the New Jersey Symphony, Paul Freeman was the associate conductor of the Dallas Symphony, and George Byrd was the assistant conductor of the American Ballet Theater.

Jazz enthusiasts during the 1960s could still enjoy the music and showmanship of perhaps the most important figure in the history of jazz, Louis Armstrong.

Music

Armstrong recorded "Hello Dolly" for the stage show in 1964, and the song soon became the top song in America. Ill health, however, caught up with Louis by 1968, and he was unable to perform for several months. When he returned to the stage, he was under doctors' orders not to play the trumpet. He passed away in 1971.

Duke Ellington, composer, pianist, and bandleader, still performed in venues from Europe to Africa to American proms. In 1969, on his 70th birthday, he was honored at the White House with the Presidential Medal of Freedom. President Richard Nixon played "Happy Birthday" to him on the piano.

Dizzy Gillespie was still playing his trumpet in the 1960s. Saxophonist Stan Getz won a Grammy Award in 1964 for "The Girl from Ipanema." In 1964 Thelonious Monk returned from several years of self-imposed absence from public performances.

A white quartet headed by pianist Dave Brubeck continued with its so-called progressive jazz in the 1960s. Brubeck's music was often labeled cool jazz, with its smooth phrasing and absence of any overt sense of the blues tradition, although Brubeck was daring in rhythm and improvisation. Brubeck was especially popular on college campuses, and one of his most famous performances occurred at the New York World's Fair in 1964. Throughout the 1960s, though, jazz was largely dominated by African American artists.

At the most daring edge of jazz in the decade were John Coltrane, Ornette Coleman, and Miles Davis. Hard bop, or funky jazz, was a reaction against cool jazz, an attempt to return jazz to its roots in black culture. Hard bop was strong, passionate, and heavily reliant on improvisation. One of the leaders of the movement was Miles Davis, a great jazz trumpeter. John Coltrane, who had worked for Davis, pushed the movement farther ahead. Coltrane had enormous range with his saxophone. He incorporated African and Asian music into his work and achieved great non-harmonic complexity. Coltrane did not identify himself as a black nationalist, and despite his deep concern with African music and civil rights he refused to define jazz as a black art form. He saw jazz as a matter of music rather than skin color, and maintained his sensitivity toward those who were suffering. When four young African American girls were killed in the bombing of the Sixteenth Street Baptist Church in Birmingham in 1963, he composed and played an elegy for them that he called "Alabama."

The next step from hard bop was free jazz, which included clarinet squeals and saxophone shrieks, a strong sense of the blues, and even more improvisation than in hard bop. The result sometimes seemed more chaotic than musical. Free jazz varied with the performer, with considerable improvisation made possible by freedom from pre-set chord progressions, abandonment of regular patterns of rhythm, use of extremes in notes, and occasional silences. Free jazz was especially energetic, with drummers and other musicians feeling free to be as irregular as the spirit moved them to be. In some cases, musicians in a group all seemed to be playing solos at the same time.

Free jazz mirrored the growing anger of black nationalists. It rejected status quo rules and traditions and conveyed passionate feelings that paralleled blacks' passion for freedom from white domination. Seen as a primitive music, free jazz appeared to hearken back to African rhythms and the primitive roots of black consciousness.

Leading the free jazz movement was saxophonist and composer Ornette Coleman, who led the Ornette Coleman Quartet. Coleman even challenged the tradition of musicians specializing in one instrument; he played the saxophone, violin, and trumpet. Coleman's *Free Jazz*, 1960, was a milestone in the history of jazz, and inspired countless musicians. It also gave a name to the new style of jazz.

Toward the end of his career, John Coltrane was influenced by Coleman and moved closer to free jazz's spirit and sound. The Coltrane's free playing sometimes sounded chaotic as the band members, including two drummers, improvised individually and sometimes drowned each other out. Miles Davis, who initially preferred what he called "controlled freedom," also began to change. His music grew more spontaneous, and he even paid his band members not to practice at home in order not to sound too polished. By 1969, Davis was combining jazz with rock; his *Bitches Brew* album sold 400,000 copies during its first year.[4]

Music

Sports

and Leisure of the 1960s

The 1960s were marked by war abroad and social upheaval at home, but the nation found itself at times able to turn away from political and social divisions to revel in playful and light-hearted pastimes. Yet so strong were the social dynamics of the decade that even play sometimes gravitated toward the ideological, and sometimes mirrored the conflicts and preoccupations that were threatening to unravel the social fabric of the country.

SPORTS

Professional Football

One of the most dominant figures in American sports during the 1960s was Vince Lombardi, the coach of the Green Bay Packers in the National Football League (NFL). "Winning isn't everything, it's the only thing," was Vince Lombardi's signature quotation, although others had made the statement before him.

Lombardi, a New Yorker, settled in a relatively small town in the football hinterlands, Green Bay, Wisconsin, where he started building a dynasty in 1960. During the next seven years, Lombardi's Packers won five NFL championships and the first two Super Bowls (1967 and 1968).

Lombardi, with his insistence on hard work and discipline and his unswerving commitment to winning, seemed to be an anomaly in the turbulent decade of the 1960s. Yet, as his biographer David Maraniss points out, he was progressive in his attitudes toward race relations and homosexuality.[1] He insisted that African American players on his team be treated the same as white players, refusing, for example, to house his team at hotels that would not accept African Americans and insisting on employing Native American caddies at a Green Bay golf course year-round when it was customary to lay them off in the summer in favor of white youngsters. When he coached the Washington Redskins later in the decade, he threatened to fire anyone who belittled a gay Redskins player because of his sexual orientation.

The two greatest players of the decade were quarterback Johnny Unitas of the Baltimore Colts and fullback Jim Brown of the Cleveland Browns. The expansion Dallas Cowboys began their rise from mediocrity to become "America's Team." The American Football League (AFL) was born in 1960, competing and finally merging with the older National Football League by 1970. The Super Bowl, conceived in competition and then cooperation between the two leagues, began its ascendancy toward its eventual status as America's most spectacular sports event. The contest that set it on that track, though, was neither of Green Bay's triumphs, but Super Bowl III, when

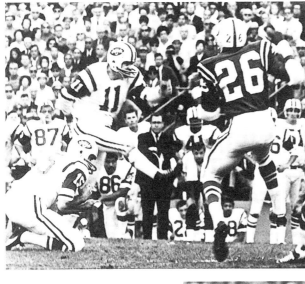

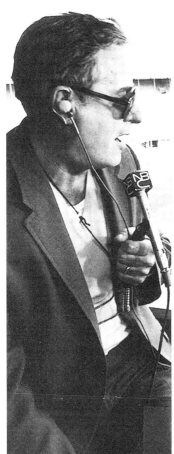

In Super Bowl III, the AFL's New York Jets scored a historic upset win over the NFL's Baltimore Colts. Clockwise from top left: Jim Turner kicks a field goal; Kyle Rote interviews Joe Namath; Namath prepares to take a snap from center; announcer Curt Gowdy covers the game. Courtesy of Photofest.

quarterback Joe Namath of the upstart AFL New York Jets predicted a victory over the NFL Colts and then made good on his promise.

The National Football League, winner of the first two Super Bowl games by decisive margins, was the prohibitive favorite to extend its winning streak in the third meeting between the league champions. Joe Namath, known as "Broadway Joe" for his flashy lifestyle, was the quarterback of the American Football League champion New York Jets. Namath, showing little respect for the older league and unfazed that his own Jets were 17-point underdogs, guaranteed victory. On January 12, 1969, Namath delivered on that guarantee, showing that the new league was the NFL's equal and setting himself on a path that would lead to the Pro Football Hall of Fame.

College Football

College football remained popular. A small number of college powerhouses ruled the gridiron. The University of Alabama won two national championships and shared a third during the 1960s, while the University of Texas won twice. The University of Southern California won two national titles and featured two Heisman winners, most notably O. J. Simpson, who would go on to a record-setting career in the National Football League and in the 1990s be the defendant in one of the most sensational murder trials in history. The University of Notre Dame, under coach Ara Parseghian, returned to prominence when the Fighting Irish captured a national title in 1966 during one of the most famous games ever: a 10–10 tie with Michigan State. This was also one of the most controversial games in college football history because Notre Dame, its starting quarterback and halfback out with injuries, elected to run out the clock.

Boxing

Muhammad Ali shares top billing with Vince Lombardi among 1960s sports figures. The young Cassius Clay, light-heavyweight gold medalist at the 1960 Olympics and heavyweight champion of the world at age 22, was an "in-your-face" fighter, predicting the round in which he would win and celebrating his greatness with whimsical verses such as his self-description, "Float like a butterfly, sting like a bee."

Clay fought Sonny Liston, a heavy favorite, in a 1964 fight for the heavyweight championship of the world. Liston had won the title with a first-round knockout of then-champion Floyd Patterson in 1962 and retained his title by again demolishing Patterson in a single round the following year. Faced with Clay's speed and taunting, though, the older fighter could not connect, and when the seventh round began, the champion remained seated in his corner. The stunning upset was followed by an even more bewildering rematch in 1965, with Liston going down for the count in the first round, victim of a "phantom" punch that no one saw land. Rumors circulated that Liston had thrown the fight.

By the second fight with Liston, Clay had converted to the Nation of Islam and changed his name to Muhammad Ali. The Nation of Islam advocated black separatism and encouraged its adherents to reject their old names, often given to their ancestors by slave masters. As Ali spoke out against racism, the media began to turn against him, even as he continued his mastery of the boxing world.

By 1967, Ali had established himself as one of the greatest, if not the best, heavyweight boxers ever. He had also become increasingly outspoken against the Vietnam War, which he saw as a racist war against another colored race. Ali was drafted into military service and sought unsuccessfully to receive a conscientious objector classification. Denied that status, he refused induction. The penalties were heavy: At the very peak of his career, Ali was stripped of his heavyweight title. He was brought to trial for refusing induction, convicted, and sentenced to five years in prison. Ali appealed the conviction, but in the meantime was deprived of his career. He traveled widely throughout the country, much in demand as a public speaker, especially on college campuses. As the decade approached its conclusion, increasing numbers of African Americans shared Ali's view, asking why they should fight in Vietnam for a government that back home refused them the rights for which they supposedly were fighting and dying to provide for the Vietnamese. As opposition to racism and the war merged in the minds of large

Sports

Cassius Clay (who changed his name to Muhammad Ali) standing over a fallen Sonny Liston in the boxing ring, 1965. Prints & Photographs Division, Library of Congress.

numbers of African Americans, Ali became an inspiring force within the Black Power movement.

In the 1970s the Supreme Court overturned his conviction and Ali returned to boxing, twice more becoming world champion. Ali continued to rise in popularity and became one of the most loved figures in America, so much so that he was invited to light the Olympic Flame at the opening ceremonies for the Atlanta Olympics in 1996.

Baseball

Professional baseball looked about the same in the 1960s as it had in previous decades except for the growing number of teams, but the winds of change were buffeting baseball.

The decade opened with Bill Mazeroski, the great defensive second baseman of the Pittsburgh Pirates, hitting a ninth-inning home run in game seven of the 1960 World Series to give his Pirates the championship and put a dent in the New York Yankee dynasty. The Yankees continued, though, to be the Yankees of old through 1964, when another Series loss, this one to the St. Louis Cardinals, temporarily ended the long run of Yankee successes.

The most important on-field baseball happening of the 1960s featured Roger Maris, the Yankees' right fielder, at a time when the greatest active Yankee hero was still Mickey Mantle. In 1961 Maris broke the beloved Babe Ruth's home-run mark, which had stood at 60 since 1927. Maris suffered under the stress of media attention and considerable fan unhappiness that the great Bambino's record had been broken. For most fans, if the record had to be broken, it should have been broken by Mantle. The commissioner of baseball, Ford Frick, a former newspaperman and ghostwriter for Babe Ruth, did his best to retain Ruth's status by adding the most famous asterisk in history to Maris's record, indicating that he had played a 162-game schedule, 8 more games than in Ruth's time.

In 1962 Maury Wills, shortstop for the Los Angeles Dodgers, took on another legendary star, Ty Cobb, outrunning Cobb's single-season stolen base record 104 to 96. The year also saw other remarkable events. A young Dodgers lefthander, Sandy Koufax, struck out 18 batters in a single game, tying the all-time single-game record. Casey Stengel, let go after the 1960 season by the Yankees, resurfaced to manage the expansion New York Mets, and lost 120 games.

From 1903 until 1953, the same 16 teams in the same 16 cities had constituted the major leagues. In the mid-1950s several teams changed residences, including the Dodgers (Brooklyn to Los Angeles) and the Giants (New York to San Francisco). In 1961, the American League added the Los Angeles Angels (who moved to Anaheim in 1966) and the second version of the Washington Senators. The Houston Colt .45's (later Astros) and New York Mets joined the National League in 1962. The Kansas City Royals and Seattle Pilots (later the Milwaukee Brewers) in the American League, and the San Diego Padres and Montreal Expos in the National League (the first inclusion

Sports

of a major league team from another country) joined the majors for the 1969 season. Also in 1962, Jackie Robinson, the first African American player in the modern major leagues, was inducted into the Baseball Hall of Fame at Cooperstown, New York. The enshrinement of Robinson was especially significant in the decade that witnessed so much striving after racial justice.

No major league team would completely replace the Yankees in the 1960s, but many would try, with the Los Angeles Dodgers coming closest. The Dodgers won the National League pennant in 1963, 1965, and 1966, and captured the World Series in 1963 and 1965. The Dodgers were led by one of the greatest pitchers ever, Sandy Koufax, who won 25 to 27 games 3 times in 4 years, struck out a then-record 382 batters in 1965, threw 4 no-hitters, including a perfect game, and captured three Cy Young and one Most Valuable Player Awards. Koufax retired at his prime with an arthritic elbow after the 1966 season.

Warren Spahn, who spent most of his career with the Boston and Milwaukee Braves, winning 20 or more games 13 times, completed his career in 1965 with 363 wins, the most ever by a left-hander. Two players won Triple Crowns in the 1960s, leading their league in home runs, runs batted in, and batting—Frank Robinson of the Baltimore Orioles in 1966 and Carl Yastrzemski of the Boston Red Sox in 1967.

In 1968, Denny McLain won 31 games for the World Series champion Detroit Tigers, the first pitcher to reach 30 since Dizzy Dean of the Cardinals in 1934. Don Drysdale of the Dodgers set a record by pitching 58⅔ consecutive innings without allowing a run. Bob Gibson of the Cardinals compiled a phenomenal earned run average of 1.12. Don Wilson of Houston recorded 18 strikeouts in a 9-inning game, and Luis Tiant of the Cleveland Indians fanned 19 in 10 innings.

The remarkable decade ended with one of the most improbable stories in baseball history. The previously hapless Mets, by now one of 24 teams playing in a divisional structure that introduced a preliminary playoff prior to the World Series, went the distance behind their great young pitcher Tom Seaver to capture the World Series.

Perhaps the most significant development in baseball during the 1960s occurred off the field.

Sports

WORLD SERIES

1960 Pittsburgh Pirates (NL), 4 games; New York Yankees (AL), 3 games

1961 New York Yankees (AL), 4 games; Cincinnati Reds (NL), 1 game

1962 New York Yankees (AL), 4 games; San Francisco Giants (NL), 3 games

1963 Los Angeles Dodgers (NL), 4 games; New York Yankees (AL), 0 games

1964 St. Louis Cardinals (NL), 4 games, New York Yankees (AL), 3 games

1965 Los Angeles Dodgers (NL), 4 games; Minnesota Twins (AL), 3 games

1966 Baltimore Orioles (AL), 4 games; Los Angeles Dodgers (NL), 0 games

1967 St. Louis Cardinals (NL), 4 games; Boston Red Sox (AL), 3 games

1968 Detroit Tigers (AL), 4 games; St. Louis Cardinals (NL), 3 games

1969 New York Mets (NL), 4 games; Baltimore Orioles (AL), 1 game

In 1966, the Major League Baseball Players Association hired Marvin Miller as executive director. Within a decade, Miller would transform a fraternal organization into one of the most powerful unions in the world. By the time the 1960s ended, Miller had negotiated a collective bargaining agreement with major league baseball. This led to the end of free agency in the following decade, with the resulting player mobility producing vast leaps in player salaries.

Basketball

Professional basketball during the 1960s was dominated by the Boston Celtics and two players huge in physical stature as well as talent. The Celtics were National Basketball Association champions every year during the decade except 1967. That year marked the first season that Bill Russell, the Celtics' center and player-coach, succeeded the legendary Red Auerbach. Russell brought his team back to the top in 1968 and 1969 before retiring. A master rebounder and defensive player, Russell brought defense into the forefront of basketball, changing the game forever. Along the way, he won five Most Valuable Player Awards and became the first African American head coach in any major professional sport in the United States.

The one blemish on the Celtics' record in the 1960s was caused by the Philadelphia 76ers, led by Wilt "The Stilt" Chamberlain, the most prodigious scorer in basketball history. In Chamberlain's first season (1960), he set a new scoring record with 37.6 points per game. He won 7 consecutive scoring titles, averaging an astronomical 50.4 points per game in 1961–1962. In one game that season, he scored 100 points against the New York Knicks. Also a great rebounder and playmaker, Chamberlain won the Most Valuable Player Award four times in his career and led his team to the NBA championship twice, once in 1967 season and again with the Los Angeles Lakers in 1972. Throughout the 1960s, the greatest matchup in the NBA was between Russell and Chamberlain, two powerful and proud individuals. Although Russell's team usually prevailed, which player was greater continues to be debated.

College Basketball

As with professional basketball, college basketball featured a dynasty in the 1960s, the University of California at Los Angeles (UCLA). The National Collegiate Athletic Association (NCAA) championship belonged to Ohio State University, the University of Cincinnati, and Loyola of Chicago during the first four years of the 1960s. In 1964, UCLA took over, ruling as NCAA champions for the rest of the decade (except 1966) under John Wooden, possibly the greatest college basketball coach of all time with 10 national titles in 12 years. After Texas Western interrupted UCLA's reign in 1966, the California university returned to the top with a new superstar, center Lew Alcindor, college player of the year in each of his three varsity seasons (1967–1969). In 1968 Alcindor became a Muslim and, as Cassius Clay had done earlier, chose a new name—Kareem Abdul-Jabbar. As the decade closed, Abdul-Jabbar, now with the professional Milwaukee Bucks, won the Rookie of the Year Award for 1969–1970 and

began a career that would last until 1989 and include six Most Valuable Player Awards, six NBA championships (one with Milwaukee and five with the Los Angeles Lakers), and the all-time career scoring record.

Hockey

Hockey was growing in popularity during the 1960s, although in most of the United States it remained behind baseball, football, and basketball. A sign of the sport's growth was the expansion of National Hockey League clubs from 6 to 12 for the 1967–1968 season. The new teams were Los Angeles, Minnesota, Oakland, Philadelphia, Pittsburgh, and St. Louis. Except for the two ends of the decade, though, Canadian teams dominated, with the Toronto Maple Leafs and Montreal Canadiens capturing the Stanley Cup. The Chicago Blackhawks won the championship in the 1960–1961 season, and the Boston Bruins in 1969–1970. The great players on U.S. teams during the 1960s included Bobby Hull and Stan Mikita of the Blackhawks, Gordie Howe of the Detroit Red Wings, and, by the end of the decade, Bobby Orr of the Bruins.

Golf

Golf took on more of a popular, if not populist, tone during the 1960s. At the beginning of the decade, golf, despite such famous stars as Slammin' Sammy Snead and Ben Hogan, was perceived as pure country club. That image faded at the skilled hands of Arnold Palmer and Jack Nicklaus. Palmer, son of a greenskeeper, won six major professional tournaments between 1960 and 1964. Palmer excited large numbers of fans, "Arnie's Army," who exulted in his patented late drives for victory, the so-called "Palmer's Charge." Although past his prime by the decade's midpoint, he continued to play good golf throughout the decade, never losing the public's goodwill.

Following Palmer into the golfing limelight was Jack Nicklaus, whose blond hair and sturdy physique earned him the nickname "the Golden Bear." In his early twenties, he won the U.S. Amateur and U.S. Open tournaments. Between 1959 and 1967, he brought home nine major titles. Like

Sports

Palmer, he continued to compete throughout the century while maintaining the respect and admiration of his fellow golfers and the public.

A number of golfers, including Julius Boros, Billy Casper, Ken Venturi, and Lee Trevino, helped golf come of age. As the decade progressed, television viewers could watch matches on the weekend, as *The Wonderful World of Golf* offered golf tournaments especially created for television. Not until the next decade, however, did women's golf, featuring Nancy Lopez, attain a level of popularity in any way approaching that of men's golf.

Billie Jean King playing at the South Africa Tennis Championship match, 1967. AP Photo.

Tennis

At the beginning of the 1960s, tennis was locked in tradition, with most of the major tournaments still played on grass and the players compelled to wear all white (the participants themselves were white). For most of the decade, only amateurs were allowed to play in major tournaments in an attempt to maintain the game's purity.

In the late 1960s, tournaments began to admit professionals in order to offer the best talent available. Metal racquets became popular with many of the top players. Meanwhile, two figures brought vitality and diversity to the sport: Billie Jean King and Arthur Ashe.

Billie Jean King helped popularize women's tennis and bring the sport closer to parity with men's tennis in terms of media attention and financial rewards. Playing an aggressive game that was copied by most top women players, King compiled a remarkable string of tournament victories, including 20 Wimbledon titles by the end of the 1970s. She won her first Wimbledon doubles title in 1961 when she was 17, and added additional doubles titles at Wimbledon in 1962, 1965, 1967, and 1968, as well as the Wimbledon mixed doubles title in 1967 and the singles title in 1966, 1967, and 1968. Among her many other victories were the U.S. Open singles, doubles, and mixed doubles in 1967. That same year she was named Associated Press Female Athlete of the Year. In 1973, she defeated Bobby Riggs in a tennis match labeled the "battle of the sexes."

Arthur Ashe, an African American, came early to tennis, then an almost totally white game. As the son of a parks supervisor in Richmond, Virginia, he had access to parks and became an outstanding tennis player when he was still a child. By the age of 10, he was touring under the sponsorship of the American Tennis Association. A tennis scholarship took Ashe to UCLA, where he became the national collegiate singles and doubles champion.

Arthur Ashe's fame was secured with his 1968 triumphs in the U.S. Open and as a member of the U.S. Davis Cup team. In a society and sport still imbued with considerable racism, Ashe became the first African American to be recognized as a top tennis player. A turning point for Ashe came in 1969 when he was denied a visa to travel to South Africa to play in a tournament. After that rejection, he became more involved in political action, increasing the public's awareness of the evils of apartheid.

Ashe spent his later years working for human rights and education. In 1988, he wrote a three-volume book entitled *A Hard Road to Glory: A History of the African-American Athlete,* 1988. After contracting AIDS through a blood transfusion while undergoing heart surgery in 1983, Ashe worked diligently to raise public awareness of the disease and its impact on those infected and their families. Arthur Ashe's impact on tennis, while great, was transcended by his contributions to the larger society. He died in 1993.

The 1960s Olympics

The three Olympics of the 1960s generated excitement that was driven as much by political issues as by popular interest in the sports themselves. The 1960 Olympics were held during the height of the Cold War, and in the middle of an international incident that seriously affected United States–Soviet Union relations. Between the winter and summer Olympics, the Russians shot down an American U-2 spy plane. Even more than usual, competition between the U.S. and Soviet teams came to be viewed as a contest for national pride and ideological supremacy.

For Americans, the highlight of the winter games was the gold medal won by the U.S. hockey team in a stunning upset of the Soviet Union and Czechoslovakia; that the match was held in Squaw Valley, California made victory all the more sweet. The U.S. basketball team, paced by future basketball immortals Jerry Lucas, Oscar Robertson, and Jerry West, took home a gold medal in the summer games in Rome. Cassius Clay (the future Muhammad Ali) won the gold as a light heavyweight boxer. Wilma Rudolph captured three gold medals in the 100- and 200-meter races, and as the anchor of the 400-meter relay event.

Wilma Rudolph had contracted polio as a child and, unable to walk, was forced to wear a brace. Gradually, she recovered, became an outstanding high school athlete, and won a bronze medal at the 1956 Olympics in Rome. She was the first African American woman to capture three gold medals in track and field, along the way setting a new record in the 100 meters. In 1962, she received the Zaharias Award, given to the individual considered the best athlete in the world.

The Olympic summer games were held in Tokyo in 1964. The Cold War continued. The U.S. team took 37 medals in swimming and diving. Joe Frazier won the gold in heavyweight boxing.

The 1968 games came as antiwar sentiment was increasing in the United States and much of the country was aflame, metaphorically and literally, over racial injustice. African American athletes threatened to boycott the Olympics if South Africa were permitted to participate, and eventually the Olympic Committee decided to ban South Africa from the games. The winter games

in Grenoble, France, were reasonably non-confrontational; U.S. figure skater Peggy Fleming and French skier Jean-Claude Killy were among the best known victors.

By the summer Olympics, held in Mexico in October, both Martin Luther King Jr., and Robert F. Kennedy had been assassinated. After Dr. King's death, riots erupted in many U.S. cities. The Tet Offensive early in the year had made it clear that victory in the Vietnam War was far away, if it were ever to come. African Americans increasingly came to the realization, as Muhammad Ali and Dr. King had done, that the Vietnam War should be seen within the context of racism.

With South Africa and its system of apartheid excluded from the games, African American athletes competed, but many still looked for a way to make a political statement. Two, Tommie Smith and John Carlos, did so very publicly. After winning the gold and bronze medals respectively in the 200-meter race, they mounted the podium shoeless but wearing black socks, each wearing a black glove on one hand to represent black power and black poverty in the United States. They raised their black-gloved hands and bowed their heads, gestures that led to their expulsion from the rest of the Olympics.

Reactions to Smith and Carlos's demonstration varied widely. The U.S. Olympic Committee promised severe penalties for any athletes who engaged in political demonstrations during the Olympics. Many others argued that the Olympics should be nonpolitical, although many who felt that way were happy to see their country capture more gold medals and more total medals than the Soviet Union in the games that year. Others saw the demonstration by Smith and Carlos as both brave and appropriate, given the continuing failures at home to establish racial equality.

There were other, less controversial medals for American athletes. For the fourth straight Olympics, Al Oerter won the gold in the discus throw. George Foreman, like Ali and Frazier a future world heavyweight champion, finished first among heavyweight boxers. Debby Meyer captured the gold in three swimming events, while Mark Spitz won four medals, two of them gold, as a prelude to his seven gold medals in the next Olympics. A U.S. athlete who did not win gold was perhaps the most important male runner of the decade. In 1964, Jim Ryun had become the first high school runner to break the four-minute mile. Although defeated in the Tokyo Olympics, he smashed the world record for the mile in 1967, running it in 3:51.1, a record that would endure for eight years; however, the high altitude of Mexico City hurt him in 1968, and he finished second.

Horse Racing

The "Sport of Kings" featured an impressive stable of horses in the 1960s but perhaps no legends. There were no Triple Crown winners in the decade, but several horses came close, winning two of the three races. Jockeys Bill Shoemaker and Bill Hartack continued to accumulate victories; Shoemaker was the top money-winner among jockeys every year from 1958 through 1964.

FADS

The 1960s included a great many fads because of the nation's general prosperity during the decade. More disposable money meant that less thought needed to be given to the long-term value of a purchase.

For example, Lava Lites were popular cylindrical lamps that contained a yellow wax that took on varying forms and hues as it was heated. The Lava Lite was not bright enough to be a reading light; its purpose was to set a mood.

The water bed, invented by Charles Hall to provide something more comfortable than the then popular beanbag furniture, became instead a major sex symbol of the late 1960s. It appealed to the counterculture and to the wealthy. Hugh Hefner established a king-sized model in his Chicago mansion. Water beds, however, had an unfortunate tendency in their early days to collapse floors and spring leaks that proved dangerous to the electrical heaters that kept the water warm.

Individuals tripping on LSD were fond of "black lights," which could be purchased in so-called headshops along with fluorescent paints and dyes. In the presence of black light bulbs, fluorescent clothes or posters created visual counterparts to the effect of LSD. Restaurants

and nightclubs installed black lights to appeal to those seeking drug (or drug-like) effects. Posters, sides of vans, guitars, and countless other types of objects were painted in Day-Glo. Since the 1960s, Day-Glo colors have been used in such everyday items as swimsuits and high-lighting markers.

Buttons that proclaimed slogans or favorite political candidates achieved a level of popularity in the 1960s never enjoyed before or since. The more serious messages on these buttons were usually antiwar or reflective in some way of social attitudes. "Make love, not war;" "Tune in, turn on, drop out;" "Kill a Commie for Christ;" and other statements expressed one's opinion and perhaps converted others'. Many slogans, such as "Cure virginity," addressed the increasingly liberal attitudes toward sex. Most popular on buttons was the peace symbol, expanded from its antinuclear origins into a somewhat abstract bomber pointed straight up. Many buttons, of course, were strictly frivolous.

At the same time, bumper stickers appeared on many automobiles. Bumper stickers were more evenly divided between the established culture and the counterculture. Individuals, often older, expressed their opposition to the new culture while affirming traditional values: "God bless America" or "Support your local police."

GAMES AND TOYS

The spirit of play in the United States continued even as the political climate of the nation changed dramatically in the second half of the 1960s. Many older games, such as cards and checkers, continued to be played by young and old. Poker and euchre were common across the age spectrum, though bridge was usually associated with an older and more upscale crowd. College students enjoyed cribbage, and increasing numbers of students and young adults turned to chess, which received a great boost from Bobby Fischer, the first chess player to become widely recognized in the United States. Robert James Fischer taught himself chess at the age of six and won the U.S. Junior Championship and the U.S. Championship by age 15. He was U.S. champion every year from 1958 to 1967 with the exception of 1962. In 1972,

Sports

he defeated Russian Boris Spassky for the World Championship.

By the middle of the decade, Tarot cards, used in fortune-telling, had become popular, in part because of a growing interest in alternative forms of spirituality. Similar impulses toward antiestablishment norms helped popularize the Ouija board, which included a planchette that, when touched, allegedly moved to point out letters on the board to spell out messages.

Adult board games introduced during the 1960s tended to mirror real-life situations and/or appeal to the supposed intelligence of adults. Acquire and High Bid were stock market games. Jeopardy posed answers and required players to supply the questions. The person with the best vocabulary was most likely to prove victorious in Scrabble. Acting out words was the point of Charades, a popular party game.

Over three million Americans were playing with slot cars by mid-decade, including Robert Kennedy and CBS anchor Walter Cronkite.[2] Universities, including several Ivy League schools, were home to slot-car teams. The small (usually two-inch) plastic slot-car derived its name from a slot in the track on which the cars were raced. A projection under the car fit into the slot, and electricity powered the vehicles. By 1967, however, the slot-car craze was over.

One of the most popular toys of the 1960s was the super ball, a small, dense ball which could bounce much longer than other balls. Wham-O produced 170,000 balls per day at the height of the craze.[3] McGeorge Bundy, National Security Advisor to President Lyndon Johnson, purchased super balls for 60 members of his staff, apparently as much to help them reduce stress as for entertainment. Skateboarders liked to bounce super balls while they skated down the street, and children used them to play jacks. Yo-yos, as well as Wham-O's Frisbee and Hula-Hoop, all of which were introduced in the late 1950s, remained popular through the 1960s.

Two very different dolls were popular in the 1960s: Barbie and G. I. Joe. Mattel produced its first Barbie in 1958. Within 5 years, 9 million Barbies had been sold and she received 500 letters a week.[4] Barbie had expensive tastes, and countless clothes and accessories were available for purchase. Some of Barbie's clothes cost more than the doll did (about three dollars). Keeping the doll inexpensive was a brilliant marketing strategy to hook youngsters and then induce continuing expenditures to keep Barbie in style.

Mattel offered friends for Barbie, the male Ken and the female Midge, both of whom also required clothes. Critics saw the Barbie phenomenon as a symbol of much that was wrong with the United States, including its commercialism and gender stereotyping.

G. I. Joe was another popular and controversial doll, created in 1963 but seemingly out of sync with the growing antiwar sentiment. By 1966, however, G. I. Joe was in 10 million homes. Sales of the doll slid toward the end of the decade, after Dr. Benjamin Spock condemned it in his *Baby and Child Care,* and the doll was marketed as more of an explorer and adventurer, though its overt combat persona was later restored. Hassenfeld Brothers created Joe's face from a composite of 20 actual Congressional Medal of Honor winners. Like Mattel with Barbie, the manufacturer kept the price of the doll low (about four dollars), while the full range of clothes, equipment, and weapons ran about $200.

Other dolls had their moments. The Troll Doll, also known as the Dammit Doll after its inventor, Thomas Dam, became a favorite among college women in the 1960s. By the end of the decade, only Barbie was outselling the Troll Doll.[5] Unlike the sexy Barbie, the Troll was an ugly gnome with big ears, long stringy hair, and a wide nose, so ugly as to be cute. College students were not the only ones who favored the doll, which was supposed to bring good luck; pilot Betty Miller had a Troll Doll co-pilot on her duplication of Amelia Earhart's 1935 flight, and Lady Bird Johnson had one in the White House.

As the equal rights movement picked up steam in the later 1960s, toy makers noticed. Baby Nancy, from Shindana, appeared in 1968. Nancy was clearly African American in features, color, and hair, and sold for five to six dollars. The Black Doll Toy Company produced "Soul Babies" and black-equivalents to previously white dolls, such as astronauts. Barbie and G. I. Joe appeared as Afro-Americans. Remco made black Baby-Grow-a-Tooth and Li'l Winking Winny, the latter with an Afro hairstyle.

Sports

Other popular toys during the decade included James Bond dolls and cars. During the early 1960s, JFK coloring books helped millions of young children learn more about the young president and his family. A child's version of disposable pop art was available with the Etch-A-Sketch. "Mr. Machine" was a robot that children could take apart and, at least in theory, reassemble without tools.

HOBBIES

Hobbies continued to occupy large numbers of Americans. The most physical of these pastimes included bowling, sailing, surfing, skateboarding, and touch football. Many men and women bowled, either informally with friends or relatives or in leagues at a local bowling alley. Teams often were sponsored by businesses, which received advertising on the backs of the team members' shirts. ABC began televising tournaments in the early 1960s.

The Kennedy administration increased the popularity of both sailing and touch football during the early 1960s. It was not unusual to see photographs of President Kennedy skippering his family sloop off Hyannis Port, family members aboard. The coastlines, rivers, and lakes of the United States meanwhile offered relaxation and adventure to millions of less famous boaters. Touch football was another Kennedy pastime, with Attorney General and later Senator Robert Kennedy often in the middle of the game. Touch football, Kennedy style, was a rugged and highly competitive endeavor shared by enthusiasts on college campuses and residential lawns.

Few outdoors activities are more associated with the 1960s than surfing. An ancient sport that almost died out in the nineteenth century, surfing was reborn in Hawaii early in the twentieth century and became popular in California during the middle of the century. Surfers comprised an important division of the counterculture of the 1960s, adopting a distinctive attire (typically striped shirts, white jeans, and sunglasses for the males), a peculiar jargon (phrases like "daddy-o" and "kook"), and enough followers to warrant their own magazines (e.g., *Surfer*, started in 1960 and still in existence). Surfing was so popular to millions—young and old who never came near a wave—that it inspired a new genre of surfing movies and gave rise to a unique kind of music (called "surf music") that was transported around the world by the Beach Boys and other groups. Among the songs glorifying surfing were the Beach Boys' "Surfin' USA" (1963) and Jan and Dean's "Surf City."(1963). (See Music of the 1960s.)

In the early 1960s, surfers devised the skateboard, an earthbound version of the surfboard, to keep in practice when they were away from the waves. The original mass-marketed skateboards were made of wood or plastic with wheels underneath; the rider controlled the board with his knees and by shifting his body weight to simulate the act of surfing.

Other outdoor activities were popular in the 1960s. A 1966 poll showed approximately 59 million bikers, 40 million volleyball players, and 36 million fishers and campers in the United States.[6] Many people also took up jogging, an activity not often seen prior to the 1960s. Many of these participants were encouraged in these activities by President Kennedy's 1961 call for Americans to exercise more and become more physically fit.

Americans who preferred their hobbies indoors had many options, one of which was collecting baseball cards. Youngsters continued to buy packages of cards with flavorless pink gum during the 1960s, as they looked for their heroes: Willie Mays, Hank Aaron, Mickey Mantle, Sandy Koufax, Tom Seaver, Frank Robinson, and many others. Al-

A popular hobby for both boys and girls in the 1960s was collecting baseball cards. Courtesy of Shutterstock.

Sports

though collecting baseball cards remained primarily a love-of-the-game hobby throughout the decade, the commercialization of card collecting had already started. The pivotal moment in this transformation was the publication of Jefferson Burdick's *The American Card Catalog* in 1967. From then on, card condition, price, and value began to shove aside the old traditions of collecting, trading, and playing imaginative games with the cards. Even young fans started to look at baseball cards as financial investments.

Building model planes and ships remained popular hobbies, primarily with boys, but also with some adults. With the space race blossoming in the 1960s, companies began offering space vehicle models. Scientifically inclined youngsters also enjoyed science kits, which were especially popular as Christmas presents from parents eager to encourage their children's academic pursuits.

Photography received a boost as a hobby in 1963 when Kodak introduced its Instamatic camera, which used a cartridge and required no real expertise. The musically inclined increasingly turned toward the guitar, in response to the resurgence of folk music among professionals.

Sports

Travel

of the 1960s

The 1960s witnessed travel on a scope never before seen as humankind explored the planets and, at the close of the decade, walked on the moon. At the same time, earthly travel also was changing; railroad travel declined, as people chose airplanes for long journeys and the automobile for shorter trips. With interstate highways increasingly available, families enjoyed new opportunities for vacations.

SPACE TRAVEL

The United States had come to think of itself as the most powerful nation in the world and the leader in all things important. It was shocking, then, when the nation's primary Cold War rival, the Soviet Union, was first in the space race when Russia launched its satellite, *Sputnik I,* into orbit in 1957. Russia became the first nation to put a man, Yuri Gagarin, into space on April 12, 1961, but the United States would soon pull ahead.

In 1961, President Kennedy declared, "I believe that this nation should commit itself to achieving the goal, before this decade is out, of landing a man on the moon and returning him safely to the earth."[1] Kennedy did not live to see his goal reached, nor did he initiate the American space program; however, he gave it the drive and focus essential to energize both the taxpaying public and the aerospace industry.

The National Aeronautics and Space Administration (NASA) was created in 1958, the year after *Sputnik I* was launched. NASA's first major space program, called Mercury after the Greek messenger of the gods, began that year with the goal of putting Americans into space. Seven astronauts were selected in 1959 to carry out the Mercury missions and instantly became America's new heroes: M. Scott Carpenter, L. Gordon Cooper, John Glenn, Virgil I. "Gus" Grissom, Walter M. Schirra, Alan B. Shepard Jr., and Donald "Deke" Slayton. Their exploits were later chronicled in the book *We Seven,* 1962. Other programs were developed to move the lunar project forward, including the Gemini and Apollo programs. Gemini consisted of two-person spacecraft designed to test systems and maneuvers necessary for space exploration, such as spacewalks and dockings with other spacecraft. The Apollo program would fulfill President Kennedy's lunar-landing goal.

Other space programs gathered important information about the moon and planets in the 1960s. Lunar Orbiter flights mapped the surface of the moon, and Surveyor craft landed on the moon's surface to gather data concerning the lunar environment. Mercury probes explored planets, principally Venus and Mars.

The United States began manned flights in 1961 with a series of Mercury launches. Less than

John H. Glenn Jr. wearing his silver Mercury pressure suit in preparation for launch, 1962. NASA image.

Liberty 7. The first American to orbit the Earth was actually a chimpanzee named Enos, who made 2 revolutions around the planet on a 3-hour 21-minute flight.

Russia claimed the first dual flight in 1962 with two cosmonauts maneuvering their vehicles close together. The Russians later put the first woman into space in 1963, launched the first multiperson flight (with three cosmonauts in 1964 aboard *Voskhod I*), and inaugurated floating in space in 1965.

The first U.S. manned orbital flight, on February 20, 1962, launched John Glenn into space. Glenn orbited the Earth three times in *Friendship 7,* seeing four sunsets before he landed, and introducing the term "splashdown" into the English language. Later that year, Scott Carpenter made another three-orbit flight and Walter Schirra circled the Earth six times. Mariner II passed by Venus on August 27, and completed the first successful interplanetary probe.

The initial unmanned Gemini test flights (1964 and 1965) tested booster and spacecraft systems; Gemini III, in 1965, was the first U.S. two-man orbit, with Gus Grissom and John Young aboard. Meanwhile, Mariner IV sent back 21 pictures of Mars, which showed Martian craters and indicated an atmosphere comprised mainly of carbon dioxide. The first commercial satellite was launched to transmit telephone and television signals. Both

a month after Gagarin's success, Alan Shepard became the first American to reach space during a 15-minute excursion aboard *Freedom 7.* Gus Grissom followed Shepard into space in July on

JOHN GLENN (1921–)

Pioneer astronaut John H. Glenn was born in Cambridge, Ohio, into what he later described as an "idyllic" childhood. Glenn became a naval pilot in 1941 and flew over 100 combat missions in World War II and Korea. Already a hero, Glenn then became a "test pilot" working with experimental aircraft for the military. Among other accomplishments, Glenn set a speed record in 1957 when he piloted an experimental plane from New York to Los Angeles in just over three hours. A renowned pilot, Glenn was one of only seven candidates selected to become astronauts in the emerging space program. In 1962, after a grueling training program, Glenn rode the Friendship 7 as the first American to orbit the earth. Though he wanted to return to space, Glenn settled for something closer to home and entered politics. Glenn was elected to the senate in 1974 and became the first Ohio democrat to win re-election four times. In 1983, Glenn made an unsuccessful bid for the presidency. In 1997, Glenn retired from politics and returned to NASA as an advisor. In 1998, Glenn (at 77 years) became the oldest person to travel into space and participated in experiments to investigate the effects of space travel on the elderly. With piloting and politics behind him, Glenn and his wife established Ohio State University's Institute of Public Service, which offered training to students interested in political service. From pilot to space pioneer and politician, Glenn spent the majority of his life in public service. In addition to his contributions to the space program and the citizens of Ohio, Glenn's life and his example have inspired a generation of Americans.

Travel

Russia and the United States managed soft lunar landings with unmanned spacecraft in 1966. In addition, Lunar Orbiter I took the first pictures of Earth from the back side of the moon.

Tragedy struck on January 27, 1967 as a three-man crew—Roger Chaffee, Gus Grissom, and Edward White—were engaging in preflight preparations for the Apollo I flight. As the three men engaged in a simulation exercise within the spacecraft, a fire broke out. The pure oxygen fire generated intense heat, and the three men died of asphyxiation from toxic gasses before anyone could open the craft's door. The Russians also lost one of their space explorers that year, a cosmonaut who died on reentry. Some Americans and scientists questioned the advisability of continuing manned space flights, not only for safety reasons but because, the argument went, unmanned flights could gather the necessary information for less cost.

Other U.S. missions were more successful in 1967. Lunar Orbiter V photomapped the lunar surface, and Mariner V passed by Venus to measure the density of the planet's atmosphere.

The prime crew of the first manned Apollo space flight, Apollo/Saturn Mission 204, is suited up aboard the NASA Motor Vessel Retriever in preparation for Apollo water egress training in the Gulf of Mexico in October 1966. Left to right, are Astronauts Edward H. White II, Virgil (Gus) Grissom, and Roger Chaffee. The three were later killed in a January 1967 accident during further training. NASA image.

The first manned Apollo flight took place October 11, 1968, when Apollo VII astronauts Walter Schirra, Donn Eisele, and Walter Cunningham carried out an 11-day test of their command and service modules. They conducted eight propulsion firings and sent back seven live television broadcasts. Apollo VIII orbited the moon on Christmas Eve. In May 1969, Apollo X came close to the moon after separating the lunar module from the command module and descending to within approximately nine miles of the moon's surface.

While preparations were under way for the first manned landing on the moon, unmanned spacecraft continued to explore more distant regions of the solar system. Mariner VI and Mariner VII transmitted images of the Martian world.

The climactic space effort of the 1960s began on July 16, 1969, with the takeoff of Apollo XI,

Astronaut Edwin E. "Buzz" Aldrin Jr. poses for a photograph beside the U.S. flag deployed on the moon during the Apollo 11 mission on July 20, 1969. NASA image.

Travel

carrying Neil Armstrong, Buzz Aldrin, and Michael Collins. On July 20, Armstrong stepped onto the lunar surface, commenting for history that he was taking "one small step for man, one giant step for mankind." Almost as memorable was Armstrong's earlier declaration when the lunar module touched down: "The *Eagle* has landed." The landing spot bore the name Tranquillity Base on the Sea of Tranquillity, names reflecting both the receptive terrain of that portion of the moon and the hope for future of peace and brotherhood among the nations of the world.

Armstrong was followed onto the moon by Aldrin; together they collected lunar rocks and soil for analysis while Michael Collins remained aboard the command module, *Columbia.* Pictures of the moon landing filled television screens throughout the world. In an attempt to keep up, Russia attempted an unmanned lunar landing at approximately the same time, but the Russian craft, Luna 15, crashed onto the moon on July 21.

One more lunar landing would occur in 1969. Apollo XII, despite being struck by lightning after takeoff, reached the moon in November. The crew, featuring astronauts Pete Conrad, Alan Bean, and Richard Gordon, brought back more moon samples.

The space programs in the 1960s reestablished America's supremacy in space even as it was being severely tested by the war in Vietnam. There were many practical benefits to the space programs. Smaller computers required for space flights led to desktop computers; miniature cameras suitable for handling by astronauts yielded more compact and efficient handheld video cameras and miniature televisions; sensors to monitor astronauts' health found important applications in hospitals. Even the fastener Velcro soon began turning up on people's clothes.

SPACE TRAVEL ON THE BIG AND SMALL SCREENS

The ultimate space film of the 1960s was *2001: A Space Odyssey,* 1968, directed by Stanley Kubrick. Minus the usual fare of science-fiction films, such as monsters from outer space, the transforming effects of radiation, or the impending destruction of Earth by approaching meteorites, and also

without any romance, the film seriously tackled the elusive concepts of time and space.

Kubrick's reliance on the visual ($6.5 million of the film's $10.5 million budget went for special effects)[2] contributed mightily to the mythic dimension of *2001.* The film asked vital questions about humankind through its images: What has humankind's creativity really wrought? Is humanity to be defined by creative tools or destructive weapons?

Planet of the Apes, directed by Franklin J. Schaffner, was also released in 1968. Far more concrete and traditional than *2001*—with a clearly defined plot, battles, and a love interest for the protagonist, astronaut George Taylor, played by Charlton Heston—the film nonetheless covered some serious social ground. In the movie, the astronauts landed, not on a distant planet, but on an Earth two thousand years in the future that had been devastated by the technological failures of the human race.

Space travel also reached the small screen in the 1960s. Producer Gene Roddenberry created *Star Trek* as a futuristic version of the western television series *Wagon Train,* 1957–1965, an approach consistent with President Kennedy's theme of the New Frontier. *Wagon Train* chronicled the journeys of American pioneers westward. William Shatner filled the role as wagonmaster, or in this case, captain of the *Enterprise.* Leonard Nimoy's Mr. Spock, DeForest Kelley's Dr. "Bones" McCoy, and other characters helped Captain Kirk "boldly go where no man has gone before." Although the NBC series lasted from 1966 until 1969 and never finished higher than 52nd in the Nielsen ratings, it spawned a huge number of dedicated Trekkies, as well as sequels on television and film (the latter featuring several of the original cast).

THE AUTOMOBILE

Americans had been driving automobiles for more than half a century when the 1960s dawned, but the decade nevertheless experienced great change. 1950s cars featured high tail fins and a lot of ornamentation, but due to the influence of smaller foreign imports, including the German Volkswagen, consumers began to prefer simpler, sleeker, more compact cars. In addition, both the number of cars and drivers grew dramatically. Car registrations increased by 25 million during the decade, and urban passenger-car travel increased by almost two hundred million miles.[3] By 1969, more than 80 percent of U.S. families owned at least one car. The four largest U.S. automakers (General Motors, Ford, Chrysler, American Motors) increased their gross revenues from about $20 billion at the beginning of the decade to nearly $47 billion by the end.[4]

One of the first automotive superstars of the 1960s was the Ford Thunderbird. Originally introduced in 1955, the Thunderbird had grown so attractive by 1961 that President-elect Kennedy requested 25 for his inaugural parade. Having sold out of its stock, Ford was not able to oblige the president. The Ford Mustang won considerable popularity in the 1960s. Launched in 1964 and billed as a young people's car, 418,000 Mustangs were sold in the first year.[5] Designed by Lee Iacocca, who would later serve as chairman and save Chrysler from bankruptcy, the Mustang came in notchback, fastback, and convertible styles with so many options that a customer could have almost an individually designed vehicle.

Another of the decade's most popular cars was the Chevrolet Corvette, long America's only sports car. Its luxurious interior, quick acceleration, and easy handling made it a favorite, especially after introduction of the Corvette Stingray. The original 1963 Stingray had a split rear window that was altered in later models. Today the 1963 Stingray is a leading collector's item.

The 1965 Oldsmobile Toronado introduced front-wheel drive, which offered greater traction and easier handling, to the American mass market. Other favorites in the 1960s were the Mercury Cougar, something of an upgraded version of the Mustang; the Chevrolet Camaro; and the Pontiac Firebird Trans Am with its distinctive sexy striping and a name borrowed from the Trans-American road race.

The most infamous car of the 1960s was the Chevrolet Corvair, first released in 1959 for the 1960 model year. The Corvair had a rear-mounted, air-cooled engine and a stylish exterior that appealed to consumers. When a convertible version appeared in 1962, the Corvair became even more

CONSUMER COUNTERCULTURE

The 1960s was a decade of great change in American society, and for many it was an era that ended the societal "consensus" of the 1940s and 1950s. In the 1960s, a larger number of Americans expressed dissatisfaction with societal norms than at any other time in history, and this freedom of dissent soon found its way into consumer culture. While some companies continued to produce advertisements that placed their products in an idealized family setting, similar to the campaigns of the 1950s, others followed the American counterculture with advertisements that stressed change, individuality, and the "hip consumerism" that came to dominate ensuing decades. The change in strategy was exemplified by companies like Volkswagen, which used a groundbreaking "think small" slogan to market the so-called beetle, with the vehicle pictured in stark imagery against a desert scene. This new approach was a complete reversal of previous trends, which used flashy images and slinky models to sell cars as glamorous accessories. Interestingly, though the methods diverged the goal was the same—to encourage consumption on a massive scale. The marketing trend extended to every industry, as consumers were encouraged to seek individual expression rather than social acceptance. In the twenty-first century, both strategies are used, with some companies stressing independence and others stressing social acceptance.

popular. However, the car seemed to suffer an unusual number of accidents. Ralph Nader, then a young lawyer only a few years removed from Harvard Law School, was so concerned about its dangers that he published one of the most influential books of the decade, *Unsafe at Any Speed: The Designed-in Dangers of the American Automobile,* 1965. The book strongly condemned the Corvair, claiming that the car's design caused it to oversteer and go out of control.

Nader, a squeaky-clean consumer advocate, readily survived investigation and harassment by General Motors (GM), who hired a private investigator to get something on him. Nader's work led to

Travel

Ralph Nader in an appearance on NBC's *The Tonight Show*, circa 1966. Courtesy of Photofest.

abandonment of the Corvair by GM and the birth of serious congressional concern for automobile safety. Nader was asked to testify before Congress, which passed the National Traffic and Motor Vehicle Safety Act in 1966 to assert federal authority over automotive design. Nader, aided by legions of idealistic young Americans known as "Nader's Raiders," took on an array of safety issues in the decade, among them dangers in the meat, natural gas, and coal industries. In response, a large body of important safety legislation came out of Congress to help the American public stay healthy.

The growing popularity of the automobile had its origins in the efforts by President Dwight Eisenhower to create a new interstate highway system for both civilian and military use. The resulting Federal Aid Highway Act of 1956 authorized a National System of Interstate and Defense Highways for 42,500 miles across the United States. As construction proceeded in the 1960s, increasing numbers of families began to vacation at considerable distances from their homes. Motels, gasoline stations, and chain restaurants mushroomed along the highways to accommodate the new tourists. Touring also became more aesthetically pleasing as the Highway Beautification Act of 1965, pushed by President Lyndon B. Johnson and his wife Lady Bird, encouraged

MOTORING IN THE MEDIA

Films and television reflected the growing popularity of automobiles during the 1960s and contributed to an image of some cars as sexy and adventurous. In addition to the red Corvette travelling along Route 66, other vehicles journeyed across the nation's screens.

In *Bullitt,* 1968, Steve McQueen pursued murderers up and down the hills of San Francisco in a wild car chase that would influence later cinematic chases. Viewers were even taken inside McQueen's Mustang and given a driver's view through camera shots outward through the windshield. Ultimately, the Mustang got the better of the criminals' Dodge Charger in the 12-minute chase. McQueen did much of the driving for the movie himself.

Viewers of *The Graduate,* 1967, especially students, envied Dustin Hoffman his graduation present, an Alfa Spider, the last car completely designed by the renowned Battista Pininfarina of Turin, Italy. James Bond drove eye-catching automobiles heavily adorned with imaginative gadgets. *Goldfinger,* 1964, featured the Aston Martin DB5, a British sports car synonymous with aristocratic style that had an ejector seat, radar, and machine guns. The James Bond film *You Only Live Twice,* 1967, starring Sean Connery, featured a Toyota convertible 2000GT, a particularly beautiful product designed to improve Toyota's image, and the Agent 007 flick *On Her Majesty's Secret Service,* 1969, with George Lazenby, showed its hero in an Aston DBS and a Mercury Cougar.

The car most associated with gadgets may be Batman's vehicle in the ABC television series *Batman,* 1966–1968. Although the vehicle was equipped for speed and fighting Gotham City evildoers, the show, starring Adam West as Batman and Burt Ward as youthful sidekick Robin, received an award from the National Safety Council because the car's occupants always buckled up before taking off. The show attained such a high level of camp that many famous actors, including Liberace, Jerry Lewis, Sammy Davis Jr., Edward G. Robinson, and former JFK press secretary Pierre Salinger, appeared on at least one of its episodes.

states to keep billboards away from highways. Terms such as "merge," "off ramp," and "exit" were introduced to drivers.

A victim of the new interstate highway system was the old one—Route 66. Dedicated in 1926 though not completed until 1937, the highway traversed eight states (Illinois, Missouri, Kansas, Oklahoma, Texas, New Mexico, Arizona, and California) and some 2,400 miles. Route 66 wound past some of the nation's most beautiful natural sites. Woody Guthrie and Pete Seeger sang of it during the Great Depression, Jack Kerouac wrote of it in the 1950s, and the Columbia Broadcasting System filmed it. Television audiences could travel the highway on the series *Route 66,* 1960–1964, with Martin Milner and George Maharis (in a red Corvette). As the highway declined and large segments closed, disappearing into dirt and grass, many fans of the romantic route sought with some success to keep Route 66 alive.

More people became commuters during the 1960s, driving longer distances to work. Automobile use encouraged movement to ever expanding suburbs, and cars also became more necessary as less of the family's life revolved around the immediate neighborhood. Businesses followed workers out of the city, and taxes followed both, creating serious economic problems for the inner cities of America. The financial problems for inner cities and neighborhood businesses accelerated as the suburban shopping mall became the place to go for purchases—as well as a favorite teen hangout. The car had transformed the life of the nation.

After oil companies lowered the prices they were paying for oil, five nations (Iran, Iraq, Kuwait, Saudi Arabia, and Venezuela) met in 1960 to address ways to restore prices and control production. They agreed to make their organization permanent. Not until the 1970s would many Americans focus on the Organization of Petroleum Exporting Countries (OPEC).

PLANES, TRAINS, AND TRUCKS

The airplane became a common mode of travel, both domestic and abroad, in the latter case largely eliminating ships as a means of crossing the oceans. What took days by ocean liner was reduced to hours by air.

The introduction of the jet plane at the end of the 1950s was crucial to expanded air travel. In 1960, airplane passengers numbered about 56 million; that number almost tripled by 1969, to over 158 million.[6]

Boeing dominated plane production with the 707 and 747. In 1966, Pan American announced an order for 25 of the new 490-seat 747s, the first plane with two aisles. The 747—able to cruise faster than other jets (at an average of 633 miles per hour) and fly farther (6,000 miles)—proved so reliable and popular that it continued in production beyond the end of the century.

One of the negative effects of increased air travel was a burst of skyjackings. In 1968 alone, 18 successful hijackings of U.S. planes occurred, and that number rose to 30 the following year.[7] Fortunately, improved security procedures at airports quickly reduced the threat, leaving the skies more crowded yet relatively safe.

As automobile and plane travel increased, train travel declined. Although the number of train passengers did not decline dramatically, trips were generally shorter, often business commutes between neighboring cities or between outlying areas and the downtown business section.

Railroad work remained labor intensive, which helped explain the industry's serious financial problems. To address these problems, the railroads attempted to make up in freight what they lacked in passengers. Although freight revenues increased slightly during the decade, by 1969 the total was only about what it had been 20 years earlier.[8]

Nonetheless, there were further efforts to stem the bleeding, including plans to develop a high-speed Northeast Corridor between New York City and Washington, D.C. Several companies tried with some success to speed up freight service and started to diversify what they carried, including trash and garbage. They also increased the practice of "piggy-back" trailer service, hauling trailers on flat cars.

The overall importance of the railroad was in decline throughout the 1960s. Where once Americans looked to the railroad as their primary means of traveling long distances and saw train travel as pragmatic, comfortable, and even romantic, they had come to see the railroad, usually when they were forced to stop their cars at railroad crossings, as at best a somewhat useful hauler of various products, but not as a conveyance for people.

Trains could not even exert dominance in hauling freight, for the 1960s was also an era of increasing truck transports. The same highways that encouraged the passenger car called forth the truck, and families and truckers came increasingly to share the highway.

Manufacturers of trucks had gained valuable experience constructing heavy trucks for use in World War II and applied their expertise to domestic vehicles in postwar years. Various technological advances in the 1950s and early 1960s also contributed to the popularity of trucks for hauling freight: power steering, especially important for large, heavy tractor-trailers; individual front suspension and variable rear suspension; the "Jake Brake" engine brake system; more powerful diesel engines; and air conditioning, tinted windows, and other advancements in providing for the comfort of the trucker on long hauls.

Certain trucking terms came into common usage by U.S. motorists and others: "rig" for the combination tractor (or cab) and trailer (sometimes dual trailers); "semitrailer" for the trailer pulled by the tractor, but usually shortened to "semi" and applied to the whole rig. As the 1960s began, a new type of enterprise arose in response to the new interstate highway system and increasing numbers of rigs on the road—large truck stops that catered especially to long-distance truckers. Tourists stopped in at the truck stops, too, when they were not flying to their destinations. Best of all, odds were good that both trucker and motorist would reach their destinations without having to stop even once at a railroad track to let a train pass.

Travel

Visual Arts

of the 1960s

As with so many areas, the 1960s were a time of tremendous variety, creativity, and aesthetic rebellion in visual art. Millions of Americans continued to love Andrew Wyeth's realistic and emotional paintings and Norman Rockwell's illustrations and paintings, especially his covers for the *Saturday Evening Post*. Many artists during the 1960s, however, not only pushed the aesthetic and conceptual envelope of art but ripped it apart. What was discovered within was troubling to some, especially traditionalists, but exciting and inspiring to many others.

ABSTRACT PAINTING

Abstract expressionism was the dominant style of painting from World War II to the 1960s. The movement included such important figures as Jackson Pollock, Franz Kline, and the Dutch-born Willem de Kooning. Abstract expressionism was the attempt to express powerful content by removing all that was ephemeral and inessential and retaining what was intrinsic and essential. Cubists earlier in the century had sought to express the essence of objects, analyze subject matter into its parts, and rearrange those elements through abstracts of familiar shapes and forms. Abstract expressionists in the postwar years borrowed these techniques from their cubist predecessors.

By the 1960s, Pollock was dead following an automobile accident, but his influence continued. Pollock popularized the concept of "action painting," in which the artist moved across a large canvas spread on the floor and dripped, squirted, and flung paint onto the surface, using such simple instruments as house-painting brushes, meat basters, and trowels. Despite the apparent randomness of Pollock's application, he maintained that he consistently remained in control of the painting process. Close examination of his paintings, such as *Autumn Rhythm,* 1950, with its complex lines and intertwined colors, bears out that claim.

Franz Kline, who died in 1962, was best known for his large black-on-white abstractions painted with the gestural strokes that supplied an alternate name for abstract expressionism—so-called gestural abstraction. Kline used house-painting brushes and gestured with them as non-artists would with their hands, to express feeling and for emphasis.

Willem de Kooning may have been the most influential of the abstract expressionists. De Kooning saw himself within a long tradition of painting, a "painterly painter." Although highly abstract, with broad gestural strokes and multilayer painting, his pictures contained recognizable images as well as references to earlier paintings. Complex and metaphorical, they seemed created to express truths regarding the painter's environment and his own condition as an artist.

By the early 1960s, a reaction had set in against abstract expressionism, especially against its use of brushwork and cubist figures to imply three-dimensional space that supposedly denied the reality of flat paintings. Increasingly, regularity was preferred to the illusion of randomness, and flat brushing or staining was preferred to heavy smearing, an approach that emphasized color or the painting as object to the artist's individually expressed ideas and feelings. The impression sought by the new generation of abstractionists practicing what sometimes was referred to as "post-painterly painting" or "post-painterly abstraction" was a detachment that came to be labeled "cool." Because of the use of bright colors in the new acrylic and the absence of obvious brushwork, the style also was called "hard-edge painting."

POP ART

Of all styles of art practiced during the 1960s, pop art remains the one most associated with the spirit of the times. It marked a radical departure from past practice, more in attitude even than technique.

Pop art grew quickly out of various antecedents, including a group of British artists impressed with post–World War II U.S. culture, transitional neo-dada artists, the American democratic spirit, and growth in American commercialism and technology in the 1950s and 1960s.

The United States, untouched directly by World War II, and with its economy booming, was growing steadily in many areas, including advertising, print and screen media, and technology. England meanwhile was struggling to rebuild after the destruction caused by German bombs. The energy of the youthful and exuberant United States appealed to a group of young artists in England who called themselves the Independent Group in the early 1950s. In 1956, the Independent Group exhibited their art in London at an exhibition entitled "This Is Tomorrow."

A collage by Richard Hamilton, *Just What Is It That Makes Today's Homes So Different, So Appealing?* served as the poster for the exhibition and introduced important characteristics of pop art to the public. It featured an assemblage of images taken from popular culture, among them the cover from a cartoon magazine entitled *Young Romance,* an advertisement for a vacuum cleaner, a canned ham, the Ford logo, a male modeling his physique, and a nude woman in a sexually provocative pose. The man was holding a Tootsie Pop forward as a phallic symbol, and the picture was one of the first to include the word "pop."

As excited as British artists were about pop art, it remained principally American in inspiration and among the most famous pop artists. England could not claim sole credit for giving birth to pop art.

Dada had grown out of World War I disillusionment with both artistic traditions and modern society. The neo-dadaists shared their predecessors' rejection of traditional artistic styles and the notion of art as elitist, but not their cynicism. Instead, despite occasional forays into irony, they tended to accept modern popular culture with its mass consumerism as, if not necessarily a good thing, at least the way life is. The line between art and life quickly began to disintegrate.

By the 1960s, perhaps the two most important neo-dadaists in the United States were Robert Rauschenberg and Jasper Johns. Rauschenberg, by borrowing the collage technique of the cubists, had developed a style of "combine" or "assemblage" painting. This approach included using three-dimensional objects, such as in the early *Bed,* 1955, which Rauschenberg created by pouring paint over his pillow and bedclothes. *Monogram,* 1955–1959, consisted of a stuffed angora goat with a tire around its stomach. The goat stood on a canvas that included painted wood, photographs, and cutout letters. During the 1960s, Rauschenberg turned to flat canvases with combinations of silk-screened images and painted additions.

Johns also helped break down the distinction between paintings and sculptures. His best known works include *Flag,* 1955, which depicted a flag painted in oil on fabric-covered plywood and included a collage of printed articles and advertisements within the red and white stripes; and *Painted Bronze II: Ale Cans,* 1964, two bronze cans heavily painted as Ballantine ale cans. The latter supposedly grew out of a joke told about an art dealer who, according to Willem de Kooning, could sell even two beer cans as art.

The heyday of pop art featured many successful and talented artists; the two best known—at least within popular consciousness—were Roy Lichtenstein and Andy Warhol.

Lichtenstein's paintings were easy to recognize because of their comic-strip approach. His subjects and techniques were borrowed from the comics, down even to the benday dots that characterized the printing process used in preparing comic books. *Whaam!*, 1963, consisted of two panels, was over thirteen feet long, and jumped into the middle of its "story" with an American jet destroying an enemy fighter. The usual balloon dialogue of comics appeared in the painting: "I PRESSED THE FIRE CONTROL…AND AHEAD OF ME ROCKETS BLAZED THROUGH THE SKY." The right panel, which depicted the exploding enemy plane, had a typical comic strip sound effect: "WHAAM!"

Aesthetically, Lichtenstein saw his painting as different from comic strips. His objective was to create a unified whole rather than engage in an extended narrative. Even when he turned to a quasi-abstract approach, as in *Yellow and Red Brushstrokes,* 1966, he continued with the comic-strip technique. Against the omnipresent dots, the brushstrokes appear as if they might have been made by an abstract expressionist, with one sweep of a brush for each color.

Andy Warhol was a series of contradictions. Like other pop artists, he sought to distance himself from his art, yet he became even more famous as a personality than as an artist. Some of his images, such as the *Big Campbell's Soup Can,* 1962, became enormously recognizable, but none as much as his own image with his bleached blond hair. He contributed to his fame with many self-portraits, associations with the rich and famous, and flamboyant behavior. He claimed that everyone would be famous for 15 minutes, but far exceeded that for himself.

Warhol's paintings also enjoyed brief fame, as he painted such everyday objects as soup cans, stamps, dollar bills, and bottles of coca cola. He filmed a man sleeping and another one getting a haircut. Yet he also chose as subjects such famous people as Marilyn Monroe, Jacqueline Kennedy, and Elvis Presley. He turned to the banal as subject matter for many of his creations, as did other pop artists, because, he felt, the banal constituted the essence of American life. Yet Warhol reassured his audience that he implied no criticism, that he merely painted what he knew best. Campbell's soup, for instance, he claimed to eat regularly for lunch. (See Art of the 1970s.)

Born to working-class immigrants in Pittsburgh, Warhol and his family struggled through the Great Depression. His father died when Andy was 14, but had set aside money for his son's schooling. Andy, who would later change his last name from Warhola to Warhol, attended the Carnegie Institute of Technology in Pittsburgh to prepare for a career as a commercial artist. Even then, he demonstrated a strong bias against the normative in art, and even created a self-portrait with his finger in his nose (1949).

Warhol moved to New York City in 1949 and became a successful illustrator for fashion magazines and department stores. By the early 1960s, he turned to fine art, with comic-strip paintings of the fictional detective Dick Tracy, highly realistic depictions of the commonplace subjects already mentioned, and portraits of celebrities. During the 1960s, Warhol established his studio in a loft that he called the Factory and turned from painting to a silk-screen process that involved photographic enlargements silk-screened onto a canvas, often in multiple images, with a layer of coloring applied. Instead of one cola bottle, *Green Coca-Cola Bottles,* 1962, for example, depicted several rows of bottles much as they would be stacked on shelves in a store. In some paintings, such as *Marilyn,* 1967, different screens were used to apply different colors, in this case, yellow hair, green eyelids, red lips, and a pink face against a green background.

At the same time, Warhol continued with commercial art and also started making films, adopting the simple approach of turning a camera on such commonplace subjects as the Empire State Building or, as mentioned earlier, a man sleeping. He explained that he saw his films as analogous to wallpaper—in other words, something one might glance at from time to time but that did not require close attention. He also adopted a rock group called the Velvet Underground, produced their first record in 1965, and filmed them on stage.

Arts

Two celebrated Warhol images based on famous actresses of the 1960s: Left, *Liz Taylor* (1964). Right, *Marilyn Monroe* (1967). Courtesy of Photofest.

In addition to the celebrity portraits, Warhol captured the decade of the 1960s in his so-called Disaster pictures. Done in his silk-screen technique, these pictures presented in multiple images such events as race riots, automobile accidents, and a suicide leap.

Many other American artists played important roles within pop art, although none equaled Warhol in fame. James Rosenquist, a former billboard painter, utilized billboard techniques in his large, flat, collage paintings, such as *President Elect,* 1960–1961, with its large partial face of President Kennedy along with fingers holding a piece of cake and an automobile fender. Claes Oldenburg, born in Sweden, combined sculpture with painting. *USA Flag,* 1960, for example, consisted of muslin in plaster over a wire frame, the whole painted with tempera. Robert Indiana produced the most famous single image to come out of 1960s pop art—the word "LOVE" in stencil-like letters imitative of signs, with the "O" tilted (1966). Indiana both painted the message and sculpted it in aluminum. The image soon appeared virtually everywhere: on posters, on buttons, on almost any object that could contain the word, and fit well with such slogans as "Make love, not war" and with the general countercultural ambiance of hippies and flower children.

No discussion of pop art should ignore the so-called pop art happenings of the 1960s. Warhol, Rauschenberg, and Oldenburg were among the pop artists who sponsored these events. Typically (although no happening was truly typical), a happening occurred in a specially created environment that might include theatrical sets, psychedelic colors, musicians, a radio or television blaring, a wind machine blowing confetti—anything that contributed to a mood of randomness and spontaneity. Participants improvised responses. The total experience shared more with the collage or assemblage approach to art than with theater, for little was plotted ahead of time

OP ART

Op art, or optical art, vied with pop art for attention during the 1960s. Op art, however, was very different from pop art, residing more in the abstract tradition than in the representational. While pop art, even abroad, was thoroughly American in inspiration, op art reached greater heights in Europe than in the United States.

Influenced by the growth of science and technology, op art sought visual effects through such techniques as repeating periodic structures or geometric figures, (like concentric circles that change in circumference and radius), the phi phenomenon (the impression that fixed images such as dots are moving), moiré patterns (superimposing one periodic structure on another to create a watery or shimmering effect), hard-edged designs to enhance contrast, and sharply contrasting colors. Some works of art created optical effects through movement (as in mobiles and other kinetic art forms), others by utilizing the impact of light on the work or even incorporating light sources into it; however, arguably the purest type of op art required the viewer to concentrate on a static work to register the illusion of movement. Many op art works were in black and white, because most of the optical effects that artists desired could be created with this contrast. Many op artists also used color to good effect, employing new acrylic and emulsion paints to create glossy surfaces that enhanced the optical illusions.

There were several fine American op artists. Josef Albers, an American immigrant mentioned earlier in this chapter, played an important role in the history of op art in the United States. While at Yale, Albers taught Richard Anuszkiewicz, a prominent figure in the American op art world, and was a major reason American op art favored color contrasts rather than the black and white that dominated European op art. Although not primarily an op artist, Albers experimented with optical illusion, especially in his paintings of squares. Anuszkiewicz was part of an international exhibit of op art in 1965 at the Museum of Modern Art, and favored, as in *Radiant Green*, 1965, interactions among colors.

PHOTOGRAPHY

The dominant style for art photography at the beginning of the 1960s was "straight photography," which presented realistic images in beautiful prints prepared with meticulous attention to light, shadow, framing, and perspective. Much of straight photography was aesthetically and spiritually uplifting, and depicted magnificent scenes of both the small details and the majestic grandeur of nature. Documentary photography of human subjects usually exhibited compassionate understanding and empathy. Operating along these traditional paths were such important photographers as Ansel Adams, Minor White, and Wynn Bullock.

Two of the most important milestones along the road to photographic innovation were books, Robert Frank's *The Americans,* which first appeared in the United States in 1960, and John Szarkowski's *The Photographer's Eye,* published in 1966. Frank took the photographs in this collection during the middle 1950s. He was concerned with subjects that other photographers had certainly explored—racism, poverty, religion—but he established a new style for the photographic documentary. Rather than praising his subject or indicting society, Frank's pictures were often slightly out of focus or idiosyncratically framed, his subjects' gestures and expressions more candid than posed.

John Szarkowski, director of the photography department at New York's Museum of Modern Art, was an influential figure in the world of art photography. That influence increased dramatically with publication of *The Photographer's Eye,* in which he reexamined the history of photography while focusing attention on photographic theory. With Szarkowski leading a critical and historical discussion of photography, and Frank leading through practice, the medium produced striking but far from conventionally beautiful photographs.

Paralleling pop art in painting, the new photographers turned increasingly to the commonplace, the banal, and the bizarre. Rather than objective representation heightened with considerable technical skill, these photographers looked to the art form as heavily subjective and at the same time clearly artifice. Thus was born the "snapshot aesthetic"—pictures that exhibited an amateur-like crudeness in lighting, focus, and arrangement.

Three of the most successful of the new photographers were Garry Winogrand, Lee Friedlander, and Diane Arbus, all three included in the important "New Documents" exhibition of 1966–1967 at the Museum of Modern Art. Winogrand was an air force photographer and later photojournalist whose work appeared in such magazines as *Sports Illustrated, Look,* and *Life.* His art photographs are especially notable for the busy, teeming numbers of people captured with wide-angle lenses. Humor, irony, even mockery appeared in many of his pictures, including those taken at the New York City Zoo and the Coney Island Aquarium and published in *The Animals,* 1969.

Arts

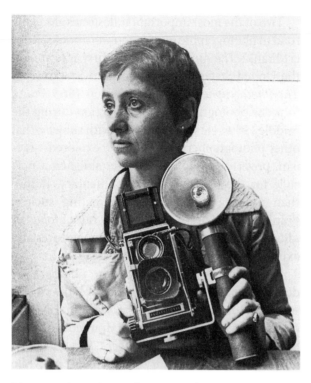

Photographer Diane Arbus poses for a rare portrait in the Automat at Sixth Avenue between 41st and 42nd Street in New York City circa 1968. Photo by Roz Kelly/ Michael Ochs Archives/Getty Images.

Friedlander's photographs often appeared to be random snapshots of urban scenes, catching whatever happened to be there that moment. The result was a collage or assemblage effect similar to much of 1960s painting. His pictures were notable not only for their detail but also for their metaphoric impact, like a church in the background behind traffic and pedestrians, a trash can and stop sign in the foreground, *Santa Fe,* 1969.

Diane Arbus is the most disconcerting of the three. She gravitated toward the bizarre, often photographing people she referred to as "freaks"— midgets, giants, transvestites, and other social outcasts.

Photojournalists, with a level of skill that blurred the line between photojournalism and art photography, captured many of the most important moments of the 1960s, and other moments that might easily have been missed had not a skilled man or woman with a camera been present. They helped shape both the public's vision of the decade and history's judgment of it. Unfortunately, many of these moments were shocking, disconcerting, even

DIANE ARBUS (1923–1971)

The photography of Diane Arbus, both beautiful and disturbing, first came to media attention in the 1960s. Arbus was born and raised in New York City, where she and her husband Alan worked as fashion photographers. Arbus first learned photography from her husband, who was trained in the New Jersey Signal Corps. After separating from her husband in the 1950s, Arbus continued working as a photojournalist, taking assignments for *Esquire* and *Harper's Bazaar.* As a photographer, Arbus had an uncanny ability to bring out the humanity in her subjects, creating portraits that were compelling and strangely disturbing. Her photography was a perfect fit with the "new journalism" movement, which sought to bring journalism closer to the artistic sensibilities of fiction. Arbus won two Guggenheim Fellowships, in 1963 and 1966, and expanded her repertoire with portraits of subjects whose physical features set them apart from the crowd, such as circus performers, transvestites, and drag queens. Arbus was one of several artists featured in the 1967 exhibit "New Documents" at the Museum of Modern Art (MoMA) in New York City, and was hailed as one of the most visionary photographers of her age. Arbus committed suicide in 1971 at age 48, after reportedly struggling with severe depression. Though her career was cut short, a posthumous exhibition of her work at the MoMA was the most popular, single-artist, photographic exhibition in the history of the museum, and a monograph of her work became one the best selling art books in history.

tragic: photographs by Robert Jackson of Jack Ruby shooting Lee Harvey Oswald, November 24, 1963; by Malcolm Browne of the Buddhist monk Thick Quang Duc burning himself to death in Saigon on June 11, 1963; by Eddie Adams of the instant when the bullet from South Vietnamese General Nguyen Ngoc Loan's gun entered the head of a Viet Cong prisoner, February 1, 1968; by Cecil Stoughton of the moment aboard *Air Force One* when the new president, Lyndon Johnson, with the new widow Jacqueline Kennedy by his side, took the oath of office on November 22, 1963.

ENDNOTES FOR THE 1960s

OVERVIEW OF THE 1960s

1. Most of the financial figures in this section are drawn from Kurian's *Datapedia of the United States.*
2. George Thomas Kurian, *Datapedia of the United States, 1790–2000* (Lanham, MD: Bernan, 1994), 144.
3. Kurian, *Datapedia of the United States, 1790–2000,* 156.
4. The following figures relating to the Vietnam War are from Harry G. Summer Jr., *Vietnam War Almanac* (New York: Facts on File, 1985).

ADVERTISING OF THE 1960s

1. George Thomas Kurian, *Datapedia of the United States, 1790–2000* (Lanham, MD: Bernan, 1994), 299.
2. Kurian, *Datapedia of the United States, 1790–2000,* 8.
3. The figures relating to African-American demographics and purchasing, and to advertising directed at the African-American community, are from D. Parke Gibson's important study, *The $30 Billion Negro* (London: Macmillan, 1969).

ARCHITECTURE OF THE 1960s

1. Robert Venturi, *Complexity and Contradiction in Architecture,* 2nd ed. (New York: Museum of Modern Art, 1977), 16.
2. Carole Rifkind, *A Field Guide to Contemporary American Architecture* (New York: Dutton, 1998), 81.
3. *The Constitution on the Sacred Liturgy,* in *The Documents of Vatican II,* ed. Walter Abbott, trans. Joseph Gallagher (New York: Guild, America, Association Presses, 1966), sections 2, 14, 48.
4. Carter Wiseman, *Shaping a Nation: Twentieth-Century American Architecture and Its Makers* (New York: Norton, 1998), 232.
5. Jane Jacobs, *The Death and Life of Great American Cities* (New York: Random House, 1961), 187.

BOOKS, NEWSPAPERS, MAGAZINES, AND COMICS OF THE 1960s

1. Robert J. Glessing, *The Underground Press in America* (Bloomington: Indiana UP, 1970).

ENTERTAINMENT OF THE 1960s

1. Marshall McLuhan, *The Medium Is the Massage* (New York: Random House, 1967).
2. George Thomas Kurian, *Datapedia of the United States, 1790–2000* (Lanham, MD: Bernan, 1994), 299.

3. United States, Bureau of the Census, vol. 2 of *Historical Statistics of the United States: Colonial Times to 1970,* Bicentennial ed. (Washington DC: U.S. Department of Commerce, Bureau of the Census, 1975), 796.
4. Newton N. Minow made this comment in a speech to the nation's broadcasters in 1961. For a more recent examination of Minow's views on television, see his and Craig LaMay's *Abandoned in the Wasteland: Children, Television, and the First Amendment* (New York: Hill and Wang, 1995).
5. Much of the information in this chapter on Emmy awards, Nielsen ratings, and related matters is based on Tim Brooks and Earle Marsh's useful reference work, *The Complete Directory to Prime Time Network and Cable TV Shows, 1946–Present,* 25th anniversary ed. (New York: Ballantine, 1999).
6. Jackie Kennedy made the connection to Camelot in an interview with Kennedy biographer Theodore H. White on November 29, 1963. White then expanded on the comment in a piece that he wrote for *Life,* "For President Kennedy: An Epilogue," which appeared on December 6, 1963.

FASHION OF THE 1960s

1. George Thomas Kurian, *Datapedia of the United States, 1790–2000* (Lanham, MD: Bernan, 1994), 8, 177.
2. Frank W. Hoffman and William G. Bailey, *Fashion and Merchandising Fads* (New York: Haworth, 1994), 270.

FOOD OF THE 1960s

1. Tremendously informative regarding a wide range of developments in the food industry is James Trager, *The Food Chronology: A Food Lover's Compendium of Events and Anecdotes, from Prehistory to the Present* (1995; New York: Henry Holt, 1997). Most of the restaurant and food statistics in this section are from Trager.
2. These statistics, as well as the following figures relating to school lunches and substances that are endangering food and the environment, are from Trager.

MUSIC OF THE 1960s

1. References to such awards in this chapter are based heavily on Irwin Stambler, *The Encyclopedia of Pop, Rock and Soul,* rev. ed. (New York: St. Martin's, 1989).
2. Stambler, *The Encyclopedia of Pop, Rock and Soul,* 559.
3. David Allen Duncan, "Music," vol. 2 of *The Sixties in America,* ed. Carl Singleton (Pasadena, CA: Salem, 1999), 506. Geoffrey C. Ward and Ken Burns, *Jazz: A History of America's Music* (New York: Alfred A. Knopf, 2000), 446.
4. Geoffrey C. Ward and Ken Burns, Jazz: A History of America's Music (New York: Alfred A. Knopf, 2000), 446.

Arts

SPORTS AND LEISURE OF THE 1960s

1. David Maraniss, *When Pride Still Mattered: A Life of Vince Lombardi* (New York: Simon & Schuster, 2000).
2. Charles Panati, *Panati's Parade of Fads, Follies, and Manias: The Origins of Our Most Cherished Obsessions* (New York: HarperCollins, 1991), 322. David Maraniss, *When Pride Still Mattered: A Life of Vince Lombardi* (New York: Simon & Schuster, 1999). Sam Chaiton and Terry Swinton, *Lazarus and the Hurricane: The Freeing of Rubin "Hurricane" Carter* (1991; New York: St. Martin's Griffin, 1999), 336.
3. Panati, *Panati's Parade of Fads, Follies, and Manias,* 320–21.
4. The statistics given here for Barbie and G. I. Joe are from Frank W. Hoffman and William G. Bailey, *Fashion & Merchandising Fads* (New York: Haworth, 1994), 27–29 and 93–94.
5. Panati, *Panati's Parade of Fads, Follies, and Manias,* 321.
6. Lois Gordon and Alan Gordon, American Chronicle: Year by Year Through the Twentieth Century (New Haven: Yale UP, 1999), 632.

TRAVEL OF THE 1960s

1. John F. Kennedy, Special Message to the Congress, 25 May 1961, published in *To Turn the Tide,* ed. John W. Gardner (New York: Harper, 1962), 74–75.
2. Louis Giannetti and Scott Eyman, *Flashback: A Brief History of Film,* 3rd ed. (Englewood Cliffs, NJ: Prentice-Hall, 1996), 347.
3. George Thomas Kurian, *Datapedia of the United States, 1790–2000* (Lanham, MD: Bernan, 1994), 267–68.
4. Peter B. Heller, "Automobiles and Auto Manufacturing," in *The Sixties in America,* ed. Carl Singleton, vol. 1 (Pasadena, CA: Salem, 1999), 52.
5. I am indebted for the statistics relating to car sales and car manufacturing specifications to Martin Buckley and Chris Rees, *The World Encyclopedia of Cars: The Definitive Guide to Classic and Contemporary Cars,* rev. ed. (New York: Hermes House, 1999).
6. Kurian, *Datapedia of the United States, 1790–2000,* 289.
7. Robert P. Ellis, "Travel," in *The Sixties in America,* vol. 3, 729.
8. Kurian, *Datapedia of the United States, 1790–2000,* 276.

Arts

1970s

Timeline

of Popular Culture Events, 1970s

1970

Richard Nixon sends U.S. troops into Cambodia.

Four Kent State University students are killed by the National Guard after a protest of the bombing of Cambodia.

Black Sabbath debuts, playing heavy metal; ZZ Top joins the Allman Brothers (debut 1969) in launching "Southern rock."

Two prominent rock singers—Janis Joplin and Jimi Hendrix—die of drug overdoses.

An estimated 20 million Americans participate in the first Earth Day commemoration.

The Environmental Protection Agency (EPA) forms.

Monday Night Football premieres on ABC.

Childproof safety caps are introduced.

California becomes the first no-fault divorce state.

Lithium is approved as a treatment for depression by the Food and Drug Administration.

Big Bird of *Sesame Street* appears on the cover of *Time* magazine.

Postal reform laws make the U.S. Postal Service self-sufficient.

1971

Swann v. Charlotte-Mecklenburg Board of Education: the U.S. Supreme Court upholds school busing as a tool to correct racial imbalances in schools.

Jim Morrison of the Doors dies of heart failure; drug overdose widely speculated.

Andrew Lloyd Webber and Tim Rice's musical, *Jesus Christ Superstar,* debuts on Broadway.

In *Reed v. Reed,* the Supreme Court rules that laws discriminating against women are illegal under the Fourteenth Amendment.

The first word processor, the Wang 1200, is invented.

Cigarette advertising is banned on radio and television.

NASA Mariner 9 circles Mars, the first time a spaceship orbits another planet; Apollo XIV lands on the moon.

Pentagon Papers, which describe U.S. war activities in Vietnam, are released to the *New York Times* by Daniel Ellsberg; *New York Times* publishes them.

Richard Nixon imposes a 90-day wage and price freeze to combat inflation.

All in the Family, starring Carroll O'Connor as Archie Bunker, debuts on television, changing the direction of programming dramatically.

Prison riots in Attica, New York, last four days more than 40 inmates and guards are killed.

MRI (Magnetic Resonance Imaging) technology is first used on humans to detect medical issues.

Charles Manson and three female followers are convicted of murdering Sharon Tate and sentenced to death.

Congress passes the 26th Amendment, which lowers the voting age to 18.

1972

Title IX bans gender discrimination at educational facilities that receive federal funds.

David Bowie's album, *Rise and Fall of Ziggy Stardust,* ushers in the era of glam-rock.

The Equal Rights Amendment (ERA) is adopted by the Senate; state ratification needed.

Richard Nixon visits Moscow, and the United States and the U.S.S.R. agree to freeze nuclear weapons at current levels; he also visits China, another historic event.

Five burglars are arrested after breaking into the Democratic National Headquarters; this becomes known as the Watergate break-in.

Gloria Steinem launches *Ms.* magazine; *Life* magazine ceases weekly publication.

Arabs terrorists storm the Olympic Village and kill 11 Israeli athletes at the Olympics held in Munich, Germany, after their demands are not met.

The Godfather, starring Marlon Brando, receives 10 Academy Award nominations; it wins Best Picture, Best Actor, and Best Adapted Screenplay.

Nike shoes debut.

The Supreme Court declares the death penalty as cruel and unusual punishment; sentences of Charles Manson, his followers, and others convicted are commuted to life in prison.

President Nixon wins his reelection bid by the largest margin since Franklin Delano Roosevelt won in 1936.

Atari's Pong begins the video game craze.

HBO launches its cable subscription service in New York.

Alabama Governor George Wallace is shot while campaigning for president; he survives but suffers from paralysis.

1973

Richard Nixon orders a cease-fire in Vietnam after peace talks begin in Paris.

The U.S. draft is abolished, and an all-volunteer military begins.

Vice President Spiro Agnew resigns after being charged with accepting bribes and falsifying federal tax returns; Gerald Ford begins serving as vice president.

OPEC enacts an oil embargo against the United States because of the military aid provided by the United States to Israel during the Yom Kippur War.

The Supreme Court hears *Roe v. Wade;* it overturns prohibitions on first-trimester abortions and eases restrictions on second-trimester ones.

The American Indian Movement seizes Wounded Knee for 71 days as a protest against the government for its treatment of Native Americans.

Billie Jean King defeats Bobby Riggs in tennis's "Battle of the Sexes."

Congress passes the Endangered Species Act.

UPC bar codes are introduced, allowing retailers to scan in information about purchases, simplifying inventory tasks.

The Exorcist, a horror film, receives five major Academy Award nominations.

1974

Publishing heiress Patty Hearst is kidnapped by the Symbionese Liberation Army.

President Richard Nixon resigns because of the Watergate scandal and an impeachment threat; Gerald Ford becomes president and he pardons Nixon for any Watergate crimes.

Hank Aaron hits his 715th home run, breaking Babe Ruth's record.

The first programmable pocket calculators become available for sale.

Naked students "streak" across college campuses; Ray Stevens's song "The Streak" becomes popular.

Eight former White House aides are indicted for conspiring in Watergate cover-up.

The U.S. Merchant Marine Academy becomes the first U.S. service academy to enroll women.

The first black model—Beverly Johnson—appears on the cover of a major fashion magazine *(Vogue)*.

The Supreme Court orders Little League to allow girls to participate.

Women are ordained as priests by the Episcopal Church.

1975

The precursor to the home computer, the Altair, debuts; assembly required.

Lynette "Squeaky" Fromme, a Charles Manson follower, attempts to assassinate Gerald Ford.

Unemployment reaches 8.9 percent, the highest since 1941.

The FBI captures Patty Hearst, who now goes by the name of Tania.

Joshua Reynolds invents and begins marketing the mood ring, a fad that sold millions.

Gary Dahl packages the Pet Rock and becomes a millionaire within a year.

Catalytic converters are introduced in cars, mitigating air pollution.

The U.S. government passes the Metric Conversion Act, stating that metric measurement is the preferred system, but people ignore its passage.

After scoring a perfect 800 on his math SATs, William Gates drops out of Harvard University to write software programs for a small computer company, Micro-Soft.

Saturday Night Live debuts on late-night television and satirizes politicians and other social phenomena.

Teamster union leader Jimmy Hoffa disappears after meeting suspected mobsters at a restaurant.

1976

On April Fool's Day, Apple Computer launches its first product, selling it for $666.66.

4.8 million people apply for a CB license; it is estimated that only half of CB users actually apply for licenses.

The New Jersey Supreme Court allows Karen Ann Quinlan's parents to remove her from life support after a long coma.

The first stand-alone Betamax VCRs are put on the market.

The United States celebrates its Bicentennial; the U.S. mint issues commemorative coins and President Gerald Ford gives a nationally televised speech.

Jimmy Carter is elected president in November after the Democratic National Convention selects him as their candidate on the first ballot.

Chicago writer Saul Bellow wins the Pulitzer Prize for his novel *Humboldt's Gift.*

The U.S. Supreme Court reverses its 1972 decision and legalizes capital punishment.

Journalist Tom Wolfe gives the decade the nickname that sticks: "The 'Me' Decade and the Third Great Awakening."

More than 200 people attending a Philadelphia convention for ex-service personnel become ill with Legionnaire's Disease; 34 die from the disease.

1977

King of Rock and Roll, Elvis Presley, dies at age 42; heart disease is named as the cause.

John Travolta stars in *Saturday Night Fever,* furthering the popularity of disco, and *Star Wars* also debuts in theaters, with its phrase "May the force be with you."

The Alaskan pipeline is completed, providing the United States with 15 percent of its oil supply.

Jimmy Carter is sworn in as president after parking his limo and walking down Pennsylvania Avenue.

President Carter grants unconditional amnesty to most of those who evaded the draft—the "draft dodgers"—to avoid serving in the Vietnam War.

The country deals with "stagflation," an economic condition consisting of continuing inflation and stagnant business activity with its corresponding high rates of unemployment.

ABC airs the hugely successful television mini-series *Roots,* based on a book written by Alex Haley.

"Son of Sam"—David Berkowitz—is arrested after a 12-month, 6-person killing spree in which he believed a black "demon" dog was instructing him to murder.

President Carter signs the Panama Canal Treaty and Neutrality Treaty, which relinquishes U.S. control of the canal by the year 2000 and guarantees its neutrality.

President Carter halts development of the B-1 bomber in favor of the development of the cruise missile.

1978

The birth of the world's first successful "test-tube baby," who was conceived through in-vitro fertilization, serves as a focal point of the science vs. religion debate.

President Carter, Egypt's Anwar Sadat, and Israel's Menachem Begin meet at Camp David to discuss peace in the Middle East.

Love Canal, New York, was declared a federal disaster after the chemical wastes dumped beneath the town leak; rates for cancer and birth defects are extremely high.

American cult leader Jim Jones of the People's Temple persuades hundreds of his followers to commit suicide in Guyana, most by drinking poisoned Kool-Aid.

Congress extends the deadline for ERA ratification, changing it from March 22, 1979, to June 30, 1982.

A sniper shoots *Hustler* publisher Larry Flynt, leaving him paralyzed.

In the *University of California v. Bakke,* the U.S. Supreme Court rules that the use of quotas is not permissible in affirmative action programs.

The former president publishes *The Memoirs of Richard Nixon.*

The first arcade game, Space Invaders, premieres in Japan.

Dallas, an evening soap opera starring Larry Hagman as J. R. Ewing, first airs on CBS.

1979

A near nuclear disaster occurs at Three Mile Island near Harrisburg, Pennsylvania; fierce arguments over the safety of nuclear energy ensue.

Militant Islamic students in Iran storm the U.S. embassy there, taking more than 90 people—65 of them Americans—as hostage; they hold 52 of these hostages for 444 days.

Fundamentalist preacher Jerry Falwell forms an organization called the Moral Majority; its aim is to reestablish traditional religious values in the nation.

The United States and China formalize diplomatic relations.

The first gay and lesbian rights march takes place in Washington, D.C.; Falwell responds by praying and saying that "God made Adam and Eve, not Adam and Steve."

The U.S. mint issues the Susan B. Anthony dollar; the coin approximates the size of a quarter and confuses many consumers.

The Sony Walkman is introduced in Japan.

The U.S. government awards the Sioux Nation $105 million in land claims.

President Carter delivers his "Crisis of Confidence" speech, telling the American people that he shares their pain.

Francis Ford Coppola's movie about the Vietnam War, *Apocalypse Now,* wins the Academy Award for Best Picture.

Overview

of the 1970s

Me Decade

NICKNAME FOR THE DECADE, 1970–1979

In the 1970s, Americans dealt with a decade of sweeping social, cultural, and political changes. Minorities continued their efforts to effect change and to institute laws that protected their civil rights. Countless women marched for their own freedoms, including economic, political, religious, social, and cultural gains. Meanwhile, the gay and lesbian cause gained momentum, with its advocates also experiencing heartbreaking setbacks.

The 1970s were also a decade of disillusionment. Many Americans lost their jobs during an era of stagflation—a combined economic disaster of inflation and stagnation. Two oil embargoes, a war in Southeast Asia, and some of the worst political scandals to ever hit the White House contributed to the sense of malaise that spread through the country.

To add to the troubles of the era, crime rates continued to increase; illegal drug use escalated. Experts increasingly attributed the causes of crimes to failures of society, and tax dollars were therefore poured into social reform and rehabilitation efforts.

Changes in the family structure echoed those of the overall society. Divorce increased and birth rates dropped. In increasing numbers, Americans left mainstream churches to seek spiritual answers elsewhere, perhaps in the growing Evangelical Christian movement, a religious group dubbed a cult, or through New Age avenues of enlightenment.

THE ECONOMY AND HEALTH CARE

The Economy

After World War II ended, Americans had come to expect a stable job market with low inflation and a steady growth of the overall economy. By the summer of 1970, though, industrial productivity had begun to decline, while unemployment rates were increasing. Interest and inflation rates were on the rise; unbalanced budgets and growing trade deficits were also warning signs of a troubled economy. In August 1971, President Richard Nixon instituted a 90-day price and wage control program, something unheard of during peacetime, with the hope that this policy would curb inflation. It did not, although many economists supported Nixon's plan at the time.

Although the United States had satisfied much of its own oil—and therefore gasoline—needs through 1950, the increasing oil and gasoline consumption during the 1960s and 1970s caused the American government to import more of these products. Much of this oil was exported out of Middle Eastern countries that had formed a cartel, the Organization of Petroleum Exporting

Countries (OPEC) in 1960. The increasing oil demands of people in the United States and other Western countries gave OPEC significant bargaining power.

Then, on October 6, 1973—Yom Kippur, the holiest day of the Jewish calendar—Arab forces attacked Israel. With the support of the United States and other Western European nations, Israel was able to rebuff these forces and a cease-fire agreement came about the following month. However, on October 17, in the middle of this short war, OPEC enforced an oil embargo on the United States, whereby Arab countries stopped selling oil to the United States in protest of its support of Israel during the Yom Kippur War.

The United States suffered from this economic retaliation; Americans were asked to turn down their thermostats, car pool to work, and otherwise limit their consumption of oil products. Gasoline prices increased from 30 cents per gallon to $1.20, drivers were eventually limited to 10 gallons of gasoline per transaction, and Sunday sales of gasoline were forbidden. OPEC lifted its punitive embargo on March 18, 1974, but significant damage to the United States economy—and the disruption of daily lifestyles—had already occurred.

Nixon pushed for the completion of the Alaskan pipeline, which would decrease the amount of imported oil purchased from OPEC. Construction of the pipeline began on March 27, 1975, and the project was finished on May 31, 1977. Just three weeks later, oil was being transported through its pipes.

Economists point to other reasons for the change in the economic picture during the 1970s. Record numbers of births during the Baby Boomer generation meant that more people's needs had to be met during a time when the average individual was consuming increasingly larger quantities of products. Some manufacturers began moving their operations overseas, where cheaper labor could be found, which meant that many American workers, especially in the Midwest, lost their jobs. Plus, with lower household incomes due to unemployment, Americans searched out lower-priced goods—which were frequently made overseas. In particular, the oil crises of 1973 and 1979 caused many Americans to purchase smaller, foreign-made cars that were more economical than their domestic counterparts. For the first time in the twentieth century, the United States imported more goods than it exported.

By 1975, the U.S. economy was clearly in a state of "stagflation," a newly coined word that described rising prices (inflation) at a time when the economy was stagnating, with high unemployment rates and an economic recession. President Gerald Ford twice proposed a combination of a massive tax cut and a spending ceiling; both times, Congress agreed with the tax cut but ignored the ceiling.

In 1979, a second oil crisis, smaller in scope yet still damaging, occurred. By this time, the phrase *energy crisis* was in common usage. This energy crisis was precipitated by the revolution in Iran. After the Shah, Mohammad Reza Pahlavi, fled Iran, the Ayatollah Khomeini took control. The Ayatollah resumed the sale of oil to the United States, but the volume was reduced. Although OPEC nations filled in much of the gap, panic ensued.

Health Care

During the 1970s, mass media focused attention on four main problems in the U.S. health care system. First was that health care costs were soaring out of control. Next was that, even though the government now provided insurance for the elderly and those on welfare, far too many Americans remained uninsured. Also, the ever-increasing number of malpractice lawsuits against doctors and hospitals brought the quality of medical care into question, and, finally, bureaucratic controls caused many patients to complain about the loss of humane medical treatment.[1] None of these problems was solved during the decade.

The term *holistic* became part of many people's vocabularies, usually in conjunction with their health. In holistic health care, the entire mind, body, and spirit is considered when diagnosing and treating problems—and, perhaps even more important, in the prevention of diseases that could be avoided by careful choices: what healthy foods and vitamins, for example, should be consumed, and what substances—alcohol, nicotine, drugs, and so forth—should be avoided or limited. Alternative treatments, including acupuncture, meditation, and herbal medicine found new followings during the 1970s.

Increasing numbers of Americans also turned to exercise during the 1970s. Jogging was a prime pursuit, while fashions such as Nike warm-up suits and running shoes were both aided and influenced by this trend.

POLITICS AND POLITICAL LEADERS

Watergate

Watergate is the scandal—perhaps better described as a series of scandals—that ended the political career of Richard Milhous Nixon and many others in Washington, D.C.; it is named after the hotel that served as the center of corrupt activity. Ever since Watergate occurred and was thusly named, other political scandals have traditionally had the suffix "-gate" attached to their names.

In June 1971, the *New York Times* and the *Washington Post* published portions of confidential government documents detailing the Vietnam War. These papers became known as the Pentagon Papers and the published excerpts showed that the government was not being forthcoming about the escalation of the war in Southeast Asia. The executive branch of the government argued that it must serve as the sole judge of what national security information should be released; the press insisted that First Amendment rights must be paramount and that the federal government wished to exercise censorship. The court ruled in favor of the press, and the newspapers were granted permission to continue to publish this material.

On September 9, a group of men known as the "plumbers" broke into the office of psychiatrist of Daniel Ellsberg, the former defense analyst who was discovered to have leaked the Pentagon Papers to the press. These men were dubbed plumbers for their ability to plug information leaks about the Nixon administration and to collect their own data on those seen as enemies of the president's policies. When the burglary came to light, the charges that the government was pressing against Ellsberg for releasing the documents were dropped.

The situation escalated dramatically on June 17, 1972 when five men, one of whom used to work for the CIA, were caught attempting to burgle the Democratic National Convention Headquarters, which were located in the plush Watergate hotel. It was later discovered that bugging devices had been planted in the Democratic headquarters in May. On June 19, the *Washington Post* indicated that a GOP security aide had been among the burglars.

On August 1, a $25,000 check earmarked for the Nixon reelection campaign was discovered to have been deposited into an account of a Watergate burglar; in September, it was uncovered that John Mitchell, former attorney general and the head of Nixon's reelection campaign, had used Republican Party funds to conduct investigations into the operations of the Democratic Party. Then, on October 10, 1972, the FBI determined that the Republicans had conducted a thorough political spy campaign against the Democrats. Meanwhile, the White House continued to deny prior knowledge of any of these events.

Despite these discoveries, Nixon won a landslide second term against Democratic candidate George McGovern, winning 520 out of the 537 electoral votes.

During the first half of 1973, members of Nixon's administration either resigned (H. R. Haldeman, John Ehrlichman, and Attorney General Richard Kleindienst), were fired (legal counsel John Dean), or were convicted of conspiracy, burglary, and wiretapping in connection with the Watergate break-in (G. Gordon Liddy and James W. McCord Jr.). During the summer of 1973, the vice president, Spiro Agnew, was being investigated on charges of extortion, bribery, and income tax evasion in connection to his term as Maryland governor. Agnew resigned on October 10, 1973, and Gerald Ford became vice president.

On May 18, 1973, the investigation began to be televised, with Archibald Cox serving as prosecutor. On June 3, former counsel to the president John Dean testified that he had discussed the Watergate cover-up at least 35 times with the president. Ten days later, a damaging memo addressed to former White House aide John Ehrlichman was found. This memo described the intent to burglarize Daniel Ellsberg's office, and thereby confirmed that Nixon's close consultants were aware of the situation beforehand.

In July, Nixon's former appointments secretary told Congress that Nixon had secretly taped all of his meetings and conversations since 1971. Nixon ordered the taping to stop, but he also refused to turn over existing tapes to investigators.

In October, Nixon fired Archibald Cox and abolished the office of special prosecutor altogether. Both the attorney general and the deputy attorney general resigned in connection with Nixon's actions. Calls for Nixon's impeachment intensified.

A Congressional committee then subpoenaed selected tapes and Nixon began reviewing them personally. The most controversial tape, one from June 20, 1972, had more than 18 minutes of conversation erased and many people now believe that Nixon's loyal secretary, Rosemary Woods, deleted portions of the tape that she feared would harm the president.

On April 30, 1974, the White House released 1,200 pages of edited transcripts. The House Judiciary Committee demanded the original recordings, and the Supreme Court ruled in favor of Congress. Within three days of receiving undoctored tapes, on July 27, 1974, Congress

passed three articles of impeachment against the president for obstruction of justice. On August 8, 1974, Nixon became the first—and so far, the only—President of the United States to resign from office. Gerald Ford assumed the office of president.

Nixon had some foreign policy successes, most specifically his breakthrough with Communist China and his détente with the Soviet Union. In February 1972, Richard Nixon became the first U.S. president to visit China. After two decades of a strained and difficult relationship between the two countries, Nixon spent a week discussing a wide variety of political topics of mutual interest with Chairman Mao Tse-tung. Moreover, the notion that the United States and China had begun to normalize relationships created the need for the Soviet Union to participate in talks with Nixon.

In May 1972 Nixon became the first president to travel to the Soviet Union, where he met with its leader, Leonid Brezhnev. The two leaders signed the Strategic Arms Limitation Talks (SALT) treaty, which limited the number of certain types of weapons and the amount of testing allowed.

Gerald Ford

As the only president not elected to office, much of Gerald Ford's presidency consisted of separating his administration from the troubles of Watergate without damaging the future of the Republican Party.

Ford's predecessor, Richard Nixon, faced criminal prosecution. A trial would occupy much of the nation's time, attention, and financial resources. Gerald Ford could prevent such a spectacle by granting Nixon a presidential pardon, especially if he did so before any formal indictments were announced. Polls, however, indicated that nearly 60 percent of American citizens opposed a presidential pardon.[2]

On September 8, 1974, Gerald Ford announced that he was giving Nixon a full, absolute, and unconditional pardon for any crimes that he may have committed while in office. Nixon did not even need to admit to any wrongdoings. Ford cited the need for national healing, and he favored focusing on recovery rather than revenge.

President Nixon addressing the investigation of the Watergate break-in at a brief news conference on April 17, 1973. Courtesy of Photofest.

In July 1976, from *Bob Hope's Bicentennial Star-Spangled Spectacular* television special to the minting of unique 1776–1976 American Bicentennial quarters, the nation stood awash in patriotism. Everywhere one looked, people celebrated 200 years of freedom. In the heartland, that celebration led to countless red, white, and blue mailboxes and a sea of flags hung from cities to farms.

Splashy TV programs unified the celebration, but local and regional activities also took place on the community level. In the nation's capital, President Gerald Ford watched as a nationally-televised fireworks display lit up the sky. The three major networks also carried a fireworks show from New York Harbor, which featured a giant "76" lit up on two barges and 3,000 shells fired from an automated control point in the World Trade Center.

In New York and Boston, visitors were invited to explore these an international collection of tall sailing ships. Some critics thought the yacht brigade served as just another less-than-dignified aspect of the national pep rally, but millions of people visited the ancient vessels, and the display of beautiful ships from many nations sailing through New York Harbor and past the Statue of Liberty was moving. The Festival of American Folklife was held on the 50 acres between the Washington Monument and Lincoln Memorial and featured ethnic celebrations of singing, dancing, and crafts, followed by a free evening concert.

Ford also faced a dire economic situation when he took office. The oil embargo had ended just five months before and stagflation was about to peak. Moreover, Ford's relationship with Congress suffered a terrible blow after the pardon—and, in the 1974 elections for the House and the Senate, the House Democrats won more than a two-thirds majority.

The Democrats newly voted into Congress became known as the "Watergate Babies." Confident in the public's vote of confidence in their party and its policies, they were aggressive in their disagreements with Ford, frequently citing their duty of "congressional oversight." None of Ford's economic plans or energy proposals were passed without significant alterations by Congress.

Running against Ford in 1976 was Georgia's Democratic governor, Jimmy Carter, a former peanut farmer who focused much of his campaign message on his outsider status in Washington. Carter won by only 56 electoral votes in an election that had the lowest turnout in nearly 30 years. Carter's victory was the first for a Southerner since before the Civil War.

Jimmy Carter

Jimmy Carter's administration became weighted down by economic troubles, struggles with Congress, and an energy crisis. Unemployment was at seven percent, inflation was between five and six percent, and the deficit was at about $66 billion. Carter believed that inflation would solve itself in a high employment nation. Carter proposed two bills that addressed the economy, but Congress did not pass either. Meanwhile, inflation skyrocketed to 13.3 percent.

The United States was importing nearly 50 percent of its oil by the time Carter took office. Carter attempted to pass an energy bill, but Congress resented its lack of input on the bill and the final result was watered down.

On November 4, 1979, Iranian militants stormed the U.S. embassy in Tehran, keeping 52 hostages for 444 days. Reasons for the hostage-taking centered on the Ayatollah Khomeini whipping up militants into a frenzy after Carter allowed the disposed Shah of Iran into the United States for cancer treatments. Carter unsuccessfully tried diplomatic solutions to resolve the crisis and to obtain the release of the hostages.

The Ayatollah swore that he would not release the hostages until the United States turned the Shah over to Iran, along with billions of dollars that the Iranians claimed he had appropriated from the Iranian people. When Marines attempted a rescue, three of the helicopters malfunctioned; one crashed, killing eight Marines and injuring three more.

In 1980, Carter lost the presidential race to Ronald Reagan. As the transfer of presidential power took place, the hostages were released.

TIME MAGAZINE "MAN OF THE YEAR"

1970 Willy Brandt (West German chancellor)

1971 Richard Nixon (37th President of the United States)

1972 Richard Nixon and Henry Kissinger (37th President of the United States and National Security Advisor)

1973 John J. Sirica (Federal judge)

1974 King Faisal (King of Saudi Arabia)

1975 American Women

1976 Jimmy Carter (39th President of the United States)

1977 Anwar Sadat (President of Egypt)

1978 Deng Xiaoping (Chinese political leader)

1979 Ayatollah Khomeini (Islamic religious leader)

Carter deregulated both the airline and banking industries, and, at the end of his term, he could truthfully state that eight million more jobs existed in 1980 than at the beginning of his term. Carter had also reduced the federal deficit and removed pricing controls from domestic petroleum to stimulate production and reduce reliance upon foreign oil.

CIVIL RIGHTS AND THE FEMINIST MOVEMENT

Civil Rights

By the early 1970s two important pieces of civil rights legislation—the 1964 act and the 1968 act—had already been passed and the initial reactions to each had died down. Discrimination based upon a wide variety of factors was declared illegal at the federal level. Throughout the rest of the 1960s and during the early part of the 1970s, courts found themselves judging cases of companies that obeyed the letter of the law, but not the spirit. To remedy this type of situation, courts needed to find ways to fight the exclusionary practices that were being used to maintain racial and/or gender imbalance. In 1971, after dealing with many of these instances, the Supreme Court ruled, in *Griggs v. Duke Power Company,* that a

company that disproportionately kept a group of workers—in this case, black employees—from inclusion, whether that was the intent or not, was involved in illegal hiring practices and must revise its employment policies.

This ruling significantly changed the scope of discrimination (civil rights) laws. Employers now needed to examine all of their hiring requirements to determine if the job qualifications they listed were actually necessary for employees to perform their job functions. For example, if a company required all employees to have a high school diploma, the company now needed to analyze whether or not the cleaning staff, for example, needed this diploma to adequately fulfill their job duties. If not, the diploma requirement was potentially discriminating.

The answer to this problem was so-called affirmative action—which created new challenges. The basic idea of affirmative action was that companies were to broaden their selection base for employee candidates and then predict, out of their pool of potential workers, what the composition of workers should be (racially, in terms of gender, and so forth). Periodically, companies would then check their actual employee demographics against their stated composition goals—and then adjust, as necessary. Even if a company's actual group of employees did not match its stated goals, if the company was hiring in good faith, the courts declared that this was enough.

Controversy ensued, with many Americans understanding the ruling to mean that companies needed to match the predicted goals—fulfill their *quotas*—or be guilty of discrimination. The situation became even more complicated when courts did order certain companies to hire precise—and rigid—numbers rather than by flexible target goals.

By the mid-1970s, employers faced another onerous problem: reverse discrimination lawsuits filed by white men who claimed that they were not hired for a job strictly because they were male and/or Caucasian. They would claim that they were better qualified for a particular position than the successful applicant, but not hired because of affirmative action constraints.

The Civil Rights Act of 1964 also empowered the federal government to force local school systems to desegregate. Many school districts in the South did not comply with court orders requiring desegregation. As a result, the 1971 Supreme Court case, *Swann v. Mecklenburg,* ruled that school districts did not need to precisely reflect the racial composition of their city, but that all-white or all-black schools must show that they did not exist due to segregation practices. Furthermore, this ruling stated that busing was a legitimate way to racially integrate school systems. Forced busing began to occur throughout the country and continued through the 1990s in some locales.

Although many people fought for civil rights during the 1970s, two deserve specific mention. One of the better-known civil rights leaders of the 1970s—the Reverend Jesse Jackson (1941–)—began his work in the 1960s, organizing marches and sit-in protests. In 1965, Jackson met Martin Luther King Jr. and began working for his organization, the Southern Christian Leadership Conference (SCLC). Jackson was with King when the civil rights leader was assassinated.

In 1970, Jackson led a march to Illinois's state capital, raising consciousness of hunger. As a result, the state increased funding for school lunches. In 1971, Jackson formed his own organization, People United to Save Humanity (PUSH), and continued to work for economic betterment for the blacks of Chicago and throughout the nation, and he kept demanding social and political improvements, as well. He conducted weekly broadcasts on the radio and created awards to honor blacks for various achievements. He also created PUSH-Excel to assist low-income black youth and help them stay in school and find jobs.

Ralph D. Abernathy (1926–1990) also fought for civil rights through most of the 1970s. In 1957, he cofounded the SCLC with Martin Luther King Jr. The two men agreed upon the philosophy of peaceful protests for civil rights, creating this phrase for their motto: "Not one hair of one head of one person should be harmed." While serving as the pastor of the Baptist Church in Montgomery, Alabama, Abernathy was extremely vocal about the need for desegregation and for equal rights for blacks.

After King's assassination, Abernathy took over the leadership role of the SCLC. In 1970,

his group formed Politics '70 for Representative Government, a platform for political gains for blacks. In 1971, Politics '70 for Representative Government worked with the National Welfare Organization and the People's Coalition for Peace and Justice to form the "War Against Repression," which was a series of mass protests that led to the restoration of welfare rights. Over the next few years, the group focused on registering new voters, which led to blacks being elected in locales that had never before had black representation. In 1976, it rallied its energies to support the Humphrey-Hawkins Full Employment program. In 1977, Abernathy resigned from SCLC to run unsuccessfully for Georgia's legislature.

The Feminist Movement

Perhaps the most hotly debated piece of legislation of the 1970s was the Equal Rights Amendment—or the ERA. The ERA's language was written to specifically state that the U.S. government must provide equal rights to both genders.

Legislators had introduced the ERA in every session of Congress, starting in 1923, with no success. That changed in 1967 when a new organization led by Betty Friedan—the National Organization for Women (NOW)—formed, pledging its dedicated and concerted efforts toward passing this amendment. The House of Representatives approved the ERA in 1971 and the Senate did the same on March 22, 1972. This approved piece of legislation included a typical phrase in the proposing clause that set a 7-year time span for 38 individual states to ratify this amendment. By 1977, 35 states had voted for ERA's passage.

Also in 1977, NOW held its first national convention in Houston, Texas. It announced that 450 groups, representing 50 million Americans, had endorsed and were supporting the amendment. NOW used this occasion to publicly request an extension of the time available for ratification; they argued that the Constitution places no limits on amendment passage, so the seven-year limit was artificial.

In 1978 NOW declared a state of emergency for the ERA and organized a march on Washington in which 100,000 supporters participated. In large part because of this march, Congress set a new deadline for ERA ratification: June 30, 1982.

Meanwhile, opponents of the ERA fought to slow down the momentum. One well-organized and vocal grassroots effort to prevent the amendment's ratification was led by social and political conservative Phyllis Schlafly, whose campaign became known as "Stop the ERA." Schlafly stated that if the ERA passed, women would be drafted to fight in wars, the government would begin to fund abortions, and same-sex marriages would become legal. These arguments were similar to those made pre-1920, when women fought for suffrage—but, this time, they were more effective. The amendment was not ratified.

Opposition to the ERA often signaled disapproval of the entire feminist movement, also called the women's liberation movement, or, simply, "women's lib." The feminist movement really was a series of overlapping movements that had one common goal: feminists were fighting for equal social, political, and/or economic rights between men and women.

Individual feminists' goals ranged from practical demands that would improve the overall conditions of life for women to more radical philosophical visions. Some women wanted economic benefits: "Equal pay for equal work," paid maternity leaves, more favorable divorce agreements, federally funded child care, and the opportunity to work in male-dominated fields. Others wanted easier access to birth control and/or legalized abortion. Still others wanted to change the structure of language, eliminating the use of "man" in words such as fireman, policeman, or mankind.

What women did not do in documented reality, although the notion is certainly well entrenched in myth and memory, is burn bras in support of the feminist movement. Many women stopped wearing bras, which would naturally lead to the apparel being thrown away—and one theory suggests that the tossing away of bras melded with the image of draft cards being burned.

A significant volume of feminist material was written in the 1970s, including Betty Friedan's *The Feminine Mystique.* In 1972, Gloria Steinem and others who identified with feminism began publishing a monthly magazine, *Ms.,* advocating their cause.

ROE V. WADE

Roe v. Wade still provokes extremely emotional reactions, decades later. At the heart of the case rests the thorny and challenging ethical question of when life begins—at conception or at birth, or perhaps somewhere in between.

During the early 1970s, people marched for and against abortion rights, and passionately debated the issue and attempted to persuade others to their viewpoints. Those who felt that abortions should be legalized called themselves "prochoice," whereas those opposing its legalization were "pro-life."

The controversial case that challenged and ultimately overturned abortion laws began simply enough when a single woman in Texas named Norma McCorvey attempted to abort her third child. At that time, Texas law stated that an abortion was legal only when pregnancy put the pregnant mother's health at risk. Although she failed in her attempts to abort, McCorvey met two attorneys—Sarah Weedington and Linda Coffee— who were willing to represent her and attempt to change the prevailing antiabortion laws.

On March 3, 1970, McCorvey's attorneys filed a complaint against the Dallas County district attorney, asking the court to declare the Texas abortion law unconstitutional and to order officials to stop enforcing this law. To protect McCorvey's privacy, the case was filed under the name of Jane Roe.

Three judges heard the case on May 22, 1970. As anticipated, the assistant district attorney claimed that McCorvey could not sue because the statutes were enforced against doctors, not against pregnant women who chose to abort. Although that was true, the court allowed the case to continue. The assistant district attorney also asked "Roe" to come forward. She declined, stating that if she were identified, she would face discrimination in future employment. Furthermore, the issue of who bears children, she claimed, is private.

Weedington and Coffee changed the status of the case to a class action lawsuit to argue the rights of all pregnant women who may choose to abort.

The state defended its law as a protection of the rights of the unborn. When the court asked

Weedington at what point she felt the state did have a responsibility to the unborn, she said it was when a fetus could live outside of its mother.

On June 17, 1970, the court overturned the Texas abortion laws, stating that they "must be declared unconstitutional because they deprive single women and married couples of their right, secured by the Ninth Amendment, to choose whether to have children."[3]

The court approved declarative relief and found the law unconstitutional, but it did not give injunctive relief, which would have ordered the state to stop enforcing the law. Because of the declarative relief provided, the state could appeal directly to the Supreme Court rather than go through the appeals process.

When the Supreme Court heard *Roe v. Wade* in December 1971, Weedington implored them to allow women to make their own decisions about bearing children, free from governmental inference. She presented the Constitution as a document that conferred rights to people at birth, not at conception. The defense disputed this interpretation, which caused the court to ask why, if abortion is murder, women seeking and receiving abortions were not prosecuted. The state admitted to not having answers to all the legal nuances.

The Supreme Court did not immediately rule on the case. With only seven justices sitting on the Supreme Court—two had recently retired—it postponed the case until October, when full court would be in session. On January 22, 1973, the Supreme Court finally ruled on *Roe v. Wade,* stating that one of the original purposes of antiabortion laws was to protect women from a dangerous procedure—abortion. That concern no longer applied. It also stated that, whether it applied the 9th or the 14th Amendment to the case, it seemed clear that a woman's reproductive rights were included in the implied right to privacy. Furthermore, the court ruled, it could not find any reference to constitutional rights applying to the unborn. As far as whether life started at conception or at birth, the judges declined to proffer an opinion.

Balancing the rights of a pregnant woman with the unborn's right to life, the court determined by a vote of 7–2 that first trimester abortions were legal. The state could regulate but not prohibit second-trimester abortions, and could deny third-trimester abortions altogether. Justices William H. Rehnquist and Byron R. White dissented over the ruling in *Roe v. Wade,* citing a lack of constitutional justification for the decision.

The court also ruled on *Doe v. Bolton,* a Georgia abortion-related case that reduced the state's control over who could receive abortions and in what facility. These two rulings caused abortions to become legal in all 50 states, invalidating laws in 46.

GENDER ISSUES

On June 27, 1969, New York police raided the Stonewall Inn, a popular gay bar in Greenwich Village. The raid itself was not unusual; typically, police would arrest some of the more flamboyant patrons as others disappeared into the shadows. The resistance to this particular raid, however, was more dramatic, and many historians mark this occasion as the official start to the gay liberation movement. Fights and riots broke out in the streets after the raid and continued for several days—and are now known as the Stonewall Riots.

Why the Stonewall reaction differed from what transpired in other similar situations is not known, although patrons were frustrated over the multitude of recent raids. Some sources suggest that the humid and hotter-than-normal weather caused tempers to become shorter. Regardless of the underlying reasons, the uprising heated up, with many protestors chanting "Gay Power" as the police attempted to regain control in the streets.

The Stonewall riots brought the gay and lesbian cause to national attention, and activists used the momentum to organize. One month after the Stonewall Riots, the Gay Liberation Front (GLF) formed. This radical leftist organization, created in New York, protested the marginalization of homosexuals and also supported other causes, such as ending racial discrimination and supporting third world countries. Other GLF organizations soon started up around the country and the world. In 1971, the Gay and Lesbian Activists Alliance formed in Washington, D.C.

On the first anniversary of the Stonewall Riots, 5,000 gay and lesbian advocates marched in commemoration. Some of these marchers gained the courage to "come out of the closet" because of the emerging public solidarity of numerous gay and lesbian movements.

Along with the growing number of organized groups and marches, the volume of publications targeted to the gay and lesbian community increased significantly, post-Stonewall. Overall, this literature helped many who felt marginalized find a sense of community, and it also helped many to "out" themselves to friends, family, and perhaps the world at large.

In the years following the riots, some larger cities created statutes that forbade discrimination based upon sexual orientation. In 1975, the Civil Service Commission eliminated the ban on homosexuals for most federal jobs, although the military remained a significant exception. Several states repealed their sodomy laws, gay community centers received federal funding to provide services, and, in 1973, the American Psychiatric Association removed homosexuality as a listed psychiatric disorder.

Religious groups struggled with the issues surrounding gay and lesbian integration. Two months before the Stonewall Riots, the United Church of Christ (UCC) publicly declared its opposition to any law that criminalized homosexual acts performed in private between consenting adults. It also stated its position that the U.S. military should not discriminate based upon a person's sexual orientation.

In 1972, the UCC ordained William Johnson, the first openly gay clergyman confirmed in a mainstream Protestant congregation. The following year, the UCC stated its openness to clergymen of all sexual orientations, and, in 1975, it stated its support of equal rights for all, regardless of orientation. In 1977, the UCC confirmed its first openly lesbian pastor, Anne Holmes. The Reformed Judaism community was also more accepting of gay and lesbian rights than many other religious groups, but in 1978, the president of the Rabbinical Alliance of America, the Orthodox Abraham B. Hecht, recommended an "all-out campaign" against the legitimacy of gay rights.

In 1975, the National Council of Churches voted to support the rights of gays and lesbians, but not for their inclusion as clergy. That same year, the Presbyterian Church agreed that homosexual behavior was not banned by the Scriptures but did not recognize the Presbyterian Gay Caucus. It also rejected the ordaining gays without the condition of celibacy. The Episcopal Church ordained an openly lesbian woman in 1977; the following year, Episcopalian bishops condemned homosexuality.

Many gays and lesbians who left other denominations formed their own churches, often under the Universal Fellowship of Metropolitan Community Churches; approximately 20,000 people joined this group by the end of the decade. The group, however, was rejected for admission by the National Council of Churches.

Overall, though, as the 1970s progressed, gays and lesbians found increasing numbers of communities, social agencies, and religious congregations that accepted their lifestyles and rights to equality.

In 1977, however, the tide began to turn, as singer, former beauty queen, and current orange juice spokesperson Anita Bryant spearheaded a public campaign to overturn legislation in Miami-Dade County, Florida, that granted civil rights to gays and lesbians. Although hers was not the first such campaign, it was the most publicized. On June 7, 1977, voters repealed the civil rights recently granted to gays and lesbians by a margin of 69 percent to 31 percent. After this repeal, the gay rights movement seemed to lose much of its momentum.

As the 1970s progressed, more distinctive identities and goals began to split some gay rights movements into ones focusing on gay men and others on lesbian women. Lesbian organizations also formed separately from gay liberation groups, with many lesbians scorning the possibility that a gay man could understand the dual challenges of being both gay and female.

From the very beginning of the decade, lesbian feminists also fought to become the core of the feminist movement. In May 1970, a radical group of 20 women who labeled themselves "Racialesbians," led by novelist Rita Mae Brown, marched onto a New York stage at the Congress to Unite Women. Uninvited, they wore shirts imprinted with "Lavender Menace" and demanded the opportunity to read their essay,

"The Woman-Identified Woman." They insisted that lesbians served as the forefront of the women's liberation movement, as they partnered with other women rather than with men.

CRIME

During the 1970s, the constitutionality of capital punishment commanded the attention of the Supreme Court—and that of the nation. When Gary Gilmore, a convicted murderer, refused to appeal his conviction and sentence, and, in fact, insisted upon receiving the death penalty in an expedient manner, the debate over executions reached a fever pitch.

The Supreme Court during this decade began requiring judges and juries to consider the offender as an individual, as well as to reflect upon the mitigating circumstances of the crime before sentencing.

In 1977, with the path cleared for judicious death penalties, the state of Utah executed Gary Gilmore. He was sentenced to die in November 1976; after announcing that he was not going to appeal his sentence, the American Civil Liberties Union (ACLU) and the National Association for the Advancement of Colored People (NAACP) fought to stay his execution, fearful of the precedent that his death would create. For two months, judicial stays were granted against the express wishes of the condemned prisoner; the ACLU fought for a reprieve up until 10 minutes before Gilmore's actual execution on January 17, 1977.

This execution deeply permeated the culture of the era. On December 11, 1976, about one month prior to Gilmore's death, the cast of *Saturday Night Live* sang "Let's Kill Gary Gilmore for Christmas," set to the tune of *Winter Wonderland*. Author Norman Mailer published a Gilmore book, *The Executioner's Song,* in 1979; in 1982, Tommy Lee Jones starred as Gilmore in a television movie, also called *The Executioner's Song.* Jones won an Emmy for his portrayal.

During an era filled with divisive opinions about capital punishment, America saw an increase in both the number of murders and in people who favored the death penalty. In 1960, 9,000 murders were committed; this number increased to 20,000 in 1975.[4] The National Association of Evangelicals (NAE)—which represented more than 10 million conservative Christians and 47 denominations—and the Moral Majority were among the religious groups that supported capital punishment sentences.

The most famous murderers of the era—those involved in the "Charles Manson trials"—benefited from divisiveness about capital punishment. On August 8, 1969, Charles Manson told his followers, a group that became known as "the Family," that it was time for "helter-skelter." Over the next two nights, the group killed seven people, including pregnant actress Sharon Tate (her husband, movie producer Roman Polanski, was in London).

After being arrested, the group showed no remorse, only an undying loyalty to Charles Manson. Prosecutor Vincent Bugliosi promised immunity to Family member Linda Kasabian, who had committed no murders—and she testified for 18 days. The defense attempted to rest without having its clients testify, but three female defendants insisted and the judge ruled that their wish to testify must be honored. Manson also testified, but without the jury present.

The jury deliberated for one week; it declared all defendants guilty of murder in the first degree and all were sentenced to death. Another Family member had a separate trial with the identical outcome. When the Supreme Court declared the death penalty as unconstitutional in 1972, however, all sentences were commuted to life sentences in prison.

After Manson was imprisoned in the summer of 1970, he handed over the control of his organization to follower Lynette "Squeaky" Fromme. On September 5, 1975, Fromme attempted to assassinate President Gerald Ford, but her gun failed to operate and the Secret Service intervened. She later claimed that she had tried to kill Ford so that Charles Manson could appear as a witness at her trial—and therefore have a venue to share his vision for the world.

Another infamous serial killer of the 1970s was David Berkowitz, better known as "Son of Sam." He killed six and wounded several others, starting in July 1976. After three murders occurred in the Bronx, police determined that the same .44-caliber gun had been used in all three. Publicity increased when, on April 17, 1977, Berkowitz murdered a young couple and then left behind a letter stating that his vampire father, named Sam, had ordered the killings. Although police did not release this letter to the general public, they allowed a few journalists, including Jimmy Breslin of the *New York Daily News,* to see the note. After Breslin dropped a few hints in his column about the murders, Berkowitz wrote to him directly and the *Daily News* labeled the still-unidentified killer the "Son of Sam."

On July 31, 1977, the killer attacked again, killing a female—his sixth victim—and injuring a male. After that shooting, however, a woman spotted someone tearing up a parking ticket and police traced Berkowitz through this ticket. Under questioning, he claimed that Sam Carr was his neighbor, and that Sam's black Labrador, Harvey, communicated Sam's requests to kill to Berkowitz. Berkowitz pled guilty to the six murders and received a prison sentence of 365 years.

One of the most publicized crime cases of the decade began with a kidnapping and ended with armed robbery. On February 4, 1974, the Symbionese Liberation Army (SLA) kidnapped heiress Patricia Campbell Hearst, aged 19, from an apartment she shared with her fiancé, Steven Weed. The group first attempted to swap Hearst for imprisoned SLA members; when that failed, it made ransom demands. The Hearst family donated $6 million worth of food to the needy, but that did not result in Patty's release.

On April 15, 1974, photographs appeared wherein Hearst participated in a bank robbery with the SLA; she held an assault rifle. Shortly thereafter, she communicated that her new name was Tania, in honor of Che Guevara's lover, and that she believed in the Marxist goals and philosophies of her kidnappers. Authorities issued an arrest warrant for Hearst, and, in September, she and her captors were arrested.

Hearst claimed that she had been brainwashed. In her trial, which began on January 15, 1976, she testified that her kidnappers blindfolded her and locked her in a closet, where they physically and sexually abused her. Her lawyers advanced the theory that because of this abuse, she began relating to her captors, who controlled her life. That strategy failed, though; in March 1976, Patty

A publicity picture that the Symbionese Liberation Army (SLA) released of the kidnapped heiress Patty Hearst in 1974 to show that she was well, had begun to agree with their philosophy, and was calling herself "Tania." Photo is from the film *Guerrilla: The Taking of Patty Hearst* (2004). Directed by Robert Stone. Courtesy of Photofest.

Hearst was convicted and sentenced to prison. President Jimmy Carter pardoned her about three years later, granting her release on February 1, 1979.

Another prominent criminal act that captured the attention of America in the 1970s occurred in Munich, Germany between a group of Arab militants and the Israeli athletes participating in the Olympics. On September 5, 1972, with only five days remaining in the Olympics, eight militant Arabs stormed the village, killing two of Israel's athletes and kidnapping nine more. They demanded the release of more than 200 Palestinian prisoners, along with two Germans jailed for terrorism. No agreement was reached; the kidnappers attempted to take the hostages to the airport, where German sharpshooters shot and killed three of the kidnappers. In the fighting and gunfire that ensued, all the hostages died.

Olympic competition ceased for 24 hours. After a memorial service attended by more than

80,000 people, the games resumed and were completed. They continued without the participation of Jewish American athlete Mark Spitz, though, who had already won seven gold medals.

WAR IN SOUTHEAST ASIA

Shortly after noon on May 4, 1970, a volley of gunfire at Kent State University in Kent, Ohio, brought the war home in a bloody and terrifying way. Kent State students were protesting the United States' involvement in the war in Southeast Asia, more specifically the invasion by American troops into Cambodia. The war had appeared to be winding down in 1969, and students were distressed over the escalation in hostilities. In response to the American invasion into Cambodia, Kent State students staged a demonstration on the Commons on May 1, 1970. Around midnight, people began tossing rocks and beer bottles downtown, breaking the window of a bank and setting off an alarm. Looting followed, and, by the time the police arrived, they encountered a group of about 100 people, some students, some not; bonfires had been set and it took an hour to disperse the crowd.

On May 2, Kent's mayor, Leroy Satrom, declared a state of emergency and asked Ohio's governor, James Rhodes, to send in Ohio's National Guard to keep order. By the time the Guard arrived, at about 10 P.M., the campus ROTC building, already slated for demolition, was on fire. A crowd of about 1,000 cheered as the building blazed; some threw rocks at firefighters and police.

The following day, nearly 1,000 Guardsmen were in Kent. Governor Rhodes compared the protesters and looters to communists, Nazis, and revolutionaries. He announced that he would take whatever steps necessary to place the area under martial law, but he did not follow through on his pledge. That night, the National Guard used tear gas to break up student demonstrations; it's possible that they believed that martial law existed—or perhaps they were fearful of yet another violent protest.

On May 4, the situation escalated out of control. University officials, believing that Rhodes had in fact declared a state of martial law, distributed 12,000 flyers stating that the war protest rally planned by students was cancelled. Nevertheless,

about 2,000 students met, and so the police and the Ohio National Guard once again attempted to disperse the crowd. Their tear gas, though, was ineffective in the wind. Some students tossed rocks at the Guard, along with empty tear gas canisters. At this point, Brigadier General Robert Canterbury ordered the National Guardsmen to load their weapons.

Some Guardsmen, with bayonets attached to their guns, attempted to advance on the protesters, but they found themselves trapped on a football field surrounded on three sides by a fence. They retreated, and, after reaching the top of Blanket Hill, 28 Guardsmen fired 61 to 67 shots into the crowd. An officer of the National Guard later said the men thought they had detected sniper fire, so they discharged their weapons.

These shots killed four students—Allison Krause, Jeffrey Miller, Sandra Scheuer, and William Schroeder—and wounded nine others. Krause and Miller had participated in the protests, while Scheuer and Schroeder were simply traveling between classes; Schroeder was in fact an ROTC member. One member of the National Guard was injured.

Intense anger erupted after the shootings, and campus authorities, fearful of further escalation by the protestors and potential retaliation by the National Guard, attempted to calm the students and entice them to disperse.

After the shootings, many colleges and universities—and even high schools and elementary schools—closed as millions of students protested the deaths. Meanwhile, Kent State itself remained closed for six weeks; during that time period, about 100,000 people marched in Washington against the war.

On October 16, 25 people—including one faculty member—were indicted on charges connected with burning the ROTC building on May 2nd or for incidents connected to the May 4th demonstration; those indicted became known as the "Kent 25." The majority of charges were dropped for lack of evidence, although one conviction, one acquittal, and two guilty pleas resulted. No charges were filed against any members of the National Guard.

In an attempt to establish ways to prevent such tragedies in the future, Kent State University created the Center for Peaceful Change in 1971. Eventually renamed the Center for Applied Conflict Management, it is the site of one of the first conflict resolution degree programs in the country.

A number of songs, books, and documentaries were created in response to the tragedy. Perhaps the most widely recognized is "Ohio," a song written by Neil Young for Crosby, Stills, Nash, and Young. The song refers to the National Guard as Nixon's "tin soldiers" and many radio stations refused to play it because of its antiwar and anti-Nixon messages.

Although America's presence in Cambodia lasted only 60 days, the United States remained entrenched in the Vietnam War until 1973. The antiwar movement remained strong with opponents coming from a wide variety of political, socioeconomic, and cultural backgrounds.

By summer 1972 Nixon was pursuing détente with both China and the Soviet Union, and he wanted to focus his energies on those initiatives, not on the stagnating war in Southeast Asia. The North Vietnamese feared their predicament if those two superpowers formed good relationships with the United States and so, by October 1972, a ceasefire agreement was crafted. In this agreement, the United States would leave Vietnam, the prisoners of war (POWs) would be returned, and a political compromise that affected South Vietnam would go into effect.

This agreement fell apart, in large part because South Vietnam's leader, Nguyen Van Thieu, was not consulted or included in the negotiations. Nixon then offered Thieu $4 billion in military equipment and he agreed to re-enter the war if North Vietnam did not abide by the peace agreement. On January 8, 1973, peace talks resumed, and all parties signed a cease-fire agreement on January 27. By March, all U.S. troops returned home, with the exception of military advisors and Marines protecting American installations. Of the 3 million men who served in Vietnam, 58,000 lost their lives, 150,000 were seriously wounded, and about 1,000 men were missing in action. The war continued between the South and North Vietnamese until Hanoi overpowered its enemy on April 30, 1975, during the "Fall of Saigon."

American veterans did not always receive the best treatment after returning home. A percentage of the people who opposed the conflict transferred their antiwar sentiments, postwar, to those who had fought in Southeast Asia. Post-traumatic stress disorder (PTSD), an anxiety disorder with debilitating recurring nightmares and flashbacks of traumatic events in Vietnam, was not unusual for returning Vietnam veterans and added significantly to their readjustment issues.

Other veterans suffered deleterious effects from the herbicide Agent Orange, which was sprayed in South Vietnam by U.S. military forces wishing to strip away jungle cover to prevent the North Vietnamese from hiding its troops. Diseases connected to Agent Orange exposure include Hodgkin's disease, multiple myeloma, respiratory cancers, and soft-tissue sarcoma, among others. Moreover, children born to men exposed to Agent Orange were at risk for many significant birth defects.

Meanwhile, other families agonized over the fate of their missing loved ones, veterans who did not return home from the war but who were not reported among the dead. In 1971, Mary Hoff, the wife of an MIA ("missing in action" soldier) created a stark black-and-white flag that symbolized the uncertain fate of the POWs and MIAs and reminded Americans to remember them and to support efforts for either their safe return or for information about their final disposition. Many Americans also wore bracelets engraved with the name of one of these soldiers, even though the wearer did not necessarily know the soldier personally.

POLLUTION

City after city, state after state, had essentially failed in their efforts to protect their air and their water, their land, and the health of their citizens. By 1970, city skylines were so polluted that in many places it was all but impossible to see from one city skyscraper to another. Rivers were fouled with raw sewage and toxic chemicals. One actually caught on fire.[5]

The date was June 22, 1969; the place was the Cuyahoga River located in Cleveland, Ohio; the speaker was former EPA Administrator Carol Browner. The fact that a river could catch on fire was seen as a sure sign that pollution was rampant, and it seemed to indicate that local and state regulations did not suffice to prevent further polluting. The burning of the Cuyahoga served as partial impetus, then, for the passage of the Federal Water Pollution Control Act of 1972, its initial three-year budget of $24.6 billion, and its Clean Lakes Program. Although the fact that rivers stopped burning was used as a symbol of the success of the act and other similar acts of Congress, the Cuyahoga—or, rather, the oil and debris floating on its surface—had caught fire numerous times before, and this had occurred at other waterways as well. In fact, cleanup efforts began well before the federal government intervened.

Awareness of environmental issues rose to the forefront in the 1960s, with the National Environmental Policy Act (NEPA) serving as baseline legislature for the onslaught of environmental laws passed by Congress in the 1970s. NEPA required all federal agencies to consider environmental factors in their decision making, including the future impact of their policies on the environment and potential alternative policies.

To continue to address overall environmental concerns, the federal government created the Environment Protection Agency (EPA) in 1970. Since that time, the EPA has served as the primary agency responsible for establishing federal environment policy.

Other actions taken by the EPA and/or Congress in the 1970s include the 1970 Clean Air Act, which regulated auto emissions and set clean air standards, and the restriction of lead-based paint in cribs and on toys (1971). In 1972 DDT, a cancer-causing pesticide, was banned and the Marine Mammal Protection Act was passed.

Congress enacted the Land and Water Resources Conservation Act of 1977 (RCA) to address farmland erosion; the Soil Conservation Service therefore began monitoring soil and water. The Forest and Rangeland Renewable Resources Planning Act of 1974 created a plan whereby the Secretary of Agriculture assessed the forests every 10 years. The Eastern Wilderness Act of 1975 added more than 200,000 acres of wild land to the eastern national forests and other bills protected more than 350,000 acres of wilderness under the National Wilderness Preservation System. Acts passed in 1976 and 1978 strengthened the legislative mandates to protect and manage these lands. Numerous laws were passed to protect farmlands, water, and wilderness areas. Industries sought to stem the tide of regulations that added significant financial burdens to their companies. The best-known clash between environmentalists and industry involved the snail darter and the Tennessee Valley Authority (TVA). During the early 1970s, the TVA spent $116 million constructing a dam on the Little Tennessee River; construction stopped in 1977, however, when environmentalists cited the 1973 Endangered Species Act and noted that the snail darter's habitat was being destroyed in the quest to build the dam. The Supreme Court sided with the environmentalists, but in 1979, President Jimmy Carter signed legislation that allowed the dam project to continue.

ENDANGERED SPECIES ACT

In 1973, Congress passed the Endangered Species Act, which considerably strengthened similar legislation from the 1960s. Lists of threatened or endangered species were created and all federal agencies were required to consider the conservation of these species in everything the agencies did; moreover, these agencies could no longer authorize, fund, or carry out any action that might jeopardize a listed species—or its habitat. The bald eagle came to represent the endangered species of the world, in large part because it also symbolized America's culture, its people, and its sense of freedom.

EARTH DAY DEBATE

According to some sources, the founder of Earth Day was John McConnell who, on October 3, 1969, submitted a proposal to the San Francisco Board of Supervisors requesting that a special date and time be set aside to honor the earth; the mayor issued the proclamation, as did officials in a few other cities in California. This resolution created a day to celebrate global unity, to share concerns about the planet's future, and to remind people of their responsibilities toward the earth. The resolution suggested that people plant trees and flowers, clean rivers and wooded areas, and observe an hour of quiet reflection.

McConnell and his committee celebrated Earth Day on March 21, the first day of spring. On April 22 of that year, the Environment Teach-In honored its own Earth Day, an event which garnered national attention. In 1971, Senator Gaylord Nelson proposed an annual Earth Week, to be honored the third week of April.

According to proponents of McConnell as Earth Day founder, the Environment Teach-In didn't turn in a proposal using the term *Earth Day* until January 1970, a couple of months after their proposal was already submitted to San Francisco officials. Those who purport that Senator Nelson actually founded Earth Day—and this includes former President Bill Clinton who awarded Nelson the Presidential Medal of Freedom as the "Father of Earth Day"—state that Nelson had announced at a Seattle conference in September 1969 that there would be grassroot environmental commemorations across the country in the spring of 1970.

According to the Environmental Protection Agency, 20 million Americans participated in Earth Day activities on April 22, 1970, including 10 million school-aged children who picked up trash in their neighborhoods and local nature spots. Congress adjourned for the day while 10,000 people celebrated by the Washington Monument.

Earth Day projects tended to focus on very specific tasks that an individual or small group of people could accomplish, such as weeding a public park and cleaning up the surrounding litter, rather than large undertakings that would require government action.

LOVE CANAL, NEW YORK

In a 36-city-block area of Niagara Falls, New York—known as the Love Canal—doctors and residents noted high rates of birth defects, miscarriages, chromosomal deformities, and cancer. Investigations revealed unusually high rates of toxins in the soil, and it was discovered that many houses and one school were built over nearly 20,000 tons of toxic chemical wastes that had been stored underground in the 1940s and 1950s in a manner now deemed illegal and dangerous. Chemicals had leaked into the soil and

risen to the surface. In 1978, the government evacuated families from the area and President Jimmy Carter declared the Love Canal a national emergency, the first man-made disaster to receive that designation.

Ironically, the Love Canal was initially conceived of as a "dream community" by William T. Love in the late nineteenth century. He intended to dig a short canal by the Niagara River so that water could power his proposed city and shipping concerns could bring commerce to his town. Workers started to dig the canal, but financial issues combined with an evolving understanding of how to transmit electricity halted his plans. The partial ditch turned into a dump site in the 1920s, and companies began storing industrial waste in the area.

In 1953, the Hooker Chemical Company covered the site with earth and sold it to the city for $1. Deed transfer papers listed both a "warning" about chemical wastes and a statement absolving Hooker from assuming any liability post-transfer. As time passed, however, new homeowners were not cautioned about potential dangers from the chemicals—or even given the information that their homes and school rested above a former chemical landfill. One hundred homes and one school building were initially constructed over the chemical dump, transforming William T. Love's vision of a dream city into one fraught with nightmares. By 1978, 800 single-dwelling homes and 240 low-income apartments existed in Love Canal.

Heavy rainfall triggered the climatic disaster. As a *New York Times* reporter who visited the site wrote, "Corroding waste-disposal drums could be seen breaking up through the grounds of backyards. Trees and gardens were turning black and dying. One entire swimming pool had been popped up from its foundation, afloat now on a small sea of chemicals. Puddles of noxious substances were…in their yards, some were in their basements, others yet were on the school grounds. Everywhere the air had a faint, choking smell. Children returned from play with burns on their hands and faces."[6]

The chemical company paid more than $20 million to the families and city officials of Niagara Falls; in 1994, the company settled with the state of New York for $98 million, and, in 1995, they agreed to pay the federal government $129 million for cleanup. Nevertheless, as a 1978 report given to the New York Legislature stated, the devastating effects of Love Canal, in terms of human suffering and environmental damage, can never be genuinely measured. Even more dire was the fact that unsafe chemical storage was not an isolated event; in 1979, 17,000 drums of leaking chemicals were discovered in a Kentucky town.

THREE MILE ISLAND NUCLEAR SCARE

Many Americans favored finding ways to supplement or replace the use of fossil fuel as energy, and this sentiment increased during the Arab oil embargo of 1973. Some believed that nuclear energy might suit this purpose, while others feared the danger of radioactive energy. *The China Syndrome* (1979), starring Jane Fonda, only increased this fear and caused many to believe that a nuclear meltdown would destroy the earth.

At 4:00 A.M. on March 28, 1979, the Three Mile Island nuclear power plant was in danger of becoming the site of a real-life radioactive disaster. Located by Middletown, Pennsylvania, the plant experienced failure in the nonnuclear portion of its site when the feed water pumps stopped working. The steam generators could no longer remove heat from the building, and the turbine and the reactor automatically shut down in response.

This increased pressure in the nuclear part of the building, and a relief valve that should have decreased this pressure did not operate appropriately and the core element overheated. The instruments that measured coolants in the core provided confusing information, and so, when alarms flashed, staff did not respond in a way that improved the situation or reduced the risk of a radioactive disaster. Approximately half of the core melted during the beginning stages of this accident, and the building was evacuated except for key personnel by 11:00 A.M. By evening, the core appeared to have cooled and stabilized.

Governmental agencies did not anticipate this near disaster and the small amounts of radiation measured outside the reactor caused significant concern. On the morning of Friday, March 30,

new worries arose when radiation was released from the auxiliary part of the building. As a safety measure, the most vulnerable population within five miles of the Three Mile Island nuclear plant, including pregnant woman and young children, were asked to evacuate the area. Throughout Saturday, March 31, experts discussed the large hydrogen bubble located in the container that held the reactor core; if this bubble exploded, the situation could become quite dangerous. By April 1, it was determined that because of a lack of oxygen in the pressure vessel, the bubble could not burn or burst; also, the experts had already succeeded in reducing the size and scope of the bubble.

According to government reporting, a combination of human error and design deficiencies caused the accident. Fortunately, the worst-case scenario—melting nuclear fuel causing a breach in the walls of the building and releasing extremely hazardous radiation—did not occur. No deaths or injuries resulted, but according to the U.S. Nuclear Regulatory Commission, the crisis did bring about significant changes in emergency response planning and training.

Post-crisis, governmental agencies and other independent bodies studied the level of released radiation and determined that the average person had been exposed to approximately one millirem of radiation, which is about one-sixth of the amount given off by a full set of chest x-rays. Nevertheless, human, animal, and plant life continued to be closely monitored. Some experts claim that Three Mile Island came within 30 to 45 seconds of a complete meltdown and more than 100,000 people rallied in Washington, D.C. to protest nuclear power as energy. And, although nine new nuclear power plants opened in 1979, 11 others—that had been planned but not yet started—were not built.

GREENPEACE

This proenvironmental group formed in the 1970s to protest the nuclear testing done by the United States in the Pacific Ocean. The members hired a boat and attempted to travel to the testing site; bad weather thwarted their trip, but also gave them national attention. In 1975, members of Greenpeace stationed a boat between whales and those hunting them from Japan and the Soviet Union—and, although they seldom stopped the hunting, their bloody documentaries encouraged the "Save the Whale" movement. This group did something similar for baby seals the following year. When they discovered that hunters clubbed these animals to death, Greenpeace members sprayed a harmless dye on the animals that rendered their fur useless for resale.

DESTROYING THE OZONE

Propellants used in deodorant and hair spray, among other items, harm the environment by slowly destroying the ozone layer that surrounds the earth. Because the ozone layer prevents harmful ultraviolet rays from reaching the earth's surface, experts in the 1970s predicted a rise in skin cancer and cataracts as the ozone deteriorated. Environmentalists therefore proposed a ban on fluorocarbon gases used in the propellants; although this was met with opposition from industry, by the time that the FDA banned the substance in 1979, most companies had already found more acceptable alternatives.

FAMILY, RELIGION, AND TRADITIONAL VALUES

Family

During the 1970s, family sizes dropped, with some experts suggesting that the uncertain economy and higher rates of unemployment caused families to decide to have fewer children. Other experts pointed to the surge of women in the workplace and the feminist movement; careers sometimes delayed—or even replaced—the urge for parenthood. Moreover, the increased availability and acceptance of birth control—and abortion—gave women more freedom in determining the sizes of their families.

Meanwhile, divorces increased significantly in the 1970s. In 1965, 480,000 divorces were recorded; this number increased to more than 1 million in 1975.[7] The rising divorce rate, in part, could be attributed to the so-called no-fault divorce laws that began to be passed in the United States. Pioneered by California and effective in that state on January 1, 1970, no-fault divorce

law prevented divorcing spouses from having to place blame on one of the parties before a divorce could be effected. With the new legislation, a couple could divorce in no-fault states by simply stating "irreconcilable differences." Over the next eight years, no-fault divorces became available throughout nearly all of the country.

Finally, more churches were accepting, albeit sometimes quite reluctantly, the realities of the increasing divorce rate in the United States. In 1973, the Episcopal Church voted to recognize civil divorces; before this vote, church members needed to go through a sometimes lengthy process with the church before they could remarry. Even the Catholic Church was relenting, as the number of annulments—which, unlike divorces, allowed Catholics to remarry in the church—increased by 77 percent from 1968 to 1981.[8]

For the first time, many experts began counseling parents that divorce was better for children than living in a conflict-filled home. Relieved of the guilt that divorce could instill, and perhaps believing that they were doing their children a favor, many parents embraced this philosophy.

The 1970s saw a rise in so-called latchkey kids, children who let themselves into their homes after school and then spent the rest of the afternoon alone or with other children. To remedy this situation, many working mothers fought for federally subsidized, or even free child care, while nonprofit organizations such as YMCAs began running latchkey kid programs, or, as they later became known, "after-school programs."

During the 1970s, couples began, in increasing numbers, living together in intimate relationships without marriage, either as so-called trial marriages or as arrangements that would not involve marriage. These relationships were dubbed POSSLQs by the Census Bureau, or Persons of Opposite Sex Sharing Living Quarters, and by 1979 approximately 1 million households fit this designation.

In 1977, the Supreme Court struck down as illegal any laws that discriminated against the children of unwed parents. Perhaps most important, this invalidated laws in some states that did not allow illegitimate children to inherit their share of their father's property unless the inheritance was expressly stated in the will.

It became popular in the 1970s for couples to create personalized wedding services to express their unique personalities, spiritual beliefs, and circumstances. Many people shunned traditional church or governmental weddings and chose to write their own vows. Some women kept their maiden names.

Religion and Traditional Values

Mainstream Christian churches struggled with many issues during the 1970s. How should they respond to women seeking greater leadership roles in the church? How accepting should each church be to gays and lesbians who were open about their sexual orientations? What about the increasing rates of divorce? How should they respond to the issue of abortion?

Most members of the clergy opposed the Vietnam War, and, by extension, many of Richard Nixon's policies. One respected preacher, though, Billy Graham, was close to Nixon, supporting him politically and conducting church services in the White House. Graham began distancing himself from the president in 1973, and later stated his deep dismay over the "dark aspects" of Nixon's personality and administration.

Despite many Americans becoming disillusioned over the responses of mainstream denominations to the controversial issues of the era, the decade witnessed a significant rise in the conservative Evangelical Christian movement. Evangelical Christians did not belong to one specific denomination. They shared several characteristics, including a more conservative religious, cultural, social, and political worldview. They also shared a belief in the power of evangelism to spread the news of their faith, and in personal conversion to Christianity and acceptance of Jesus Christ as their Lord and Savior. They believed the Bible to be inerrable and everlasting, adamant that its wisdom and guidance should be applied to the questions and challenges of the day.

The rise in television evangelism—or televangelism—greatly increased preachers' ability to spread the news of the gospel. Advances in cable television created new channels that needed content, and so time was purchased by televangelists. By the time the 1970s began, Pat Robertson had created his own network—the Christian Broadcasting Network (CBN)—a strategy followed by Jim and Tammy Faye Bakker with their PTL (Praise the Lord and/or People That Love) Network. Other televangelists of note included Oral Roberts, Jimmy Swaggart, and Robert Schuller.

Funding these shows was expensive, so these programs included impassioned pleas for viewers to send money. In 1978, amid suspicions that not all televangelists used this donated money appropriately, Billy Graham helped create the Evangelical Council for Financial Responsibility, an organization that ministries could choose to join to be open about their financial collecting, spending, and reporting.

Reverend Jerry Falwell created the Moral Majority in 1979. The Moral Majority served as a political and religious force for conservative fundamentalist factions in the country. Platforms included prayers in public schools, and the group opposed several causes, including the Equal Rights Amendment, abortion rights, and rights for gays and lesbians. Falwell pushed for a return to what he defined as America's traditional social values.

The Moral Majority also advocated teaching creationism—the Biblical explanation of creation—in schools. In the middle of the decade, courts upheld the notion that creationism should not be taught as an alternative scientific explanation of the creation of the world and its creatures.

In 1978, Pope John Paul died after only 34 days as pontiff. His successor, Pope John Paul II, was Polish and the first non-Italian pontiff since 1522. In his 1979 visit to the United States, John Paul II expressed fairly liberal political and economical views, but stressed traditional and conservative positions on sexual issues. He extolled Catholics to reject birth control, abortion, homosexuality, divorce, and nonmarital sex; he also reiterated the positions that women could not become priests and that male priests must remain celibate. Overall, the Pope was well received, and crowds of hundreds of thousands greeted him.

In reality, Catholics in the United States were using birth control in increasing numbers despite the pronouncements of the pope. Some of the tension between Catholic theology and Protestant beliefs eased, though, when the restrictions on Catholics marrying outside the faith were lessened in 1970, as were the strictures on raising children of these marriages in the Catholic Church.

Cults

Several so-called cults came to national attention during the 1970s. These religions were labeled cults because the groups were usually led by one charismatic leader, and participants made their religions the central part of their lives, often leaving behind family, friends, college, and jobs, donating personal possessions to the group, and living with other followers in a communal setting.

Many people outside of these religious groups, including concerned parents, perceived this intense influence as brainwashing; they would sometimes hire "deprogrammers" to track down their "thought-controlled" loved ones. Once found, these cult members would sometimes forcibly be removed from their communal settings, and the deprogrammers would attempt to dissuade them from following the cult's beliefs. Parents formed support groups to assist their families in deprogramming processes and courts heard numerous cases on the subject.

Religions dubbed as cults during the 1970s included the International Movement for Krishna Consciousness, a theology begun in India; called Hare Krishnas in the United States, this movement began in America in the 1960s and continued through the 1970s. Perhaps the image that still resonates is that of Hare Krishnas dressed in robes, sporting unusual haircuts, and soliciting money from people in airports.

People flocked to hear the teachings of Transcendental Meditation—or the TM movement. This movement was spearheaded by the Maharishi Mahesh Yogi, and approximately 10,000 Americans visited his training centers monthly during the early part of the decade. After being assigned a *mantra,* a word or phrase which a person could repeat and focus upon, a follower could practice the techniques of meditation.

In 1971, the Reverend Sun Myung Moon from South Korea visited the United States, recruiting for Moon's Unification Church. Later known for participating in massive weddings, where hundreds of couples were married at the same time, the followers became known by outsiders as "Moonies." By the end of the decade, the Internal Revenue Service had begun an investigation into Moon's wealth.

In 1977, the Federal Bureau of Investigation conducted an investigation into another religion with cultlike features: Scientology, founded by science fiction writer L. Ron Hubbard in the 1950s. In the 1970s, the FBI suspected that some members of the church had attempted to infiltrate governmental investigative agencies in order to destroy church members' records; some of those who were arrested were convicted in federal court.

The biggest—and most deadly—cult story of the decade is the Peoples Temple and its leader, Jim Jones. Initially Pentecostal, Jones originally affiliated the church that he created, the Peoples Temple, with the mainstream Disciples of Christ. By the mid-1970s, though, he began telling his followers that he was God; meanwhile, his politics became increasingly radical along the socialist-Communist spectrum. He moved his followers to Guyana in South America, the "Promised Land," where political beliefs better matched his own. U.S. officials heard disturbing stories about gun-running and irregular bank transactions by the Peoples Temple. By 1978, Jones was holding "White Nights" during which his followers practiced the techniques of mass suicide.

In November 1978, Congressman Leo Ryan of California traveled to Guyana to observe the Peoples Temple for himself. Some of Jones's followers asked to leave with Ryan; they were permitted to do so, but their plane was attacked on the trip home, and Ryan and all of the former followers were killed. When investigators arrived at the commune to question Jones, they found 914 dead bodies, including that of Jones; most of the deceased had drunk Kool-aid laced with cyanide, although some had been shot.

Finally, no overview of the 1970s can be complete without mentioning the New Age followers, who turned away from traditional religions to find individual truth. Some New Age followers focused their spiritual energies on angels, while others studied reincarnation, crystals, or chanting.

Advertising

of the 1970s

Significant changes took place in the advertising world in the late 1960s and early 1970s, in large part because of the increasing concern for consumer protection. Consumer rights issues rose to the forefront largely because of activist lawyer Ralph Nader, who published a significant number of investigative books that questioned the appropriateness, thoroughness, and safety of many contemporary laws, guidelines, and regulations in America. In 1971, Nader founded a group called the NGO Public Citizen that focused even more attention on health and environmental issues.

Changes that affected the advertising world included the 1969 ban on cyclamate—a sugar substitute—used in many diet drinks and food products; this ban required an immediate reaction by advertising firms. Three out of four American households regularly purchased products containing cyclamates, and advertisers moved quickly to assure them that their clients had found healthful and tasty ways to honor the ban. Advertisements during the 1970s often contained the phrase "contains no cyclamates."

Similar upheavals took place in the tobacco industry as strictures continued to become more stringent during the decade.

Advertising firms also needed to walk a new tightrope to appeal both to working women and stay-at-home mothers and homemakers. Advertisers also needed to consider women who worked outside the home but still identified their primary roles as homemakers and/or wives and mothers.

Advertising firms therefore needed to consider both evolving legislation and changing societal roles. Rather than simply changing how they marketed a particular product, though, many companies altered their strategy in a more radical manner by focusing more on a point of view than a specific service or product. As another trend, top corporations switched advertising agencies to create new and hopefully more intriguing marketing campaigns.

These changes surely played a role in the alteration of the advertising world and contributed to the increasing number of creative and innovative marketing ideas of the 1970s. The transition from 60-second to 30-second commercials was accepted as standard, which also resulted in a larger variety of advertisements. Finally, advertisers also needed to contend with and consider the emerging presence of cable television.

SUPERSTARS OF ADVERTISING AND ADVERTISING PHENOMENA

In 1977, Xerox created what ESPN has named the fourth-best Super Bowl commercial ever, one that—because of its irreverence—serves as "the

Advertising

prelude to every boundary-pushing pitch you see now."[1] In this commercial, Brother Dominic, a humble-looking monk, completes the duplication of an ancient manuscript; he then learns that 500 more sets are needed. Slipping through a secret passageway, Dominic returns to his modern-day shop that boasts the Xerox 9200, a marvelous machine that can create two copied pages per minute. When he returns to the monastery with his completed task in hand, the head monk proclaims Dominic's work "a miracle!"

When *Advertising Age* named the top 100 advertising campaigns of the entire twentieth century, this commercial was ranked no. 85, and 20 of the advertisements on this list—one out of every five—originated during the 1970s. The number one criteria for making the list was changing the advertising business or pop culture in a significant way. Other benchmarks include propelling the brand to number one in its industry or simply being unforgettable. Although some of the earlier ads on this list appeared in print or on radio, by the 1970s, ads also appeared on television—either solely or as part of a cross-medium advertising campaign.

Two commercial campaigns in the *Advertising Age* top 10 list originated in the 1970s: McDonald's "You deserve a break today" ads and Miller Lite beer's "Tastes great, less filling." Both slogans are readily recognizable even today; the former campaign gave mothers—many of whom were trying to juggle parenthood and a career, and facing criticism because of it—permission to take their children to fast-food restaurants without feeling guilty.

The Miller Lite ads transformed the entire perception of a product. Prior to this campaign, beers with lower alcohol content were perceived

ADVERTISING SLOGANS OF THE 1970s

"Leggo My Eggo!" Eggo Waffles, 1970s

"You deserve a break today," McDonald's, 1971*

"Tastes great, less filling," Miller Lite beer, 1974*

"It's the real thing," Coca-Cola, 1970*

"Our L'eggs fit your legs," L'eggs pantyhose, early 1970s

"Have it your way," Burger King, 1973*

"This Bud's for you," Budweiser, 1970s*

"It takes a tough man to make a tender chicken," Perdue chicken 1971*

"Reach out and touch someone," AT&T, 1979*

"He likes it! Hey, Mikey!" Life cereal, 1972*

"Do you know me?" American Express, 1975*

"The ultimate driving machine," BMW, 1975*

"It's a miracle," Xerox, 1977*

"Take a bite out of crime," McGruff the Crime Dog, National Crime Prevention Council, 1980

"A mind is a terrible thing to waste," United Negro College Fund, 1972

"When it absolutely, positively has to be there overnight," Federal Express, 1982

"Be a Pepper," Dr Pepper, 1977

"We bring good things to life," General Electric, 1979

"Stuck on me/Stuck on Band-Aid," Band-Aid, 1975

"B-O-L-O-G-N-A," Oscar Meyer, 1974

"The incredible edible egg," American Egg Board, 1977

"Because I'm worth it," L'Oreal, 1973

"Like a good neighbor, State Farm is there," State Farm Insurance Companies, 1971

"The quicker picker-upper," Bounty paper towels, 1970

"It's not nice to fool Mother Nature," Chiffon margarine, early 1970s

"Don't leave home without it," American Express, 1975

"How do you spell relief? R-O-L-A-I-D-S," Rolaids, 1970s

*Among Advertising Age's "The Advertising Century: Top 100 Advertising Campaigns," http://adage.com/century/campaigns.html.

as having less value and/or were products for women and dieters only; the catchy slogan transformed the reduced alcohol and calorie content of the brand into assets, and this strategy was later mimicked by other beer companies. In the Miller commercials, retired athletes such as Bubba Smith, Bob Uecker, and Dick Butkus debate whether the taste or the calorie level—the tastes great, less filling argument—was the primary asset of this beverage. These advertisements are credited, to a significant degree, with making Miller Lite the number one light beer in the nation.

Some of 1970s advertising campaigns that made the century's best 100 list—and the number assigned to them—include:

- Alka-Seltzer, various ads during 1970s, including "Plop, plop, fizz, fizz, oh, what a relief it is" (13)
- American Express, "Do you know me?" 1975 (17)
- Burger King, "Have it your way" 1973 (18)
- Keep America Beautiful, "Crying Indian" 1971 (50)
- 7-Up, "The Uncola" 1970s (61)
- Life Cereal, "Hey, Mikey" 1972 (64)
- Jell-O, Bill Cosby with kids, 1975 (92)

See "Advertising Jingles of the 1970s" sidebar for more examples.

Technically, the "Crying Indian" ad was a public service announcement (PSA) created by the Advertising Council and the Keep America Beautiful organization. During these spots, a tear rolls down the cheek of Iron Eyes Cody after he rows his boat through a polluted waterway and then has a box of old food tossed by his feet along a highway; the message of this PSA was that "People start pollution…people can stop it. Keep America Beautiful." The campaign was so popular that stayed on the air from 1971 to 1983.

This emphasis on nature and the natural extended beyond the plea for pollution control. Dow Chemical claimed to use nothing that God didn't make—this in spite of the fact that they once manufactured napalm—and both cigarette and alcohol companies shared the "naturalness" of their products with their audiences.[2] Makeup ads assured women that their products were "nearly invisible" and "natural," thus sidestepping

Georgia Governor Zell Miller accepts a poster of Iron Eyes Cody, the "Crying Indian" whose tears helped fuel the environmental movement in the early 1970s, during a ceremony in his capitol office in Atlanta 1998, when Georgia began a "Keep Georgia Beautiful" campaign. AP Photo/HO, Curtis Compton.

the issue of whether a truly liberated woman would feel the need to wear makeup.

During the 1970s, John Wayne taped his own PSA wherein he talked about his lung cancer and urged others to see their doctors for a checkup.

No cigarette ads from the 1970s appeared on the top 100 list; this is to a large degree because commercials hawking cigarettes were banned from television on January 2, 1971, a year after the Federal Trade Commission established strict truth-in-advertising standards for the tobacco industry.

This ban also applied to radio advertising, so the tobacco industry changed its focus to advertising in magazines, newspapers, billboards, rapid transit advertising venues, and sponsoring sporting events. The people who appeared in cigarette ads now tended to be stylish, attractive women.

The use of women in advertising was a hot topic during this decade. In a well-publicized reversal of the expected, a camera panned a pair of pantyhose-clad feet, calves, and thighs—which turned out to be those of New York Jets football player and celebrity Joe Namath wearing a pair of Hanes. The punch line? "I don't wear pantyhose, but if Beauty Mist can make my legs look good, imagine what they'll do for yours." Although Namath managed to instill a sense of lighthearted fun into his commercial, more radical feminists expressed feelings of outrage about how women were portrayed in advertisements.

Feminist leader Gloria Steinem therefore faced a difficult dilemma when she spearheaded *Ms.* magazine in 1972. Although she wished to share news of liberated women, she also needed funds from advertisers to publish her magazine. Controversy existed from the beginning; the first issue of *Ms.* sported a large ad of a slender, beautiful, bikini-clad blonde who advocated the use of Coppertone suntan lotion, and many readers wrote to protest the ad's appearance. Steinem never did stop running beauty ads in her publication; in fact, she sought out sponsorship from Revlon, a major cosmetic corporation.

Revlon itself responded to the trend of feminine liberation by creating a cologne named "Charlie" that was advertised to the "new woman;" ads portrayed a single career woman who was thrilled to be wearing this fragrance. Perhaps Charles of the Ritz even more successfully captured the essence of the times via its perfumes. The ad for a scent called "Enjoli" showed a woman singing, "I can bring home the bacon, fry it up in a pan, and never, ever let him forget he's a man." This seemed to portray women's dual roles during this transitional decade in a way that other advertisements could not.

More traditional portrayals of women still saturated the media, however; although nearly 50 percent of women held jobs by the mid-1970s, many advertisements still portrayed them as overwhelmed homemakers. To address these disparities, the National Advertising Review Board (NARB) met in 1975 to create a set of standards to avoid stereotyping women in advertising. According to these standards, the following were to be avoided:

- belittling language such as "gal Friday," "lady professor," "weaker sex," or "ball and chain"
- double entendres, especially focusing on sex or female bodies
- unrealistic promises, such as that a perfume would lead to instant romance.[3]

While advertisers struggled to change their portrayal of women, Mexican Americans or "Chicanos" also fought against stereotypes in advertising. Their efforts were somewhat successful, as they forced Arrid deodorant to stop using a Chicano in an ad in which the message was, "If it works for him, it will work for you," as well as the "Frito Bandito" ads that "portrayed Mexican Americans as indolent, criminal, and filthy."[4]

Black Americans also protested the way they were portrayed on television, including in advertisements. A 1978 study conducted by Michigan State University underscored the consequences of inaccurate portrayals on television. According to its research:

- Black children believed that television was "very true to life."
- Forty-six percent of elementary school children believed that blacks on television were representative of blacks in real life.
- Commercials were more believable for black children than white children.
- More than 50 percent of all black children between the ages of 5 and 12 believed that commercials presented true and accurate information.[5]

The question, then, is how accurately were black Americans portrayed in advertisements? In research published in 1970 (culled from 1967–1968), only two percent of 11,000 advertisements contained black models. The researcher, Keith Cox, concluded, though, that the portrayal of black Americans had improved; in 1949–1950, media references showed this demographic group in lower-skilled jobs such as maids and cooks, but the 1967–1968 ads did not.[6] In research published in 1972 by David Colfax and Susan Sternberg, that conclusion was refuted; the duo felt that because half of the blacks in the advertisements Cox had studied were musicians displaying their album covers, the shift of the portrayal of black Americans was nowhere near as dramatic as what he had reported.[7]

Later in the decade, Dr. George Gerbner reviewed 2,556 television commercials (1977–1979) and discovered that advertisements with white actors were shown 7 out of 10 times; commercials with black actors were aired fewer than 2 out of 100 times.[8]

Another study compared 1,431 advertisements in *Time, Sports Illustrated, Women's Day, Newsweek, Vogue,* and *Esquire* in the years 1959, 1969, and 1979. 95.9 percent of the advertisements featured white actors; out of the 48 ads with black models, they posed with white actors in 39 of them, leaving only 9 ads with solely black actors. Marilyn Kern-Foxworth, in *Aunt Jemima, Uncle Ben, and Rastus: Blacks in Advertising, Yesterday, Today, and Tomorrow*[9] concluded that without pressure from civil rights organizations, this representation of blacks would continue in the media. So, although scholars were looking at the role of black actors and models in advertising during the 1970s, no significant progress was made toward a more realistic depiction of this population.

Meanwhile, another group—the working class—was also receiving short shrift in advertising. Research conducted by Robert Goldman indicated that the only commercials from the 1970s that portrayed the working class were truck ads and beer ads, and the most common worksites in ads were auto assembly lines and building construction sites. However, those commercials did present workers in a positive light, as they showed coal miners and construction workers as the core of American society.

During the latter part of the decade, overall, industry tried hard to overcome its image of employing an increasingly disinterested workforce, one that no longer cared about quality. Automobile manufacturers perhaps felt this negative perception most keenly, and, in a clever dual marketing move, a Budweiser ad featured a black foreman in a car manufacturing plant. The foreman was competent and solved problems well, and his peers accepted him and applauded his accomplishments.

Meanwhile, the oil industry tried a different tactic to improve its image, which suffered because of rising energy prices: it began sponsoring programs on the Public Broadcasting System (PBS) with Mobil's *Masterpiece Theatre* hosted by Alistair Cooke serving as a prime example. The show debuted in January 1971. In 1977, when oil company funding for public television had increased 10 times since the beginning of the decade, cynics began suggesting that PBS really stood for "Petroleum Broadcasting Service." Print ads for *Masterpiece Theatre, Mystery!,* and *Upstairs, Downstairs* appeared in the *New York Times* and the *Washington Post,* thanks to oil industry

sponsorship, and Mobil Information Center spots appeared before the news broadcasts. These spots discussed the pro-growth philosophies of off-shore oil drilling and other pro-energy policies that were often protested by environmental groups and frequently restricted by governmental legislation.

Although the oil industry used print ads to its advantage, newspaper and magazine ads were in fact declining. Perhaps the high visibility of television during the 1970s—plus internal issues with magazine publishing—caused advertisers to turn away from print publications. To recover, the magazine industry developed an increasing number of special-interest—or niche—publications, a trend that continues today. Advertising in these publications allowed advertisers to target their audiences more effectively. As another strategy, magazine companies began advertising on television, and usually offered incentives to purchase their products. Successful cross-pollination among industries occurred; for example, a 1979 television commercial for Coca-Cola that featured football player "Mean" Joe Greene being unexpectedly kind to a child later served as the basis for an NBC movie.

During the 1970s ads for sugary cereals dominated the Saturday morning cartoon time. In fact, by 1976, 43 percent of the commercials on Saturday mornings were for breakfast cereal, followed by candy ads and promotions for fast-food restaurants. Toys were often placed in cereal boxes to entice children to ask for them. In an interesting twist, Quaker Oats selected three freckle-faced boys to feature in its Life Cereal ad; the theme was that, even though the cereal was "good for you," it still tasted good. In the commercial, the two older boys refused to sample the cereal, instead pushing it in front of their youngest brother, Mikey, who "hates everything." To their surprise, Mikey devoured the Life Cereal and the older brothers exclaimed, "He likes it! Hey, Mikey!" This successful ad ran for 15 years.

In 1970, Action for Children's Television attempted to have all commercials eliminated from children's programming; although that initiative was not successful, legislation became effective on January 1, 1973 that reduced ads during children's television programs from 16 minutes per hour to 12. Advertisers also could not mention specific commercial products in a program or use cartoon characters or other recognizable show hosts during youth programming. Further restrictions occurred in 1975 when nonprogram material (advertisements) was limited to 10 minutes per hour during weekend children's programming.

THE NEW MARKETS

Another competitor to network television was actually invented during the 1940s but was seldom used until the 1970s: Community Antenna Television, or, as it is better known, cable TV. Cable TV's original function was to bring programming into communities where poor or nonexistent reception prevented the more standard form of television from airing—and, in fact, the FCC attempted to keep cable television in rural areas only. As regulations loosened during the 1970s, though, increasing numbers of households subscribed. In 1975, 10 million viewers and 3,506 cable systems existed; 10 years later, there were 40 million cable television subscribers. The dizzying choice of channels, each boasting its own demographics, presented advertisers with a whole new set of challenges and choices.

Throughout the 1970s, another form of "free-floating billboards,"[10] existed. T-shirts proclaimed political statements and religious beliefs, while bands and sports teams sold shirts in mass quantities as a form of promotion. In 1975, Anheuser-Busch gave away shirts with the Budweiser beer logo to college students on spring break in Miami and San Diego. The success of this promotion paved the way to shirts featuring any number of products—and the shirts were no longer given away for free. People began paying for shirts that advertised their favorite products.[11]

Meanwhile, an increasing number of cars displayed bumper stickers, many of them identifying the driver with a certain political or ideological group; others attempted to turn common sentiments upside down.

Architecture

of the 1970s

Architecture during the 1970s followed, in general, one of two movements: international modernism or postmodernism. The first style employed glass, steel, and concrete as materials in buildings that had regular geometric shapes and open interiors. Using this style, architects designed a series of buildings, each of which successively became the world's tallest structure. These included the John Hancock Center in Chicago; the twin towers of the World Trade Center in New York City; and the Sears Tower, also in Chicago. In postmodernism, architects attempted to insert the unexpected into buildings in ways that were both whimsical and thought-provoking. The familiar was turned upside down—figuratively, of course, but sometimes almost literally as well. Architects might select symbolic shapes and features, or they might choose a particular element simply to be fanciful. Architects including William L. Pereira, Charles Moore, I. M. Pei, Philip Johnson, and Frank Gehry continued to be influential.

Economic difficulties during the 1970s, including the dual energy crises, caused many architectural firms to close their doors. Business costs were rising at a time when their potential clients' budgets were also tightening. To partially address rising heating costs, architectural firms attempted to employ energy-saving solutions, such as wind and solar energy options, in homes and offices as they analyzed the advantages and disadvantages of passive systems, which use no moving or motorized parts, versus the more traditional active heating systems.

During the 1970s, architects experimented with offbeat building shapes, using unusual—and sometimes recycled—materials. Meanwhile, another movement gained momentum in the United States: the preservation of historic buildings.

LEADING FIGURES OF AMERICAN ARCHITECTURE

William L. Pereira

Chicago-born architect William L. Pereira (1909–1985) completed more than 400 projects during his illustrious career, including the pyramid-shaped Transamerica Building (1972) in San Francisco. Many residents resisted his notion of the pyramid structure, but Pereira stood by his professional opinion that the shape would allow more light and air into the surrounding area.

Pereira became well known for his futuristic designs as well as for his ability to envision and plan entire cities. Credited for developing much of Orange County, he designed a number of unique buildings at the University of California at Irvine that featured unusual concrete patterns.

The Transamerica Pyramid building in San Francisco, foreground, designed by William Pereira and built in 1972, and the Bank of America building, back, which, until the Transamerica building was built, had been the tallest building west of the Mississippi River. AP Photo.

When designing the campus buildings, he imagined a place where a diverse group of people from different socioeconomic backgrounds could live together and mutually respect their environment. Perhaps he achieved this to an even greater degree than he had anticipated, for not only did humans populate the area, but in 1972 the movie *Conquest of the Planet of the Apes* was filmed at the university, with the campus serving as "Ape City." Perhaps it wasn't surprising that Pereira's buildings served as the set for a Hollywood movie, for he began his architectural career in the 1930s by designing movie sets. Moreover, he won three Oscars, including an Academy Award in 1942 for best special effects in *Reap the Wild Wind.*

Pereira strongly believed that people must respect nature while building their towns and cities and that city planning must also focus significantly on its transportation systems, as well as its educational, technological, and scientific aspects. Leisure activities, Pereira believed, were also vital to a community's well-being. His architectural firm created concepts that became commonplace, including zero lot lines and a combination kitchen and family room located at the rear of houses.

Charles Moore

Architect Charles Moore (1925–1993) embodied a sense of gleeful fun in the work that he did—and even in his own home. Features that Moore added to the once-nondescript structure that became his home included a wave-topped gate, a boxy wooden tower, a variety of lighting fixtures above jam-packed bookcases that created a sense of columns, a floor that was painted with geometric shapes, a fireplace mantel surrounded by palm trees, and a conversation area filled with pillows.

Moore designed more than 180 buildings during his career. A Smithsonian writer dubbed him the Frank Lloyd Wright of this era. He mentored aspiring architects, who frequently traveled with him to Mexico, and encouraged them to incorporate vigorous colors and vivacious details in their work.

I. M. Pei

Ieoh Ming (I. M.) Pei (1917–), Chinese by birth and educated at the Massachusetts Institute of

Technology (MIT) and at Harvard University, is known for his architectural work with stone, concrete, glass, and steel, as well as for his sophistication, large-scale vision, and bold and high-tech geometric designs. He rose to national prominence after Jacqueline Kennedy selected him to design the John F. Kennedy Library in Boston in 1964.

Pei, who designed the Rock and Roll Hall of Fame (1998) in Cleveland, Ohio, has been credited with the transformation of the museum concept from a highbrow and exclusive institution to a welcoming and educational type of community center where people can gather to learn about pop culture and overall society. Pei served on many art and cultural boards of directors, including the Metropolitan Museum of Art, and 16 prestigious universities granted him honorary doctorate degrees.

He received many awards during the 1970s as well, including membership to the American Academy and Institute of Arts and Letters in 1975; only 50 living members are allowed into this academy. In 1978, he became the first architect to serve as this prestigious organization's chancellor. When selected as the Pritzker Architecture Prize Laureate in 1983, Pei was recognized by the jury for his ability to create beautiful architecture by incorporating a skillful—even poetic—use of materials.

Philip Johnson

Born in Cleveland, Ohio, Johnson (1906–2005) was a Harvard-educated architect whose first job of significance was as the Director of the Department of Architecture at the Museum of Modern Art in New York. Johnson was no stranger to controversy. His advocates described his work as brilliant, but his detractors labeled him as uninspired. Prone to stirring up debate about his architectural skills, Johnson worried that his personal life might cause him to lose work. In 1977, he asked *New Yorker* magazine to omit reference to his homosexuality, for fear that AT&T might send its business elsewhere.

In 1978, Johnson won the Gold Medal of the American Institute of Architects, and in 1979, he was the first architect selected to receive the

Pritzker Architecture Prize, which was created to encourage "greater awareness of the way people perceive and interact with their surroundings." Johnson was selected because of his 50 years of imaginative designs of a wide range of public buildings, including libraries and museums, as well as houses and office space.

PUBLIC BUILDINGS

Postmodern architects figuratively turned the familiar upside down, and I. M. Pei's most famous structure from 1978 almost literally stands upside down. Constructed out of concrete and glass, and serving as the city hall building for Dallas, Texas, it has been described by observers as a right triangle with a point turned down. The ground-level floor of the city hall is, unlike in most buildings, smallest in size; each floor is then larger than the one below, creating a unique, jutting appearance. The upper floors of the building thereby create shade from the hot Texas sun for those waiting by the front door. Pei also created a park—including a fountain—around this structure to create a welcoming atmosphere for this city's central building.

Another Pei-designed building is the East Building of the National Gallery of Art in Washington, D.C. John Russell Pope had designed the West Building, which was completed in 1941, in a classical style. Pei and his partners needed to keep the shape and style of the West Building in mind as they created more than 150 drafts of their proposed designs for the East Building. Meanwhile, they faced a significant challenge: the space allotted for their building was shaped like a trapezoid. After they solved this problem and a design was chosen, Pei and his partners constructed an "H-shaped" building; the American Institute of Architects selected this unique 1979 structure as one of the 10 best buildings in the United States.

Some of Charles Moore's most famous buildings were also constructed in the 1970s, including the Piazza d'Italia, located in New Orleans (1976–1979). This glorious mixture of arches and pillars and steps honored the Italian contribution to the city of New Orleans. Moore crafted the Burns House in Santa Monica Canyon in 1974; its stucco colors include ochre, orange, and mauve.

He built the home on a steep slope, and right outside the lower level is a swimming pool and terrace. Another famous building of his design is Kresge College at the University of California at Santa Cruz. Built in 1973, the "L-shaped layout rambles through a redwood forest, widening, narrowing, twisting along its central 'street' in his version of the 'Italian hill town.'"[1]

One of Phillip Johnson's best-known buildings erected during the 1970s is the Pennzoil Plaza located in Houston, Texas. In this building, two towers, each 36 stories in height, are located in triangular-shaped plazas. The towers are crafted from bronze glass and dark brown aluminum, a significant contrast to the roof's painted white steel trusses, which are decorated in a filigree pattern. Johnson also used significant whimsy while designing the AT&T Building—now the Sony Building—in New York City in 1979. Using granite panels of pinkish-brown rather than glass, he topped off the building with a shape that reminded some of the top of a Chippendale highboy chest, while still others saw in it a car grille or the top of a grandfather clock.

A public building that was designed using the postmodern technique of recreating ancient archeological styles is the Getty Museum in Los Angeles, California. Modeled after a first-century Roman country house, and including columns and quaint gardens, the museum showcased ancient Greek, Roman, and Etruscan art. Two other museums built in the 1970s are the Kimball Art Museum in Fort Worth, Texas, designed by Louis Kahn, and the National Air and Space Museum in Washington, D.C., designed by Gyo Obata.

The design of the Kimball Art Museum has been called timeless, with its vault-like structure, and Kahn's perfectionism has been compared to that used in creating classic Greek architecture. Funding for Obata's project—the National Air and Space Museum—was delayed because of the Vietnam War, but groundbreaking took place in 1972. Design challenges for this project were daunting: Obata needed to create a building that would accommodate huge crowds and appropriately display enormous aeronautical equipment. Obata chose to use pink granite as the exterior to match the West Building of the National Gallery of Art, located nearby; he echoed the same basic geometry of that building, as well. Reinforced truss structures were constructed to support the heavy displays and marble blocks were used to create floor display space.

Another public building constructed in the 1970s that was considered among the country's best was the Marin County Civic Building in California. This building was designed by Frank Lloyd Wright in 1958 but not completed until 1972. Nearly a quarter of a mile long, the building consists of a series of arches and is said to resemble a Roman aqueduct.

HOMES, STORES, AND OFFICES

Architects during the 1960s built primarily in the modernism style, and as the decade progressed, buildings became even more sleek and contemporary. Near the end of the 1960s, though, builders also began to resurrect more traditional forms of housing, borrowing elements from a variety of eras and cultures for inspiration; this phase is now called *Neo-Eclectic*. These homes could be Neo-French, for example, or Neo-Colonial, Neo-Tudor, Neo-Mediterranean, Neoclassical Revival, or Neo-Victorian. Regardless of genre, the builder or developer would select a few historically relevant features to add style and character to the homes. Houses such as these were built in suburbs throughout the country, as were apartment buildings. Architects were not significantly involved in designing these developments, as builders chose basic building designs and then added appropriate details to create the desired look.

Some experts question whether postmodern structures should in fact be called part of a style, because the term *Neo-Eclectic* refers to the revival of an architectural style from the past. In fact, Neoclassical Revival architecture made its third appearance in America in the 1970s. Overall, clients appreciated these designs, which were remarkably different in style from the sleek and streamlined modernism structures from the previous decade. This resurgence also occurred at a time when many Americans were becoming more interested in the historical preservation movement.

Also popular in the 1970s were Tudor A-frame houses, especially for vacation and beach homes and for rural getaway retreats. In Tudor A-frames,

the side walls were angled to create a sharp peak at the roof. Second-story rooms were often loft-like in design but more spacious than they appeared from the outside.

The self-designed Frank Gehry House in California deserves special mention. Gehry, a professional architect, created structures out of scraps of material, including plywood and corrugated metal and eventually concrete. This resulted in a collage-like appearance in his buildings that some compared to architectural sculpting.

The Gehry House has been described as a collusion of parts. After acquiring the structure, Gehry first removed much of its interior, exposing the rafters and studs. He then surrounded the home with plywood, glass, and metal, including aluminum siding and chain-link fencing. Not surprisingly, the architect also designed a line of furniture crafted from corrugated cardboard. In 1979, Gehry used chain-link fencing when constructing the Cabrillo Marine Museum to connect the structures in the 20,000-square-foot compound.

Two stores built in the 1970s are well known for their architectural ingenuity. First is the Best Products Showroom located in Houston, Texas. The store is built out of white brick, and the bricks in the front of the building appear to be tumbling down toward the heads of shoppers entering the building. Intended to symbolize the overpackaging of America's consumer society, this concept was described as "de-architecturisation." The other store known for its creative design is the Pacific Design Center in West Hollywood, California. Very large—with more than 100 million cubic feet of space—and constructed of blue glass, the store became known as the "Blue Whale."

PRESERVING HISTORY

In 1966, the National Historic Preservation Act (NHPA) codified federal policies to help preserve historic structures in America. According to this act, the federal government would increase its efforts to aid governmental and private agencies, as well as individuals, to accelerate historic preservation programs and activities. Overall, legislation passed during the 1960s began the shift in focus from the preservation of single homes to the creation of historic districts across the nation.

This trend continued when President Gerald Ford signed into law the Housing and Community Development Act of 1974, wherein Community Development Block Grants (CDBGs) were created. Under this system, local communities could decide how their allotted funds should be spent through a series of public hearings. Frequent CDBG choices included improvements in a community's infrastructure and property rehabilitation loans. Savannah, Georgia, and Charleston, South Carolina, especially benefited from revolving loans given for house rehabilitation. Successful projects of significance include Ghirardelli Square in San Francisco, Quincy Market in Boston, and Pike Place Market in Seattle.

In 1974, a national lobbying group called Preservation Action formed. Representatives of this group, which included local community activists and preservation experts, historians, and civic and commercial leaders, monitored federal legislation

World Trade Center, 1971. Shown: the Twin Towers under construction. Courtesy of Photofest.

THE WORLD TRADE CENTER

For almost three decades, New York's World Trade Center complex, or the "Twin Towers" as it was affectionately known, was a symbol of New York's success and leadership in American commerce, industry, and culture. The New York State legislature first initiated plans to build what was then called a "world trade mart" in the 1940s, but the plan didn't come to fruition until Chase Manhattan Bank leader David Rockefeller put his financial muscle behind the idea in the early 1960s. Construction was delayed by protests from residents who objected to the destruction of existing neighborhoods. Architect Minoru Yamasaki's building design was accepted in 1964 and construction began in 1966. The complex, which consisted of two towers and four peripheral buildings, took several years to complete. The south tower was the first to be completed in 1971 followed by the north in 1973. The Twin Towers were the first skyscrapers built without masonry, using a revolutionary drywall and steel core design. The World Trade Center was widely credited with reversing the degradation of lower Manhattan, which had become one of the most dilapidated districts of the island.

Over the more than two decades of their existence, the twin towers became symbolic of New York City and were featured in innumerable films and photographs. The towers, which housed more than 200 businesses, were destroyed in the terrorist attacks of September 11, 2001, and thus became the center of one of the most devastating tragedies in modern American history. A contest was held in 2002 to find an architect to construct a new financial center at the site of the former twin towers. A winner was eventually chosen and construction began in 2006 on the "Freedom Tower," which will be one of the tallest skyscrapers in existence at over 1,700 feet. Though the twin towers' history ended in tragedy, their emergence in the 1970s as one of the most innovative building projects of the age, and their eventual acceptance as an iconic element of New York's famed skyline, have cemented the towers as monuments in American history.

that might affect the historic preservation movement. In 1976, Congress passed the Tax Reform Act, which eliminated the incentive that had existed for people who demolished older buildings. The 1978 Revenue Act furthered the advantages of restoring older buildings by establishing a tax credit for property owners who rehabilitated historic properties. These pieces of legislation, along with the enthusiasm growing for the United States Bicentennial, fueled an interest in many people to adapt older structures for modern living.

Annual surveys conducted by the National Trust for Historic Preservation, Mainstreet programs, and tourism organizations in the 1970s spurred local governments to join in this preservation effort. The surveys indicated that cities and towns that focused on historic preservation benefited economically. Locales with historic districts tended to witness increased property values, both residential and commercial, with homes and businesses within the historical districts experiencing the greatest increases. Historic districts, studies determined, created specialized local jobs and encouraged tourism. Furthermore, people were generally more willing to invest in their neighborhoods, the studies concluded, because they perceived the value in such an investment.

People remodeling homes could, starting in 1973, refer to the *Old House Journal.* This magazine provided information to those wishing to renovate, maintain, and decorate homes that were more than 50 years old, and offered practical, step-by-step information for those new to the process.

Not everyone was pleased with preservation legislation. In 1978, the Supreme Court heard a case that would determine the legitimate power of historic district designation and its corresponding standards. The case was *Penn Central Transportation Co. v. New York City.* Penn Central wished to erect an office skyscraper above the 1913 Grand Central Terminal that was considered an historical landmark under New York's Landmarks Preservation Law. This proposed skyscraper met all zoning laws, but Penn Central needed permission from the Landmarks Preservation Commission as well. The commission rejected the request, as the proposed building would damage part of the Grand Central Terminal.

When the case made it to the Supreme Court, Penn Central testified that it would lose millions of dollars annually if it could not build this skyscraper, but the court ruled six to three for the city of New York and the skyscraper was not built.

Books

Newspapers, Magazines, and Comics of the 1970s

Literary novels published during the 1970s tackled challenging issues, including those associated with the feminist and civil rights movements, political disillusionment, violence, and changing family roles. Characters became alienated from their spiritual roots and disconnected from their places within the family unit and society as a whole.

Short stories frequently focused on characters who had no discernable motives for their actions, people who performed tasks and lived life without any sense of meaning or purpose. *New York* magazine was a prime publishing spot for these types of stories.

The push toward new journalism, a genre of nonfiction that incorporated elements of fiction, continued through the first half of the decade, both as a practice and as a source of great debate.

Writers of both fiction and nonfiction received conflicting messages about the definition of obscenity and its legal strictures. In 1970, the Commission on Obscenity and Pornography issued a 700-page report in which the majority of participants agreed that the government should not interfere with the adults' rights to read, obtain, or view explicitly sexual materials involving other adults. The committee did not reach consensus, however, and 250 pages of the report contained dissenting opinions. President Nixon called the report "morally bankrupt."[1] The Senate voted 60–5 to reject the report, and the debate over what was obscene continued, with inconsistent rulings continuing to be made in the court system.

Poets continued to pursue many of the same experimental avenues as they did during the 1960s, with surrealism a key area of exploration. Magazine publishers began targeting more and more niche audiences; underground and alternative newspapers and magazines set up and then folded throughout the decade.

From a business standpoint, publishing was evolving, and for the first time, the marketing function surpassed the editorial function in book publishing houses.

FICTION

Literary Fiction

Joyce Carol Oates is a prolific and award-winning author who, during the 1970s, published seven novels, along with a number of novellas, short story collections, dramas, and poetry anthologies.

Oates's characters attempt to find a niche within a world without security, and they struggle to meet that challenge. These characters, on the whole, are ordinary people who endure the random violence of modern-day life and for whom these acts of violence are not climactic moments; rather, they are commonplace events that are absorbed without significant importance placed on them. Although Oates was not identified as a feminist writer, her focus on women who persevere resonated with many readers.

John Updike was another major literary figure of the 1970s. In 1960, Updike published *Rabbit, Run*. His main character, Harry Angstrom, is a former basketball player who struggles with middle-class married life; early in his marriage, he has an affair that indirectly causes the death of his infant daughter. In 1971, Updike released the sequel to this novel, setting *Rabbit Redux* in 1969 and using two historical events, Apollo 11 and the Vietnam War, as a backdrop.

In the sequel, Angstrom learns of his wife's affair while watching the Apollo launch on a television located in a bar, and he envisions the rocket going into a great emptiness, a metaphor for his own sense of loss. In a plot twist, two people enter Harry's life and home: 18-year-old Jill, who is fleeing her rich parents' home in search of sex, drugs, and radical politics; and Skeeter, a fundamentalist who imagines himself as a black Jesus. Throughout the book, Angstrom attempts to find his place in the world and within his relationships. Updike uses the themes of space and war to illustrate Angstrom's emotional upheavals.

Another author—Kurt Vonnegut Jr.—was also established in the 1960s. In his 1970s works, Vonnegut began to use his public persona—represented as a character named Kilgore Trout—as the narrator in his novels. This practice began with *Breakfast of Champions* in 1973; in this novel, a Midwest car dealer believes that Trout's novels are not fictional at all, but are in fact real. Most critics point out a sometimes overwhelming sense of pessimism in Vonnegut's world perspective as he writes about contemporary society and its pervasive sense of emptiness.

Toni Morrison also emerged as a major writer of the 1970s, during which she published her first three novels. The first, *The Bluest Eye*, shares the story of Pecola Breelove, who prays for blue eyes because she believes that her horrible life will improve when her eyes change hue. The second book, *Sula*, explores the intense relationship between two black women who are bound together by a terrible secret. The third novel, *Song of Solomon*, won the National Book Critics Award; in this book, a character named Milkman searches for a hidden treasure of gold. Although he never finds those riches, he does discover important family traditions.

Another novel, this one focusing on a former slave, also captured the attention of American readers: *The Autobiography of Miss Jane Pittman* by Ernest J. Gaines. Gaines writes the story from the perspective of a 110-year-old Pittman reminiscing about her life and memories.

Saul Bellow had already received numerous awards before the 1970s began. In 1970, he won the National Book Award for *Mr. Sammler's Planet*, and he was the first writer to win this prize three times; in 1975, he won the Pulitzer Prize for *Humboldt's Gift*, and, in 1976 he won the Nobel Prize for literature.

Other 1970s writers of note include Gore Vidal (*Two Sisters, Burr, Myron, 1876,* and *Kalki*) and Tom Robbins (*Another Roadside Attraction* and *Even Cowgirls Get the Blues YEARS*).

Philip Roth, whose 1969 novel *Portnoy's Complaint* brought him recognition, published several novels during the 1970s, including *Our Gang: Starring Tricky and His Friends*, 1971, *The Breast*, 1972, *The Great American Novel*, 1973, *My Life as a Man*, 1974, *The Professor of Desire*, 1977, and *The Ghost Writer*, 1979.

Finally, it seems appropriate to complete this listing of award-nominated and award-winning authors by discussing one who refused to accept a prize. In 1973, Thomas Pynchon published *Gravity's Rainbow*, which won the National Book Award for fiction in 1974. The book was also selected for the Pulitzer Prize, but the advisory board overruled this choice, calling the book "unreadable," "turgid," "overwritten," and "obscene." The following year, the book received the Dean Howells Medal of the American Academy of Arts and Letters; however, after stating that the award was a great honor, Pynchon declined to accept, saying that any further imposition on the part of the Academy would make him look rude. Pynchon stopped publishing for several years after that refusal, and his whereabouts were not well known.

Books

NOTABLE BOOKS

Deliverance, James Dickey, 1970

Love Story, Erich Segal, 1970

Jonathan Livingston Seagull, Richard Bach, 1970

Rich Man, Poor Man, Irwin Shaw, 1970

Bury My Heart at Wounded Knee, Dee Brown, 1971

The Day of the Jackal, Frederick Forsyth, 1971

The Exorcist, William Peter Blatty, 1971

Fear of Flying, Erica Jong, 1973

Centennial, James Michener, 1974

Watership Down, Richard Adams, U.S., 1974

All the President's Men, Carl Bernstein and Bob Woodward, 1974

Jaws, Peter Benchley, 1974

Shôgun, James Clavell, 1975

Ragtime, E. L. Doctorow, 1975

Roots: The Saga of an American Family, Alex Haley, 1976

Interview with the Vampire, Anne Rice, 1976

The Thorn Birds, Colleen McCullough, 1977

The Complete Book of Running, Jim Fixx, 1977

The Shining, Stephen King, 1977

Moosewood Cookbook, Mollie Katzen, 1978

Scruples, Judith Krantz, 1978

The World According to Garp, John Irving, 1978

The Executioner's Song, Norman Mailer, 1979

Sophie's Choice, William Styron, 1979

The Right Stuff, Tom Wolfe, 1979

Popular Fiction

Readers interested in less intellectual material could enjoy fast-paced fiction, ranging from romance to horror, from pulp fiction to political thrillers.

Barbara Cartland and Phyllis A. Whitney were two key romance writers of the decade. Cartland, a British writer with a wide American readership, was known as the "Queen of Romance"; she published more than 700 novels, many of them during the 1970s. She specialized in historical romances with chaste females, and her books included such titles as *The Innocent Heiress, The Penniless Peer,* and *The Devil in Love.*

Whitney was also a prolific writer; an American who spent her childhood in Japan, China, and the Philippines with her missionary parents, she set her novels in a wide variety of exotic locales. She frequently wove supernatural elements into her tales, and her 1970s releases came with titles such as *The Vanishing Scarecrow, Mystery of the Scowling Boy,* and *The Glass Flame.*

Rosemary Rogers, who was to become known as the "Queen of Historical Romances," began her career in the 1970s. She published books such as *Wicked Loving Lies,* a story with a pirate theme, and *Wildest Heart,* set on the New Mexico frontier.

During this decade, Harlequin Enterprises, a publishing house, began to focus almost solely on romance novels. It sold its mass market paperbacks on what were called "job racks" at grocery stores, in beauty salons, and at other locales that were not previously regarded as likely places to buy books. To attract the attention of housewives, Harlequin began paying special attention to cover design and made its covers more eye-catching; this successful strategy was soon imitated by other category houses, particularly by those producing westerns, crime fiction, and horror fiction.

Mystery novels also abounded during the 1970s. James Crumley published two mystery novels during the decade: *The Wrong Case,* 1975, and *The Last Good Kiss,* 1978. Tony Hillerman began publishing his Joe Leaphorn and Jim Chee series in 1970, beginning with *The Blessing Way.* Hillerman used this series to explore the challenges that can occur when modern-day culture clashes with the traditional beliefs of more ancient cultures. Other novels from the Leaphorn and Chee series include *The Fly on the Wall,* 1971, *Dance Hall of the Dead,* 1973, and *Listening Woman,* 1978.

Marcia Muller began her Sharon McCone mystery series in 1977 with *Edwin of the Iron Shoes,* and, in 1979, Anne Perry began her Thomas Pitt series with *The Cater Street Hangman.*

The horror field was dominated by Stephen King, an author who revived the genre in the 1970s.

King's first novel, *Carrie,* debuted in 1974 and features a taunted teenager who uses telekinetic powers to exact revenge. The film version appeared in 1976, as did his second novel, *Salem's Lot,* wherein small-town residents find themselves transformed into bloodthirsty vampires. In 1977, King penned *The Shining;* the movie based on this novel was directed by Stanley Kubrick and was memorable for numerous disturbing scenes of a family isolated in a resort hotel high in a snowbound mountain pass and threatened by a father who is going progressively psychotic.

Dean Koontz wrote dozens of suspense novels during the decade, including several under the pen names of K. R. Dwyer, Brian Coffey, Deanna Dwyer, Anthony North, John Hill, and David Axton. As Koontz established his reputation as a writer, these novels were reissued under his own name.

Another writer, Mary Higgins Clark, a New York housewife-turned-novelist, wrote suspense novels such as *Where Are the Children,* 1975 and *A Stranger Is Watching,* 1978. Known as the "Queen of Suspense," Higgins Clark played on the commonality among her readers' fears. In *Where Are the Children,* a woman must start life over after the macabre deaths of her two children. She remarries and has two more children; one day, though, when she looks out the window to check on the children from her new marriage, all she sees is a red mitten. Her nightmare begins again. In Higgins Clark's second novel, a man is to be executed for a murder he didn't commit; the family of the victim, who believes that their nightmare will be eased after the death sentence is carried out, is wrong. Their nightmare will also occur anew.

Peter Benchley's *Jaws* is perhaps better remembered in movie form, but the book sold more than 20 million copies and spent more than 40 weeks on the *New York Times* best seller list.

Glitz and glamour pulsed through the "trash fiction" novels of Harold Robbins and Judith Krantz, among others. Money, sex, and power served as dominant themes. *Scruples,* for example, Krantz's bestselling novel from 1978, was set in the world of high fashion, of champagne and designer clothing.

In a twist that evoked the darker side of personal relationships, Judith Rossner's *Looking for Mr. Goodbar* delved into realities created by the sexual revolution from the perspective of a single parent. Rossner based this book on a real woman who, although brought up in a strict Catholic environment, decides to find sexual partners in New York bars. Although she decides to stop this practice, she does so too late.

Harold Robbins, whose sensational 1961 novel *The Carpetbaggers* was loosely based on the life of eccentric billionaire Howard Hughes, continued his career throughout the 1970s. A 1979 novel, *Memories of Another Day,* tells the story of a fictional union leader with close connections to the real life Jimmy Hoffa—a labor boss who had disappeared under mysterious circumstances just a few years before. Another novel, *The Betsy,* 1971, was made into a movie starring Laurence Olivier, Robert Duvall, and Tommy Lee Jones.

Political espionage novels and spy thrillers found a ready audience in the 1970s, perhaps because after the Watergate scandal, people were disillusioned by their own leaders and governments. By the time Robert Ludlum published his first book, *The Scarlatti Inheritance,* in 1971, he already had an extensive playwriting career behind him. His novel features Nazis working hand-in-hand with international financiers; his next thriller, *The Osterman Weekend,* (1973), focuses on a news executive recruited by the CIA to break up a Soviet spy ring.

One of the most successful examples of historical fiction based on a broadly factual construct was *Roots* by Alex Haley. Writing about his ancestors in Africa and their forced journey to America as slaves, Haley saw his book form the basis of television's first true miniseries.

The American Bicentennial revived an interest in American history, and James Michener, venerated author of the widely popular *The Source* and *Hawaii* in earlier decades, came out with *Chesapeake,* a novel that focuses on several generations of a family living in Maryland from 1583 to the present. His next book, *Centennial,* was set in Colorado in the 1870s and was later filmed as a miniseries.

During the 1970s, Larry McMurtry published two western novels: *Moving On,* 1970, and *All My Friends Are Going to Be Strangers,* 1972. He also received an Academy Award for the screenplay he penned in 1971 for the filming of his 1966 novel, *The Last Picture Show*. Overall, fewer people read western novels during the 1970s than in previous decades. One of the few prolific writers in this genre was Louis L'Amour, a man who saw himself as a simple storyteller. His work has been translated into dozens of languages and his books serve as the basis for 30 movies.

Feminist novels became a significant focus of publishing during the 1970s; authors include Joan Didion, Erica Jong, Marilyn French, Alison Lurie, Marge Piercy, Joanna Russ, and Alix Kate Shulman. Didion and Jong were known for their literary fiction, while the others published more commercial books.

Another novel that captured the attention of the American public include *Jonathan Livingston Seagull,* Richard Bach's parable about an outcast seagull; its spiritual tone was especially appealing in the 1970s. Erich Segal's *Love Story* examines the relationship between a collegiate athlete and his dying girlfriend. The first edition paperback print run was 4,350,000; Ryan O'Neal and Ali McGraw starred in the subsequent movie. As yet another example of a novel turned into a movie, William Peter Blatty's *The Exorcist* climbed to the top of the *New York Times* best seller list. In it, a priest exorcises demons from a young female patient, played by Linda Blair in the 1973 film.

CREATIVE NONFICTION

New journalism put a fresh twist on traditional nonfiction writing by incorporating elements of fiction writing: using dialogue in a conversational style; listing everyday, mundane details in the setting; developing characters through the use of third-person point of view and unique narrative voices; and crafting scenes rather than simply sharing information in a more linear manner. Some believe that new journalism rose to prominence during the 1960s and 1970s because a strictly factual recounting could not possibly impart the nuances of—and passions attached to—the Vietnam War, civil rights, women's lib, and gay rights, among other events and causes. Journalists increasingly began focusing on emotional truth as much as or more than imparting information in their essays and articles.

It is generally accepted that Tom Wolfe officially ushered in the era of new journalism in 1965 with his book *The Kandy-Kolored Tangerine-Flake Streamline Baby*—although it wasn't until 1973 that he published an anthology with the title *The New Journalism,* thereby making that phrase even more familiar to writers, editors, and savvy readers.

New journalism authors included Tom Wolfe; Truman Capote, whose book, *In Cold Blood,* 1966, was an early example of this genre; Norman Mailer; Gay Talese; Hunter S. Thompson; and Joan Didion.

In 1975, Wolfe published *The Painted Word,* an inside look at America's art world. In 1979, he published *The Right Stuff,* which investigates why astronauts put themselves at risk during space exploration and focuses on the first seven men chosen by NASA, the "Mercury Seven," as well as Chuck Yeager, who broke the sound barrier but was never selected by NASA to serve as an astronaut.

Mailer wrote several books during the 1970s, including *The Prisoner of Sex,* 1971, wherein he suggests that gender determines how a person interprets reality. He received criticism from feminists for this viewpoint. His 1975 book, *The Fight,* details the boxing match between Muhammad Ali and George Foreman. He also published two biographies during the decade: one on Marilyn Monroe and one on convicted murderer Gary Gilmore and his refusal to appeal his death sentence. Mailer received his second Pulitzer Prize for the latter book, titled *The Executioner's Song.*

In 1971, Talese published *Honor Thy Father,* an in-depth look at the New York Bonanno crime family. Known for his willingness to investigate so-called unreportable stories, such as the inside story of the Mafia, Talese was admired by his readers for his in-depth research. Whenever a topic captured his attention, he returned to it again and again, finding new angles to explore.

Hunter S. Thompson became well known for taking new journalism a step further—into gonzo journalism. Some say that a *Boston Globe* reporter dubbed Thompson with that designation, "gonzo" being a term for the last person standing after an all-night drinking marathon. Another explanation for the term is that a friend told Thompson

Journalist Hunter S. Thompson sits on his Penton motorcycle with his rifle over his shoulder on his ranch circa 1976 near Aspen, Colorado. Photo by Michael Ochs Archives/GettyImages.

that his writing was "totally gonzo," which may be a bastardization of the Spanish term *gonzagas,* loosely translated as "fooled you." Thompson immersed himself in the stories he told, lacing his sense of humor throughout the adventurous telling of his stories. Two books published by Thompson during the 1970s were *Fear and Loathing: On the Campaign Trail '72* (1974) and *The Great Shark Hunt* (1977).

Although many of new journalism's stars were men, it was not an exclusively male club. Joan Didion published a significant amount of material, including the nonfiction book *The White Album* in 1979. Writer Carolyn Wells Kraus quotes Didion expressing her personal philosophy of writing, that as "nonfiction writers, we interpret what we see, select the most workable of the multiple choices"[2] and therefore present the world through authorial lenses. Kraus and Didion point out the risk of autobiographical intrusion into new journalism-style essays and books; although all writers must make critical selections of what to include and what to leave out of their work, new journalism puts writers in an especially vulnerable position.

Maya Angelou, although not identified with the creative nonfiction/new journalism movement, became well known for the story of her often-terrifying childhood. She published *I Know Why the Caged Bird Sings* on the cusp of the 1970s; although reviews were mixed for this book, some critics have compared her work to Frederick Douglass's autobiography, as both authors share their experiences as African Americans facing racism.

True crime novels found a ready market in the 1970s; Vince Bugliosi's and Curt Gentry's *Helter Skelter* is a prime example. The two write of Bugliosi's experiences when he prosecutes Charles Manson for the murder of Sharon Tate, and the title is that of a Beatles' song Manson liked. In *The Onion Field,* Los Angeles police officer Joseph Wambaugh describes the murder of a police officer and the effect the crime had on his surviving partner—as well as its impact on the men who committed the crime.

Maya Angelou, circa 1970. Photo by Michael Ochs Archives/Getty Images.

Other books that tackled serious subjects include *Bury My Heart at Wounded Knee* by Dee Brown, which discusses how white settlements have affected Native Americans And *All the President's Men* and *The Final Days,* both by *Washington Post* reporters Bob Woodward and Carl Bernstein. Both books reveal behind-the-scenes details of the Watergate scandal and Richard Nixon's presidency. Woodward and Bernstein, their boss executive editor Benjamin Bradlee, and their employer the *Washington Post* are often credited with bringing the Nixon administration to its end. The popularity of *All the President's Men* led to a popular movie of the same title in 1976, with Robert Redford as Bob Woodward and Dustin Hoffman as Carl Bernstein. Journalism departments at colleges and universities experienced a noticeable increase in students majoring in journalism thereafter.

Several other popular bestselling nonfiction books focused on ways to feel better, ranging from *Everything You Always Wanted to Know about Sex (But Were Afraid to Ask)* by Dr. David Reuben, *The Joy of Sex: A Cordon Bleu Guide to*

Lovemaking by Alex Comfort, and *Your Erroneous Zones* by Wayne Dyer. The third book attempted to simplify concepts of psychology to help people find ways to live happier lives. Yet another book, *The Complete Book of Running* by James Fixx, encouraged people to become healthier and feel better through a particular form of exercise.

POETRY

Confessional poetry—or the "I" poetry—seemed especially appropriate for the Me Generation, although it had its roots in the earlier poetry of Anne Sexton, Allen Ginsberg, and Sylvia Plath, among others. Confessional poets shared raw and private feelings about topics that were previously taboo: death, sex, depression, and the like.

Protest poetry, more commonly associated with the 1960s, continued during the 1970s. This form focused on challenging bodies of authority or "the establishment," which often translates into the government; poets often used shocking language or ideas to startle readers into awareness of the cause being championed.

In 1971, a new form of poetry, known as L-A-N-G-U-A-G-E poetry, emerged. It first appeared in a magazine called *This*. Seven years later, the magazine was renamed L-A-N-G-U-A-G-E. Bernadette Mayer employed the philosophy in her poetry and suggested that those new to L-A-N-G-U-A-G-E poetry try these exercises: read an index as a poem; write a poem using only prepositional phrases; and attempt to write in an unsettled state of mind. Bruce Andrews and Charles Bernstein were key figures of this poetic movement.

Poetry also served as a vehicle for minorities to express their unique viewpoints. Maya Angelou first rose to prominence in 1969 with the publication of the autobiographical *I Know Why the Caged Bird Sings* and the book's subsequent National Book Award nomination. She also published three collections of poetry during the decade, including *Just Give Me a Cool Drink of Water 'fore I Die,* for which she received a Pulitzer Prize nomination in 1972. She divided this collection into two sections: poems of love and poems of racial confrontation. Angelou published two other poetry collections in the 1970s, *Oh Pray My Wings Are Gonna Fit Me Well* and

And Still I Rise, which describes city life for black Americans.

Another poet, Rod McKuen, stayed true to more traditional forms of poetry and enjoyed unparalleled commercial success, selling more than 65 million copies of his poetry collections and seeing them translated into one dozen languages. His poetry tapped into feelings common among people everywhere, love and hope and fear, and some have compared the atmosphere of his poetry readings to that of a rock concert. During the 1970s, McKuen published 11 collections of poetry with titles such as *Caught in the Quiet, Fields of Wonder,* and *Come to Me in Silence.*

MAGAZINES

Three magazines that captured the attention of a significant portion of America's reading audience—*Ms., Hustler,* and *People*—first appeared in the 1970s, but each of these magazines appealed to a considerably different set of demographics.

The first to debut was *Ms.,* a magazine founded by Gloria Steinem and a small group of others dedicated to the feminist movement. The very name of the magazine caused controversy as, during the early portion of the decade, debate flourished about the appropriate title for women. Heated discussions began when some women pointed out that "Mr." did not designate the marital status of a man, whereas "Miss" indicated an unmarried woman and "Mrs." designated those married or widowed—and these women demanded a title comparable to "Mr." Although "Ms." had been suggested as a neutral feminine title 10 years earlier, it was Steinem's magazine that brought the choice to the forefront.

In 1971, *New York* magazine inserted a mini version of *Ms.* into its publication. In January 1972, Clay Felker, the editor of *New York* magazine, sponsored the first independent issue of *Ms.,* and, starting in July 1972, the magazine appeared monthly, funded by Warner Communications. By 1978, the Ms. Foundation for Education and Communication had begun publishing *Ms.*

This magazine was controversial on several fronts. Some despised the magazine for the feminist beliefs that it espoused, while many advocates of feminism protested the ads that *Ms.*

NEW MAGAZINES

Essence, 1970

National Lampoon, 1970

Smithsonian, 1970

Travel + Leisure, 1971

Money, 1972

Playgirl, 1973

Ms., 1972

People, 1974

National Geographic Kids, 1975

Soap Opera Digest, 1975

Country Living, 1978

Inc., 1979

Self, 1979

carried, which included a bikini-clad woman as an advertisement for Coppertone suntan lotion. Nevertheless, the magazine enjoyed significant support from its advocates and subscribers, and it provided practical information to those curious about the feminist movement.

Shortly after *Ms.* debuted, a radically different type of publication began: Larry Flynt's *Hustler* newsletters, which were intended to promote his strip clubs. By 1974, the newsletter format evolved into a glossy magazine that featured raw and explicit sexual photos, along with graphic—and some say vulgar—satires and commentaries.

Hustler was not the first magazine to feature female nudity outside of Triple X bookstores; *Playboy* could stake an earlier claim. Striking differences, though, existed between the two publications. *Playboy* highlighted the nude female form as something seductively beautiful and something to be admired, and its editors artfully prevented female genitals from appearing in photos; Flynt, meanwhile, posed his models in ways that shocked many Americans: covered with excrement or involved in male-dominated rape scenes. He became especially vilified by detractors and applauded by fans in 1975, when he featured photos of a topless Jackie Kennedy Onassis.

Flynt never claimed that *Hustler* was a literary publication, but *Playboy* aspired to such a

Gloria Steinem, publisher of the magazine *Ms.*, holds a mock-up of that publication's January 1978 cover while standing in front of the White House on December 16, 1977. The issue rates President Carter's first year in office from a feminist perspective. AP Photo.

Books

WORDS AND PHRASES

ageism (discrimination against the elderly)

biofeedback

blahs

body language

boogie board

boss

brainiac

chemo

choice

ditsy

dyn-o-mite

easy-peasy

-gate (from Watergate, suffix used to denote a scandal)

gross out

hacky-sack

high-maintenance

improv

jazzercise

no-brainer

no-no

pigout

rad (radical)

right on (interjection to express approval)

sicko

skeevy

streaking

to trash (to vandalize, especially as an act of protest)

trekkie

wacko

wicked

wuss

designation, and the latter publication did feature high-quality essays, thus giving rise to the tongue-in-cheek claim that one only bought *Playboy* for the articles.

The third major magazine that debuted in the 1970s, *People,* seemed tame in comparison to *Ms.* and *Hustler,* and perhaps its lack of controversy is what allowed it to become so popular so swiftly. First appearing on March 4, 1974, *People* quickly became a top source of popular culture news, focusing on the personal and professional lives of the country's celebrities. The first issue featured actress Mia Farrow who was appearing in the movie *The Great Gatsby.* Unlike "gossip rags" that told scurrilous secrets about stars, *People* served as a source of public relations for them and allowed the general American public to glimpse their favorite celebrities wearing beautiful gowns and dashing tuxedos, getting married, showing off their babies, and performing in their chosen fields of entertainment.

Another magazine launched in 1970—*National Lampoon*—targeted a smaller audience. This sharply satirical publication skewered political and pop culture figures and served as the basis of a comedy troupe and live radio show. Although the publication was influential during the 1970s, the National Lampoon concept ended shortly after the decade did.

The 1970s also saw the budding of computer-based magazines, such as *Computer Graphics World* in 1977.

NEWSPAPERS

Television transformed American society in the 1950s and 1960s and that influence continued into the 1970s. Built on the foundation of its coverage of the Vietnam War, TV news became a more central part of viewers' lives. The growing importance of television news eventually led to the demise of newspapers' traditional afternoon editions as network newscasts replaced print as people's primary source of evening news.

This shift to television forced the newspaper industry to change, and the limited nature of news delivery via the small screen enabled newspapers to take on an important role in providing in-depth coverage and local information. Newspaper evolved as consumers looked to papers for different aspects of their news and information diets, such as cost-saving coupons for use at local stores and classified ads. Suburbanization also forced newspapers to adapt to new realities. People looked for news outside of metropolitan areas.

Two events that reestablished the newsgathering prowess of papers took place in the 1970s—the "Pentagon Papers" and Watergate. In 1971, the *New York Times* published a series of articles on the Pentagon Papers, a secret Department of Defense history of the Vietnam War. The classified documents were leaked by Daniel Ellsberg, a State Department insider, who secretly photocopied the papers. The Nixon Administration obtained a court order barring the *New York Times* from publishing further installments, but other newspapers, including the *Chicago Tribune* and *Washington Post,* responded by printing the series.

Perhaps the most important event in journalism history took place when the enterprising *Washington Post* reporting team of Bob Woodward and Carl Bernstein uncovered the Nixon administration's illegal activities, dubbed "Watergate." The investigative work done by Woodward and Bernstein led to Nixon's 1974 resignation. As a result, enterprising reporters across the nation took up the investigative cause. Into the twenty first century, almost all political scandals, particularly ones involving government figures, have been given the "-gate" suffix in recognition of Watergate's importance.

Overall, newspapers continued to grow in the 1970s, in large part because of the country's expanding population. Newspaper advertising revenue leaped from $5.7 billion in 1970 to $14.8 billion 10 years later. Unions lost labor battles, printing technologies improved, and newspapers became "big business."

Comics and Cartoons

The late 1960s had revealed the power of comic books as standalone products and advertising tools. The 1970s continued this trend, with Marvel and DC, the two top publishers, battling for supremacy. Although DC featured the iconic Superman and Batman characters, Marvel sold more books. From 1970 to 1979, Marvel sold more than 5 million copies a month. Even three lesser companies had astronomical sales in the decade, with Harvey's averaging about 3.5 million monthly, Archie's at 3.5 million, and Gold Key at about 3 million. All told, these five companies sold more than 19 million comic books a month across the decade.

The 1970s remained heavy on superheroes, but other stories that included creatures such as ghosts and swamp monsters gained in popularity. Adult-themed tales of terror and vampire stories aimed at adults and young people were also popular. Many of the adult-themed comic books were actually changed to circumvent the Comics Code Authority, which tightened restrictions on comic book content in 1954 and basically served as a censor. To avoid these restrictions, publishers issued these works in a magazine-size, black-and-white format dubbed "Picto-Fiction," a new form of adult entertainment. These comics were more expensive than traditional ones, and usually cost 35 to 50 cents per issue.

Snoopy, with Woodstock on his head, being happily carried by the Peanuts gang in a scene from the movie, *Snoopy Come Home* (1972). Courtesy of Photofest.

The 1970s also witnessed comic books introducing and addressing social issues that plagued the real world. In 1972, for example, Marvel introduced Luke Cage, a black, urban mercenary who operated both within and outside the law. Spider-Man also dealt with drug issues in the early 1970s, even though Marvel had to issue the series without Comics Code approval, since it did not allow such content at the time.

Films based on comic book characters often sparked renewed interest in superheroes, just as some popular movie characters became stars of comic books. In 1978, the box office smash "Superman" starred a young, unknown actor named Christopher Reeve as the man of steel. Using advanced special effects and other film techniques to make it seem like Superman could actually fly, the film grossed more than $300 million worldwide and led to a series of sequels in the 1980s.

Charles M. Schulz's *Peanuts* comic strip continued to be popular, with the droll beagle Snoopy and his rich fantasy life (as a World War I flying ace among other characters) coming more to the forefront of interest in the 1970s. Dozens of books featuring collections of *Peanuts* strips were published; stuffed animals of Peanuts characters, especially Snoopy and his bird friend Woodstock, were sold; and a full length movie, *Snoopy Come Home* (1972), was released.

Entertainment

of the 1970s

The 1970s were a comeback decade for movies. Although television had gobbled up increasing numbers of America's leisure hours, a combination of blockbuster movies and technological advances such as Panavision and Dolby sound, and more believable special effects such as those seen in *Star Wars* and *Jaws,* enticed people to return to the movie theater. Young filmmakers, including Francis Ford Coppola, George Lucas, Martin Scorsese, and Steven Spielberg, also revived the movie industry. Other top directors were Woody Allen, Robert Altman, and Michael Cimino. Another movie trend of the 1970s was the film as art.

Meanwhile, television continued to evolve to meet America's needs. For the first time, sitcoms and other shows focused on social consciousness, tackling pressing issues of the day, often in a satirical manner. By 1972, for the first time, half of U.S. households owned a television set, so shows were finding a broader audience. Soap operas became increasingly popular, and this decade also saw the rise of the television miniseries, the made for TV movie, and cable.

Disco dominated the dance scene from the middle of the decade until its end, when it suffered a significant backlash. Broadway saw the rise of more African American musicals and endured a spate of controversy over so-called sacrilegious material.

FILMS

The image of John Travolta as Tony Manero is burned into our public consciousness. Decked out in a three-piece white leisure suit with his shirt collar wide open, his hand points toward the heavens as the lighted disco floor glares below him. Tony, a disaffected, disillusioned youth from Brooklyn, New York, sees the disco as the only way out of a dead-end life that includes a low-paying job at the local paint store; his boss, already devoured by cynicism, provides no encouragement.

Strutting through the swirling lights of the disco, though, Tony swaggers with confidence and people move aside in silent tribute to watch him dance.

He and his dance partner—a woman named Stephanie who has ambitions beyond what Tony can yet comprehend—win a highly competitive dance contest that confers prestige in Manero's world, but even that doesn't bring joy because he knows that the Hispanic couple who competed against them was better. Spurred on by Stephanie, Tony longs to move to Manhattan where he vaguely perceives that a better life may exist. As the movie winds down, Tony stumbles toward his dream and we want to believe that, somehow, he will "make it."

Audiences flocked to disaster and horror films in the 1970s. *Towering Inferno, Earthquake, Poseidon Adventure, Airport, Jaws, Amityville Horror, Alien,* and the *Exorcist* attracted large numbers of viewers, and many could even be labeled with the emerging term of "blockbuster." *Jaws* was the first movie ever to make more than $100 million for its studio. Changes in technology permitted movie producers to create credible-looking disasters that cause audiences to scream, rather than laugh at the poor quality of the special effects.

The first well-known disaster movie of the decade was *Airport,* 1970, with a stellar cast of Burt Lancaster, Jean Seberg, and Dean Martin. In this movie, the manager attempts to keep his airport open during a snowstorm; meanwhile, someone is attempting to blow up an airplane. As a rule, disaster movies have large casts with multiple subplots and personal and dramatic interactions occurring among characters—and *Airport* followed that formula. The personal dramas are interwoven along the main thread of the plot, which involves characters attempting to prevent or escape from a disaster; sometimes they're also forced to cope with the disaster's aftermath. Some disaster films use nature as the enemy and force of reckoning, while others point toward technology and human error.

In 2004, a group of cinema buffs voted *Airport* as the fourth-best disaster film of all time. Two other 1970s movies—*Poseidon Adventure* and *The Towering Inferno*—ranked first and third, respectively. In the *Poseidon Adventure,* starring Gene Hackman, a tidal wave turns a luxury liner upside down, and passengers must work together to find their way to the top to survive. Some succeed; others do not. As one woman is dying after saving another person from drowning, she passes on a pendant that she wants her grandchildren

The Rocky Horror Picture Show (1975). Directed by Jim Sharman. Shown: Tim Curry (center) sings "Sweet Transvestite." Rear (left to right): Little Nell Campbell, Patricia Quinn, and Richard O'Brien. Courtesy of Photofest.

to have and she tells potential survivors that life matters, very much. In contrast, in Paul Newman and Steve McQueen's *Towering Inferno,* people do want to survive and don't need encouragement; in fact, some may value life too much.

Although each of these disaster movies thrilled and entertained moviegoers, the films didn't necessarily change viewers' behavior patterns outside the theater. The disaster film *Jaws,* however, did have such an effect, and caused many beach goers to fear entering the water. This movie's effect spread even further as posters advertising *Jaws,* the movie, were imitated by political and social parodies using the *Jaws* theme: the State of Liberty was menaced by the CIA, Americans by tax bites, inflation, the energy crisis, and unemployment.

Other films addressed the Vietnam War issue, including *Coming Home, The Deer Hunter,* and *Apocalypse Now.* Each film—and others like them—presented a unique twist to the challenges presented by the war. The first movie explores the changing relationships between the men who fought in Vietnam and the women they left behind; the second involves three friends who are drafted, captured, and imprisoned, and must break all rules to escape; and the third focuses on a special forces officer sent into the jungle to capture and kill the U.S. military leader who has created his own renegade army.

Other films tackled social issues, such as divorce and child custody (*Kramer vs. Kramer*); intolerable work conditions and the resistance to union organization (*Norma Rae*); caring for those with psychological problems (*One Flew over the Cuckoo's Nest*), and the collapse of a presidency (*All the President's Men*), among others. Still other movies were inspiring, sentimental, and/or nostalgic. These include *Rocky, Grease,* and *American Graffiti.* Comedies that continue to air long after the decade ended include *The Rocky Horror Picture Show* and *Animal House.* No listing of 1970s movies would be complete, though, without mentioning *The Godfather* (I and II) and *Star Wars.*

Many movie reviewers and film experts consider *The Godfather* and its first sequel to be masterpieces. Directed by Francis Ford Coppola, the original film features an all-star cast, including Marlon Brando, Al Pacino, and James Caan.

CULT CLASSIC: THE ROCKY HORROR PICTURE SHOW

Written and directed by Richard O'Brien and Jim Sharman, *The Rocky Horror Picture Show,* 1975, follows the plight of two newlyweds stranded in rural England (played by Barry Bostwick and Susan Sarandon) who stumble upon a rural castle in search of shelter. Once inside, they become entangled with a mythic group of transvestites from the city Transsexual on the planet Transylvania, led by their larger than life leader, Dr. Frank-n-Furter (played by Tim Curry). This over-the-top drama and all its subsequent hilarity ensue as the film leads the audience through a series of intentionally silly horror and science fiction inspired storylines aimed at challenging gender roles and encouraging sexual freedom.

But the road from the box office to cult classic would not be an easy one. Universally panned by critics for its overt sexual content combined with initially low ticket sales, the film was pulled from marquees across the country within weeks of its release. It wasn't until over a year after its first screening that the film began to find a following with a run of surprise sold-out shows at the Waverly Theatre in New York City where moviegoers would sing along with film. The midnight time-slot combined with a participation-encouraged motto proved to be a recipe for success. Since then, The *Rocky Horror Picture Show* has continually attracted a raucous audience and become one of the only theatrical musicals in history where attendees attend screenings in full costume and take part in a highly choreographed act and stage show that encompasses nearly every scene of the 98-minute film.

The movie brought about public awareness of the Mafia, and much of what we know about the subculture came from these movies. Phrases from the movies such "sleeping with the fishes" and "I'll make him an offer he can't refuse" became part of American culture.[1] When we first meet the Godfather, he is immaculately dressed, receiving visitors in his darkly impressive office while others celebrate his daughter's wedding outside in the sunshine. We immediately know that he is powerful, a force to be reckoned with. The first movie focuses on the attempted assassination of the leader of the Corleone family and his family's response. In the second movie, which also stars Robert DeNiro, we watch the maturation of the upcoming Godfather of the Corleone family. *The Godfather* and its sequel won the Academy Award in 1972 and 1974.

In another blockbuster movie series that began in the 1970s, the *Star Wars* trilogy, the lead character finds himself bereft of family and must create new ties to sustain himself. The 1977 science fiction film opens with Luke Skywalker, a orphaned young man living with his aunt and uncle, longing for adventure. His uncle needs him at home, though, and so he stays. Soon, disaster strikes Luke's homeland, and all ties are broken. Luke meets up with adventurer Han Solo and together they attempt to rescue Princess Leia from the clutches of the evil Darth Vader, whose dark empire intends to take over the galaxy.

Star Wars examines the concepts of good and evil and juxtaposes the notions of technology and humanity. Surrounded by combative robots and other mechanical creatures who will do whatever the dark empire bids them, the humans triumph—although even they also rely upon a couple of their own robotic friends, plus the deep wisdom and intense tutelage of Jedi Master Obi Wan Kenobi. In the movie, good clearly wins out against evil, although the ending provides a hint that victory is only temporary and that evil will rise again.

Woody Allen began to make his mark in films in the 1970s, with films such as *Bananas, Everything You Wanted to Know about Sex but were Afraid to Ask, Sleeper, Love and Death, Annie Hall, Interiors,* and *Manhattan.*

Another movie theme or genre from the 1970s was "blaxploitation films." In 1971, Melvyn Van Peebles produced an independent film called *Sweet Sweetback's Baadasssss Song,* a movie described

Star Wars (1977). Directed by George Lucas. Shown from left: Peter Mayhew (as Chewbacca), Mark Hamill (as Luke Skywalker), Alec Guinness (as Ben Obi-Wan Kenobi), and Harrison Ford (as Han Solo). Courtesy of Photofest.

Star Wars Goes International

By the time the movie blockbuster *Star Wars* opened outside North America in October of 1977, audiences around the world were primed and ready for it. In the six months since its American premiere, media outlets had devoted numerous stories to the frenzy the film had generated in the United States—its box-office records, its tie-in products, the long lines outside theaters—and audiences in Europe, Asia, the Middle East, and elsewhere were just as receptive. The film earned $460 million in the U.S. and $337 million in other markets, making it one of the biggest moneymakers of all time.

Unlike other American pop-cultural juggernauts, *Star Wars* provoked little resistance from cultural watchdogs in other countries. Perhaps this was due to the otherworldly nature of its setting in "a galaxy far, far away." The tropes of science fiction made the film less recognizable as an American product. Perhaps it was the threads of myth and legend that writer/director George Lucas had worked into the story, which gave his tale a classic feel that people of many cultures could appreciate. It didn't hurt that Lucas was quick to credit his cinematic sources and influences, including the samurai films of Japan's Akira Kurosawa.

The tremendous worldwide success of *Star Wars* ushered in an era of "global filmmaking" as movie studios vied to produce splashy, action-packed entertainments that would play in many markets.

NOTABLE ACTORS OF THE 1970s

Woody Allen, 1935–

Marlon Brando, 1924–2004

Charles Bronson, 1921–2003

Clint Eastwood, 1930–

Sally Field, 1946–

Jane Fonda, 1937–

Dustin Hoffman, 1937–

Glenda Jackson, 1936–

Diane Keaton, 1946–

Jessica Lange, 1949–

Steve McQueen, 1930–1980

Paul Newman, 1925–2008

Jack Nicholson, 1937–

Ryan O'Neal, 1941–

Al Pacino, 1940–

Richard Pryor, 1940–2005

Robert Redford, 1937–

Christopher Reeve, 1952–2004

Burt Reynolds, 1936–

George C. Scott, 1927–1999

Sylvester Stallone, 1946–

Barbra Streisand, 1942–

John Travolta, 1954–

John Wayne, 1907–1979

as an "angry, violent screed about the racist persecution of a poor black everyman."[2] In *Song*, a pimp named Sweet Sweetback is celebrated as a cult figure after killing two white police officers who have abused their authority in the black community. Van Peebles's film cost $500,000 to produce—and then grossed $20 million within its first few months of release. In 1971, Hollywood was suffering financially and this skyrocketing success caused studios to focus on creating more blaxploitation movies. Approximately 40 movies were made during the first half of the 1970s, and three—Van Peebles's *Song,* plus *Shaft* and *Superfly*—became quite successful. In all three movies, black heroes fight against and beat the white system.

These films starred black actors and deliberately targeted black audiences. The actors expressed sexuality and served as heroes who survived the system and escaped the ghetto. Ironically, these films were frequently produced and directed by white professionals, although both *Shaft* and *Superfly* had African American directors. Despite the appropriation of black expression by white-run studios, these films allowed a greater black presence in the theater and created

ACADEMY AWARD WINNERS

1970 Picture: *Patton*

Director: Franklin J. Schaffner, *Patton*
Actor: George C. Scott, *Patton*
Actress: Glenda Jackson, *Women in Love*

1971 Picture: *The French Connection*

Director: William Friedkin, *The French Connection*
Actor: Gene Hackman, *The French Connection*
Actress: Jane Fonda, *Klute*

1972 Picture: *The Godfather**

Director: Bob Fosse, *Cabaret*
Actor: Marlon Brando, *The Godfather*
Actress: Liza Minnelli, *Cabaret*

1973 Picture: *The Sting*

Director: George Roy Hill, *The Sting*
Actor: Jack Lemmon, *Save the Tiger*
Actress: Glenda Jackson, *A Touch of Class*

1974 Picture: *The Godfather, Part II*

Director: Francis Ford Coppola, *The Godfather, Part II*
Actor: Art Carney, *Harry and Tonto*
Actress: Ellen Burstyn, *Alice Doesn't Live Here Anymore*

1975 Picture: *One Flew Over the Cuckoo's Nest*

Director: Milos Forman, *One Flew Over the Cuckoo's Nest*
Actor: Jack Nicholson, *One Flew Over the Cuckoo's Nest*
Actress: Louise Fletcher, *One Flew Over the Cuckoo's Nest*

1976 Picture: *Rocky*

Director: John G. Avildsen, *Rocky*
Actor: Peter Finch, *Network*
Actress: Faye Dunaway, *Network*

1977 Picture: *Annie Hall*

Director: Woody Allen, *Annie Hall*
Actor: Richard Dreyfuss, *The Goodbye Girl*
Actress: Diane Keaton, *Annie Hall*

1978 Picture: *The Deer Hunter*

Director: Michael Cimino, *The Deer Hunter*
Actor: Jon Voight, *Coming Home*
Actress: Jane Fonda, *Coming Home*

1979 Picture: *Kramer vs. Kramer*

Director: Robert Benton, *Kramer vs. Kramer*
Actor: Dustin Hoffman, *Kramer vs. Kramer*
Actress: Sally Field, *Norma Rae*

* Highest grossing.

Entertainment

OTHER NOTABLE MOVIES

*M*A*S*H* (1970)

A Clockwork Orange (1971)

The Poseidon Adventure (1972)

American Graffiti (1973)

The Exorcist (1973)*

Chinatown (1974)

Jaws (1975)*

The Rocky Horror Picture Show (1975)

All the President's Men (1976)

Carrie (1976)

Network (1976)

Taxi Driver (1976)

Close Encounters of the Third Kind (1977)*

Saturday Night Fever (1977)

Star Wars (1977)

Grease (1978)*

Halloween (1978)

National Lampoon's Animal House (1978)

Superman (1978)

Alien (1979)

Apocalypse Now (1979)

The China Syndrome (1979)

The Muppet Movie (1979)

Star Trek: The Motion Picture (1979)

* Highest grossing.

new stars such as Jim Brown, Ron O'Neal, Richard Rowntree, Tamara Dobson, and Pam Grier. As the genre developed, critics pointed out how later films focused on the sexual and aggressive features of the genre to the degree that they overshadowed development of black identity. As more movies were made, they became more formulaic and stereotypical. By 1976, the movement crashed for two reasons. One, the market was so targeted that it became difficult for studios to make a profit, even though blacks comprised 12 percent of the country's demographics; and two, a segment of the black population began protesting the pimp and/or junkie connotations portrayed by the (anti) heroes of these movies.

TELEVISION

Sitcoms

Groundbreaking is a word frequently used to describe new television shows, to the degree that the term loses meaning and emphasis. One show that does deserve this label, though, is *All in the Family,* which first aired on January 12, 1971, and starred Carroll O'Connor as Archie Bunker; Jean Stapleton as his wife, Edith; Sally Struthers as their grown daughter, Gloria Stivic; and Rob Reiner as her husband, Mike. Because Mike is a college student, he and Gloria live with Archie and Edith.

In the pilot program, Archie and Edith's 22nd anniversary is approaching, so Gloria and Mike decide to plan a surprise Sunday brunch. Archie does not appear grateful for their efforts and misunderstandings ensue. From this plot summary, it's easy to infer that a series of slapstick twists and turns will occur to the sound of canned laughter, and that all will be solved within the confines of 30 minutes.

That, however, didn't happen. Instead of dealing with trivial disagreements that could be quickly resolved during the brunch, Archie and Mike argued passionately about prejudice, politics, and religion, a focus that was radically different from previous sitcoms.

Besides being innocuous, sitcoms of the 1960s—some of which carried over from the 1950s—employed significant elements of fantasy and implicitly asked viewers to not question the impossibility of their premises. These shows include *Mr. Ed; My Mother, the Car; Lost in Space; Flying Nun; Gilligan's Island; Bewitched; Get Smart;* and *I Dream of Jeannie.*

On the cusp of the 1970s, though, Norman Lear and his partner Bud Yorkin (Tandem Productions) decided to smash through the blandness that had served as entertainment on television. Using the British show *Till Death Do Us Part* as his model, Lear created a script wherein the Bunker family would bring social issues such as racism, sexism, abortion rights, homosexuality, and menopause to prime TV in a comic fashion. Persuading ABC to air the program, though, proved impossible. After taking his pilot to CBS, Lear needed to compromise with the head of the station's standards and practices department, William Tankersley, who believed that the 1960s model of programming was appealing to all and offended no one. Surprisingly, though, Tankersley and Lear came to an agreement, wherein Lear would remove scenes such as the one when Mike came downstairs while zipping up his pants but be permitted to keep all politically controversial material in his script—and thus the show aired in January 1971.

O'Connor's character, Archie Bunker, was key to the show's premise. Archie worked as a foreman on the docks and drove a cab on the side. His world view was narrow and bigoted, and he called people "wops," "yids," "coons," and "Hebes;" when reminded that Jesus was, in fact, Jewish, he responded, "Only on his mother's side." He called his son-in-law "that no-good, lunk-headed Polack" and "Meathead." He nicknamed his wife "dingbat" and, whenever she talked too much or said something that upset him, Bunker told her to "stifle"—and yet, despite all these intolerant and hurtful statements, O'Connor portrayed a man who, deep down, loved his family and was even tender-hearted.

Jean Stapleton's Edith provided a perfect foil for Archie; Edith Bunker was patient and tolerant, and her sunny nature defused situations. Gloria Bunker Stivic, played by Sally Struthers, often had to mediate between her conservative and bullheaded father and her liberal and passionate husband; Mike Stivic, played by Rob Reiner, was earning his sociology degree while living in the Bunkers' household and his opinions were nearly always the polar opposite of his father-in-law's. Their next-door neighbors, the Jeffersons, also played an important role in the show. George Jefferson was as biased toward the white race as Archie was about the black; George's wife, Louise (or Weezie) was open-minded and warm-hearted—and Edith's best friend. Their son Lionel rounded out the family; a friend of Mike's, he made low-key and witty observations about his family's situation.

Viewer reactions to Archie's character varied widely. Some proffered that, because Archie was the butt of most jokes, the show exposed bigotry as ridiculous. Many people applauded the show for promoting tolerance, but other viewers enjoyed watching Archie Bunker because they agreed with what he said.

All in the Family was revolutionary and the *Washington Post* credited the show for paving the way for another new show, *Sanford and Son*.

Debuting a year after *All in the Family*, *Sanford and Son* was set in Watts, the site of a recent race riot. The plot and humor frequently centered on conflicts between the father, Fred Sanford (Redd Foxx), and the grown son, Lamont (Desmond Wilson). Fred's character was outspoken and somewhat manipulative; if not given what he wanted, he would clutch his chest and talk of having "the big one," a heart attack that would send him to heaven to reunite with his deceased wife. Lamont played a straightforward character who attempted to reason with his curmudgeonly father as he blustered his way through various get-rich-quick schemes that invariably failed.

All in the Family, on CBS television, ran from 1971 to 1979 and broke new ground in a comedy by covering such social issues as bigotry and sexism. Shown from left: Rob Reiner, Sally Struthers, Jean Stapleton, and Carroll O'Connor (as Archie Bunker). Courtesy of Photofest.

Entertainment

Entertainment

> ### NOTABLE TV SHOWS
>
> *All in the Family*
>
> *The Bob Newhart Show*
>
> *Charlie's Angels*
>
> *The Flip Wilson Show*
>
> *Happy Days*
>
> *Laverne & Shirley*
>
> *Little House on the Prairie*
>
> *The Mary Tyler Moore Show*
>
> *M*A*S*H*
>
> *One Day at a Time*
>
> *Roots* miniseries
>
> *Sanford and Son*
>
> *Saturday Night Live*
>
> *60 Minutes*
>
> *Three's Company*
>
> *The Waltons*

Another new show that year that relied on humor and focused on the behavior of black Americans was the *Flip Wilson Show*. This was America's first successful variety show hosted by an African American. Clerow "Flip" Wilson first appeared on the *Tonight Show*, the popular late-night talk show hosted by Johnny Carson. After receiving national exposure on the *Tonight Show*, Wilson was offered his own show on which he shared jokes and humorous stories and portrayed characters such as the wildly dressed Geraldine Jones. Wilson partially based Geraldine on the Butterfly McQueen character (Mammy) in *Gone with the Wind*, making Geraldine unrefined but honest, flirtatious without being trashy, demanding of—and receiving—respect from her off-screen boyfriend, Killer. Wilson also hosted well-known guests on his show.

The program won two Emmys its first year—for the best variety show and for the best writing in a variety show—and relied on outrageous humor for its success. Meanwhile, Norman Lear created yet another successful television show: the *Jeffersons*, an *All in the Family* spin-off featuring the Bunker family's black neighbors.

Successful as these producers were, another duo provided them with competition for the title of top television producers: Mary Tyler Moore and her husband, Grant Tinker (MTM Enterprises). Their breakout program, the *Mary Tyler Moore Show*, featured Mary as a single woman working at a television studio in Minneapolis. Mary was originally to be a divorcee, but CBS feared that viewers wouldn't separate Mary's new character from the one she played in the 1960s' *Dick Van Dyke Show*—and would therefore assume that Mary had left the beloved Van Dyke. Therefore, Mary was portrayed as a single woman who'd just suffered through the breakup of a longtime romance.

Although this idea does not seem daring today, it was of significance then because of the feminist resurgence that was occurring in the country. The show debuted in September 1970, shortly after the August 26, 1970, "Women Strike for Equality" demonstration during which women marched in protests across the country—most notably in New York—to both honor the 50th anniversary of the ratification of the Nineteenth Amendment, which granted women the right to vote, and to protest the continuing oppression of women.

According to author Bonnie J. Dow, the *Mary Tyler Moore Show* was the first successful program to portray the influence of the women's movement. Although Mary was not the first working woman to appear on television, she was the first to have a satisfying career. Moreover, her profession was not one where she was subservient to men or where she had to put the needs of others before her own. Mary was novel because she had a position of authority, was unmarried, and lived alone. She had personal freedom.

Another strong female starred as the lead of an early 1970s sitcom; yet another spin-off from *All in the Family*, the title was simply *Maude*. Played by Bea Arthur, Maude was the strong-willed, determined, and opinionated foil to Archie Bunker; her viewpoints were liberal and she seldom shied from sharing them.

Maude was already divorced from her fourth husband when the plotline began, and she lived with her current husband, Walter, and her divorced daughter. In the series, Walter and Maude deal with his alcoholism, and they decide to abort a late-in-life pregnancy.

Lear also produced *One Day at a Time,* which debuted in 1975 and featured a recently divorced professional mother who was raising two head-strong teenaged daughters.

Finally, no 1970s sitcom listing would be complete without mentioning *M*A*S*H,* a show set in a field hospital in Korea during the Korean War. Doctors and nurses used humor, sometimes dark, sometimes absurd, to deal with the horrors of war. Although Alan Alda is generally considered the star, it was the interactions of the various characters that brought richness and texture to this ensemble show. One of the most memorable characters may be the cross-dressing Max Klinger, played by Jamie Farr; this character hoped that dressing in outrageous clothing, including dresses and feather boas, would label him unsuitable for duty and would therefore get him sent home. The show debuted on September 17, 1972, and outlasted the decade. Some consider *M*A*S*H* the finest ever produced for television.

From the mid-point of the decade on, a degree of fantasy returned to television shows such as *Mork and Mindy, Charlie's Angels,* and the *Love Boat.* Nostalgia also reigned, as evidenced by *Little House on the Prairie,* starring Michael Landon and telling the story of a pioneer family in Minnesota; the *Waltons,* starring Richard Thomas and focusing on an idealized version of family life during the Great Depression; *Happy Days,* starring Ron Howard and Henry Winkler, and the ensemble show, *Brady Bunch.*

Soap Operas

In 1970, another television genre was reaching fruition: the soap opera. That year, 20 million people watched one or more of the 19 serial shows wherein plotlines continued from show to show. At the beginning of the decade, soap operas aired from 11:30 A.M. to 4:30 P.M., and each show lasted 30 minutes, Monday through Friday. On January 6, 1975, *Another World* expanded to one hour; shortly thereafter, *Days of Our Lives* and *As the World Turns* followed suit.

Although soap operas were traditionally considered programming for housewives, a study indicated that 30 percent of early viewers of *All My Children,* a soap opera that rose to prominence in the 1970s, were either males or younger viewers.

By 1976, soap operas were so popular that *Time* magazine devoted a cover story to *Days of Our Lives,* with the headline "Soap Operas: Sex and Suffering in the Afternoon." University level courses were taught on the genre and the 1970s saw the creation of many new programs. For example, *All My Children* (Agnes Nixon, ABC) premiered as a half-hour program on January 5, 1970, and dealt with social issues ranging from child abuse to Vietnam War protests. Highlights include the Emmy Award won by Mary Fickett in 1972; Fickett's character, Ruth Parker Brent, criticized the Vietnam War after her on-screen son was drafted. This was the first Emmy awarded to a daytime actor. In 1974, *All My Children* aired an episode wherein Brent's son, Phil, was shot and then dragged away by a young Vietnamese boy; this was the first war scene aired on daytime television.

Also in 1973, Erica Kane (Susan Lucci) underwent an abortion because she did not want a pregnancy to affect her modeling career, an option that was legal because of the recent *Roe vs. Wade* decision. Fan mail supported Erica's choice—one that was made against the advice of her soap opera husband—but the writers still had the character suffer from septicemia so she would not escape punishment for her decision.

Variety Shows

Flip Wilson created the first successful variety show featuring a black American. Other successful variety shows of the 1970s include:

Sonny and Cher (CBS): Debuting on August 1, 1971, this show featured a married couple who sang duets, hosted guests, and bickered. Cher became well known for her outrageous outfits and she even exposed her belly button, a first in television history. Personal troubles marred the show's success. At the end of the 1973–1974 season, with the show still rated eighth on television overall, Sonny filed for divorce and the show ended. Sonny and Cher each created a variety show without a partner, but both shows flopped—causing the divorced couple to try, once again, to perform on television together. So, on February 1, 1976—with Cher pregnant with her estranged rocker husband Greg Allman's baby—the new show debuted. Problems quickly cropped up, though; producers didn't think that Cher, a recent divorcee, should wear outlandish costumes; legal battles prevented skit routines from being revamped; and the quality of new writing was uneven.

Donny and Marie (ABC): Donny and Marie Osmond were a brother-sister team from a large Mormon family; the boys of the family performed together as the Osmond Brothers and Donny was the most popular. Donny and Marie's first television special aired in November 1975; it was so successful that their variety show began appearing in January 1976. The most popular segment of the show was called "A Little Bit Country, A Little Bit Rock & Roll," during which Marie would perform country vignettes, while Donny would provide the rock & roll. They also bantered with one another on screen.

Saturday Night Live (Dick Ebersol and Lorne Michaels, NBC): "Hi. I'm Chevy Chase—and you're not." Teenagers and young adults flocked to the late-night antiestablishment comedy show to hear punch lines such as this. Originating on October 11, 1975, this show featured satiric skits that thumbed figurative noses at convention and often mocked politicians and other top public figures. Stars included Chevy Chase, John Belushi, Dan Aykroyd, Jane Curtin, Gilda Radner, Garrett Morris, Bill Murray, and Laraine Newman. Ongoing skits focused on the Coneheads, Land Sharks, and the Samurai Deli. The show featured a different celebrity guest host each week, and guest bands—some quite popular, others cutting-edge—performed on the show. Although the show has undergone countless changes, most specifically in talent, it still airs today.

News

News reporting evolved during the 1970s; for the first time, a news program—CBS's *60 Minutes*—successfully competed against prime-time programming. This show featured thought-provoking and controversial interviews and viewers responded to its quality.

Moreover, despite pressure from the Nixon administration, television stations—most notably CBS—aggressively reported on the Watergate scandal and subsequent presidential resignation. Horrifying and mind-numbing updates of the Vietnam War also caused anxious viewers to tune in for details. Meanwhile, morning news shows continued to gain acceptance. Starting in 1976, presidential debates became an anticipated ritual.

The Miniseries

In 1977, ABC aired the eight-part miniseries *Roots*. Based on a book written by Alex Haley, the series shared a broad yet intimate look at an African American family whose ancestor Kunta Kinte was kidnapped, sold into slavery, and brought to the United States against his will. He is maimed as the result of several attempts to escape, but finally settles down on his owner's plantation, marrying the cook and having a daughter—who is eventually sold to another owner. Viewers watch 200 years of historical events unfold through the eyes of Kinte, played by LeVar Burton, and his descendants.

Television executives compressed this series into the shortest number of days possible, fearful of not garnering enough audience, but nearly half the population of the United States at the time, 100 million people, watched the conclusion of the series while 130 million viewers watched at least part of this historical drama. This miniseries was so successful that it helped launch ABC into first-place ratings and revenues for the first time, and it spurred an interest in many Americans to search for their own roots.

At the time of the airing, speculation arose about how the series would affect race relations in the United States. *Time* summarized observations this way: "Many observers feel that the TV series left whites with a more sympathetic view of blacks by giving them a greater appreciation of black history"—and yet, "the same article reported that white junior high school students were harassing African Americans and that black youths assaulted four white youths in Detroit while chanting, 'Roots, roots, roots.'"[3] Post-airing, many also speculated about the degree of truth portrayed in the miniseries. Haley himself called it "faction," or a blend of fact and fiction.

Overall, *Roots* was the impetus of the successful television miniseries, helping to solidify it as a viable format for television.

Made for TV Movies

Many made for TV movies were designed to appeal to female viewers, many of whom—because of a purchase of a second television set—gained control over what they viewed. One of the first successful and well-done made for TV movies was *Duel.* Produced by Steven Spielberg and starring Dennis Weaver, this 1971 movie eventually appeared in European cinemas. Overall, made for TV movies tended to have lower budgets and fewer actors; many focused on melodramatic subjects, leading to a derisive nickname of "disease of the week" movies; plots were often written to reach cliffhangers that coincided with commercial breaks.

Cable Television

The notion of cable television providing a deluxe—or extra—service for additional pay was first introduced in November 1972, when Service Electric first aired Home Box Office (HBO) in the Wilkes-Barre, Pennsylvania, area. Only a few hundred households had subscribed by the time the channel aired, but it quickly gained more subscribers. By 1975, 3,506 cable systems existed, serving nearly 10 million subscribers. These viewers could select from numerous channels, as compared to the three or four channels available to viewers of broadcast-only television.

In 1975, HBO aired the well-touted Joe Frazier-Muhammad Ali heavyweight boxing match. The following year, Ted Turner's WTBS Atlanta channel broadcast throughout much of the country via cable television, as did the channel eventually known as the Family Channel. Viacom's Showtime debuted in March 1978—and ESPN, which began airing sports programming around the clock, first appeared in 1979 under the name Sports Programming Network. Its popularity was quite high, even from its inception, and reached more than 57 million homes. 1979 also saw the debut of the children's cable channel, Nickelodeon, and the Movie Channel. Ted Turner's supernews channel, Cable News Network (CNN), was only a year away.

The most obvious transformation wrought by cable was the plethora of programming choices; shows and channels were becoming both more abundant and more niche. Parents could, for example, allow their children to watch Nickelodeon or the Family Channel, safe in the knowledge that sex and vulgar language would not be part of the programming. Sports lovers no longer needed to wait for specific times to watch athletic activities, and movie fans could enjoy films in the convenience of their own homes, day or night. Satellites made live shows from around the nation and the world possible.

PUBLIC TELEVISION

Network television also faced competition from public broadcasting. In 1969, the Public Broadcasting Service (PBS), which replaced National Educational Television (NET), began its broadcast service. This form of programming depended upon corporate sponsorships and private donations rather than funds collected from companies that paid to run advertisements during commercial breaks. Viewers therefore had a choice that included watching programming—albeit limited at first—that did not feature slick commercials. One of the initial PBS programs was the Children's Television Workshop's *Sesame Street,* an award-winning children's program that aimed to teach preschool children the basic skills needed for kindergarten. Characters included Jim Henson's muppets Ernie and Bert, Big Bird, Cookie Monster, Grover, and Oscar the Grouch, among others. The show continues in the twenty-first century and has helped countless children (and their parents) learn about numbers, letters, and concepts. In 1975, AT&T began sponsoring PBS news programming; initially called the *Robert McNeil Report,* the show became better known under its revised name, the *McNeil-Lehrer Report.*

Disco

Disco music tends to be upbeat with a regular rhythm. Disco dances range from choreographed line dances, often created for one particular song, to freestyle movements that fit the beat of the music being played. Dance floors in the 1970s were frequently crowded; colored lights flashed, often around a large silvery disco ball. Men and women alike wore flashy outfits, including tight

Entertainment

spandex pants, glittery tops, and platform shoes—and the music thumped throughout the room in an insistent bass beat.

It is difficult to separate disco as dance from disco as music, as the beat of the music fueled the dance—and the two are so intertwined that the same word—disco—is used to describe both the songs and the corresponding dance steps. Disco in the 1970s first became popular in the middle of the decade with people dancing to songs such as "Rock the Boat" by the Hues Corporation. Donna Summer's music epitomized the disco scene later in the decade, with songs such as "Love to Love You, Baby," "Hot Stuff," "Heaven Knows," and "Last Dance."

Identifying the first disco song ever created is difficult. Various musical genres contributed to the culmination of the sounds and steps of disco, including funk and soul, rhythm and blues, and Motown and jazz. During the late 1960s, various male counterculture groups, most notably gay but also heterosexual black and Latino, created an alternative to rock 'n' roll, which was dominated by white—and presumably heterosexual—men. This alternative was disco, and, by the mid-1970s when it became mainstream, it was an amalgamation of the talents and influence of many subgenres.

In 1977, after the movie *Saturday Night Fever* debuted, dancers would disco in the style showcased in that extraordinarily popular film. In the movie, partners danced the steps of the hustle in a couple format, borrowing heavily from salsa and swing and adapting that to the continuous disco beat. In this dance, the male spins his female partner quite frequently, drawing her close to him and then pushing her away. In the movie, characters danced to songs of the Bee Gees, including "Staying Alive" and "How Deep Is Your Love," and people all around the country attempted to duplicate those snazzy moves.

Near the end of the decade, though, disco suffered from an enormous backlash. People criticized the disco scene for numerous reasons. The music was too feminine, it was meaningless, and the disco lifestyle was too connected with sex and drugs.

Drama

The 1970s witnessed an upswing of African American musicals, including *Raisin,* which won the Tony Award for best new musical; Virginia Capers won a best actress award for her performance. In this play, an extended family waits for an insurance check after the death of a family member and each has a different reason for wanting that check.

In 1975, *The Wiz,* a play based on Frank Baum's *Wizard of Oz,* won seven Tony awards and ran for 1,672 high-energy performances. The cast urbanized the story; the most popular song was *Ease on Down the Road,* which was sung by characters as they danced down the Yellow Brick Road. The following year, *Bubbling Brown Sugar* celebrated the Golden Years of Harlem, which received six Tony nominations, and a new production of *Porgy and Bess* appeared on stage. In 1978, Nell Carter won the Best Actress in a Musical Tony for *Ain't Misbehavin'.*

In 1970, for the first time ever, the Equity Council allowed someone—the New York Public Library—to tape performances for archival purposes; at the end of that year, an off-Broadway strike over pension fund issues affected 17 shows.

NOTABLE THEATER

Sleuth, 1970 (1,222 perfs.)

Jesus Christ Superstar, 1971 (711 perfs.)

Grease, 1972 (3,388 perfs.)

Pippin, 1972 (1,944 perfs.)

The Magic Show, 1974 (1,920 perfs.)

A Chorus Line, 1975 (6,137 perfs)

Same Time, Next Year, 1975 (1,453 perfs.)

The Wiz, 1975 (1,672 perfs.)

Oh! Calcutta! (revival), 1976 (5,959 perfs.)

Annie, 1977 (2,377 perfs.)

Gemini, 1977 (1,819 perfs.)

Ain't Misbehavin', 1978 (1,604 perfs.)

The Best Little Whorehouse in Texas, 1978 (1,584 perfs.)

Dancin', 1978 (1,774 perfs.)

Deathtrap, 1978 (1,793 perfs.)

Evita, 1979 (1.567 perfs.)

In 1975, nine Broadway shows shut down over a musicians' strike that lasted 25 days.

A rock opera—*Jesus Christ Superstar*—caused controversy. Created by Tim Rice and Andrew Lloyd Webber, it first appeared in 1970 and highlighted personal struggles between Jesus and Judas Iscariot. The play opens with Judas confronting Jesus, telling him that his popularity is getting out of control. Mary Magdalene then massages Jesus with ointment, further angering Judas, who doesn't think that Jesus should hang around with a former prostitute. The play first appeared on Broadway on October 12, 1971, and received mixed reviews, along with criticism from Andrew Lloyd Webber. Some religious groups also condemned the play, aghast at Jesus's portrayal as man, not God; the omission of the resurrection, they said, was sacrilegious. In 1976, the opera began a national tour, which continued until 1980.

In 1975, *A Chorus Line* by Michael Bennett first appeared on Broadway. This play featured a group of 25 desperate dancers vying for eight spots on a chorus line and it ran for 6,137 performances, becoming the longest-running show in Broadway history; it received the New York Drama Critics Award, the Pulitzer Prize, and nine Tony Awards, as well. All this was accomplished with no real scenery, except mirrors, and no costumes except for leotards and a "few spangles for the finale."[4] This, contrary to what worked for most plays, was truly an ensemble with no discernable star.

In 1979, Andrew Lloyd Webber and Tim Rice premiered *Evita,* which depicts Juan Peron's rise to power as president of Argentina and the significant role played by his wife in this event. Both *Evita* and *Jesus Christ Superstar* were inspired by musical albums. In *Evita,* the lyrics were partially based upon *Evita: The Woman with the Whip,* which drew upon stories told by her enemies and victims. After the play appeared, a more sympathetic biography of Evita was written.

The play *Evita* illustrates how mediums blended together and borrowed inspiration from one another in the 1970s: A biography inspired songs— that inspired a play. In another example, a 1979

play *The Elephant Man* told the real-life story of Joseph Merrick, a man who suffered from a disease that horribly deformed his face. Shortly after that play appeared, a character on a popular television Show discovered that he, too, had the disease.

RADIO DEBUTS OF THE 1970s

"American Top 40" (1970): weekly countdown of the top songs on the national pop charts, hosted by Casey Kasem.

"All Things Considered" (1971): public radio's afternoon news and public affairs program, emphasizing long-form, in-depth features and interviews.

"Earplay" (1972): innovative radio drama series, presenting adapted and original radio plays on National Public Radio.

"A Prairie Home Companion" (1974): variety show hosted by Garrison Keillor, featuring old-time music, comedic skits, and stories about the fictional town of Lake Wobegon.

"CBS Radio Mystery Theater" (1974): mystery anthology in the style of the old-time dramas of radio's golden age.

"King Biscuit Flower Hour" (1974): live rock music, featuring performances by Bruce Springsteen, the Rolling Stones, Eric Clapton, the Who, Fleetwood Mac, U2, and many others.

"Dr. Demento" (1974): syndicated music program focused on novelty songs, rock parodies, and unusual instrumentals.

"The General Mills Radio Adventure Theater" (1977): children's drama anthology hosted by Tom Bosley, part of the short-lived "Golden Age of Radio" revival.

"The Larry King Show" (1978): lengthy interviews, listener call-in, and commentary hosted by Larry King.

"Morning Edition" (1979): National Public Radio's daily news program featuring headlines, commentary, newsmaker profiles, and reports on politics, the arts, science, and business.

Fashion

of the 1970s

People in the United States had a relaxed attitude about clothing styles during the 1970s, the decade of athletic shoes and warm-up suits as fashion statements, of denim as high style. T-shirts were plentiful and jewelry was funky. Even one of the more formal pieces of attire—the leisure suit—was known by a name that implied the casual.

In the 1970s, the work of U.S. fashion designers appeared on the Parisian stage—albeit for charity fundraising purposes. Although Americans shed French designers' looks, they incorporated style elements from Africa, Asia, and the Near East. Younger—and some older—Americans embraced the more extreme fashions of the decade, wearing the tallest of shoes and the skimpiest of outfits, while rockers introduced outrageous new looks that became known as punk and glam fashions.

AMERICAN INFORMALITY

Nothing says American informality like Nike—both the athletic shoes bearing that trade name and the company's embroidered "swoosh" symbol. Prior to the rise of Nike, the notion of athletic shoe as fashion statement would have seemed absurd. In 1971 though, Portland State University instructor Phil Knight paid advertising student Caroline Davis $35 to design a logo for the lightweight athletic shoes that he was selling out of

the trunk of his car—and thus the brand of Nike was born.

Whether the fitness and running boom skyrocketed the sales of Nike shoes—or Nike expedited the exercise trends of the 1970s—the fact is that a simple pair of shoes became strongly connected to a cultural transformation. "Working out" was more than a fashion statement; it became a way for people to concentrate on themselves—on their identities as athletes and on their bodies—and what could more appealing than this intense self-focus during the "Me Decade?"

By the spring of 1972, consumers could buy a shoe complete with Nike's swoosh—and Knight raked in $3.2 million in sales that year alone. Each year throughout the decade, sales doubled, and, as more and more Americans wore athletic shoes—even people who weren't necessarily athletes—it became a status symbol to at least appear as someone who exercised.

What precisely, though, did one wear with Nike shoes? In a clever marketing move, the company created a Nike T-shirt that actually debuted before the shoes with the swoosh. Sweatsuits were also fashion statements in the 1970s. In 1972, *Sports Illustrated* declared the warm-up suit one of the hottest fashions around, one worn by people of all ages, genders, and shapes. Warm-up suits came in a wide variety of colors and were generally at

FASHION HIGHLIGHTS OF THE 1970s

Fashion in the 1970s included a variety of styles as individuals dressed more for personal preference than as dictated by designers.

Women wore Laura Ashley fashions with dropped waists and Victorian-inspired dresses. Some wore the prairie look—full ruffled skirts, and high necked blouses with puffy sleeves. Other preferred the Annie Hall look—layered menswear with trousers, vests, and wide ties. Shirtdresses, bodysuits, and slacks with matched blazers were also popular, as were hot pants, jeans tucked into boots, ponchos, halters and tube tops, satin pants, and clogs. The Dorothy Hamill wedge haircut was popular, as was the Farrah Fawcett hairstyle—flowing, layered curls.

Young women and men wore punk styles—Doc Martens boots, body piercings, and dyed, spiked hair. Bell bottoms were common. Young people also wore designer jeans, T-shirts, platform shoes, hipster pants, and bodysuits, until mid-decade. Warm-up suits were in. Men favored open-necked, big-collared shirts, leisure suits, and sideburns.

least 50 percent polyester, thereby keeping their form better than those made entirely from cotton; people wore them with coordinating headbands.

JEANS

Although people considered denim as acceptable work or leisure wear prior to the 1970s, denim became downright fashionable throughout the first half of the decade. People often personalized the "bell" portion of their bell-bottomed jeans by adding metal eyelets and studs, antiwar graffiti, embroidery, and iron-on transfers. Once a pair of jeans became too tattered for wear, people cut off the lower legs to make shorts or purses; squares of denim material were also sewn together to make duffle bags, patchwork skirts, and quilts.

Jeans lost much of their individuality—but garnered even more popularity—when two New York garment makers chose the name "Jordache" for their new line; the designers selected this word because it sounded both French and classy.

Almost instantly, rhinestones and other embellishments disappeared from fashionable jeans, replaced by sleek, straight-legged and simple denims with the Jordache symbol on the right rear pocket. Out went the low-cost pair of pants, and in came "designer jeans" such as those created by Gloria Vanderbilt, Calvin Klein, and Sassoon—with prices as high as $55 per pair. The old stand-bys, jeans made by Levi's and Wranglers, remained popular, however.

The popularity of blue jeans in the decade cannot be underestimated. By the end of the decade, it was difficult to find anyone—young or old—who didn't wear blue jeans, and, as more sophisticated design choices became increasingly available, jeans were a status symbol that didn't require wearers to give up comfort. Meanwhile, the plethora of T-shirt choices—ranging from ones purchased at rock concerts to those making a statement about political, spiritual, or environmental beliefs—made completing outfits a cinch. Tie-dyed shirts were also part of the mix, as were sleeveless tank tops and other halter-style shirts. Footwear choices included clogs and earth shoes.

JEWELRY

Jewelry in the 1970s was often crafted from elements in nature and could be worn with informal clothing. Teenagers often gave their sweethearts silver ID bracelets with their names engraved on the front.

Other popular jewelry trends in the 1970s included puka shells (or beads); silver-and-turquoise "squash blossom" pieces; and spoon rings.

Puka beads or shells are doughnut-shaped, light-colored, hard substances found in Hawaii. Manufacturers would string them tightly on a short cord, just long enough that the necklace rested above the line of clothing; because the style was open-collared shirts, these necklaces made a distinct fashion statement. Some followers of this trend began wearing pukas after teen idol David Cassidy—who played Keith on the television show *The Partridge Family*—wore them.

Others fell in love with puka beads after actress Elizabeth Taylor wore a necklace containing these shells. Another popular—and more exotic—fashion trend in the 1970s was to wear Native

American "squash blossom" jewelry, pieces that consisted of hand-crafted silver and turquoise and generally weighed five or six pounds. Perhaps a jewelry item boasted only one chunk of turquoise, or perhaps several stones formed a blossom; in either case, the jewelry was treasured because each piece was unique and "the color and veining of the turquoise, along with the intricate tooling of the silver, were like individual fingerprints."[1] Others wore spoon rings, which were fashioned from the top portion of eating utensils. The various silverware patterns allowed for a wide variety of designs, and a significant number of Americans wore these rings.

LEISURE SUITS

The quintessential moment of fashion in the 1970s, or at least the most memorable, may have been the white polyester leisure suit—which consisted of a casual jacket and matching pants—that John Travolta wore in *Saturday Night Fever*, 1977. In the most famous still photo from this movie, Travolta is poised beneath the bright lights of the Brooklyn disco, surrounded by darkness and with one hand pointing boldly and confidently toward the sky; that moment, for many, epitomizes the culture of the entire disco era.

This movie both illustrated and contributed to another 1970s fashion curiosity. For the first time in many decades, people paid attention to men's fashion rather than just women's. Who remembers what Travolta's dance partner, Karen Lynn Gorney, wore during that famous scene? The outfit—a bright red, knee-length, scoop-shouldered, swirling dress that twirled with her every move—certainly wasn't subtle, and, had Travolta's outfit not so fully commanded our attention, would have been quite memorable.

As men's fashion began appearing in the spotlight, some women began donning startlingly masculine fashions. After the move *Annie Hall*, 1977, debuted, some women began wearing tweed jackets, neckties, and derby hats. This development echoed Diane Keaton's style in the movie, wherein she wore exaggerated and mismatched male fashions, often oversized. This movie premiered during years of intense feminist debate; it isn't really surprising, then, that some women

literally usurped the shirts off men's backs—or that men's and women's clothing styles blurred and crossed over as traditional gender roles themselves shifted and became less distinct.

Apropos of a decade that abolished the autocratic rules of fashion, other women wore soft and romantic dresses, old-fashioned and loosely flowing.

FOREIGN INFLUENCE

The 1970s were a time of individual expression, of clashes and emerging identities; women wore a wide spectrum of clothing styles throughout the decade. Perhaps skirt length best represents this variety, as some women continued to wear the short miniskirt of the 1960s while others followed the dictates of Parisian fashion and chose to don the midi; still others wore loose flowing skirts—maxis—that draped nearly to the floor, and were often called "granny skirts."

Fashion buyers in America panicked at this broad scope of skirt-length options, having heavily invested in the midi after assuming that American women would—as they had in the past—desire what had been fashionable in Europe just six months prior. Younger women especially disliked the midi and refused to give up their miniskirts for the new style; furthermore, hot pants—a pair of shorts that were skimpier than the mini—gave women an even more daring fashion alternative, so the Parisian midi faced significant challenges.

French designers of note during the 1970s included Yves Saint Laurent, Christian Dior, Hubert de Givenchy, Emanuel Ungaro, and Pierre Cardin. These designers all influenced Americans in their fashion choices, especially among those who wanted a "designer" look. On November 28, 1973, these five designers showed their latest styles at the Palace of Versailles to raise money for the Versailles Restoration Fund. Several American fashion designers also participated in the fundraiser. These included Anne Klein and her assistant Donna Karan; Stephen Burrows; Henri Bendel; Bill Blass; Oscar de la Renta, who began his career by designing for a Parisian couture house; and Halston.

Although individuals and designers in the United States declared a degree of independence from Parisian haute couture, they did not create a fashion culture free from global influences; rather they incorporated elements from Africa, Asia, and the Far East. During the 1970s, many people searched for their ethnic and cultural roots, which helps explain why this decade witnessed a mixture of clothing styles and trends from around the world. From the mid to the late part of the decade, loose flowing garments, including caftans and kimonos, which were available in a wide variety of exotic fabrics, appeared on the fashion scene.

Asian influences appeared as well, as women began wearing quilted jackets reminiscent of Tibetan and Chinese styles. Sometimes these jackets were worn over cotton voile dresses imported from India. Colors ranged from brilliant pinks to mossy greens and sky blues, often accented with gold. Other times, these jackets were paired with gently pleated patchwork skirts.

Fashion gurus imported macramé bags—and even bikinis—from the Greek Isles, along with shawls from Spain. Light cotton gypsy-style blouses also found favor in the 1970s, as did gypsy dresses. Peasant blouses incorporated sleeves so full that they resembled bell-like *engageantes* from the Victorian era of England. Another British fashion influence appeared when petticoats peeked from underneath peasant-styled skirts. Native American looks were imitated, too, especially in lightweight loose shirts and wide dresses.

THE YOUTHFUL LOOK

Platform shoes were among the most distinguishing features of 1970s fashions, and were embraced by teenagers and young adults throughout the country. Soles and heels were cork, wood, plastic, or rubber; by 1975, the sole needed to be at least two inches thick to be considered

In *Cleopatra Jones* (1973), a movie where she plays a sexy drug agent, Tamara Dobson wears a number of outfits showing some more extreme 1970s fashion: platform shoes, wide-legged pants, and flowing skirts. Courtesy of Photofest.

fashionable, with the heel portion reaching five inches in height. Dress shoes, sandals, and even sneakers were modified to the platform style, as were thigh-high lace-up boots. Fans of platform shoes sought out the most original and offbeat designs, which included floral and fruit embellishments, glitter, painted rainbows, stars and moons—and even goldfish in a clear and detachable sole.

Extremes also existed outside of footwear. The summer of 1974 saw the advent of string bikinis. All was string except for the minute triangles that covered women's breasts and another that covered the genitals. String bikinis cost $35–$45, which was somewhat pricey, yet Bloomingdale's in New York sold out of them within two weeks of their arrival.

Hot pants—those short shorts that didn't cover much more of one's bottom than a traditional bathing suit—debuted in the United States about the same time as the string bikini. Boots completed the look. Boots might be shiny and slick, made of textured fabric, covered with rhinestones and beads, or psychedelic in appearance.

Young men often wore their hair at shoulder length, although the trend toward ethnic fashion inspired many of them to sport Afros. Some wore quite extravagant Afros, which led to a 1970s-inspired flashback scene in the *Naked Gun 33 1/3: The Final Insult,* 1994. In this film, a character played by O. J. Simpson could not walk though a doorway because of the hugeness of his 'fro.

Women also wore Afros, and after Bo Derek starred in the movie *10* in 1979, many women copied her look and had their stylists put cornrows—numerous rows of very tight braids with wide spaces between rows—into their hair, a style that African American women had developed. Derek was not the only celebrity to braid her hair with cornrows, but she is the person credited for opening up this style to white women. In 1972, African American actress Cicely Tyson appeared on television with intricate Nigerian braids—and funk and soul musician Rick James also wore cornrows, pre-Derek. Another extremely popular look for women in the 1970s was the Farrah Fawcett hairdo with large rollers used to feather hair back from the face.

ANTIESTABLISHMENT WEAR

Finding a look that startled or offended the "establishment" was difficult during the 1970s, when psychedelic prints, plaid sports jackets, afros, miniskirts, and hot pants were popular.

British rocker David Bowie—and his wife, Angie—were certainly up to that challenge. Almost by accident, the duo gave birth to the Ziggy Stardust look in February 1972. Bowie's manager, recognizing how David enjoyed incorporating elements of cross-dressing—such as skintight catsuits—into his attire, suggested that he wear a costume and makeup every time he left the house. Angie thought David also needed a haircut that stood out from the long straight hair predominating rock culture. Flipping through *Vogue* magazine, they decided on short hair on the top of his head and in the back, with two points of hair traveling down the sides of his face. Angie persuaded David to color his hair red. The following day, he panicked, so they added peroxide and a German dye known as "Red Hot Red."

By the time they were finished, Bowie's hair was spiked and as pinky-orange as it was red. Suddenly, Bowie was the idol of countless teens and young adults who wanted to be part of the antiestablishment in both his native England and the United States.

Other performers who wore glam fashions include Elton John—whose oversized and glittery pairs of glasses and extreme platform shoes helped define the style; KISS, well known for their outrageous red, black, and white face makeup; and Rod Stewart, a British rocker who appears a bit tame next to his counterparts. Perhaps Tim Curry's performance as the transvestite Dr. Franken Furter in the *Rocky Horror Picture Show* best typifies the excessive nature of the glam fashion movement. (See Entertainment of the 1970s.)

Around the time Bowie was creating Ziggy Stardust, punk was emerging as a musical form and lifestyle. Those who identified with this movement made deliberate attempts to startle—and perhaps even antagonize and alienate—others with their wardrobes. Typical outfits included ripped or even slashed clothing pieced together again with oversized safety pins. Wardrobe items clashed with one another; delicate fishnet

The Sex Pistols, with the punk look in the 1970s: spiky hair, plenty of metal, safety pins, leather, and torn clothes. Shown (left to right): Sid Vicious, Steve Jones, Johnny Rotten, and Paul Cook. Courtesy of Photofest.

stockings, for example, might be paired with clunky and masculine-looking combat boots. People incorporated vinyl and other elements of S&M (sadism and masochism) and bondage fetishes in their wardrobes. Hair might be dyed a bright and obviously unnatural shade; spiked; or cut in odd, asymmetrical ways. Accessories ranged from razor blades to chains, and from Nazi armbands to spiked dog collars.

Punk fashion originated in England, and fashion designer Vivienne Westwood and her partner Malcolm McLaren are credited for originating the style. The couple opened a shop named Sex; a band managed by McLaren, the Sex Pistols, purchased outfits from them—and followers imitated their look. Although the punk movement already existed, the Sex Pistols greatly influenced the wardrobe needed to be part of the punk rock scene.

Observers of the fashion noted how carefully the disparate wardrobe elements were juxtaposed against one another; this antifashion was clearly not randomly put together from thrift shop items. Punk's movement, though, was not composed of working class or underprivileged youth; rather nearly one-third of those playing in punk rock bands were former or current art students.[2]

The punk look associated with Vivienne Westwood and the Sex Pistols dominated antiestablishment fashion from about 1975–1978. About a year after this look began appearing, other more subtle ensembles sprang up, perhaps consisting of straight-legged pants and collarless shirts, or combat fatigues. Near the end of the decade, some punk aficionados donned black studded leather jackets and bondage trousers, ironically mimicking a look chosen by more traditional rock and rollers.

During the 1970s, some who embraced the punk rock culture made significant changes to their looks, perhaps putting a controversial tattoo where it could not be hidden or easily erased, or making some other kind of permanent bodily alternation. These "hardcore" punks also slashed their hair into dramatic styles that could not grow out quickly.

Fashion

Food

of the 1970s

As women entered the workforce in increasing numbers in the 1970s, they needed to find ways to balance the demands of their homes, families, and jobs. Convenience foods and fast foods offered convenience and speed of delivery at a relatively low cost. Although warnings about the high fat content and low nutritional value of the meals had already started to surface, the benefits outweighed those concerns for an increasing number of Americans.

Some of the new foods introduced during the decade became entrenched in the American diet, while others were mere fads. Americans explored both European and Asian cuisine, and manufacturers created new appliances to aid these cooks in their exploration of ethnic foods. The desire to return to a more natural lifestyle in the 1970s is reflected in the trend of using more "health foods."

Congress became more involved in farming, rural living, and agricultural issues, changing its philosophy on how best to help farmers and encouraging exports of American crops. Environmental issues rose to the forefront, as well, both on farms and in the country as a whole, and legislators also attempted to address these concerns.

PRODUCT DEBUTS AND TRENDS

Rumors had it that Mikey, the freckle-faced kid from the Life cereal commercials who hated everything, met a dastardly fate in the mid-1970s. Mikey, as the story was told, accepted a dare to fill his mouth with Pop Rocks—a fad candy that shattered or "popped" in your mouth—and then he guzzled a Pepsi. Once Mikey did so, pundits declared, his stomach simply exploded. This urban legend, though, was simply not true.

Although the story was fabricated, Pop Rocks were quite real—and also quite popular when introduced in 1974. Pop Rocks consisted of sugar, corn syrup, and flavoring that was cooked to a hard consistency and that contained trapped carbon dioxide gas bubbles; as the candy dissolved, it snapped inside the mouth. Pop Rocks were reminiscent of Fizzies, the tablets, introduced in 1957, that created a carbonated drink out of water. The fizz in a mouthful of Pop Rocks has been compared to only one-tenth of the carbonation ingested with one single sip of a cola beverage.

Food-related trends that emerged during the 1970s and continued long after the decade ended included gourmet cooking that began on the West Coast and that promoted the use of regional and organic ingredients. Anything that was perceived as "natural" was considered to be "good," even if the natural ingredients were honey and other sweets. Granola, a snack or cereal made from oats, nuts, spices, sweeteners, and various other additions, and a favorite of hippies and college

CANDIES, SWEETS, AND GOODIES OF THE 1970s

Orville Redenbacher's Gourmet Popping Corn (1970);

A&W Root Beer in cans, Jell-O Pudding Treats, and Rolos Candy (1971);

Snapple (1972);

Honey Maid Cinnamon Grahams (1973);

Soft frozen yogurt (1974);

Famous Amos Chocolate Chip Cookies (1975);

Starburst Fruit Chews, Country Time Lemonade, Jelly Belly Jelly Beans, and orange M&Ms (1976);

Mrs. Fields Cookies and Twix Cookie Bars (1977);

Ben & Jerry's ice cream and Reese's Pieces (1978).

Other new foods made cooking easier for women who were focusing more of their attention on the workplace, including Eggo Waffles, Morton's Salt Substitute, and Hamburger Helper (1970); smoked Spam and McCormick's "Roast in a Bag Kit" (1971); Top Ramen, Stove Top Stuffing, Quaker Oats 100% Natural, Celestial Seasonings Herbal Teas, and Tuna Helper (1972); Cup O'Noodles (1973); French Bread Pizzas (1974); and Yoplait Yogurt (1977).

FOOD HIGHLIGHTS OF THE 1970s

1970 Southern California boasts more than 300 health food stores and 22 organic restaurants.

1971 Publication of *Diet for a Small Planet* by Frances Moore Lappé. The book, which sold 2 million copies, points out the heavy toll that meat consumption takes on the earth's resources and advocates combining plant food sources to create "complementary proteins."

1971 An iconic Coca-Cola commercial features a group of attractive young people of various ethnicities gathered on a hilltop in Italy singing "I'd Like to Buy the World a Coke."

1972 The Henson family sells its Hidden Valley Ranch salad dressing business. Dude rancher Steve Henson had created the so-called ranch dressing for his dude ranch clientele in the early 1960s by mixing mayonnaise, buttermilk, and dried herbs.

1974 Adelle Davis, author of *Let's Eat Right to Keep Fit* and other works and an early and tireless crusader for the benefits of eating whole, unprocessed foods and avoiding additives, dies of cancer at age 70.

1975 Per capita consumption of beef, which has risen till this year, begins to decline among both men and women, in large part over concern about the impact of cholesterol on heart disease.

1977 Americans spend 35 percent of their food budget on fast food, up by 10 percent from 1954.

1979 Chef Paul Prudhomme opens K-Paul Louisiana Kitchens in New Orleans, showcasing his blackened redfish dish and igniting a nationwide fad for Cajun-style cooking.

Food

students everywhere, skyrocketed to popularity as one such naturally good food. Practically every major cereal company produced some sort of granola breakfast food.

Salad bars began appearing in restaurants, starting in Chicago in 1971. Vegetarian cookbooks continued to emerge, while ingredients such as brown rice, whole grain breads, and yogurt appeared in more and more recipes. People bought canning supplies to save money during a time of an energy crisis and recession, and 1973 ushered in the Cuisinart food processor, also a help to the frazzled cook. Other appliances purchased by Americans included woks, fondue sets, crock pots, microwave ovens, yogurt makers, bread machines, rice steamers, coffee makers, and food dehydrators. In the 1970s, the spork—a combination spoon and fork—and the first soft drinks in plastic bottles debuted.

Ingredients in diet soft drinks changed and/or were challenged throughout the decade. By 1970, the FDA had banned the use of cyclamates in diet drinks and various food products upon receiving information that the substance caused cancer

President Jimmy Carter, 1976, and his grandson, Jason, with a box of granola cereal on the table. (The president's mother, Lillian Carter, sits to the left.) Although many people made granola themselves, it became available in prepackaged form once it gained popularity. Courtesy of Photofest.

in lab rats. In 1977, the FDA was under pressure to ban saccharin for similar reasons, but it exercised caution and waited for more studies to be conducted.

Shopping experiences changed when the bar code—a series of lines that identified a grocery product—was standardized in 1970. This was the beginning of an improved inventory system for grocers, and, more immediately, it allowed cashiers to rapidly serve and check out customers. Plastic bags first began appearing in grocery stores, as well, slowly replacing the familiar brown paper sacks. In 1974, the FDA and USDA began their voluntary nutrition labeling program, as well as one that required nutrition labels on foods with added nutrients or those that made claims about nutritional value.

Consumers made somewhat different grocery purchases overall during the decade. For example, at the beginning of the 1970s, 34 percent of an average household's food budget was spent on snacks and meals eaten away from home; by the end of the decade that figure increased to 39 percent.

Other dietary factors differed from today's menu. Vegetarianism was not yet embraced by mainstream cooks. Eggs featured more prominently while the composition of dairy products differed from latter decades. More people drank milk in the 1970s—and 81 percent of milk sold was whole, not skim or reduced in fat—but yogurt consumption was only one-sixth of what it was by the 1990s.

Grain consumption differed in comparison, as well. In 1970, the average person consumed 136 pounds of flour in his or her diet; that increased to 200 pounds in the 1990s. Snack food sales—such as pretzels, popcorn, and crackers—increased 200 percent in that time frame, while ready-to-eat cereal sales increased by 60 percent.

COOKBOOKS AND DIETS

A new version of *The Joy of Cooking* by Irma S. Rombauer was quite popular, while Betty Crocker cookbooks arrived in people's homes every year. More tongue-in-cheek cookbooks mocked the Watergate scandal and popular recipes included Watergate Salad and Watergate Cake. The salad featured pistachio-flavored pudding, crushed pineapple, marshmallows, nuts, and whipped topping, while one Watergate cake recipe involved putting green food coloring into an angel food cake mix and adding nuts. According to one newspaper article, the full name of the cake included icing as a "cover up."

Dr. Robert Atkins first presented his high-protein, low-carbohydrate eating plan in 1972 with the release of *Dr. Atkins' Diet Revolution.* His advice ran contrary to what many medical experts and dieticians advised. Dr. Herbert Tarnower formulated his own diet, which consisted of a 7- to 14-day plan; Tarnower stated that a one pound a day weight loss was not unreasonable, given a controlled diet. His plan listed very specific foods in specific proportions to achieve this reduction, and followed a formula of 43 percent protein, 22.5 percent fat, and 34.5 percent carbohydrates.

ELEGANT EATING

More stylish options existed for those entranced by "Nouvelle Cuisine" or "Cuisine Minceur" trends. Nouvelle Cuisine—or new cuisine—advocated that food presentation was very important, as food should engage all five senses and not just the taste buds. Cooks used herbs and spices to lighten up sauces so that the individual flavors were not overpowered. Dishes tended to be simple, but elegant. This cooking style boasts French origins, as does cuisine minceur—or cooking light, low-calorie meals.

According to the International Association of Culinary Professionals, popular foods of the 1970s included homemade breads; Beef Wellington; French foods, especially quiche and crepes; fondue; slow cooker chili; buffalo chicken wings; pasta primavera; Szechwan cuisine; Bundt cakes; and cheesecakes. Cooks concerned with presentation added garnishes to plates, using scallions, tomatoes, parsley, radishes, and carrots in creative and attractive ways.

FAST-FOOD RESTAURANTS

"You Deserve a Break Today . . . at McDonald's"

In 1970, McDonald's reported $587 million in sales from nearly 1,600 restaurants located throughout the United States and in four other countries; that same year, one single franchise, located in Bloomington, Minnesota, racked up $1 million in sales. Just two years later, McDonald's broke the billion-dollar mark. In 1976, McDonald's boasted the sale of its 20 billionth hamburger. In 1977, more than 1,000 chains reported sales topping $1 million, with 11 of them exceeding $2 million.

In 1972, McDonald's debuted the Egg McMuffin, its ham, egg, and cheese breakfast sandwich. In 1975, Sierra Vista, Arizona, hosted the first drive-through McDonald's restaurant, and, in 1977, the fast-food restaurant began targeting to its youngest consumers with its Happy Meals; test-marketed in St. Louis, this product became available nationwide in 1979 as part of McDonald's "Circus Wagon" campaign.

"Have It Your Way . . ."

McDonald's wasn't the only fast-food game in town. Overall, Americans spent $6 billion in fast-food items in 1970 alone, which was 28.6 percent of the total "eating out" funds spent. Burger King ranked second in sales and began offering franchises in the 1960s. It claimed to have offered the first fast-food dine-in service, and it opened up its first drive-through windows in 1975. Its mascot, the Burger King, first appeared in the 1970s, sporting a magnificently jeweled crown and an ostentatious royal robe. Other marketing characters included the Duke of Doubt; Burger Thing; Sir Shakes-a-Lot; and the Wizard of Fries. This decade also saw the invention of the Kids' Club, whose young members could receive discount coupons—and a special surprise on their birthdays.

Food

"Quality Is Our Recipe..."

Dave Thomas opened the first Wendy's Old Fashioned Hamburgers Restaurant in Columbus, Ohio, on November 15, 1969; he named his restaurant after his youngest daughter's nickname. When he opened a second site in Columbus just one year later, he included a pick-up window, the precursor to the drive-through windows of today. The pick-up window even had its own grill, expediting service. Thomas sold his first franchise in 1972 and the restaurant's growth was phenomenal: by March 1979, there were 1,500 Wendy's restaurants. In November 1979, Wendy's claimed to have become the first national chain restaurant to include a salad bar, and the decade ended with 1,767 restaurants located in the United States (including Puerto Rico), Canada, and Europe.

Other Options

A number of other fast-food operations strengthened and expanded their markets in the 1970s. By the early 1970s, Kentucky Fried Chicken was already a publicly held corporation, with more than 3,500 locations. On July 8, 1971, Heublein, Inc. purchased KFC Corporation for $285 million. Glen Bell's Taco Bell became a publicly held corporation in 1969; in 1978, the company and its 868 locations were sold to PepsiCo. Burger Chef peaked shortly before the 1970s began; in the 1960s, though, it was the second most lucrative fast-food restaurant, with only McDonald's being more successful. Burger Chef also stakes a claim to creating the first fun meal for kids. Still other fast-food chains of the 1970s include Hardees and Roy Rogers. In 1971, Pizza Hut became the number

Jack in the Box, the fast food restaurant with an eye-catching sign, is shown in Los Angeles, November 1970. AP Photo/David F. Smith.

one pizza chain in the world, both in number and in sales figures. In the late 1960s, Ralston Purina purchased the small San Diego-based Jack in the Box hamburger restaurant chain, and during the 1970s, they expanded the chain significantly into the Midwest and East of the United States. In 1971, the original Starbucks opened in Seattle, although it did not develop into a chain until well after the decade ended.

Music

of the 1970s

Not surprisingly, songs of the 1970s reflected the social movements of the day, and a number of feminists adopted Helen Reddy's song, "I Am Woman (Hear Me Roar)" as their rallying cry. Although initial sales were mediocre, female fans began requesting to hear the song on radio stations; Reddy won a Grammy Award for this song. In a similar manner, country singer Johnny Paycheck typified the frustrations of blue-collar workers when he sang David Allen Coe's song "Take This Job and Shove It."

Also in the 1970s, some bands began filling up large arenas for their performances. Previously, artists put out albums or they sang in live venues, and this new supersized option amplified the latter choice. Bands and artists who filled stadiums included the Beatles, the Rolling Stones, and the Who. Later on, bands such as Queen, Pink Floyd, Boston, Foreigner, Journey, KISS, and Genesis followed suit, as did some heavy metal bands.

The decade served as a gateway to crossover tunes, wherein artists that appealed to one fan base could also begin to break onto the charts of another.

Teenyboppers worshipped young stars such as Donny Osmond, David Cassidy, Bobby Sherman, and the Jackson 5, which featured the young, talented Michael Jackson. Easy listening fans could enjoy the Carpenters, the Commodores, and Barry Manilow, while those in search of a funkier beat listened to Stevie Wonder's tunes.

FOLK MUSIC

The original folk singers were balladeers who told rhythmic stories set to music. Folk songs shared the struggles and triumphs, the joys and sorrows, of the "common folk." These songs were passed along orally; as generations passed, the music evolved and it isn't unusual to hear several versions of the same song. During the 1960s and 1970s, "folk singers" often wrote their own music, which differed from the more primitive songs that were entirely oral, but contemporary singer-songwriters held true to the spirit of the folk song as they sang heartfelt stories.

Folk singers from the 1960s, such as Bob Dylan, Woody Guthrie, Paul Simon and Art Garfunkel, and Joan Baez, inspired the music of the 1970s, which included the spirituality seeking song, "My Sweet Lord," written and sung by former Beatle George Harrison, and the music of Fleetwood Mac and Bruce Springsteen.

A trend during the 1970s was for singers to write their own songs, often from a first-person perspective. These songs tended to be introspective and were often called "confessional" in tone and content. Carole King experienced

SINGER-SONGWRITER CAT STEVENS

It is hard to fathom how someone could walk away from the money, fame, and success that stardom offers—but that's exactly what Cat Stevens, a pop/folk singer, did in the 1970s. Born Steven Demetre Georgiou to a Greek father and a Swedish mother, Stevens gained a steady following during the 1960s. Near the end of that decade, though, a bout of tuberculosis and a lukewarm reception to some of his new music sent Stevens on a spiritual quest. He wrote two songs in 1970 that reflected that search: "Mona Bone Jakon" and "Tea for the Tillerman," the second of which reached number one on music charts in the United States.

In 1971, Stevens released a successful album, *Teaser and the Firecat,* which included a song called "Peace Train." Many embraced this song as a plea for the Vietnam War to end; Stevens, though, saw the symbolism of the train's journey as something deeper, stating that the locomotive was rolling along the edge of darkness without a known destination.

Over the new few years, Stevens continued his pursuit of the sacred, rejecting life as a Buddhist monk, Zen, Christianity, and various New Age options. He nevertheless released three highly successful albums: *Catch Bull at Four,* 1972, *Foreigner,* 1973, and *Buddha and the Chocolate Box,* 1974.

His brother David gave Stevens a translation of the Koran. Stevens found what he called the "true religion" within its pages. While studying Islam, he released two more albums, *Numbers,* 1975, and *Izitso,* 1977; after officially converting to Islam and choosing a new name, Yusuf Islam, he recorded one last album as Cat Stevens, *Back to Earth.* He then married and focused on his religion, but he recorded one more album, An Other Cup, in 2006 as Yusuf Islam.

significant success in this genre; her 1971 album *Tapestry* sold 11 million copies and garnered four Grammy Awards. King wrote or co-wrote every song on *Tapestry;* some had already been successfully performed by other singers, including Aretha Franklin with "You Make Me Feel Like a Natural Woman" and the Shirelles with "Will You Still Love Me Tomorrow?"

In 1970, singer-songwriter James Taylor released his second album, *Sweet Baby James.* The success of the hit song, "Fire and Rain" brought attention back to his first album and its single, "Carolina in My Mind." In 1971, Taylor released *Mud Slide Slim and the Blue Horizon* and won a Grammy Award for performing Carole King's song, "You've Got a Friend." Taylor continued to release albums during the 1970s, with another significant hit with "How Sweet It Is (To Be Loved by You)." His greatest hits album, released in 1976, sold more than 11 million copies.

Carly Simon, another singer-songwriter, married James Taylor in 1972, shortly after launching her solo career with an album, *Carly Simon* followed by *Anticipation.* In 1972, she released a highly successfully album, *No Secrets,* that featured her signature song, "You're So Vain;" this song admonished an unnamed former lover for his vanity, leading to decades of speculation about who had inspired this song. Simon continued releasing albums on a regular basis throughout the 1970s.

Still other well-known singer-songwriters of the 1970s include Harry Chapin, best known for his singles, "Taxi" and "Cat's in the Cradle." Jackson Browne released albums steadily through the decade, with "Doctor My Eyes," his first hit single, and "Running on Empty," his biggest. Jim Croce became well known for "Time in a Bottle" and "Big Bad Leroy Brown," while Gordon Lightfoot released such songs as "If You Could Read My Mind," "Sundown," and "Wreck of the *Edmund Fitzgerald.*" Joni Mitchell became known as the "female Bob Dylan" for her body of work, although she did not use that label.

COUNTRY MUSIC

One show consistently delivered country music to television audiences throughout the 1970s. "*Hee-Haw*" began in 1969. (See Entertainment of the 1960s.) Featuring celebrity guests who performed country music tunes, "*Hee-Haw*" interspersed corny comedy shticks, often performed by women in scanty and stereotypically rural outfits, in between songs. The show was hosted by musicians Roy Clark and Buck Owens, and was cancelled by CBS in 1971 after executives determined that, although the program showed respectable ratings, it appealed to less affluent demographics. Producers therefore syndicated the program throughout the 1970s and beyond.

The list of well-known country music performers and bands that appeared on the show is lengthy. Bands included Alabama, a group that received its first recording contract in 1977; the Bellamy Brothers, whose 1976 song, "Let Your Love Flow," became an international hit; and the Nitty Gritty Dirt Band, perhaps best known for their 1970 rendition of "Mr. Bojangles."

Individual performers ranged from rising stars to those in the prime of their careers, such as Roy Acuff. By the time Acuff appeared on "*Hee-Haw*," he had been singing on the Grand Ole Opry radio program, which aired on Saturday nights in Nashville, Tennessee, for more than 30 years. In 1974, the radio program moved to the 4,400-seat Grand Ole Opry House, which was adjacent to the country music theme park, Opryland USA.

Other well-established country music stars who appeared on "*Hee-Haw*" include Johnny Cash, the "Man in Black" who sold more than 50 million albums; Conway Twitty, who had 55 singles reach number one on various music charts; and Roy Rogers, known as the "King of the Cowboys," and who appeared in more than 100 movies.

Hee-Haw hosted a wide spectrum of country subgenres—including outlaw country—that became popular in the 1970s. Led by such singers as Waylon Jennings, Johnny Cash, Johnny Paycheck, Merle Haggard, David Allen Coe, Willie Nelson, and Kris Kristofferson, the term outlaw country arose from a song, "Ladies Love Outlaws," sung by Jennings in 1972. In 1976, Jennings and Nelson recorded country's first platinum album, which was titled *Wanted: The Outlaws!* Outlaw country singers often wore their hair long and dressed in faded denims and leather. They often drank hard, got into brawls, and, in some cases, even spent time in prison. They brought a raw hardness back into country music.

After releasing "Ladies Love Outlaws," Jennings's career continued with *Lonesome, On'ry and Mean,* and *Honky Tonk Heroes,* both released in 1973 and both huge hits. Other albums included

The Ramblin' Man and *This Time,* 1974; *Dreaming My Dreams,* 1975; and *Ol' Waylon,* 1977, which included another duet with Nelson. In 1978, the two coproduced an album called *Waylon and Willie* that contained their biggest hit: "Mamas, Don't Let Your Babies Grow Up to Be Cowboys." Jennings then released *I've Always Been Crazy,* 1978, and a greatest hits album in 1979. Nelson, meanwhile, also released several solo albums in the 1970s, including *Shotgun Willie,* 1973, *Phases and States,* 1974, *Red Headed Stranger,* 1975, and *Stardust,* 1978.

Meanwhile, Merle Haggard could genuinely claim to be an outlaw. Sent to prison for 15 years in 1957 on a burglary charge, he continued his rebellious ways inside prison, planning escapes that he never attempted and running a gambling ring from his cell. In the 1970s, Haggard's hits included "Someday We'll Look Back," "Carolyn," "Grandma Harp," "Always Wanting You," and "The Roots of My Raising."

Kris Kristofferson released a solo album, *Kristofferson,* in 1970; this album contained new songs and ones performed in the 1960s. The reception was lukewarm, but when the album was rereleased the following year under the title of *Me & Bobby McGee,* people bought it. Kristofferson's other 1971 album, *The Silver Tongued Devil and I,* was very successful and established him as a recording artist. He won several Grammy nominations in 1972, and he continued to release albums.

In 1971, George Jones, a veteran country music singer, and his new wife, Tammy Wynette, became two of country's biggest stars, selling out concerts across the country. Jones, who had previously sung in a honky tonk style, switched to singing smooth ballads, and in 1972 had a solo hit with "We Can Make It," a song celebrating his marriage to Wynette. Shortly thereafter, their duet "The Ceremony" made the charts. Although the two were finding musical success, their marriage was sometimes described as a soap opera as Jones fought alcoholism and drug abuse; Wynette filed for divorce in 1973, but she quickly withdrew her petition. Their personal life continued to be played out in their songs, with their next hit titled, "We Gotta Hold On." Jones also sang "The Grand Tour," a song about a broken marriage, and "These Days (I Barely Get By)." Shortly after he recorded the latter song, Wynette left Jones again, and, this time, they divorced. Continuing as a singing duo, they still made the country music charts.

Other male country music stars of the decade included Charlie Pride, Charlie Rich, Boxcar Willie, Don Williams, and Hank Williams Jr. Meanwhile, female stars chalked up their own musical successes, with Loretta Lynn receiving fame as the "Coal Miner's Daughter," a hit song released in the 1970s. Lynn used that title for her 1976 biography, and in 1980, Sissy Spacek starred in a film based on Lynn's life, also with that title. Lynn penned songs that detailed the challenges of women's lives, such as 1971's "Wanna Be Free," which showed divorce in a positive light.

Lynn's younger sister, Brenda, who went by the stage name Crystal Gayle, also forged a country music career. Known for her waist-length curtain of shining dark hair, she released her fourth album in the 1970s; her 1977 hit single, "Don't It Make My Brown Eyes Blue," became a number one hit on U.S. country charts and reached number two on the pop charts, as well. Gayle was the first female country artist to have an album reach gold.

Barbara Mandrell also boasted a list of number one country hits, earning millions of dollars from record sales around the world. Her most recognizable songs include "Sleeping Single in a Double Bed," "Standing Room Only," "Years," "One of a Kind Pair of Fools," "I Was Country When Country Wasn't Cool," and "If Lovin' You Is Wrong (I Don't Want to Be Right)."

Dolly Parton incorporated many traditional elements of folk music into her songwriting. After singing duets with Porter Wagoner for many years, she began to record as a solo artist and 1971's "Joshua" became her first number one hit. In 1974, five of Parton's singles in a row became number one: "Jolene," "I Will Always Love You," "Please Don't Stop Loving Me," "Love Is Like a Butterfly," and "The Bargain Store." In 1976, she starred in her own syndicated television program, "Dolly." Her 1977 album, *Here You Come Again,* sold more than 1 million copies and her songs appeared on country and pop charts simultaneously; by this point, her songs were deliberately crafted for crossover appeal to gain pop chart success. For her 1977 album, she also won a Grammy Award.

Post-1970s, Parton sang duets with Kenny Rogers, who also had a significant number of crossover hits on the country and pop charts. Rogers was perhaps the most successful "crossover artist" of the decade, as he found fans in both genres and opened the doors for other easy listening artists to follow this route.

After singing in pop bands in the 1960s, Rogers had his first solo hit, "Love Lifted Me," in 1976. This was followed by a major hit on the country charts, "Lucille." The latter song won the Country Music Association's single of the year award—and also reached number five on the pop charts. Rogers followed this dual success with "Love or Something Like It," "The Gambler," "She Believes in Me," "You Decorated My Life," and "Coward of the County."

POP AND ROCK

April 10, 1970—For pop and rock fans in many countries around the world, shock, anger, and sadness reverberated after Paul McCartney announced that the Beatles had broken up. In December 1970, McCartney sued the other three Beatles—John Lennon, Ringo Starr, and George Harrison—to officially dissolve the group. Throughout the 1970s, rumors circulated that the group was getting back together, but that reunion never happened.

The dissolution of the Beatles was much bigger than the breakup of a band; it was, for a significant demographic of America, the shattering of the symbol of youth as a force to be reckoned with.

Fans could still listen to the "King of Rock 'n' Roll," Elvis Presley. Influenced by the blues, soul music, and gospel, Presley incorporated elements of country and rock 'n' roll to create his unique brand of entertainment. Already a musical superstar by the 1970s, his "Aloha from Hawaii" concert aired on NBC on January 14, 1973, as the first performance broadcast live by satellite; it reached 1.5 billion viewers. After performing a wide variety of hits, including "Burning Love," "Blue Suede Shoes," and "Suspicious Minds," and ending with "Can't Help Falling in Love," Presley completed his show by dramatically flinging his cape into the audience.

Music fans suffered a second loss, though, when Elvis Presley was found dead in his bathroom on August 16, 1977 at the age of 42. People talked about where they were when they heard the news of his death, much as they did when John F. Kennedy died almost 14 years earlier. During his career, Presley had 94 gold singles and more than 40 gold albums, and even though he stopped recording new rock and pop songs during the 1970s, he still sold out concert venues. His death created a gaping hole in the world of music.

The dissolution of the Beatles and the death of the King, though, opened up a vast field of opportunity for aspiring rock singers. In 1969, a struggling singer released an album, *Empty Sky*, in hopes of finding commercial success—but the reception was lukewarm and nothing about the album's sales indicated the level of success that Reginald Dwight and songwriter Bernie Taupin would reach during the 1970s. Dwight began using his musical pseudonym, Elton John, and became known throughout the world for his music, but also for his flamboyant style of dress—which included extraordinarily high and extravagant platform shoes and oversized, glittery, and glamorous glasses—and his melodramatic concert performances.

His first top 10 single, "Your Song," hit the charts in 1970. Thereafter, John had a steady row of hits on the musical charts, including "Levon," "Rocket Man," "Honky Cat," "Crocodile Rock," "Daniel," "Bennie and the Jets," "Goodbye Yellow Brick Road," "Candle in the Wind," and "Saturday Night's Alright for Fighting."

In 1974, Elton John collaborated with John Lennon. Elton John performed "Lucy in the Sky with Diamonds," a Beatles song, and John Lennon's "One Day at a Time;" he and his band were also featured on Lennon's "Whatever Gets You thru the Night" record. The duo performed these songs along with "I Saw Her Standing There" at Madison Square Garden. It was Lennon's last live performance; a deranged fan killed him in 1980.

In 1975, John released *Captain Fantastic and the Brown Dirt Cowboy,* an album containing autobiographical material that detailed how he and Taupin struggled to find musical success. His best song on the album, it is generally conceded, is "Someone Saved My Life Tonight," which referred to a friend persuading John not to marry his fiancée. In 1976, John revealed that he was bisexual. The album reached number one on the charts, as did his greatest hits album. John recorded the song

"Tommy" for the movie of the same name, and he filled stadiums throughout the world wherever he performed.

Other hit singles included "Sorry Seems to Be the Hardest Word" and "Don't Go Breaking My Heart." In 1979, John became the first Western pop/rock star to tour the Soviet Union.

Rock musicians and bands that found success in the 1970s included Peter Frampton, Bob Seger, Bruce Springsteen, Rod Stewart, Meat Loaf, Billy Joel, Chicago, the Eagles, and Journey. Frampton had played live rock 'n' roll prior to releasing his breakout album, but it was his 1976 *Frampton Comes Alive!* album that propelled him to stardom. Selling more than six million copies, the record included such hit singles as "Do You Feel Like We Do," "Baby, I Love Your Way," and "Show Me the Way." His follow-up album, *I'm in You,* sold nearly one million copies.

Bob Seger formed his Silver Bullet Band in 1974, and the group steadily produced albums throughout the 1970s. Seger's themes often focused on blue-collar workers, particularly in the Midwest. His album, *Night Moves,* with a title track of the same name, helped Seger get significant air time play; other songs of note include "Hollywood Nights," "We've Got Tonight," and "Old Time Rock and Roll."

Even better known for his songs about working-class trials, tribulations, and occasional triumphs is Bruce Springsteen. Part folk singer and part rocker, his 1975 hit, "Born to Run" quickly made Springsteen a household name; the song has since become a rock classic. Years later, *Rolling Stone* magazine called the release of this song one of rock's most important moments. Other songs from the album, also called *Born to Run,* were "Thunder Road" and "Jungleland."

Springsteen and his E Street Band toured across the country playing these songs and new ones that Springsteen was writing. In 1978, they released *Darkness on the Edge of Town;* this album contained "Badlands" and "The Promised Land."

Meanwhile, British rocker Rod Stewart had a mammoth hit called "Maggie May" in 1971; the Rock and Roll Hall of Fame later listed this song as one of the world's 500 most influential rock tunes. That album, *Ever Picture Tells a Story,* also contained a harder rock song, "Every Picture Tells a Story (Don't It)," which garnered significant

Music

attention. In 1975, Stewart moved to the United States, creating such hit songs as "This Old Heart of Mine," "Tonight's the Night," "The First Cut Is the Deepest," and "The Killing of Georgie." As the decade progressed, he continued to churn out hit singles, including "You're in My Heart," "Hot Legs," "I Was Only Joking," and "Do Ya Think I'm Sexy?"

Billy Joel has sold more than 100 million albums and won six Grammy Awards during his musical career, kick started by his first big hit, "Piano Man," released in 1973. Other highly successful singles include "Just the Way You Are," "My Life," "Big Shot," and "Honesty." His song, "Only the Good Die Young" stirred controversy, as it featured a worldly male attempting to seduce an innocent Catholic female.

A rock singer who went by the moniker Meat Loaf released an album in 1977—*Bat Out of Hell*—that has sold an estimated 34 million copies. Featuring songs such as "You Took the Words Right out of My Mouth," "Heaven Can Wait," "All Revved Up with No Place to Go," "Two out of Three Ain't Bad," and "Paradise by the Dashboard Light," the entire album has become a classic and the songs still receive significant attention today.

Chicago named their albums in a practical manner, using the appropriate Roman numeral to indicate the sequence of albums they had released. Hits of the 1970s include "Saturday in the Park," "Just You and Me," "Feelin' Stronger Every Day," "I've Been Searching So Long," the Grammy Award–winning "If You Leave Me Now," and "Baby, What a Big Surprise."

The Eagles, led by singer Glenn Frey, found tremendous success in the 1970s, most notably with their 1976 album, *Hotel California;* this album contained hit singles such as "New Kid in Town," "Hotel California," "Wasted Time," and "The Last Resort." Other hits of the decade included "Best of My Love," "One of These Nights," "Take It Easy," "Lyin' Eyes," "Witchy Woman," and "The Long Run."

In October 1977, the progressive rock band Journey hired a new lead singer, Steve Perry, who brought a new style to the band. In 1978, the group released an album called *Infinity,* which featured the song "Lights" written by Perry. This song was played on many radio stations and elevated Perry to rock star status.

Finally, a quartet from Sweden, ABBA, reached a global market and released two of the decade's biggest pop hits: "Waterloo" and "Dancing Queen."

PROGRESSIVE ROCK

The 1970s opened with the deaths of three promising young rocks stars, including Jimi Hendrix, Janis Joplin, and Jim Morrison. Hendrix, electric guitarist extraordinaire, died on September 18, 1970, at the age of 27. Janis Joplin, a gravelly voiced singer who sang powerfully emotional ballads, died three weeks later, on October 4, also at the age of 27. In 1979, Bette Midler played a character based on Joplin in *The Rose* and won an Oscar for her performance. Jim Morrison of the Doors died on July 3, 1971, at the age of 27. He is perhaps best known for his haunting song, "Light My Fire." Joplin's death was clearly attributed to a heroin overdose, while Morrison appeared to have died of heart failure; Hendrix's cause of death was more uncertain, although drugs appeared to have played a role.

Meanwhile, several bands of the 1960s continued with their concerts and studio recordings in the 1970s, including the Rolling Stones, the Who, and Black Sabbath. The Rolling Stones are led by the campy and dramatic singer Mick Jagger and hard-living guitarist Keith Richards, who struggled with drug addiction throughout the decade.

HIT SONGS OF THE 1970s

"Coal Miner's Daughter" (Loretta Lynn)—1970

"Whole Lotta Love" (Led Zeppelin)—1970

"Bridge Over Troubled Water" (Simon & Garfunkel)—1970

"It's Too Late/I Feel the Earth Move" (Carole King)—1971

"You're So Vain" (Carly Simon)—1973

"Dancing Queen" (ABBA)—1976

"Dreams" (Fleetwood Mac)—1977

"The Gambler" (Kenny Rogers)—1978

"Stayin' Alive" (Bee Gees)—1978

"Bad Girls" (Donna Summer)—1979

Music

Their albums during the first half of the 1970s received lukewarm reviews and members of the group pursued individual musical opportunities as the band struggled to regain the momentum they enjoyed in the 1960s. They reunited for an album in 1978, *Some Girls,* the hit single "Miss You" reached number one on the U.S. charts, and the Rolling Stones were back in business.

The Who, featuring guitarist Pete Townsend, vocalist Roger Daltrey, bass player John Entwistle, and drummer Keith Moon, were well known for their extremely energetic live performances that included plenty of Townsend's improvised riffs. During the 1970s, they recorded hit singles such as "Won't Get Fooled Again." In 1978, they returned to their harder rock roots, releasing *Who Are You.* Although this album reached platinum status and served as their comeback album, the band was derailed when drummer Moon died of a drug overdose on September 7, 1978. The other members continued to play together as a band, but the group's identity basically dissolved after Moon's death. On December 3, 1979, their concert in Cincinnati, Ohio, was the impetus for the most deadly rock event ever, as 11 fans were crushed to death in an uncontrollable throng.

Meanwhile, Black Sabbath, fronted by singer John "Ozzy" Osbourne, continued their trademark heavy metal play. In 1971, *Paranoid* sold more than four million copies, their most commercially successful album yet; the most popular song, "Iron Man," fueled sales. The band continued to churn out successful albums that sold more than one million copies—including *Master of Reality,* 1971, *Black Sabbath, Vol. 4,* 1972, *Sabbath Bloody Sabbath,* 1973, and *We Sold Our Soul for Rock 'n' Roll,* 1975. Late in the decade, Osbourne and Black Sabbath parted ways; in the 1980s, he became notorious for biting off the head of a bat during a concert.

The 1970s also witnessed the explosion of several new superstar rock bands. These bands included Aerosmith, AC/DC, KISS, Led Zeppelin, Blue Oyster Cult, Queen, and Van Halen. Aerosmith, fronted by singer Steven Tyler and guitarist Joe Perry, formed in 1970. Their debut album, *Aerosmith,* received respectable attention with "Dream On" played regularly on radio stations. Other hits such as "Train Kept a Rollin'"

also added to the success of the record. Their 1975 album *Toys in the Attic* catapulted them to international stardom and included such hits as "Sweet Emotion," "Walk This Way," and a remixed version of "Dream On." Their next album, *Rocks,* included songs such as "Back in the Saddle" and "Home Tonight." Aerosmith's song "Come Together" became a classic rock anthem.

KISS, a band that played a hybrid of rock and glam music, formed in 1973 with lead singer Gene Simmons and guitarist and vocalist Paul "Ace" Frehley the best known of the band members. Easily recognizable by the face paint they wore during concerts, which included stark white all over with black and red embellishments, their live performances included fire breathing, smoke, and lasers. In 1975, they recorded their breakthrough *KISS Alive* album, which eventually achieved

KISS, circa 1970s. Shown from left: Peter Criss, Gene Simmons, Paul Stanley, (front) Ace Frehley. Courtesy of Photofest.

Music

quadruple platinum status; on this album, they added a guitar solo to their song, "Rock and Roll All Nite," creating a classic rock anthem. A rock ballad, "Beth," from their next album reached number seven on rock charts. In 1977, a Gallup poll listed KISS as America's favorite band.

Led Zeppelin, led by singer Robert Plant and guitarist Jimmy Page, enjoyed significant success during the 1970s, and released one of rock's all-time favorite songs in 1971: "Stairway to Heaven." Meanwhile, Blue Oyster Cult released two of the decade's hard rock favorites: "Don't Fear the Reaper" and "Godzilla."

The British band Queen released two albums before they first toured America. They found significant success with their 1975 album, *A Night at the Opera;* this album included "Bohemian Rhapsody," which became a hit single in many countries. Their 1976 album, *A Day at the Races,* contained the hit "Somebody to Love," which reached number 11 on U.S. singles charts; their 1977 album, *News of the World,* included "We Will Rock You" and "We Are the Champions," songs that are still played at international sporting events.

Lead guitarist Eddie Van Halen of the band Van Halen dazzled the rock world with his skill and innovation with his electric guitar on the band's first album (*Van Halen,* 1978), setting a new standard for rock guitarists nationwide. Employing a variety of techniques, some self-taught, that created animal and machine sounds from his instrument, Van Halen displayed a creativity that was astounding. Lead singer David Lee Roth understood the nuances of showmanship and the band established themselves as forerunners in the 1970s rock world. Within three months, their first album had gone gold; five months later, it reached platinum and eventually sold more than six million copies. Single hits from the album include "You Really Got Me," "Jamie's Cryin'," and "Runnin' with the Devil." The following year the band released *Van Halen II;* their song "Dance the Night Away" hit the Top 20 Singles list.

REGGAE AND DISCO

Reggae

Seldom does one single artist or band represent a movement in the way that Bob Marley and his band, the Wailers, did for Jamaican reggae in the United States in the 1970s. This form of reggae created a unique sound by merging American soul music with traditional African and Jamaican folk music and incorporating elements of *ska* music, which is Jamaican folk music influenced by rhythm and blues. The music relied on bouncy rhythms and an ensemble of musical instruments, most notably the electric guitar and the electric bass.

Themes of reggae songs included love and sexuality, political and social commentary, and the Rastafari movement. The latter advocated that the former emperor of Ethiopia, Haile Selassie I, was the Messiah promised in the Bible.

Bob Marley and his band released *Catch a Fire* in 1973, following it up with *Burnin';* the latter contained songs such as "Get Up, Stand Up" and "I Shot the Sheriff," later recorded by Eric Clapton. After releasing these two albums, the group broke up. Band member Peter McIntosh continued to record under the name Peter Tosh; Bunny Livingston became Bunny Wailer. Bob Marley kept recording, as well, under the name "Bob Marley & the Wailers," releasing his first international hit in 1975: "No Woman, No Cry." In 1976, he released *Rastaman Vibration,* an album that stayed on the top 10 Billboard charts in the United States for a month.

Other reggae performers included Burning Spear, Toots and the Maytals, and Jimmy Cliff. Burning Spear combined political anger against repression with a focus on spirituality, with hits such as "Joe Frazier (He Prayed)" in 1972. Cliff's most popular album in the United States was released in 1975: *Follow My Mind.* International hits by Toots and the Maytals were "Funky Kingston" in 1973 and "Reggae Got Soul" in 1976.

Disco

Disco became so deeply engrained in American pop culture in the 1970s that even classic music icons such as Beethoven and Mozart found themselves posthumously associated with the disco movement, with songs such as "Rock Me, Amadeus" playing on the radio.

Disco as music is deeply intertwined with disco as a dance form. (See Entertainment of the 1970s.) Disco songs were upbeat, in direct contrast to many of the darker rock songs or introspective first-person folk songs written during the 1970s. The music pulsed at quick and steady rhythms and it fused funk and soul with rhythm and blues, Motown, jazz, and swing. Lyrics were teasing and often distinctively sexual.

One of the most popular disco songs, by Van McCoy, urged listeners to "do the hustle." McCoy later stated that "The Hustle" was a last-minute addition to his album, *Disco Baby.* McCoy won a Grammy Award for this song and it was his only song to reach the Top 40.

Yet another disco classic is "Disco Inferno" by the Trammps, while KC and the Sunshine Band provided discothèques with plenty of singles for dance aficionados, including "Get Down Tonight," "That's the Way (I Like It)," "I'm Your Boogie Man," "Shake Your Booty," and "Keep It Comin', Love."

Women who recorded popular disco songs were identified as "disco divas," with Donna Summer surely serving as the queen. In 1975, Summer released a 17-minute version of a song that she wrote: "Love to Love You, Baby." Complete with suggestive moans, the song reached number one on dance charts and quickly became gold. Many radio programs refused to air this song because of its sexually suggestive background sounds.

In 1977, Summer incorporated techno sounds into "I Feel Love," an innovative use of electronic enhancements in music. The following year, she released "Last Dance," another disco hit for which she received her first Grammy. Later that year, she released a live album, *Live and More,* which featured her first number one pop single, "MacArthur Park." In 1979, she released the album for which she is perhaps most famous: *Bad Girls.* This album boasted two number one singles, "Bad Girls" and "Hot Stuff." The album sold more than seven million copies and reached number one on the charts.

Gloria Gaynor had two disco hits of significance: "Never Can Say Goodbye" (1974) and "I Will Survive" (1979). The latter song reached number one on the Billboard Hot 100 list and was adopted as an anthem for the feminist movement, as well as the gay movement. Anita Ward's "Ring My Bell" perhaps served as disco's closing hymn, receiving prominent air play in 1979 before the disco movement began to self-destruct.

The Bee Gees. Left to right: Maurice, Robin, and Barry Gibb. Courtesy of Photofest.

In 1978, a musical group called the Village People performed a song, "YMCA," which detailed gay encounters in YMCA dormitories. Other hit songs included "Macho Man" (1978), "In the Navy" (1979), and "Go West" (1979). One of the band's four singers was openly gay, while the others did not discuss their sexual orientations. Three albums went gold, selling more than 500,000 copies, and four went platinum (selling more than 1,000,000 copies each).

In disco music, the Bee Gees dominated the scene. They were a trio of English brothers, Barry, Maurice, and Robin Gibb, who had moved with their family to Australia. In the early and middle 1970s, they were known for their soft rock harmonies in such songs as "How Can You Mend a Broken Heart" and "Jive Talkin'," but in the late 1970s, they became known for their songs that were played as background music on the soundtrack of *Saturday Night Fever,* the ultimate disco movie. Three singles"—"Stayin' Alive," "How Deep Is Your Love," and "Night Fever" reached number one. A song they wrote for Yvonne Elliman for the movie, "If I Can't Have You," also reached number one. More than 30 million copies of this album sold, but this unprecedented success also had a backlash; as popular as disco was during much of the decade, by the end of the 1970s, few people admitted to being swept into this manic music form—and the Bee Gees suffered from this reversal.

Sports

and Leisure of the 1970s

WOMEN AND SPORTS

Pre-1972, educational institutions were not required to provide equal program activities to its students based on gender. On June 23, 1972, however, this changed when President Richard Nixon signed into legislation Title IX of the Educational Amendments of 1972. This law prohibited gender-based discrimination in any educational program that received any federal funding whatsoever. Although little controversy arose when the act first passed, heated debate soon began. Prompted by concerns stated by the National Collegiate Athletic Association (NCAA), a significant portion of American citizens soon expressed the viewpoint that male sports programs would suffer if funds were diverted to either begin or strengthen athletic programs for females.

In 1974, Senator John Tower proposed the "Tower Amendment," excluding any revenue-producing sports from the act; the amendment was rejected but the debate didn't die. On July 21, 1975, President Gerald Ford signed into legislation language that specifically prohibited gender discrimination in athletics, giving educational institutions three years in which to fully comply. Legislators continued to introduce amendments that would limit the scope of Title IX. Nevertheless, Title IX significantly changed the landscape of women's sports.

Tennis player Billie Jean King was a symbol of female athletic ability during the tumultuous early days of Title IX. Shortly after its passage, King was challenged by Bobby Riggs to a televised match that became known as the "Battle of the Sexes."

Riggs became a world-class tennis player in 1939, when he was just 16. Although his tennis career basically ended in the 1950s, he returned to the spotlight early in 1973 when he challenged—and beat—tennis player Margaret Court; he then announced that women could never beat men in the athletic arena and demanded a match with the "women's lib leader," Billie Jean King, who was 29 years old to his 55. Riggs had already won 20 Wimbledon titles, but King had won the Associated Press's Woman Athlete of the Year award in 1967 and 1973; and she was also *Sports Illustrated's* Sportswoman of the Year in 1972. King, who resented the fact that male tennis players were paid so much more than female champions, accepted this challenge eagerly. Prematch, Riggs wore T-shirts asking for "Men's Liberation," and, during interviews, proclaimed that if he was going to symbolize a male chauvinist pig, he would ensure that he was the biggest male chauvinist pig ever.

On September 20, 1973, approximately 50 million people watched the Riggs-King match on prime time television. Riggs arrived in a carriage pulled by women while University of Houston football players carried King onto the court. Billie Jean King subsequently beat Bobby Riggs in three straight sets (6–4, 6–3, and 6–3), and Riggs credited King's speed and overall excellence for the results.

King was not the only successful female tennis player of the decade. Chris Evert was another powerhouse; in 1970, when she was just 15 years old, Evert beat the world champion, Margaret Court, in a tournament. One year later, Evert reached the semifinals of the U.S. Open, the youngest tennis player to ever accomplish this feat. Keeping amateur status until 1973, Evert had earned $1 million in tennis by 1976—again the first woman tennis player to reach this benchmark. In 1978, she won the U.S. title for the fourth time, the first tennis player to accomplish this since the 1930s.

OLYMPICS, 1972

Three truly memorable events occurred during the 1972 Olympics held in Munich, Germany. Eight terrorists killed two Israeli athletes and took nine more as hostages; all were killed by the following day. Included among the dead was 26-year-old David Berger, a dual-citizenship American who had returned to Israel. Another American, Mark Spitz, was also Jewish, left Germany after the act of terrorism. His Olympic performance before the tragedy was the second memorable aspect of the 1972 games. Before his departure, Spitz had already won four individual gold medals in swimming and had participated in three gold medal relay events; all set world records, giving him a total of seven gold medals, the most anyone had won during a single Olympics Games.

The final event, extremely controversial when it occurred, still causes debate. After the U.S. basketball team lost the gold medal game against the Soviet Union—the first basketball game ever lost in the Olympics by Americans—the U.S. team refused to accept the silver medal. The players felt that they had lost unfairly; they had been winning the game until officials granted the Soviet team three chances to convert an inbound pass. On the third attempt, the Soviets succeeded in their attempts, winning the game with a score of 51–50. Olympic competition was intense between the United States and the Soviet Union during the Cold War era under the best of circumstances, and this controversy added significant fuel to the fire.

OLYMPICS, 1976

The 1976 Winter Olympics were held in Innsbruck, Austria. Interestingly, the games had been awarded to the city of Denver, Colorado, but a state vote against using public funds to help present the Olympics forced the games to move to Austria.

Perhaps the most spectacular performances of the 1976 Summer Olympics (held in Montreal, Canada) were given by 14-year-old Romanian

Bruce Jenner set a world record in the 1976 Olympics with 8,634 points in the decathlon. Courtesy of Photofest.

gymnast Nadia Comaneci, who scored seven perfect 10s and won three gold medals. Nevertheless, four American athletes established themselves as world-class athletes, as well; these include decathlete Bruce Jenner and three boxers: "Sugar" Ray Leonard, Michael Spinks, and his brother, Leon Spinks.

Jenner set a world record by scoring 8,634 points in the decathlete, causing some to label him the "World's Greatest Athlete." He received the Sullivan Award, given to the greatest amateur athlete of the year, and his photo appeared on Wheaties boxes.

Leonard won a gold medal in the Olympics and went on to win the 1979 welterweight championship. He was named "Fighter of the Decade" in the 1980s. Michael Spinks turned professional the year after he won his gold medal in the 1976 Olympics; he is now considered among the four best light heavyweight boxers in American history. Meanwhile, Leon Spinks, post-gold, briefly took away Muhammad Ali's heavyweight boxing title.

BOXING

Heavyweight boxing was dominated by three superstars in the 1970s: Muhammad Ali, Joe Frazier, and George Foreman, and it witnessed the rise of another star, Larry Holmes. "The Fight of the Century," took place on March 8, 1971, between Ali—who was born Cassius Marcellus Clay, but who often went by the moniker, "the Greatest"—and Frazier, who was the reigning heavyweight champion. Ali, who also called himself the "People's Champion," claimed that Frazier couldn't truly be champ until he had beaten Ali—which is just what Frazier did in the 15th round of their match-up at Madison Square Garden; the decision was unanimous.

In January 1973, George Foreman, who was known for his sheer brute strength, challenged Frazier for the title in the first boxing match aired by HBO. Broadcaster Howard Cosell's comments during the culmination of this fight, when Foreman clinched the heavyweight title, are still among the sport's most memorable. Repeated in an emphatic, staccato tone, Cosell simply said, "Down goes Frazier…Down goes Frazier…Down goes Frazier…"

In 1974, Ali, who could "float like a butterfly, sting like a bee," captured the heavyweight crown from Foreman. The fight took place in the Congo and was known as the "Rumble in the Jungle." Ali used his "rope-a-dope" strategy, wherein he rested against the ropes of the ring and allowed Foreman to attack him, hoping that he would wear himself out in the process—which Foreman did.

On October 1, 1975, Ali and Frazier boxed against each other one more time, with 28,000 people in the arena and an estimated 700 million television viewers. Ali, well known for his pithy sayings, promised that the fight would be a "killa and a thrilla and a chilla when he got the gorilla in Manila." Ali won the fight.

BASEBALL

Powerhouse teams of the 1970s include the 1970 Baltimore Orioles, Cincinnati's "Big Red Machine" in 1975, and the Oakland A's during the early part of the decade. In 1970, the Orioles put up a 108–54 record, winning their division by 15 games. The team beat Minnesota in three straight games to win the American League Championship—and then captured the World Series title against the Cincinnati Reds in just five games. The following year, the Orioles' roster included four pitchers who had each won at least 20 games.

In 1975, the Reds duplicated the 1970 Orioles' win-loss record. The team's star-studded lineup included Pete Rose, nicknamed "Charlie Hustle" for his boundless enthusiasm and can-do attitude, and Johnny Bench, arguably the sport's greatest catcher. During the 1970s, a Cincinnati player won the Most Valuable Player award six times; Bench won two of them. Joe Morgan's MVP season in 1975 helped lead the team into the World Series, where it beat the Boston Red Sox in seven games.

The A's boasted stars such as pitcher Rollie Fingers and outfielder Reggie Jackson, and the team won the World Series in 1972, 1973, and 1974. Jackson, after being traded to the New York Yankees, hit four consecutive home runs against the Dodgers during the fifth and sixth games of the 1977 World Series; Jackson's nickname was "Mr. October."

WORLD SERIES

1970 Baltimore Orioles (AL), 4 games; Cincinnati Reds (NL) 1 game

1971 Pittsburgh Pirates (NL), 4 games; Baltimore Orioles (AL), 3 games

1972 Oakland A's (AL), 4 games; Cincinnati Reds (NL) 3 games

1973 Oakland A's (AL), 4 games; New York Mets (NL), 3 games

1974 Oakland A's (AL), 4 games; Los Angeles Dodgers (NL), 1 game

1975 Cincinnati Reds (NL) 4 games; Boston Red Sox (AL), 3 games

1976 Cincinnati Reds (NL) 4 games; New York Yankees (AL), 0 games

1977 New York Yankees (AL), 4 games; Los Angeles Dodgers (NL), 2 games

1978 New York Yankees (AL), 4 games; Los Angeles Dodgers (NL), 2 games

1979 Pittsburgh Pirates (NL), 4 games; Baltimore Orioles (AL), 3 games

There was also controversy in baseball during the 1970s. On January 16, 1970, player Curt Flood filed a lawsuit protesting a trade deal that he did not wish to fulfill. He requested free agency and the ability to make his own choices, and he compared baseball's system of owners deciding which players played on which team to the system of pre–Civil War slavery. The Supreme Court did not buy that argument or the antitrust one, and ruled in favor of organized baseball.

On April 1, 1972, players went on strike, demanding more health benefits and a better pension plan. The season was delayed by nine days and 86 games were canceled before owners satisfied the players' demands. Although the season was played to its conclusion, spring training was delayed in 1973 until March 1, as players and owners attempted to hash out more contractual details. Salary arbitration, one feature that was newly granted to the players and their union, radically changed the power balance between team owners and players, as players could request arbitration after two years of major league play, and owners were bound by the decisions.

TENNIS

Billie Jean King and Chris Evert featured prominently in women's tennis; men's tennis included Arthur Ashe, who was already an established star after winning both the U.S. Open and U.S. Amateur championships in 1968. In 1975, he beat reigning champion Jimmy Connors, who was a full decade younger than Ashe, at Wimbledon. That year, Ashe ranked number one in the United States and fourth in the world; in 1976, he ranked number two in the United States.

John McEnroe sprung into prominence later in the decade, perhaps as well known for his aggressive, tantrum-like behavior on the court as for his stellar play. Nicknamed "Superbrat," he qualified for Wimbledon in 1977 at the age of 18, the youngest to do so. He reached the semifinals where he lost to Connors, who was ranked number one in the world every year from 1974–1978. McEnroe won his first U.S. Open in 1979.

FOOTBALL

The Pittsburgh Steelers, with its "Steel Curtain" defense, was the powerhouse National Football League team in the 1970s, making the playoffs eight times and winning Super Bowl titles in 1974, 1975, 1978, and 1979; nine of its players ended up in the Football Hall of Fame. Led by quarterback Terry Bradshaw and NFL Defensive Player of the Year in 1972 and 1974, "Mean" Joe Greene, other outstanding players included Franco Harris, Lynn Swann, John Stallworth, Mel Blount, Jack Lambert, Jack Ham, and Mike Webster. In 1974, the team selected four Hall of Famers in one year (Webster, Swann, Stallworth, and Lambert). Coach Chuck Noll led all four Super Bowl teams, the only NFL coach to win four of these titles.

Football fans were able to watch games broadcast live when "Monday Night Football" first aired on September 21, 1970. The first commentators included Keith Jackson, Howard Cosell, and Don Meredith; after the first season, Jackson

Sports

was replaced by Frank Gifford. Alex Karras, Fran Tarkenton, and Fred Williamson also served as commentators during the 1970s.

BASKETBALL

Spectacular teams from the decade include the 1969–1970 New York Knicks, which boasted players such as Willis Reed, Walt Frazier, Dick Barnett, Dave DeBusschere, Bill Bradley, and Cazzie Russell. The team's winning percentage of .732 fueled its effort to make the NBA Championship Series for the first time in Knickerbocker history. Two inspirational baskets, made by injured team captain Willis Reed during the decisive game of the championship, sealed the team's first league victory.

Another team of significance was the 1971–1972 Los Angeles Lakers, with Gail Goodrich, Jerry West, Wilt Chamberlain, Jim McMillian, and Happy Hairston capturing the first Laker championship with an .841 winning percentage. The team won 33 consecutive games that season, breaking the NBA record for consecutive wins.

The 1974–1975 season ended with one of the sport's most exciting championship playoffs, as the Boston Celtics played against the Milwaukee Bucks and that team's star player, Kareem Abdul-Jabbar. The series went all the way to seven games, and Boston won it.

The end of the decade marked the beginning of the Boston Celtics rivalry—led by Larry Bird, Kevin McHale, and Robert Parish—with the Los Angeles Lakers, including multitalented rookie Earvin "Magic" Johnson and veteran player Abdul-Jabbar, with his amazing sky-hook shot.

Another player of note is Julius Erving—or "Dr. J."—who eventually scored more than 30,000 career points. Erving began his professional career during the 1970s and incorporated mid-air twists and turns and slam dunk shots into his play, a style sometimes called "show time."

LEISURE TRENDS

Certain fads of the 1970s—such as Mood Rings and Pet Rocks—instantly captured Americans'

Sports

HOW OTHERS SEE US

Pet Rocks Go Around the World

The Pet Rock was perhaps the quintessential American fad of the 1970s with its quick rise to public consciousness, huge profits, and equally fast collapse. Its meteoric flash also offers a glimpse into the national psyches of two other historically linked but culturally disparate nations, Great Britain and Australia.

The goof gift of the 1975 Christmas season, the Pet Rock was a marvel of marketing and packaging. It was a rock, no more or less, nestled in a bed of straw and tucked into a box complete with air holes and a 36-page care-and-feeding manual. Its sales in the U.S. were in the millions.

The British public held itself proudly aloof from the craze, which was widely but dismissively covered in the press. Reporters and commentators took a mockingly chiding tone in these stories; one could almost hear their tongues clucking over the silly thing that the Colonists had been suckered into this time. Decades later, "pet rock" remained a code phrase among British journalists for "foolish foreign fluff."

Australians, on the other hand, plunged into the fad with cheerful abandon. Both the original version and knock-off imitators were sold there by the hundreds of thousands and enjoyed a popularity that paralleled that in the United States. In the 1990s, a popular local rock band called themselves the Pet Rocks, and newspapers ran stories about the nostalgic memories that Australians had of the "fun" they'd had with their "pets" 20 years before.

attention; other trends, including the Little People Originals—eventually renamed Cabbage Patch Kids—were invented in the 1970s but didn't receive widespread acclaim until the following decade. Still other trends, such as the ubiquitous smiley face, were conceptualized in earlier times, but became hallmarks during this decade.

Some fads, such as toe socks, had practical value. Toe socks were knee-high in length and were often colorful, with bright stripes and glittery threads in their design. They kept a person's feet, including the spots between the toes, and legs warm. Other fads, such as clackers, were not quite as cozy and safe as toe socks. Clackers were basically two pool ball–sized marbles connected by a string that held a ring. Users slipped a finger into the ring and swung the balls together, "clacking" them and attempting trick moves with the toy. Unfortunately, the glass versions shattered and caused injuries; subsequent plastic versions never caught on.

FADS

Mood Rings

If the 1970s truly were the "Me Decade"—as journalist Tom Wolfe declared in 1976—then no fashion or fad could better represent these years than "Impulse Stones"—or, as they were better known, Mood Rings. Created in 1975 by Josh Reynolds—a direct descendent of one of England's greatest portrait painters, Sir Joshua Reynolds—mood rings were basic bands of metal connected to large oval-shaped pieces of glass that either contained thermotropic liquid crystals or were coated on the back with the substance. These crystals changed color in response to the ring wearer's body heat, which caused the "jewel" of the ring to also change hue—and, by consulting a chart provided with the purchase of the ring, the person wearing the jewelry could determine his or her mood. According to the literature provided with the rings, the following colors corresponded, more or less, with the following moods:

Dark blue: Happy, romantic, or passionate
Blue: Calm or relaxed
Blue-green: Somewhat relaxed
Green: Normal or average
Amber: A little nervous or anxious
Gray: Very nervous or anxious
Black: Stressed, tense, or feeling harried

Even if a ring-wearer did not feel that the results garnered by mood rings were scientific, the rings at least served as conversation starters on the subject of feelings and emotions.

People could purchase basic (plastic look-alike) mood rings for as little as $2, while those with genuine gold settings cost $250. By December 1975, more than $15 million worth of rings had been sold. After the first flush of success caused the initial stock of mood rings to sell out in New York, imitators created other products, including more masculine-looking rings, a "mood watcher" that both kept time and monitored moods, mood pendants, and nail polish that contained the liquid crystals. Mood shirts were sold and manufacturers also attempted to sell handbags with stones in the straps and belts complete with mood buckles.

Famous owners of mood rings included Sophia Loren, Barbra Streisand, Paul Newman, and Muhammad Ali—who even wrote a poem about the object.

The crystals used in these mood-detecting devices usually maintained their effectiveness for one or two years—the shelf-life of this fad.

Pet Rocks

The "Pet Rock" concept has come to represent the ultimate exception in marketing; rather than satisfying an obvious need or filling an important niche, the Pet Rock seemed to create its own demand—and then filled it en masse. In April 1975, Gary Dahl, an advertising professional from California, socialized with friends after work. Conversation turned to the high maintenance required by traditional pets such as cats, dogs, and birds, and Dahl informed his pals that pets made too much of a mess; they misbehaved, and they cost too much money. As a tongue-in-cheek alternative, he suggested owning a rock.

Dahl then wrote a training manual that described how to have a good relationship with your pet rock and how to make your pebble sit, stay, roll over, play dead, and be housetrained. After creating his manual, Dahl bought a supply of round gray pebbles from a building store in San Jose, California for one penny each. He packed each individual rock in a gift box that looked like a pet carrying case—complete with air holes—and he marketed the stone, gift box, and pet rock manual at a gift show in San Francisco in August 1975 and later at a show held in New York. For publicity, he sent out a quirky press release of himself surrounded by Pet Rocks.

Almost immediately, Neiman-Marcus bought 500 rocks, and *Newsweek* published a story about the concept. By the end of October, Dahl shipped

Sports

out about 10,000 rocks daily. He appeared on the *Tonight Show* twice, and by Christmas Dahl had sold two and a half tons of rocks. His product appeared in editorials and newspaper articles across the country. Within a few months, Dahl had sold more than 1,000,000 Pet Rocks at $3.95 each, making him a nearly instant millionaire.

Copycat products inundated the market; some boasted painted-on facial features and others comprised a cluster of rocks that represented a pet rock family. Others hoping to cash in on the fad offered obedience lessons for pet rocks or burial at sea services for rocks that had perished. The demand for this product, though, evaporated almost as quickly as it began.

Streaking

Another fad of the decade was streaking—or darting through a public place while nude, usually for the shock value and/or to entertain an audience. Ray Stevens song "The Streak" began playing on radio stations in 1974. A significant portion of streakers were college students running naked across some portion of their campus. Had Stevens's song not become a huge hit, perhaps the effects of this trend would have been more contained; however, it became a number one song—and awareness of streaking hit the national landscape. The thrust of the lyrics was the singer's attempts to prevent his wife—Ethel—from seeing the full frontal view of a male streaker. His cautions of "don't look" apparently fell on deaf ears, though, as at the end of the song, the narrator demands that Ethel get her own clothes back on…

One infamous streaker is Robert Opal, who in 1974 raced across the stage of the 46th Academy Awards at the peak of the streaking fad. He flashed a peace sign at the cameras that were broadcasting nationally; NBC quickly cut away to avoid a frontal nudity shot. Host David Niven is also well remembered for his response: "The only laugh that man will ever get in his life," he quipped, "is by stripping…and showing his shortcomings."

GAMES, TOYS, AND HOBBIES

The 1970s saw the invention of a wide range of innovative toys, including Star Wars action figures

in 1977. Based on the popular movie of the same name, these action figures were slightly less than four inches in length, much smaller than the Barbie dolls and GI Joes from previous generations. Because they were smaller, they were less expensive and children could more feasibly collect the entire set. Not surprisingly, the main characters of the movie (including Darth Vader, Luke Skywalker, Princess Leia, and Han Solo) had their own action figures, but so did the background aliens—many of whom didn't even have names until they were needed on the toy's packaging.

The year after the Star Wars action figures premiered, Milton Bradley Company invented a game—SIMON—that contained electronic lights and sounds and introduced it at New York discotheques, including the ultrachic Studio 54. The black, plastic, circular-shaped toy was divided into four sections, each with a red, blue, green, or yellow light that flashed on and off in random patterns. The player had to correctly repeat the ever-increasing complexity of the pattern—or lose the game.

SIMON—which was an electronic version of the old childhood game, Simon Says—had a big impact on society. People threw SIMON parties, and, early in the morning, extremely dedicated players would show up at FAO Schwartz to play before work. *People, Money, Esquire, GQ,* and *Newsweek* published articles about the game. The game sold out during the 1978 Christmas season and remained popular. Perhaps for the first time, a game intended for children became a pop culture phenomenon for adults—and for the country as a whole.

Television Console Games

On January 27, 1972, Magnavox introduced the first-ever home video game system: the Odyssey. Invented by Ralph Baer, an employee of a defense contractor, the original notion was to create a "television gaming apparatus" that would help develop the reflexes of those serving in the military. Baer shared his invention with Magnavox in 1970, and he signed a licensing agreement with them. The original Odyssey cost $100 and allowed users to play games that used basic black-and-white graphics as a game board. During the first three years, 200,000 units sold. Perhaps more would have been purchased, but Magnavox implied in its advertising that the Odyssey would only work on Magnavox televisions; this was not true, but the company hoped to fuel television sales.

Nolan Bushnell saw an early version of the Odyssey's tennis game, and he invented his own game—PONG—for rival Atari. People first played this coin-operated game on machines in bars and arcades, and then Atari partnered with Sears and Roebuck to create a television-based version of the game. This system also cost $100—and more than $40 million of Atari game systems sold during the 1975 Christmas season.

After Atari's success, Coleco released Telstar and Magnavox created Odyssey 100, each of which found some sales. In October 1977, Atari released a $199 programmable video game system that sold more than 25 million units. Programmable meant that the games themselves were contained on devices separate from the actual hardware of the game system. Many consider the Atari unit the beginning of "true" home video games; these included Space Invaders, Asteroids, and Pac-Man.

Small Computer Beginnings

When the decade debuted, teens and adults interested in electronics were building games, radios, and other light-controlled devices, much as they had been for the past two decades. Early in the 1970s, though, they could begin purchasing integrated circuit boards at a reasonable price, thereby greatly extending the options available for their experimentation. This enabled hobbyists to create increasingly more sophisticated devices—at younger and younger ages.

When Intel began selling the 8080 microprocessor in the mid-1970s, people first attempted to build their own computers; MITS, Inc. sold kits for $395 each. The January 1975 issue of *Popular Electronics* featured this do-it-yourself project—which snagged the attention of Paul Allen and Bill Gates. Those two young entrepreneurs moved into the building where these computer kits were being sold and established their original software company of Microsoft. About the same time, Steve Jobs, Steve Wozniak, and Ronald Wayne were beginning to develop the Apple computer. Throughout the decade, electronics

hobbyists could find increasing numbers of books and magazines that described computer building projects. Although the notion of computer kits was short-lived, the computer itself was still in its toddler stage. (See Overview of the 1980s for moreon personal computers.)

Citizens Band Radio

The Citizens Band (CB) radio had existed since 1947, but its usage did not become popular until the mid-1970s when long-distance truckers used CB radios to communicate information to one another—about traffic conditions, detours, or "speed traps" set up by police officers—and to chase away the loneliness during long hauls. A CB radio consisted of a microphone, a speaker system, and a control box. These radios were relatively easy to set up and to use, and they served as a precursor to cellular phones. Moreover, the cost of technology had become more affordable by the 1970s, which fostered even wider usage.

Users created special names and slang to solidify their subculture: "Smokey" indicated a police officer; "negatory" was a lively way to say "no;" and "10–4" signified that a listener had received a message.

C. W. McCall (pseudonym of Bill Fries) fueled the CB craze with his song "Convoy"(1975), in which a CB user dubbed "Rubber Duck" organizes a powerful bumper-to-bumper conglomeration of vehicles. More than 11.3 million units sold in 1976 alone.[1] Movies such as *Smokey and the Bandit,* 1977, starring Burt Reynolds, Sally Field, and Jackie Gleason further shared "trucker culture" with society at large.

Dungeons and Dragons

In 1971, Gary Gygax and Jeff Perren invented a fantasy game called Chainmail that involved the use of medieval warfare miniatures. The game soon evolved into Dungeons and Dragons (D&D), which also incorporated significant role playing. On the one hand, D&D was deceptively simple and straightforward. Game boards and playing pieces were optional, and there were no traditional winners or losers in the noncompetitive activity. On the other hand, successful players needed to possess strong imagination and intellect.

Sports

"Dungeons & Dragons" in 1979. AP Photo.

In D&D, the central player of the game, the Dungeon Master (DM), creates an imaginary world peopled with characters that are evil and good, weak and strong. The DM also develops a fantasy landscape complete with castles and dungeons, monsters and treasures. The DM must know all agreed-upon rules and monitor the actions of the players as they further develop their assigned medieval characters and attempt to escape from the make-believe dungeon while obstacles, ranging from goblins to physical obstructions, stand in their way.

Games could last for hours, weeks, months—or even years. Devotees of the game—who were often either teenagers or college students—purchased countless manuals and accessories to further their ability to play the game. By the end of the decade, creator Gary Gygax estimated that 250,000 Americans engaged in D&D play, while other estimates ranged up to 300,000.

Controversy, however, surrounded D&D. Some parents applauded their children's participation, calling the game challenging and hailing it as an effective way to work out psychological issues using imaginative solutions to unexpected problems. Other parents worried, though, about signs of depression in their children after their character died in the game.

GENEALOGY AND THE SEARCH FOR ETHNIC/CULTURAL IDENTITY

By the mid-1970s, the *Los Angeles Times* estimated that half a million Americans pursued genealogy as a hobby. Many of these people belonged to one or more of the 700 genealogical clubs and societies in the country; at that time, genealogy ranked as the country's third most popular hobby. According to the *Chicago Tribune,* the intense interest in genealogy and the search for ethnic, cultural, and familial history could be attributed to four factors: a yearning for family ties in an increasingly mobile society; the greater amount of leisure time afforded post–World War II; the Bicentennial; and the increasing number of adopted children seeking information about their biological family.

In response, libraries, schools, and YMCAs offered genealogy classes, while publishers began printing books and magazines on the subject. Alex Haley's *Roots* was the most easily recognizable of these printed materials. The book, which became a television miniseries, helped fuel an interest in genealogy, particularly among African Americans. (See Entertainment of the 1970s.)

Roots, though, was not the first foray into family history in the 1970s. Richard Gambino's *Blood of My Blood* shared his Italian heritage, while Irving Howe's *World of Our Fathers* explored the first-generation Jewish American experience in New York City.

In 1974, Congress approved the Ethnic Heritage Studies Program and provided nearly $6 million to allow citizens the opportunity to research their roots and for Americans of all ethnic backgrounds to learn about others' background; this act helped initiate ethnic studies programs at universities around the country. The resumption of diplomatic discussions between China and America allowed Chinese Americans the opportunity to finally visit the homes of their ancestors. The Church of Jesus Christ of Latter-Day Saints (Mormons) also continued to add to its genealogy collection during this decade. By the mid-1970s, Mormon structures housed more than 130,000 volumes of family genealogies along with more than 1 million rolls of microfilm containing census records, birth and death certificates, probate documents, and countless other minutiae from around the world.

Sports

Travel

of the 1970s

On the cusp of the 1970s, many experts believed that more Americans than ever before would travel during the decade. Factors for this enthusiasm included the advent of the first jumbo jet—the Boeing 747—that was anticipated in 1970; the increase in ship cruise options; and the lower airfares being predicted. Furthermore, American Express announced that it expected travel to Europe to double.

Lower airfares did occur because of a rate war among airlines, and, once the 747 became available for commercial flight, airlines dramatically slashed ticket prices, making international travel much more feasible. To compete with the Boeing 747, cruise ship operators ramped up their advertising and their special deals.

High travel expectations in the 1970s dimmed, though, for a variety of reasons, including an oil embargo that caused gasoline prices to increase significantly and an overall sluggish economy with rapid rates of inflation, high unemployment figures, and slow growth that caused the average American's budget to tighten.

On a more positive note, although space travel did not continue at the fever pitch of 1969, Americans did make significant strides in space voyages and research. The 1970s saw automobile innovations, including the first American-made, fuel-efficient subcompact car. The founding of

Amtrak saved a disintegrating passenger railway system from possible extinction.

SPACE TRAVEL

When the 1970s began, the country had recently celebrated the successes of extraordinary, seemingly superhuman undertakings in space. John Glenn had walked on the moon, broadcasting his historic step for all mankind throughout the world, and people's imaginations flourished, anticipating lunar colonies—or ones on Mars—as the answer to overpopulation, pollution, or any number of other social ills.

In January 1970, *Science* magazine dedicated an entire issue to the analysis of Apollo 11 lunar samples. It was the first time the magazine had devoted all of its pages to a single topic, and this attention from the well-respected *Science* seemed to reinforce that the world—led by the United States of America's efforts—was on the verge of a new galactic age. This flush of success was not limited to the scientific, either; the moon landing was, for the United States, also a political coup.

Astronauts were heroes for most Americans; in a time when many questioned the "establishment," those who succeeded as astronauts had, as Tom Wolfe defined the phenomenon, the "right stuff." To qualify, these men needed superb physical stamina and health; they underwent a battery of psychological tests, as well, so that America could boast of the strongest and best astronauts in the world.

Hopes for an expansion of the space program quickly faltered in the 1970s, though, as economic troubles and other concerns—ranging from the Vietnam War to feminist and civil rights struggles—took precedence. The American psyche took yet another hit when the space program lost momentum—and when the first Apollo launch of the decade nearly turned tragic.

On April 11, 1970, NASA launched Apollo 13, hoping to land on the Fra Mauro highlands of the moon. Fifty-five hours later, an oxygen tank exploded on board, putting the entire crew in extreme danger. Astronauts Jim Lovell, Jack Swigert, and Fred Haise aborted their mission and used the resources located on their lunar lander to survive, including its oxygen, radio, and engines. Four days later, the rocket reentered Earth's orbit and landed safely.

The following summer, Alan Shepard led Apollo 14 into space. Shepard was America's first space traveler, but an ailment had prevented him from participating in space flight since 1961; because of a successful surgery, though, he could command the Apollo 14. When he did, he walked on the moon's Fra Mauro highlands.

Apollo 15's astronauts explored the moon's mountains using a Lunar Rover. They discovered a rock dating back 4.5 million years, nearly the estimated age of the moon; they named the rock "Genesis." Apollo 16 explored the moon's highlands using new technology known as the ultraviolet camera and spectrograph. Apollo 17 furthered the knowledge of the moon's origins significantly. All told, 12 astronauts walked on the moon during 6 lunar landings. After Apollo 17, though, budget cuts caused this particular space program to cease operations.

Soviet cosmonauts also landed on the moon, starting in 1970, and they also created automated rovers. In 1971, they attempted to claim the world's first space station, Salyut 1, but all three cosmonauts died after the cabin suddenly lost pressure. In 1973, the Soviets succeeded in a similar scientific mission, as the Cold War continued to be waged in outer space.

Exploration of Mars also occurred in the 1970s. NASA's Mariner 9 began photographing the planet in 1971. In 1976, two Viking landers touched down on Mars and gathered data; an attempt was made to find microbial life, but nothing was discovered. Mariner 10, employing gravity assist, used the pull of Venus to direct itself toward Mercury; three successful "flybys" occurred. Meanwhile, Soviets succeeded in a Venus landing and discovered 900°F temperatures. The U.S. Pioneer 10 and 11 flew by Jupiter and Saturn, while Voyager 1 and 2, both launched in 1977, began a space tour that would ultimately lead to the outer solar system.

Perhaps the most remarkable accomplishment, diplomacy-wise, happened in 1975 when a U.S./Soviet cooperative effort created the Apollo-Soyuz Test Project (ASTP). Through this initiative, the two countries studied launching and docking protocol; after spacecraft launched from each of the countries, the crews met in space for two days to conduct more experiments.

SKYLAB

Using Apollo and Saturn technology, NASA created a space platform from which trained scientists and astronauts could gather information; they would, while in space, examine the sun, photograph the earth, and study weightlessness. The creation of Skylab cost less than $3,000,000,000, and the space station was ready for a test run by 1973.

Skylab suffered from technical difficulties, though, during its unmanned experimental flight on May 14, 1973. Just 63 seconds after blasting off, atmospheric drag ripped off a shield intended to protect Skylab's workshop. After NASA repaired Skylab, three sets of three men lived in its workshop space while orbiting Earth. All 3 flights were successful and these 9 men lived in Skylab for a total of 171 days during 1973 and 1974. The 3 trips lasted 28, 59, and 84 days, respectively.

These men continuously pointed a sophisticated observation device, called the "Apollo Telescope Mount," at the sun to gather data. The crew, who were both scientists and astronauts, carefully selected targets on the sun to observe and watched for its active regions; they then filmed those areas to record the radiation released during the flare-ups.

These men conducted nearly 300 scientific experiments while in space, trying to determine how humans adapted to zero gravity; they also continued to study the Earth and the sun. For the first time ever, refueling successfully occurred in space, and, on July 11, 1979, five years after the project had ceased operations and the men had safely returned home, pieces of Skylab fell back down to Earth.

THE AUTOMOBILE

Legislation

In 1965, consumer advocate Ralph Nader published *Unsafe at Any Speed*, which listed a substantial number of charges against the car manufacturing industry and its alleged unwillingness to spend money on safety features in cars. The car manufacturing industry and Nader clashed furiously over his claims; meanwhile, a public outcry arose, demanding that these safety features be installed in cars. Ironically, when the National Safety Council mounted seat belt education campaigns in both 1972 and 1973, no significant changes in behavior were noted.

Nevertheless, largely in response to these demands, the federal government passed significant safety-related legislation in the automobile industry in the latter part of the 1960s and during the 1970s. One area of concern was cars' bumpers. Effective September 1, 1972—for 1973 models—bumpers were required to withstand minimal impacts without damage to headlights or fuel systems. In October 1972, Congress passed an act that created a federal bumper standard.

The notion of passive restraint systems in cars was debated as well. The National Highway Traffic

Skylab space station, occupied by American astronauts during 1973–1974. NASA image.

Travel

Safety Administration set a deadline of 1974 for passive restraint systems in cars; after industry executives lobbied Richard Nixon, the deadline was extended until 1976. When that deadline loomed, Gerald Ford's transportation secretary agreed to cancel the requirement after car manufacturers agreed to voluntarily install safety air bags in selected cars. In 1977, Jimmy Carter's transportation secretary reversed that decision and gave car manufacturers a new deadline of 1984 to include passive restraints or air bags in cars.

Car manufacturers experimented with safety air bags even before legislation definitively required them to install the devices in selected cars. The Oldsmobile Toronado came equipped with air bags in 1973. That same year, General Motors built 1,000 Chevrolets with air bags for testing purposes; in the first recorded air bag fatality, an infant in the front seat of a car died after an air bag deployed during a wreck. In 1974, General Motors offered air bags as an option in selected Cadillacs, Oldsmobiles, and Buicks from 1974 through 1976. Hoping to sell 100,000 cars with air bags during that three-year period, sales were a disappointing 10,000, and so General Motors abandoned the project.

In 1975, Volvo conducted an experiment to determine the safety of putting young children in front seats of cars that had air bag safety features. The company used pigs in place of the children; 8 of the 24 pigs died and all but 3 of the surviving pigs were injured. This experiment helped lead to the conclusion that children should stay in the back seats of cars that came equipped with air bags.

Two significant technological improvements occurred during the decade; the first was Chrysler's invention of the electronic ignition in 1972. Four years later, Volvo introduced cars with catalytic converters that greatly reduced harmful emissions into the environment. The following year, California passed strict new legislation that limited the acceptable levels of the three most harmful emission types.

American Subcompact Cars

American Motors Company (AMC) premiered the Gremlin, the first American subcompact, on April 1, 1970. This vehicle was created by AMC to compete with imported cars from Japan and Germany.

Although the car's appearance received some criticism, the Gremlin had one important factor going for it—the very reasonable price. A two-seated Gremlin cost $1,879, while the four seater hatch-back cost $1,959. Furthermore, the car boasted decent mileage, which would become an important factor during the oil crisis. Perhaps to combat the criticism of its appearance—and certainly to capitalize on America's love of denim—the 1972 Gremlin came in a "Levi edition," which included copper rivets and soft-brushed denim-colored nylon in the interior.

Starting with 1971 models, Americans could choose from three domestic subcompacts: the Gremlin, the Ford Pinto, and the Chevrolet Vega. *Motor Trend* named the Chevy Vega as car of the year in 1971. The Ford Pinto, though, was in the news for less happy reasons.

Numerous Pintos were involved in car fire fatalities, in large part because the fuel tank placement seemed to make it especially vulnerable in rear-end collisions. Ford received significant criticism after 27 fatalities, and it was alleged that Ford Motor Company memos indicated the company would rather pay the expenses of lawsuits than spend the money to fix the problem.[1] More recently, though, a 1991 law review paper suggested that, because more than 2,000,000 Pintos were built, this car was no more dangerous, percentagewise, than many others of the era.[2] Regardless, the Pinto was perhaps the most controversial car of the 1970s.

Although the creation of the American subcompact car preceded the oil embargo crisis of 1973, and was in fact built to challenge the success of smaller imported cars, appreciation of these fuel-efficient vehicles increased as gas prices skyrocketed. As a comparison, large cars got only about eight miles per gallon, while compacts could get as many as 35 miles per gallon. Gas prices climbed from 30 cents per gallon to 60 cents during the 1973 embargo, and lines at gas stations stretched down the block.

In 1974, more by coincidence than by deliberate preplanning, Ford Motor Company was ready to introduce a smaller Mustang with a more fuel-efficient four-cylinder engine at a price of $2,895.

Although this model was enthusiastically received, 1974 was a bad year for the automobile industry. Sales were down 3,000,000 units from 1973 and no relief was in sight. In 1975, manufacturers modified designs to make cars look more compact—perhaps to give the impression that they were more fuel-efficient. Chevrolet introduced the Monza, a line of subcompact cars that were more substantial than the Vega, but still economical and fuel-efficient. The oil crisis also led to a brief interest in Hybrid Electric Vehicles, but that enthusiasm died once the panic over oil abated. Post-crisis, car manufacturers enjoyed a couple years of rebounding sales—but another, albeit less severe oil crisis, occurred in 1979 and once again focused interest on the smaller, more fuel-efficient subcompact car.

Oil Crisis Effect

Prior to the oil crisis of 1973, American car manufacturers focused significantly on improving vehicle performance, each trying to outdo previous efforts, surpass domestic competitors, and prevent imported cars from securing more of a market share in the United States. During the early part of the 1970s, the so-called muscle car, with its oversized engine and large body, remained popular. The rapidly increasing gas prices caused by the oil crisis made muscle cars significantly more expensive to operate—and significantly less socially acceptable in an era concerned with the environment—and so their popularity waned.

Imported Cars

Imported cars, generally still called "foreign cars" during the 1970s, sold well during the decade. In 1970, more than half a million German Volkswagens sold in the United States, as did nearly 185,000 Toyotas from Japan. American consumers still tread somewhat cautiously when buying Japanese products, though, as the phrase "made in Japan" was considered a putdown. Meanwhile, sales of American-made cars and light trucks fell. On February 3, 1975, because of sluggish sales, one-third of the workforce in Detroit's auto industry lost their jobs. By the end of the 1970s, Japanese manufacturers out-produced their American counterparts.

Cars were also used as diplomacy tools. During each of the three peace summits between the United States and the Soviet Union, Richard Nixon gifted Leonid Brezhnev with a car. In 1972, he gave the Soviet leader a Cadillac limousine, valued at $10,000. The following year, Brezhnev received a Lincoln Continental, also valued at $10,000. In 1974, the year that Nixon's domestic political situation was quite shaky, he gave a Chevy Monte Carlo, a car that retailed at $5,578. Although that lesser gift might seem to indicate a falling of Nixon's fortunes or a falling out in the relationship, Brezhnev in fact requested that car as a gift after *Motor Trend* named it the car of the year.

PLANES, TRAINS, AND TRUCKS

Boeing 747: Jumbo Jet

The success of Boeing's jumbo jet known as the 747 actually began with a failure several years prior. In the mid-1960s, Boeing lost its bid on a U.S. Air Force contract for a very large plane but, through that process, the company identified a market for a jumbo-sized jet. Furthermore, Boeing could use research material collected for the bidding process to design such a plane, and it began work on the project in 1966.

The first test flight was scheduled for February 9, 1969. The Federal Aviation Administration (FAA) warned Boeing that these planes must be substantially quieter than ones currently flying; this requirement marked the first time that federal authorities imposed noise criteria on airlines.

Boeing's first jumbo jet weighed 355 tons and cost $20 million to build. Capable of carrying 490 passengers on a 6,000-mile flight, the flight speed of the test run was anticipated to be 300 mph, and the maximum speed was gauged at 625 mph. The plane was two and a half times the size of current commercial planes, with three times the seating capacity and twice the cargo space. Airports needed to modify their facilities to accommodate the jumbo jets, and, because of safety concerns related to flying on such massive planes, insurance companies mulled over how to modify their policies.

Travel

The jumbo jet's test flight was scheduled to last four hours, but it was cut short by an hour and 15 minutes because of wing flap difficulty; all otherwise progressed well. The take-off was quiet and the landing was smooth, as well. To ensure safety, no passengers flew on this test run; to approximate the weight of passengers, 176 barrels, each containing 55 gallons of water, were placed on seats.

The plane's advent was anticipated with awe. An average jumbo jet would contain 12 lavatories, with plumbing available for 17. Between 12 and 18 flight attendants would be assigned to each flight. Meanwhile, experts talked about the psychological effect these huge planes would have on residents living near the airports.

On June 3, Boeing's jumbo jet successfully flew to Paris, its first overseas test. More than 2,000 Parisians toured the plane and its six movie theaters,

spiral staircase leading to the upstairs lounge, and six different decorating schemes.

Boeing received clearance for public use of its 747 on December 30, 1969. In January 1970, the 747–100 began service with Pan American.

Deregulation

During the latter part of the 1970s, airline companies struggled beneath the weight of hefty regulations. The system of the era has been described as both inflexible and cumbersome; for example, lengthy Civil Aeronautics Board (CAB) hearings were required for two affiliated airlines to receive permission to wear similar uniforms.

CAB determined what prices airlines could charge and what routes they could take. Following their belief that consumers would not pay full price if they only needed to travel a short distance,

Travel

Thousands of employees and guests surround the Boeing 747 wide body jetliner shortly after its rollout at Boeing's Everett, Washington, plant. The new jumbo jet was the world's largest commercial jetliner at the time. AP Photo.

they set lower prices for short-haul markets and higher prices for long-haul markets. Opponents of this philosophy stated that this policy inhibited the growth of air travel—and therefore of the entire airline industry.

In 1978, Congress voted to deregulate the airlines, which allowed the companies to determine their own pricing structures and to openly compete with other companies. Consumers hoped for lower prices and better service as airlines attempted to woo them; overall, studies indicate that deregulation accomplished those goals. However, before deregulation, airline tickets were generally fully refundable and consumers could change flights without penalty, so the decision contained both advantages and disadvantages.

Amtrak

Passenger train usage began to decline during the 1930s as increasing numbers of people purchased automobiles. It dropped even further in the 1950s, when long-distance travelers had the option of flying to their destinations, and when improved highways systems made driving easier and more pleasant. In October 1967, the U.S. Postal Service began transporting first class mail by truck and plane, relegating only second and third class mail to the passenger trains. In the face of such fierce competition, many passenger train systems folded.

Shortly after the postal service withdrew its first-class contracts with the railways, an attorney named Anthony Haswell formed a lobbyist group, the National Association of Railroad Passengers, to persuade the federal government to solve the problem of declining railway passenger transportation. It lobbied Congress, the Department of Transportation, and the Federal Railroad Administration.

Concurrent with the lobbyist group forming, two major railway systems—the Pennsylvania Railroad and the New York Central Railroad—merged on February 1, 1968, to create the Penn Central Railroad system. This mammoth new railway system was expected to solve many of the railway's problems. Instead, on June 21, 1970, the Penn Central railroad system filed for bankruptcy—the largest bankruptcy to date. Penn

Central's failure was agonized over and analyzed in depth. When the Penn Central Transportation Company crashed, it had 100,000 creditors and more than 118,000 stockholders, and the railway system simply collapsed beneath these demands.

Although Congress recognized the need for a solution to the passenger railway crisis, it was not united in the specifics. The collapse of the Penn Central, though, deepened the state of emergency, and, on October 14, 1970, Congress passed the Rail Passenger Service Act to revitalize passenger railroads in the country. On October 30, Richard Nixon signed the bill that authorized the National Railroad Passenger Corporation (NRPC) to operate the railroad system. Eight presidential appointees plus key members from the Federal Railroad Administration and the Department of Transportation spearheaded the planning; their goal was to operate a quality system while maintaining freedom from regulation.

The law created a quasi-public corporation—originally to be named Railpax, but changed to Amtrak. The name Amtrak stood for "American Travel by Track" and the red, white, and blue inverted arrow that came to symbolize Amtrak was designed.

Private rail companies had until May 1, 1971, to either merge with Amtrak or decide to remain independent. Private railroad systems kept control of the more lucrative freight service, causing many policymakers to assume that passenger service would eventually fade from American culture. To join the NRPC, private passenger railways could pay a fee in cash, provide equipment and services based on half of the company's losses for 1970, or purchase an agreed-upon amount of common stock in the new corporation. In exchange, the company no longer bore the financial burden of running a passenger service. Almost all services opted to join NRPC, but four chose to remain independent: Southern, Rio Grande, Rock Island, and Georgia Railroad.

Prior to the grand opening, Amtrak issued press releases promising many great things for the future. Promises included clean cars, precise adherence to schedules, quality meals, and an overall pleasant travel experience. On May 1, 1971, half of the country's railways made their final private enterprise journey and the first train of Amtrak, clocker number 235, left New York's Penn Station at 12:05 A.M., heading to Philadelphia. Initially, Amtrak used 184 trains, covering 314 destinations along 21 key routes, each route traveling between 2 major cities. Even-numbered trains were to travel north and east; odd-numbered were assigned routes to the south and west. Because Amtrak absorbed old railway systems, though, it also kept a few numbering systems that clashed with the new organizational chart, including those from the Santa Fe Railroad and some of the Empire Corridor routes.

On the first day of operations, 184 trains covered 23,000 miles, about half of the area covered by private enterprises just the day before, and many locales had no service, whatsoever. Other problems existed, including technical incompatibility as equipment from several companies attempted to merge. Amtrak had begun its operations by leasing older coach and sleeper cars from freight railroads in the eastern portion of the country, connecting them with newer equipment from companies on the West Coast, leading some to label the first few years of Amtrak as the "Rainbow Era."

By 1974, Amtrak had purchased much of its own equipment and painted it with a consistent color theme. Throughout the 1970s, Amtrak attempted to improve its image and its service; as the decade progressed, other private railway systems—ones that had previously declined to merge with Amtrak—became part of the system, as well.

Trucks

Starting in 1977, the trucking industry saw a movement toward deregulation, which resulted in easier entry into the industry and relative freedom for companies to set their own rates. Although many positive benefits arose from this movement, safety sometimes suffered. Truckers often communicated by CB (citizens band) radios, each of which consisted of a microphone, speaker system, and control box; these were relatively easy to set up and to use. By 1977, the airwaves became so crowded that 17 additional channels were set up, for a total of 40. (See Sports and Leisure of the 1970s.)

Visual Arts

of the 1970s

In 1971, portrait painter Andrew Wyeth created the first of more than 240 portraits of his neighbor, Helga Testorf. This project lasted 15 years and Wyeth kept the sketches and paintings a secret from everyone, including his wife, as he focused on the study of light and how it affected Helga's appearance. Wyeth sometimes focused on the light hitting Helga's reddish hair; other times, he emphasized a shadow on her body. Although the Helga series has intrigued untold numbers of spectators since Wyeth first made the work available to the public, it was not the typical type of visual art being produced during the 1970s. What was typical in the 1970s, though, is somewhat difficult to define.

No major movement surfaced in the world of painting or sculpture during the 1970s. Instead, many established artists continued their work from the 1960s developing compelling—and sometimes controversial—works of art and stretching the limits of artistic expression. The 1970s was a decade wherein artistic mediums blended and merged, as painters used film, music, and video to complement their work, and as performance art came to the forefront as a form of legitimate social expression.

Improved technology served as the impetus for a controversial art form—one that some critics say wasn't really a form of art, at all. Starting in the early 1970s, graffiti artists began using newly invented aerosol spray cans of paint to scrawl text and create sketches on public property. Although graffiti certainly wasn't new, the 1970s saw an explosion of colors and designs, especially in subways. The United Graffiti Artists formed in 1972; in 1975, the association displayed an exhibition of graffiti in New York, thus causing some to label this type of work as "urban folk art" rather than random vandalism. Graffiti artists usually developed so-called tags, which could be visual or textual symbols, to identify themselves to their followers—and to their competitors.

Street photographers captured gritty portraits of everyday life, especially in New York, while war photojournalists memorialized even bloodier scenes from Southeast Asia. Meanwhile, a new brand of photography was coalescing, wherein selected photographers who took photos of celebrities became famous themselves. Photographic technology improved during the 1970s, as digital photography allowed people to create prints from negatives; prior to this, the majority of photographers used slide or chrome film, which required a slide projector for viewing.

In 1973, the National Endowment for the Arts began a program with a goal to make the arts available to everyone in the country, using public broadcast television as a communications medium.

Hugo Martinez, right, head of a group called Graffiti Artists United, discusses a new floor-to-ceiling exhibition of graffiti in December 1972 at New York College. AP Photo.

ABSTRACT PAINTING

Abstract art does not contain recognizable subjects; it does not attempt to replicate real world objects. Some abstract art is geometric and patterned, while other examples are more fluid and unregimented.

By the 1970s, several experimental art forms of the twentieth century had merged into the genre generally known as abstract act. The richness of the multitude of artistic movements inherent in the abstract form allowed painters from the 1970s to select from and play around with a wide range of philosophies and styles, including Cubism. French artist Georges Braque and Spanish artist Pablo Picasso first experimented with this art form in about 1908, after being influenced by the work of painter Paul Cezanne. The name of this artistic movement comes from painter Henri Matisse's comment that one of Braque's paintings consisted of "petits cubes," or "little cubes."

Advocates of Cubism believe that an artist can capture the essence of an object by showing it from multiple angles within the same painting.

To accomplish this effect, the artist breaks up the representation of the actual object and then reassembles it in an abstracted form, following Cezanne's advice to express nature via three forms: the cylinder, the sphere, and the cone. In one of the earlier examples of this art form, Picasso's *Girl with Dark Hair,* viewers can see the front of her face as well as the side, all at the same time. Perhaps Cubism mimics the way in which the human brain actually processes visual data, as a number of glances at an object merge to create an overall perception. Italian artists influenced by Cubism became part of the Futurist movement, wherein technological force and movement inspired their paintings. In turn, Futurism contributed its own facets to the overriding concept of abstract art.

The school of Abstract Expressionism began in the 1940s in the United States, with Jackson Pollock its best-known advocate and practitioner. Abstract Expressionism, in many ways, was more of an attitude than a precisely defined style. Its advocates valued individuality,

Arts

spontaneous improvisation, and freedom of expression; some of them emphasized the physical act of painting, while others focused on the exploration of color. They believed that inspiration could be found from the unconscious mind, and that a spontaneous approach to their work would serve them well in this pursuit. Abstract Expressionism was the first significant art form that developed most fully in America and then spread to other parts of the world; prior to this, painters in the United States learned techniques and philosophies that were first developed in Europe.

Most American artists of the 1970s chose to either continue experimenting with the multiple possibilities inherent in Abstract Expressionism or to join an art form that was newer and quite different: Pop Art.

POP ART

One of the best-known examples of Pop Art is Andy Warhol's red-and-white Campbell's Soup can, created in 1964; his silk screens of the deceased movie star, Marilyn Monroe, also created during the 1960s, are other examples. Pop art incorporates popular cultural and consumer icons and objects, including advertisements, household goods, and television features to make its artistic statement. This movement began in Britain during the 1950s, made its way to the United States in the 1960s, and continued to influence the art world throughout the 1970s and beyond. Although the death of the movement was predicted as early as 1965—a rapid rise-and-crash that seemed fitting for an art form that celebrated the built-in obsolescence of modern consumerism—the form continued to reinvent itself well past its anticipated demise.

The early popularity of the art form was said to be a reaction against the Abstract Expressionist movement. Pop Art focused on features of everyday life, and was "unemotional, deliberate, systematic, impersonal, ironic, detached, non-autographic and amoral—a 'cool' or classical style."[1] Although some artists kept working in the Abstract Expressionism style during the 1960s and 1970s, pop moved to the forefront of the art world.

Some critics accused pop artists of plagiarism, of merely copying items available in the commercial world.

Warhol, the unofficial spokesperson of Pop Art, worked with a group of assistants in a studio called the "Factory" and specialized in art that used a silk background and had varieties of a master image imprinted upon it in multiple fashions. Some critics say that Warhol attempted to critique middle-class America through his art, while others claim that his work celebrated pop culture in the United States. Starting in 1970, he focused more frequently on portraits, usually of friends or figures of pop culture, and his work, in fact, began to more closely resemble Abstract Expressionism—or it at least blended aspects of the two forms.

One critic points out Warhol's uncanny ability to discern the trends of the moment—which, during the 1960s and 1970s, included symbols of consumerism and celebrity—and to then re-create them in his art. By doing so, he not only reflected the fads of popular culture, he reinvented them, illuminating elements for historians. Although Warhol's work rebelled against what had previously been considered art, many museums embraced his art and showed his paintings and silk screenings in special exhibitions worldwide.

Another American pop artist of note was Roy Lichtenstein, who created his first well-known piece of art in 1956: his print of the 10-dollar bill. He then experimented with Abstract Expressionism for three years. After returning to the field of Pop Art, he created a painting of Disney characters Mickey Mouse and Donald Duck—the type of comic strip art for which he became famous.

Although comic strip art became a significant focus for Lichtenstein, cartoons did not turn into his sole center of attention. He also painted people and created paintings using dots, attempting to prevent any visible brush strokes. He preferred that his paintings appear machine-made.

Swedish-born pop artist Claes Oldenburg set up *Lipstick (Ascending) on Caterpillar Tracks,* 1969, on the campus of Yale University This particular piece of art became a focus of student protests. In 1976, he installed *Clothespin* in downtown Philadelphia; since then, he and his spouse Coosje van Bruggen have created and placed more than 40 large-scale pieces of art in urban

Arts

Artist Roy Lichtenstein. Courtesy of Photofest.

areas throughout the United States and the world. Oldenburg chose to create such colossal pieces to intensify the presence of the object; he selected outdoor urban locales because he saw the city as his tablecloth.

Other pop artists of the era include Jim Dine, Red Grooms, Philip Guston, Keith Haring, Jasper Johns, Peter Max, Mel Ramos, Larry Rivers, Edward Ruscha, and Wayne Thiebaud.

Closely related to Pop Art was the school of Photorealism, in which painters sought to create such precise detail that their paintings appeared to be photos. The subject matter of Photorealism was often mundane, similar to what might appear in a random photo. Labels such as Superrealism and Hyperrealism were also used, and this form of art harkens back to the Illusionism of earlier, pre-photography centuries. Artists associated with this movement include John Salt, Richard Estes, and Chuck Close.

Some artists took the notion of realism even further, using their own bodies as the medium for expression in an art form called performance art. Performance artists incorporated many other art forms in their work, including music, song, story-telling, video, and sculpture. Performance art took on political overtones during the 1970s, and often served as a venue for feminist, gay and lesbian, and minority messages. Although enthusiastically received by some audiences, other critics and spectators questioned how performance art differed from theater and other visual performances.

PHOTOGRAPHY

During the 1930s, a group of photographers aligned themselves with the social realism movement and focused on capturing the hardships of society with their cameras. Perhaps one of the best-known social realists of the 1970s was Allan Sekula, who focused on people in the midst of economic or political struggles. As one example, Sekula photographed factory workers as they were leaving their shift at General Dynamics, preserving the dull monotony of the moment. In 1972, he created a series of slides from these photos, calling his collection the "Untitled Slide Sequence." In 1973, he exhibited another series of photos called "Performance under Working Conditions."

Sekula used many of his own experiences to create his art. In 1974, he shot a series of photos that he named "This Ain't China" that focused on the working conditions in a restaurant where he was once employed. Starting in 1978, he began work on "School Is a Factory," photographs of night school students who were attending the classes he taught, and the working conditions of a generation that Sekula believed had become detached from their lives. Sekula was virulently antiwar and staged photos to symbolically express his viewpoints, such as one of a man publicly slinking on his belly while wearing a straw hat and carrying a toy gun.

Sekula often employed a street photography approach to his work, capturing real-life moments as they randomly occurred in urban locales. Some street photographers used panoramic cameras to create large-scale photos, and their work, by definition, captured everyday life in the streets. Street photography interested artists around the globe, many of whom came to New York because of the challenges and possibilities inherent in such a crowded and diverse venue. Photographers Robert Frank and William Klein dominated street photography during this era; Frank published his second book of photography in 1972, titled *Lines of My Hand,* and focused on creating montages with words and images directly scratched on the photos' negatives. Klein spent much of the 1970s experimenting with film documentaries.

The 1970s also witnessed the work of war correspondents, including Dick Swanson, who photographed scenes in Vietnam. Swanson spent five years there working for *Life* magazine. After marrying a woman from Vietnam, he was transferred to Washington, D.C. in 1971. He continued to travel between the two countries for the next four years and returned to Saigon in April 1975 to help his wife's family escape before the city fell.

Finally, in an era that celebrated celebrity, it isn't surprising that photographers who snapped pictures of celebrities sometimes found themselves accorded with some of that same status. Annie Leibovitz is a prime example of this phenomenon. She began her career at *Rolling Stone* magazine in 1970 and became the chief photographer in 1973. She first took black-and-white photographs for the magazine until the magazine switched to color in 1974 and Leibovitz adapted her craft. Her assignments included taking photos of John Lennon and serving as the official photographer for the Rolling Stones' 1975 world tour.

In 1979, Leibovitz took a now-famous photo of singer and actor Bette Midler lying in a bed of roses. Because Leibovitz focused her work on celebrities and pop culture, she received some criticism for creating commercial work; however, she always strove to capture the essence of the celebrity's public persona.

ENDNOTES FOR THE 1970s

OVERVIEW OF THE 1970s

1. Max Heirich, *Rethinking Health Care: Innovation and Change in America* (Boulder, Colo.: Westview Press, 1998), 5.
2. Stephanie Slocum-Schaffer, *America in the Seventies* (Syracuse, NY: Syracuse University Press, 2003), 37.
3. "Roe v Wade," Thomson Gale, 1997. Available at: http://www.gale.com/free_resources/whm/trials/roe.htm (accessed July 14, 2006).
4. David Frum, *How We Got Here: The 70's—The Decade That Brought You Modern Life (for Better or Worse)* (New York: Basic Books, 2000), 16.
5. Jonathan H. Adler, "Fables of the Cuyahoga: Reconstructing a History of Environmental Protection," *Fordham Environmental Law Journal* 14, p. 89. Available at: law.case.edu/faculty/adler_jonathan/publications/fables_of_the_cuyahoga.pdf (accessed July 22, 2006).
6. Eckardt C. Beck, "The Love Canal Tragedy," *EPA Journal,* January 1979. Available at: http://www.epa.gov/history/topics/lovecanal/01.htm (accessed July 22, 2006).
7. Frum, *How We Got Here,* 73–74.
8. Frum, *How We Got Here,* 80.

ADVERTISING OF THE 1970s

1. "Best Super Bowl Commercials," Page 2, ESPN.com, 2006. Available at: http://espn.go.com/page2/s/list/sbcommercials.html (accessed July 15, 2006).
2. Peter N. Carroll, *It Seemed Like Nothing Happened: America in the Seventies* (New Brunswick, N.J.: Rutgers University Press, 2000), 312.
3. Nancy Artz, Jeanne Munger, and Warren Purdy, "Gender Issues in Advertising Language," *Women and Language* 22, no. 2(1999): 20.
4. Peter N. Carroll, *It Seemed Like Nothing Happened: America in the Seventies* (New Brunswick, N.J.: Rutgers University Press, 2000), 207.
5. Marilyn Kern-Foxworth, *Aunt Jemima, Uncle Ben, and Rastus: Blacks in Advertising, Yesterday, Today, and Tomorrow* (Westport, Conn.: Praeger, 1994), 132.
6. Kern-Foxworth, *Aunt Jemima, Uncle Ben, and Rastus,* 133.
7. Kern-Foxworth, *Aunt Jemima, Uncle Ben, and Rastus,* 133.
8. Kern-Foxworth, *Aunt Jemima, Uncle Ben, and Rastus,* 134.
9. Kern-Foxworth, *Aunt Jemima, Uncle Ben, and Rastus,* 134.
10. Carroll, *It Seemed Like Nothing Happened,* 296.
11. Gail B. Stewart, *A Cultural History of the United States through the Decades: The 1970s* (San Francisco: Lucent Books, 1999), 72.

ARCHITECTURE OF THE 1970s

1. Marvin Trachtenberg and Isabelle Hyman, *Architecture from Prehistory to Post-Modernism* (Englewood Cliffs, NJ: Prentice-Hall, 1986), 568.

BOOKS, NEWSPAPERS, MAGAZINES, AND COMICS OF THE 1970s

1. Paul Boyer, *Purity in Print: Book Censorship in America from the Gilded Age to the Computer Age* (Madison: University of Wisconsin Press, 2002), 307, 309.

Arts

2. Carolyn Wells Kraus, "Hurting People's Feelings: Journalism, Guilt, and Autobiography," *Biography* 26, no. 2 (Spring 2003): 283–297.

ENTERTAINMENT OF THE 1970s

1. Mary Ann Mannino, "The Godfather and American Culture: How the Corleones Became 'Our Gang,'" *MELUS*, 2003, p. 218ff. Available at: http://www.findarticles.com/p/articles/mi_m2278/is_3_28/ai_110473975 (accessed July 29, 2006).
2. Thomas Elsaesser, Alexander Horwath, and Noel King, *The Last Great American Picture Show: New Hollywood Cinema in the 1970s* (Amsterdam: Amsterdam University Press, 2004), 117.
3. "Alex Haley," Africanamericans.com, 2005. Available at: http://www.africanamericans.com/AlexHaley.htm (accessed July 29, 2006).
4. "A Chorus Line," PBS.org, 2004. Available at: http://www.pbs.org/wnet/broadway/musicals/chorus.html (accessed July 29, 2006).

FASHION OF THE 1970s

1. Gail B. Stewart, *A Cultural History of the United States through the Decades: The 1970s* (San Francisco: Lucent Books, 1999), 64.
2. Roger Sabin, *Punk Rock, So What? The Cultural Legacy of Punk* (London: Routledge, 1999), 96.

SPORTS AND LEISURE OF THE 1970s

1. Carol Ting, Johannes M. Bauer, Steven S. Wildman, "The U.S. Experience with Non-traditional Approaches to Spectrum Management: Tragedies of the Commons and Other Myths Reconsidered." Prepared for presentation at the 31st Research Conference on Communication, Information and Internet Policy, Arlington, VA, September 19–21, 2003. Available at: http://quello.msu.edu/wp/wp-03–05.pdf.

TRAVEL OF THE 1970s

1. Matthew T. Lee, "The Ford Pinto Case and the Development of Auto Safety Regulations, 1893–1978," Department of Sociology and Criminal Justice, University of Delaware. Available at: http://www.h-net.org/~business/bhcweb/publications/BEHprint/v027n2/p0390-p0401.pdf (accessed July 29, 2006).
2. Gary T. Schwartz, "The Myth of the Ford Pinto Case," *Rutgers Law Review* 43 (1991). Paper first presented at the Third Annual Lecture in the Pfizer Distinguished Visitors' series, Rutgers School of Law–Newark, November 14, 1990. Available at: http://www.pointoflaw.com/articles/The_Myth_of_the_Ford_Pinto_Case.pdf (accessed July 29, 2006).

VISUAL ARTS OF THE 1970s

1. John A. Walker, *Art in the Age of Mass Media* (Boulder, Colo.: Westview Press, 1994), p. 31.

1980s

Timeline

of Popular Culture Events, 1980s

1980

United States hockey team beats the USSR. at the Winter Olympics in Lake Placid, New York.

A two-year sting, Operation Abscam, where FBI agents passing as Arab businessmen offered bribes to government officials in exchange for political favors, indicts 1 senator, 7 Congressmen, and 22 other officials.

President Jimmy Carter sets in motion the boycott of the Summer Olympics by the United States in protest of the Soviet invasion of Afghanistan.

Toxic Shock Syndrome linked to women's super-absorbency tampons.

Ronald Reagan is elected president, defeating incumbent Jimmy Carter and independent candidate John B. Anderson.

The "Who Shot J. R.?" episode of prime-time soap *Dallas* draws 83 million viewers.

John Lennon is murdered in front of his apartment building in Manhattan; a disturbed fan, Mark David Chapman, is tried for his murder.

Bruce Springsteen's *The River* is the number one album of the year.

The Empire Strikes Back opens in movie theaters, shattering box-office records.

On the best seller list: *The Official Preppy Handbook* edited by Lisa Birnbach.

On Television: *The Cable News Network* (CNN), ABC's *Nightline, Magnum, P. I., Too Close for Comfort,* and *Bosom Buddies.*

In stores: 3M's Post-It Notes, cordless telephones, and Rollerblades.

Ordinary People wins the Oscar for Best Picture; Robert De Niro named Best Actor (*Raging Bull*); and Sissy Spacek named Best Actress (*Coal Miner's Daughter*).

1981

July 29: Prince Charles, heir to the British throne, marries Lady Diana Spencer.

October 6: Egyptian President Anwar Sadat is assassinated in Cairo, while reviewing troops.

After 444 days the 52 hostages held at the American Embassy in Tehran are released.

John Hinckley Jr. shoots President Reagan on March 30 outside the Washington Hilton; Press Secretary James Brady is shot in the head, along with two other agents.

The Columbia, America's first space shuttle, makes its maiden voyage.

Pope John Paul II is shot and seriously wounded in Saint Peter's Square, Rome; Mehmet Ali

Agca. A Turkish radical, is tried for the attempt.

The Center for Disease Control publishes a report naming a new disease Acquired Immune Deficiency Syndrome (AIDS).

Wayne B. Williams is arrested for 20 serial murders involving black children in Atlanta, Georgia.

Sandra Day O'Connor named the first female Supreme Court justice, by President Reagan.

President Reagan fires striking air traffic control workers en masse, after they defy a return-to-work order.

On television: *Music Television* (MTV), *Dynasty,* and *Hills Street Blues.*

In stores: IBM personal computers; Nutra-Sweet; Pac-Man.

Chariots of Fire wins the Oscar for Best Picture; Henry Fonda named Best Actor (*On Golden Pond*) and Katharine Hepburn named Best Actress (*On Golden Pond*).

1982

Seventy-seven people die when Air Florida flight 90 crashes into the Potomac River after taking off from Washington National Airport.

Seven people die in the Chicago area after taking Tylenol caplets laced with cyanide; after the massive recall of the pills, the FDA authorizes the creation of tamper-proof containers for foods and drugs.

Barney Clark, a Utah dentist, becomes the first recipient of an artificial heart; he lives for 112 days after the operation.

Disney's EPCOT Center opens in Orlando, Florida.

Elizabeth Carr, America's first test-tube baby, is born to Judy and Roger Carr.

On the best seller list: *Real Men Don't Eat Quiche* by Bruce Fierstein; *The Color Purple* by Alice Walker; *North and South* by John Jakes.

On television: *Family Ties; Cheers; St. Elsewhere; Late Night with David Letterman; Cagney and Lacey; Newhart.*

In stores: Diet Coke; *USA Today;* the Sony Watchman (miniature TV).

The Vietnam Veterans Memorial, designed by 21-year-old Yale student Maya Lin, is opened and dedicated in Washington D.C.

Gandhi wins the Oscar for Best Picture; Ben Kingsley named Best Actor (*Gandhi*); Meryl Streep named Best Actress (*Sophie's Choice*).

1983

Karen Carpenter, 32, dies of a heart attack, calling attention to eating disorders such as anorexia nervosa and bulimia.

Star Wars—the network news' term for the Strategic Defense Initiative—unveiled by President Regan.

Sally K. Ride becomes the first woman in space when she blasts off with four crewmates aboard the space shuttle *Challenger.*

A truck bomb explodes outside the Marine compound in Beirut, killing 200 U.S. Marines sent to maintain peace between Muslims and Christians in Lebanon.

Vanessa Williams becomes the first African American to win the "Miss America" competition; Williams resigns the title 10 months later when *Penthouse* publishes nude photos of her, taken years before.

Lech Walesa, a Polish trade union worker, awarded the Nobel Peace Prize for securing the right for workers in Poland to organize.

"Just Say No" drug campaign launched by First Lady Nancy Reagan.

On television: *The A-Team; Night Court; Hotel; Scarecrow and Mrs. King.*

In stores: *Trivial Pursuit;* the compact disc; the contraceptive sponge.

Terms of Endearment wins the Oscar for Best Picture; Robert Duvall named Best Actor (*Tender Mercies*); Shirley MacLaine named Best Actress (*Terms of Endearment*).

1984

October 24: United States invades the tiny island of Grenada after its Prime Minister is ousted during a coup; President Reagan uses the fact that there are a number of American medical students studying there to justify the attack.

Geraldine Ferraro becomes the first woman to run for vice-president on a major party ticket when Walter Mondale selects her to be his running mate.

"Where's the Beef?" becomes the latest catch phrase when 83-year-old Clara Peller begins appearing in television spots for Wendy's restaurants.

"Baby Fae" is the recipient of a baboon heart during an experimental heart transplant operation; she dies three weeks later.

President Reagan wins re-election carrying 49 states, posting the greatest Republican landslide in history.

Bhopal, India becomes the site of the world's worst industrial disaster as toxic fumes from a Union Carbide plant leak into the water supply; 2,000 die as a result.

Alec Jeffreys develops "genetic fingerprinting," the ability to link an individual to a crime by tracing his or her DNA.

On the best seller list: *Bright Lights, Big City* by Jay McInerney; *The Unbearable Lightness of Being* by Milan Kundera; *What They Don't Teach You at Harvard Business School* by Mark H. McCormick.

On television: *The Bill Cosby Show; Miami Vice; Murder, She Wrote.*

In stores: The Chrysler minivan; Apple's Macintosh computers; CD-ROM.

Amadeus wins the Oscar for Best Picture; F. Murray Abraham named Best Actor (*Amadeus*); Sally Field named Best Actress (*Places in the Heart*).

1985

October 2: Rock Hudson dies of AIDS at age 59—the first public figure to acknowledge that he was dying of the disease.

"We Are The World" becomes an instant number one single after 45 rock stars get together to cut the record to raise money for famine victims in Africa.

Mikhail Gorbachev coins the phrase "glasnost" (openness) to reflect his plan for "perestroika" (reconstruction) between the Soviet Union and the rest of the world.

New Coke is introduced, the first altering of the soft-drink in its 99 year history; 10 weeks later, the old *Coke*, now termed *Coca-Cola Classic*, is brought back in response to the

millions of complaints against the new product.

A TWA jet is skyjacked by Shiite Muslims, with 41 passengers aboard; after the jet lands in Beirut and the terrorists kill one passenger, the United States arranges a trade, releasing the remaining hostages in exchange for Lebanese prisoners held in Israel.

Economic sanctions are announced against South Africa in response to the country's continued policy of apartheid.

Pete Rose makes hit number 4,192, breaking Ty Cobb's 57-year record for most hits during a career.

Willie Nelson organizes the first Farm Aid concert in Urbana, Illinois, to benefit farmers at risk of foreclosure.

A hole in the ozone layer is discovered in the atmosphere over Antarctica.

On the best seller list: *The Accidental Tourist* by Anne Tyler; *Lake Woebegon Days* by Garrison Keillor.

On television: *Moonlighting; Spenser for Hire; Dynasty II: The Colbys; The Golden Girls.*

In stores: Microsoft Windows software; Nintendo entertainment systems; the Ford Taurus.

Out of Africa wins the Oscar for Best Picture; William Hurt named Best Actor (*Kiss of the Spiderwoman*); Geraldine Page named Best Actress (*The Trip to Bountiful*).

1986

January 29: The space shuttle *Challenger* explodes 73 seconds after liftoff, killing all seven crew-members including Christa McAuliffe, the first teacher in space.

Martin Luther King Jr.'s birthday is celebrated as a national holiday (though it is not until 2000 that all 50 states celebrate the holiday).

August: Chernobyl, Ukraine becomes the site of the world's worst nuclear accident, killing 30 people but spreading radiation across northern Europe.

"Hands Across America" raises $100 million for the poor and homeless, as people link hands from Long Beach, CA to New York City.

The Supreme Court upholds affirmative action hiring quotas for minorities and women.

The Iran-Contra Affair reveals that the Regan administration illegally funded covert operations by the Contras (Communist Nicaraguan forces) with money raised in an arms-for-hostages deal with Iran.

Microsoft, co-founded by Bill Gates, goes public.

Prince Andrew weds Sarah Ferguson in Great Britain; Maria Shriver weds Arnold Schwarzenegger; Caroline Kennedy weds Edwin Schlossberg; Tatum O'Neal weds John McEnroe.

On the best seller list: *The Handmaid's Tale* by Margaret Atwood; *All I Really Need to Know I Learned in Kindergarten* by Robert Fulghum.

On television: *L. A. Law; Alf; The Oprah Winfrey Show.*

In stores: Microwave pizzas; nicotine chewing gum; Honda Acura; Polaroid Spectra; digital audiotape.

Platoon wins the Oscar for Best Picture; Paul Newman named Best Actor (*The Color of Money*); Marlee Matlin named Best Actress (*Children of a Lesser God*).

1987

October 18: "Black Monday," the stock market plunges 508 points.

Rev. Jim Bakker admits that he committed adultery and stole money from his ministry on his PTL (Praise the Lord) televangelist network; his wife Tammy Faye weeps copiously as she forgives him on television.

The "Baby M" case goes to court as Mary Beth Whitehead, a surrogate mother artificially inseminated under a contract with William Stern, decides she wants to keep her baby. The courts decide in favor of the Sterns.

Gary Hart, a married, Democratic party hopeful to run for president, is photographed with his then-girlfriend Donna Rice; after the *National Enquirer* publishes the photo, Hart withdraws from the race.

Lt. Col. Oliver North appears before the House Judiciary Committee investigating the Iran-Contra Affair; he claims his actions in organizing the mission were authorized by his superiors.

"Baby Jessica" McClure, an 18-month old child, falls down a well in Midland, Texas; millions watch her rescue on television.

The United States and Soviet Union sign the INF Treaty (on intermediate-range nuclear missiles). The treaty eliminates all ground-launched nuclear missiles with a range of up to 3,400 miles.

"The California Raisins" appear on television singing "I Heard It Through the Grapevine" to plug the raisin industry.

On the best seller list: *Beloved* by Toni Morrison; *Presumed Innocent* by Scott Turow; *And the Band Played On* by Randy Shilts; *Bonfire of the Vanities* by Tom Wolfe.

On television: *thirtysomething; Married...with Children; Beauty and the Beast.*

In stores: disposable cameras; Prozac; soymilk.

The Last Emperor wins the Oscar for Best Picture; Michael Douglas named Best Actor (*Wall Street*); Cher named Best Actress (*Moonstruck*).

1988

Jimmy "The Greek" Snyder is fired by CBS Sports when he tells a television reporter that "the black is a better athlete to begin with because he's bred to be that way."

Jimmy Swaggart, another televangelist, confesses on his television broadcast that he is guilty of sin; his sobbing confession is broadcast globally.

The U.S. cruiser Vincennes mistakes an Iranian airliner for a warplane, and shoots it from the sky, killing all 290 passengers.

The Reverend Jesse Jackson makes a strong bid for the Democratic presidential nomination with his "Rainbow Coalition."

Discovery, the new space shuttle, launches successfully; it is the first attempt since the *Challenger* disaster.

George Bush and Dan Quayle beat Michael Dukakis and Lloyd Bentsen for the presidency of the United States.

Pan Am flight 103 explodes over Lockerbie, Scotland, killing 259 passengers. Investigators later reveal that a terrorist bomb aboard the plane caused the explosion.

On the best seller list: *Love in the Time of Cholera* by Gabriel Garcia Marquez; *A Brief History of Time* by Stephen Hawking; *Breathing Lessons* by Anne Tyler.

On television: *Murphy Brown; Roseanne; The Wonder Years; Wiseguy.*

In stores: Disposable contact lenses; Rogaine hair restorative.

Rain Man wins the Oscar for Best Picture; Dustin Hoffman named Best Actor (*Rain Man*); Jodie Foster named Best Actress (*The Accused*).

1989

The Ayatollah Khomeini issues a death threat to author Salman Rushdie (*The Satanic Verses*) for supposedly insulting the Islamic faith.

The *Exxon Valdez,* an oil tanker, runs aground in Prince William Sound, dumping 11 million gallons of crude oil into the ocean.

The United States invades Panama after Manuel Noriega usurps the presidency; he later flees the country, only to be convicted of drug-trafficking, money laundering, and racketeering in Florida.

Students stage a protest as they demonstrate for reform in Beijing's Tiananmen Square; estimates of those killed when the army fires at the crowds range from 700 to 7,000.

A Robert Mapplethorpe photography exhibit, funded by the National Endowment for the Arts, draws much criticism in Cincinnati; a subsequent showing scheduled by the Corcoran Gallery is canceled.

General Colin Powell becomes the first African American chairman of the Joint Chiefs of Staff.

Pete Rose is banned from baseball and is ruled ineligible for the Baseball Hall of Fame for betting on major-league games.

Leona Helmsley, billionaire hotelier, is convicted of income tax evasion; she receives a sentence of four years and a fine of $7.1 million.

Hurricane Hugo strikes the Carolinas, killing 70 people and causing $4 billion in damage, leaving thousands homeless.

Driving Miss Daisy wins the Oscar for Best Picture; Daniel Day-Lewis named Best Actor (*My Left Foot*); Jessica Tandy named Best Actress (*Driving Miss Daisy*).

Overview

of the 1980s

Go-Go Eighties

NICKNAME FOR DECADE, 1980–1989

GOVERNMENT

For some, the 1980s represented an era of grand prosperity, characterized by President Ronald Reagan, who symbolized a nostalgic 1950s view of America—patriotism, conservative family values, and conspicuous consumption. For those at the other end of the socioeconomic scale, such as the large number of homeless people and the countless ill felled by a new, unknown virus, the decade represented a time of great despair. Reagan's ability to make others feel confident about their futures blinded many people to the difficult realities the United States faced.

Reagan's easy charm, calm voice, and call for a return to a better time in American history resonated with the public, particularly those in the middle class. He laid out a vision of America in simple terms that warmed listeners, in stark contrast to the seemingly endless and confusing challenges of the 1970s.

A 1985 poll conducted by the *New York Times* showed Reagan's resiliency and ability to steady the course. He deflected criticism with charming retorts and an "awe-shucks" persona, which earned him the nickname the "Teflon president." As the president's approval rating soared, pollsters determined that the public accepted him as a leader, whether or not they agreed with his posi-

tions. By the end of Reagan's term, many people could not even remember what he had done or not while in office. Still, Reagan set a mood for the nation that people found comforting, particularly when they asked themselves the important question: "Am I better off now than I was four years ago?"

It is safe to say that the 1980s began on November 4, 1979, when Reagan was elected President. The end of the 1980s is not as easily identified. Some would argue that the decade unofficially closed October 19, 1987—so-called Black Monday—when the stock market lost 22.6 percent of its total value in one day; others usher the decade out on the heels of President George H. W. Bush's defeat in the 1992 presidential election to Arkansas Democrat Bill Clinton, who used the rocky economy and the public's fear of further economic calamities to oust the Republican incumbent.

Ronald Reagan

Some eras in American history have been defined by the events that unfolded in the period, while others have been closely linked to the president who presided over the time. Certainly, Ronald Wilson Reagan served as the most pervasive icon of American life in the 1980s. He became the 40th President of the United States in 1980, and was the first man to serve two terms in office since fellow Republican Dwight D. Eisenhower. Reagan's election initiated a conservative political movement that swept the country, and his powerful rhetoric ushered in a renewed sense of patriotism across the land. Reagan's Hollywood charm, blended with his blunt criticism of the Carter administration, helped him win the election by a 10-point margin.

By 1980, the Republican party needed change and readily adopted Reagan's optimistic, pro-America approach. Debating and campaigning on a conservative platform that put America first, Reagan swept into the White House, pinning the disastrous economy and the lengthy hostage crisis in Iran squarely on the Carter administration. Reagan's simple message, delivered with a grandfatherly air, captured the public's imagination and gave them a renewed sense of hope.

Under Reagan's watch, the administration began a series of reforms that marked some of the most significant economic and social policy changes in half a century. A key moment in Reagan's first term took place on March 31, 1981, when John W. Hinckley, a deranged loner trying to impress actress Jodie Foster, fired a volley of bullets at Reagan's entourage from close range. Although it initially seemed that the president had escaped harm, one bullet exploded into Reagan's chest, while another seriously wounded White House Press Secretary James Brady, leaving him paralyzed. Reagan survived the ordeal, using hospital bed photo ops to push his conservative agenda through Congress when public sympathy was at an all-time high.

During the next two years, economic recovery from the Carter years began in earnest: unemployment numbers dropped, interest rates remained stable, and tax cuts benefited upper-income taxpayers. Reagan's charisma, toughness, and willingness to speak directly to the American people in language that they understood led to an overwhelming victory against Walter Mondale in 1984. Mondale's running mate, Geraldine Ferraro, was the first woman to be nominated for vice president by a major political party. Mondale only carried Massachusetts and the District of Columbia, giving Reagan one of the most resounding re-election victories of all time.

The president called the "Great Communicator," Ronald Reagan, ca. 1985. Prints & Photographs Division, Library of Congress.

Reagan earned the nickname "The Great Communicator" for his uncanny knack of understanding the public's concerns and responding in an optimistic, believable manner. His carefully crafted speeches and effective presentation method made him appear grandfatherly and appealed to the masses that bought into his so-called family values campaign. Reagan's conservatism gave the public a sense of calm after decades of strife, from the lingering pain of Vietnam and Watergate to the psychological scars of the Iran hostage crisis and faltering economy of the 1970s, evidenced by a nationwide gas shortage and soaring interest rates.

The public forgave Reagan because he earned their trust. The president's campaign commercial "Morning in America" encapsulated his philosophy—the American values that connected patriotism, family, and moral conviction were what separated America from the rest of the world, particularly the Soviet Union's so-called Evil Empire.

However, Reagan's Republican party did not do so well in the 1984 election, and a Democratic

TIME MAGAZINE "MAN OF THE YEAR"

1980 Ronald Reagan (40th President of the United States)

1981 Lech Walesa (Polish Solidarity leader)

1982 The Computer

1983 Ronald Reagan (40th President of the United States) and Yuri Andropov (Soviet leader)

1984 Peter Ueberroth (organizer of the L.A. Olympic games)

1985 Deng Xiaoping (Chinese political leader)

1986 Corazon Aquino (President of the Philippines)

1987 Mikhail Gorbachev (Soviet leader)

1988 Endangered Earth

1989 Mikhail Gorbachev (Soviet leader)

majority blocked one of his more ambitious plans: the Strategic Defense Initiative—dubbed "Star Wars" by the media—an arsenal of satellites to render useless any nuclear attacks waged by the Soviets. In hindsight, however, Reagan's legacy consisted of an enormous debt, a booming economy that collapsed as soon as he left office, and a reputation for not really being in control.

THE *CHALLENGER* DISASTER

A blue sky and surprisingly crisp 27-degree morning greeted spectators gathered on January 28, 1986, in Cape Canaveral, Florida. Despite the cool air, conditions were nearly perfect for the lift-off of the 10th flight of the space shuttle *Challenger*. This special flight carried the first civilian astronaut, a social studies teacher from Concord, New Hampshire, 37-year-old Christa McAuliffe.

McAuliffe's presence attracted special attention to the *Challenger* flight. Networks across the nation televised the event. Millions of schoolchildren waited to see America's first teacher in space guide them through the ultimate lesson plan.

The lift-off seemed perfect, and for 73 seconds, all seemed to go as planned. Then, in a puff of smoke that trailed an orange fireball some nine miles above, it was over. Two crisp trails of smoke

followed the path of the separated booster rockets as the remains of the shuttle plummeted to earth. The unthinkable had happened—the space shuttle *Challenger* was gone, and its seven-member crew were gone with it.

The tremendous publicity surrounding McAuliffe had forced NASA officials to carefully orchestrate the flight. A mother of two, the teacher had competed with 11,000 applicants to win the coveted seat after President Reagan had announced in 1984 that he wanted a teacher to be the first civilian in space.

While McAuliffe taught via close-circuit television, the other six members of the Challenger crew: Dick Scobee, Michael Smith, Judith Resnick, Ellison Onizuka, Ronald McNair, and Gregory Jarvis, planned to launch a new $100 million communications satellite into orbit and conduct a series of experiments involving the ozone layer. McAuliffe endured months of training for the mission, worked with the assigned crewmembers, and gradually became a member of the NASA family.

Her immediate family, including her mother and father, traveled from New Hampshire with 18 members of her seventh-grade class to see the lift-off in person. As the crew walked to the craft with the eyes of the world on them, McAuliffe gave the "thumbs up" sign to her family.

It would be years before the cause of the explosion was found—a set of faulty O-rings. That evening, however, among the many questions, President Reagan postponed his sixth State of the Union address to the nation, knowing he must wait to incorporate word of the tragedy in his remarks. His speechwriter Peggy Noonan then wrote one of his most memorable speeches, which incorporated lines from John Gillespie Magee's 1941 poem, "High Flight" at the end:

And I want to say something to the schoolchildren of America who were watching the live coverage of the shuttle's take-off. I know it's hard to understand, but sometimes painful things like this happen. It's all part of the process of exploration and discovery. It's all part of taking a chance and expanding man's horizons. The future doesn't belong to the fainthearted; it belongs to the brave. The Challenger crew was

The space shuttle *Challenger* exploded shortly after lifting off from Kennedy Space Center Tuesday, January 28, 1986. Here, some of the wreckage is retrieved. NASA image.

pulling us into the future, and we'll continue to follow them....

We will never forget them, nor the last time we saw them, this morning, as they prepared for their journey and waved good-bye and "slipped the surly bonds of earth" to "touch the face of God."[1]

FOREIGN POLICY

Reagan's foreign policy centered on two tightly linked ideas: virulent anticommunism and expanding America's military might around the world—represented physically by more troops and psychologically by nuclear weapons. The administration once again hoped to bolster the nation's confidence by harkening back to the early Cold War when American might was unquestioned, while at the same time, pointing to the

technological future when automated weapon defense systems would protect the nation.

Moving toward a more antagonistic relationship with the Soviet Union, Reagan's efforts emulated the containment strategy used at the height of the Cold War. He began an anti-Soviet public relations effort deliberately designed to battle the enemy psychologically. The president harshly criticized the Soviet Union in his first press conference, claiming that the nation would advance world communism by any means necessary, including lying and cheating. In March 1983, Reagan labeled the Soviet Union an "evil empire," which then became the mantra of the administration's anticommunism efforts. More direct efforts at influencing world opinion took place as Reagan took steps to strengthen the United States Information Agency (USIA), Voice of America, Radio Free Europe, and other media outlets.

Reagan called for a dramatic increase in military spending, while simultaneously labeling many worldwide revolutionary movements as either Soviet-backed or outright terrorism. Fighting off the lingering doubts about sending troops overseas—based on the nation's experience in Vietnam—Reagan ordered increased support for Afghanistan rebels fighting a Soviet invasion, sent Marines into Lebanon, and armed counterrevolutionaries in Nicaragua.

The Reagan administration quickly moved to restore the nation's military confidence by increasing defense spending. In 1980, the military budget stood at $134 billion. Five years later, it was $253 billion. Much of the additional budget went toward building conventional forces at home and abroad, increasing the airpower and sea power of the Air Force and Navy, and modernizing technological advances.

The ultimate expression of Reagan's efforts to prove America's strength overseas unfolded on the tiny Caribbean island of Grenada. On October 25, 1983, the United States invaded the island in the first use of direct force since Vietnam. In the view of the administration, communists could not take power in Grenada lest they create a network of anti-American governments in the area with Cuba and Nicaragua.

A bloody coup broke out in Grenada on October 13 and threatened American citizens on the island, most notably the 800 medical students studying there. Reagan authorized the American strike on October 22. The next day terrorists attacked a Marine barracks in Beirut, Lebanon, killing 244 American soldiers. Despite the worry that the Grenada invasion would look like an attempt to divert attention from the attack in Beirut, the president proceeded with the invasion.

An initial force of 1,200 American troops swarmed into Grenada and met stiff resistance. Quickly the U.S. force grew to more than 7,000 and overwhelmed the enemy, many of whom fled into the mountains or surrendered. Documents uncovered on the island proved Grenada's close ties with the Soviet Union and Cuba, and thereby vindicated the American invasion.

The success of the Grenada invasion gave the administration newfound strength in negotiations with the Soviet Union and Soviet leader Mikhail Gorbachev. Reagan stood firm in directing Gorbachev toward an agreement that would destroy land-based intermediate and short-range nuclear missiles.

The administration's far-flung efforts to eliminate communism led it into hot water when the stage turned to Nicaragua. As 1986 approached, the news media uncovered a tie between administration officials and the Contras, an antigovernment guerrilla movement in Nicaragua. In an effort to undermine the Sandinista government, Reagan officials secretly supplied the Contras with weapons, training, and financial aid.

The funding came in an "arms for hostages" deal that undermined the administration's get-tough policies. The scheme worked out by officials in the Reagan administration involved the government selling weapons to Iran (an avowed enemy of the United States), then using the money to fund the Contras. In exchange for the weapons, Iran would exert its influence to free American hostages held by terrorists in Lebanon.

Congressional hearings began in 1987, and television cameras recorded the testimonies of the two central ringleaders, Lieutenant Colonel Oliver North and Admiral John Poindexter, both Pentagon officials who acted as national security advisors. While Congress tried to link the plan to the White House, both North and Poindexter denied that they had informed the president of their actions. In the end, only North and Poindexter served prison time, yet both were accorded "hero" status for defending America by any means possible.

The scandal marred the end of Reagan's term, but not his immediate reputation. He handpicked his successor, George H. W. Bush, who won the election and guaranteed conservative representation in the Oval Office for another four years.

BUSINESS AND THE ECONOMY IN THE 1980S

One of the most highly charged debates concerning the Reagan legacy is the former president's long-term impact on economic policy. The basic tenets of Reagan's economic philosophy included freeing Americans from big government, implementing massive tax cuts for businesses and individuals, and increasing the national debt to build a stronger military. Reagan believed that easing the financial burdens of wealthy Americans would place more money into the system, which would gradually "trickle down" through the lower classes.

Reagan's tax cuts did improve the nation's economy in the short term and led to increases in both personal income and consumption. However, these gains were offset by larger budget deficits, lower levels of personal savings, and sluggish business investment. Ultimately, Reagan's supply-side economic policies weakened the foundation of the economy by relying on a massive federal deficit to bankroll America's spending spree.

The economic expansion that took place between 1982 and 1987—and that produced $20 trillion in new wealth—gave Americans new hope in the form of lower inflation, falling interest rates, job creation, and an expanding stock market. The Reagan recession yielded to the Reagan recovery, which enabled businesses and households to gain the stability that had been missing from the economy for years.

Black Monday and Insider Trading

Although some observers believe that the 1980s did not ideologically pass until Bill Clinton's election to the presidency in 1992, others consider the decade's end as Monday, October 19, 1987, when the stock market crashed 508 points—the largest one-day percentage collapse in history. On that one day, the Dow Jones Industrial lost 22.6 percent of its value—roughly $500 billion dollars. For administration critics, the break down revealed the hidden flaws in the Reaganomics infrastructure.

The stock market flourished in the mid-1980s. Trading stood at an all-time high, having continued the growth initiated by the bull market of 1982. A series of hostile takeovers, leveraged buyouts, and a form of merge-mania fueled the events taking place on Wall Street.

As the market boomed, Wall Street culture changed. Formerly the country club of established elites trading in near secrecy, a young breed of traders backed by new money had a different objective—to get rich quick. Wall Street players in the 1980s saw themselves as economic cowboys tackling a new frontier. They played hard and drank hard. They wore "power suits" with bold red or yellow ties, slicked back their hair, and walked with a swagger. They played fast and loose with government regulations as well.

Insider trading, or the act of gaining an unfair advantage buying or selling securities based on nonpublic information, had plagued Wall Street from its earliest days. Prior to the formation of the Securities and Exchange Commission (SEC) in 1934 in response to the stock market crash of 1929, insider trading had occurred frequently. Since the mid-1930s, the SEC regulated trading and attempted to make the stock market a trustworthy system.

Although insider trading is usually associated with illegal activity, it also happens when corporate officers, directors, and employees buy and sell stock within their own companies. Legal insider trading occurs every day and is permitted within the rules and regulations of individual companies and government regulations that govern this kind of trade, which must be reported to the SEC.

Illegal insider trading gained great notoriety in the 1980s, epitomized by the criminal charges brought against junk-bond king Michael Milken and financial speculator Ivan Boesky. Oliver Stone's hit motion picture *Wall Street* centered on insider trading. Tom Wolfe's bestselling novel

Bonfire of the Vanities also employs a Milken-like figure as its main character. (See Entertainment of the 1980s and Books, Newspapers, Magazines, and Comics of the 1980s, respectively.)

One of the new breed of Wall Street guru, Milken worked his way up the ladder and eventually landed at Drexel Burnham, one of the Street's revered firms. In 1986, at the height of his power, Milken earned a bonus of $550 million. The venerable *Wall Street Journal* even proclaimed Milken the most influential financier since J. P. Morgan, virtually creating a $125 billion market.

Milken's early junk-bond deals were used to finance several new high tech companies, which by their very nature exposed investors to greater risk. Some of these companies went on to great heights, despite the risk involved in their inceptions. For example, Milken's financing helped launch Ted Turner's Cable News Network (CNN) and McGraw Cellular, an early innovator in cellular telephone service.

At the same time, another so-called Master of the Universe, Ivan Boesky, privatized public companies through leveraged buyouts (LBOs). The corporate raider bought stock in companies targeted for takeover, and then sold his share when the deal took place. After taking a $24 million loss on an oil deal, Boesky built a network of insiders (bankers, brokers, and executives) who supplied him with information on new deals in exchange for cash.

The SEC launched an investigation into Boesky's dealings, and on November 14, 1986, announced his confession to numerous security law violations. In exchange for a reduced sentence (ultimately three years in prison), Boesky turned government informant. The biggest name he revealed was Milken, and government prosecutors zealously pursued him.

Ultimately, Milken pleaded guilty to six counts (of 98) filed against him and received a whopping $600 million fine, the most ever levied against an individual.

In the midst of the 1980s boom, many companies, grew, in essence, by purchasing smaller companies. Companies orchestrated leveraged buyouts by raising massive amounts of capital by selling junk bonds (with higher risk, but the possibility of greater reward through higher interest rate payouts) to the public. Business executives then used the money to purchase targeted companies.

Another form of capital acquisition occurred when a company "went public." For instance, companies in the high tech industry launched initial public offerings (IPOs) in the 1980s, because analysts forecasted robust personal computer sales. The investing public caught a sort of mania and the release of these new commodities made the market soar. The rapid growth caught the SEC off-guard. The regulating body could not properly monitor the many IPOs, or the buying and selling frenzy that was happening across the corporate world.

In early 1987, however, the SEC uncovered a large insider trading operation and found many of the involved companies liable. In addition, the Federal Reserve raised short-term interest rates to temper a rise in inflation, which also tempered activity on Wall Street. In response, many trading firms resorted to using portfolio insurance as protection from dips in the market. This practice used futures contracts as an insurance policy—those that held futures contracts could make

money if the market crashed, thereby offsetting losses in the stock market. In order to counteract the federal government's interest hikes, many institutions began trading on their portfolio insurance futures, taking in billions of dollars in a matter of minutes and causing both the futures market and the stock market to crash simultaneously. The dark cloud of "Black Monday" fell over Wall Street.

Within a 24-hour period, $500 billion dollars simply evaporated from the index. The crash created a domino effect, causing similar collapses across the globe. Individuals blamed their brokers, and when circuits jammed as a result of millions of phone calls, some people took the law into their own hands and shot brokers in their offices for not pulling out in time.

Panic ensued and a global recession looked imminent. Though caught up in the chaos, many small investors could not even begin to understand what had happened. They had trusted their financial advisors and Wall Street, and had ignored the potential risk to gain their share of the healthy returns.

YUPPIES

In the 1980s, "Young Urban Professionals" (better known simply as Yuppies) were more than just an emerging marketing demographic, they constituted a pseudo-movement, a mindset, and for some, a religion. Yuppies focused on upward mobility, status, income, proximity to power. Primarily high-income professionals, they possessed a singular concern regarding affluence. Flashy was the style of choice, whether that meant Armani suits or cherry red sports cars.

Washington, D.C. served as one of the primary Yuppie hot spots in the 1980s. In the nation's capitol, the number of Baby Boomers, those born between 1946 and 1965, increased greatly during the decade. They flocked to urban neighborhoods like Adams Morgan, a culturally diverse, trendy part of town filled with bookstores, antique shops, and a host of ethnic restaurants from Ethiopian to Caribbean and everything in between. Yuppies filled high-paying posts in the federal government, corporations, associations, and other organizations in the D.C. metro area. Many were positioned in the halls of power.

The Yuppie mentality flourished in the 1980s on the back of the growing disparity between the wealthy segment of society and everyone else. While the elites gained in the market-driven economy, the rest of the population felt the squeeze. The notion gained currency in the 1980s to the point that *Newsweek* deemed 1984 "The Year of the Yuppie." Yuppie characters also infiltrated the decade's fiction, including Jay McInerney's *Bright Lights, Big City,* 1984, and *The Bonfire of the Vanities,* 1987, by Tom Wolfe. Both were later released as major films.

The stereotypical 1980s Yuppie male worked in finance, wore bright yellow "power" ties, suspenders, and expensive suits, all designed to emulate (and in some cases outdo) firm partners. Basically, these Yuppie powerbrokers were young men simply searching for a way to look grown up.

The federal government responded quickly to the melee by lowering short-term interest rates the next day in an effort to curtail a depression and banking crisis. The market surged once more, recovering much more quickly than it had following the Crash of 1929. One long-term gain from this particular crash was the installation of a circuit breaker system to electronically stop stock trading if prices dropped too rapidly, thus preventing a similar crash in the future.

REAGANOMICS, THE ECONOMY, AND POVERTY

So-called Reaganomics had a profound impact on the American economy. The massive federal deficit drove interest rates higher, ensuring that little extra funds existed for social programs designed to help the poor and needy. The administration targeted welfare programs, believing that the work to eliminate poverty in earlier decades had failed. Reagan decimated food stamp benefits, job service programs, and low-income housing funds. The rhetoric coming from the White House waged psychological war against welfare programs and recipients, attaching a stigma to those who needed help to survive.

The tax cuts Reagan championed dropped the top individual tax rate from 70 percent, where it had been in the previous decade, to 28 percent in 1986. Working-class Americans assumed the burden of paying a higher proportion of their incomes in taxes, particularly when rising state and Social Security taxes factored into the equation.

The official poverty line stood at $12,675 for a family of four, but the ranks of those below that figure swelled into a "hyper poor" class that barely eked out an existence on the fringes of society. By the end of the decade, more than 12 million people (1 of every 20 Americans) made less than half the poverty line standard. Single females headed 60 percent of the families in this category. The number of black children in this class leaped 52 percent in the 1980s. Studies revealed that 62 percent of the hyper poor lived outside cities and 43 percent were in the South.

By mid-decade, 50 percent of America's towns saw a decrease in population as more people flocked to big cities. The travails for farmers and farm families intensified. Approximately 500,000 farms disappeared in the 1970s, and 267,000 more went under over the next 10 years. Although Reagan preached a sermon of nostalgia and recalled the simpler days of the past, the nation grew steadily more urban.

THE WORKPLACE

During the 1980s, Republican economic policies enabled the richest 20 percent of the population to increase its income by one-third, while the total income of the lowest 60 percent fell in real dollars. Out of this environment grew the notion of the "working poor," with 33 percent of working Americans earning annual incomes below the poverty line.[2]

Downsizing

The recession during Reagan's first term devastated many working-class families and communities. Many of these never recovered, even after the economy rebounded. Cities in the Midwest and Middle Atlantic—reliant on heavy manufacturing—suffered through successive plant closings. In 1982, mass layoffs eliminated 1.25 million jobs in the region, turning America's manufacturing base into a giant "Rust Belt."

The recession and resulting unemployment (11% of the total workforce) had lasting psychological consequences on Americans, particularly those male breadwinners who had lost their jobs. Depression, alcoholism, and even violence followed this life-changing experience. Few men over 40 years old who had been forced out of their companies later found work at the same income level or were able to update their job skills to qualify for a career change.

Layoffs among white-collar employees found a new name in the 1980s—downsizing. Although the exact origins of downsizing are open to interpretation, this term is now part of the American business lexicon. The practice has even become part of popular culture, showing up as a topic on the syndicated hit television show *Roseanne* and the Dilbert cartoon strip.

In 1996, the *New York Times* ran a series of articles looking at the phenomenon; the paper used

DOWNSIZING AS GOOD BUSINESS

Former General Electric Chairman and CEO Jack Welch's early tenure at GE in the early 1980s institutionalized downsizing. Under his direction, the company eliminated more than 100,000 jobs, earning Welch the nickname "Neutron Jack"—like the bomb, he turned people into dust, but left buildings standing.

The massive layoffs overturned GE's corporate culture and changed the business world. GE's stock went up, causing other CEOs to follow Welch's lead.

Welch's brand of corporate capitalism, in which shareholder return is the only measure of success, also set in motion a cruel system of constant dread—fear about job loss and the economic and psychological destruction it causes.

Welch's sole focus on shareholder return and hitting or surpassing analyst expectations each quarter won him rave reviews as a tough-minded leader. However, given closer examination, these pursuits may be seen as a magician's bag of tricks. An obsession with quarterly earnings ahead of long-term planning led GE to cut corners and not think about the environmental consequences of dumping PCBs (polychlorinated biphenyls) into the Hudson River.

Welch's personal aggressiveness was replicated throughout GE in the 1980s, implementing a winner-take-all attitude that rewarded profit and nothing else. Other corporate executives began using mass layoffs as a way to cut costs, take restructuring charges against earnings, and meet quarterly earning estimates. The tick upward in stock price benefited those with the largest number of shares…almost always the leadership team.

Bureau of Labor Statistics reports to conclude that 43 million people had been laid off between 1979 and 1995.

PERSONAL COMPUTERS

By the early 1980s, technological advances transformed computers from unwieldy behemoths into smaller, more efficient business and personal tools, and two companies, Microsoft, and Apple Computer, were instrumental in making small computers—often called "microcomputers" to distinguish them from the large "main-frame" computing machines already in use in science and industry. By 1983, these small computers, had become so important, and so commonplace, that *Time* magazine named "The PC" its "Man of the Year." Apple and IBM worked in competition through the 1970s, and each came to the marketplace of the 1980s ready to make the computer an essential component of the modern world.

The 1980s were banner years for IBM, which introduced the industry standard for the personal computer in the 1970s. In 1980, the corporation teamed with Paul Allen and Bill Gates to develop an operating system for their new lines of computers—the system DOS became the industry standard. Later that year, Gates's new company Microsoft received a contract from IBM to create a series of languages for its new systems. The four languages developed by Microsoft—BASIC, FORTRAN, COBOL, and Pascal—enabled the corporation to release its new personal computer in early 1981, called the IBM-PC, which ran with its new system, MS-DOS.

By 1982, Microsoft developed another language, "Multiplan" for use with the Apple II computer, developed by Apple Computer, whose founders were Steve Jobs, Steve Wozniak, and Ronald Wayne. Meanwhile, a competitor to Microsoft, WordPerfect Corporation, unveiled its new word-processing system, "WordPerfect." The company's Version 1.0 soon became the most popular word processing system in the world. By 1983, Microsoft had joined IBM in developing "Windows," a file management system for the personal computer.

As Microsoft's MS-DOS systems kept speed with new variations, IBM continued issuing newer, faster models to openly compete with the Apple computer. By 1985, Microsoft and IBM were seen as a unit, developing newer products for the growing demands of the decade. In 1987, IBM's PS/2 personal computer allowed a clearer

An August 1981 photo of an IBM Personal Computer (PC), which is outfitted with a monitor, printer, and two disk drives. AP Photo.

variety of graphics and a smaller disc size—3.5, which again quickly became the industry standard.

The Apple II is considered to be the first "personal computer" marketed for in-home use. Built in a factory, Apple's PC gave users a relatively inexpensive and easy-to-learn machine. With its extensive software capabilities and cheap "floppy discs," the Apple II was the first personal computer capable of color graphics and an easy-to-use interface. By 1982, Apple became the first PC company to reach $1 billion in annual sales.

In 1983, Apple introduced a more powerful unit, the Apple IIe. Containing 64 kilobytes of RAM, the one megahertz 6502 processor sold for $1,400 retail and ran on its new language, Applesoft BASIC. It began to be widely used in schools. In 1986, Apple released its next incarnation, The Macintosh, which contained one megabyte of RAM and a newly designed keyboard. It originally sold for $2,600.

Of course, the competition between Apple and IBM was not always friendly. In 1988, Apple filed a copyright infringement suit against Microsoft for its Windows 2.03, claiming that it was basically stylized after their program for the Mac. The lawsuit was ultimately thrown out of court.

Other popular personal computers were developed mainly for the youth market. The Commodore 64 became the best selling personal computer in history, costing only $299.00 from the start. Using the television for its monitor, the Commodore 64's large memory capacity (64 kilobytes), high quality graphics, and inexpensive discs, made it a favorite among teens. Atari Models 400 and 800 were considered the best personal computers for games and color graphics. Though the machines were capable of high quality graphics and varieties of games, their inability to accommodate business software made them obsolete quickly. By 1985, they were replaced with the Nintendo game systems, which accommodated a wider variety of games and graphics.

By the end of the decade, no office was complete without a computerized system, and millions of homes owned and operated some form of personal computer. Understanding of the workings of both the computer and the varieties of

1980s PERSONAL COMPUTERS

For children born in the late 1980s and the 1990s, the personal computer is a way of life. From social networking and online dating to massive multiplayer online gaming communities and e-commerce, the personal computer revolution is arguably the most important development in everyday culture of the twenty-first century. Personal computers originated in the 1950s, when giant machines functioning by means of punch cards gave the first glimpse into the potential of computing technology. By the 1970s, computers were much faster than their predecessors, miniscule by comparison, and were gradually appearing in the home. By 1983, the total number of computers in the United States exceeded 3 million. It was during this time that businesses first began adopting computer systems in large numbers. The days of paper filing and organization were replaced by catalogues of "floppy disks." Other companies saw the opportunity for profit and began creating peripheral equipment, like disks and printers; instructional literature and industry magazines further fueled the industry's growth. While the computers of the 1980s were as different from modern computers as bicycles are to sports cars, the decade set the tone and constant improvements, utility, and enthusiastic adoption have carried the computer into the modern age. Given its impact on daily life, the development of the computer can be viewed as similar in scope to the advent of paper or the automobile.

languages and graphic capabilities soon became an expectation in job interviews—the rapid rise of the personal computer changed the ways we did business, the words and methods we used to communicate, and the future for industry, business, and the home.

CELLULAR TELEPHONES

The development, marketing, and resulting universal use of the cellular telephone, all in less than 20 years, makes it one of the world's most popular innovations. Once merely toys for wealthy businessmen and the rich, cell phones are now a part of everyday life. The roots of cellular phones stretch back to the crude origins of mobile radio usage in vehicles. Police and emergency use pushed early development, which progressed slowly. Researchers gave little thought to public applications for mobile phones. AT&T, which built the vaunted Bell System in the United States, showed little interest in mobile phones.

In the late 1940s, technological innovations such as low cost microprocessors and digital switching, made mobile telephones more practical. The first public mobile telephone system in the United States began in St. Louis in 1945 with three channels. The St. Louis experiment was also made possible by the increased pool of skilled radio personnel after World War II and the use of radio communications in the armed services.

D. H. Ring, a Bell Laboratories scientist, originated the cellular concept in 1947. Ring and his colleagues realized that by using small geographic service areas (or "cells"), combined with low powered transmitters and radio spectrum frequency reuse, the capacity of mobile phones would be greatly increased.

Few people believed the cellular system had a commercial application, and the Federal Communications Commission (FCC) decided to limit the frequencies, thus squelching further work. Under increasing pressure from AT&T and the general public, the FCC reconsidered its position in the late 1960s. The Bell Labs once again took the lead in proposing a cellular system of numerous low-powered broadcast towers, each covering a cell only a few miles in radius. By 1977, AT&T built and operated a model cell system. The next year, after the FCC approved Illinois Bell's request, testing began in Chicago with over 2,000 customers. In 1979, the first commercial cell phone system opened in Tokyo.

In 1981, Motorola and American Radio started a second test in the Washington, D.C. area. The next year, the FCC finally permitted commercial cellular service in the United States. The FCC's 1982 decision to break up AT&T's regulated monopoly also stymied additional research and development. Ameritech provided the first commercial service the next year in Chicago, while Motorola followed up in Baltimore and Washington, D.C.

Over the next several years, consumer demand exploded. There were more than one million subscribers by 1987. The airwaves quickly became overcrowded, forcing the FCC to open the 800 MHz band. This decision stimulated growth in the cell phone industry and forced further research.

While it took decades for the cellular phone industry to develop, the acceptance of cell phones worldwide was nearly immediate. The first profile of cell phone users was generated in 1987 and found that they were primarily male, 35–50 years old, managers or entrepreneurs who spent a great deal of time in their cars and had income in excess of $35,000. Most users had mobile phones installed in their cars for business use. In fact, the average mobile phone cost $1,000 that year, with portables reaching $2,000. The biggest complaints, however, were battery weight, short battery life, and lack of privacy on cell phones. The FCC even denied a petition filed by the Washington Legal Foundation requesting that a privacy label be placed on the devices, saying it would not serve public interest.

As the 1980s progressed, the CTIA and cellular carriers embarked on a program to raise mainstream awareness of cellular phones. In 1988, the cellular industry began testing retail sales channels, such as Sears and Kmart, and audio manufacturers like Clarion and Sanyo entered the market. It would take several years before cellular phones regularly appeared in retail stores.

RELIGION

The twin pillars of American disappointment—Vietnam and President Nixon and his Watergate scandal—continued to influence the 1980s. As a matter of fact, the nation would continue to grapple with the legacy of these challenges well into the twenty first century. The loss of faith in America's military might and its political system had strange consequences for the public. In many cases, this loss of faith seemed to lead some back to religion with newfound fervor. In the political arena, for example, a renewed sense of faith became an important character trait and led to a candidate's moral standing developing into a primary rationale for support. People believed that closely examining a presidential candidate's

position on religion and character would excise Nixon's ghost.

The Democratic party turned away from evangelical audiences, despite the fact that 80 percent of Americans claimed religion was a central part of their lives and the genuine religious tenets proclaimed by President Jimmy Carter. The Republicans, led by Reagan, courted this audience relentlessly, particularly as abortion became a more important political topic. In response, Republican party leaders built the disparate conservative religious groups into a voting block.

Like so much of the 1980s, a sleazier side coincided with the grassroots religious movement. Televangelist Jim Bakker and his sidekick, wife Tammy Faye Bakker, exemplified the worst aspects of the constant desire for glitz and money in the decade. The Bakkers built a theme park, dubbed "Heritage USA," as a money-generating arm of an international organization seemingly devised to bilk worshippers out of their money.[3] They built a television network to broadcast their show, The PTL Club, which is reported to have attracted upwards of 12 million viewers a week and drawn more than $1 million a week in donations. Journalists sought out Bakker for quotes, since he had little modesty in comparing himself to Jesus and claiming that Jesus would use TV evangelism if he was alive in the 1980s.

Eventually, financial shenanigans caught up with the Bakkers. In early 1987, investigators discovered that nearly $300,000 in payoff money had been given to a former employee named Jessica Hahn to ensure that she would not discuss a sexual relationship she had had with Bakker. This scandal forced Bakker's resignation. Later, in 1989, a jury indicted Bakker on a series of counts, including mail fraud and wire fraud. A judge sentenced him to 45 years in jail and a $500,000 fine. The decade was not kind to other corrupt televangelists, including Jimmy Swaggart, who provided plenty of fodder for comedians when he renounced his visit to a prostitute in a weepy apology to his congregation in 1988.

AIDS

On July 5, 1981, *The New York Times* ran its first story on a "gay cancer" identified as Kaposi's sarcoma. At the time, only 71 people in the United States had what is now known as Acquired Immune Deficiency Syndrome (AIDS). However, two and a half years later, 1,922 Americans were diagnosed with AIDS.[4]

When AIDS first surfaced, it appeared to be concentrated in the gay community, which caused most media outlets to ignore the details of the growing epidemic. The first activists and medical personnel to fight AIDS emerged early in the epidemic. Don Francis of the Center for Disease Control, Selma Dritz of the San Francisco Board of Health, and Marc Conant from the University of California, worked to secure funding for research and support for closing the bathhouses in San Francisco and New York City, where the disease was easily spread through unsafe sexual practices. The gay community had Bobbi Campbell, the self-proclaimed "poster boy"; Larry Kramer, the advocate/playwright; Paul Popham, who assisted Kramer in founding Gay Men's Health Crisis in New York City; and Bill Kraus, the San Francisco legislator who fought for AIDS funding. As AIDS spread into the heterosexual community, others joined the call for government assistance, including Randy Shilts, whose book *And the Band Played On* chronicled the early years of the epidemic; Cleve Jones, whose NAMES Project created a memorial to victims lost to the disease in the form of a giant quilt; and Elizabeth Taylor, actress and founder of AmFAR, still a major contributor to the research efforts to eradicate the disease.

It was not until 1985, however, that the nebulous disease acquired a notable face in the form of movie star Rock Hudson. During his 37-year career as a film star and matinee idol, Hudson had maintained secrecy concerning his sexual orientation. He was cast as a strong, quiet type in a series of woman's pictures during the 1950s. His biggest success came in the early 1960s in a series of light, screwball comedies with Doris Day and Tony Randall, namely *Pillow Talk* (1959), *Lover Come Back* (1962), and *Send Me No Flowers* (1964). During the 1970s, Hudson teamed with Susan St. James in the comic crime series *MacMillan and Wife* (1971–1976), and he returned to television to play Daniel Reese on *Dynasty* during the 1984 season.

During his stint on *Dynasty,* the tabloids began to report on Hudson's appearance—he appeared gaunt. In July 1985, Hudson was diagnosed with the disease, and his trip to the Pasteur Institute for treatment with experimental drugs not available in the United States created a media circus; when he flew back to the United States seven days later, on a stretcher, news cameras from around the world recorded his image. Hudson went public with his homosexuality and his fight against AIDS when he appeared with Doris Day, helping her to launch her cable show *Doris Day and Friends,* a show to support her activities as an animal rights activist. At the time of his death, on October 2, 1985, AIDS was finally surfacing as an acceptable topic for the nightly news. Five years later, it had become the *cause celebre,* as celebrities started the practice of wearing red ribbons at awards shows.

The AIDS crisis paved the way for many broad reaching initiatives that have had far-reaching social impact on American society. Early posters advocating "Silence = Death" and "Safe Sex" created by ACT UP (AIDS Coalition to Unleash Power) helped to institute a broader, franker discussion of sexuality in America's schools.

Responses to the pandemic brought the gay community together in its efforts to make the Reagan/Bush administrations assist in the fight. Actor's Equity created "Broadway Cares," a group dedicated to assisting the sick in the artistic community. The group gathered media attention when they began to ask celebrities attending awards shows to don red ribbons to symbolize the continuing struggle against indifference. Other notable artistic responses include Robert Mapplethorpe's and Keith Haring's art (see Art of the 1980s), Gran Fury's "Bloody Hands" posters, and the AIDS Memorial Quilt, unveiled for the first time in October 1987. The quilt's debut on the Mall in Washington, D.C. illustrated the deep loss felt by the American community, as each of its 1,920 panels represented a person who had died of the disease.

Interestingly, Hollywood did not respond to the crisis in a significant manner until 1993 with the release of *Philadelphia,* which won Tom Hanks an Academy Award for best Actor for portraying a lawyer fired because he had AIDS. During the 1980s, the theater made the most notable contribution to the awareness of the epidemic by turning plays into political manifestos demanding action, including Larry Kramer's *The Normal Heart* (see Entertainment of the 1980s) and William Hoffman's *As Is*. On television, one of the first films to portray the ravages of the disease and its effect on the family was *An Early Frost* (ABC, 1985), a daring-for-its-day melodrama. The movie tells the story of a Chicago lawyer (Aidan Quinn) who returns to his New England family (headed by Ben Gazarra and Gena Rowlands) to tell them he is both gay and dying of the AIDS virus.

Despite the tragedies of the AIDS pandemic, it has had a positive aspect. Not only has it made sexual orientation a much more open topic in mainstream America, it has also proved that people can come together to fight injustice. Other health issues, such as breast and colon cancer, have replicated the activities of these groundbreaking protests to find broader support.

Advertising

of the 1980s

The notion of consumer culture in the United States came of age in the 1980s. At the upper reaches of the economic ladder, flashy advertising sold images of success. Lower down the scale, advertising promised a better life, if only a person bought the right clothes, shoes, cigarettes, beer, or automobile.

Many high-profile campaigns featured celebrity endorsers and were designed to add an air of familiarity and pizzazz to the promotions. One of the nation's most popular celebrity spokesmen was Bill Cosby, an African American comedian who starred in the mega-hit television program *The Cosby Show*. (See Entertainment of the 1980s.)

Advertisers had long realized that success meant selling the perception of a better life. Creating buyers' aspirations led to a deeper connection with the product, from Nike and Michael Jordan with "Just Do It" to Miller Brewing Company's "High Life" campaigns. Linking celebrities to products added the luster that 1980s consumers desired.

Although the advertising industry gained important new outlets in the 1980s, particularly with the increasing number of cable television stations, the total money companies spent on advertising remained static for most of the decade.

Many ads from the decade became pop culture staples. The One Club for Art and Copy declared Ally & Gargano's 1982 Federal Express television commercial "Fast Talker" the best ad of the 1980s. The commercial features a typical, overworked office manager talking at a nearly imperceptible speed, but FedEx intervenes and gives him time to slow down.

Advertising executives viewed the 1980s as dominated by television, feel-good marketing, and style over substance. For example, Chiat/Day/Mojo's commercial for Apple's Macintosh computers "1984" did not discuss the features of the product or how it differed from its competitors. Instead, the commercial showed computer users as Orwellian automatons who would be freed from their black-and-white, drab world by using Apple's more user-friendly computer.

While many campaigns played on consumers' aspirations, others stuck to tried-and-true formulas that had worked in the past, or simply rehashed successful campaigns from the past, including those for Campbell Soup and Timex. Consumers felt comfortable with familiar slogans like Timex's "Takes a licking and keeps on ticking."

NIKE

No company in the 1980s rode the confluence of popular culture, fashion, and fitness more effectively than Nike. Decades later, the Nike story

ADVERTISING SLOGANS OF THE 1980s

"Absolut [something]," Absolut Vodka, 1980*

"Soup is good food," Campbell's Soup, 1980

"Visa. It's everywhere you want to be," Visa, 1985

"Just do it," Nike, 1988*

"Be all that you can be," U.S. Army, 1981*

"It keeps going and going and going…" Energizer batteries, 1989

"A different kind of company. A different kind of car," Saturn, 1989

"Know what comes between me and my Calvins? Nothing," Calvin Klein, 1980*

"Where's the beef?" Wendy's 1984*

"We'll leave the light on for you," Motel 6, mid 1980s*

"Recommended by Dr. Mom," Robitussin cough medicine, 1986

"The heartbeat of America," Chevrolet, 1986

"Just for the taste of it," Diet Coke, 1982

"Coke is it!" Coca-Cola, 1982

"The best part of waking up is Folger's in your cup," Folger's coffee, 1984

"Michelin. Because so much is riding on your tires," Michelin, 1985

"Beef. Real food for real people," Beef Industry Council, 1987

"Pork. The other white meat," National Pork Producers Council, 1987

"The fabric of our lives," Cotton, Inc., 1989

"The choice of a new generation," Pepsi-Cola, 1984

"Hefty, hefty, hefty, wimpy, wimpy, wimpy," Hefty trash bags, 1983

"Star of the American road," Texaco, 1988

"Quite possibly the world's most perfect food," Chiquita Bananas, 1989

"Choosy mothers choose Jif," Jif peanut butter, early 1980s

---

*Among Advertising Age's "The Advertising Century: Top 100 Advertising Campaigns," http://adage.com/century/campaigns.html.

is commonplace, but in the 1980s its dominance of the shoe market could hardly have been imagined. Throughout the early decade, Reebok, Adidas, Keds, Converse, and Pony crowded into the shoe market, making Nike just another choice among many.

Riding the jogging craze in the late 1970s and 1980s, Nike's first successes were with running shoes. Nike co-founder Phil Knight realized that by glamorizing athletes and athleticism, sports and fitness could be used as tools to measure a person's worth. Consumers that emulated sports stars would then buy products endorsed by those athletes. Nike's mission statement pushed this analogy even further, claiming, "to bring inspiration and innovation to every athlete in the world" and redefining "athlete" to mean anyone who had a body.[1]

In 1982, Dan Wieden and Dave Kennedy left their jobs and began their own advertising agency, Wieden+Kennedy. Nike was their first client. Later that year, Nike ran its first national television ads during the New York Marathon.

The decisive move for Nike in the 1980s was signing Michael Jordan to a five-year, $1.25 million contract. At the time, Jordan was a heralded basketball star from the University of North Carolina, but hardly a household name. No one realized that Knight and his executive team had bet the company's future on Jordan. Only three games into the 1984–1985 basketball season, the NBA banned Jordan's red and black Nike shoes because they did not conform to the Chicago Bulls uniform. The ban was widely reported in the media, and this, combined with Jordan's spectacular ability, increased interest in the shoes that had caused so much uproar. Suddenly, everyone wanted Nike shoes—basketball players and non-players alike.

Nike's daring commercials, directed by Spike Lee and starring Lee's "Mars Blackmon" character from the film *She's Gotta Have It* (1986), propelled Jordan and Nike to new heights. In 1988, Nike announced its "Just Do It" slogan, again understanding and somehow bottling the national zeitgeist. As Jordan's fame grew, he not only signed as a spokesperson with more companies (Wheaties, Coca-Cola, Gatorade, Wilson, McDonald's, and more), but the Chicago Bulls were regularly featured on network and cable television. Jordan and the Nike swoosh became one symbol, forever linked by success and millions of dollars in marketing. In 1986, thanks in part to Jordan, Nike total revenues surpassed $1 billion for the first time.

Nike also introduced the idea of technology into the sneaker industry, a notion that caught on among buyers. At first, customers did not understand the company's "air" concept, used to create a better feel in its running and basketball shoes. Nike designers responded by adding a "window" into the side of the shoe that allowed a view of the air bag inside.

Nike's air cushioning was practical and made shoes more comfortable, but it also drove up the price. It helped that "Air" was one of Michael Jordan's nicknames, based on his apparent ease in defying gravity while playing basketball. Other shoe companies responded with their own innovations and gimmicks. Reebok, for example, introduced "The Pump" in 1989, which allowed wearers to use a tiny air inflation system embedded in the sneaker to make it tighter, then later push a release valve to deflate the shoe. Reebok sold the sneaker for $170. Nike countered with its own tech-laden shoe, Nike Air Pressure, which sold for $175. Nike supplied a mini-pump that buyers used to inflate the ankle portion of the shoe.

At the end of the decade, Reebok captured the high-end sneaker market with The Pump. The company spent $3 million advertising the product, much of it showing NBA stars demonstrating how the shoes worked.

Typical buyers of The Pump were on opposite ends of the socioeconomic spectrum—inner-city youngsters and yuppie businessmen. The Pump's design helped Reebok beat Nike in this category. People did not want to have to carry an extra pump, as required with the Nike version. The battle between Nike and Reebok drove tennis shoe industry revenues to $5 billion in 1989, a 20 percent jump over 1988.

CALVIN KLEIN

The mastermind behind marketing fashion to men was Calvin Klein, whose erotic advertising set the stage for a complete rethinking by Madison Avenue. In 1980, Klein created a suggestive advertisement using a 15-year-old Brooke Shields with the copy "Nothing comes between me and my Calvins." Though the ad sparked controversy over using the combination of a young teenage girl and sex to sell blue jeans, Klein's jean empire took off, and he followed with a campaign featuring his new line of men's underwear.

For the new campaign, Klein hired fashion photographer Bruce Weber to photograph Olympic pole-vaulter Tom Hintnaus, posed against a white wall and sunbathing in nothing but his briefs, on the Greek isle of Santorini. Weber focused his lens between the model's legs, and the photograph, which captured the quiet, rugged sexuality of a Greek god, made history. When the campaign was unveiled in 1982, sales for the product soared, and the photograph, which Janice Castro claims is now acknowledged as one of the most successful advertisements ever, became iconic—on par with "The Marlboro Man." Klein's efforts swiftly galvanized his reputation as a mover in the advertising business.[2] Klein employed even racier tactics for his campaigns for "Obsession," a new fragrance line for both men and women. The advertisements for the women's perfume situated a woman, usually in bed, between two men, turning her into the power figure, rather than a victim. She was often photographed facing the camera, while the naked men appeared fragmented. The ads for the men's fragrance of the same name featured more androgynous types, men with longer hair and no facial hair, partially clothed, relating the fragrance to more mysterious tastes. In some of the more famous two-page spreads, Klein featured both nude men and women in a variety of poses, almost as if they were pieces of sculpture, linking the product name with good taste and classic design.

SWATCH

Swatch is the trademark of a Swiss-based watch designer and retailer whose marketing strategy typified the materialism of the 1980s. The Swatch is a plastic watch with Swiss craftsmanship that comes in a variety of colors and designs. The idea was to mass-produce inexpensive watches in such a way that they became a fashion statement when one wore more than one. Though plastic,

opponent Gary Hart and then President Reagan. Just as Wendy's retooled its commercial image to start another series of commercials featuring Peller, she signed on to a Prego Spaghetti Sauce ad, proclaiming that she had found the beef in the sauce—Wendy's immediately terminated her contract.

NEW COKE FIASCO

The Coca-Cola Company made news worldwide in April 1985 when it introduced New Coke, which to most people tasted sweeter and more bland than the "old Coke." Within three months, customer outrage forced the company to bring back the original drink, which the company now marketed as "Coca-Cola Classic." By April 1986, Coke's top corporate customers (McDonald's and Kentucky Fried Chicken) announced that they were reverting back to original Coke. New Coke bombed worldwide. Despite the utter failure of New Coke, however, the $8 billion company attained record sales and profits in 1985.

A fiasco like the introduction of New Coke would have destroyed many companies and kept them scrambling to regain market share for years. A *New York Times* reporter called the debacle "one of the greatest marketing fiascos of modern times."[3] Coke, however, had decades of consumer goodwill built up and spent about $400 to $600 million a year on promotion and advertising. The introduction of the new cola cost Coke overall market leadership to Pepsi for 1985, but Coke rebounded the following year. New Coke's failure stands in stark contrast to the 1982 launch of Diet Coke. The drink quickly became the best-selling diet soft drink in the country and helped its parent company increase market leadership.

Rather than rely on its strong heritage and classic advertising, New Coke introduced an electronic character "Max Headroom," designed to appeal to younger consumers. The new wave character was Coca-Cola's attempt to counter the "Pepsi Generation" campaign that featured hot pop stars like Michael Jackson and Lionel Ritchie. Coke's slogan, "Catch a Wave" referred to the wavy line that ran from the top to the bottom of the redesigned Coke can.

Throughout the tumultuous era, Coke continued to develop its marketing and advertising campaigns, first around the 1982 slogan "Coke Is It!" As the decade ended, the focus shifted to "Can't Beat the Real Thing," which played on a general nostalgic feeling that swept the nation and harkened back to simpler times. The ubiquity of Coke as a popular cultural icon showed as Coke bottles, machines, signs, and other paraphernalia appeared in movies such as *About Last Night* (1986), *American Gigolo* (1980), *Bronco Billy* (1980), and *Urban Cowboy* (1980).

Architecture

of the 1980s

Although not to the extent of the heyday of the 1920s, when architects built vast palaces in homage to the nation's business leaders, America's fixation on success and money in the 1980s influenced architecture. Titans of industry hired the decade's leading architects to reinvigorate commercial architecture. In turn, the resulting glare from these high-profile jobs turned architects into celebrities. Before long, it wasn't uncommon to see architects' faces (along with their buildings) on the covers of magazines and in the society pages.

Many of the decade's new buildings—designed using computer-aided graphics and innovation—were glitzy and added to the personal fame of the profession's leading thinkers. The developers and city officials who commissioned these works of art were part of the game, raising the publicity stakes as high as possible. Good public relations equaled higher prices per square foot and higher occupancy rates.

Donald Trump's sudden rise as a real estate genius in Manhattan found its way onto the New Jersey shore as he used gambling casinos to turn the economically depressed coastline of Atlantic City into one of the most lucrative real estate ventures of the century. Soon, properties in the bedroom communities of New Jersey, Connecticut, and upstate New York were selling for much more than what they previously returned. Real estate in Manhattan, particularly apartments, sold for millions of dollars. Trump's ventures created a need for more glamorous architecture to reflect these times of economic prosperity, such as the Trump Taj Mahal, a "themed hotel" located on the boardwalk in Atlantic City, for which construction began in the late 1980s; it opened in 1990.

Not all architects and firms bought into the fame and publicity of the 1980s. Others attempted to restrain the developers, yet still make an influential mark on the field. Rather than mimic the designs from earlier in the century, simply building corporate temples higher into the sky, architects in the 1980s found interesting ways to fit breathtaking buildings into odd-sized and odd-shaped lots using rounded facades and vibrant colors.

One of the first iconic buildings designed and built in the 1980s based on these principles was 333 Wacker Drive (1983), on the edge of downtown Chicago at the bend in the Chicago River. The firm Kohn Pedersen Fox built the 35-story greenish-blue mirrored building on a triangular lot bordering the river. The curved face of 333 Wacker mimics the gentle turn of the waterfront. The bottom features horizontal stripes of gray granite and green marble and a two-story main entrance.

The 42-story Trump Taj Mahal Casino Resort looms over the boardwalk before its opening in Atlantic City, New Jersey, on March 28, 1990. AP Photo.

By 1986, the postmodern effects of the 1970s were considered passé. Looking back to the grand scale of buildings such as the Chrysler Building (1930) and the Empire State Building (1931), I. M. Pei & Partners (see Architecture of the 1970s) put a 1980s twist on the skyscraper. The firm purposely moved away from the traditional rectangular cage construction when designing Fountain Place (1986) in Dallas, Texas. The resulting building looks like a gigantic, light green glass sculpture with a diagonal slice taken off the top. Rather than build in the heart of the downtown business district, the architects, led by Henry Cobb, placed the 60-story building a bit further out so that it would attract more attention and give visitors to Dallas a better view. One part of Fountain Place juts up from the street like a triangle with spaceship wings coming out the sides. The top of the building looks like an oblong glass diamond that has somehow slid down atop the triangle and been perfectly melded together. Viewed from different perspectives, Fountain Place seems to transform at the blink of an eye. Even the sheared top looks like it comes to a point from some angles and not from others.

Not content to simply design and build a fantastic skyscraper, landscape architect Dan Kiley developed an urban oasis at the building's ground level. The plaza features intricate water art comprised of 172 bubbler fountains in the pools and 360 fountainheads in the Central Court Fountain. In addition, Kiley brought in more than 200 Texas bald cypress trees to decorate the plaza.

Architecture in the 1980s, however, did not stop with ornate corporate towers. In Washington, D.C., Benjamin Thompson & Associates built a marketplace in the renovated Union Station. Suddenly, train passengers mixed and mingled among the many restaurants, retail stores, and boutique shops that filled the space. The two-story central kiosk is topped with Roman-inspired arches and lined with columns. Although still a working train station and Metro subway stop, Union Station's beauty gave visitors a calming respite amid the hustle of the nation's capital.

LEADING ARCHITECTS

Michael Graves

Born in Indianapolis in 1934, Michael Graves studied architecture at the University of Cincinnati and Harvard University. In 1960, Graves won the Rome Prize, which allowed him to study in Italy for two years. He founded his own architectural firm in 1964 in Princeton, New Jersey, he served as the Robert Schirmer Professor of Architecture at Princeton University from 1965 to 1995. While at Princeton University, Graves taught and guided the latest trends in American design during the 1980s.

Graves went on to win a number of prestigious awards, including the 2001 Gold Medal of the American Institute of Architects, the 1999 National Medal of the Arts, and the $50,000 Frank Annunzio Award from the Christopher Columbus Fellowship Foundation.

During the 1980s, Graves's design for The Humana Building in Louisville, Kentucky, won many accolades, not only named one of "The 10 Best Buildings" of the decade by *Time* magazine, but recipient of the AIA Design Award as well. Other buildings designed by Graves include Disney's corporate headquarters in Burbank, California; the headquarters of the Ministry of Culture at the Hauge; the Federal Reserve Bank in Houston; and the Philadelphia Eagles' football stadium. In addition, Graves designed the World Bank Group's International Finance Corporation at Washington Circle in Washington, D.C.

The Portland Public Services Building (1982) was Graves's crowning achievement. The building's triple tier structure and rectangular shapes imbued with deep earthy colors called to mind classical structures for banks and courthouses, as it blended the old and the new.

The 15-story skyscraper attempted to elevate the often drab government building to new heights and redefine what a public service building could be. Graves's block design and square windows gave the building an imposing look, but it was his use of dramatic colors (blue, brown, and a deep rust red) that made it iconic and controversial. Both *Newsweek* and *Time* featured the Portland Public Services Building on their covers.

Time has not been kind to the Portland Building. City residents and architectural critics now label the building a failure. Office workers don't like the small offices in the building and the lack of natural light. In addition, many structural problems have surfaced over the past two decades, including major cracks in concrete and plaster. Many of these criticisms have been directed at Graves, but in retrospect, the city's constant budget cuts enabled some shoddy workmanship on the part of contractors. Despite these criticisms, however, the Portland Building remains one of postmodernism's most prominent structures.

Robert Venturi

Robert Venturi (1925–) continued to excel in architecture in the 1980s. A graduate of Princeton University in 1947, he received an MFA there three years later. In 1954, Venturi continued his studies as a Rome Prize Fellow, traveling there to study architecture before returning in 1956 to begin teaching at the University of Pennsylvania.

His designs include the Milwaukee County War Memorial Center. In 1966, he published his first book, *Complexity and Contradiction in Architecture,* which pondered the place of the architect in the modern world of design.

Venturi's rebel views rocked the architecture world. His theories paid homage to architecture of the past, blending these attributes with the basic tenets of modernism, yet still exemplifying the importance of human use, memory, comfort, and entertainment. In 1969, he founded his own design office, now called VSBA (Venturi, Scott Brown and Associates), with his wife, Denise Scott Brown. The couple continue to work there. In 1972, in a book titled *Learning From Las Vegas,* Venturi joined his wife and Steven Izenour to explore the impact of the desert city on the architecture of America.

Venturi was named to the list of the American Institute of Architecture's 25 top architects. Some of his work from the 1980s includes the Molecular Biology Building at Princeton University (1983–1985), the Art Museum of Seattle (1988–1991), and the Sainsbury Wing of the National Gallery in London (1988).

Andres Duany and Elizabeth Plater-Zyberk

In 1980, Andres Duany (1949–)and Elizabeth Plater-Zyberk (1950–) joined forces in Miami to found one of the top architectural design companies in the United States, Duany Plater-Zyberk & Company. Since then, the married couple and their firm have designed more than 250 residential communities, redefining the scope and scale of urban development. In 1989, *Time* magazine selected their community at Seaside, Florida, as one of the "Best of the Decade."

Duany and Plater-Zyberk's method integrates their master plans with project-specific design codes and regulations and their choice to work within the southeastern United States and the Caribbean. Today, the firm is recognized as one of the leaders against the proliferation of suburban sprawl. (In 2001, after the publication of *Suburban Nation,* a book that articulates their theories, Duany and Plater-Zyberk were awarded the Vincent Scully Prize.)

Maya Ying Lin

The 1981 competition to design a memorial commemorating American dead and missing from the Vietnam War drew 1,425 entries. The winner, 21-year-old Yale architecture student Maya Ying Lin, designed a powerful memorial unlike any that had come before it. Rather than make the building itself the center of attention, Lin made the names of the dead and missing men and women the focus, a fitting idea for a memorial to a war that continued to divide many Americans.

The young Yale student hardly seemed old enough to put forth such a mature vision for the memorial. Lin grew up in Athens, Ohio, and her parents taught at Ohio University—her mother literature and her father art. These influences fused with her identity as an Asian American and resulted in a strong respect for nature and the earth. These tenets of Lin's thinking were clearly represented in the Vietnam Memorial.

Lin proposed a v-shaped, black granite wall that eased up from the ground at one end and back down into the ground at the other. The names of 58,253 dead and missing Americans were listed on the wall chronologically. Even more emotional than the list of names is the way the black walls reflect the onlooker's image as he or she views the wall. Through Lin's design, visitors become more than onlookers, and are basically drawn into the memorial.

Constructed in 1982, the walls of the Vietnam Memorial are each 246-feet, 8-inches long. The v-shape comes together at an angle of 125 degrees, 12 minutes, and point directly at the northeast corners of the Washington Monument and Lincoln Memorial. The walls are supported by 140 concrete pilings, driven down approximately 35 feet to bedrock.

Architect Maya Ying Lin and the Vietnam Memorial. Washington D.C. Photo by James P. Blair/National Geographic/Getty Images.

Although the announcement of Lin's winning design drew a great deal of criticism, today the Vietnam Memorial is the capitol's most visited site, with thousands leaving mementos and tributes to loved ones. Lin's idea stretched the notion of how a memorial should look beyond people's natural thought processes.

ARCHITECTURE AT HOME

The changing demographics of the 1980s—a sharp increase in smaller, nontraditional families—started to influence the way people thought about standard housing and living spaces. Yet homebuilders and apartment designers still built places as if nuclear families were the norm. If there was a concession to the nontraditional at all, it was usually to make a house smaller, not change the basic design.

At an earlier time in history moving to the suburbs may have been considered fulfillment of the American dream. In the 1980s, however, the suburbs isolated families and family members, particularly children stung by divorce or the after-school loneliness with both parents in the workforce. For single-parent families, however, neither the suburbs nor the city offered the kind of after-school programs, daycare, or social services needed to care for school-age youngsters. Thus, changing family demographics served as both a social problem and a design challenge.

The growing disparity between society's "haves" and "have-nots" also played a role in housing for millions of Americans. In a rapidly growing city like Stamford, Connecticut, which was home to many large businesses, two distinct societies sprouted up. On one side stood the prosperity of suburban life in the 1980s—those who could afford $300,000 single-family homes. These families found themselves elevated to a higher economic rung by corporate paychecks. Those on the other end of the scale were pushed further and further down the economic ladder, making too much money to qualify for subsidized housing, but barely making enough to scrape by as housing prices skyrocketed.

Crime-ridden ghettoes across America were real-life examples of how large numbers of people lived in the 1980s. These were the places that affluent white males, like those from gilded Fairfield County, ventured into to buy drugs and engage in illegal prostitution.

During the day, Stamford and other cities teamed with businesspeople and commerce. At night, however, corporate workers fled back to the suburbs and left empty shells of cities behind. In Stamford, the gap between affluence and poverty caused drug arrests to double over a 10-year period and led to a greater number of drug-related muggings.

Affluent Homeowners

Given staggering interest rates and a sluggish economy in the early 1980s, homebuilders did not stray far from traditional ideas. The changes in basic home construction that did take place featured a return to historical styles, particularly a Victorian revival, an idea replicated in the nation's politics and socioeconomic thinking. As a result, front porches became more central meeting and entertaining places at the expense of backyards.

One option for smaller, affluent families was purchasing a condominium. In 1980, there were more than two million condo units in the United States. These homes—bigger than most apartments, but smaller than traditional single-family homes—gave people more privacy and space than apartments, but without the maintenance or high price of detached houses.

In Chicago, for example, condominium construction increased in the 1970s because building owners feared rent control and discovered that they could make greater profits by converting apartments to condos. City hotspots, such as the Loop, Lincoln Park, and Edgewater, witnessed the greatest growth in condo sales. By 1980, 50 percent of the housing in the Loop was condos. Building new condos and converting older apartments remained steady throughout the decade. Given the exorbitant cost of owning a home in the Chicago region, the area also experienced heavy condo growth in the suburbs.

In San Jose, California, by mid-decade one of the five most expensive real estate markets in the nation, an influential British builder in the United States, Barratt, identified how much affluent singles and young couples could afford for a condo. Barratt then built units they called "Studio Solo" and "Studio Duo" to meet these criteria. Although incredibly small (some units were as little as 486 square feet), buying a mini-condo was a better option than renting.

When filling the San Jose condos with amenities, Barratt designers purposely avoided giving the units an apartment feel. Therefore, they placed a washer and dryer in each condo, so occupants would avoid the college dorm experience of a shared laundry room. They also gave the condos full-sized bathrooms, large closets, garages, and small patios or decks. These minor upgrades played directly on the dweller's emotional desire to be a homeowner, not a renter, even in a place as expensive as San Jose.

Traditional home styles allowed the newly wealthy to show off their houses—precursors to today's so-called McMansions. For the affluent, homes increased in size, not only in terms of square footage, but also in terms of ornamental elements, such as intricate towers, gables, and latticework.

Many builders crammed houses full of upgrades, such as security systems, intercoms, central vacuum systems, and built-in appliances. The larger, luxurious homes—often referred to as "custom houses"—turned the kitchen into the most expensive room in the house with solid oak cabinetry, tile or wood floors, skylights, sink islands, and breakfast nooks.

Although the most money went into kitchens in affluent homes, bathrooms were often the most glamorous. A custom builder in Columbia, Maryland noted that nearly every home they built in the $100,000 to $500,000 range had a Jacuzzi tub or spa bath. The new spotlight on the tub forced builders to separate it from the shower, thus enabling the shower to receive its own attention. Fancy toilets, bidets, sinks, walk-in closets, and separate compartments for the commode also boosted the price of bathrooms in luxury homes.

The bathroom upgrade was a cornerstone of the rise in "master suites" in the 1980s. The combination of bedroom, bathroom, and sitting room came together to form a separate part of the house reserved for adults and a kind of sanctuary from the rest of the house, including children. Master suites often featured cedar-lined, walk-in closets, fireplaces, and entertainment centers.

The role of the architect in private home design usually occurred in homes priced at more than $200,000. For those at the top of the economic ladder, hiring a renowned architect or firm meant that the American Dream had been fulfilled. Architects not only fit a building to the land, but married the interior and exterior, making full use of the surrounding environment.

Books

Newspapers, Magazines, and Comics of the 1980s

In the 1980s, cultural critics, such as E. D. Hirsch and Secretary of Education William Bennett, argued that American literary culture had declined. However, a closer analysis reveals that books remained highly popular in the decade, as readers branched out into new genres and embraced best-selling authors in droves.

Commentators like Hirsch and Bennett simply did not approve of what people read, particularly writers they deemed "low brow," like Stephen King, Tom Clancy, and Danielle Steele, who sold millions of books in the decade. The appearance of serious literature by Alice Walker, William Kennedy, and Toni Morrison on *The New York Times* list of top selling books further diminished the argument of the cultural elites.

Nonfiction books also took on a very different cast during the decade. Instead of biographies of famous politicians and movie stars, people purchased the life stories of business executives, such as Donald Trump and Lee Iacocca, reading about their lives in an effort to discover insider formulas for getting rich. Along similar lines, investment primers and money management books also gained in popularity.

The publishing world replicated the rest of the decade with the ascendancy of the corporation. In earlier times, publishers may have taken a chance on quality writers who sold modest numbers of works early in their careers and then slowly built a dedicated readership over time. In the 1980s, as publishers became part of large, multinational corporations, the bottom line eliminated risk-taking. Publishers, despite critical acclaim or quality, frequently dropped authors who did not sell.

BEST SELLERS

The most successful writer of the 1980s in terms of sales and readership was Stephen King. During the decade, King hit the number one spot on the *New York Times Best Seller List* with five novels, four of these the top seller in its respective year. King's novels are long and involved, but his use of the everyday world and its confrontation with the unthinkable makes his books popular. By 1985, 50 million copies of his books were in print. Four years later, he added another 50 million copies to his total.

King's *Misery* (1988) is an example of his deft storytelling and his attention to novelistic form—two items that his critics constantly berated him for not employing. What sets *Misery* apart from King's other novels is his witty use of self-reflexivity to challenge his detractors. At the outset of the book, writer Paul Sheldon completes what he calls his "first serious novel"; he has made a fortune from writing romance novels featuring

NOTABLE BOOKS

The Bourne Identity, Robert Ludlum, 1980

Cosmos, Carl Sagan, 1980

A Confederacy of Dunces, John Kennedy Toole, 1980

Masquerade, Kit Williams, U.S., 1980

Jane Fonda's Workout Book, Jane Fonda, 1981

The Color Purple, Alice Walker, 1982

Hollywood Wives, Jackie Collins, 1983

Christine and *Pet Sematary*, Stephen King, 1983

Ironweed, William Kennedy, 1983

The Hunt for Red October, Tom Clancy, 1984

Lincoln, Gore Vidal, 1984

Lee Iacocca: An Autobiography, Lee Iacocca, 1984

Bright Lights, Big City, Jay McInerney, 1984

The Unbearable Lightness of Being, Milan Kundera, 1984

Lake Wobegon Days, Garrison Keillor, 1985

Lonesome Dove, Larry McMurtry, 1985

The Accidental Tourist, Anne Tyler, 1985

All I Needed to Know I Learned in Kindergarten, Robert Fulghum, 1986

I'll Take Manhattan, Judith Krantz, 1986

The Prince of Tides, Pat Conroy, 1986

Beloved, Toni Morrison, 1987

Presumed Innocent, Scott Turow, 1987

The Bonfire of the Vanities, Tom Wolfe, 1987

Battle Cry of Freedom, James M. McPherson, 1988

A Brief History of Time, Stephen Hawking, 1988

Love in the Time of Cholera, Gabriel Garcia Márquez, U.S., 1988

Clear and Present Danger, Tom Clancy, 1989

A Time to Kill, John Grisham, 1989

The Joy Luck Club, Amy Tan, 1989

The Seven Habits of Highly Effective People, Stephen R. Covey, 1989

The Satanic Verses, Salman Rushdie, 1989

Stephen King, whose popularity began to soar in the 1980s. Courtesy of Photofest.

his heroine, Misery Chastain, a noblewoman of eighteenth-century America.

In the book, Sheldon has grown weary of his romance franchise and killed off his heroine in his last release, *Misery's Child*. Sheldon then sets out to compose something that matters. Sheldon's thoughts certainly mirror those of many serious critics of King's fiction, who berated him for not turning his talent to something "important."

Sheldon then crashes his car on a remote Colorado mountainside, and his "Number 1 fan" Annie Wilkes rescues him. Annie is sad in her lonely struggle to maintain, yet crazed to obsession when things do not go her way. With the incapacitated Paul in her guestroom and the arrival of Paul's new volume, she is elated.

However, Annie's mania turns murderous when she realizes that Sheldon has killed off his

STEPHEN KING (1947–)

Stephen King was born in Portland, Maine, where he and his brother David were raised by their mother. King had an early interest in science fiction and fantasy, and as a child he read voraciously, taking inspiration from the science fiction pioneers of the 1940s and 1950s. King's own writing expanded on this influence, with stories that featured a variety of fantastic and often disturbing themes. King's first published work was a short story that appeared in a 1965 issue of *Comics Review* magazine, but it was not until 1974, after college and several years of failed manuscripts, that King published his first novel, *Carrie,* to critical acclaim. Over the next two decades, King published prolifically and his novels were so successful that many, including *Carrie,* were made into films. King eventually became known as the "Master of Horror," though he might more aptly be called a master of suspense, for it is his uncanny ability to build suspense that has captivated generations of readers. From 1965 to 2008, King published 50 bestselling novels and hundreds of stories, and his works have been translated into over 30 languages. King's stories appeal to the part of the human psyche that is attracted to the dark and mysterious, and his success testifies to the widespread appeal of the supernatural. Over the years, King published in other genres, and in 2000 King published an autobiographical book *On Writing,* in which he speaks about his unique approach to characters and plot.

heroine. In retaliation, Annie makes Paul destroy his draft of his new novel and begin a new *Misery* novel—one that resurrects its heroine. Once, when Annie leaves the house, the recovering Paul gets out of his bedroom prison to find that Annie was once tried for and acquitted of murdering a number of babies in a Colorado maternity ward, where she had been a nurse. When Annie discovers Paul's foray out of his room, she drugs him, ties him to the bed, and methodically hobbles him. Paul fights back from this new injury fueled by his own brand of revenge, fought in the novel's final pages. The novel was made into a movie (1990) that won a Best Actress Oscar for Kathy Bates.

Another popular novel of the early 1980s was *The Name of the Rose,* 1983, Umberto Eco's tale of a medieval Benedictine monk who uncovers a murder. Prior to writing this novel, Eco was a world-class intellectual, a semiotician embraced for his discussions of signs and symbols in linguistics. However, with its detective/monk seeking to solve the puzzling murder, the novel shot to the top of the charts after being translated from Italian by William Weaver.

Scott Turow, a lawyer with a bent for storytelling, began a successful literary career when he published *Presumed Innocent,* 1987, a crime drama he claimed he wrote on yellow legal pads on the Chicago subway system. The novel told the story of Rosate "Rusty" Savage, a successful Assistant District Attorney accused of murdering his mistress. Turow's adherence to the crime genre's structure made for a splendid reading experience, and the novel's complicated turn of events revealed a masterful control over the many characters and plots. However, the solution of the murder, once Rusty is acquitted, is a marvelous twist of the conventions of the crime novel—instead of the customary capture/confession/explanation, Turow forces Rusty to face a serious ethical dilemma of his own creation. For this reason, *Presumed Innocent* is recognized as a classic of modern crime fiction.

One of the biggest surprises of 1985 came when journalist Tom Wolfe turned to fiction. His first novel, *The Bonfire of the Vanities,* chronicled the worlds of Wall Street finance, Brooklyn politics, and Harlem's disadvantaged. The three-plot narrative captures the glamour of 1980s high society and the pitfalls of believing that once one rises to the top, one cannot tumble.

Wolfe's novel was truly one of the 1980s grandest reads. The novel opens with the first plot, contemplating the world of Sherman McCoy, a Wall Street broker who sees himself as a "Master of the Universe." McCoy's limited perspective from his $10 million Park Avenue apartment and his office suite downtown prevents him from objectivity.

He allows his spoiled wife and child to pamper themselves while he conducts an affair with Maria Ruskin, a trash-talking Southern belle married to a corporate mogul who made his money of-fering discount trips to the Holy Land for Jew-ish families. After picking Maria up at the airport one night, Sherman makes a wrong turn toward the Bronx, where he mistakes two black youths for gang members. In escaping the scene, Maria, who is driving the car, hits Henry Lamb, one of the teens, and knocks him into a coma. McCoy finds himself embroiled in a scandal when Maria refuses to take responsibility.

The novel's second plot involves the District Attorney's office and the politicians who seek jus-tice on Henry's behalf. Foremost is Larry Kramer, a 30-ish lawyer who longs for the spotlight and a lifestyle like Sherman's. On his tiny salary, Kramer is left to dream until his boss, Abe Weiss, hands him the Lamb case. Kramer seeks to use the Lamb case as his stepping stone to fame.

The third plot focuses on a reporter for a New York City tabloid paper, *The City Light*. Simon Fal-low is a drunk, disorderly refugee from England, where his stories on the Royal Family won him fame and fortune. Now, nearly broke, he seeks the one story that will put him back on top, and he finds his opportunity with the Lamb case. Under his by-line, Henry Lamb goes from being a good, honest kid of the Bronx to a former honor student whose potential has been cut short by careless, upper-class white society.

The plots intertwine throughout the novel as they reveal the corruption based within the Amer-ican society. One of the novel's most brilliant mo-ments follows Sherman through a socialite party. Wolfe's keen eye and sharp pen assist the reader in understanding this outrageous world of excess as Sherman watches his wife interact within "the hive" of this social order.

Wolfe shows that Sherman comprehends the superficiality of the culture, but realizes that this is what he deserves, as he will not extract himself from it. A savage indictment of Reagan's America, *The Bonfire of the Vanities* is a powerful novel that exposes all three worlds in an effort to prove that very little separates the "haves" and the "have-nots." The subsequent 1990 film adaptation of the novel starring Tom Hanks, Bruce Willis, and Melanie Griffith, directed by Brian De Palma, was roundly denounced by critics as a poor represen-tation of the book.

Author Tom Wolfe in a publicity photo for writing and narrating *Marshall McLuhan: The Man and His Message* (PBS special, 1984). Courtesy of Photofest.

E. L. Doctorow's *Billy Bathgate* (1989) uses the past to speak volumes about the present. The novel follows a 15-year-old boy as he matures under the tutelage of legendary mobster Dutch Schultz. The complexity of the novel is in its characterizations, as Billy navigates the grimy crime world and the glittering society worlds of the gangster and his many associates.

Salman Rushdie's *The Satanic Verses* (1988) was the most controversial novel of the decade. Radical Muslims decreed the book blasphemous due to its depiction of Muhammad. Many Mus-lim nations banned the book within months of its release. Iranian leader Ayatollah Ruhollah Kho-meini called for Rushdie's assassination, going so far as to offer a $3 million bounty. The death threats forced Rushdie into hiding for most of the decade. Although no one carried out the assas-sination, reaction to the book caused a great deal of violence. Riots broke out in Turkey and India. Radicals firebombed a bookstore in Berkeley,

TOM WOLFE (1931–)

American novelist Tom Wolfe was one of the founders of a literary non-fiction movement of the 1960s and 1970s, sometimes called the "new journalism." The new journalism movement combined elements of journalism with elements more commonly associated with fiction, including evocative descriptions and character development. (See Books, Newspapers, Magazines, and Comics of the 1970s.) Wolfe was born and raised in Richmond, Virginia, attended some of the nation's leading schools, and worked as a journalist for ten years, lending his talents to the *New York Herald Tribune* and *New York* magazine. His first book, *The Kandy-Kolored Tangerine-Flake Streamline Baby,* a collection of stories about 1960s culture, was released in 1965 and hit the best seller list. Wolfe's later writings built upon his success and included a provocative exploration of LSD use and the surrounding culture. While many of his works focused on the counterculture, Wolfe also wrote books with a more general appeal. In 1977, Wolfe released *The Right Stuff,* which had been in the works for over six years and provided a fascinating inside look at the relationships and tensions of the space program of the 1960s. The book was enormously popular and, in 1983, was converted into a blockbuster film. Wolfe surprised audiences in the 1980s when he released his first novel *Bonfire of the Vanities,* which was produced in serial installments in the pages of *Rolling Stone* magazine. Wolfe's novel remained on best seller lists for more than a year and was recognized as one of the best American novels of the decade. Wolfe continued producing popular works throughout the nineties and into twenty-first century, and is widely recognized as a quintessential modern American writer. Whether dealing in fiction or fact, Wolfe helped a generation of readers and journalists realize a greater connection between life and art.

Muslim students display a drawing of author Salman Rushdie in a noose during a demonstration calling for his death, outside the former British Embassy in Tehran, Iran. AP Photo.

California. Rushdie's Japanese translator, Hitoshi Igarashi, was stabbed to death near Tokyo.

Rushdie's novel retells the biblical story of Gabriel (renamed Gibreel) as a satanic avenger. Chamcha, a hapless victim, encounters Gibreel as they both fall from grace, encountering an array of characters that mirror the political and historical world of the 1980s.

SERIOUS LITERATURE

Marilynne Robinson's debut novel, *Housekeeping* (1981), follows a girl named Ruth, a wide-eyed dreamer who has lost both her parents—her father in a car accident, and her mother to suicide. What is so unique about the novel is that it chronicles Ruth's slow unraveling as she is passed from relative to relative, seeking a new home where love will help her cope with her inner pain.

John Updike concluded his Rabbit trilogy in 1981 with *Rabbit Is Rich* (Knopf), a chronicle he began in 1960 with *Rabbit, Run,* and followed in 1971 with *Rabbit Redux.* The trilogy concludes with Rabbit still running the Toyota agency left to him by his father-in-law, and still married to wife Janice, now celebrating their 23rd wedding anniversary.

Schindler's List (1982) by Thomas Keneally is perhaps best known as an Oscar-winning film directed by Steven Spielberg in 1993. The novel, published by Simon & Schuster, chronicles the real-life struggle of Oskar Schindler, a Nazi industrialist who realizes he could save lives by foregoing profits. The novel captures the drama of the Nazi rise to power and their gradual redefinition of the Jewish people as they were first segregated, and then slowly, mechanically, decimated.

Once he realizes that the Nazis were murdering innocents, Schindler orchestrates a plan to purchase lives from one crooked commandant. Eventually, Schindler saves 1,300 Jews, helping them not only to escape, but to begin life anew.

Cathedral (1983), Raymond Carver's collected short stories, made the Seattle writer a household name, as his poignant stories of middle-class Americans found an audience among the masses. Carver's stories follow the paths of men and women who work hard, and who cannot communicate their desire for love. Marriages collapse, jobs are lost, and dreams are shattered as the outer world blithely crushes the hopes of each subject.

William Kennedy's *Ironweed* (1983) was the final novel in his Albany trilogy, an extended story of the Phelan family. After the success of the first two, *Legs* (1981) and *Billy Phelan's Greatest Game* (1982), *Ironweed* not only became a best seller, but also won the Pulitzer Prize for literature. The plot follows protagonist Francis Phelan during his return to Albany on Halloween night, 1937, to a town and a family he left after accidentally causing his youngest son's death. Francis encounters a number of spirits from his past—particularly men he killed to survive—but nothing prepares him for his return to the family he had abandoned 17 years before.

Toni Morrison, with her 1987 novel *Beloved*, became the first African American to win the Pulitzer Prize for literature. The novel recounts the struggles of a fugitive slave woman, Sethe, who commits infanticide against one of her four children rather than see her subjected to slavery. While everyone simply believes Sethe is crazy, she knows that she committed the atrocity out of love—she had planned to kill all of her children, rather than see them in bondage. The story focuses on Sethe's existence in 1873, when the spirit of the dead child rematerializes as a 17-year-old girl who has the mind of the infant. In addition to haunting Sethe, the spirit befriends Denver, the baby Sethe had in her arms as she killed the three-year-old Beloved.

Gradually, Denver begins to realize the "haunt" is seeking revenge for being the only child murdered. Sethe's guilt compromises her ability to understand this, and her sincere love for the child makes her feel complete, allowing her to succumb to Beloved's spell. As Denver starts work in the town that has ostracized her family, she learns that the black community holds Sethe at arm's length because of her actions. In an effort to save her mother, Denver convinces the community to come to her mother's rescue. Blending folklore with the complexities of the postmodern narrative, Morrison created a truly unique reading experience.

NEW WRITERS FOR A NEW GENERATION

Two young writers made names for themselves during the 1980s by writing hard-hitting, postmodern novels that bristle with irony and disdain directed toward the "Me Generation." Jay McInerney was born in Hartford, Connecticut and graduated from prestigious Williams College. Following writing fellowships at both Princeton and Syracuse, McInerney burst on to the literary scene with a short, scathing novel of life in Manhattan.

Bright Lights, Big City (1984) chronicles the fall of its main character, Jaime Conway, as he loses his family, his wife, and his career in a haze of cocaine. Written in the second person throughout, the novel's accusing tone places the reader in Jaime's position and assaults the sensibilities with a cynical morality.

At the outset, Jamie has already lost two of the most important people in his life—his mother, who had died of cancer the summer before, and Amanda, his young wife who has turned her virginal country look into a lucrative modeling career. Jamie's one friend, the socialite Tad Allagash, supplies Jamie with drugs and provides other hedonistic outlets. Jamie's goal of becoming a serious writer is impossible to empathize with as he gropes his way to his job each day—with a hangover—at the Department of Factual Verification at a conservative magazine. Jamie's self-indulgence causes him to lose his job, and his frustrated efforts to speak to ex-wife Amanda, now in New York with her photographer boyfriend, only cause Jamie to embarrass himself again in an alcoholic, cocaine-laced stupor. McInerney's novel clearly sought to capture the club-based life of the self-indulgent youth of this generation. His stark, accusing tone gave the novel power in a vibrantly new fashion.

The second writer to make a sensation writing about the trappings of this privileged generation was Bret Easton Ellis, whose novel *Less Than Zero* (1985) took on the members of the "Me Generation" on the west coast. Born in Los Angeles and educated at Bennington College, Ellis appeared to parrot the cynicism of McInerney. However, Ellis employed a singularly different structure, breaking the narrative action repeatedly, mirroring a music video, to relate the tale of Clay, a young college student returning to his California roots during his first midterm break.

In returning home to see his friends Blair and Julian, Clay senses the need to connect with them, to hold on to the past that, in his mind, was innocent and honest. Over the course of his journey, however, Clay discovers his own bisexuality, and finds that during his four months away, Blair has turned to booze and dope and Julian snorts cocaine each morning to just get going and has turned to a life of male prostitution to supply his needs. In one chilling sequence, Clay accompanies Julian to a meeting and watches in stunned paralysis as Julian subjects himself to humiliation—all for the promise of a fix.

Ellis's narrative structure mirrors the cutting of MTV videos—short, staccato-like paragraphs that capture Clay's observations, but not his emotional core. This is because he, himself, is afraid of merging—an appropriate metaphor for this privileged group of selfish, materialistically spoiled youths. The novel ends with Clay's disillusioned return to college, hoping to find the soul that he so desperately believes he lost.

NONFICTION

Many nonfiction readers in the 1980s switched from histories and biographies to self-help books that focused on dieting and exercise and autobiographies of those people who could show others how to succeed in business by staying true to conservative roots.

The most successful self-help book proved to be *Jane Fonda's Workout Book,* which sold 693,000 copies in 1982 alone (see Sports and Leisure of the 1980s). However, looking good and feeling better about yourself was also behind the popularity of Judy Mazel's *Beverley Hills Diet* (1981's best seller) and Robert E. Kowalski's *The 8-Week Cholesterol Cure* (1988's best seller). Each of these books focused on diet and exercise as a way of staying fit and remaining young—two components very important in the age of beauty. Jim Fixx's popular *Book of Running,* 1980, went into multiple editions as a jogging craze swept the nation.

As for autobiographies, two of the best sellers told rags-to-riches stories with homespun humor, furthering the notion that one could learn from the mistakes and advice of another. Lee Iacocca's story, *Iacocca: An Autobiography* remained the bestselling volume of nonfiction for 1984 and 1985, selling a combined total of 2,565,000 volumes. What made Iacocca's story so appealing, however, was not simply the tale of his life, but his inspirational discussion of how he saved the Chrysler corporation and how he proposed to do the same for New York City, which was experiencing similar financial troubles.

The second writer who turned his life story into a profitable series of books was Bill Cosby, the creative genius behind *The Cosby Show* (see Entertainment of the 1980s). Cosby's advice books *Fatherhood* (1986) and *Time Flies* (1987) sold a total of 3,861,000 copies over the same two-year period that *The Cosby Show* was number one in the Nielsen ratings. Cosby's humorous tales of rearing children and his anecdotes about growing old reached across racial boundaries to speak to average Americans.

Investment and management books were also popular during the decade, particularly those that explained how the average person could make a financial windfall from the growing stock market. Books like Douglas R. Casey's *Crisis Investing* (1980) and Thomas J. Peters and Robert H. Waterman's *In Search of Excellence* (1983) made stock trading and commodities brokering look manageable and profitable.

Books

The most stirring nonfiction book to come out of the 1980s has to be Randy Shilts's examination of the AIDS crisis, *And The Band Played On: Politics, People and the AIDS Epidemic* (1987). Shilts, a columnist for the *San Francisco Chronicle,* had been writing about the crisis in his native city for seven years when he began uncovering what he saw as the glaring irresponsibility of the federal government to halt the epidemic. While navigating these political waters, Shilts also reportedly found that the American research facilities, headed by Dr. Robert Gallo, and those of the French Pasteur Clinic were constantly battling over the rightful discoverer of the HIV virus. The first part of the volume follows Shilts as he blends an investigative tone with an attention to human detail to make heroes out of Doctors Marcus Conant, Don Francis, and Mary Guinan of the Center for Disease Control (CDC); Selma Dritz of the San Francisco Board of Health; and gay activists Bobbi Campbell, Gary Walsh, Bill Kraus, Larry Kramer, and Cleve Jones.

Perhaps most interesting, Shilts includes in this section a hypothesis he credits to Mary Guinan concerning Gaetan Dugas—the infamous "Patient Zero." Dugas, according to Shilts, was a flight attendant with a healthy sexual appetite. Shilts argues that Dugas was particularly key to spreading the virus between New York City and San Francisco. By the time he died in 1986, Dugas estimated that he had been with 1,100 to 20,000 men during his active sexual life, and when the figures were compiled on a cluster diagram at the CDC, it was found that "[a]t least 40 of the first 248 gay men diagnosed with GRID in the United States, as of April 12, 1982, either had had sex with Gaetan Dugas or had had sex with someone who had."[1]

The second part of the book follows a trail of blame, painting the Reagan administration, Ed Koch's mayoral office in New York, and the San Francisco Board of Health as villainous cretins. Included in this section is a detailed examination of the on-going rivalry between Dr. Robert Gallo, the director of the U.S. National Institutes of Health, and the Pasteur Clinic. The squabbling was over the right to name the virus discovered to be causing AIDS, now known as HIV. Shilts chronicles

WORDS AND PHRASES

air guitar

as if

carbo-loading

channel surf

chill pill

comb-over

cred

cyberspace

dweeb

e-mail

freakazoid

gag me with a spoon

gangsta

geekfest

geeky

gobsmacked

grody to the max

hip-hop

ka-ching (noun and interjection)

McJob

metal-head

mommy track

my bad

party animal

power walking

problemo

rightsize (for layoffs)

road rage

shopaholic

snowboarder

trash talk

uni-brow

valley girl

wannabe

wilding (packs of teens making violent attacks)

Yuppie (young urban professionals)

these petty political and academic arguments as he relates the human drama that was overlooked as the bureaucrats fought—the tainted blood supply that put surgery patients and hemophiliacs at risk. By the end of Shilts's volume, one senses that the catastrophe that still plagues the world 20 years later might have been avoided if politicians had tried to save lives, and if the doctors on the battle front had been listened to by those in the conference rooms holding the purse strings.

MAGAZINES

The combination of print and photographic innovation and abundant advertising dollars expanded the magazine industry in the 1980s. In addition, the growing popularity of personal computers led to the launch of niche magazines that focused on the new computer user. The industry confronted an interesting dichotomy—on one hand, more specialty magazines appeared, while at the same time general interest books faced stiff competition and increasingly distracted consumers who spent more time watching television than reading.

TV Guide, launched in 1953, turned into a big business as Americans spent more time in front of the tube. In 1988, media mogul Rupert Murdoch

purchased Triangle Publications for $3 billion, specifically to acquire the magazine. Bringing *TV Guide* into the News Corporation family guaranteed that Murdoch's Fox television network would be listed. As Fox grew, network officials used *TV Guide* to feature its programming.

One magazine launched in the 1980s in response to the nation's changing culture was *Shape,* directed at female athletes and fitness enthusiasts. Each month *Shape* offered readers workout, diet, and beauty tips. The power of young women as consumers led to a resurgence in magazines targeting them, including *Sassy, Seventeen, 'Teen,* and *YM. Sassy,* in particular, aimed at mature young people, not only offering updated fashion styles and tips, but also more openly confronting controversial issues such as teen sexuality.

NEWSPAPERS

What people read in the decade changed, as well as the way they acquired information. One invention that catered to the rapid pace of American life was the founding of *USA Today* in 1982 by Allen H. Neuharth in McLean, VA. Hoping to cash in on America's need for quick information, Neuharth created a 64-page paper that could be easily perused during an average commute to work. The first edition was published on September 15, 1982 and quickly surfaced as a major news source, boasting a circulation of 2,280,760 by the end of its first 12 months.

Although newspaper readership dropped in the 1980s, more women became print journalists and television newscasters. In 1982, 66 percent of journalists were male, down from 80 percent in 1971. The competition from TV also led to greater technological innovation, such as improvements in photo quality, including color, and concentration on local news and events. The most important innovation took place as newsrooms adopted computers to compose and edit stories, as well as to lay out and print copy.

Additional economic factors forced the newspaper industry to cut costs. Many advertisers turned to television rather than traditional print sources. The late 1980s witnessed an overall slowing in ad spending across the board, which led to

NEW MAGAZINES

Shape, 1981

PC World, 1982

PC Magazine, 1982

Vanity Fair, 1983

MacWorld, 1984

Elle, 1985

Spin, 1985

Spy, 1986

Cooking Light, 1987

Men's Health, 1987

Parenting, 1987

First for Woman, 1989

Sports Illustrated KIDS, 1989

lower ad revenues for newspapers. Classified ad spending dropped sharply as a result. While daily circulation dropped, many weekly papers actually increased subscribers as consumers looked for hyper-local (community-level) news.

In the 1980s, most newspapers sold for 25 cents or 35 cents. Daily newspaper readership dropped in the decade, from 66.9 percent in 1980 to 63.6 percent in 1989. Sunday paper readership remained basically unchanged.

COMICS

The success of the 1970s continued into the 1980s as comic book publishers remained an influential part of popular culture. Although the average cost of an individual title jumped from 40 cents to 60 cents in the decade, monthly sales totals continued to rise, with Marvel titles dominating the top 20 lists. *X-Men* and *Spider-Man* often topped the annual best seller lists.

More and more young artists and writers flocked to the industry in the 1980s, including Frank Miller, Walt Simonson, and Bill Sienkiewicz. Many top titles focused on violence and aggressive, vigilante justice, reflecting the gritty reality of urban life in the 1980s. Marvel's character Punisher was a one-man death squad, and DC introduced Vigilante in 1983.

The art of selling comic books also changed in the 1980s. Traditionally, comic books were sold at newsstands. During the 1980s, however, comic shops replaced newsstands as venues for selling comics. Casual fans and extreme aficionados, dubbed "fanboys," flocked to shops packed with comic books and related merchandise. One series, the Teenage Mutant Ninja Turtles, appealed to young children, which led to a hit animated television show, toy sales, and hundreds of merchandising byproducts. The creative duo behind the Teenage Mutant Ninja Turtles, Kevin Eastman and Peter Laird, became multimillionaires.

In 1989, big-budget feature film *Batman* starred Michael Keaton as a brooding, psychologically-scarred caped crusader battling the maniacal Joker, played by Jack Nicholson. The film touched off "Batmania" and fueled more than $750 million in merchandise. Globally, Batman grossed $411 million at the box office and another $150 million in home video revenue. The success of *Batman* led the movie studios to release a series of comic books based in the 1990s.

Books

Entertainment

of the 1980s

The performing arts underwent a series of challenges in the 1980s as television, films, and theater all responded to the more conservative political climate infiltrating the middle class. Television comedies played off of these distinctions, showcasing both black and white families wrestling with their differences in ideology. Television dramas made the most of the conspicuous consumption of the era, launching nighttime serials that basked in the glossiness of new wealth. Even police shows tapped into this ethic, with some cops parading about in the latest fashions.

Films, always a reflection of their times, appeared to take an opposite turn as most of the successful features of the decade were escapist in nature—big budget comedies, sequels, and science-fiction action pictures dominated the filmic landscape, leaving only the melodrama, which continued to reflect the changing mores of America, caught between the idealistic liberal politics of the previous generation and the conservative ideology of the middle class.

The theater world, devastated by the AIDS crisis, took on a more volatile tone in every manner. While gay playwrights confronted the disease in a number of brave political plays, female playwrights continued to make the strides they had during the 1970s by staging poignant plays that detailed their own dramas.

TELEVISION

Situation Comedies (Sitcoms)

Cheers aired on NBC from 1982 to 1993 on Thursday evenings. Even though the show received critical acclaim and landed in the Nielsen "Top 10" for 7 of its 11 seasons, *Cheers* had a rocky start, facing cancellation in its first season. By 1985, however, the show often rated first in the weekly Nielsen's. Its final episode, which aired May 20, 1993, received the second highest rating in television history for a situation comedy. *Cheers* received a record 111 Emmy nominations, and gathered 26 Emmy Awards during its 274-episode run.

Produced by Glen Charles, Les Charles, and James Burrows, *Cheers* began the practice of employing the episodic "cliffhanger" at the end of the season, similar to that employed by serial dramas. These serial elements also added a note of drama to the sitcom, causing the audience to follow the weekly exploits of the central characters. Set in Boston, Massachusetts, at "Cheers," a neighborhood bar "where everybody knows your name," the show featured bar owner, Sam Malone (Ted Danson), a former Red Sox pitcher who turned to bartending after he was forced to retire due to his problems with alcohol.

The popular regulars at the bar included customers Cliff Claven (John Ratzenberger), a middle-aged, trivia-playing, mailman who still lived with his mother; Frasier Crane (Kelsey Grammer), Diane's priggish, one-time fiancé; and Norm Peterson (George Wendt), a tax accountant married to Vera. The central plot of the show was Sam and Diane's on-again/off-again relationship. The on-going romantic tension that ran through the first four seasons allowed the characters to develop gradually, and permitted plot lines for the other characters involving their personal lives. Frasier Crane had a successful spinoff, *Frasier*, NBC, 1993–2004, which followed Crane's life in Seattle.

The Cosby Show was one of the biggest surprise hits of the 1980s, dominating the Thursday night line-up on NBC from 1984 to 1992. Inspired by a monologue performed by comedian Bill Cosby on the *Tonight Show*, the show was produced by Marcy Carsey and Tom Werner. The series placed in the Top 3 of the Nielsen's during its first season; for the next four, it was the number one program watched in America. In its remaining years, *The Cosby Show* never fell from the Top 10.

The show revolved around the daily lives of the Huxtable family: Cliff (Bill Cosby), a successful obstetrician, Claire (Phylicia Rashad), a partner in a New York law firm, and the couple's five children. These traits created something seldom seen on television—a solidly middle-class, African American family. The show was innovative in its refusal to use one-liner jokes; instead it found humor in the reality of daily life. *The Cosby Show* stressed racial pride through a variety of techniques, including a strong nuclear family with a successful, active father figure; caring, professional parents still very much in love with one another; an emphasis on education; a secondary cast that represented a connection to a multigenerational family; and multiracial friends and colleagues. The show was a classy alternative to the stereotypical depictions of African Americans on shows like *Sanford and Son,* 1972–1977, *Good Times,* 1974–1979, and *The Jeffersons,* 1975–1985.

Family Ties (NBC, 1982–1989) revolved around Elyse (Meredith Baxter-Birney), an architect, and Steven Keaton (Michael Gross), a station manager for a local PBS station in Ohio. The couple met while serving in the Peace Corps after their activist days protesting the Vietnam War. They

TOP TV SHOWS

Cheers

The Cosby Show

Dallas

Dukes of Hazzard

Dynasty

Family Ties

The Jeffersons

Knight Rider

MacGyver

M*A*S*H

Miami Vice

Murder, She Wrote

Roseanne

60 Minutes

were the parents of three children: Alex P. Keaton (Michael J. Fox), Mallory (Justine Bateman), and Jennifer (Tina Yothers). The conflict between Alex's conservative notions and his parents' more liberal ideas took shape once the show began to solidify an audience during its first season. Fox became the breakout star, and his antics, particularly when they conflicted with his credo, became the real focus of the show.

Police Dramas

Cagney and Lacey (CBS, 1982–1988) blended the typical police drama with the melodramatic elements of the woman's serial to create a unique series that attained a cult following. The show never surfaced in the Nielsen "Top 25," although its stars won the Emmy Award for Best Actress each year of its run. The series began as a made-for-television movie, starring Loretta Swit and Tyne Daley as the female police detectives, when creators Barbara Corday and Barbara Avedon could not sell the idea as a feature film. Once CBS picked up the show, Swit could not commit. Instead, Meg Foster was cast in the role as Christine Cagney. Foster had played a lesbian in an earlier television role and CBS threatened to cancel the series unless Foster was replaced. She was replaced by Sharon Gless, a more conventionally feminine blonde.

Blending police action with a women's drama caused further problems with the network executives. Once Daly began to put on weight and severely cut her hair, questions of her appearance became paramount in both board meetings and in the tabloids. Story lines that involved rape, incest, abortion, breast cancer, alcoholism, and middle-aged sexual relations caused the network to threaten cancellation on more than one occasion. Once the series performed well at the 1983 Emmy Awards, however, CBS backed off, and renewed the series.

Another item that singled out *Cagney and Lacey* from standard dramas of the time was the structure of each episode. Each episode entwined three narrative strategies. The first thread involved the trials of women navigating the male-dominated work force. The second thread focused the action on a particular crime or investigation that could be resolved by the end of the hour. The third thread related this crime to a significant social problem that confronted the women in a more resounding fashion than it could if they were men.

Hill Street Blues (NBC, 1981–1987), created by Steven Bochco, blended the procedural elements of a police drama with more conventional cumulative series elements. The show was a critic's darling and had a small but extremely loyal fan-base. The series won six Emmy Awards in its first season and won the award for Outstanding Drama Series for the next four years.

The basic formula set the action in the Hill Street police station, an orderly home base in the midst of a criminally chaotic Los Angeles. Each episode opened with the morning roll call by desk sergeant Phil Esterhaus (Michael Conrad) and closed on a familiar note: "Let's be careful out there." After dismissal, the partnered police would filter out into the city. The regular teams included Hill and Renko (Michael Warren and Charles Haid), LaRue and Washington (Keil Martin and Taurean Blacque), and Coffee and Bates (Ed Marinaro and Betty Thomas).

The show also focused on the captain of the Hill Street unit, Frank Furillo (Daniel J. Travanti), who battled bureaucrats and criminals alike to secure a moral center in the city. One of the bureaucrats

Furillo battled was Public Defender Joyce Davenport (Veronica Hammell), a tough, contentious attorney who carried on a secret, intimate relationship with Frank. The writers maintained the secrecy of the affair from the other characters for three seasons, until Furillo asked Davenport to marry him. Of course, the professional antagonism never left the couple, so the intersection of the personal and professional became a staple of the series. *Magnum, P. I.* (CBS, 1980–1988) proved another successful departure from the standard police show with its colorful Hawaiian locale and its tough, yet loveable hero. The show appeared in the Nielsen Top 20 each year it was on the air, and won Tom Selleck, its star, an Emmy for Outstanding Lead Actor in a Dramatic Series in 1984.

Set in Honolulu, the series featured Thomas Magnum (Selleck) as a former Navy Intelligence officer serving as a private investigator. *Magnum, P. I.* began as a standard cop drama and evolved into a more sophisticated character study of the central character and his colleagues, all veterans of the Vietnam conflict. When not investigating, Magnum served as the security officer on the estate of Robin Masters, an author never seen on-screen. Masters's estate overseer, Jonathan Higgins III (John Hillman), cynically commented on what he saw as Magnum's carefree existence.

The show's use of Vietnam helped to position it as a different series. Many episodes revolved around the idea that a gesture or an incident would trigger a memory flash that grew from war experiences. The creators gradually introduced this sub-plot. They focused initially on Magnum's adjustment to the culture of the 1980s, and, after attracting a sizable audience, began to blend war elements into the storylines to explain Magnum's behavior. The strategy worked, and the show paved the way for other series to begin to seriously dissect the effects of the conflict.

Murder, She Wrote (1984–1996), was an innovative detective series that broke new ground by employing as the protagonist a 60-plus woman. Angela Lansbury, who created and produced the show with her son, Peter S. Fisher, found an untapped audience with a made-for-television movie about a mystery writer who finds herself an amateur sleuth along the coast of Maine. When the

Entertainment

movie proved popular on CBS in 1984, the network asked for a weekly series.

The premise was simple. Jessica Fletcher (Lansbury), a retired, widowed high school English teacher, writes mystery novels under the name J. B. Fletcher. As her books begin to sell, she becomes a celebrity in Cabot Cove, Maine, where she bikes around town and gossips with her longtime friends Sheriff Amos Tupper (Tom Bosley), Dr. Seth Hazlitt (William Windom), and Mayor Sam Booth (Richard Paul). Each show began with a crime. All the clues to who committed said crime were presented within the first 20 minutes of the show. Viewers could play along with Jessica as she solved the puzzle.

As the series became more successful, Jessica's popularity in the fictional world grew as well, and the author found herself solving crimes in New York City, London, and San Francisco. Lansbury became a major celebrity. She became a

spokesperson for elderly rights and also took on the Hollywood moguls by speaking out against the notion that television was a young persons' medium, populating the series with older movie stars. The show maintained high ratings throughout the 1980s, winning its Sunday-night time slot for 10 straight years.

Serial Dramas

Dallas was the first "prime time soap." Originally airing as a five-episode arc in 1978 on CBS, the show focused on Bobby Ewing (Patrick Duffy) and Pamela Barnes (Victoria Principle), the children of rivals "Jock" Ewing (Jim Davis) and "Digger" Barnes (David Wayne). When the series debuted that fall, the focus shifted to the Ewing clan's conspicuous existence at Southfork, the family's Texas homestead, and the elder brother J. R. Ewing's (Larry Hagman) shenanigans. For

Dallas, shown on CBS from 1978 to 1991. Shown from left: (back) Patrick Duffy, Victoria Principal, Jim Davis, Larry Hagman, Linda Gray, Steve Kanaly; (front) Barbara Bel Geddes, Charlene Tilton. Courtesy of Photofest.

the next 12 years, Dallas dominated CBS's Friday night line-up, consistently placing in the Nielsen Top 10.

J. R.'s popularity as a villainous cad created a new kind of villain—one that was fun to watch, no matter how despicable he was. He was openly abusive to his wife, Sue Ellen (Linda Gray), a former Miss Texas, now a drunk; he openly detested brother Bobby's ethics, and his own nemesis, "Digger's" son Cliff Barnes (Ken Kercheval) proved a weak, incompetent boob; audiences tuned in just to see what fresh hell J. R. could create.

The big budgets invested in high fashions, rich sets for homes and offices, and glossy exteriors shots added to the glamour of the series, making a keen ideological statement as the show began to reflect the real world of corporate monopolies and the dreams of young men and women seeking careers in big business.

The second full season ended with a cliffhanger: J. R. shot in his office, lying unconscious in a pool of blood. The mystery as to "Who Shot J. R.?" created a frenzy as the suspects remained too numerous to offer easy answers. Seventy-six percent of all television sets in America tuned in for the season premiere to find out the answer (the culprit was Kristin Shepard [Mary Crosby], one of J. R.'s many girlfriends). The success of this episode made the cliffhanger a staple of the series, and each season ended with a series of unanswered questions. *Dallas* set the standard for the serial melodramas, such as *Knots Landing* (a *Dallas* spinoff) and *Falcon Crest*.

Dynasty (ABC, 1981–1989) was the other significant prime-time serial of the 1980s. Beginning as a three-hour made-for-television movie, the creators turned it into a series almost immediately, capturing an audience similar to that of *Dallas* and often surpassing *Dallas*' numbers in the early years.

In many ways, *Dynasty's* central plot of followed that of *Dallas,* revolving around the family of Blake Carrington (John Forsythe), a wealthy Denver oil magnate; his second wife, Krystle (Linda Evans), a former model; and Blake's children. Blake's ex-wife Alexis Carrington Colby Dexter (Joan Collins) surfaced to take on the role of villain, aided by her sexy husband, "Dex"

HOW OTHERS SEE US

Big Money, Big Hair: "Dallas"

"Dallas," the massively popular prime-time soap opera that focused on a wealthy Texas oil family, became famous for its elaborate, back-stabbing plots, cliffhanger endings, and an entire season that turned out to be a dream. The show ran from 1978 until 1991 and continued in syndication internationally. Translated and dubbed into 67 languages and shown in more than 90 countries, the show achieved unprecedented levels of international success. The show's characters, including oil magnate JR Ewing in his giant cowboy hat, the elegant ladies that surrounded him, and their luxury cars and giant estates typified the nouveau riche oil culture of Texas, at least in the minds of viewers around the world.

References to the show appeared in international pop culture throughout the 1980s. Swedish disco icons ABBA sang about "Dallas" in their song "The Day Before You Came," and Irish and British television comedies of the period, such as "Father Ted" and "The Young Ones," joked about its pervasive popularity.

In many countries, the immense reach of "Dallas" raised serious concerns about the undue influence of American popular culture on local culture. At a time when leaders such as France's Francois Mitterand sought measures to ensure the integrity of French culture and language, "Dallas" came to symbolize the encroachment of American culture and its fetishization of opulence, greed, and consumerism. (Ironically, President Mitterand was reported to be a huge fan of the show himself, allegedly knowing all its characters and story lines.) Meanwhile, the DAAD German Research Foundation, seeking a scientific basis for its thesis that American imports such as "Dallas" were having a corroding effect on German culture, undertook a series of ultimately inconclusive studies on the question.

Dexter (Michael Nader), who soon turned to support Blake because of Alexis's antics, which often forced her three children to take sides against their father.

With Collins came a higher weekly budget; the show spent $1.2 million per episode (with an estimated $10,000 per episode spent on clothing alone), and the plotlines took on a campier, exaggerated quality. *Dynasty* offered style over substance: one season, 1984–1985, ended with Blake's daughter being abducted by aliens. *Dynasty* is noteworthy for a few unique contributions to 1980s television. The series included one of the first gay male characters in Steven Carrington; although he was briefly married and fathered a son, he enjoyed a long-term relationship with Luke Fuller (William Campbell). In another first, Diahann Carroll joined the cast as Dominique Devereaux, a chanteuse once involved with Blake. She became the first African American to appear as a series regular on a major serial drama. In another play for ratings, Rock Hudson took on the role of Daniel Reese for two seasons to woo Krystle from Blake. The role proved to be Hudson's last, and tabloids quickly splashed their covers with stills from his open-mouthed kissing scenes with Evans once his AIDS diagnosis became public in 1985.

Other serial dramas focused on middle-class worlds in a more realistic manner. These shows included *St. Elsewhere* (1982–1988), which detailed the day-to-day lives of doctors and nurses at Boston's St. Eligius Hospital; *Knots Landing* (1981–1991), which chronicled the interconnected lives of three families living in a southern California cul-de-sac; and *thirtysomething*, (1987–1991), which followed the domestic and professional struggles of young urban professionals outside of Philadelphia.

FILM

The New Musical

Musicals evolved into a new form in the 1970s, first with films like *Saturday Night Fever* (1977) and *Grease* (1978). The plots concerned young teens combating societal odds for acceptance, and music—whether performed by the protagonist or played as part of a soundtrack—proved popular. The soundtracks for these films, often produced by the film production company, helped to make this new brand of musical film popular among the youth market, playing into teenagers' needs for both acceptance and financial independence. For example, *Flashdance* (1983), earned $94 million—and the soundtrack not only went platinum, but its theme, "What A Feeling" sung by Irene Cara, won the Oscar for "Best Song" in 1984.

The plot follows Alex (Jennifer Beals), who works as a welder for a Pittsburgh construction company by day, and has aspirations of being a ballet dancer. At night she works as a cocktail waitress and exotic dancer. Eventually, Alex auditions for a big city company, and, is not only cast, but allowed to star. Artistic success and money are hers in return for her hard work and effort—a 1980s fairy tale.

In *Footloose* (1984), Ren (Kevin Bacon) moves into a mythical Midwestern farming community where the local minister (John Lithgow) has banned dancing and rock n' roll music. The minister's daughter, Ariel (Lori Singer) joins with Ren to stage a prom where all the students can express themselves through dance. The soundtrack had eight Top 10 singles, while the film itself reached $80 million at the box office.

Another blockbuster appealed to audiences seeking a link back to the early days of rock n' roll. *Dirty Dancing* (1987), combined teenaged romance with a rebel against authority genres to create a dance-infused vehicle that struck box-office gold, grossing $60 million. Francis "Baby" Houseman (Jennifer Grey) and her family vacation at resort in the Catskills. Baby (her father's nickname for her) hears boisterous tunes coming from the staff quarters and discovers a band of would-be dancers heating their cabins with a new form of dance, termed dirty dancing—a blend of salsa, rumba, and tango. She falls for the head dance instructor, Johnny Castle (Patrick Swayze).

Baby's father (Jerry Orbach) does not approve of Johnny or of the dance, so Johnny and Baby practice their own moves in the woods. After a series of misunderstandings, the couple gets to perform their routine to enthusiastic raves. The soundtrack and the MTV-inspired editing made the film a real hit with female audience members.

The soundtrack, blending new and older tunes, went platinum in a matter of weeks, and spawned four number one hits.

The Return of the Sequel

The 1980s, full of nostalgia for the previous decades, was ripe for sequels. A variety of sequel series—from science fiction to horror to comedy—proved to be popular with audiences.

Science Fiction/Fantasy

The most successful series of the 1980s was the *Star Wars* trilogy, launched in 1978 by director George Lucas. At the time of its release, *Star Wars* was the most successful film of all time, bringing in a total box office of $100 million. The second in the series, *The Empire Strikes Back* (1981), once more followed Luke Skywalker (Mark Hamill) and his efforts to secure his planet from the dark forces of the Empire, led by Darth Vader (David Prowse, voiced by James Earl Jones). Continuing to assist him from the first feature was Princess Leia (Carrie Fisher), the rightful ruler of the land, and Han Solo (Harrison Ford) a charismatic smuggler. Of added assistance were the nonhuman characters, made loveable by their human emotions: R2D2 (Kenny Baker), C3PO (Anthony Daniels), and Chewbacca (Peter Mayhew). Joining the forces for good against the Empire were Lando Calrissian (Billy Dee Williams), an old partner of Solo's, and Yoda (Frank Oz), a tiny green swamp creature who trains Luke in the ways of the Jedi knights. The success of the franchise was unparalleled, with merchandising money coming from the sale of *Star Wars* action figures, clothing, and commercial tie-ins (with Burger King).

Another popular sequel franchise was *The Terminator* films, produced and directed by James Cameron and starring Arnold Schwarzenegger as the android from the future. *The Terminator* (1984) is a cyborg sent from the future to kill Sarah Connor (Linda Hamilton), an innocent woman who is to mother John Connor, who will, in the future, lead a successful revolution to wipe out the cyborg species. The seemingly unstoppable cyborg, played by Schwarzenegger, wrecks everything in his path in his attempt to kill Sarah. Ironically,

The Terminator ultimately kills the man helping Sarah flee, Kyle Reese (Michael Biehn), but only after he fathers John. Reese's efforts help halt the insurrection and render the Terminator useless by the film's end. *The Terminator* was followed in 1991 by a sequel, *Terminator 2: Judgment Day,* which proved even more successful at the box office, aided in part by even more spectacular special effects.

Director Robert Zemeckis tapped into the popularity of television's *Family Ties* in casting Michael J. Fox as the earnest protagonist of the *Back to the Future* series, a series that blended a Frank Capra-like vision of America with the sci-fi genre to create a magically comic franchise. The first film, *Back to the Future* (1985), opens in the present as Marty McFly (Fox) navigates the terrain of teenaged hell. Marty is the eldest son of George (Crispin Glover) and Lorraine McFly (Lea Thompson)—George is a corny nerd, and Lorraine is a closet alcoholic. Biff Tannen (Thomas F. Wilson), the prototypical bully, and Marty fall for the same girl, Jennifer (Elizabeth Shue).

Paradoxes and predicaments ensue as Marty comes into his own town 30 years in the past, where he helps his father take on the family bully and fends off his mother's advances. Marty helps his father become a confident man and brings his parents together before returning to his present. The film was followed by two sequels, *Back to the Future II* (1989) and *Back to the Future III* (1990). In *Back to the Future II,* Marty travels to the future to find himself married with a family (his wife played by Lea Thompson) in an age similar to *The Jetsons. Back to the Future III* follows Marty and Doc Brown together to the past, some 100 years before, as they save their township from villainous cowboys. Combined, the franchise made more than $400 million, solidifying Fox's star power and making Amblin Entertainment, Steven Spielberg's production company, one of the real powers of 1980s movie-making.

Undoubtedly, the biggest science fiction/fantasy film of the decade was *E.T.: The Extra-Terrestrial* (1982), Steven Spielberg's film of a lost space being and his efforts to return to his home with the assistance of Elliot (Henry Thomas), a typical American 11-year-old. Even though he loves Elliot,

E.T. still desires to return home—particularly after government agents discover him. The film's total of $800 million in world-wide receipts still makes it one of the most popular films in history. The fact that Spielberg's film rests on the shoulders of his harmless little creation is a true testament to his filmmaking.

Horror

In the late 1970s, writer and director John Carpenter created the disturbing *Halloween* franchise starring Michael Myers, who not only pursued his sister (Jamie Lee Curtis) through eight films (1978–2002), but killed every teenager who got in his way.

An imaginative take on the horror villain as protagonist genre, *The Nightmare on Elm Street* series (1984–1994) followed the exploits of Freddy Krueger (Robert Englund) as he visited teens in their dreams and murdered them while they slept. In the first film, Freddy's main goal is to murder Nancy Thompson (Heather Langenkamp) simply because she is the daughter of the local police chief (John Saxon) who stood by and watched as kids taunted and killed Freddy some years before. While Nancy emerges as the heroine and victim of the film, having to use her wits not only to fight off Freddy but the many adults who do not believe her, Freddy, with his own wit and evil laugh, makes audiences root for him to succeed.

Comedy Franchises

The two most successful comedy sequels of the 1980s began with the casting of *Saturday Night Live* alumni in the central roles. *Beverly Hills Cop* (1984) cast Eddie Murphy as the wisecracking Axel Foley, a Detroit police detective who travels to California to avenge the murder of a friend. Instead of a smart social satire that had the denizens of white Rodeo Drive contending with this black ubercop, the action film went for broader laughs, and director Martin Brest and producer Jerry Bruckheimer succeeded in creating a movie that was critically panned, but financially rewarding. In its opening weekend, *Beverly Hills Cop* brought in $14.4 million and the number one album in the country, from which came five number one singles.

The sequel, *Beverly Hills Cop II* (1987), directed by Tony Scott, reunited Axel with the Beverly Hills cops from the first feature. This time, Axel travels to Beverly Hills to avenge the shooting of a friend by Brigitte Nielsen. The caper brought in over $153,000,000.

Ghostbusters (1984) featured a screenplay by *Saturday Night Live*'s Dan Aykroyd and *Second City* alum Harold Ramis and was directed by special effects wizard Ivan Reitman. The film blended horror with quick-witted dialogue to produce an entertaining story. Using New York City as its background, Drs. Peter Venkman (*Saturday Night Live*'s Bill Murray), Ray Stanz (Aykroyd), and Egon Spengler (Ramis) open a "Ghostbusters" business to combat the many goblins and ghosts in Manhattan's major buildings. When Dana Barrett (Sigourney Weaver) begins to see signs of spirits in her apartment, she calls the team, who discovers that her apartment building is the gateway to the underworld. Armed with their nuclear powered artillery, the team fights the many demons, including the Stay-Puft Marshmallow Man, who takes on Manhattan like King Kong. The film grossed $238 million in its initial release.

The plot of the sequel *Ghostbusters II* is similar, though the special effects do not blend with the comic antics of the team as readily. The film grossed $112 million in its initial release.

Action/Adventure

Another popular serial from Producer George Lucas was the *Indiana Jones* trilogy. This series of three pictures, harkening back to the serial dramas of the 1930s, was directed by Steven Spielberg and starred Harrison Ford as Indiana Jones (Indy), a professorial archeologist who fought a variety of criminals out to secure the world's art treasures for their own selfish reasons.

In the first film, *Raiders of the Lost Ark* (1981), Indy travels around the globe to secure the lost Ark of the Covenant, now in the possession of a rival of Jones's who works for Hitler's Nazis. A former girlfriend, Marion Ravenwood (Karen Allen) joins Indy. In the deserts of Egypt, the mysteries of the Ark are uncovered to horrific result.

The action never lets up, and Indy and Marion find themselves assaulted by tarantulas, runaway boulders, poisoned spears—and a bevy of snakes in a sequence marked as one of the best in the action genre. Rescuing themselves from these fates, Indy and Marion chase the Nazis in one sequence that involves one truck, a horse, and a motorcycle, and ends with a nail-biting sequence where Jones crawls along the axel of a speeding army vehicle.

The second film, *Indiana Jones and the Temple of Doom* (1984), is more noteworthy for its gratuitous gore than for the comically adventurous chase sequences that characterize the first film. The dark sequences came under much discussion by conservative parents' groups, who argued that such violence was not entertainment.

TOP ACTORS

Warren Beatty, 1937–

Glenn Close, 1947–

Tom Cruise, 1962–

Robert De Niro, 1943–

Michael Douglas, 1944–

Clint Eastwood, 1930–

Sally Field, 1946–

Harrison Ford, 1942–

Jodie Foster, 1962–

Michael J. Fox, 1961–

Tom Hanks, 1956–

Dustin Hoffman, 1937–

Eddie Murphy, 1961–

Bill Murray, 1950–

Jack Nicholson, 1937–

Burt Reynolds, 1936–

Arnold Schwarzenegger, 1947–

Sissy Spacek, 1949–

Sylvester Stallone, 1946–

Meryl Streep, 1949–

Kathleen Turner, 1954–

Robin Willliams, 1951–

TOP MOVIES

The Empire Strikes Back, 1980*

Raging Bull, 1980

The Shining, 1980

The Cannonball Run, 1981

Raiders of the Lost Ark, 1981*

E.T.: The Extra-Terrestrial, 1982*

Fast Times at Ridgemont High, 1982

An Officer and a Gentleman, 1982

Tootsie, 1982

The Big Chill, 1983

Flashdance, 1983

Return of the Jedi, 1983*

Risky Business, 1983

Scarface, 1983

Beverly Hills Cop, 1984*

Ghostbusters, 1984*

Indiana Jones and the Temple of Doom, 1984

The Karate Kid, 1984

Police Academy, 1984

The Terminator, 1984

Back to the Future, 1985*

The Breakfast Club, 1985

Aliens, 1986

Ferris Bueller's Day Off, 1986

Top Gun, 1986

Dirty Dancing, 1987

Fatal Attraction, 1987

Lethal Weapon, 1987

Wall Street, 1987

Die Hard, 1988

Who Framed Roger Rabbit, 1988

Batman, 1989*

Born on the Fourth of July, 1989

Field of Dreams, 1989

Glory, 1989

Indiana Jones and the Last Crusade, 1989

The Little Mermaid, 1989

When Harry Met Sally, 1989

*Highest-grossing movies of the decade.

Entertainment

ACADEMY AWARD WINNERS

1980 Picture: *Ordinary People*

Director: Robert Redford, *Ordinary People*
Actor: Robert De Niro, *Raging Bull*
Actress: Sissy Spacek, *Coal Miner's Daughter*

1981 Picture: *Chariots of Fire*

Director: Warren Beatty, *Reds*
Actor: Henry Fonda, *On Golden Pond*
Actress: Katharine Hepburn, *On Golden Pond*

1982 Picture: *Gandhi*

Director: Richard Attenborough, *Gandhi*
Actor: Ben Kingsley, *Gandhi*
Actress: Meryl Streep, *Sophie's Choice*

1983 Picture: *Terms of Endearment*

Director: James L. Brooks, *Terms of Endearment*
Actor: Robert Duvall, *Tender Mercies*
Actress: Shirley MacLaine, *Terms of Endearment*

1984 Picture: *Amadeus*

Director: Miloš Forman, *Amadeus*
Actor: F. Murray Abraham, *Amadeus*
Actress: Sally Field, *Places in the Heart*

1985 Picture: *Out of Africa*

Director: Sydney Pollack, *Out of Africa*
Actor: William Hurt, *Kiss of the Spiderwoman*
Actress: Geraldine Page, *The Trip to Bountiful*

1986 Picture: *Platoon*

Director: Oliver Stone, *Platoon*
Actor: Paul Newman, *The Color of Money*
Actress: Marlee Matlin, *Children of a Lesser God*

1987 Picture: *The Last Emperor*

Director: Bernardo Bertolucci, *The Last Emperor*
Actor: Michael Douglas, *Wall Street*
Actress: Cher, *Moonstruck*

1988 Picture: *Rain Man*

Director: Barry Levinson, *Rain Man*
Actor: Dustin Hoffman, *Rain Man*
Actress: Jodie Foster, *The Accused*

1989 Picture: *Driving Miss Daisy*

Director: Oliver Stone, *Born on the Fourth of July*
Actor: Daniel Day-Lewis, *My Left Foot*
Actress: Jessica Tandy, *Driving Miss Daisy*

Indiana Jones and the Last Crusade (1989) returned to the earlier formula of witty secondary characters who could banter with the ironic professor and the evil Nazis. In this installment, Indiana Jones's long estranged father and fellow archeologist, Dr. Henry Jones (Sean Connery) joins with Marcus Brody (Denholm Eliot) and Sallah (John Rhys-Davies), a Middle-eastern assistant from Indy's glory days, to fight off the Nazis, this time in pursuit of the Holy Grail.

The comical squabbling between Indy and his cantankerous father never detracts from the riotous chase sequences. All comes to a climax when one Nazi officer shoots Jones Sr., and Indy must use all the teachings his father once instilled in him to secure the Grail from its repository. With Henry healed from the Grail's holy water, and the Nazis destroyed by their own heresy, the four ride off into the sunset bickering—a fitting "end" to the trilogy. The three *Indiana Jones* films together

grossed nearly $720 million in their initial releases and have achieved classic status on home video. In 2008 the highly-profitable franchise was resurrected with the release of *Indiana Jones and the Kingdom of the Crystal Skull*.

The War Film

The war film was represented by a very successful serial: *First Blood* (1982), directed by Ted Kotcheff from a screenplay written by movie star Sylvester Stallone. Viewers relived the horrors of the Vietnam Conflict, and, via a revisionist story, experienced winning the conflict. In the first installment, John Rambo (Stallone) is a Vietnam veteran trained in Green Beret tactics who is mishandled by policemen after returning home a hero. He wages war on the police using the same tactics that made him a killing machine during the war. The central action involves the police tracking the warrior through the forests of the Pacific Northwest to a predictable, cliff-side battle. *First Blood* made $7 million in its opening weekend in only 900 theaters.

In the second film, *Rambo: First Blood II* (1985), penned by Stallone and James Cameron, and directed by George P. Cosmatos, Rambo returns to Vietnam to rescue a group of veterans who have been labeled "Missing In Action" by the U.S. government. Fighting off Vietcong, Rambo leads the men to freedom. Despite uniform critical panning, audiences flocked to see the film; receipts totaled $25 million in its opening weekend.

Another kind of war film blended the passions of youth, the technical wizardry of action film editing, and the patriotic verve of Reagan's America; *Top Gun* (1986) was a stylish crowd-pleaser that extolled the virtues of America's powerful men in uniform. Pete "Maverick" Mitchell (Tom Cruise) is a hot-dog pilot who risks his life for his country. He joins an elite flight school connected to the Navy's "Top Gun" program, set on preparing America's best pilots for aerial dogfights with the enemy. At this secret academy, the school's top graduate each year is named "Top Gun," distinguishing his record with assignments that test his abilities.

The film's patriotic flair had audiences cheering in the aisles as the Russian pilots were sent scampering. Not only did *Top Gun* gross $176 million in its initial release, it solidified Tom Cruise's status as a box-office draw.

The Business Film

The 1980s marked a time for big business ventures, and Hollywood released films that not only celebrated the possibilities of wealth through big business, but also told stories where American values, such as hard work and moral living, would eventually help one to succeed.

In Oliver Stone's *Wall Street* (1987), the film's protagonist Bud Fox (Charlie Sheen) works as a commodities broker. Bud's tenacity gets him an audience with Gordon Gekko (Michael Douglas), a ruthless multimillionaire whose earnings afford him a most fabulous life that Bud aspires toward. Gordon senses Bud's hunger and rewards his faithfulness with perks—an upper-Eastside pent-house, $2,000 suits, and a gorgeous decorator girl friend. Gekko's unscrupulous philosophy is revealed when he delivers the film's most famous line, "Greed is good" to a group of disgruntled stockholders.

When Bud comes to Gekko with some insider trading information involving a small airline that Bud's father, Carl (Martin Sheen), oversees as union president, Gekko lets Bud overtake the interests, but then leaves Bud hanging out to dry when it comes time to dump the stocks. Humiliated by being arrested at his office, Bud is forced to turn state's evidence against Gekko, who will undoubtedly beat the charges. In creating this morality tale of the times, Stone actually celebrated the greed and excess of the era.

In *Working Girl* (1988), Tess McGill (Melanie Griffith) is engaged and has everything that her friend Cyn (Joan Cusack) desires for her life. But Tess wants more. She believes she has found a role model when she begins a new job as an assistant for a female executive, Katharine Parker (Sigourney Weaver). Tess then learns that her boss has stolen one of her own ideas, and has passed it off as her own. Tess proves to Oren Trask (Phillip Bosco), a player from a partner corporation, that Katharine is the true plagiarist. Trask rewards her with an entry-level position with her own secretary, and Jack Trainer (Harrison Ford) rewards her with his love.

Marital Relations

In the 1950s and early 1960s, marriage films revolved around the pursuit by single men and women to marry by film's end. Films of the 1970s began to explore marriage itself, and those of the 1980s examined the destruction of the institution, becoming cautionary tales about the evils of infidelity and not communicating.

Robert Redford's directing debut, *Ordinary People* (1980) focuses on the Jarreds—an affluent family that appears to have everything. Based on Judith Guest's novel, the film focuses on how the inability to speak freely can corrode a marriage and family. Before the film opens, the Jarreds lose a son in a boating accident. The youngest son, Conrad (Timothy Hutton), survived the accident, but still holds himself accountable for his

The Breakfast Club (1985). Directed by John Hughes. Shown from left: Judd Nelson (as John Bender), Emilio Estevez (as Andrew "Andy" Clark), Ally Sheedy (as Allison Reynolds), Molly Ringwald (as Claire Standish), Anthony Michael Hall (as Brian Ralph Johnson). Courtesy of Photofest.

JOHN HUGHES

John Hughes wrote and directed several of the most successful comedies for teens of the era. Hughes's films were set in America's Midwest. His protagonists were most often middle class and white, but their discontented malaise endeared them to teen audiences. Hughes refused to speak down to his audience—his characters were witty and intelligent, and their problems really mattered to them. Hughes's skill at finding comedy in the kind of "everyman" teenager, then deriving larger messages from their experiences, gave his films their power.

Hughes launched out on his own by directing his own screenplay of *Sixteen Candles* (1984), the story of Samantha (Molly Ringwald), a girl whose sister is to be married on the same weekend as Samantha's sixteenth birthday. His next film, *The Breakfast Club* (1985), was an even bigger hit with the youth market. The film taps into the idea that authority tangles with the lives of teens in a manner that cripples identity and forces conformity. The plot revolves around five students at a typical Midwestern high school who, for various reasons, attend a Saturday detention. To the outside world and those inside the school, each student fits neatly into a stereotypical clique: Andrew (Emilio Estevez) the jock, Brian (Anthony Michael Hall) the brain, Bender (Judd Nelson) the stoner, Claire (Molly Ringwald) the princess, and Allison (Ally Sheedy) the neurotic. After spending the detention together and learning about each other as individuals the five teens bond.

Hughes followed his early hits with *Ferris Bueller's Day Off* (1986), *Pretty in Pink* (1986), and *Some Kind of Wonderful* (1987). Each film portrayed real teen problems and made young people more than just cardboard cutouts, unlike most movies and television shows in the decades leading up to the 1980s.

RADIO DEBUTS OF THE 1980s

"Rock of the Eighties" (1980): a format pioneered by KROQ in Los Angeles that emphasized punk, new wave, and modern rock, paving the way for similar radio stations across the country, as well as for MTV.

"Dick Clark's Rock, Roll, and Remember" (1982): oldies and classic rock tunes, hosted by TV and radio personality Dick Clark.

"Loveline" (1983): call-in show about relationships and sexuality, hosted since 1984 by Dr. Drew Pinsky.

"Whad'Ya Know?" (1985): comedic quiz show that also incorporates celebrity and audience interviews.

"The Howard Stern Show" (1986): nationally syndicated morning show featuring the raunchy comedy of this influential "shock jock."

"Cruisin' America" (1987): oldies music introduced by Cousin Brucie, a top radio deejay of the 1960s.

"Car Talk" (1987): call-in public radio program offering the auto-repair advice and corny comedy of mechanics Tom and Ray Magliozzi.

"Rush Limbaugh" (1988): political news and commentary from a conservative perspective, the first of many nationally syndicated right-leaning radio talk shows.

"Marketplace" (1989): National Public Radio's global business and economic news program.

"Coast to Coast AM" (1989): callers and expert guests discuss the occult, paranormal experiences, conspiracy theories, UFOs, cryptozoology, and similar topics.

family's loss—so much so that Conrad tries to kill himself. On the surface, Beth Jarred (Mary Tyler Moore) looks like she has survived these traumas as well as can be expected; however, her composure is all façade. It is left to Calvin Jarred (Donald Sutherland), Beth's husband and Conrad's father, to hold the family together.

Beth and Cal attend a birthday party, where Calvin tells others about Conrad's psychiatrist. On the return home, Beth erupts, telling Cal he drinks too much and that he should not discuss private matters in public. It is in these brutal conversations that Redford carefully reveals how fragile the Jarred family situation is.

Conrad begins the slow process of forgiving himself and Beth abandons the family. Redford's film is a telling reminder of the early 1980s concern with family values—here is the perfect family on the outside, falling apart from within.

Director Adrian Lyne brought family values to the forefront in a *Fatal Attraction* (1987), a thriller about a family man who has a one-night affair with a woman who becomes obsessed with him. Even though most critics hated the ending, believing that Alex's character was sacrificed for gratuitous audience pleasure, the ending made the film a real crowd pleaser, grossing $156 million in its initial release. The film was nominated for six Academy Awards, including Best Picture, but won none. Ideologically, *Fatal Attraction* is a fascinating film because it vilifies the career woman; Dan is never held responsible for what happens to Alex, even though he willingly engaged in the affair, and murders not only Alex but their alleged unborn child.

THEATER

Female playwrights made significant gains in the theater during the 1980s, creating plays that pushed male characters to the sidelines (or completely off stage) and placed the women center stage. The first of these plays was by Beth Henley, a first-time playwright who blended the trappings of her Southern Gothic background with the complexities of sisterhood. Her play *Crimes of the Heart* won the Pulitzer Prize for Drama while it still played off-Broadway. The play's subsequent success on Broadway and beyond certainly proves that her message was clearly understood.

Another playwright, Marsha Norman, took a vastly different approach in her 1983 Pulitzer-Prize winning play '*night, Mother*. The play opens on the last night in the life of Jessie Cates, a woman in her late 30s who announces to Thelma, her mother (and the play's only other character), that in two hours she will commit suicide by firing her father's gun into her own brain. Clocks onstage help build the tension as Jessie prepares for her

NOTABLE THEATER

Amadeus, 1980 (1,181 perfs.)

42nd Street, 1980 (3,486 perfs.)

Dreamgirls, 1981 (1,521 perfs.)

Cats, 1982 (7,485 perfs.)

Torch Song Trilogy, 1982 (1,222 perfs.)

Brighton Beach Memoirs, 1983 (1,299 perfs.)

La Cage aux Folles, 1983 (1,761 perfs.)

Me and My Girl, 1986 (1,420 perfs.)

Les Misérables, 1986 (6,680 perfs.)

The Phantom of the Opera, 1988 (8,350 perfs.)*

Grand Hotel, 1989 (1,017 perfs.)

*Still running.

final act. Jessie cannot make her mother understand that her death is the one thing in her life she can control. The play ends with Jessie retreating to her bedroom and the sound of a gun going off.

David Mamet's Pulitzer Prize winning *Glengarry Glen Ross* takes place in a second-rate real estate office, where the salesmen use whatever crafty line they can dream up to "Always Be Closing." Mamet's focus on the male social order through work helps his audience come to terms with the effects of Reaganomics—a world where ethics fly out the window for the almighty buck—a world where male camaraderie is not worth the price of a lead. Schoolyard competition and bullying are admirable traits; male bonding is something to be abused for the good of the sale.

Harvey Fierstein's *Torch Song Trilogy* won the 1983 Tony Award for drama—the first openly gay play to win the award. Writer and star Fierstein also won the award for Best Actor, and the play ran to packed houses for three years. Critics praised the play for its postmodern structure and its unconventional use of stereotypes to explode myths of homosexual relationships. Fierstein proved that a homosexual story was a human story, first and foremost.

The overall play strings three one-act plays together with a torch-singer performing blues numbers between the "acts," commenting on the action just staged. The protagonist, Arnold, is a middle-aged drag performer looking for love. He encounters Ed, a bisexual teacher, in a local bar. The first play ends as Ed leaves Arnold for a conventional marriage to Laurel.

Between the acts, Arnold meets Alan, a young model. Alan and Ed hook up for a fling that Laurel does not know about. The act draws parallels between the two couples, outlining the lack of difference between homo- and heterosexual relations—each is characterized by infidelities, arguing, and loving, tender moments. Arnold overlooks the infidelity, and "marries" Alan, while Laurel leaves Ed.

The third playlet takes place five years later. Alan and Arnold have adopted a troubled youth, David, but on the eve of moving to a new apartment, Alan is killed in a gay bashing. Ed now lives with them, but he sleeps on the sofa. This action takes on the tone of a situation comedy, openly revealing that "gay domesticity" is nothing more than "domesticity"—David refers to Arnold as "Ma."

Upon the arrival of Arnold's mother, the tone of the play turns serious, as she disparages Arnold's lifestyle. The conversation resonates with the LGBT (lesbian, gay, bi-sexual, and transgender) rights movement, as gay men and women were fighting for equal protections and escalates toward a climax where Arnold confronts his mother's homophobia once and for all.

The AIDS crisis ushered a new brand of theater, addressing the immediacy of confronting the pandemic while making a call to arms to the audience. Larry Kramer's autobiographical, episodic drama, *The Normal Heart,* recounts the founding of Gay Men's Health Crisis, one of the first community efforts to battle the stigma of the disease. The play focuses on Kramer's efforts to bring the gay community together to create this organization and to combat the white, heterosexual establishment who turned their backs to the onslaught of the disease. Kramer not only recreates the struggle with the heterosexual community, but dissects the struggles within the gay male community through these years.

Fences tells the story of Troy Maxon, a former baseball player who once played for a Negro league after being denied a spot in the legitimate white league. Troy allows this one experience to define him in his life, and his constant squabbles with his wife, Rose, and their two sons, Lyons (a small-time piano player and pimp) and Cory (a promising football player), reveal how this single rejection destroyed his vision of a true American Dream for him and for his family.

Wendy Wasserstein's *The Heidi Chronicles* explores the positive and negative effects of 1970s feminism. The "chronicles" of the play's title episodically reveal that the protagonist, Dr. Heidi Holland, grows to have faith in herself rather than in the revolutions that bonded her to the feminist movement and in the men who promise only to be there if Heidi will compromise her ambition.

Wasserstein structures the play in an interesting fashion—Heidi is presenting a lecture to her class on Women Artists at Columbia University. Heidi presents herself as confident, articulate, and personable with her students. However, as the lecture continues, the action of the play flashes back to pivotal moments in Heidi's education: meeting her life-long gay friend; meeting her life-long love; and her burgeoning awareness of feminist thought and its ideological effects. Heidi is constant in her efforts to have men in her life and belong to a sisterhood conflict through her career as she works toward fulfillment.

As the play progresses, Heidi adopts a baby and defines herself for the first time—on her own terms. The play ends with Heidi bringing her lecture to a close, selecting as her last slide a photograph of her holding baby Judy "triumphantly" in front of a banner for a Georgia O'Keefe retrospective. Heidi learns that she can have both a professional and a personal world.

Musical Theater

Certainly the most consistent experimental voice in the theater during the 1980s was Stephen Sondheim's. For Sondheim, the decade began with *Merrily We Roll Along* (1981), his follow-up to the success of *Sweeney Todd* (1979). The production closed after 16 performances, marking it as one of the biggest musical flops in recent memory. However, since 1981, *Merrily* has been revised and restaged a number of times, most recently, as the crowning glory of a summer long celebration of Sondheim's work in Washington, D.C.

Sondheim did not give up on bending the rules of the Broadway form, and in 1983 he embarked on a fascinating project with playwright and director James Lapine that certainly bent the rules. *Sunday in the Park…* is based on George Seurat's painting *A Sunday Afternoon on the Island of Grande Jatte.*

The critics were impressed with this new team, but mixed in their response to the show. That year, while the play lost all the major Tony Awards that it was nominated for, Sondheim and Lapine were awarded the Pulitzer Prize for Drama, an honor that makes *Sunday in the Park…* one of the highlights of 1980s theater.

With a critical hit under their belts, Sondheim and Lapine looked for another project; they found it in the story books Lapine read to his daughters at bedtime. In the innovative *Into the Woods* (1987), Sondheim and Lapine defy the traditional values embodied in the romantic musical comedy, which generally ends happily. *Into the Woods* challenges the audience's assumptions not only about marriage, but also about the ideology of the romantic musical narrative. It interweaves four familiar folk tales that combine the quest motif and the marriage motif to explore the ramifications of "Happily Ever After."

Sondheim and Lapine selected three popular tales from the Brothers Grimm, "Cinderella," "Little Red Riding Hood," and "Rapunzel," as well as the popular English folk tale "Jack and the Beanstalk." They then undercut the "timeless moralities" of these tales with an original one of their own, "The Baker and His Wife." In order to produce progeny, the couple interact with their fantastic folk community to present a unified critique of how the musical predisposes the audience to unthinkingly accept marriage as a form of closure.

Ideologically speaking, the entire first act, which follows the pursuit of each character's goal, confirms the selfish, yet simplistic, motives of each storybook figure. The Baker and His Wife compromise their values by stealing, lying, and cheating the other characters out of the possessions they need. Their actions illustrate the problems and entanglements that occur when the ideology of community does not figure into the actions of each individual. The show was embraced by critics and audiences, and *Into the Woods* received numerous awards. More importantly, these musicals marked a new era for Broadway—the days of the Rogers and Hammerstein musical were gone, taken over by a new type of show that could make people think while they were being entertained.

Fashion

of the 1980s

The dichotomies of the 1980s influenced the world of fashion. Fashion in the 1980s ran the gamut from haute couture glamour to street-smart punk; from the star power trends set by Madonna, the boys of *Miami Vice,* and the *Flashdance*-ing Jennifer Beals to the conservative guidelines set by *The Ultimate Preppy Handbook.* With the percolating economy in full bull-market mode, fashion met the challenge by altering advertising trends to emphasize male beauty. Designers also drew inspiration from the new threads being sported by pop stars on MTV.

Women ditched the stringy, long hair of the 1970s, instead opting for perms and hairspray, teasing their hair into incredible walls, emphasizing the new look with two-toned eye shadows and glossy lipsticks. Males appropriated a variety of looks to emulate their role models, all in an effort to reflect their own ideas of control and power.

Since the early years of the twentieth century, entertainers, first stage stars and singers then celebrities from the film industry and later television, influenced fashion trends. What is so telling about the fashion trends of the 1980s is the influence of big business on the industry, not only in respect to styles and trends, but in regard to the market economy.

Wall Street's corporate look—long considered the stuffy, refined appearance of another generation with tweed jackets and conservative vests—suddenly found itself at the center of the fashion universe. Designers turned out their own variations of the business suit, tailoring the look for all occasions. Some of the decade's influential fashion trendsetters aped the corporate world on television, like the vixens and villains on the hit television shows *Dallas* and *Dynasty.*

For men, the new business look meant paisley or power red ties worn with fashionable suspenders or silk vests. Mimicking Michael Douglas's Gordon Gekko character in Oliver Stone's film *Wall Street,* many real-life brokers wore powder blue dress shirts with white collars and cuffs. Other trends included the return of the double-breasted suit (usually in dark blue) and oversized suit jackets with wide, padded shoulders.

By the end of the decade, however, a new look swept offices nationwide—casual Fridays. In the pressure-filled work world, giving workers a chance to relax their everyday formality by taking off their ties or wearing casual pants seemed revolutionary. Within a decade, most offices turned completely "business casual," cemented by the dot.com craze of the late 1990s. However, after the boom went bust, a return to formality made a comeback in the early 2000s. Today, the corporate world is a mix of business casual and more reserved dress.

MADONNA, MTV, AND FILM FASHION

Films were not the only trendsetters in the 1980s—the onset of Music Television (MTV) in 1983 found a youth market with money to spend, and the clothes and the looks of the rock stars whose videos were played on the 24-hour music station created a demand for high-end trends and thrift store rejects.

Madonna influenced styles in many ways via her music videos (see Music of the 1980s). Her changing styles with each new album earned her the label "chameleon;" however, by decade's end, the public was very aware that her style alterations were part of her own marketing savvy. With the release of her first album, *Madonna,* in 1982, Madonna's style was part guttersnipe, part mall chick with short, tight skirts, fishnet stockings, gloves, heavy eye make-up, mismatched earrings, and bows tied up in her two-toned hair. The look marked her as not only a renegade, but as a product of a commodified culture—appropriating discarded clothing to create a new style.

Madonna, as Susan in the movie *Desperately Seeking Susan* (1985) showed her eclectic style, which carried through to young women. Courtesy of Photofest.

This became more evident with the release of her second album, *Like A Virgin,* 1984. For a concert promoting this album and for her appearance on the first MTV Music Video Awards program, Madonna appeared in a restyled wedding gown with veil—the dress hem was cut mid-thigh—black lingerie, and a large crucifix. This look, much like the first, was soon replaced by a sense of glamour—a Marilyn Monroe persona with tight satins and beautifully coiffed hair for her "Material Girl" video.

With the release of her albums *True Blue,* 1987, and *Like a Prayer,* 1989, Madonna transformed herself using male-fantasy costumes of leather to take on a more dominatrix persona. In the video "Open Your Heart," she performs for men in a strip joint. The two-toned hair had been replaced by a short, sassy bleached bob. By the time she released *Like A Prayer,* the short hair had become synonymous with the performer, but her appropriation of male attire, designed by Jean Paul Gautier, for her video "Express Yourself" showed a more conscious playfulness. In this video, Madonna sports a double-breasted men's suit with slits cut in the front to accommodate—and to accentuate—her golden lingerie beneath. Possibly

Fashion

FASHION HIGHLIGHTS OF THE 1980s

Power dressing was the style of the 1980s: big shoulder pads, big hair, and power ties. Styles were also influenced by movies, television, and a book (preppy style). By the end of the decade, business casual was beginning to appear in some workplaces.

Women favored big shoulder pads and tight slim skirts.

Men often wore preppy styles, including polo and oxford shirts, power ties, crew neck sweaters, khaki pants, loafers/boat shoes.

Women wore *Flashdance-* inspired ripped sweatshirts and leg warmers; men emulated *Risky Business* with Ray Ban Wayfarer sunglasses and tousled hair; and men copied *Miami Vice* styles with T-shirts under unconstructed jackets in pastel colors.

Jeans and T-shirts remained popular. Females wore leggings with oversize sweaters or T-shirts.

Russian Youth and the Pop-Culture Rebellion

The mid-1980s were a pivotal period for the Soviet Union. Within the governing elite, elderly Communist Party hard-liners gave way to a younger group, led by Mikhail Gorbachev. His policies of *glasnost* (openness) and *perestroika* (restructuring) would eventually result in the dissolution of the USSR. At the same time, Soviet young people looked to the United States and the West to develop a sense of fashion and style that clearly separated them from older generations.

Cracks in the Soviet system were appearing in 1981, as its young people looked to American pop culture as never before. At first the changes were incremental. The "golden youth," children of high-level government bureaucrats, set trends with their American blue jeans and leather boots. Western-influenced Russian rock bands, long an underground phenomenon, ventured into the mainstream. Groups such as Aquarium and others released their first studio albums—but to the black market, not through the state's official record label.

By 1984, these trends had filtered throughout the country, and according to Western reporters, "for the first time, young people in Russian cities are beginning to look like young people anywhere else." Jeans were ubiquitous, T-shirts sported the logos of American products and even the American flag, and Adidas sneakers were in style. Rock music was played openly with little fear of reprisal. Kids adapted English phrases freely—*diski* for records, *dzhinsi* for jeans, *dzhaz* for jazz—and created their own Russian/English hybrid terms, like *khailaifist*, or "high-life-ist," one who reveled in high-end Western goods.

All this grated on Russians of an older generation. A 1984 edition of *Pravda* published sharply divergent views on American music and fashion. Traditionalists called for a ban on rock music, saying it would destroy Russian culture "like a Colorado beetle," and denounced young people who wore American emblems. The youth fired back: "When you can make jeans better than Levi's, that will be the time to start talking about national pride," one wrote. Clearly, fashion played a complex role in loosening Soviet culture and helped pave the way for additional Western influences.

Fashion

more than any other rock performer in history, Madonna set the fashion trends for the young women of the 1980s, changing the styles forced upon women for decades into the frisky accoutrements of empowered women.

For men, the 1980s were a time of appropriation as well, but of another sort. In addition to Armani's and Lauren's stylish cuts, men appropriated formal clothing for play as demonstrated in a number of music videos from England (namely those by Duran Duran, ABC, and Spandau Ballet), rolling up the sleeves of sport jackets and turning up the collars of their blazers to turn their formal wear into action wear. The hit show *Miami Vice* (NBC) took this trend one step further, replacing the shirt and tie combo with a delicate, silk T-shirt in a pastel color.

Other fashion trends became popular as a result of films. Women began wearing designer fitness wear everywhere. Bodysuits in bright flashy colors, topped by a ripped sweatshirt dangling off one shoulder a la *Flashdance*, 1983, with matching leg warmers and headbands became popular. Men began wearing Ray Ban sunglasses once Tom Cruise strutted his stuff in *Risky Business*, 1980; during a pivotal moment in the film, Cruise, wearing an Oxford shirt, white briefs, and his Ray Bans, dances to Bob Seger's "Old Time Rock n' Roll," a sure sign of desire for a limited rebellion.

TELEVISION FASHION

Miami Vice quickly earned its nickname "The MTV cop show" after its debut in 1984; it ran on NBC on Friday nights until 1989. The show acquired this nickname because of its innovative use of popular rock music to string together its episodes: its pulsating theme written by Jan Hammer reached number one on Billboard's "Hot 100" in a matter of weeks. The show's cinematography and editing techniques—quick, montage effects that contributed to the fast-pace and glossy look of the pastel-colored city—mirrored the process of the music video, made famous by MTV in 1981.

The series' stars contributed to this look as well. The two male leads, Sonny Crockett (Don Johnson) and Ricardo Tubbs (Philip Michael Thomas) donned colorful, fashionable clothes as they drove around Miami's glossy underbelly in cool cars and on pristine boats to capture drug lords in violent exchanges. The show was shot on-location in Miami, which added to the crisp, distinct look that the producers wanted in contrast to the criminal underworld that shaped each plot.

Other television shows featured less action, but just as much fashion. Dramas such as *Dallas* and *Dynasty* featured elegant stars often in full formalwear. *Dallas* mixed several styles, from urban cowboy chic to corporate boardroom formality as J. R. Ewing and his family mixed business and pleasure at the Southfork Ranch. *Dynasty* ushered in the shoulder-pad look that soon found its way into everyday wear for women nationwide.

Dynasty debuted on ABC on January 12, 1981, and stayed on the air until 1989. The show centered on Blake and Krystle Carrington (played by John Forsythe and Linda Evans). Evans dressed in sparkling gowns with opulent earrings that peeked out from under her frosted hair. Joan Collins played villain Alexis Colby, Krystle's archenemy. Collins wore flashier clothing, often including bright colored feathers and large jewels.

As *Dynasty* soared in the ratings, tie-in products hit the nation's shelves. One of the most successful was Evans's "Forever Krystle" perfume. Producers realized that many people tuned in each week just to see the latest fashions, so they hired a fashion designer, the first series to do so. Thousands of women contacted ABC to find out what designers Collins and Evans wore and where they could buy similar outfits.

Hairstyle and jewelry played an important role in the way *Dynasty* actresses portrayed their characters. Although Evans stuck closely to her feathered look, the other women on the show teased their hair to give it volume. The "big hair" look on *Dynasty* took the nation by storm and ushered in the style everywhere. Jewelry on the show was not confined simply to hands, fingers, and ears. Many

The television show *Dynasty* (1981–1989) ushered in the big hair, big shoulder style to the television-watching public in the 1980s. Shown from left: Joan Collins (as Alexis Morell Carrington Colby Dexter Rowan), John Forsythe (as Blake Carrington), Linda Evans (as Krystle Grant Jennings Carrington). © ABC-TV. Courtesy of Photofest.

Fashion

of the formal dresses were adorned with beads and sparkles that added an air of sophistication to the designs. The jewelry itself featured gaudy pieces, oversized earrings, and large gemstones (costume or real), which spoke to its owner's wealth.

Television shows continued to play an important role in setting fashion trends in the 1980s. In the beginning of the decade, the Farrah Fawcett long feathered hairstyle remained popular. However, the fitness craze mid-decade ushered in shorter styles, which many television stars mimicked. The fitness craze also brought leg warmers, headbands, and miniskirts back into vogue. Actresses on popular TV shows helped popularize these fads, like Lisa Hartman wearing headbands on the drama *Knots Landing* in the early 1980s.

TV shows even played a role in determining the kind of underwear people wore. Female actresses, such as *Moonlighting* star Cybill Shepherd, often wore the one-piece teddy, and baseball star Jim Palmer popularized men's Jockey underwear in commercials.

BUILDING RETAIL BRANDS

Two distinctly different kinds of stores dominate much of America's retail history—ornate department stores and discount stores, such as Woolworth's five-and-dimes. In the 1980s, shopping malls helped lead to the popularity of specialized retail stores. Suburbanization and more disposable income for middle-class Americans combined to give rise to malls both as meccas to consumerism and as places for teens to meet up with friends. Driven by young people's desire for affordable, yet fashionable clothes, companies that had had narrow audiences in the past suddenly became household names (and mall staples), including The Gap, Benetton, Ann Taylor, Banana Republic, and The Limited.

The Limited, founded in 1963 by Leslie Wexner, took off in the 1980s, becoming the largest, fastest-growing fashion chain in the country. By 1986, the Columbus, Ohio-based store sold more women's clothes and accessories than any other merchant in the world, leaving traditional stores such as J. C. Penney, Sears, and Kmart far behind. That year the company rang up sales of $2.4 billion in its 2,400 stores, with sales rising at an annual rate of 55 percent.

The Limited, the flagship store in Wexner's retail conglomerate, determined what was fashionable for millions of women. In 1983, when company buyers saw European teens buying bulky yachting sweaters in Florence, Italy, The Limited launched a line of their own under the private

Fashion

Shopping became a major form of entertainment and excursion for young women in the 1980s. A movie, *Valley Girl* (1983), directed by Martha Coolidge and featuring Elizabeth Daily (as Loryn) and Deborah Foreman (as Julie Richman), illustrated the interests of teenagers in suburban Los Angeles as wells as their fashions. Courtesy of Photofest.

label Forenza. The sweaters took the nation by storm and became mainstays in the wardrobes of women across the nation. Its goal of producing clothes that shoppers wanted to buy led The Limited to invest heavily in market research and testing, similar to other consumer companies, but quite revolutionary in the retail business. As a result, The Limited produced 200 million items of clothing in 1985, or 3 for every single woman in the United States between the ages of 15 and 55.

Ann Taylor, another national chain, also thrived in the decade. By mid-decade, the company had 65 stores in 17 states with sales growing 500 percent.

The Ann Taylor chain knew its target customer well—the woman who wanted to keep up with fashion, but not necessarily be a trendsetter, at reasonable prices. The company's typical shopper was female, aged 25 to 40 years old, with an income of $25,000 to $60,000. Demographically, Ann Taylor benefited from the size and purchasing power of the Baby Boomer generation.

In 1980, Benetton, the flagship store in Italy's fastest-growing fashion empire, opened a store in New York City. Within four years, the upscale chain, which catered to younger consumers, had 180 stores nationwide. For a company like Benetton, marketing to young women with disposable income determined its ultimate success, particularly in the fickle fashion market. However, the chain could trace much of its success to a highly efficient computerized inventory system, which linked its stores and revealed changing purchasing patterns.

Benetton's founder, Luciano Benetton, made clothing that was not only fashionable, with bright colors and interesting designs, but also relatively affordable. The worldwide success of Benetton powered its move into the United States. From 1980 to 1983, revenues jumped more than 50 percent to $271 million. Benetton also began a striking advertising campaign that promoted racial harmony and challenged authority.

Seattle-based Nordstrom solidified its place among 1980s retailers by becoming the national leader in customer service. The company performed this task so well that it changed the way its competitors dealt with its customers. From a financial point of view, the focus paid off. Nord-

strom's sales grew tenfold over the course of the decade, reaching $2.3 billion in 1988. The company also went national, expanding from 15 to 42 stores.

Nordstrom made simple moves that had dramatic effects on its customers. Rather than approach shoppers after 10 minutes, like most retailers, salespeople on the floor got to them in less than two minutes. They provided liberal merchandise returns policies. Nordstrom also put its salespeople on commission, which fostered a different mindset among the staff and reemphasized the importance of the customer.

In direct competition with retailing stalwarts Macy's and Bloomingdale's, Nordstrom stood out by providing a more relaxed atmosphere—open and airy—rather than the glitzy and glamorous that department stores usually employed. Nordstrom also provided small touches that customers enjoyed, such as a real pianist entertaining shoppers on a Baby Grand. From a fashion point

---

THE PREPPY LOOK

According to the *Official Preppy Handbook,* one is born a preppy. Following the fashion trends set by Ralph Lauren, the preppy look was a style characterized by name-brand clothing, always monogrammed, in fetching contrasts (such as pink and green), hair styled in the manner of the latest country club set, and tastes that ran from "Bloodies" in the morning to knowing the right taverns and restaurants at which to eat dinner (preppies never cooked).

The phenomenon that Lisa Birnbach spoofed in the *Handbook* was a real craze that came with the 1980s, mainly as a result of the conspicuous consumption many teens could enjoy with their affluence. Retail and designer names such as Ralph Lauren, L. L. Bean, and Izod became staples of the preppy wardrobe. Top-siders, loafers, and cuffed trousers were the staples of the blazer set. Typified by Michael J. Fox's character Alex P. Keaton on television's *Family Ties,* preppies were interested in making names for themselves in business (with their Ivy-League MBA) and marrying into the right families, preferably from the Connecticut suburbs, who had summer homes along the coast.

METALHEADS

Much the opposite of the Preppy, Metalhead was another style that became popular during the decade. Taking their name from the rock bands they adored, metalheads listened to what MTV branded "Heavy Metal"—a kind of rock music played by male bands, characterized by wailing guitars and loud, brash lyrics. The teens who listened to this music sought an alternative to pop music. They embraced the guitar-based, aggressive music because of its rebellious quality. Popular bands falling into this category include Motley Crue, Def Leppard, Bon Jovi, and Van Halen.

Rebelling against the pretty, synthesizer-based groups in constant rotation on MTV, headbangers wore T-shirts emblazoned with the logos of their favorite bands. Often they cut the sleeves off, turning them into "muscle shirts." Some metalheads mimicked the tight spandex clothing of their rock heroes and wore tight jeans adorned with various bandanas and holes. What the tattoo is to youth of the early 2000s, the earring was to teens in the 1980s. Headbangers pierced their ears and wore a variety of diamond studs, fish hooks, and dangling crosses.

The most popular hairstyle among rockers was long and teased with hairspray. Others let the back grow long, while keeping the front and sides shorter. This style became known as the "mullet." Headbangers imitated the hairstyles they saw on their heroes, such as the bushy manes of Van Halen frontman David Lee Roth or Jon Bon Jovi, which were actually rather androgynous.

of view, Nordstrom did not stray far from designers that appealed to its upper middle-class customers, such as Calvin Klein, Gianni Versace, and Donna Karan.

The customer service payoff for typical Nordstrom employees (young and college educated) included the opportunity to make upwards of $30,000 a year. Nordstrom often served as a first step in a retail career, either with the Seattle company or elsewhere in the industry. Tales of

extraordinary achievement, called "heroics" by execs, were trumpeted throughout the chain and served to build company lore. The same leaders, however, also pushed the sales staff to meet quotas and maintain the level of service that made the company famous.

Top Nordstrom salespeople earned the label "Pacesetters," which some people thought akin to earning varsity letters. In many respects, company officials used the analogy of a sports team at a pep rally to build camaraderie, but also to build internal competitions among the sales staff.

HAIRSTYLES OF THE 1980s

For many who lived in the decade, the 1980s is a fashion period that is best forgotten. While the fashion of the 1960s and 1970s was tied to a cultural revolution that began the "counterculture" movement, fashion in the 1980s was more ambiguous in origin and seemed to move in a multitude of directions at once. In the playground of hairstyle, the 1980s were a time of creativity and tremendous eccentricity. Following the comparative simplicity of hair fashion in the 1960s and 1970s, a variety of new hair styles were invented in the 1980s, and products of various kinds were used to create spikes, twists, and bangs that seemed to stretch into the atmosphere. The dominant theme was to make the hair seem big, both in extent and impact. Vibrant colors flooded the hair dye market, with blues, pinks, and magenta streaking across women's and men's hair. A variety of styles seemingly inspired from tribal fashions, like the "mohawk" and "liberty spikes," entered the mainstream on the heels of music and cultural movements. In more mainstream circles, men and women seemed dissatisfied with the standard division between short and long, giving rise to the "mullet" and other hairstyles that combined short bangs with a free-flowing hair in the back. In the twenty-first century, the hairstyles of the 1980s seem like a humorous side note in history, though the inventiveness of the era's stylists left its mark on history. Still, many now look at the eccentric styles of the age and can't help but ask, "What were they) thinking?" or worse, "What was *I* thinking?"

LEADING DESIGNERS OF THE 1980s

Giorgio Armani

Born in Italy in 1934, Giorgio Armani attended medical school for two years before signing on to complete his military requirements and taking up the hobby of photography. After the army, Armani worked in the famed La Rinascente, a department store, where he was first introduced to the possibilities of fashion as a career, designing their windows with his instinctive taste. He signed on to work with Nino Cerruti as a designer from 1961 to 1970, and embarked on a solo career as a designer shortly thereafter. His women's wear label was founded in 1970; he began designing his menswear label in 1974.

Armani's designs reached international popularity in the late 1970s, but his casual wear was not launched until 1981, setting off a global demand for his "designer jeans." In 1982, in addition to launching his first fragrance line, Armani began selling his designs for underwear and swimwear, gradually moving into accessories and eyewear by 1987.

Armani's clothes became the fashions of choice throughout Hollywood, and his style enhanced a number of films in the early 1980s. His costumes for Richard Gere in *American Gigolo* (1980) set the standard, and men everywhere wanted the sleek two-piece suit that Gere wore throughout his escapades as a male gigolo. Seven years later, Armani designed the costumes for Brian DePalma's remake of *The Untouchables* (1987), and his Depression-era suits, with large fedoras and vicuña coats, set the stage for a retro look that padded the shoulders of men's jackets and tapered their double-breasted suits.

Ralph Lauren

Born Ralph Lifshitz in New York City in 1939, the man who became "Ralph Lauren" never attended design school. He worked in the fashion industry as a retailer until 1967, when he launched his own line, Polo—named for the game that promotes an ideal of "discreet elegance and style." Lauren is credited with widening the men's tie, making it a more flamboyant article of clothing. By 1968, he was designing an entire menswear line of tailored suits in the style of European fashion designers.

By the 1980s, Lauren and his "Polo" emblem had transferred themselves into a multimillion dollar conglomerate with the popular mesh shirt in 24 colors in 1972, the fragrance and women's accessories line in 1973, and the women's wear line in 1974. The 1980s saw the creation of Lauren's home-style line, introducing home décor, luggage, and furniture to his ever-growing boutiques. The need for a central locale led Lauren to purchase the famous Rhinelander mansion on Madison and 72nd Street in New York and convert it into a showcase for his designs. The mansion, pushed into receivership after being neglected for almost 100 years, became the flagship store of Lauren's empire in 1986.

Lauren's approach to advertising has its roots in his love of film and photography. After opening his first boutiques, which were exclusively for men, in 1969, Lauren capitalized on his approach to style in a variety of 20-page ads beginning in 1974. This also coincided with his selection as chief costume designer for Jack Clayton's *The Great Gatsby* for Paramount Studios. By 1979, the ads had become a standard of the industry, and were used to sell Lauren's lines of casual clothes as well as his professional attire. The ads were considered revolutionary because they emphasized the ideal that clothes are as important as the lifestyle they characterize and because they used little to no copy—only the company's trademark. Lauren's success is predicated on his determination that Americans want to feel that they are part of the American Dream; his clothes and his trademark lifestyles have brought the glamorous life to every corner of the world.

Fashion

Food

of the 1980s

The changes taking place in the 1980s extended to the foods people ate and the methods they used to prepare meals. Americans were on the go, so their eating habits reflected society's increased speed. Fast food's popularity continued to grow and few homes were without a microwave oven. Microwaves and fast food made life easier for children home alone after school to make a quick snack or for single mothers or working parents to pick up or prepare meals. In the 1980s the traditional nuclear family was harder to find, and many households ate meals while watching television or playing video games.

A 1989 poll conducted by the Gallup Organization revealed that only about one in three adults dined at home with other people and engaged in conversation during meals without distractions. Most people—a whopping 64 percent—did some other activity while eating, such as watching television, working, or reading. Nearly half of the respondents said that their typical meal was frozen, packaged, or take out.

Large food corporations were quick to offer frozen foods suitable for microwaving. From 1984 to 1988, sales of frozen foods increased more than 300 percent, from $49 million to $153 million. Kraft, Campbell Soup Company, Hormel, and Betty Crocker led the way, putting frozen cakes, hamburgers, soup, finger foods, and hot dogs on the market.

One of the early movements toward healthy living, and fueled by America's need to look good, created a need for an artificial sweetener that did not prove as toxic as saccharin. In 1982, Nutra-Sweet was unveiled with great fanfare, causing sales of diet foods to skyrocket. Soon, almost every product on the shelves contained Nutra-Sweet, virtually turning any item—even ice cream and candy—into a dieter's delight.

Although Nutra-Sweet found its way into a multitude of products, the fitness craze that swept the 1980s caused people to look more closely at the foods they were consuming. Concern about additives and preservatives created a new market for organic produce, particularly among vegetarians, boosting the need and sales of items such as soymilk. America's taste became refined, and many people wanted more natural foods, which created avenues for newer, faster, and tastier products.

Changing lifestyles transformed the way people cooked in the decade. America's two-income families created a niche for microwave foods, which were easier for children and for working parents to prepare as meals. Everything from specialty dinners to pizzas became "microwavable." The appliance soon became a staple in every home.

FOOD HIGHLIGHTS OF THE 1980s

1982 Taco Bell replaces its logo—a sleeping Mexican in a sombrero—and removes any cultural references to Mexico from its décor when market research shows Americans distrust "Mexican" restaurants as being unhygienic.

1983 Meeting the trend for microwavable foods, Hot Pockets brand stuffed sandwiches arrive on the market. By 2008, the product line includes 22 different flavors.

1983 There are nearly 123,000 fast food establishments in America, triple the number that existed in 1963.

1984 American Popcorn Company, headquartered at One Fun Place, Sioux City, Iowa, introduces its first flavor of Jolly Time microwaveable popcorn.

1987 The California Raisin Advisory Board comes up with the California Raisins, animated singing and dancing raisins who not only become the board's spokesfruit, but spin off into children's books, musical recordings, a cartoon series, toys, and lunchboxes.

1988 Oscar Mayer launches Lunchables and creates a new food category, the lunch combination. Loosely based on the Japanese bento lunchbox, the prepackaged cheese, meat, and cracker lunches have wide appeal among time-pressed working parents who need to pack school lunches in a hurry.

1989 When asked by a Gallup poll what they were having for dinner, more than half of respondents said they were eating a packaged, frozen, or take-out meal.

FOOD CONSCIOUSNESS

It is no wonder that in a decade labeled the "Me Generation," people were consumed with the way they looked and felt. As a result, the public paid closer attention to the foods they ate and started reading and studying food labels. Dieting became a constant topic of office chatter and talk-show filler. The government and health organizations responded with efforts to educate the public by publishing a variety of guidelines and reports.

By releasing a series of frightening reports about the risks of unhealthy living, these agencies (both public and private) made food education an important issue. In 1980, for example, the National Research Council released "Toward Healthful Diets," a tract that linked dietary factors and chronic disease. At the end of the decade, the 10th Edition of the *Recommended Dietary Allowances* provided detailed information about the role of wholesome eating and long-term health. Perhaps for the first time in the country's history, the general public understood the consequences of an unhealthy diet.

Scientific evidence supported the research findings. By linking these figures to eating habits, then presenting them to a willing audience, officials informed the public about the evils of heart disease and other ailments. More than 1.25 million people had heart attacks each year, resulting in 500,000 deaths, but the number of deaths decreased in the 1980s because of medical innovations and changes in lifestyles. The government facilitated this decrease with the 1984 Coronary Primary Prevention Trial, which showed that lowering cholesterol levels greatly reduced fatal heart attacks. The results of this study were highlighted on a March 1984 cover of *Time* magazine, which showed a face made of two fried eggs and a frowning piece of bacon. The cover brought the discussion of cholesterol into the mainstream.

The government promoted the idea of cutting fat to prevent heart disease throughout the decade. The Surgeon General's office spearheaded the charge, along with the National Heart Lung and Blood Institute. Foods that aided in lowering cholesterol levels (bran, oatmeal, omega-3 acids, and so on) were featured in television commercials and other forms of advertising. Companies helped educate consumers, which led to increased sales.

The government worked to publicize heart disease, but also attacked the second leading cause of death in the 1980s—cancer—afflicting nearly 1,000,000 people annually and killing 400,000. The National Cancer Institute commissioned an early study examining the link between cancer and diet. Published by the Committee on Diet, Nutrition, and Cancer in 1982, the study showed that one-third of all cancer deaths are related to diet.

Major food companies responded to the increased education taking place by offering alternatives to traditional fare. Kraft, the second largest food company in the world in the decade, launched several "low fat" options in the late 1980s. The company developed Light French Dressing, Cholesterol Free Mayonnaise, and other healthy options in hopes of appealing to weight conscious customers. In 1983, Kraft introduced Planters Lite peanuts, which used a technological innovation that reduced the caloric content of peanuts by one-third.

DIETING

Dieting became a multibillion dollar industry in the 1980s. Bestselling book lists were filled with books that promised unwanted pounds would melt away. At least 24 diet books attained best seller status, with titles like *Fit for Life,* 1985, *Dr. Berger's Immune Power Diet,* 1985, and *The Beverley Hills Diet,* 1981. Countless fitness gurus, from actress Jane Fonda to Richard Simmons, promised to get people moving again, sweating or dancing away pounds. Ironically, in a decade filled with public education campaigns, many people trusted clearly misleading or erroneous advice found in many of the era's diet tomes.

The constant concern with dieting led to people losing, and then regaining weight, at an alarming rate. Researchers called these people "crash" or "yoyo" dieters. They were almost set up to fail, because the body's response to starvation is to slow metabolism, thus making it even more difficult to lose weight. When Oprah Winfrey appeared on her show in size 10 jeans claiming that she had lost 67 pounds on a liquid diet, countless women flocked to similar fads.[1]

Entire industries sprouted up to fulfill people's desire to lose weight. Managed weight loss centers, such as Weight Watchers, Nutri/System, and Jenny Craig, ran nearly constant commercials during daytime television hours, hoping to lure women into their pricey programs. Some people attempted to manage weight loss on their own, turning to meal replacement shakes and drinks, such as Medifast and Ultra Slim-Fast.

Oprah Winfrey shows off her new figure in 1988. She credited her 67-pound weight loss to a liquid diet and exercise. Her goal was to fit into size 10 blue jeans, which she wore for the first time on her national television show. AP Photo.

FAST FOOD

Ironically, in a decade so consumed with health and wellness, fast-food restaurants became a major staple of many Americans' diets in the 1980s. The nation's 130,000 fast-food restaurants rang up $60 billion in sales in 1988. The notion of quick, cheap food came into its own, developing into the modern fast-food industry that we see today.

Speed, rather than taste or nutrition, seemed the most important factor in the expansion of the fast-food industry. The widespread acceptance of the microwave in people's homes significantly increased the competition for customers. Restaurant executives realized that consumers didn't have to wait in lines to microwave food at home, and that the whole notion of what *fast* meant had changed dramatically; as a result, they altered their businesses significantly. Thus, fast-food chains searched for innovative ways to cut down on ordering time by using computer technology and even changing their physical appearance, removing seating areas that were basically unnecessary for customers on the go.

Rather than simply waiting for customers to come into fast food restaurants, many looked for new ways to reach people. Kentucky Fried Chicken and other restaurants toyed with the idea of home delivery. Pizza Hut, which prided itself on fast delivery, built mini-ovens and placed them where consumers would be, such as in student cafeterias, hospitals, and malls. It even attempted a nationwide, toll-free number so people wouldn't have to waste time looking in the phone book for the number of the closest branch.

Most of the 1980s witnessed double-digit sales growth in the fast-food industry. However, many corporations expanded too quickly, and the market became oversaturated. Labor, construction, real estate, and advertising costs squeezed some of the chains. Restaurants stopped at nothing to win market share, whether it meant changing their menus to appeal to health conscious eaters with salads and roasted chicken or beginning breakfast service. Pizza Hut began serving "personal" pan pizzas to bring in a larger lunch crowd, while Burger King introduced "Burger Bundles," bite-sized hamburgers sold in three- or six-packs. Companies outside the fast-food business also fought for customers by capitalizing on the notion of speed and convenience. Not only did McDonald's compete with Wendy's and Burger King, but convenience stores such as 7-Eleven offered an alternative with deli counters and microwavable entrees.

McDonald's grew into the industry leader, with sales in excess of $14 billion and providing service to 17 million customers a day at its 10,000 restaurants nationwide. The burger chain even became the second largest in chicken sales with the introduction of "Chicken McNuggets." The company's ongoing success allowed it to continue building stores in the best locations and to invest money into new innovations, such as the double-sided grill that cooked both sides of the hamburger at once. Its profitability also gave McDonald's more

HOW OTHERS SEE US

Fast Food, Slow Food

From 1967 into the 1980s, as McDonald's expanded as a global brand, reactions to the opening of franchises in Toronto, Paris, London, Hong Kong, Rome, and elsewhere varied widely. Where some saw "burger imperialism" and a capitalistic steamrolling of local custom and cuisine, others saw modernity and progress. ("It's like the coming of civilization to Moscow," said a Russian man as he polished off his first Big Mac in 1990.)

Italian journalist Carlo Petrini, on learning that the first Italian McDonald's was set to open in Rome's famous Piazza di Spagna, chose resistance. In 1986 he formed Arcigola, a group dedicated to the promotion and enjoyment of Italy's own foods, wines, and specialty dishes. Three years later, this Greenpeace-for-gourmands went international with a new name, Slow Food, and new chapters in Zurich, Brussels, Copenhagen, Stockholm, Vienna, Fez, New York, and San Francisco.

Rejecting critics' charges of elitism, snobbery, and anti-American bias, Petrini insisted that the trend toward mass-produced fast food was damaging nutritionally, socially, and ecologically, and that locally produced "slow foods" could be made accessible to people of all classes, at all income levels. "I'm not trying to overthrow the system," he said. "I'm hoping we can offer an alternative to the fast life. We won't throw bombs at McDonald's." Nearly two decades later, the movement had grown to encompass more than 83,000 members in 800 local branches around the world. "It's revolution with a spatula, not a Kalashnikov," as one reporter put it.

funds for marketing campaigns and signing celebrity endorsers.

NEW COKE

One of the most unsuccessful food changes involved an American tradition. Invented in 1886 by Dr. John Pemberton, Coca-Cola was the world's reigning soft drink in the early 1980s. Even with the advent of Pepsi Cola, Coke had maintained a popularity unsurpassed in the world of soft drinks, and its CEO Roberto Goizueta had proved a genius when in 1982 he introduced Diet Coke—a lower calorie version of Coca-Cola with a similar taste. In the mid 1980s, Goizueta had diversified Coke's assets into the acquisition of Columbia Pictures, adding to its cache as a major American corporation.

However, by 1985, Pepsi created a marketing campaign that centered on toppling Coke as the number one choice. "The Pepsi Challenge" ads, featuring celebrities like Michael J. Fox, Michael Jackson, and, for a very short time, Madonna, proved effective with the growing youth market. By mid-year, Coke sales, for the first time in history, trailed Pepsi sales by 1.7 percent—one third of Coke's total sales. Even though Coca-Cola's advertising budget surpassed $100 million that year, the soft drink began to feel that the challenge was threatening their hold on the American mindset. With the approaching centennial of Coca-Cola, Goizueta knew that a radical idea was necessary to help Coke triumph.

Therefore, Goizueta authorized the creation of a "New Coke," permitting the existing formula to be tampered with in order to create a new taste sensation. Conducting blind taste tests in their laboratories, scientists found that a slightly modified version of Coke proved more successful than Pepsi—sometimes by 18 points. With this sketchy result, the product was immediately marketed for wide distribution—even when the press, which had found out about the experiment, pointed out that their studies proved that most Americans objected to the experiment in the first place.

On April 23, 1985, "New Coke" was released—and almost immediately rejected. By mid-June, sales plummeted, and the reaction was swift and humiliating to the company. According to Michael Bastedo, the press likened the taste of New Coke to "sewer water, furniture polish" calling it "Coke for wimps" and likening the taste to that of "two day old Pepsi."[2] *Newsweek* likened the altering of the formula to "spitting on the flag;"[3] *Time* recorded the response to the drink in an interview with one Coke drinker: "At first I was numb.

Bottles and cans of "New Coke" from Coca-Cola are shown May 5, 1986. The release of the new version of Coke was a spectacular failure. AP Photo.

Then I was shocked. Then I started to jump and scream and run up and down."[4]

Immediately, "Old Coke" (as it was called by aficionados) became a luxury item. People began stockpiling cases of it in their homes, paying upward of $30 a case for it. Others used Fed-Ex to ship it to relatives in Canada. One Hollywood executive rented a $1,200 wine cellar to hold his 100 cases of Old Coke.[5]

Obviously, the strategy backfired, making the corporate heads at Coca-Cola look foolish. While the executives believed that the tampering would simply improve the product, the public outcry showed them immediately how wrong they were. By the end of 1986, when the company announced it would stop the production of the new product and return to making "Classic Coke," even Congress approved—"This is a very meaningful moment in the history of America," said Arkansas Senator David Pryor, "It shows some American institutions cannot be changed."[6]

NOUVELLE CUISINE

Characteristic of the 1980s, Nouvelle Cuisine became the staple of most trendy restaurants in America's big cities. Yet, while the concept appears to represent the faster pace of America's corporate world, the idea of carefully placing a small amount of food on a plate and charging exorbitant amounts for it had its birth many years earlier.

In 1969, Andre Gayot, Andre Gault, and Christian Millau founded a culinary magazine called *Le Nouveau Guide,* a monthly publication devoted to food and wine for chefs. First distributed in France, and eventually around the world, the magazine revealed the new strategies the chefs had concocted in their world-famous French kitchens. Seeing themselves as cultural revolutionaries, the chefs used their magazine to unveil a new way of thinking about food, wine, and presentation.

This magazine ran a manifesto, of sorts, unveiling a series of principles in food preparation and presentation. "First, a dinner was an opportunity to satisfy all our senses, beginning with sight."[7] Food was to be presented in an artistic fashion, taking color, texture, and form into consideration—almost as if the plate was the chef's canvas and the food his paint. Second, new methods of preparation were to be utilized, including food processors and state-of-the-art ovens. Third, quality and freshness of the food were paramount, minimizing the need for heavy sauces. Not only did this method go against the nineteenth-century notions of cooking and overloading, but also it blended well with the new American lifestyles emphasizing fitness and health.

QUICHE

Undoubtedly, the most maligned food of the 1980s was the quiche—the savory cheese pie made from eggs, Swiss cheese, bacon, onions, and cream. Quiche became a symbol of all that was wrong with the redefined ideas of masculinity in the 1980s. Historically, the dish was a favorite of the French. When it was introduced to Americans in the late 1970s, restaurants began to experiment with the pie, adding mushrooms, tomatoes, asparagus, and broccoli to the egg mixture, making it a vegetarian dish.

In 1982, author Bruce Feirstein released his humorous "guidebook to all that is truly masculine," *Real Men Don't Eat Quiche.* The book sold millions of copies, becoming an overnight best seller on the *New York Times* list and steering sensitive men toward the path of rugged individualism. Correlating the quiche to effeminate behavior branded it as something un-American.

Later in the book, in the chapter titled, "The Real Man's Nutritional Guide," Feirstein spelled out the ingredients of a properly masculine diet. Though the book's humor makes as much fun of the "Real Man" as the effeminate man, it is clear to see that the homophobic jokes of the text still paint a seriously skewed impression of the 1980s—a time when a simple dish like a quiche caused an entire gender to think twice about what they ordered at a restaurant.

Food

Music

of the 1980s

Several technological innovations in the 1980s changed how people listened to music. The most significant change came with the development of the Compact Disc, or "CD," a plastic, metallic disc that could not only hold more music than a traditional vinyl album, but also protect musical purity. The creation of the CD-player made the record player with its diamond-tipped stylus obsolete and turned "record stores" into very different places than they had been previously. Another change was that small transistors made music more mobile. Consumers sported "Walkmen"—personal stereos that played audio tapes or CDs—as they jogged, rode the subways, or walked.

In 1983, the music scene in America was changed forever when a new television station, Music Television (MTV), began broadcasting from Manhattan. Blending "the music of today" with the cinematic possibilities of videotape, the joint venture between Warner Communications and American Express created a 24-hour television station devoted to airing 1,000 video titles in its first year. The music television phenomenon caught on quickly.

MTV transformed the music industry almost immediately, but also had larger implications. The cable station turned into a true capitalist phenomenon, given its ability to market and sell to America's youth. Videos had began as promo-clips

in Europe in 1976, designed to sell bands to disco dancers and television viewers in suburban areas. When the video came to America, however, big budgets found a way to create stars of band members. The rules for success in the music business changed quickly. Traditionally, a new group built a fan base by constantly touring. With the rise of MTV, a band had to have "video potential" in addition to musical talent as record companies quickly budgeted for this new medium.

In short order, videos affected music sales. Few bands proved the power of videos more than British pop sensation Duran Duran. The band featured heavily synthesized dance beats and catchy lyrics, but more important in the MTV age, good looks and high fashion. *Newsweek* magazine's Eric Gelman reported that prior to the risqué video for "Girls on Film," Duran Duran's album *Rio* couldn't even break into the Billboard Top 100 albums. The publicity generated by the video, however, led MTV executives to put the group's next release into heavy rotation. After four months on the music network, *Rio* broke into the Billboard Top 10 and sold more than 1 million copies.

The fact that videos exposed bands and sold records made record company budgets soar as each one tried to capitalize on the trend. Record companies were willing to sink large sums into videos because successful videos dramatically

POP MUSIC IN THE 1980s

When it comes to musical eccentricity, few periods can match the experimental flavor of the 1980s. Pop music of the 1980s combined newly emerging electronic instrumentation with the fashion and sensibilities of the British punk and post punk music scenes. A number of British artists, like Pink Floyd and David Bowie, rivaled domestic artists in terms of both mass appeal and influence. The 1980s has been called the "forgotten decade" because so much of the cultural development, from clothing and hairstyles to music, seems like more of a cultural pit stop than a period of significant importance. In contrast to this popular view, many songs of the 1980s have remained remarkably popular for over 20 years. While early electronic instruments may sound dated by modern standards, the integration of new technology was certainly innovative at the time. As the computer age was reaching its adolescence, American pop joined in for the ride as a variety of beeps, clicks, and synthesized instruments replaced the guitar, bass, and drums of earlier decades. It was also during this decade that the video became popular, fueled by the emergence of MTV (Music Television), and sparked a worldwide phenomenon in the combination of visual and musical media. Though 80s pop is sometimes laughed at for its eccentricity, the pop music of the day has left an impression on the industry and on the culture, encouraging a generation of artists not to fear experimentation.

improved CD sales. MTV provided the boost that the sagging record companies needed, and it created a number of music video stars who became household names.

MICHAEL JACKSON

For many, Michael Jackson epitomizes the 1980s. His album *Thriller,* released in 1982, spawned seven Top 10 singles and eight Grammy awards. Songs like "Billie Jean" and the title track, "Thriller," defined the era, not only reinvigorating dance music in mainstream America, but

taking music videos to new heights. When *Rolling Stone* magazine released its list of the 500 greatest albums of all time in 2003, *Thriller* came in at number 20, based largely on its 37-week stay at number one and sales of 26 million.

Born in 1958 in Gary, Indiana, Michael Jackson was the fifth son in a large working-class family. The boys were urged to sing by their mother, who sang in the church choir, and their father Joe, who played guitar part time in a small blues band. In 1970, Joe traveled to Detroit with his sons to form The Jackson 5, who eventually released 13 albums on the Motown record label. The Jackson 5 had a string of hits, and many people considered the group the premier rhythm and blues/soul band in the country. The Jackson 5 became a popular culture phenomenon, even launching a Saturday morning animated cartoon. Michael, the youngest and "cutest" Jackson, served as the group's front man, dazzling audiences with his singing and dance moves.

In 1977, the group signed with Epic Records and changed their name to "The Jacksons," but they were unable to maintain their popularity. In 1979, Michael recorded his first solo effort *Off the Wall,* with producer Quincy Jones.

Thriller (1983 video short). Directed by John Landis. Shown: Michael Jackson. Courtesy of Photofest.

Jones also produced Jackson's second solo album, *Thriller*. The album catapulted Jackson into the limelight for both the quality of the songs and the frequent playing of the videos on MTV. Jackson quickly transformed from pop star to music legend.

Jackson's videos for *Thriller* were legendary because of the performer's street-wise beats and his amazing dancing. The first single, "Billie Jean," narrates a story about a one-night stand that results in a baby. The video's stylish look splits the screen into thirds and showcases Jackson's modern look and his incredible abilities as a dancer. It is in this video that Jackson sports a single sequined glove on one hand and wears matching socks. The singer's tuxedo, made of shiny black leather and outfitted with a purple satin bowtie, suits the moody look of the video. In one of the more memorable elements of the video, the panels

of the sidewalk light up as Jackson dances across them, providing the only bright light in the piece. "Billie Jean" proved a phenomenal hit and set the bar for videos that followed.

Loosely based on *West Side Story*, the video of the album's second release, "Beat It," features Jackson taking on the persona of a negotiator between two rival gangs. He struts about dressed in red leather, while the song pulsates with an urgency that culminates in him leading both gangs into a dance that is both physically challenging and masculine. Soon after the release of "Beat It," many kids, even those in suburban white neighborhoods, began sporting a single sequined glove and red leather jackets.

The release of Jackson's epic video for "Thriller" turned into a worldwide event, which MTV milked for publicity. Directed by John Landis, the 17-minute video paid homage to horror films by

Beat Street (1984), told the story of young hip hop artists trying to break into show biz. Here Robert Taylor demonstrates some excellent breakdancing. Courtesy of Photofest.

BREAKDANCING

The urban dance craze known as "breakdancing" had its roots in the "hip hop" urban culture of the late 1970s. Featuring a blend of movements inspired by traditional African dancing, modern jazz, ballet, tap, and acrobatic moves that resemble martial arts, breakdancing started as a "street" dancing style. Breakdancers performed in clubs and in the streets, where breakdancing developed into a type of battle dance, halfway between street fighting and ballet, with breakdance "crews" competing for bragging rights and respect. From the inner city streets, breakdancing was popularized by hip hop artists of the early 1980s like Afrika Bambaataa of the Universal Zulu Nation. The obvious passion and athletic skill of breakdancing allowed the style to become popular far from the inner city streets of New York and Los Angeles. Some breakdancing moves, like the "moonwalk" that was famously performed by pop star Michael Jackson, began seeping into mainstream pop culture. Within a few years, breakdancing moves were popular everywhere from middle school dances to modern jazz performances. Though breakdancing peaked in the 1980s, it remained part of hip-hop and urban culture into the twenty-first century and played a role in the development of the next generation of street dances, including the "clown" and "krump" dancing of the Los Angeles dance scene.

opening in a theater where Jackson and his date watch *I Was a Teenage Werewolf* starring Jackson on the big screen in the Michael Landon role.

The video featured state of the art computer graphics and cinematography. In one scene, Jackson "morphs" from human to werewolf using computer graphics to make the transformation seem smooth and therefore more frightening. As Jackson and his date leave the theater, they find themselves surrounded by ghouls, who join Jackson in a stylish dance number, reminiscent of old film musicals.

MTV announced the times the video would play throughout the day, intensifying the movie-like feeling. "Thriller" made an important contribution to MTV's legacy—the video was released on VHS home video with a behind-the-scenes documentary that recorded how the video was made. The 60-minute tape sold millions of copies, making it the first such venture of its kind. *Thriller* not only revealed that MTV was a commodity that people wanted, but it ensured that it was here to stay.

MADONNA

Like Michael Jackson, Madonna defines the 1980s. Seemingly overnight, she emerged from nowhere to become a music icon. Madonna's music has been purchased by hoards of fans and maligned by industry critics since she first appeared on the scene in 1983. No artist of the 1980s had a larger effect on the cultural landscape than Madonna.

Born in Michigan, Louise Ciccone moved to New York City with dreams of becoming a ballerina in 1977. After studying with Alvin Ailey, she joined a few Village repertory dance companies before signing on to Sire Records as a solo performer. Adopting her mother's maiden name, "Madonna" quickly made a name for herself in the bustling club circuits with her first singles in 1982.

Madonna's self-titled debut album was released in 1983. The first single, "Holiday," was a catchy dance number that emphasized the beat and downplayed Madonna's tinny voice. "Holiday" enjoyed some success, but it was Madonna's video for MTV, "Borderline," that pushed her into the stratosphere. When the song broke the Top 10 in March 1984, it became the first of her 17 consecutive Top 10 hits—an industry record for a female solo performer.

The songs from Madonna's first album have a frisky, disco dance quality that appealed to a variety of consumers. The carefully packaged videos introduced Madonna to the world decked out in leather, lingerie, and two-toned hair, lace gloves, high-heeled boots, and a belt buckle emblazed with "Boy Toy."

Fun and sexy, the videos from Madonna's second album *Like a Virgin* playfully maligned the role of men in the world. The album sent young female teens, called "wannabes," to thrift shops in droves hoping to find styles that mimicked Madonna, further establishing her as a cultural lightning rod. (See Fashion of the 1980s.) Selling millions of records solidified her status as a major force in the record industry.

Madonna caused an uproar among conservatives when she appropriated religious and virginal wedding attire for the video to "Like A Virgin." In a live performance of the song on the "MTV Music Awards," Madonna slithered across the floor, dripping sexuality. Many parents of teenage girls were up in arms over Madonna's influence and her videos. Her freewheeling sexuality challenged societal norms.

The second release from the album *Material Girl* solidified Madonna's reputation as a chameleon, as she transformed herself from "guttersnipe" to a Marilyn Monroe look-alike in a video that employed a visual pastiche of Monroe's number "Diamonds Are A Girl's Best Friend," staged by Howard Hawks for the film *Gentlemen Prefer Blondes* (1953). The video's parallel structure allowed Madonna to be seen as both a man-eating "material girl" and a more down-to-earth alter ego. Many popular culturists read Madonna through this video as the symbol of the affluent, self-centeredness that pervaded the culture. That was the power of MTV—its immediate link to the popular culture and the populace. Madonna learned early to use it to her advantage, and her stardom shows how careful she was to control the process.

In 1986, Madonna courted more controversy with the first videos from her new album *True Blue.* The best of these was the video for "Open Your Heart," directed by Louis Malle. Famed still photographer Herb Ritts, who took the cover photograph for the album, shot the video, giving it a cinematic feel and emphasizing Madonna's newly shorn and bleached hair. The video showcased Madonna's training as a dancer and her willingness to become the center of attention. In it, Madonna performs in a peep show wearing a black leather bustier and fish net stockings, spinning about a bentwood chair *à la* Bob Fosse.

Of course, controversy surrounded the video, mainly because the character Madonna played in the video had the charge of a small, seemingly innocent Italian boy who waited for her outside while she "worked"—Malle employed a cross-cut technique to show that while she dances inside, he struts about outside imitating her suggestive movements in front of a poster advertising her performances. As she leaves work for the evening, she joins him outside, bestowing a long, sensuous kiss on his lips. The two dance off together into the sunset in a nod to the innocent "road movies." However, the image of this young boy being entrusted to this type of woman sent many into a panic.

With the release of *Like a Prayer* (1989), Madonna once more found herself in controversy, as the video for the title track toyed with her Catholic heritage and her questioning of organized religion. Pepsi-Cola, the soft-drink giant, entered into a multimillion dollar contract with the singer to back a tour for the new album, in return for the use of "Like a Prayer" as a commercial tie-in. The ensuing controversy, orchestrated by right-wing conservatives, caused Pepsi to back out of the contract. In the video accompanying the song, Madonna—now brunette—performs with a black gospel choir on stage, simulating a passion play of sorts. Again, the structure employs a dual narrative: in one, Madonna pauses before a statue of a black Christ, kisses his feet, and receives his suggestive embrace as he comes to life; in the second, Madonna witnesses an attempted rape perpetrated by white skinheads and the same black man is arrested for the crime.

Feminists embraced the video for its overt confrontation of the Catholic Church and its reach toward social responsibility, as the Madonna character tells the police what happened, freeing the young black. Yet, the conservative public demanded punishment, pressuring Pepsi to pull out of its obligation.

HAIR METAL

In the 1980s, heavy metal musicians, raised on bands like Led Zeppelin, Kiss, and Black Sabbath, fused hard rock with an overt image consciousness to form the hair metal (or glam metal) wave. Strong on guitar licks and melodic choruses, but cognizant of costumes and hair spray, groups like

Mötley Crüe, Van Halen, Def Leppard, and Bon Jovi exploded onto the scene, promoted almost equally by MTV and tales of bad-boy escapades.

In the early part of the decade, two bands dominated the scene: the U.K.'s Def Leppard and Van Halen from the United States. In 1983, Def Leppard released *Pyromania.* The first single, "Photograph," sparked a headline tour across the country. Sales for the album surpassed seven million in America alone. Def Leppard almost came to an end the next year when drummer Rick Allen lost his left arm in an auto accident. Allen, however, surprised audiences by learning to drum one-handed, and the band played on.

Def Leppard remained a musical force throughout the 1980s, but took a secondary position for several years after *Pyromania* as young, Los Angeles-based bands stole the spotlight. The band retooled its sound, getting bigger and more anthem-like. In late 1987, Def Leppard put out *Hysteria,* led by the single "Pour Some Sugar on Me." Def Leppard played 227 shows to promote the album in 1987 and 1988. The album had a total of seven hit singles and constant rotation on MTV, which led to 16 million albums sold worldwide.

In the late 1970s, the group Van Halen rose from the streets of Los Angeles, led by front man David Lee Roth and guitarist Eddie Van Halen. The group released its self-titled debut album in 1978, which set off a string of five bestselling albums, culminating in *1984,* which sold 10 million copies. Van Halen had a unique sound, but also rode the music video wave, first with a fun-filled romp through "Jump," then in a hilarious take on the single "Hot for Teacher." Roth's video persona

Glam metal band Mötley Crüe. Nikki Sixx, Mick Mars, Vince Neil, Tommy Lee. Courtesy of Photofest.

Music

"Diamond Dave" wore multicolored tights, did high-flying karate kicks on stage, and sported long, bleached blond hair. His larger-than-life antics were countered by Van Halen's blistering guitar and ever-present smirk.

Despite reigning over the rock world since their influential debut album, animosities between Roth and Eddie Van Halen split the band apart. The original Van Halen lineup broke up in 1985. Van Halen replaced Roth with Sammy Hagar, a successful solo artist who shared their artistic influences and freewheeling lifestyle.

Van Halen released *5150* in 1986, and the disk quickly climbed to number one on the Billboard album charts, a first for the band. A string of singles, including "Why Can't This Be Love," "Dreams," and "Best of Both Worlds," introduced Van Halen fans to a new sound, which some found too much like the era's pop music, particularly with the heavy use of keyboards and synthesizers. Two years later, Van Halen (dubbed by many "Van Hagar" to distinguish it from earlier days) released *OU812,* another pop-driven album that fans bought in droves, but that further alienated many early Van Halen devotees.

The successes of Van Halen and Def Leppard paved the way for other hair metal bands, but many used MTV's influence and stories of wild partying to establish themselves. Los Angeles served as one proving ground for glam metal groups, with Motley Crue opening doors for later acts such as Poison and Guns N' Roses.

Mötley Crüe released a string of multiplatinum albums, including *Shout at the Devil,* 1983, *Theatre of Pain,* 1985, *Girls, Girls, Girls,* 1987, and *Dr. Feelgood,* 1989, which became the group's only number one album. Early in the band's career, its members wore heavy androgynous makeup and looked nearly feminine. As the glam wave spread, however, Mötley Crüe adopted a tougher look, though still with multicolored leather clothing and teased locks. Hair bands could not afford to look too soft and possibly offend male fans who drove their sales.

Fueling Mötley Crüe's power was the way the band mastered videos, gaining a wide audience among the MTV crowd. Mötley Crüe also embodied the rock star lifestyle of drugs, partying, sex, and decadence.

Glam rock continued to do well in the 1980s, but a change loomed on the horizon. Hair metal lost its edge as it gained in popularity. Too many fans turned away from the pop-oriented songs and ballads being churned out by second-rate bands like Europe, which hit number one with the schmaltzy single "The Final Countdown" in 1986.

Guns N' Roses (GN'R) helped close the door on hair metal by revealing a darker side to the music that groups like Bon Jovi, Cinderella, and Poison could not duplicate. Led by front man W. Axl Rose and guitarist Slash, Guns N' Roses released the seminal *Appetite for Destruction* in 1987. Riding the wave of hair metal, but providing a grittier version, the disk hit number one and eventually sold 20 million copies. Three singles ("Welcome to the Jungle," "Sweet Child O'Mine," and "Paradise City") spent time in the top 10 and were popular videos in constant rotation on MTV. Tales of excess followed GN'R around the world as the band toured to promote the album.

In 1988, Guns N' Roses caused an uproar with the song "One in A Million" on its *G N' R Lies* CD. The lyrics included references to "niggers" and "faggots," which Rose claimed reflected the societal problems in America. Critics, however, took the band to task for its words and actions. The adverse publicity fueled the band's notoriety and record sales. Guns N' Roses churned out new songs as the decade ended, releasing two separate albums on the same date in 1991, *Use Your*

Music

HIT SONGS OF THE 1980s

"Another Brick in the Wall" (Pink Floyd)—1980

"(Just Like) Starting Over" (John Lennon)—1980

"Billie Jean" (Michael Jackson)—1983

"Every Breath You Take" (The Police)—1983

"Jump" (Van Halen)—1984

"Like a Virgin" (Madonna)—1984

"We Are the World" (USA for Africa)—1985

"Walk Like an Egyptian" (Bangles)—1986

"I Wanna Dance With Somebody (Who Loves Me)" (Whitney Houston)—1987

"With or Without You" (U2)—1987

Illusion I and *Use Your Illusion II.* The gimmick paid off as the disks debuted holding the top two spots on the Billboard charts.

THE NEW BRITISH INVASION

Duran Duran

In 1962, The Beatles released their first album and made their first tour of America, bringing with them a new sound that quickly galvanized America's youth. In 1983, as MTV began in America, videos had already been circulating in the clubs of Europe, making record producers and industry critics agree that the Brits had, once more, cornered the initial market, producing clever, meaningful videos that celebrated the culture and sold bands.

The new British Invasion benefited groups like Duran Duran, who excelled at producing modern pop music and stylish, popular videos. Founded as a punk-oriented band in 1978 in Birmingham, England, the initial members—Nick Rhodes, John Taylor, Andy Taylor, and Roger Taylor—played in small pubs with one major disadvantage; these talented musician/songwriters needed a lead singer. In 1980, they met an acting student in London named Simon Le Bon.

As the newly-energized group began to make a global name for themselves, they exerted more control over their video efforts, pushing the form in a number of positive ways, including the use of computer-generated animation.

The group became an international sensation with the advent of MTV and their video for "Hungry Like the Wolf." Filmed in an exotic jungle setting, the video places the band in tropics reminiscent of *Raiders of the Lost Ark,* dressed in safari outfits as they stalk the "wolf"—a bevy of beautiful models sporting day-glow lines painted all over their bodies. The song's catchy dance rhythm and haunting lyrics blend with the vibrant colors and lush splendor. In 1983 the video won the first Grammy Award for a video.

As the 1980s progressed, Duran Duran began to take more risks, creating a body of video work that is still viewed by many as groundbreaking. For their next album, *Seven and the Ragged Tiger,* the group blended animation with live performance to create the video for "The Reflex," a song that quickly went to number one. Their video for the "The Wild Boys" is one of their more ambitious videos. It is a celebration of boisterous activity—those boyish antics that defy authority. The video opens in a classroom, and the "boys" sit dressed in their Etonian best, listening to a teacher. As the song picks up momentum, the boys begin to rebel, smashing their desks about the room, embracing the freedom of anarchy.

These images are intercut with those of a futuristic series of male warriors dancing in unison as members of the band seek to rescue lead singer, Simon Le Bon, who is tied to a windmill that spins him about, ducking his head under water as it goes around. The singer continues to lip-synch the song as he boldly looks into the camera, obviously defying his captors. Once the band frees him, Le Bon enters the water, only to be assaulted by some *Alien*-like creature. As the song ends, and the camera pans the destroyed, abandoned classroom and the warriors return to their dance, the video registers as an apocalyptic reminder of the fine line between chaos and control.

George Michael

Born Georgios Kyriacos Panayioutou in 1963, George Michael grew up in a working class ghetto of London. After playing in a number of street bands, he formed a partnership with another student named Andrew Ridgley, and together they recorded as Wham. The duo's first album *Fantastic* hit number one in the United Kingdom, and their second effort *Make It Big* hit number one in the United States as well. *Make It Big* scored as a direct result of the fun, campy video for "Wake Me Up Before You Go-Go," a joyfully banal celebration of life.

After the second album, George decided to leave the group to perform as a solo artist. His first album, *Faith,* helped redefine the capabilities of video performance, which re-invented Michael's image from clean cut and carefree to black leather chaps and a three-day stubble. The album sold eight million copies and spawned four number one singles, earning Michael a 1988 Grammy for Album of the Year.

Music

The videos for *Faith* are directly responsible for Michael's success. Using his good looks to his advantage, the videos position him as a masculine sex object. For instance, the video for the cover single shows glimpses of parts of his body: a strong profile in one shot, his ever-present stubble upon his chin; a flash of his derriere in another, shaking to the beat of the song, clad in tight jeans. In the video for another hit, "I Want Your Sex," Michael courted controversy, appearing naked as he scrawls "Explore Monogamy" across the back of his female lover in red lipstick. The video for "Father Figure" brought Michael the most fame as the ballad hauntingly recounts a tale of dominant desire. Filmed in muted colors with stop-action photography, the images cut between Michael driving a cab, and a female model, haunted by the memory of their coupling, deciding to move on to a more successful photographer. The "Father Figure" video experiments with openly using images to complicate the song rather than overtly illustrating it.

Michael rejected his music company's plan for further sexualized videos toward the end of the 1980s, and did not appear in videos for his next album *Listen Without Prejudice*. Interestingly, the album failed.

MALE SOLO PERFORMERS

In addition to creating icons, MTV affected the gender roles in America, in some cases strongly delineating the stereotypical roles of men and women, and in others blurring the lines between women and men by celebrating androgyny.

Bruce Springsteen

The persona that Bruce Springsteen honed during the 1970s served him well in the 1980s, helping him become one of the most respected musicians in history. His album *Born in the USA* (1984) contributed to his iconographic image as a masculine ideal.

Born in Freehold, New Jersey in 1949, Springsteen grew up in a fairly typical middle-class environment, beginning guitar lessons in high school. After he graduated, he traveled to New York City, where he tried to make it big in the folk music scene of the Village. His failure to do so brought him back to Ashbury Park, New Jersey, where he began performing in small bands until one of his own creation, the E-Street Band, found a spot on the local venue.

Their first album, *Greetings from Asbury Park, NJ* (1973) won critical praise, but little audience attention. In 1974, he released his next album *Born to Run,* which became a hit as his sound began to filter into the rock scene.

Springsteen opened the 1980s with a double album, *The River,* which went platinum in a number of weeks due to the instant success of his first number one single, "Hungry Heart." In 1984, the album *Born in the USA* sold 20 million copies and launched a world tour that lasted two years. This album brought "The Boss" to MTV and the videos he made for the singles reveal much about the masculine ideal the singer represented.

Some of the videos for the *Born in the USA* album emphasized Springsteen performing with his band, strutting across the stages of America in front of thousands of cheering fans. In "Dancing in the Dark," Springsteen pulls a young woman from the audience (a young Courtney Cox) to dance to the song, every concert-goer's dream. The video for the title track was also this type of performance video, but with a savage political edge, intercut with images of the Vietnam Memorial and close-ups of Vietnam vets in the audience. As the song speaks of the irony of being "Born in the USA" to a land of privilege and freedom, the images sharply illustrate the plight of the veterans, crippled and forgotten by the policies of the Reagan administration.

The video's closing image of Springsteen facing an American flag, dressed in white T-shirt and blue jeans (as on the album's cover) and looking back over his shoulder, became one of the most charged political images of the 1980s. In it, "The Boss" looks directly into the camera—at his audience—daring them to remain complacent.

However, the video also provides an interesting illustration of the generation gap caused by MTV. For his 1984 re-election campaign, Ronald Reagan's strategists began playing "Born in the USA" at rallies, hoping to incorporate it into a new campaign anthem. Missing the irony of the lyrics completely, the Republicans only heard the song's refrain, believing it suited Reagan's message of a better tomorrow. They only ceased using the song when Springsteen threatened to sue the Republican National Committee. Springsteen's image as a political rebel, a masculine man-of-the-people, and as a common man was eventually embraced by the Democrats—a party more suited to Springsteen's personal ideology—when they worked to elect Bill Clinton in 1992.

Prince

Prince stood on the other end of the masculinity barometer on MTV. The artist fused an urban funk beat with pop and rock to reshape the musical terrain in the 1980s. His soundtrack from his feature film debut, *Purple Rain,* made him one of the most celebrated artists of the decade, bringing him both a Grammy and an Oscar. Prince's videos for *Purple Rain* were mainly pulled from the film and revealed a different kind of American masculinity. Prince created an image more androgynous and street-smart savvy than Springsteen's "common man."

Prince's 1982 album *1999* sold more than 3,000,000 copies and the videos for his songs "Delirious" and "Little Red Corvette" introduced him to America's living rooms. The soundtrack for *Purple Rain* (1984) spent 20 weeks at number one, and yielded four Top 10 singles.

The videos that accompanied Prince's *Purple Rain* were mainly advertisements for the film—trailers with additional footage of the provocative performer in various states of undress ("When Doves Cry") or in performance ("Let's Go Crazy"). Despite adopting an androgynous persona, including heavy makeup and eyeliner, Prince exuded heterosexual sexuality and manliness. Although the nation seemed to skew toward conservative thinking in the 1980s, the music industry had room for different brands of masculinity, represented on different ends by Springsteen and Prince. Ultimately, the viewing public demanded this variety, nudged along by what MTV programmers thought would sell.

Prince's video for "When Doves Cry" featured a supposedly naked Prince in a bathtub, gazing into the camera while singing the opening lyrics. His hair is long and curled and his mascara evident, even though the room is filled with steam. After cutting to scenes from the film, the video returns to the star, who is this time crawling across the floor like a cat. The video intercuts this crawling with more scenes from the film before cutting completely away from the bath to a performance space, where Prince performs with his band, all of whom are dressed in glittery tailcoats and frilly blouses. Prince's own outfit is a skin-tight, lime green bolero jacket and tight trousers, and he wears a large purple hat with a veil. Again, his features are heavily made-up with mascara and eye shadow, much like the other members of his band. The video, however, shows the star as sexy, provocative, and daring.

Prince's adoring fans interpreted his appearance as more punk and funk influenced than feminized. Prince's effect on the ideas concerning masculinity is almost as important as his contribution to the music of the era—he offered another look at man, one that embraced a desire for show and glamour, but that was still heterosexually charged.

FEMALE SOLO PERFORMERS

MTV redefined common perceptions of women with the rock-music video. In a 1985 *Newsweek* article, Jim Miller argued that 1980s female musicians were firmly ensconced in the day's gritty reality, no longer willing to sing mindless songs about pretty rainbows or first loves. The music world began to change for women after only two years of MTV. More importantly, their music and style helped transform the way Americans thought about women.

Cyndi Lauper

Born in New York, Cyndi Lauper learned the guitar at an early age and began singing professionally after dropping out of high school. After touring with a few small bands in the 1970s, she began a solo career in 1980 and released her first album, *She's So Unusual,* in 1983. The album sold nine million copies in the United States and garnered four Top 10 singles. Lauper won a Grammy in 1984 and many "Best New Artist" awards. After a world tour in 1985, she released a second album, *True Colors.* Her new, more mature sound did not mix well with the MTV crowd, so the album did not sell as well. However, the title track ballad went platinum.

Lauper's first single, "Girls Just Want to Have Fun," became an anthem for young women across America. Lauper's outrageous appearance–bright red dyed hair, shaved on one side, tons of costume jewelry, and dressed in an outfit half thrift store chic and half remnants from a fire sale, drew in young MTV fans who wanted to emulate her style. Lauper's friends in the video come from all walks of life—girls dressed in colorful, daring clothes with hair dyed every color of the rainbow. As they dance about the streets, joined here and there by handsome boys, the video clearly illustrates the song's intended message: that girls—young women—deserve just as much right to "have fun" as young men, without society thinking less of them.

Lauper's other releases from this album also became anthems of the MTV crowd, but her video for "She Bop" rocked the censors as it proclaimed women's rights to not only talk openly about reading pornography, but masturbate to it as well. The video for "She Bop" ends with a variety of people, from all walks of life, attempting to dance a Busby Berkeley production number.

The humor increases as each person turns around to show that they are wearing dark glasses and wielding walking sticks for the sight impaired. Lauper's primary agenda seemed to defy the moral majority. Her work of the 1980s paved the way for young women to take control of their lives and enjoy themselves.

Tina Turner

Tina Turner, the former Anna Mae Bullock from Nutbush, Tennessee, already reigned as a rock-and-roll legend in the 1980s. After leaving Tennessee for St. Louis, she teamed up with her husband Ike Turner and his band, the Kings of Rhythm, to become The Ike and Tina Turner Review, a mainstay of rhythm and blues throughout the 1960s. Tina recorded as a member of the Revue until Phil Spector approached her to release a single of her own, "River Deep, Mountain High" (1969). After opening successfully for the

Rolling Stones, the Revue had a major hit with their cover of the Credence Clearwater Revival song "Proud Mary."

Ike's temper, however, corrupted the working relationship between the band members and his marriage to Tina. Evidence of abuse finally destroyed the union, although the wider world would not learn the full details until the 1993 film *What's Love Got to Do with It?* Tina left Ike in 1976, securing enough money for a divorce two years later.

In 1980, Tina signed with manager Roger Davies, who helped reshape her career and move her away from the second-rate Vegas-styled career she maintained on her own. Their first album together, *Private Dancer,* sold 10 million copies and scored a number one hit with "What's Love Got To Do With It?" in addition to four other Top 10 hits. The song went on to win four Grammys, and in the next three years, Turner won three more.

The video for "What's Love Got to Do With It?" introduced a different kind of femininity, based in the personal life of the singer herself, to the MTV audience. Turner returned to the music scene at the age of 54, and the video showed her looking like a much younger sexual goddess, decked out in a mini skirt, denim jacket, fishnet stockings, and six-inch heels. Her new trademark was a big, blonde hairdo, a startlingly funky change from the stylish wigs she wore when performing with Ike. The song itself allowed Turner to use her low, gravelly voice to call attention to the fact that she was on the prowl, looking for a man who could satisfy her, and not try to control her. She strutted about Manhattan, gazing at men like they routinely gaze at women in most videos, actively turning the tables to show a woman as the owner of the gaze. Turner's toughness made her a *cause celebre,* and her style revealed that women could make it big in a man's world.

Paula Abdul

Born in Los Angeles, Paula Abdul began her career as a dancer and choreographer. For a time, she was a cheerleader for the L.A. Lakers, which got her noticed, and she slowly began to parlay that attention into jobs with artists who needed dance choreography for their music videos.

LIVE AID

Contrary to the "Me Generation" label, young people in the decade had a growing awareness of the world's problems and their roles in changing society for the better. The response to the famine that rocked Ethiopia in 1984 is a perfect example of how Americans could be moved to help.

During that year a million Africans perished due to a severe drought and lack of international aid. British pop star Bob Geldof (lead singer of the Boomtown Rats) decided to use his celebrity to fight the famine. With singers from the British groups Midge Ure and Ultravox, Geldof wrote a song released in December 1984 called "Do They Know It's Christmas?"—a ballad that spoke of the need for mankind to pay attention to the Ethiopian victims.

On November 25, 1984, 40 pop stars from the British recording industry, including Sting, Phil Collins, George Michael, Bono, members of Duran Duran, Culture Club, and Bananarama, recorded the song, hoping to raise $150,000 for relief. The record went multiplatinum worldwide, raising $16 million for famine relief. This effort was followed in America with "We Are The World," a song written by Michael Jackson and Lionel Ritchie, performed by 75 rock stars in America on the night of the Grammy Awards in February 1985.

Geldof worked to stage an intercontinental concert that would raise more funds and increase awareness of African starvation. "Live Aid" was staged on July 13, 1985 at Wembley Stadium, London, and at JFK Stadium, Philadelphia. The roster of performers was staggering: Elton John, Madonna, Sting, Queen, U2, Eric Clapton, Spandau Ballet, The Four Tops, Run DMC, David Bowie, Bryan Adams, the Beach Boys, Billy Joel, and Tina Turner. Phil Collins performed in London that morning for a crowd that included Prince Charles and Lady Diana and then flew aboard the Concorde to play with Sting and Eric Clapton in Philadelphia. The event was carried live all day on both CNN and MTV, and the youth of America watched in record numbers, raising another $80 million for famine victims.

Abdul choreographed the dance sequences for a number of big stars in the music business, including Janet Jackson, Duran Duran, and Tracy Ullman. Gradually, Abdul convinced industry insiders to take a chance on her as a singer. Her first album *Forever Your Girl* soared after the video for the first single "Straight-Up" jumped into heavy rotation on MTV. The album went on to sell 10 million copies and had three additional number one songs.

Abdul's highly stylized videos carefully showcased her beauty and dancing ability. The video for "The Way That You Love Me," for instance, intercut a series of material objects—fine wines, CD players, sleek auto interiors—with the glowing image of Abdul, singing directly to the camera: "It ain't the money or diamond rings/Honey, I don't care about material things/It's just the way that you love me."

In the video, the portrayal is that of a man who needs material objects to satisfy his ego. However, the beautiful woman argues that it is not the things that make the man, but the man himself—a stylish lesson for the materialism of the decade.

THE DEATH OF JOHN LENNON

The assassination of former Beatle John Lennon on December 18, 1980, outside the Dakota, his Manhattan home, marked the end of an "age of innocence" for many Americans. A self-proclaimed peace advocate, Lennon, who orchestrated the break-up of The Beatles with his marriage to Yoko Ono, died from a single gunshot to the head, fired by Mark David Chapman, an obsessed fan.

In the years since the demise of the Beatles, Lennon had taken the lead of the anti-war movement, mobilizing hoards of young men and women to rally against the Vietnam War in 1972, and Richard Nixon in particular. Nixon's paranoia set off an FBI investigation into Lennon's activities that lasted until he died. Ono refused to let her husband's death pass without meaning. Throughout the 1980s, she used the incident to lobby for tighter gun control restrictions. Lennon's message of a world filled with peace resonated throughout the 1980s as a call to the rebels of the 1960s and 1970s to not forego the battle against aggression.

Music

Sports

and Leisure of the 1980s

America's long preoccupation with sport and leisure activities changed during the 1980s. While millions jogged and aerobicized themselves into better shape during the decade, millions more became fixated on the sofa, watching sports, playing videogames, and learning DOS on their new computers. America's notion of leisure changed during the decade, influenced once more by the melding of technology and the advertising convictions of Madison Avenue bent on assuring Americans that they could not get along without more commodities.

A series of fads swept the nation, from the Rubik's Cube to Cabbage Patch Dolls. Millions of Americans took to the malls, sometimes just to window shop or meet up with friends. Often, however, a trip to the mall included a movie at the burgeoning multiplexes.

AMC Theaters, founded in the 1920s and headquartered in Kansas City, Missouri, helped build the multiplex industry. In the 1960s and 1970s, the company built multi-screen theaters close to or attached to shopping malls, convinced that moviegoers wanted the added convenience. In the early 1980s, AMC realized that by combining many screens under one roof, movie theaters became more efficient and profitable.

The cost savings enabled AMC to introduce new innovations in technology and marketing.

AMC developed the automated projection system, which revolutionized the industry. In 1981, the company installed the first cup-holder armrests. It also bumped up the number of screens in each location from 5 or 6 to 8 or 12.

SPORTS

The sporting world's hold on the nation broadened as technological innovations such as cable television gave audiences more opportunities to watch sports. Television catapulted athletes to new heights of wealth and fame. The professional athletic leagues used different methods to promote their sports on television, ranging from the NFL's emphasis on winning teams, such as the Dallas Cowboys and San Francisco 49ers, to the NBA focusing on its marquee players, like Michael Jordan, Larry Bird, and Magic Johnson.

With little original programming, cable networks traditionally relied on network reruns and old movies to fill space. In the 1980s, cable television executives realized that sports would attract audiences and build loyalty among viewers. For example, early NBA playoff coverage on Ted Turner's TBS network drew record ratings across all cable programming.

ESPN started as an alternative to the short sports segments in standard television news broadcasts and the information found in "Sports" sections of newspapers. ESPN started out fairly small and often had to broadcast unorthodox sporting events, such as tractor pulls; international sports relatively unknown in the United States, such as Australian Rules Football; as well as the short-lived United States Football League (USFL), to attract viewers.

In 1987, ESPN landed a contract to show National Football League games on Sunday evenings, an event which transformed ESPN from a smaller cable TV network into a marketing empire and a cornerstone to the enthusiastic "sports culture" it largely helped to create. The major networks soon followed with increased sports programming.

Advertisers used this newfound intimacy between athletes and fans to promote their products, turning sports stars into mega-celebrities. In the 1960s, less than 10 percent of all ads featured sports figures. In the 1980s, however, that figure climbed to 20 percent.

Corruption also intervened in the sports world in often harsh ways in the 1980s. Many of the episodes were driven by greed on the part of franchise owners or players, while others revolved around illegally bending the rules to gain a competitive advantage.

Other incidents were more tragic. University of Maryland basketball star Len Bias died of a cocaine overdose before ever getting to don a Boston Celtics jersey as the team's first round draft choice. Olympic diving champion Greg Louganis and Los Angeles Lakers basketball star Magic Johnson each contracted the HIV virus, opening the world of AIDS to the American public like never before.

BASEBALL

In the 1980s, nine different Major League Baseball (MLB) teams won the World Series, which made the decade interesting for fans. Rather than the dynasties that had dominated baseball in past decades, a handful of teams had a legitimate chance at winning the title. Baseball fans also saw numerous individual and career achievements during the 1980s. In 1985, for example, Pete Rose passed Ty Cobb as baseball's all-time hit leader, a mark that many observers thought would

WORLD SERIES

1980 Philadelphia Phillies (NL), 4 games; Kansas City Royals (AL), 2 games

1981 Los Angeles Dodgers (NL), 4 games; New York Yankees (AL), 2 games

1982 St. Louis Cardinals (NL), 4 games; Milwaukee Brewers (AL), 3 games

1983 Baltimore Orioles (AL), 4 games; Philadelphia Phillies (NL), 1 game

1984 Detroit Tigers (AL), 4 games; San Diego Padres (NL), 1 game

1985 Kansas City Royals (AL), 4 games; St. Louis Cardinals (NL), 3 games

1986 New York Mets (NL), 4 games; Boston Red Sox (AL), 3 games

1987 Minnesota Twins (AL), 4 games; St. Louis Cardinals (NL), 3 games

1988 Los Angeles Dodgers (NL), 4 games; Oakland A's (AL), 1 game

1989 Oakland A's (AL), 4 games; San Francisco Giants (NL), 0 games

stand forever. Three years later in 1988, millions watched as Kirk Gibson hobbled off the bench on injured knees to hit a homerun off Oakland A's star closer Dennis Eckersley to lead the Los Angeles Dodgers to a World Series title.

THE OLYMPICS

The Olympic Games of the 1980s took on a political air not seen since Jesse Owens ran at the 1936 Munich Games; participation and medal counts were seen as a reflection of a nation's power.

1980 Olympic Games

Protesting the USSR invasion of Afghanistan in December 1979, President Jimmy Carter announced that if Soviet troops did not withdraw before February 20, 1980, he would refuse to allow the American teams to participate in the Moscow Olympics. The Soviets called his bluff, justified their invasion to the world, and waited for America's official withdrawal. Carter signed

Sports

the order withdrawing the American delegations, and the world—including the American teams—turned against Carter. The International Olympic Committee announced that the Games should be above politics; however, West Germany, Japan, Canada, and China joined the U.S. boycott, which set the stage for Soviet domination of the Games; they won 197 medals, 80 of them gold.

This action by the United States made the Winter Games at Lake Placid, New York, all the more interesting. The Soviets, still in Afghanistan, sent their delegation to participate, and the showdown over the new world order took place on a hockey rink, rather than on a battlefield. The U.S. team, coached by Herb Brooks, emerged the victor in a series of stunning upsets over Sweden and Czechoslovakia. A showdown with the heavily-favored Soviet team loomed for the underdog Americans. The teams battled furiously, understanding the political and cultural ramifications of the game. They skated to a 3–3 tie at halftime. Then, team captain Mike Eruzione scored a third period goal that allowed the American team to beat the Soviets. Sports fans around the nation celebrated the victory as if it had been the gold medal game.

The final victory over the Finnish team gave the United States its first gold medal in hockey—a "miracle" that resonated as a victory for democracy.

Another highlight of these Games was Eric Heiden winning five gold medals in speed skating—taking first place in each of his races. Heiden set Olympic records for the 500-meter, the 1,000-meter, the 1,500-meter, and 5,000-meter races and a world record for the 10,000-meter race. Heiden's sister Elizabeth won the bronze medal in the Women's 3,000-meter speed-skating race.

1984 Olympic Games

The 1984 Summer Games in Los Angeles boasted its share of American athletic heroes in a variety of sports, partially because the USSR boycotted these games. Texas native Carl Lewis won four goal medals in the track-and-field competition, tying Jesse Owens's record set in 1936. Lewis would defend his medals in the 1988 Olympics.

Diver Greg Louganis became the first American in 56 years to win two gold medals for diving, in the springboard and the 10-meter platform events. Louganis had won a silver medal at the 1976 Rome Games, and he was the first diver to receive a perfect score of 10 at the 1982 World Championships. He was prepared to win the gold in Moscow when the Americans pulled out of the competition. He became the first diver to pass 700 points in both events in the same Olympics, and his total of 710.91 points remains the most number of points awarded to a diver in Olympic history.

American gymnast Mary Lou Retton became "America's Sweetheart" as she won five gold medals at the Summer Games. In addition, she won a silver medal for her performance on the vault, and two bronze medals in the floor exercise and the parallel bar events. Her impressive back somersault with a backward twist from the vault won her the gold medal for best all-around gymnastic competition; she became the first American gymnast to win that prize. In addition, her silver medal awarded for team competition made her one of America's most decorated gymnasts in the history of the Games. She retired from competition in 1986, but worked as a television commentator during the 1988 Games.

1988 Olympic Games

The 1988 Summer Games were held in Seoul, South Korea, and no nations boycotted the competition. Lewis defended his long jump title with a jump of 28′ 7¼″. His attempt to defend his 100-meter title was the center of much greater controversy, and Lewis lost the crown of "world's fastest man" to Ben Johnson of Canada in a dramatic race. Sparks erupted after the race, however, when Johnson tested positive for steroids. Olympic officials stripped Johnson of the medal and awarded Lewis the gold.

Greg Louganis faced difficult competition in defending his medals as well. Going up against 14-year-old Xiong Ni of China, Louganis attempted a reverse somersault pike and hit his head on the diving board, shocking the world. The gruesome video of the accident was replayed countless times. After receiving stitches, the American

Sports

Olympic athletes often go on to perform in other venues, including entertainment. Here, figure skater Dorothy Hamill (who won a gold medal in the Winter Olympics of 1976), and diver Greg Louganis (who won gold medals for diving in both 1984 and 1988), are seen in 1986 on CBS-TV's *The Eleventh Annual Circus of Stars*. Courtesy of Photofest.

diver came back the next day to nail all 11 dives perfectly and regain his title. Louganis became only the second American diver in history to win back-to-back titles.

The thrilling Olympic victory after such a horrendous accident was overshadowed by the revelation that Louganis was HIV-positive at the time, revealed the following year in his autobiography, *Breaking the Surface*. Many speculated that the diver's injury put other contestants at risk, but doctors agreed that the chances of that were minimal.

Wearing hot pink spandex running suits and brandishing multicolored, 5-inch nails, Florence Griffith Joyner appeared more like a fashion plate than an Olympic athlete. However, "Flo Jo" took the world by storm, winning gold medals for the 100-meter, the 200-meter, and the 4 × 100-meter relay. She also won a silver medal in the 4 × 400-meter relay with her teammates.

FADS

Like most things connected to the 1980s, extreme fads reveal much about people. While Americans lived healthier due to avid interests in jogging, weightlifting, rollerblading, and aerobic exercise, the advent of the videogame and the personal computer tied people, particularly youngsters, to the couch and led to a rise in obesity.

Fads such as Cabbage Patch Dolls and Care Bears, and action figures such as Go-bots and Transformers, made shopping for Christmas a nightmare. In malls across the nation, desperate crowds stampeded stores in hopes of acquiring these toys for their children. In an image conscious decade, these toys became status symbols, even to the very young. For some parents, acquiring the toys became an end in itself and much more important than the impact the toy would have on the child getting it.

The biggest fad of the 1980s came in the form of a toy. The Coleco Toy Company launched their "Cabbage Patch Dolls" in 1983. Originally the dolls were part of an elaborate art show mounted by Xavier Robert, a sculptor from Cleveland, Georgia. Robert used them in an art show he mounted in a local gallery, where he and his assistants dressed as maternity room attendants. The basic design of each doll was the same—they were all chubby with pudgy faces and close-set eyes. However, Roberts made every doll distinct. He dressed them differently and provided a birth certificate for every one, offering them for "adoption" rather than for purchase.

After Coleco purchased the initial design from Roberts, they used computers to assign each doll a distinction, in order to comply with Roberts's original intent. The demand soon overwhelmed the factory, with sales reaching $60 million in 1983, the first year on the market. Shortages caused mass stampedes at shopping malls and fistfights in the aisles as a Cabbage Patch Dolls craze broke out during the 1984 Christmas shopping season. By 1985, sales reached $500 million, and many stores held lotteries for customers to secure orders. By the next year, however, the fad had passed.

Physical fitness became another fad that tapped into an America that wanted to look good and feel healthy. The foremost guru for the fad came from an unlikely source—Jane Fonda, actress and political advocate. Unveiling a video titled *Jane Fonda's Workout,* the 44-year-old actress demonstrated an aerobic style exercise regimen that women could perform along with the actress. Her video sold millions of copies, and Fonda became the poster girl for clean and healthy living. Her *Workout* book, complete with diet plan, was number one on the *New York Times* Best Seller List for months, and Fonda was named one of the most influential women of 1984 by the *World Almanac*—ahead of Sandra Day O'Connor and Nancy Reagan. By the end of the decade, Fonda had starred in and produced 10 other fitness videos for every kind of woman—from pregnant and elderly women to those in the working world.

Fonda's video bonanza was just the first in a long line of fitness related ventures that made physical fitness a legitimate, billion-dollar industry. Women began aerobicizing and jazzercizing in gym classes and with other videos, like Richard Simmons's *Sweating to the Oldies.* The film *Flashdance* ushered in a new trend in fitness clothing for women—sweatshirts—frequently ripped—worn off the shoulder, with leotards, leg warmers, and headbands becoming the latest gym fashions. The new emphasis on the male physique brought about by Calvin Klein's underwear advertisements made men more conscious of how they looked as well. Instead of three martini power lunches, some men retreated to the gym to jog or to power lift in clubs outfitted with new Nautilus training equipment. Because of a renewed interest in holistic healing, spas began to experience a surge in attendance for massages, tanning facilities, and saunas. A gym membership became a badge of honor, and memberships to some establishments in New York City cost about $2,000 a year.

One example of the fitness craze appeared on the *Billboard* charts with Olivia Newton John's single "Physical." The song climbed to number one in three weeks and remained there for much of 1982. The video for the song, one of the first in heavy rotation on MTV, showcased Newton John's new image, worlds away from the simple country girl she had portrayed in earlier work. With "Physical," Newton John transformed into a confident, sexy woman of the world, prowling about a trendy gymnasium dressed in a body suit with matching headband and leg warmers, posing between muscle-bound weight lifters and encouraging out-of-shape men.

GAMES

A number of new games became popular during the decade—some old-fashioned and others acutely electronic. Jenga, distributed by Milton Bradley, was one party game advertised as a game of skill. Wooden blocks fit together to form a tower of 18 levels—each level comprised of three blocks at right angles, intersecting with the previous layer. The object of the game was to pull out the blocks one at a time without toppling the tower. The person who toppled the tower lost.

Another board game that became an instant sensation was *Trivial Pursuit,* advertised as a "party in a box" when it debuted in 1982. Initially, the game caused only a minor stir when unveiled at the American International Toy Fair in 1982. Its creators, Scott Abbott, a Canadian sports writer; Chris Haney, a photo editor for the *Montreal Gazette;* Chris Abbott, a former hockey player; and Ed Werner, an attorney, devised the game in Canada after trying to stump one another with trivia questions. They sank all their money into producing the prototype unveiled at the Fair, but were disappointed by the initial results. Soon, however, word of mouth spread and the game became a Christmas season sensation, selling more than 20 million games in 1984 alone.

Given the widespread interest in Trivial Pursuit, the team then produced specialized versions, such as the "Silver Screen" and the "All Sports" editions. In 1988, Parker Brothers purchased the rights to the game. The company increased the variety of specialized versions to include a popular culture version and a children's version. Across all the different versions, the goal of the game remained the same—to fill in your "pie" by answering trivia questions correctly from five categories, each represented by a different color wedge: Geography

Sports

(blue), Arts and Entertainment (pink), History (yellow), Literature (brown), Science and Nature (green), and Sports and Leisure (orange). The player who fills his pie, then returns to the center of the board and answers a question in a category picked by his opponent, wins the game.

Another hot item was the Rubik's Cube, a plastic puzzle cube with six different sides each made up of nine colored squares. Players attempted to align the sides of a jumbled Rubik's Cube so that each side featured its original solid color. The best players nimbly whirled the cube at near blinding speed, in a frenzy of clicking, until they completed the puzzle regardless of how jumbled it had become.

The game was invented in 1974 by Erno Rubik, a professor of Interior Design at the Academy of Applied Arts and Design in Budapest. The model for the cube was the basis of one of Rubik's lectures and consisted of a three-dimensional cardboard cube he had constructed to assist his students in figuring square footage and other useful theories. When the students enthusiastically responded to the cube as a game, Rubik applied for a patent in 1975, and the leading toy firm Politechnika released the game to Budapest toy stores in 1977.

Rubik's Cube mania spread quickly in Hungary, and word of the puzzle reached Ideal Toys in 1979. Unveiled at the International Toy Fair of London in January 1980, the Rubik's Cube made an enthusiastic debut in the West, making the cover of *Scientific American* that same month. Orders for the Rubik's Cube surpassed expectations in the United States. Although Ideal

Sonoma State University's (California) Space Invaders Club (1980), shows the popularity on college campuses of early video game enthusiasts. Courtesy of Photofest.

Sports

VIDEO GAMES

The video game industry had its roots in 1952, when Cambridge University Researcher A. S. Douglas created the first graphic computer game, a version of tic-tac-toe, for his dissertation on human-computer interactions. From Douglas's game to the 1970s, video games remained simple, with basic graphics and controls and little complexity in terms of plot. The 1970s was a major decade in computer design and saw a number of innovations, including the first arcade games (1971), the first home gaming console (1972), and the first multi-game console, the Atari 2600 (1977). In under a decade, the video game industry accelerated from a crawl to a sprint. It was in the 1980s, however, when home gaming evolved from a minor pastime into a national obsession. Game systems became smaller and more reliable, and increased graphical capabilities made games more engaging. Along the way, video games attracted controversy, including attempts at censorship because of adult content or because of fear that violence in video games would have negative psychological effects on players. In most cases, judges chose to protect video games with other forms of media under First Amendment provisions guaranteeing free speech. Though some continued to criticize video games as a lower form of art, millions of gamers around the world objected and still say that video game designers and writers are innovators and should be credited with creating new worlds of creative entertainment.

considered renaming the game before its release, the company decided to keep the original name, and launched the game in May 1980 with a Hollywood party hosted by actress Zsa Zsa Gabor. Over the next two years the Rubik's Cube sold more than 100 million units, puzzling children and adults alike.

Board games appealed to traditional fans, but electronic-based video games transformed leisure time in the 1980s and soon became an integral part of many people's childhoods. The most exciting game to come along was Pac-Man, a video arcade game invented in 1977 by Toru Iwatani, who claimed that his inspiration had come from a slice of pizza.

Pac-Man, the yellow chomping circle pursued by evil ghosts, arrived in American arcades in 1980, the first video game targeted toward pre-adolescents. By 1982, there were 100,000 machines in arcades across the country, and Pac-Man was a household word. Not only did the video game inspire its own novelty song "Pac-Man Fever," it spawned other versions, including Ms. Pac-Man and Professor Pac-Man.

Travel

of the 1980s

Travel in the 1980s reflected the desire for bigger and better methods of transport, affecting everything from the family automobile to the largest corporate jets. During this time, Chrysler unveiled its new minivan, marketing it for suburban families on the go. Honda and Toyota, Japanese corporations, brought out new cars promising better gas mileage than any American-made car on the market. In an effort to keep pace with these foreign vehicles, Ford released its Taurus, a newly designed sedan.

In an era of high stakes business deals and one-upmanship, tried and true foreign car manufacturers such as BMW, Saab, Volvo, and Mercedes, made pricey, foreign cars that became status symbols in corporate America and among the wealthy.

HOME FOR THE HOLIDAYS

The convenience of air travel made Americans more mobile than ever. This mobility became most apparent during the holiday season. More than 22 million passengers traveled during the holiday season in 1988, a record at that time. The chaotic atmosphere intensified as the regular business and corporate travelers were joined by vacationers, college students, and military personnel.

As the holidays grew nearer, the headaches increased for the airlines. At Chicago's O'Hare Airport, United Airlines reported that it escorted 900 children from one plane to the other on a busy day. Not only were the airlines moving an influx of travelers, they also shipped countless tons of mail; some airlines lugged up to one million pounds of mail a day. Checked and carry-on luggage increased during the holidays as well.

Despite the record number of air passengers in the 1980s, the airlines did not make profits commensurate with the influx. Passengers used new computerized airline ticketing systems to book several different flights, often without letting the airlines know which ones they were not taking. As a result, flights that should have been full were often less than half full. The 15 to 20 percent of all passengers that were "no shows" during regular times of the year jumped to 60 or 70 percent during the holidays. Pan American World Airways hedged its bets by forcing customers to prepay for tickets and did not give refunds for no shows.

Some days and destinations were sure bets for the airlines. Around Christmas, Hawaii stood as vacationers' number one destination. In response, United added 74 additional roundtrips to and from the islands, which added nearly 30,000 new seats between Christmas and New Year's. Even a single-day event like the Rose Bowl could

John Z. DeLorean answers reporters' questions at his news conference in New York on February 19, 1982. AP Photo.

bolster airline profits. United added four extra 254-passenger DC-10 trips between Los Angeles and Detroit, specifically catering to University of Michigan boosters.

AMERICAN AIRLINES

The passage of the Airline Deregulation Act of 1978 had far-reaching consequences for air travelers and the industry. The act removed government control of air routes and ticket prices and encouraged new airlines to enter the market. The regulatory changes meant that large companies could expand routes into new parts of the nation and overseas. However, it also opened the skies to smaller, cut-rate airlines that could sell tickets for much less than their larger competitors.

Realizing it needed a new kind of management to deal with the changes taking place in the industry, American hired Robert L. Crandall as president and chief operating officer in 1980. Crandall had previously worked at TWA and Bloomingdale's before joining American, and he had a reputation for innovative uses of technology

THE DELOREAN

One symbol of affluence was the limited edition DeLorean. John Z. DeLorean was born and raised in Detroit, Michigan, son of an autoworker at the local Ford plant. After graduating with an MBA and working for Packard Motor Company, DeLorean worked for General Motors as chief engineer of the Pontiac, where he reworked the "old ladies' sedan" to make it more powerful and more affordable. When the GTO sold 31,000 units in 1964, DeLorean was hailed a genius.

After parting ways with GM in 1975, DeLorean founded his own motor company in Detroit, eventually moving to Park Avenue. Set to unveil a product that catered to the newly affluent, DeLorean hired the top designers from Porsche, Renault, and BMW, but the development of the car itself proved a formidable task. Unveiled in 1978, the distinct features of the car included gull-wing doors, a rear-mounted, PRV-6 engine, and a 304-grade stainless steel body. In addition, the car's stainless steel body was not painted to avoid rust, making it appear a sleek silver bullet as it sped along the roads of America.

Early purchasers paid $1,000 down for the privilege of being one of the first owners, but projected costs were off, and the car that was initially set to cost $12,000 actually cost $28,000 by the time it was complete in 1981. Consumer groups rated the car low, but advertising paid off, and sales of the car were good for the first year.

In 1982 a sting operation in Los Angeles found DeLorean (some say he was framed) in a cocaine bust, linking him to drug trafficking. Although he was eventually acquitted, the series of trials left the company bankrupt. According to the DeLorean Owners Association, 6,539 cars were produced in 1981, 1,126 in 1982, and 918 in 1983, making it a highly sought after collectible. The DeLorean also achieved fame as the vehicle used as Doc Brown's time machine in the Back to the Future films. (See Entertainment of the 1980s.)

that drove greater efficiencies. Crandall became American Airlines' Chairman and CEO in 1985.

In January 1979, American Airlines took advantage of deregulation (see Travel of the 1970s) to introduce new flights to a wider selection of cities in the United States and across the Caribbean. The same year, the airline also took a bold step, moving its headquarters from New York City to Dallas/Fort Worth, Texas. The new complex also housed a training facility for employees and pilots and a reservations office.

In 1981, as more people took to the skies for business and leisure travel, American Airlines introduced AAdvantage travel awards program, a marketing program to reward frequent fliers. The same year, the company also brought out its "AAirpass," an early corporate travel card that offered guaranteed fixed air travel costs. The company continued its marketing efforts in the face of the many competitors battling for market share.

In 1985, American introduced "Ultimate Super Saver" fares, which offered passengers up to 70 percent discounts, a direct assault against its smaller competitors. American also attempted to draw in older travelers with its Senior SAAVers Club, which gave discounts to senior citizens.

These attempts to deal with increased competition went beyond marketing campaigns. In 1984, American introduced the American Eagle system, a network of regional airlines that linked small communities to large cities through connections to and from American Airlines.

AIR TRAFFIC CONTROL STRIKE

One of the most serious tests to labor laws concerning the travel industry came early in Ronald Reagan's first term. The Professional Air Traffic Controller's Organization (PATCO) believed that the Federal Aviation Agency (FAA) had never

Two striking air traffic controllers stand on a picket line as an airliner taxis on the runway behind them at New York's La Guardia Airport, 1981. AP Photo.

seriously addressed their concerns about working conditions in the industry. PATCO had argued its case and registered complaints against the agency in years past, but the continued threat of a strike was never believed to be real until 1980. At this time, concerns about fair labor practices and compensation were simply rebuffed once more, and the union believed they had enough votes to finally make the threat a reality. On August 3, 1981, the Controllers gained the votes necessary for a walk out, and 13,000 air traffic controllers went on strike, following talks that had begun the preceding December.

Robert Poli, PATCO President, explained that the union's three major demands included a $10,000 across the board raise, a 32-hour work week (down from 40 hours), and a substantially improved retirement package. The press, generally, was not sympathetic to the union demands, and made much of the raise in pay. PATCO had hoped it would be able to avoid the strike by pushing the federal mediators into negotiations, but the talks failed.

Most historians consider President Reagan's handling of the striking air traffic controllers the crowning achievement of his first administration: Within 48 hours of the walkout, Reagan simply fired 11,350 workers on the basis that they had each taken an oath not to strike. He insisted that not one of the fired air traffic controllers be re-hired, even if a contract was signed. Although the action was thought extreme, the public rallied around the President, believing that the air traffic controllers should not be able to walk out.

While studies showed that job stress for air traffic controllers was high, the FAA's "Rose Report," named for Dr. Robert Rose, did not find the job as problematic as alleged. Reagan's firing of the workers forced the FAA to hire inexperienced workers to fill time slots. These new workers created a new union by 1987, the National Air Traffic Controllers Association (NATCA), and Reagan was credited with crushing the old organization. The long-lasting effects of the Air Traffic Controllers' Strike changed the way unions went about making demands on management. The strike also revealed the need for more advanced technology, which has steadily become more available in the subsequent years.

FAMILY VACATIONS

High gas prices for the period and memories of national gas rationing in the late 1970s placed a damper on many family vacations in the early 1980s. As the decade progressed, though, gas prices dropped and more families hit the nation's highways. Fluctuations in gas prices often determined the length of vacations and the distances families travelled from home. During the 1980s, gas prices ranged from a high of about $1.38 in 1981 to a low of about $0.93 in 1986.[1] Nearly 83 percent of all summer travel took place in motor vehicles in 1989, with 273 million vacationers traveling in the 14-week holiday season between Memorial Day and Labor Day.[2]

Many family vacations took place at the country's national parks. In the early 1980s, the most visited park was the Great Smoky Mountains National Park on the Tennessee/North Carolina border. In 1980 the park had 8.4 million visitors, but that number jumped to more than 9 million the next year. Throughout the decade, about 240 million

DISNEY

In the mid-1980s, the Walt Disney Company undertook an aggressive marketing campaign to regain its place among the nation's top vacation spots. In 1984, Michael Eisner was named chairman of the entertainment conglomerate. He sparked a campaign to reinvigorate Disneyland, Walt Disney World, and Disney's motion picture division. The full-blown branding operation included getting the "Disney Sunday Movie" back on network television and sending its main characters (Mickey Mouse, Donald Duck, and others) on a 120-city tour that included hospitals and local parades. In October 1986, company executives sent Mickey to China on a publicity tour and then brought Chinese journalists to Disneyland to promote the company.

Disneyland celebrated its 30th anniversary in 1985 with record-setting attendance, surpassing 11.5 million guests. The park celebrated by giving away a new car to every 30,000th visitor and a free watch to every 30th person entering the gate.

Travel

people vacationed at the country's national parks each year.

The concept of the long weekend really took hold in the 1980s as more families had both parents working outside the home. The increased pressure at work and the uncertainty about downsizing and layoffs also made workers apprehensive about taking long vacations.

The changing workplace also contributed to the way employees approached vacations. As technology made workers more efficient, some companies responded by giving workers more freedom in establishing their own hours, and did not necessarily require 9-to-5 or 40 hours a week. In other organizations, particularly hospitals and critical care facilities, employees worked fewer, but longer, shifts.

ATTRACTING FOREIGN TRAVELERS

States strong in tourism sought to offset the economic ups and downs of the decade by attracting foreign vacationers. American travel companies and state chambers of commerce and development produced slick marketing brochures and magazines designed to promote tourist sites to overseas audiences. Pacific Gateways, a firm based in Portland, published Japanese language *Colorado Gaido* ("Colorado Guide") and *Oregon Treiru* ("Oregon Trail") for sale on newsstands in cities such as Tokyo, Nagoya, and Fukuoka.

Local tourist attractions added signage in Japanese so tourists would feel more comfortable staying (and spending money) in the United States. Casinos in Vegas also catered to Japanese visitors by adding Asian games of chance, such as Sic Bo and Pai Gow. With traditional Western industries (mining, railroads, forestry) on the decline, many states worked to build tourist attractions.

The Mountain West states created a promotional organization, called "Visit USA West," in an attempt to build the same momentum with Asian tourists as Hawaii, California, and Alaska had in earlier decades. In Wyoming, 8,000 Japanese tourists visited in 1989, double the number that had visited the previous year. Ski resorts in Utah went from almost no Japanese visitors to 3,000 in only two years. In Deer Valley, Utah, Asian guests found Japanese-speaking ski instructors and Japanese-language restaurant guides.

Travel

Visual Arts

of the 1980s

The art of the 1980s reflected the turbulent times of the world that produced it. Art was no longer the paintings or sculptures purchased to match the sofa—art was seen as the viably relevant statements of a disenfranchised portion of the social culture. The world of museums had relevance within the American culture, and art was seen as a purveyor of the cultural climate.

As in many aspects of life in the 1980s, greed, speculation, and the lure of a quick profit defiled the art world. By the end of the decade, the art boom, fueled by Wall Street's money culture and a strong Japanese yen, which enabled foreign investors to enter the market, lost steam. Some paintings still received record bids at auction houses like Sotheby's and Christie's, but far more failed to reach their estimates.

What changed in the art world were the buyers, not necessarily the artists themselves. Newly rich investors sought to treat art like just another commodity that could be bought low and sold high. Pop artists like Andy Warhol opened up the art world to the masses, for better and worse. Public outrage became commonplace in a sensationalized media environment. The hoopla surrounding Robert Mapplethorpe's Cincinnati exhibit culminated in sanctions against the use of taxpayer money for artistic exhibits, but it was not the only public outburst of the decade. Public

art, like Maya Lin's Vietnam Memorial, spurred hotly contested debates about art's place in society. It seemed that as new money flooded into the art world, sensationalism swept in with the backwash. Using art as trading cards was one way to commodify it. Using outcry over supposed indecency as political fodder further debased the business.

The financial security of the 1980s critically affected the art world, throwing art into the speculative realm of the stock market. This operated in two significant ways. First, *nouveau riche* collectors on Park Avenue and from around the world began to pay outrageous prices for masterworks. At the start of the 1980s, the highest prices ever paid for paintings at a public auction were: Turner's *Juliet and Her Nurse* for $6.4 million; Velazquez's *Portrait of Juan de Pareja* for $5.4 million; and van Gogh's *Poet's Garden* for $5.2 million.[1]

By 1988, these prices would appear cheap as a Japanese insurance conglomerate paid $35 million for van Gogh's *Sunflowers;* another investor paid $47 million for Picasso's *Yo Picasso;* and Australian broker Alan Bond paid $53.9 million for van Gogh's *Irises,* which was later purchased by the Getty Foundation for its private collection.[2] By the end of the 1980s, with the bottom of the stock market tapped dry, the art market dried as well.

The second effect the 1980s had on the art world involved the artists themselves, who became new celebrities, with agents assisting them in securing multimedia deals to show and sell their work. The icon most budding artists held up as their role model was Andy Warhol, the pop artist of the 1960s who had revolutionized the art scene with his concept art, focusing everyday commercial images in his work.

A series of events came together in the 1980s that enabled talented young artists to rapidly climb the art ladder—a larger art audience, an upwardly mobile Baby Boomer generation, summer trips to Europe, and more disposable income and sources of credit to finance purchases. Young artists, potential superstars in the making whose works were still under $50,000, reaped the benefits. The market itself ballooned. In 1970, there were 73 galleries listed in New York City, but 15 years later, the number approached 450.

ERIC FISCHL

The paintings of the 1980s characterize a commitment on the part of the artist toward revealing the phoniness of the middle-class world. Eric Fischl used bright colors to convey the coldness of the suburban world. His most famous work, *Sleepwalker,* shows a typical young teen masturbating in a wading pool.

The painting's use of cool blues appears soothing against the vivid greens of the grass and the lawn furniture. The boy's creamy skin, highlighted with only touches of pink and white, starkly blends with the blues of the pool water—the figure of the young man is in profile, not completely turned away from the viewer's perspective. He almost dares us to watch, maybe even to participate in this bold defiling of the innocent children's pool. This is not the shameful act of American lore from the 1950s, but a bold exhibition—a liberation that entices the spectator to join in the exploration of sexual freedom. In essence, the scene assaults the vision of suburbia, protector of the wholesome American middle class, for its title, *Sleepwalker,* does not refer to the masturbating young man but to the adults who have left the lawn chairs empty—it is adult America that wanders about in a coma while the youthful spirit assaults the safe images of childhood.

JEFF KOONS

In his television series *American Visions,* Robert Hughes visits the "factory" of Jeff Koons, the last of the artists created by the boom of the 1980s. In Hughes words, Koons was a "starry-eyed opportunist par excellence," his art a painful homage to the Pop Art movement of the 1960s. Koons, a former commodities trader, openly reveled in his personal assault on the art world. On the day Hughes visited him, Koons showed Hughes how he mass produced his gigantic sculptures.

In one of his more famous pieces of the period, *Michael Jackson and Bubbles,* 1988, Koons captured through his ceramic and gold leaf creation the superficial, plastic ideal of 1980s celebrity. The reclining Jackson, dressed in a gold Sgt. Pepper-like band uniform, has only his eyes and lips painted in color, making him appear to be a Kabuki geisha rather than the innovative rock and soul talent he was at the time. Koons appeared to comment on the shallowness of the MTV-generation with the piece.

In one of his catalogues, Koons dared his critics and patrons to embrace the trashy, gaudy side of their personalities. He believed that everyone had a superficial side that is at once obnoxious, at another filled with bravura. He felt that embracing this aspect permitted a social persona to emerge, elevating the spirit toward a new level of success—his art typified the flaunting quality of the pop culture experience.

KEITH HARING AND JEAN-MICHEL BASQUIAT

The graffiti movement began in the late 1970s and rose to prominence in the mid-1980s, quickly fading soon thereafter. Begun as a form of self-expression on the subway cars of Manhattan, the movement was chiefly characterized by two Village artists, Keith Haring and Jean-Michel Basquiat. Both men died at the peak of their careers (Haring of AIDS and Basquiat from a heroin overdose), their work profiting by their youthful

Arts

"Ushering in Banality," 1988. Artist Jeff Koons describes this piece and others like it as both satirizing and celebrating trite images. AP Photo.

exuberance and carefree attitudes toward stereotypes and artistic codes.

Haring used the whimsical characters and bold primary colors found on the subways to relate an alternative, highly politicized message articulating a rage against the conservative politics of the Reagan era.

Basquiat symbolized the way artists were marketed in the 1980s. At 18 years old, the young artist (never formally trained) was homeless, and often slept on friends' couches. Five years later, he sold paintings for up to $25,000. His clients included Richard Gere, Paul Simon, and the Whitney Museum of American Art. Basquiat's works were heavy in color and words, like a modern montage of edgy images and symbols. His first solo show was held at the Mary Boone Gallery in New York City in early 1984.

Basquiat gained early fame as a graffiti artist in the SoHo section of New York. He signed his works "SAMO" and developed a reputation for witty, slightly anarchistic drawings. Quickly, Basquiat gained a reputation in New York and

Europe. He left behind the SAMO persona and produced more mainstream pieces.

Basquiat drew inspiration from a variety of sources, particularly Picasso and boyhood hero Andy Warhol. The latter became a friend and mentor to the young artist, encouraging him, providing direction, and giving him exposure. Warhol also worked with Basquiat on a series of projects that combined their two styles—the older with familiar symbols and the younger with figures, words, and pictures.

ANDRES SERRANO

Photography would be the artistic arena that would test the stamina of the public taste and attitudes concerning American art in the 1980s. The first test came in the form of an exhibition of work funded by the National Endowment for the Arts (NEA), a government resource designed to promote the arts for the masses via grants to artists. One photo in the exhibit, by Andres Serrano, was entitled *Piss Christ* and consisted of a cibachrome

Arts

Keith Haring sits in his Broome Street apartment in New York, 1983, surrounded by some of his art. AP photo.

photograph of a plastic crucifix swimming in a bottle of the artist's own urine.

The photo itself is a brilliant orange color, due to the process of development. The crucifix, of white plastic, glows through the vibrant orange. The photo certainly embraces the artist's identity politics, which challenge the sanctity of the icon; however, there is another way to read this. By immersing the sacred artifact in his own waste, Serrano reminds the viewer of the real Jesus

Christ—a man whose good deeds are celebrated through the tenets of organized religion.

In placing him on a pedestal, organized religion has forsaken the notion that Jesus was a real man, with real loves and real fears—the urine represents this common attribute of all humanity. Therefore, the photograph does not denigrate Christ, but reminds us of his basic humanity—his mission to treat all men and women with equal esteem.

Arts

Unfortunately, Congress used the photograph as evidence in hearings about public spending on art that ultimately stripped the NEA of its funds for artists in 1995. Soon thereafter, the NEA lost its ability to fund major exhibitions, public broadcasting series, and humanities projects (books, lecture series, films) that might be seen as unpatriotic.

ROBERT MAPPLETHORPE

In 1990 in Cincinnati, Ohio, an NEA-sponsored exhibition of Robert Mapplethorpe's photographic art was to be staged. The curator, refusing to section off a room for what became "the Cincinnati seven"—photographs by Mapplethorpe that openly displayed the sadomasochistic side of gay culture—was arrested on obscenity charges, charges that were ultimately thrown out of court when the case was spot-lighted by the national media. This instance is a fitting example of how politically charged the art arena became in the 1980s; it is also an appropriate capstone to this particular artist's notorious career.

In 1988, Mapplethorpe gathered 111 of his photographs and, with NEA monies, staged a traveling exhibition of his most controversial work. His exhibition opened at the Whitney Museum of American Art in August, 1988, moved to the Institute of Contemporary Art in Philadelphia that December, the Art Institute in Chicago, the Boston Museum of Fine Arts, and finally ended up at the Corcoran Gallery in Washington, D.C. However, before the show arrived in Washington, Mapplethorpe died of AIDS, and the hysterical response to the show by conservatives, bent on shutting down the NEA, forced the Corcoran to cancel it. The Corcoran cancellation set the stage for the curator of the Cincinnati Museum of Fine Arts to accept the show, paving the way for his own legal entanglements and the glare of the national spotlight.

Mapplethorpe's work, though mainly completed from 1978 to 1980, was a fitting response to the conservative juggernaut that believed that art should entertain—and not teach. For instance, Mapplethorpe's *Self Portrait,* 1980, confronts the spectator with the artist's direct stare. However, upon close examination, this is not simply a photograph of the artist, sitting shirtless—make-up applied delicately to his eyes and mouth feminize his features, and his coiffed hair, styled as if by a curling wand, helps to further this androgyny, calling into question the masculine image of the artist. This new artist, embracing both the masculine and the feminine, celebrates the honest possibilities of portraiture. In his other photos of body parts: *Chest,* 1986; *Vibert,* 1984; and *Ken and Tyler,* 1985, the male body is objectified by being dissected and revealed in close-up body parts, thus commenting on the common practice of objectifying the female body.

These abstract photos of a chest, a back, and a pair of dancers' legs and buttocks, suggested that male beauty, transfigured by tropes of hypermasculinity, had been lost to contemporary society. The photographs blurred the gender lines between the masculine and the feminine to reveal the male body in its own beauty—delicate yet strong.

Mapplethorpe's other homoerotic photographs were more objectionable than his artsy gender-bending photos. Four photographs in particular captured the immediacy and drive of his assault on contemporary mores. *Self Portrait,* 1978, shows the artist leering from over his shoulder at the spectator; the artist stands with his chaps-clad, naked buttocks in the photo's center, a bullwhip inserted between his cheeks. The image was daring in a playful manner. Mapplethorpe openly questioned the gendering of sexual pleasure by showing a man at play with himself, inviting the spectator to join him in this daring venture.

In *Brian Ridley and Lyle Heeter,* 1979, the artist took on another photographic genre and photographed a homosexual couple as a new form of wedding photo. The couple are photographed in their middle-class home decked out in the leather accoutrements of their sexual predilection. The dominant, bearded figure wears a leather captain's hat and stands to the side of a wing chair beside an end table on which rest a tasteful lamp and clock; he holds a chain that entraps a beardless man who is sitting in the chair wearing a collar, handcuffs, and leg braces that bind him to the standing figure. This obvious take on family photos was another humorous riff on middle America, instructing us all that behind each suburban façade, sexual games takes place, be it between men and women, men, or women. In this world, sexual roles are prevalent, yet part of the fun.

In *Elliot and Dominic,* 1978, one man stands shirtless, facing the camera, holding a cigarette in his right hand. His hand is by his fly, as if we have interrupted his undressing. In his left hand, he grasps the genitals of his partner, naked and bound upside-down, feet tied together with hemp, his arms bound in cuffs and tied to large hemp cords. A single chain runs from this man's neck to his genitals, disappearing behind the clutched hand of the standing figure. This image brought to the forefront a variety of gender roles, as neither man appears "feminine" as in the other photo—both exhibit rugged muscles and much body hair. However, the upside down man, trussed like an animal or dangling in an inverted crucifix, is rendered helpless, vulnerable because of his inversion. The steely grin on his face deflects any thoughts of danger—this is a pleasurable position for him. Instead of depicting patriarchal dominance, the photo reflects the joy of mutual gratification; like *Brian Ridley and Lyle Heeter, Elliot and Dominic* depicted a new way of thinking about relationships between men—an aesthetic that sharply questioned the normative heterosexist values of the dominant culture.

RICHARD SERRA

Sculptor Richard Serra (1939–) was born in San Francisco, where he spent much of his young life working in steel mills to support himself while attending college. It was in the San Francisco steel mills where Serra learned metalworking and welding, which he would later apply to his art. Serra studied painting and sculpture with some of the most famous artists of the 1940s and 1950s and his early works were in keeping with the mainstream art of the day. During his involvement in the New York art scene of the 1960s, however, Serra began to develop a different approach to sculpture, using nontraditional materials such as fiberglass and rubber. Serra is best known for his minimalist sculpture, utilizing only a few materials folded or constructed in such a way as to emphasize the qualities of the materials themselves. During the 1980s, his large, bold sculptures caught the eye of aficionados and critics alike, and Serra became a favorite of urban designers. Serra was asked to install

his sculptures in galleries across the world, including in New York, London, and Nova Scotia. One of his most famous pieces, "Tilted Arc," was prominently displayed in the Federal Plaza of New York City. While Serra was best known as a minimalist sculptor, his influence is also present in the rise of "process art," wherein the construction process is as important as the finished work, bringing the active process of artistic creation to the forefront.

ENDNOTES FOR THE 1980s

OVERVIEW OF THE 1980s

1. Michael Waldman and George Stephanopoulos, *My Fellow Americans: The Most Important Speeches of America's Presidents, from George Washington to George W. Bush* (Naperville, IL: Sourcebooks MediaFusion), 266.
2. Joshua Freeman, et al. *Who Built America: Working People and the Nation's Economy, Politics, Culture, and Society* (New York: Pantheon, 1992), 638.
3. Richard N. Ostling, "Jim Bakker's Crumbling World," *Time,* December 19, 1988.
4. Tom Morganthau, "Gay America in Transition," *Newsweek,* August 8, 1983, 30.

ADVERTISING OF THE 1980s

1. Kelly McMasters, "Nike and Popular Culture." *Basketball in America: From the Playgrounds to Jordan's Game and Beyond.* Ed. Bob Batchelor. (New York: Haworth, 2005), 53.
2. Janice Castro, "Calvin Meets the Marlboro Man." (*Time,* 21 October 1985), C1.
3. Randall Rothenberg, "The Media Business: Advertising," *New York Times* (November 9, 1989), D1.

BOOKS, NEWSPAPERS, MAGAZINES, AND COMICS OF THE 1980s

1. Randy Shilts, *And The Band Played On: Politics, People and the AIDS Epidemic* (New York: Penguin, 1987), 147.

FOOD OF THE 1980s

1. Janet Helm, "EN Looks at the 80's: A Decade Devoted to Counting Cholesterol, Beating Obesity and Preventing Cancer," *Environmental Nutrition* 12 (December 1989).
2. Michael Bastedo, "God, What a Blunder: The New Coke Story," *Cola Fountain* (August 3, 2004), 3.
3. Bastedo, "God, What a Blunder," 32.
4. Bastedo, "God, What a Blunder," 48.

Arts

5. Bastedo, "God, What a Blunder," 3.

6. John Greenwald, "Coca-Cola's Big Fizzle: Consumer Revolt Forces the Company to Bring Back the Old, Familiar Flavor," *Time* (July 22, 1985), 48.

7. André Gayot, "Of Stars and Tripes," *Gayot.com* (August 23, 2003). Available at: http://www.gayot.com/restaurants/features/nouvellecuisine.html.

TRAVEL OF THE 1980s

1. Energy Information Administration. U.S. Department of Energy. "Retail Gasoline Historical Prices." http://www.eia.doe.gov/oil_gas/petroleum/data_publications/wrgp/mogas_history.html.

2. "Analysts Predict More Vacation Driving, But Shorter Trips Due to Rising Gas Prices." *Los Angeles Times* (May 27, 1989), 10.

VISUAL ARTS OF THE 1980s

1. Robert Hughes, *American Visions* (New York: Knopf, 1997), 591.

2. Hughes, *American Visions,* 593.

Resource Guide

PRINTED SOURCES

Ali, Muhammad, with Richard Durham. *The Greatest: My Own Story.* New York: Random House, 1975.

Allen, Geoffrey Freeman. *Railways, Past, Present and Future.* New York: Morrow, 1982.

Amburn, Ellis. *Pearl: The Obsessions and Passions of Janis Joplin: A Biography.* New York: Warner, 1992.

Archer, Michael. *Art Since 1960.* New York: Thames and Hudson, 1997.

Armstrong, Neil. *First on the Moon: A Voyage with Neil Armstrong, Michael Collins and Edwin E. Aldrin, Jr.* Boston: Little, Brown, 1970.

Ashe, Arthur. *Days of Grace: A Memoir.* New York: Alfred A. Knopf, 1993.

Assayas, Michka. *The Beatles and the Sixties.* New York: Holt, 1996.

Atwan, Robert. *Edsels, Luckies and Frigidaires: Advertising the American Way.* New York: Dell, 1979.

Bailey, Beth L., and Dave Farber. *America in the Seventies.* Lawrence: University of Kansas Press, 2004.

The Beatles Anthology. San Francisco: Chronicle Bks., 2000.

Bernstein, Leonard. *The Infinite Variety of Music.* New York: Simon and Schuster, 1966.

Bertrand, Michael T. *Race, Rock, and Elvis.* Champaign, IL: University of Illinois Press, 2000.

Beschloss, Michael R. *The Crisis Years: Kennedy and Krushchev, 1960–1963.* New York: Edward Burlingame, 1991.

Bigsby, C.W.E. *Modern American Drama, 1945–1990.* New York: Cambridge University Press, 1992.

Birnbach, Lisa. *The Official Preppy Handbook.* New York: Workman, 1980.

Bloom, Alexander, ed. *Long Time Gone: Sixties America Then and Now.* New York: Oxford University Press, 2001.

Booth, Stanley. *Dance with the Devil: The Rolling Stones and Their Times.* New York: Random House, 1984.

Bowles, Jerry G. *A Thousand Sundays: The Story of* The Ed Sullivan Show. New York: Putnam, 1980.

Branch, Taylor. *Parting the Waters: America in the King Years, 1954–1963.* New York: Simon and Schuster, 1988.

Brock, Ted, and Larry Eldridge Jr. *Twenty-five Years: The NFL Since 1960.* New York: Simon and Schuster, 1985.

Brooks, Tim, and Earle Marsh. *The Complete Directory to Prime Time Network and Cable TV Shows 1946–Present.* 7th ed. New York: Ballantine, 1999.

Bugliosi, Vincent. *Helter Skelter: The True Story of the Manson Murders.* New York: Norton, 1974.

Burne, Stewart. *Social Movements of the 1960s: Searching for Democracy.* Boston: Twayne, 1990.

Campbell, Dorothy. *Poverty in the United States During the Sixties: A Bibliography.* Berkeley: University of California Press, 1970.

Canaday, John. *Mainstreams of Modern Art.* New York: Simon and Schuster, 1962.

Carr, Ian. *Miles Davis: The Definitive Biography.* New York: Thunder's Mouth, 1998.

Carroll, Peter N. *It Seemed Like Nothing Happened: America in the Seventies.* New Brunswick, NJ: Rutgers University Press, 2000.

Carson, Clayborne. *In Struggle: SNCC and the Black Awakening of the 1960s.* Cambridge, MA: Harvard University Press, 1981.

Carson, Rachel. *Silent Spring.* Boston: Houghton Mifflin, 1962.

Cash, Johnny. *Cash: The Autobiography.* San Francisco: HarperSanFrancisco, 1997.

Chamberlain, Wilt. *A View From Above.* New York: Villard, 1991.

Chapman, James. *License to Thrill: A Cultural History of the James Bond Films.* New York: Columbia University Press, 2000.

Child, Julia. *The French Chef Cookbook.* New York: Knopf, 1968.

———, Simone Beck, and Louisette Bertholle. *Mastering the Art of French Cooking.* 2 vols. New York: Knopf, 1961–1970.

Clark, Dick. *Rock, Roll & Remember.* New York: Crowell, 1976.

Connikie, Yvonne. *Fashions of a Decade: The 1960s.* New York: Facts on File, 1990.

Cosby, Bill. *Fatherhood.* New York: Berkeley, 1986.

———. *Time Flies.* New York: Bantam, 1988.

Davis, Flora. *Moving the Mountain: The Women's Movement in America since 1960.* New York: Simon and Schuster, 1991.

Dickstein, Morris. *Gates of Eden: American Culture in the Sixties.* 1977; Cambridge, MA: Harvard University Press, 1997.

Dobrow, Larry. *When Advertising Tried Harder: The Sixties: The Golden Age of American Advertising.* New York: Friendly, 1984.

Douglas, George H. *All Aboard: The Railroad in American Life.* New York: Paragon House, 1992.

———. *Skyscrapers: A Social History of the Very Tall Building in America.* Jefferson, NC: McFarland, 1996.

Dow, Bonnie J. *Prime-Time Feminism: Television, Media Culture, and the Women's Movement since 1970.* Philadelphia: University of Pennsylvania Press, 1996.

Draper, Hal. *Berkeley: The New Student Revolt.* New York: Grove, 1965.

Edelstein, Andrew J., and Kevin McDonough. *The Seventies: From Hot Pants to Hot Tubs.* New York: Dutton, 1990.

Elderfield, John, ed. *American Art of the 1960s.* New York: Museum of Modern Art, 1991.

Ellington, Duke. *Music Is My Mistress.* Garden City, NY: Doubleday, 1973.

Ellis, Bret Easton. *Less Than Zero.* New York: Penguin, 1985.

Fisch, Shalom M., and Rosemarie T. Truglio. *"G" Is for "Growing": Thirty Years of Research on Children and Sesame Street.* Mahwah, NJ: Lawrence Erlbaum, 2001.

Fixx, Jim. *The Complete Book of Running.* New York: Random House, 1981.

Flink, Christopher. *The Car Culture.* Cambridge, MA: MIT, 1975.

Flowers, Ronald B. *Religion in Strange Times: The 1960s and 1970s.* Macon, GA: Mercer University Press, 1984.

Fonda, Jane. *Jane Fonda's Work-Out Book.* New York: Simon and Schuster, 1981.

Franklin, John Hope, and Alfred A. Moss. *From Slavery to Freedom: A History of African Americans.* 8th ed. New York: Knopf, 2000.

Friedan, Betty. *The Feminine Mystique.* New York: Norton, 1963.

Frum, David. *How We Got Here: The 70's—The Decade That Brought You Modern Life (for Better or Worse).* New York: Basic Books, 2000.

Garrow, David J. *Bearing the Cross: Martin Luther King, Jr., and the Southern Christian Leadership Conference, 1955–1968.* New York: W. Morrow, 1986.

George, Nelson. *Where Did Our Love Go?: The Rise and Fall of the Motown Sound.* New York: St. Martin's, 1986.

Gitlin, Todd. *The Sixties: Years of Hope, Days of Rage.* Rev. ed. New York: Bantam, 1993.

Goodwin, Doris Kearns. *Lyndon Johnson and the American Dream.* New York: Harper & Row, 1976.

Gordon, Linda. *Woman's Body, Woman's Right: A Social History of Birth Control.* New York: Grossman, 1976.

Graham, Hugh Davis. *The Civil Rights Era: Origins and Development of National Policy, 1960–1972.* New York: Oxford University Press, 1990.

———. *The Uncertain Triumph: Federal Education Policy in the Kennedy and Johnson Years.* Chapel Hill: University of North Carolina Press, 1984.

Gruen, Victor. *Shopping Towns U.S.A.: The Planning of Shopping Centers.* New York: Van Nostrand Reinhold, 1960.

Hallin, Daniel C. *The "Uncensored War": The Media and Vietnam.* New York: Oxford University Press, 1986.

Harrington, Michael. *The Other America: Poverty in the United States.* New York: Macmillan, 1962.

Heinrich, Thomas and Bob Batchelor. *Kotex, Kleenex, Huggies: Kimberly-Clark and the Consumer Revolution in American Business.* Columbus: Ohio State University Press, 2004.

Hoffman, Elizabeth Cobbs. *All You Need Is Love: The Peace Corps and the Spirit of the 1960s.* Cambridge, MA: Harvard University Press, 1998.

Hollowell, John. *Fact & Fiction: The New Journalism and the Nonfiction Novel.* Chapel Hill: University of North Carolina Press, 1977.

Iacocca, Lee. *Iacocca: An Autobiography.* New York: Bantam, 1984.

Ingles, Ian, ed. *The Beatles, Popular Music and Society: A Thousand Voices.* New York: St. Martin's, 2000.

Isaacs, Neil David. *All the Moves: A History of College Basketball.* Philadelphia: Lippincott, 1975.

Jackson, John A. American Bandstand: *Dick Clark and the Making of a Rock 'N' Roll Empire.* New York: Oxford University Press, 1997.

Jacobs, Jane. *The Death and Life of Great American Cities.* New York: Random House, 1961.

Jacobus, John. *Twentieth-Century Architecture: The Middle Years 1940–65.* New York: Frederick A. Praeger, 1966.

Jakle, John A. *Fast Food: Roadside Restaurants in the Automobile Age.* Baltimore: Johns Hopkins University Press, 1999.

James, David E. *Allegories of Cinema: American Film in the Sixties.* Princeton: Princeton University Press, 1989.

Kaiser, Charles. *1968 in America: Music, Politics, Chaos, Counterculture, and the Shaping of a Generation.* York: Grove, 1988.

Karnow, Stanley. *Vietnam: A History.* Rev. ed. New York: Penguin, 1991.

Kennedy, Pagan. *Platforms: A Microwaved Cultural Chronicle of the 1970s.* New York: St. Martin's Press, 1994.

Kennedy, Robert F. *Thirteen Days: A Memoir of the Cuban Missile Crisis.* New York: Norton, 1969.

King, Billie Jean. *We Have Come a Long Way: The Story of Women's Tennis.* New York: McGraw-Hill, 1988.

Kluger, Richard. *Simple Justice: The History of Brown v. Board of Education and Black America's Struggle for Equality.* 1975. New York: Knopf, 1976.

Kowinski, William S. *The Malling of America.* New York: Morrow, 1985.

Kroc, Ray, and Robert Anderson. *Grinding It Out: The Making of McDonald's.* Chicago: Contemporary Bks., 1977.

Levy, Peter B. *The New Left and Labor in the 1960s.* Urbana: University of Illinois Press, 1994.

Linden-Ward, Blanche, and Carol Hurd Green. *American Women in the 1960s: Changing the Future.* New York: Twayne, 1993.

Louganis, Greg. *Breaking the Surface.* New York: Random House, 1995.

MacDonald, J. Fred. *Black and White TV: African Americans in Television Since 1948.* 2nd ed. Chicago: Nelson-Hall, 1992.

———. *Who Shot the Sheriff?: The Rise and Fall of the Television Western.* New York: Praeger, 1987.

Mailer, Norman. *Pontifications: Interviews.* Ed. Michael Lennon. Boston: Little, Brown, 1982.

Marable, Manning. *Race, Reform, and Rebellion: The Second Reconstruction in Black America, 1945–1990.* 2nd ed. Jackson: University Press of Mississippi, 1991.

Maraniss, David. *When Pride Still Mattered: A Life of Vince Lombardi.* New York: Simon and Schuster, 1999.

Marc, David. *Comic Visions: Television Comedy and American Culture.* 2nd ed. Malden, MA: Blackwell, 1997.

Marcus, Eric. *Making History: The Struggle for Gay and Lesbian Equal Rights, 1945–1990: An Oral History.* New York: HarperCollins, 1992.

Mariani, John F. *America Eats Out.* New York: Morrow, 1991.

Marqusee, Mike. *Muhammad Ali and the Spirit of the Sixties.* New York: Verso, 1999.

Marwick, Arthur. *The Sixties.* 1998. New York: Oxford University Press, 1999.

May, Elaine Tyler. *Homeward Bound: American Families in the Cold War Era.* Rev. ed. New York: Basic Books, 1999.

McInerney, Jay. *Bright Lights, Big City.* New York: Vintage, 1984.

McKeen, William. *Tom Wolfe.* New York: Twayne, 1995.

Melody, William. *Children's TV: The Economics of Exploitation.* New Haven, CT: Yale University Press, 1973.

Miller, James. *Flowers in the Dustbin: The Rise of Rock and Roll, 1947–1977.* New York: Simon and Schuster, 1999.

Morris, Edmund. *Dutch: A Memoir of Ronald Reagan.* New York: Random House, 1999.

Morrison, Toni. *Beloved.* New York: Vintage, 1987.

Nader, Ralph. *Unsafe at Any Speed: The Designed-in Dangers of the American Automobile.* New York: Grossman, 1965.

Nicklaus, Jack. *Jack Nicklaus: My Story.* New York: Simon and Schuster, 1997.

Ozersky, Josh. *Archie Bunker's America: TV in an Era of Change, 1968–1978.* Carbondale: Southern Illinois University Press, 2003.

Palmer, Arnold. *A Golfer's Life.* New York: Ballantine, 1999.

Peck, Abe. *Uncovering the Sixties: The Life and Times of the Underground Press.* New York: Pantheon, 1985.

Peterson, Theodore. *Magazines in the Twentieth Century.* 2nd ed. Urbana: University of Illinois Press, 1964.

Phillips, Gene D. *Stanley Kubrick: A Film Odyssey.* New York: Popular Library, 1975.

Pichaske, David R. *A Generation in Motion: Popular Music and Culture in the Sixties.* New York: Schirmer Bks., 1979.

Pinsker, Sanford. *Jewish-American Fiction, 1917–1987.* New York: Twayne, 1992.

Pollack, Howard. *Aaron Copland: The Life and Work of an Uncommon Man.* New York: Henry Holt, 1999.

Polsky, Richard M. *Getting to Sesame Street: Origins of the Children's Television Workshop.* New York: Praeger, 1974.

Rielly, Edward J. *Baseball: An Encyclopedia of Popular Culture.* Santa Barbara, CA: ABC-CLIO, 2000.

Rudolph, Wilma. *Wilma.* New York: New American Library, 1977.

Sandler, Irving. *American Art of the 1960s.* New York: Harper & Row, 1988.

Schulman, Bruce J. *The Seventies: The Great Shift in American Culture, Society, and Politics.* Cambridge, MA: Da Capo Press, 2001.

Shaughnessy, Dan. *Ever Green: The Boston Celtics: A History in the Words of their Players, Coaches, Fans, and Foes, from 1946 to the Present.* New York: St. Martin's, 1990.

Sheppard, Dick. *Elizabeth: The Life and Career of Elizabeth Taylor.* Garden City, NY: Doubleday, 1974.

Shilts, Randy. *And The Band Played On: Politics, People and the AIDS Epidemic.* New York: Penguin, 1987.

Slocum-Schaffer, Stephanie. *America in the Seventies.* Syracuse, NY: Syracuse University Press, 2003.

Spigel, Lynn, and Michael Curtin, eds. *The Revolution Wasn't Televised: Sixties Television and Social Conflict.* New York: Routledge, 1997.

Spitz, Bob. *Dylan: A Biography.* New York: McGraw-Hill, 1989.

Sterritt, David. *The Films of Alfred Hitchcock.* New York: Cambridge University Press, 1993.

Stewart, James B. *Den of Thieves.* New York: Simon and Schuster, 1991.

Stich, Sidra. *Made in the U.S.A.: An Americanization in Modern Art, the '50s and '60s.* Berkeley: University of California Press, 1987.

Troy, Gil. *Morning in America: How Ronald Reagan Invented the 1980s.* Princeton: Princeton University Press, 2005.

Venturi, Robert. *Complexity and Contradiction in Architecture.* 2nd ed. New York: Museum of Modern Art, 1977.

————. *Learning from Las Vegas: The Forgotten Symbolism of Architectural Form.* Rev. ed. Cambridge, MA: MIT, 1977.

Viorst, Milton. *Fire in the Streets: America in the 1960s.* New York: Simon and Schuster, 1979.

Wolfe, Tom. *The Bonfire of the Vanities.* New York: Farrar, Straus and Giroux, 1987.

Wood, Robin. *Hollywood from Vietnam to Reagan.* New York: Columbia, 1986.

Wooden, John R. *They Call Me Coach.* Rev. ed. Chicago: Contemporary Bks., 1988.

Wright, John W., ed. *The Commercial Connection: Advertising and the American Mass Media.* New York: Dell, 1979.

MUSEUMS, ORGANIZATIONS, SPECIAL COLLECTIONS, AND USEFUL WEB SITES

The John F. Kennedy Presidential Library and Museum. Columbia Point, Boston, MA, 02125. http://www.jfklibrary.org/.

> The John F. Kennedy Presidential Library and Museum is dedicated to the memory of the nation's 35th president. The purpose of the institution is to advance the study and understanding of President Kennedy's life and career and the times in which he lived. Located on a 10-acre park, overlooking the sea that President Kennedy loved and the city that launched him to greatness, the library stands as a vibrant tribute to his life and times.

The Lyndon Baines Johnson Library and Museum. 2313 Red River St., Austin, TX, 78705. http://www.lbjlib.utexas.edu/.

> The Lyndon Baines Johnson Library and Museum is one of 12 presidential libraries administered by the National Archives and Records Administration. The library houses 45 million pages of historical documents, which include the papers from the entire public career of Lyndon Baines Johnson and also from those of close associates. These papers and the vast administrative files from the presidency are used primarily by scholars. The museum provides year-round public viewing of its permanent historical and cultural exhibits. Special activities and exhibits are sponsored by the LBJ Foundation.

Nixon Presidential Library and Museum. 18001 Yorba Linda Blvd., Yorba Linda, CA, 92886. http://www.nixonlibrary.gov.

> For researchers, the Nixon Presidential Library offers a wealth of White House tapes and audiovisual materials. The largest portion of the collection is the 46 million pages of textual information. Visitors can tour the museum, situated on nine acres in southern California. In addition to exhibitions, the grounds include President Nixon's helicopter and birthplace. Visitors are also invited to see the special exhibit galleries, which show a variety of rotating exhibits related to the museum's mission as a national institution and local landmark.

Ronald Reagan Presidential Library and Museum. 40 Presidential Drive, Simi Valley, CA, 93065. http://www.reaganfoundation.org/.

> The Ronald Reagan Presidential Foundation is a nonprofit, nonpartisan organization that sustains the Ronald Reagan Presidential Library and Museum, the Center for Public Affairs, the Presidential Learning Center, and The Air Force One Pavilion. The library houses over 55 million pages of gubernatorial, presidential, and personal papers and over 100,000 gifts and artifacts chronicling the lives of Ronald and Nancy Reagan. It also serves as the final resting place of America's 40th president.

The Watergate Story. The Washington Post Web site. http://www.washingtonpost.com/wp-srv/politics/special/watergate/index.html. The Washington Post Company, 2008.

> A Web site maintained by *The Washington Post* examines the Watergate scandal from the early investigatory work conducted by its reporters Bob Woodward and Carl Bernstein through the unmasking of Deep Throat in 2005. The site offers a wealth of information on the national crisis, including many audio and video clips, in addition to interviews with many of the key players.

VIDEOS/FILMS

Apocalypse Now: The Complete Dossier. Produced by Francis Coppola. 355 minutes. 2 DVDs. Distributed by Paramount Home Entertainment, 2006. Release of the original 1979 film with added features, including *Apocalypse Now Redux.* The powerful tale, inspired by Joseph Conrad's *Heart of Darkness,* is the story of a United States Army officer/trained assassin, played by Martin Sheen, who is sent into the depths of a southeast Asian jungle to seek out a renegade colonel, played by Marlon Brando, during the Vietnam War.

Cold War. Produced by Jeremy Isaacs. 1,120 minutes. 8 VHS. Distributed by Warner Home Video and CNN Productions, 1998. The 24-part documentary series examines the Cold War and its influence on history, culture, technology, economics, and the modern psyche.

Dr. Strangelove or, How I Learned to Stop Worrying and Love the Bomb. Produced by Stanley Kubrick. 95 minutes. DVD. Distributed by Columbia TriStar Home Entertainment, 2004. The DVD release of the original 1964 dark comedy. Chaos erupts when a general orders an attack on the Russians, which will subsequently trigger the Russian "Doomsday Device." The president and his aides struggle to find a way to stop the impending doom. The film features a memorable scene with actor Slim Pickens riding a bomb as if it were a bucking bronco.

Fast Times at Ridgemont High. Produced by Irving Azoff and Art Linson. 90 minutes. VHS. Distributed by MCA Home Video, 1996. The VHS release of the original 1982 motion picture parodies the life of teens in San Fernando Valley of Los Angeles, the center of the Valley Girl lifestyle in the 1980s. The movie focuses on a group of teenagers (featuring Sean Penn in one of his first movie roles) as they deal with independence, success, sexuality, money, maturity, school, and particularly with just making it through the formative years.

Reagan. Produced by Adriana Bosch and Austin Hoyt. 263 minutes. 2 VHS. Distributed by Warner Home Video, 2000. Originally airing in 1998, the two-part documentary tells the story of Ronald Reagan's life, with comments by contemporaries and historians.

Valley Girl. Produced by Wayne Crawford and Andrew Lane. 99 minutes. VHS. Distributed by MGM Home Entertainment, 1983. The film chronicles 1980s teenage angst in the San Fernando Valley of Los Angeles when a Valley Girl, played by Deborah Foreman, falls for a Hollywood punk, played by Nicolas Cage. The movie ends with a quintessentially 1980s moment: a limo ride by the two main characters driving past the Sherman Oaks Galleria as the Modern English song "I Melt With You" plays.

Vietnam: A Television History. Produced by Judith Vecchione, Andrew Pearson, Martin Smith, et al. 780 minutes. 7 VHS. Distributed by Sony, 1987. The documentary depicts events in Vietnam from 1945 through 1975. The primary focus is on America's intervention in the Vietnam War.

When We Were Kings: The Untold Story of the Rumble in the Jungle. Produced by Keith Robinson and Vikram Jayanti. 94 minutes. DVD. Distributed by Universal, 2005. The 1997 Academy Award, Best Documentary Feature winning film focuses on the famous 1974 "Rumble in the Jungle" boxing match between Muhammad Ali and George Foreman in Zaire, Africa.

Index

ABBA (singing group), **III:**204

Abbey, Edward, **III:**42–43

ABC of the Teeth (Colgate Company), **I:**17

Abdul, Paula, **III:**312–13, **IV:**175

Abernathy, Ralph D., **III:**136

Abie's Irish Rose (Nichols), **I:**277

Abstract Expressionism, **II:**242–43, 380, **III:**226–27

Abstract painting, **III:**117–18, 226–27

Academy Award winners: 1920s, **I:**286; 1930s, **II:**51; 1940s, **II:**193; 1950s, **II:**303; 1960s, **III:**64; 1970s, **III:**179; 1980s, **III:**282; 1990s, **IV:**54; 2000s, **IV:**180

Academy of Motion Picture Arts and Sciences, **I:**286

Acadia, Florida, **I:**14–15

Accessories, fashion: 1900s, **I:**53, 59; 1910s, **I:**169; 1920s, **I:**298–99; 1930s, **II:**75–76; 1940s, **II:**198–99; 1950s, **II:**330–31; 1960s, **III:**67, 71; 1970s, **III:**193; 1980s, **III:**253–54; 1990s, **IV:**65

Acquired Immune Deficiency Syndrome (AIDS), **III:**248–50, 270, 286, 315, **IV:**13–14, 93–94, 108–9, 218. *See also* Human Immunodeficiency Virus

Action adventure movies, **III:**280–82

Action figure toys, **IV:**96

Actors' Association for Clean Plays, **I:**277

Actors' Equity Association, **I:**154

The Actors Studio (New York), **II:**181

Acuff, Roy, **II:**220–21

Adams, Ansel, **II:**149

Adams, Scott, **IV:**140

Ad Council (War Advertising Council), **II:**154–55

Adelphia Communications, **IV:**139

Adidas Shoes, **IV:**226

Adler, I., **I:**179

Adolph Coors Brewing Company, **II:**90

Adventure (magazine), **I:**272

The Adventures of Ellery Queen (TV show), **II:**284

The Adventures of Ozzie and Harriet (TV show), **II:**318

Adventure travel, **IV:**102–3

Advertising Age (magazine), **III:**151

Advertising (1900s): agencies, **I:**20–23; industrialism and, **I:**16; merchandising in, **I:**18–20; progressive nature of, **I:**23–24; slogans, **I:**17, 20; of soft drinks, **I:**20

Advertising (1910s): on billboards, **I:**121; communication through, **I:**123–24; effectiveness of, **I:**124–27; Madison Avenue and, **I:**122–23; in magazines, **I:**121, 215; modernization of, **I:**120–21; in newspapers, **I:**121; slogans, **I:**121; of soft drinks, **I:**124–25; for WWI, **I:**127–28

Advertising (1920s): as "anti-modern," **I:**244; industry trends in, **I:**241–42; in magazines, **I:**249–50; photography for, **I:**356; publicity stunts, **I:**247–48; racism in, **I:**247; on radio, **I:**250–51, 289–90; size of, **I:**229; slogans, **I:**242; spokespersons for, **I:**245–47; strategies for, **I:**242–45, 341; swindles, **I:**251; venues, **I:**248–51

Advertising (1930s): art in, **II:**16–17; effects of Great Depression, **II:**14–16; gender specific, **II:**18; music in, **II:**99; racism in, **II:**19–20; on radio, **II:**18–19, 62–63; slogans, **II:**18; for smoking, **II:**20–21; trends, **II:**16–18

Advertising (1940s): Coca-Cola, **II:**158; for "common man," **II:**157–58; corporate, **II:**156–57; futurism and, **II:**158–59; institutional, **II:**156; "Rosie the Riveter" in, **II:**155–56; single-product campaigns, **II:**160–61; slogans, **II:**158; of soft drinks, **II:**158; for war effort, **II:**154–55, 159–60

Advertising (1950s): to children, **II:**270–71; jingles, **II:**266; media messages in, **II:**268–69; to men, **II:**271; to minorities, **II:**271–72; in print, **II:**265–66; public relations of, **II:**273–73; on radio, **II:**266, 311; slogans, **II:**269, on television, **II:**266–68; trading stamps for, **II:**273; to women, **II:**269–70

Advertising (1960s): innovations in, **III:**21–22; to minorities, **III:**20–21; new markets for, **III:**18–20; notable people in, **III:**22–24; slogans, **III:**19; to women, **III:**20–21

Advertising (1970s): new markets for, **III:**155; slogans, **III:**151; superstars in, **III:**150–55; women in, **III:**152–53

Advertising (1980s): icons, **III:**255–56; to men, **III:**253; shoes, **III:**251–53; slogans, **III:**252; by sports figures, **III:**315

Advertising (1990s): anti-drug campaigns, **IV:**21; business of, **IV:**16; by celebrities, **IV:**18–19; to children, **IV:**20–21; infomercials, **IV:**18; innovation in, **IV:**17–18; niche marketing, **IV:**22; online, **IV:**22–23; political, **IV:**21–22; product placement in, **IV:**19–20; slogans, **IV:**17; by sports arenas, **IV:**94; by telemarketing, **IV:**18; trends in, **IV:**16–17

Advertising (2000s): by celebrities, **IV:**152–53; future of, **IV:**153–54; marketing education in, **IV:**146–47; media transformation in, **IV:**148–50; mega agencies in, **IV:**151–52; politics in, **IV:**150–51; reactions to, **IV:**147–48; slogans, **IV:**145; on television, **IV:**174–75; values in, **IV:**144–46

Advice columnists, **II:**293–94

Advocacy advertising, **II:**157

Aerosmith (singing group), **III:**205

Affirmative action, **III:**135

AFL-CIO (trade union), **I:**12

African Americans (1900s): in books, **I:**39–42; in boxing, **I:**80–81; jazz music of, **I:**73–74; lynching of, **I:**12; music influenced by, **I:**69; ragtime music of, **I:**72–73; as visual artists, **I:**97–98

African Americans (1910s): blues music of, **I:**189–91; in boxing, **I:**199; in films, **I:**163; jazz music of, **I:**189–91; magazines for, **I:**122; music influenced by, **I:**182, 183–84; racism and, **I:**110–11; ragtime music of, **I:**188–89; theatrical parody of, **I:**154; in WWI, **I:**113

African Americans (1920s): as actors, **I:**285–86; as authors, **I:**278–79; in baseball, **I:**328; black nationalism and, **I:**232; blues music of, **I:**319–21; fashions for, **I:**298; jazz music of, **I:**318–19, 323; in musicals, **I:**316; as record buyers, **I:**321; as visual artists, **I:**354–55

African Americans (1930s): employment status of, **II:**9; homeownership by, **II:**166; jazz music of, **II:**93; as magazine entrepreneurs, **II:**176; in music, **II:**92–94; at Olympic Games, **II:**106; as poets, **II:**175; radio portrayal of, **II:**63–64; as visual artists, **II:**128

African Americans (1940s): as authors, **II:**171–72; in baseball, **II:**225; in basketball, **II:**229; in football, **II:**229; jazz music of, **II:**222–24;

unemployment of, **II:**147; in WWII, **II:**146, 147–48, 230; in zoot suit riots, **II:**203

African Americans (1950s): advertising to, **II:**271–72; jazz music of, **II:**348; unemployment of, **II:**256

African Americans (1960s): advertising to, **III:**20–21; as authors, **III:**36; in classical music, **III:**94; fashion trends of, **III:**72–73; in football, **III:**96; in tennis, **III:**102

African Americans (1970s): advertising portrayals of, **III:**153–54; hair influences, **III:**192; in movies, **III:**177–79, 180; in musicals, **III:**174, 186; reggae music of, **III:**206; in television, **III:**182, 184

African Americans (1980s): in advertising, **III:**251; as authors, **III:**268; dance influence of, **III:**305; poverty of, **III:**244; in television, **III:**274

African Americans (1990s): in advertising, **IV:**22; hair products for, **IV:**66; in middle class, **IV:**5–6; in music, **IV:**83, 85; racism and, **IV:**46, 73, 80

African Americans (2000s): in advertising, **IV:**146; in music, **IV:**215; racism and, **IV:**135–37; in sports, **IV:**225; as visual artists, **IV:**249, 254

Agee, James, **II:**129, 246

Agent Orange herbicide, **III:**143

The Age of Innocence (Wharton), **I:**40

Age of Opulence (1910s), **I:**108

Agnew, Spiro, **III:**132

Agricultural issues, **II:**8–9, **III:**80–81

AIDS. *See* Acquired Immune Deficiency Syndrome

Aiken, Clay, **IV:**213

Aiken, Conrad, **I:**267

Air bags in cars, **III:**220

Airflow line (Chrysler Motors), **II:**30–31, 114

Air Jordan shoes, **IV:**62

Airline Deregulation Act, **III:**322

Airline travel: 1900s, **I:**91–92; 1910s, **I:**207–8; 1920s, **I:**348–51; 1930s, **II:**120–23; 1940s, **II:**238–40; 1950s, **II:**377; 1960s, **III:**115; 1970s, **III:**221–23; 1980s, **III:**322–24; 1990s, **IV:**100, 101–2; 2000s, **IV:**238–39;

Airport (Hailey), **III:**40

Airstream Trailer Company, **II:**117–18

Air traffic controller's strike, **III:**323–24

Akron (dirigible), **II:**121

Alaskan pipeline, **III:**131

Albers, Josef, **III:**121

Albers Super Mkts., Inc. (supermarket), **II:**82–83

Albom, Mitch, **IV:**38

Alcoholic beverages: 1900s, **I:**42; 1910s, **I:**112, 233–34; 1920s, **I:**233–35, 308, 312; 1930s, **II:**89–90; 1940s, **II:**221; 1950s, **II:**343–45; 1960s, **III:**76; 1970s, **III:**151–52; 1980s, **III:**254–55; 1990s, **IV:**75–76; 2000s, **IV:**236

Aldrin, Buzz, **III:**112

Alexander's Bridge (Cather), **I:**143

Ali, Muhammad (Cassius Clay), **III:**98–99, 101, 210

All-America Football Conference (AAFC), **II:**229

All-American Girls Professional Baseball League, **II:**225

Allen, Gracie, **II:**64, 318

Allen, Ian, **IV:**252–53

Allen, Ida Bailey, **I:**251

Allen, Paul, **III:**215, 245

Allen, Woody, **III:**177

All in the Family (TV show), **III:**180–81

All My Children (TV show), **III:**183

All the King's Men (Warren), **II:**174

All the President's Men (1976), **III:**169

Allure (magazine), **IV:**41

Al Qaeda (terrorist group), **IV:**129–30

Alternative rock music, **IV:**80–82

Altman, Robert, **IV:**55–56

Amahl and the Night Visitors (1951), **II:**355

Amateur Athletic Union (AAU), **I:**82

Amateur Golf Association, **I:**81

Amateur photography, **II:**381–82

Amateur *vs.* professional athletes, **I:**326–27

The Amazing Adventures of Kavalier & Clay (Chabon), **IV:**168

Amazing Stories (magazine), **I:**272

Amazon.com (online bookstore), **IV:**32, 166

AMC Theaters, **III:**314

American Airlines, **III:**322–23

American Airways, **I:**351

American Association of Plastic Surgeons, **IV:**67

American Ballet Theatre, **II:**179, **III:**61

American Bandstand (TV show), **II:**328, 354–55, **III:**60–61, 88

American Baseball League, **I:**195–96

American Basketball League (ABL), **II:**104

American Broadcasting Company (ABC), **III:**53

American Broadcast System (ABC), **II:**188

American Civil Liberties Union (ACLU), **I:**237, **III:**140

American Express (credit card), **II:**257

American Federation of Labor (AFL), **I:**11, 114

American Film Institute, **IV:**56

American Flyer wagon (toy), **II:**110

American Football League (AFL), **III:**96

American Gladiators (TV show), **IV:**90

American Gothic (Wood), **II:**125–26

American Guide series (FWP), **II:**35–36

American Idol (TV show), **IV:**175–76, 213–14

The American Indian Movement (AIM), **III:**12

American Institute for Cancer Research, **IV:**203

American Institute of Architects (AIA), **I:**131

American Institute/Society of Interior Decorators, **II:**26–27

American League (AL), **I:**77–78

American Motors Company (AMC), **III:**220

American Painters and Sculptors (AAPS), **I:**218

American Ping-Pong Association, **II:**109

American Professional Football Association (APFA), **I:**330

American Scene painting, **I:**354

American Society of Composers, Authors, and Publishers (ASCAP), **I:**186

American Tobacco Company, **I:**180, 245

America Online (AOL), **IV:**15, 127–28

Amos 'n Andy (radio show), **I:**290, **II:**20, 63–64

AM radio broadcasting, **II:**355

Amtrak trains, **III:**223–24, **IV:**106. *See also* Railroad travel

Amusement parks, **II:**375–76

Anderson, Gilbert, **I:**159

Anderson, Maxwell, **II:**68

Anderson, Sherwood, **I:**143–44

And God Created Woman (1956), **II:**310

The Andromeda Strain (Crichton), **III:**40

And The Band Played On: Politics, People and the AIDS Epidemic (Shilts), **III:**270–71

The Andy Griffith Show (TV show), **III:**54

Andy Hardy movies, **II:**58–59

Angelou, Maya, **III:**168, 169–70

Animal comics, **II:**46–47

Animated cartoon movies (animation), **I:**288, **II:**160

Animorphs series (Applegate), **IV:**40

Aniston, Jennifer, **IV:**184–85

Annenberg, Walter, **II:**290

Annie Allen (Brooks), **II:**175

Annie Get Your Gun (1950), **II:**305

Annie Hall (1977), **III:**190

Ann Taylor (retail store), **III:**293

Anthony, Susan B., **I:**40

Antibiotic usage, **II:**357

Anti-drug advertising, **IV:**21

"Antiestablishment" fashion, **III:**192–93

Anti-modern advertising, **I:**244

Antiperspirant usage, **II:**78

Apollo-Soyuz Test Project (ASTP), **III:**218

Apollo space flights, **III:**110–12

Appalachian Spring (1944), **II:**180

Appia, Adolphe, **I:**151

Apple, Fiona, **IV:**82

Apple Computer, **III:**215, 245–46

Applegate, K. A, **IV:**40

A&P (supermarket), **II:**82, 83

Aquitania (ocean liner), **I:**348

Arbuckle, Roscoe ("Fatty"), **I:**239

Arbus, Diane, **III:**121–22

Arby's (fast food restaurant), **III:**79

Archie comics, **II:**295

Architecture/architects (1900s): Burnham, Daniel, **I:**26–27; challenges of, **I:**25; interior design and, **I:**28–29; residential, **I:**27–28, 29–30; of skyscrapers, **I:**25–27; Sullivan, Louis, **I:**25–26, 29; Wright, Frank Lloyd, **I:**25, 29–31

Architecture/architects (1910s): Arts and Crafts movement, **I:**135–37; city planning and, **I:**131; of college campuses, **I:**133; École des Beaux-Arts, **I:**131–32; form *vs.* meaning in, **I:**129–31; interior design and, **I:**129–30; International Style, **I:**133; modern materials in, **I:**131; of private buildings, **I:**134; of public buildings, **I:**132–34; of public monuments, **I:**133–34; residential, **I:**134–37; of skyscrapers, **I:**129, 132; Wright, Frank Lloyd, **I:**134–35

Architecture/architects (1920s): as advertising, **I:**249; Art Deco, **I:**252–53, 261; of churches/temples, **I:**255; of gas stations, **I:**259; of government buildings, **I:**256; Hood, Raymond M., **I:**261–62;

interior design and, **I:**261–62; International Style, **I:**253; Kahn, Albert, **I:**261; manufacturing/industrial, **I:**256–57; mimetic, **I:**259–60; of movie palaces, **I:**258–59; residential, **I:**260; of restaurants, **I:**257; of skyscrapers, **I:**253–55; styles, **I:**252–53; of universities, **I:**255–56; Van Alen, William, **I:**262; Williams, Paul Revere, **I:**262; Wright, Frank Lloyd, **I:**262

Architecture/architects (1930s): Art Deco, **II:**22–23, 30; of fairs/expositions, **II:**27–30; of gas stations, **II:**27; interior design and, **II:**26–27, 30; International Style, **II:**23–25; Johnson, Philip, **II:**24; mass housing, **II:**26; period revivals in, **II:**26–27; Pope, John Russell, **II:**23–24; residential, **II:**26; of skyscrapers, **II:**23; Wright, Frank Lloyd, **II:**25–26

Architecture/architects (1940s): innovation in, **II:**167; interior design and, **II:**165; International Style, **II:**167; Mies van der Rohe, Ludwig, **II:**167–68; of prefab housing, **II:**163–64; of quonset huts, **II:**163–64; residential, **II:**163–64; of shopping centers, **II:**166; of skyscrapers, **II:**167; of suburban developments, **II:**164–66

Architecture/architects (1950s): commercial, **II:**275; of fallout shelters, **II:**281; interior design and, **II:**281–82; International Style, **II:**275; residential, **II:**277–79; of roadside services, **II:**276; of shopping centers, **II:**275–76; for signs, **II:**276–77; Wright, Frank Lloyd, **II:**278

Architecture/architects (1960s): of churches, **III:**31–32; Gropius, Walter, **III:**25; historical preservation through, **III:**33–34; interior design, **III:**30; Kahn, Louis, **III:**26; residential, **III:**30–31; of skyscrapers, **III:**28, 30; of stores/offices, **III:**27–30; Venturi, Robert, **III:**26–27; Wright, Frank Lloyd, **III:**25

Architecture/architects (1970s): historical preservation through, **III:**160–62; interior design and, **III:**160; Johnson, Philip, **III:**158–59; Moore, Charles, **III:**158; Pei, I. M., **III:**158; Pereira, William L., **III:**156–58; of public buildings, **III:**159–60; residential, **III:**160; of skyscrapers, **III:**161, 162

Architecture/architects (1980s): Duany, Andres, **III:**259; Graves, Michael, **III:**258–59; Lin, Maya Ying, **III:**260–61; Plater-Zyberk, Elizabeth, **III:**259; residential, **III:**261–62; of skyscrapers, **III:**258, 259; Venturi, Robert, **III:**259

Architecture/architects (1990s): Gehry, Frank, **IV:**25–26; glass in, **IV:**26–27; "green," **IV:**27; museums, **IV:**27–28; Pei, I. M., **IV:**26–27; residential, **IV:**28–29; of suburban developments, **IV:**28–29; technology in, **IV:**24–25; in urban renewal, **IV:**29–30

Architecture/architects (2000s): Gehry, Frank, **IV:**156, 158–59; interior design and, **IV:**162–64; residential, **IV:**160–62; of skyscrapers, **IV:**158–59; trends in, **IV:**155–57; in urban centers, **IV:**159–60; of World Trade Center, **IV:**157–58

The Argosy (magazine), **I:**272
Armani, Giorgio, **III:**295, **IV:**59
Armory Show (art), **I:**216–19
Armstrong, Louis, **I:**74, 319, **II:**93, **III:**94–95
Armstrong, Neil, **III:**80, 112
Arnaz, Desi, **II:**263, 279, 317
Arness, James, **II:**320
Arrested Development (rap group), **IV:**84
Arrowsmith (Lewis), **I:**264
Art Deco style, **I:**252–53, 261, **II:**22–23, 30
The Arthur Murray Party (TV show), **II:**328
Arts. *See* Visual arts
Arts and Crafts movement, **I:**28–29, 135–37
The Ashcan School (artists), **I:**95–96, 216, 217, 220, 353–54
Ashe, Arthur, **III:**102, 211, **IV:**93
The Asphalt Exodus (postwar), **II:**240
Associated Advertising Clubs of America, **I:**123, 251
The Associated Press (AP), **II:**42
Association of Licensed Automobile Manufacturers (ALAM), **I:**212
Astaire, Fred, **II:**54–55, 70, 123–24, 331
Astronauts, **III:**217–18
Atari Games, **III:**215
Atkins, Chet, **III:**87
Atkins, Robert C. (Atkins Diet), **III:**197, **IV:**77, 203
Atlantic Monthly (magazine), **I:**33
Atlas, Charles, **I:**338
Atomic bomb. *See* Nuclear bomb
Aunt Jemima (advertising figure), **I:**247, **II:**20
Aunt Sammy's Radio Recipes (radio show), **I:**251, 306
Austin, Gene, **I:**317
Austin, Steve "Stone Cold," **IV:**89–90
The Autobiography of Miss Jane Pittman (Gaines), **III:**164
Auto camping, **I:**345–46, **II:**116
Automobiles, 1900s, **I:**89–91; 1910s, **I:**204–5, 210–11; 1920s, **I:**340–43; 1930s, **II:**30–31, 31, 114–16; 1940s, **II:**235–37; 1950s, **II:**367–69, 371–73; 1960s, **III:**112–15; 1970s, **III:**219–21; 1990s, **IV:**104–6
Auto racing, **I:**333, **IV:**90–91
Autry, Gene, **II:**53, 98, 214–15
Avalon Theatre (Chicago), **I:**259
The Awakening (Chopin), **I:**13
A&W food stand, **I:**310
Axene, Harry, **II:**210–11

B. F. Goodrich Company, **I:**250
Babbit (Lewis), **I:**264
Baby boom generation, **II:**151–53, 256, 257, 373, **III:**131, **IV:**142, 221
Bach, Richard, **III:**167
Bacharach, Burt, **III:**88
The Backstreet Boys (singing group), **IV:**87
Back to the Future (1985), **III:**279
Bacon, Henry, **I:**133–34
Bad Boy Records, **IV:**83–84
Baez, Joan, **III:**84–85, 199

Bagatelle (board game), **II**:108–9

Baker, Kermit, **IV**:163

Bakker, Jim & Tammy Faye, **III**:248

Balanchine, George, **II**:180, **III**:61

Baldwin, James, **III**:36

Baldwin Hills Village (Los Angeles), **II**:162–63

Ball, Lucille, **II**:263, 279, 317

Ballet: 1910s, **I**:157; 1920s, **I**:279, 309, 321; 1930s, **II**:54; 1940s, **II**:179–80; 1960s, **III**:61

Baltimore Orioles, **III**:210

Banana Republic (retail store), **IV**:62

Bancroft, Anne, **III**:50

Bannister, Roger, **II**:361

Bara, Theda, **I**:160, 298

Barbecue fad, **II**:338

Barbie doll (toy), **II**:365, **III**:105, **IV**:96

"Bar" foods, **IV**:70–71

Barlow, Janelle, **IV**:206

Barn dances, **I**:322

Barnes & Noble Bookstore, **IV**:31, 32, 74

Barney Baxter in the Air (comic strip), **II**:122

Barratt builders, **III**:261–62

Barton, Bruce, **I**:265

Barton, Ralph, **I**:274

Baseball: 1900s, **I**:77–79; 1910s, **I**:195–99; 1920s, **I**:327–28; 1930s, **II**:101–3; 1940s, **II**:225–28; 1950s, **II**:357–58; 1960s, **III**:99–100; 1970s, **III**:210–11; 1980s, **III**:315; 1990s, **IV**:92–93; 2000s, **IV**:228–29

Basketball: 1910s, **I**:199; 1920s, **I**:331–32; 1930s, **II**:104; 1940s, **II**:229–30; 1950s, **II**:358–59; 1960s, **III**:100–101; 1970s, **III**:212; 1980s, **III**:315; 1990s, **IV**:91; 2000s, **IV**:224–27

Basketball Association of America (BAA), **II**:229

Basquiat, Jean-Michel, **III**:327–28

Bathing suits, **II**:74–75, 77

Batman (1989), **III**:272

Batman (comic book character), **II**:177

Batman (TV show), **III**:55

Batten, Barton, Durstine, and Osborne (advertising firm), **II**:274, **III**:20

Battle Dome (TV show), **IV**:90

Bay Area Laboratory Cooperative (BALCO), **IV**:229

Bay of Pigs incident, **III**:16

Baywatch (TV show), **IV**:44

The Beach Boys (singing group), **III**:88–89, 106

Beanie Baby craze, **IV**:96

Beany and Cecil (TV show), **II**:363–64

Beard, James, **II**:212

Beastie Boys (rap group), **IV**:84–85

Beat Generation, **II**:286–87

The Beatles (singing group), **III**:57, 68–69, 89–90, 202

Beatnik culture, **II**:203, 287

Beaton, Cecil, **II**:246

The Beats (literary group), **III**:35–36, 43

The Beauty Myth: How Images of Beauty Are Used Against Women (Wolf), **IV**:68

Beauty pageants, **IV**:68

Beaux-Arts style, **I**:28

Beavis and Butt-Head (TV show), **IV**:50

Beckett, "Sister" Wendy, **IV**:109

Beck (singer), **IV**:85

Beech-Nut gum advertising, **II**:20

Bee Gees (singing group), **III**:207

Beetle Bailey (comic strip), **II**:294

Beetle (Volkswagen), **IV**:104–5, 162

Beijing, China, **IV**:230

Beisbol (Cuban baseball), **I**:79

Belafonte, Harry, **II**:353

Belasco, David, **I**:153

Bel Geddes, Norman **II**:30

Bellow, Saul, **II**:174, **III**:36, 164

Bellows, George, **I**:95–96, 353

Beloved (Morrison), **III**:268

BeltLine (Atlanta), **IV**:156

Benchley, Peter, **III**:166

Bendix Trophy (airplane racing), **II**:122

Benetton (retail store), **III**:293

Bennett, Tony, **III**:87–88

Benny, Jack, **II**:185

Benson, Frank Weston, **I**:94

Benton, Thomas Hart, **II**:125–27

Berkeley, Busby, **II**:53–54

Berkowitz, David ("Son of Sam"), **III**:140–41

Berle, Milton, **II**:188, 189–90, 285

Berlin, Irving, **I**:48, 187–88, **II**:74, 215–16

Berlin Olympics (1936), **II**:231

Berlin Wall, **IV**:101

Bermuda shorts, **II**:332, 335

Bernbach, William, **III**:22–23

Bernhardt, Sarah, **I**:47, 158–59

Bernstein, Carl, **III**:172

Bernstein, Leonard, **II**:217, 220, 355, **III**:94

Berry, Chuck, **II**:350–51

Best-selling authors: 1900s, **I**:33; 1910s, **I**:145; 1920s, **I**:264–66, 275; 1930s, **II**:33–35; 1940s, **II**:172; 1950s, **II**:284–87; 1960s, **III**:39–41; 1970s, **III**:165, 263–57; 1980s, **III**:263–67; 1990s, **IV**:34; 2000s, **IV**:167

Betty Crocker, **II**:19, 270, 338, **III**:197

The Beverly Hillbillies (TV show), **III**:55

Beverly Hills Cop (1984), **III**:280

Beyond the Horizon (O'Neill), **I**:152

Bicentennial, U.S., **III**:134, 166

"Big Air" competition, **IV**:221

Big bands, **II**:93–94

Big business economy, **I**:7–10, 229–30

The Big Hangover (1950), **II**:344

Big Jim McLain (1952), **II**:301

Big Little Books (comics), **II**:47–48

Big Lots (close-out retailer), **IV**:192

Billboard advertising, **I**:121

Billboard (magazine), **II**:214

Bill Haley and His Comets (singing group), **II**:349

Bill posters in advertising, **I**:121

Billy Bathgate (Doctorow), **III**:266

Binge Eating Disorder (BED), **IV**:202

Bingo (board game), **II**:108

bin Laden, Osama, **IV**:129, 130

Bioengineering food, **IV**:77–78

Biograph Films, **I:**163

Biplanes, **I:**207, 208

Birdseye, Clarence (Birdseye Foods), **I:**178, 305, **II:**84

The Birth of a Nation (Griffith), **I:**164

Birth rates, **II:**151, **IV:**5

Bisquick Company, **II:**84

Blachford, Erik, **IV:**240–41, 242

Blackbirds (Leslie), **I:**279

The Blackboard Jungle (1955), **II:**300, 349–50

The Black Bottom (dance), **I:**280–81

Black Boy (Wright), **II:**173

Black Mask (magazine), **I:**272

Black Monday (stock market loss), **III:**237, 241–44

Black nationalism, **I:**232

The Black Panthers, **III:**12

Black Power movement, **III:**11, 99

Black Sabbath (singing group), **III:**205

Black Sox scandal, **I:**327

The Blair Witch Project (1999), **IV:**52

Blanks, Billy, **IV:**88

Blaxploitation films, **III:**177–78

Bleach (1989), **IV:**79

Blendtec ads, **IV:**149

The Blob (1958), **II:**307

Blockade (1938), **II:**60

Blogging/blogs, **IV:**172

Blondie (comics), **II:**46

Blow, Charles M., **IV:**137

Blue jean fashions, **II:**72, 332–33, **III:**71–72, 74, 189, **IV:**60–61, 194

Blues: An Anthology (Handy), **I:**320

Blues music. *See* Rhythm and blues

The Bluest Eye (Morrison), **III:**164

Blu-ray disc, **IV:**183

Bly, Robert, **III:**44

"B" movies, **II:**300

Board games: 1930s, **II:**108–10; 1950s, **II:**363; 1960s, **III:**104–6; 1970s, **III:**214; 1980s, **III:**318–20

"Bobby soxers" fashion trend, **II:**200

The bob (hairstyle), **I:**297

The Bob Mathias Story (1954), **II:**361

Bodybuilding fad, **I:**338

Body Count (rap group), **IV:**84

Boeing Airplane Company, **I:**351, **II:**377, **III:**115, 221–22

Boesky, Ivan, **III:**242

Bogart, Humphrey, **II:**200

Bok, Edward W., **I:**23, 42, 64

Bolden, Charles ("Buddy"), **I:**73–74

"Bollywood" (Indian film industry), **II:**309

The Bolshevik Revolution, **I:**112, 115, 154, 230

Bonanza (TV show), **III:**55–56

Bonds, Barry, **IV:**228

The Bonfire of the Vanities (Wolfe), **III:**265–66

Bonnie and Clyde (1967), **III:**51

Bono (singer), **IV:**218

Boo, Elizabeth, **IV:**103

Boogie Nights (1997), **IV:**54

Book-of-the-Month Club, **I:**263

Books/literature (1900s): African Americans in, **I:**39–42; best-selling authors, **I:**33; comics/cartoons, **I:**43–44; fiction, **I:**33; global economy of, **I:**32; magazines, **I:**38, 42–43; muckrakers and, **I:**37–39; naturalism in, **I:**34–37; nonfiction, **I:**32; poetry, **I:**37, 41; public response to, **I:**37; racism in, **I:**42; realism in, **I:**34–37; women of, **I:**39–40

Books/literature (1910s): about WWI, **I:**144–46; best-selling authors, **I:**145; comics/cartoons, **I:**147–49; fiction, **I:**138, 141–42; magazines, **I:**139–40; Midwestern Renaissance, **I:**142–44; "New Criticism," **I:**140–41; newspapers, **I:**147–49; nonfiction, **I:**139–40; poetry, **I:**146–47; popular novels, **I:**141; realism in, **I:**138–40, 141; trends in, **I:**141–42

Books/literature (1920s): best-selling authors, **I:**264–66, 275; comics/cartoons, **I:**275–76; cookbooks, **I:**265, 306; fiction, **I:**263–64; Harlem Renaissance in, **I:**268–69; illustrations in, **I:**274–75; magazines, **I:**269–73; modernist fiction, **I:**266–67; newspapers, **I:**273–74; nonfiction, **I:**265–66; poetry, **I:**267; science fiction, **I:**272, 275–76, 284

Books/literature (1930s): best-selling authors, **II:**33–35; comics/cartoons, **II:**44–48; Federal Writers Project, **II:**35–36; fiction, **II:**35, 37; magazines, **II:**36–41; monthly clubs for, **II:**35; newspapers, **II:**41–44; nonfiction, **II:**35; poetry, **II:**43; science fiction, **II:**46

Books/literature (1940s): best-selling authors, **II:**172; censorship of, **II:**171; comics/cartoons, **II:**177–78; fiction, **II:**172–74; magazines, **II:**175–76; monthly clubs for, **II:**169, 232; movie adaptations of, **II:**170; newspapers, **II:**176–77; nonfiction, **II:**169–71; poetry, **II:**174–75; transitions in, **II:**171–72; true crime, **II:**169

Books/literature (1950s): best-selling authors, **II:**284–87; censorship of, **II:**296–97; comics/cartoons, **II:**294–97; cookbooks, **II:**337–38; fiction, **II:**284; magazines, **II:**289–92; newspapers, **II:**292–94; nonfiction, **II:**288; paperbacks, **II:**283–84; poetry, **II:**287–88; science fiction, **II:**290–91

Books/literature (1960s): best-selling authors, **III:**39–41; comics/cartoons, **III:**46–47; cookbooks, **III:**76–78; creative nonfiction, **III:**35, 41–43; fiction, **III:**35–37; magazines, **III:**44–46; metafiction, **III:**35, 37–38; newspapers, **III:**44–46; nonfiction, **III:**35, 41–43; poetry, **III:**43–44; science fiction/fantasy, **III:**46, 57

Books/literature (1970s): best-selling authors, **III:**165, 263–57; comics/cartoons, **III:**172–73; cookbooks, **III:**197; creative nonfiction, **III:**167–69; fiction, **III:**163–65; magazines, **III:**170–72; newspapers, **III:**172–73; nonfiction, **III:**163, 167–69; poetry, **III:**169–70; science fiction, **III:**177–78

Books/literature (1980s): best-selling authors, **III:**263–67; comics/cartoons, **III:**272; fiction, **III:**267–68; magazines, **III:**271; newspapers, **III:**271–72; new styles in, **III:**268–69; nonfiction, **III:**269–71; science fiction, **III:**279–80

Books/literature (1990s): best-selling authors, **IV:**34; for children, **IV:**39–40; comics/cartoons, **IV:**41–43; fantasy, **IV:**35–36; fiction, **IV:**36–38, 39–40; films of, **IV:**34–35; literary fiction, **IV:**38; magazines, **IV:**40–41; memoir, **IV:**38; mystery, **IV:**36–37; newspapers, **IV:**40–41; nonfiction, **IV:**32, 38; online buying/publishing of, **IV:**31–32; Oprah effect, **IV:**32–34; poetry, **IV:**38; romance, **IV:**37–38; science fiction, **IV:**35–36; self-help, **IV:**38–39; superstores for, **IV:**31; true crime, **IV:**36–37; for TV, **IV:**34–35

Books/literature (2000s): best-selling authors, **IV:**167; blogs on, **IV:**172; comics/cartoons, **IV:**168, 183; fiction, **IV:**166–67, 167–70; magazines, **IV:**171–72; newspapers, **IV:**172; nonfiction, **IV:**170–71; poetry, **IV:**169

Boone, Pat, **II:**353

Bootleggers, **I:**233–34

Bop music, **II:**222–23

Borders Bookstore, **IV:**31

Borglum, Gutzon, **I:**356–57, **II:**130

Born in the USA (1984), **III:**310–11

Boston Braves, **II:**357

Boston Brewing Company, **IV:**75

Boston Celtics, **III:**100–101, 212

The Boston Cooking-School Cook Book (Farmer), **I:**306

Boston Red Sox (Beaneaters), **I:**78, 196, 327, **III:**100

"Boston Strangler" (Edward DeSalvo), **III:**13

Boston Symphony, **I:**70

Botox use, **IV:**67, 197

Bottled water craze, **IV:**203–4

Bouffant hairdos, **II:**331–32

Bourke-White, Margaret, **II:**128–29, 246

Bovine growth hormone (rBGH), **IV:**78, 206

Bow, Clara, **I:**245, 287, 298

Bowie, David, **III:**192

Bowling (1950s), **II:**359

Boxing: 1900s, **I:**79–81; 1910s, **I:**199; 1920s, **I:**328–29; 1930s, **II:**105; 1940s, **II:**230–31; 1950s, **II:**359–60; 1960s, **III:**98–99; 1970s, **III:**210; 1990s, **IV:**93, 94; 2000s, **IV:**220, 229

Bradford, Mark, **IV:**254–55

Brady, "Diamond Jim," **I:**175

Brady, James, **III:**238

Branch Davidian cult, **IV:**11

Branded Customer Service (Barlow), **IV:**206

Brando, Marlon, **II:**262, 299–300, 305, 334

Brautigan, Richard, **III:**38

Brazil, **II:**212

Breakdancing, **III:**305

Breakfast of Champions (Vonnegut), **III:**164

Breaking the Surface (Louganis), **III:**317

Breast enhancement surgery, **IV:**67, 195

Breck, John, **II:**76

Breedlove, Sarah, **I:**170

The Breen Office (movie censorship), **II:**52

Brezhnev, Leonid, **III:**221

Brian Ridley and Lyle Heeter (Mapplethorpe), **III:**330–31

Brice, Fanny, **I:**317

Bridge (game), **II:**110

Bright Lights, Big City (McInerney), **III:**268–69

Brinkley, David, **II:**323

Britain. *See* United Kingdom

British Overseas Airways Corporation (BOAC), **II:**377

Broadway entertainment: 1900s, **I:**46–48; 1910s, **I:**153–54; 1920s, **I:**277–78, 315–16; 1930s, **II:**67–68, 99; 1940s, **II:**180–84; 1950s, **II:**326–27; 1960s, **III:**64–65; 1970s, **III:**186–87; 1980s, **III:**285–87; 1990s, **IV:**56–58; 2000s, **IV:**186

Brooklyn Dodgers, **II:**357

Brooks, Garth, **IV:**85–86

Brooks, Gwendolyn, **II:**175

Brotherhood of Sleeping Car Porters, **II:**148

Brown, Dan, **IV:**166–67

Brown, Helen Gurley, **III:**45

Brown, Jake, **IV:**221

Brown, James, **III:**93

Brown, Jim, **II:**360

Browne, Jackson, **III:**200

The Brownie camera, **II:**129

Brown v. the Board of Education, **II:**258

Brubeck, Dave, **III:**95

Bryan, William Jennings, **I:**237

Bryant, Kobe, **IV:**225

Bubble gum invention, **I:**311

Buck Rogers in the 25th Century A.D. (comic strip), **I:**275–76

Budd, Ralph, **II:**238

Budge, Don, **II:**104

Buffy the Vampire Slayer (TV show), **IV:**49

Bungalow construction styles, **I:**136–37

Bunyan, John, **I:**38

Burdick, Eugene, **III:**40

Bureau of Motion Pictures (BMP), **II:**159

Bureau of Public Roads, **II:**368

Burger King (fast food restaurant), **III:**78, 197, 299, **IV:**20, 72

Burleigh, Harry, **I:**184

Burlesque entertainment, **I:**48–50

Burma-Shave advertising, **I:**248, **II:**17

Burnham, Daniel, **I:**26–27

Burns, George, **II:**64, 318

Burns, Tommy, **I:**80

The Burns and Allen Show (TV show), **II:**318

Burns House (Santa Monica), **III:**159

Burroughs, Edgar Rice, **I:**142, 272

Burroughs, William S., **II:**287, **III:**36

Burton, Richard, **III:**51

Bush, George H. W., **III:**237, 241, **IV:**7, 193

Bush, George W., **IV:**128–29, 150, 203

Business attire, **IV:**60

Business travel, **IV:**100

Bus transportation, **I**:343, **IV**:106
Butch Cassidy and the Sundance Kid (1969), **III**:51
Butts, Alfred M., **II**:363
Byam, Wally, **II**:117–18
The Byrds (singing group), **III**:85
Byrne, Rhonda, **IV**:170

Cabbage Patch Dolls (toy), **III**:317
Cable cars, **I**:209
Cable News Network (CNN), **III**:242, **IV**:13
Cable television, **III**:155, 185, **IV**:178–79, 207
Cafeterias (quick-service restaurants), **I**:309
Cagney and Lacey (TV show), **III**:274–75
Calder, Alexander, **II**:381
Caldwell, Erskine, **II**:33
California Fluid Milk Processor's Advisory Board
  (CFMPA), **IV**:17
California Pizza Kitchen (restaurant chain), **IV**:74
The California Raisins, **III**:255
California style homes, **III**:30
Cambodia, **III**:142–43
Camelot (1960), **III**:62
Cameron, Lucille, **I**:199
Camhi, Leslie, **IV**:248
Camp, Walter, **I**:200
Campbell, Glen, **III**:87
Campbell Soup Company, **I**:67, 244–45, **II**:341,
  III:76
Campers. *See* Trailers/campers
Camping sport, **I**:207, 346, **IV**:102
Canasta (card game), **II**:363
Cancer concerns, **III**:298
Candid Camera (TV show), **III**:57, **IV**:177
Candy/sweets: 1910s, **I**:178–79; 1920s, **I**:310–12;
  1930s, **II**:84
Canfield, Jack, **IV**:39
Canseco, Jose, **IV**:228
Cantor, Eddie, **I**:317
Cape Cod style, **II**:280
Capital punishment, **III**:140
Capone, Al ("Scarface"), **I**:234
Capote, Truman, **III**:41–42
Capp, Al, **II**:234
Capra, Frank, **II**:56–58, 116, 230
Capri pants, fashions, **II**:335–36
Captain America (comic book character), **II**:178
Captain Kangaroo (TV show), **II**:326
Captain Marvel (comic book character), **II**:177
Captain Midnight (TV show), **II**:270
Captain Video (TV show), **II**:364
The Carbohydrate Addict's Diet (Heller, Heller), **IV**:77
Cardin, Pierre, **III**:67
Cardini, Caesar (Caesar salad inventor), **I**:306
Care Bears (toy), **III**:317
Carey, Mariah, **IV**:85
Caricature art, **I**:275
Carlos, John, **III**:103
Carnegie, Andrew, **I**:7–8
Carnegie, Dale, **II**:35
Carney, Art, **III**:62

Carnivals, **I**:83–85
Carousel (1945), **II**:217
Carson, Johnny, **III**:58, 182
Carson, Rachel, **III**:82
Carter, Jimmy, **III**:134–35, 141, 238, 248, 315–16
The Carter Singers, **I**:323
Cartland, Barbara, **III**:165
Caruso, Enrico, **I**:70
Carver, Ray, **III**:268
Casablanca (1942), **II**:191
Cash, Johnny, **III**:87
Cassatt, Mary, **I**:94
Cassini, Oleg, **III**:66
Castle, Vernon & Irene, **I**:156–57, 172, 186
Castro, Fidel, **III**:9, 16
Casual dining, **IV**:206
Casual wear, **IV**:60–62
Catalina Swimwear, **I**:295
The Catcher in the Rye (Salinger), **II**:285, 344
Catch-22 (Heller), **III**:38–39
Cathedral (Carver), **III**:268
Cather, Willa, **I**:142–43
The Catholic Church (Catholicism), **III**:16,
  148–49, **IV**:143
Cavalcade of Stars (TV show), **II**:317
CDs. *See* Compact discs
Celebrities: as athletes, **IV**:94–95; as chefs,
  IV:69, 73–74; endorsements from, **I**:245–47,
  IV:16–19, 152–53, 230; fashion of, **IV**:194–95;
  obsessions with, **IV**:235–37
Celestial Seasonings (teas), **IV**:71
Cellular phones, **III**:247–48, **IV**:15, 124
Censorship, **II**:52, 171, 296–97, 310
Centers for Disease Control (CDC), **III**:270, **IV**:13
Central Intelligence Agency (CIA), **II**:146,
  III:45, **IV**:131
Cezanne, Paul, **III**:226
Chabon, Michael, **IV**:167, 168
Chain letters/jokes, **II**:107–8
Chain stores, **I**:18–19
Challenger (space shuttle) disaster, **III**:239–40
Chamberlain, Wilt ("The Stilt"), **III**:101
Chandler, A. B. Happy, **II**:226
Chandler, Asa, **I**:124
Chandler, Raymond, **II**:169
Chanel, Gabrielle ("Coco"), **I**:294–95, 299, **IV**:60
Chaney, Lon, **I**:286
Channel One (satellite TV service), **IV**:21
Chapin, Harry, **III**:200
Chaplin Charles ("Charlie"), **I**:156, 160–62, 285
Chapman, Roy, **I**:327
Charles, Ezzard, **II**:359
Charles, Ray, **III**:86, 92–93, 94, 255
The Charleston (dance), **I**:280–81, **II**:70
Charlie Chan films, **II**:52
Chase, Edna Woolman, **I**:172–73
Chase, William Merritt, **I**:94–95
Chautauqua movement, **I**:206–7
Chávez, César, **III**:80–81
Checkered Cab Manufacturing Company, **I**:344

Cheers (TV show), **III:**273–74, **IV:**50

Chekov, Anton, **I:**150

Cheney, Dick, **IV:**128–29

Chesnutt, Charles W., **I:**41–42

Chesterfield cigarettes, **II:**21

The Chesterfield Supper Club (TV show), **II:**318

Chevrolet, Gaston, **I:**333

Chex Party Mix, **II:**339

Chicago, Illinois: architectural challenges in, **IV:**156; as jazz center, **I:**318; skyscrapers of, **I:**26; South Park system, **I:**194; vaudeville theaters in, **I:**156; World's Columbian Exposition, **I:**72–73

Chicago Bears football team, **I:**330

Chicago Hope (TV show), **IV:**48

Chicago Poems (Sandberg), **I:**146

Chicago School of architecture, **I:**142

Chicago (singing group), **III:**204

Chicago Temple of the First Methodist Episcopal Church, **I:**255

Chicago White Sox (baseball team), **I:**197

Chicago World's Fair (1933–1934), **II:**27–28

Chicken Soup for the Soul series (Canfield), **IV:**39

Child, Julia, **III:**76–77, **IV:**207

Children/child issues: 1900s, **I:**51, 67; 1910s, **I:**109–10, 117, 149; 1920s, **I:**236, 247, 275, 302; 1930s, **II:**59–60, 78–79; 1940s, **II:**151, 177, 186, 207; 1950s, **II:**270–71, 325–26, 336; 1960s, **III:**17, 58–59, 70; 1970s, **III:**147–48, 153–55; 1980s, **III:**272, 296, 317; 1990s, **IV:**20–23, 39–40, 70, 72, 95–99; 2000s, **IV:**142, 166, 200, 201, 220

Children's Online Privacy Protection Act, **IV:**23

Chili's (restaurant chain), **IV:**73

China, **III:**133, 216, **IV:**230

Chinese food, **I:**309

Chipotle (restaurant), **IV:**206

Chocolate trends, **I:**178–79, 310–11

Cholesterol concerns, **III:**297

Chopin, Kate, **I:**13

Chopra, Deepak, **IV:**39, 170

A Chorus Line (1975), **III:**187

Choynsky, Joe, **I:**80

Christianity, **I:**236–37, **III:**148

Chromatic abstraction in art, **II:**243

Chrysler Building (New York), **I:**253–55, **II:**23

Chrysler Motors, **I:**341, **II:**30–31, 114, 368, **III:**220, 321

Chubby Checker (singer), **III:**60

Churchill, Winston, **II:**145

The Church of Jesus Christ of Latter-Day Saints (Mormons), **III:**216

Church/temple architecture, **I:**255, **III:**31–32

Cigarettes: 1900s, **I:**127; 1910s, **I:**179–80; 1920s, **I:**242, 245, 288; 1930s, **II:**20–21; 1940s, **II:**213; 1950s, **II:**272; 1960s, **III:**7–8, 20; 1970s, **III:**152; 1980s, **III:**254–55; 1990s, **IV:**20

Cimarron (Ferber), **I:**264–65

Cincinnati Reds (baseball team), **I:**77, **II:**101, **III:**210

CinemaScope films, **II:**299

Cinerama Corporation, **II:**298–99

The Circular Staircase (Rinehart), **I:**265

Citizen Kane (1941), **II:**190–91

Citizens Band (CB) radio, **III:**215, 224

The City Light (Wolfe), **III:**266

Civic art, **IV:**109

Civil Aeronautics Board (CAB), **III:**222

Civilian Conservation Corps (CCC), **II:**115, 237–38

Civil rights: 1900s, **I:**41; 1910s, **I:**111; 1920s, **I:**232; 1940s, **II:**148, 226; 1950s, **II:**257–58; 1960s, **III:**10–12, 84, 93; 1970s, **III:**130, 135–37, 139, 154, 163, 167; 1990s, **IV:**5, 7

Civil War, **I:**34

Clackers (toy), **III:**213

Clairol hair coloring, **II:**331, **III:**20–21

Clancy, Tom, **IV:**34

Clark, David Little, **I:**179

Clark, Dick, **II:**354–55, **III:**60–61, 88

Clark, Mary Higgins, **III:**166

Clarke, Conor, **IV:**204

Clarkson, Kelly, **IV:**213

Classical music: 1900s, **I:**68, 70; 1910s, **I:**182, 184; 1920s, **I:**323–25; 1930s, **II:**98–99; 1940s, **II:**220; 1950s, **II:**355–56; 1960s, **III:**94–95

Classicism style, **I:**27–28

Clay, Cassius (Muhammad Ali), **III:**98–99, 101

Clef Club Symphony Orchestra, **I:**185–86

Clemens, Roger, **IV:**228

Cleveland, Grover (U.S. President), **I:**9

Cleveland Indians, **II:**357

Cline, Patsy, **II:**349, **III:**86–87

Clinton, Bill, **III:**145, 237, **IV:**7–10, 21, 29, 128

The Cliquot Club Eskimos (radio show), **I:**250

Cloche hats, **I:**298–99

Cloning attempts, **IV:**77

Clooney, George, **IV:**183–84

Clowes, Dan, **IV:**43

Coast Guard Women's Reserve (SPARS), **II:**149

Cobain, Kurt, **IV:**79–80

Cobb, Henry, **III:**258

Cobb, Tyrus Raymond ("Ty"), **I:**77–78, 196, 328, **III:**99

Coben, Harlan, **IV:**167

Coca-Cola Company (Coke), **I:**19–20, 125–26, 249, 312–13, **II:**90–91, 132, 158, 345, **III:**21, 79, 80, 154, 256, **III:**299–300, **IV:**19, 21

Cocktail parties, **II:**343–44

Coffee, Linda, **III:**137–38

Coffee/tea: 1900s, **I:**29; 1910s, **I:**167, 177, 181; 1920s, **I:**312; 1930s, **II:**91; 1940s, **II:**208, 209, 227; 1950s, **II:**343, 345; 1960s, **III:**80; 1990s, **IV:**74–75; 2000s, **IV:**203–4

Cohan, George, **I:**46, 187

Colbert, Claudette, **II:**56–57, 77, 116

Cold War: movies about, **II:**301–2, **III:**51; newspapers and, **II:**293; during Olympic Games, **II:**361; *vs.* WWII, **II:**144–46

Cole, Fred, **I:**295

Cole, Nat King, **II:**219

Coleco Toy Company, **III:**317

Coleman, Ornette, **III:**95

Colgate-Palmolive company, **I:**17, **II:**272

Collage art style, **III**:118

Collectible card games, **IV**:98–99

College campus architecture, **I**:133

College football, **I**:329, **III**:98

College pranks, **II**:361

Collegiate men's fashions, **I**:301

Collier's (magazine), **I**:23, 147, **II**:291

Collins, Floyd, **I**:239

Collins, Michael, **III**:112

Colonial revival style, **I**:28–29, 260

Colonial Williamsburg, **II**:27

Color television, **II**:314

Coltrane, John, **III**:95

Columbia Broadcasting System (CBS), **I**:289, 315, **II**:62, 66, 187–88, 261, 314, **III**:53

Columbia Phonograph Company, **I**:70, 315

Columbia Records, **II**:347

Columbine High School massacre, **IV**:12–13

Comaneci, Nadia, **III**:210

Combat films, **II**:192

Combs, Sean "P. Diddy" (rapper), **IV**:83, 195, 216

Comcast cable, **IV**:178

Come Back, Little Sheba (1952), **II**:309

Comedy entertainment: 1900s, **I**:48–50; 1910s, **I**:152–53, 154; 1920s, **I**:250, 284–85, 332; 1930s, **II**:56–58, 63–64; 1940s, **II**:184, 190, 216; 1950s, **II**:316–17; 1960s, **III**:54, 57–59, 62; 1970s, **III**:172, 176, 184, 200; 1980s, **III**:280; 1990s, **IV**:49–51; 2000s, **IV**:182

Comics/cartoons: 1900s, **I**:43–44; 1910s, **I**:147–49; 1920s, **I**:249, 275–76; 1930s, **II**:44–48; 1940s, **II**:177–78; 1950s, **II**:294–97; 1960s, **III**:46–47; 1970s, **III**:172–73; 1980s, **III**:272; 1990s, **IV**:41–43; 2000s, **IV**:168, 183

Comics Code Authority, **II**:296, **III**:172

Comiskey, Charles, **I**:197–99

Commercial air travel, **I**:208, 348–49, 350–51

Commercial architecture, **II**:275, **III**:159–60

Commercialism, **I**:108, **III**:46

Commercial theater (1910s), **I**:152–53

Commission on Obscenity and Pornography, **III**:163

Committee on Sustainable Development, **IV**:103

"Common man" advertising, **II**:157–58

The Common Sense Book of Baby and Child Care (Spock), **II**:151–52, 171, 289, **III**:8

Communication advances, **I**:123–24, **IV**:15

Communism: campaign against, **II**:293; decline of, **IV**:101; fears of, **II**:262–63; McCarthyism and, **II**:261–62

Communist Party of the United States of America (CPUSA), **II**:146

Como, Perry, **II**:218

Compact discs (CDs), **III**:302, **IV**:212–13

Complexity and Contradiction in Architecture (Venturi), **III**:27

Composers, orchestral, **I**:68–69

"Composographs," **I**:274, 356

Computer-aided design (CAD), **III**:257, **IV**:25, 65

Computer games, **IV**:24, 35, 96–98

Computers, **III**:215, 245–47, **IV**:6–7, 14–15, 51–52, 65, 111–13

Coney Island, New York, **I**:84–85

Confessional poetry, **III**:169

Confessions of a Nazi Spy (Warner Brothers), **II**:60

The Confessions of Nat Turner (Styron), **III**:39

Congress of Industrial Organizations (CIO), **I**:12

Conn, Billy, **II**:230

Connolly, James, **I**:82

Connolly, Maureen, **II**:360

Conrad, William, **II**:320

Consciousness in food, **III**:297–98

Consumerism: 1900s, **I**:16–17; 1910s, **I**:201; 1920s, **I**:241; 1930s, **II**:17; 1940s, **II**:240–41; 1950s, **II**:266–67; 1960s, **III**:19, 113; 1970s, **III**:227; 1980s, **III**:277, 292; 2000s, **IV**:227

Convair Corporation, **II**:155

Conversations with God (Walsch), **IV**:39

Cookbooks, **I**:265, 306, **III**:76–78, 197

Cooking devices, **I**:176

The cookout craze, **II**:339

Coolidge, Calvin, **I**:228, 349

"Coon" songs, **I**:183

Cooper, Gary, **II**:131

Coors Brewing Company, **II**:345

Copeland, Aaron, **II**:99, **III**:94

Corliss, Richard, **IV**:186

Coronary Primary Prevention Trial, **III**:297

Correll, Charles, **I**:290, **II**:63–64

Corset fashions, **I**:166, 168–69, 172, 296

Corvette (General Motors), **II**:369

Cosby, Bill, **III**:269, 274

The Cosby Show (TV show), **III**:274

Cosell, Howard, **III**:210

Cosmetic/plastic surgery, **IV**:67

Cosmetics: 1900s, **I**:57; 1910s, **I**:169–70; 1920s, **I**:298; 1930s, **II**:75–76; 1950s, **II**:332; 1970s, **III**:192; 1980s, **III**:288; 1990s, **IV**:65; 2000s, **IV**:197

Cosmonauts (Soviet astronauts), **III**:218

Cosmopolitan (magazine), **I**:33, 122, **III**:45

Costco stores, **IV**:167, 189–90

Costume jewelry, **I**:299

Coubertin, Pierre de, **I**:82, 83

Coué, Emile, **I**:338

Coughlin, Charles E. ("Father"), **II**:66

Coulter, Catherine, **IV**:37

Council of National Defense (CND), **II**:235

The Country Girl (1954), **II**:309

The Country Life Movement, **I**:109

Country music: 1950s, **II**:348–49; 1960s, **III**:86–87; 1970s, **III**:200–202; 1990s, **IV**:85–86; 2000s, **IV**:216

"Country Swing" music, **II**:98

Covan, Willie, **I**:157

Cowboy poetry, **IV**:38

Cowell, Simon, **IV**:175–76

Cowles, Gardner, Jr, **II**:38

Cox, Archibald, **III**:132–33

Cox, Keith, **III**:153

Craft brew market, **IV**:75–76

Craft Master kit, **II**:380–81

Crafts (hobby), **II**:366

The Craftsman (magazine), **I**:29

Craig, Gordon, **I**:151

Cram, Ralph Adams, **I**:133

Crane, Clarence, **I**:179

Crawford, Francis Marion, **I**:37

Crawford, Joan, **III**:52

Crayola crayons, **I**:334

Creative nonfiction, **III**:35, 41–43, 167–69, **IV**:172

Credit card purchases/debt, **II**:256–57, **III**:6, **IV**:138, 191, 192–93

Creel, George, **I**:127

Creole Jazz Band, **I**:318–19

Cresswell, Luke, **IV**:57

Crewdson, Gregory, **IV**:253–54

Crichton, Michael, **III**:40, **IV**:36, 184

Crime: 1910s, **I**:112; 1920s, **I**:234–35; 1930s, **II**:7, 11–12; 1940s, **II**:151, 211; 1950s, **II**:300; 1960s, **III**:13–14; 1970s, **III**:140–42; 1980s, **III**:261; 1990s, **IV**:10, 125; 2000s, **IV**:252

Crime shows, **II**:323

Crimes of the Heart (Henley), **III**:285

Croce, Jim, **III**:200

Crocker, Betty (advertising figure), **I**:247

Crockett, Davey, **II**:364

Crosby, Bing, **II**:96, 216, 218, 219, 347

Cross Word Puzzle Book (Simon & Schuster), **I**:265–66

Crossword puzzles, **I**:335

Crow, Sheryl, **IV**:82

The Crucible (1953), **II**:327

Crumley, James, **III**:165

"Cry" (1951), **II**:346

Cuban Missile Crisis, **III**:16

Cubism (Cubist art), **I**:352, **III**:117–18, 226

Cubist Realism. *See* Precisionism

Cugnot, Nicholas, **I**:89

Cults, **III**:149

A Current Affair (TV show), **IV**:13

Currier, Nathaniel, **I**:93

Curry, Tim, **III**:192

Curtiss, Glenn H., **I**:208

Cuyahoga River fire, **III**:143–44

Cyber criminals, **IV**:125

Czolgosz, Leon, **II**:6

Dadaist movement, **I**:352

Dahl, Gary, **III**:213–14

Dairy Queen (restaurant), **II**:210

Dalhart, Vernon, **I**:322

Dalí, Salvador, **II**:242

Dallas, Texas City Hall, **III**:159

Dallas (TV show), **III**:276–77, 291

Dana House (1902), **I**:30–31

Dance Dance Revolution (video game), **IV**:232

Dance entertainment: 1900s, **I**:51–52; 1910s, **I**:156–57; 1920s, **I**:279–81, 316, 335–36; 1930s, **II**:70, 97, 107; 1940s, **II**:179–80; 1950s, **II**:327–28; 1960s, **III**:59–61; 1970s, **III**:174,

185–86; 1980s, **III**:278; 1990s, **IV**:57; 2000s, **IV**:214

Dangling Man (Bellow), **II**:174

Darin, Bobby, **III**:88

Darna (comic book character), **II**:178

Darrow, Charles, **II**:110

Darrow, Clarence, **I**:237, 239

Daughtry, Chris, **IV**:213

Dave Matthews Band (singing group), **IV**:82

Davies, Arthur B., **I**:218

Davies, Roger, **III**:312

The Da Vinci Code (Brown), **IV**:166–67

Davis, Bette, **III**:52

Davis, Miles, **II**:224, **III**:95

Davis, Stuart, **I**:220

Davis Cup (International Lawn Tennis Challenge Cup tournament), **I**:81

Day, Doris, **II**:331, 344, **III**:249

The Day the Earth Stood Still (1951), **II**:306

DC Comics, **II**:178, **IV**:41, 43

DDT pesticide (dichloro-diphenyl-trichloroethane), **III**:82, 144

Dean, James, **II**:300, 334

Dean, John, **III**:132

"Death metal" music, **IV**:82

Death of a Salesman (Miller), **II**:181, **IV**:57

Death penalty, **III**:140

Death Row Records, **IV**:83–84

De Beers Diamond Company, **II**:157–58

Debussy, Claude, **I**:182, 189

The Decoration of Houses (Wharton), **I**:40

Deep Blue (computer game), **IV**:98

The Deep End of the Ocean (Mitchard), **IV**:32–33

Def Leppard, **III**:307

DeLorean, John Z. (DeLorean car), **III**:322

DeMille, Cecil B., **I**:283, **II**:306

"Democracity" (Dreyfuss), **II**:30

Democratic National Convention Headquarters, **III**:132

Dempsey, Jack, **I**:199, 329, 353

Denishawn School of Dance, **I**:279

Dennis the Menace (comic strip), **II**:294

Denny's (restaurant chain), **IV**:73

Department of Homeland Security, **IV**:130–31

Department of Justice (DOJ), **IV**:14

Department stores: 1900s, **I**:18; 1910s, **I**:171, 176; 1920s, **I**:294; 1930s, **II**:15

Deregulation of airlines, **III**:222–23

Derek, Bo, **III**:192

DeSalvo, Albert ("Boston Strangler"), **III**:13

Desegregation in schools, **III**:135–36

Detective fiction, **II**:169

Detective Story Magazine, **I**:271–72

Detroit Automobile Company (Ford Motors), **I**:90

Development Block Grants (CDBGs), **III**:161

Dewey, Thomas, **II**:146

Diamond Comics Distributors, **IV**:42

Dick Tracy (1990), **IV**:51

Dick Tracy (comics), **II**:44, 46

Dick Van Dyke Show (TV show), **III**:182

Didion, Joan, **III**:168

Diesel truck travel, **III**:116, 224

Dietary habits: 1900s, **I**:62–63, 66–67; 1910s, **I**:174–75; 1920s, **I**:307; 1930s, **II**:80–82; 1940s, **II**:206, 208, 212; 1950s, **II**:339–41; 1960s, **III**:79, 80; 1970s, **III**:197; 1980s, **III**:298; 1990s, **IV**:69, 76–77; 2000s, **IV**:202–3

Digital music player (MP3), **IV**:211

Digital photography, **IV**:110–11

Digital video discs (DVDs) technology, **IV**:165

Digital video recorder (DVR) technology, **IV**:181

Dilbert (comic strip), **IV**:140

DiMaggio, Joe, **II**:226–28, 357

Dime novels, **I**:33, 43

Dimension X (radio show), **II**:312

Dinah Shore Show (TV show), **II**:318, 373

Diner's Club (credit card), **II**:256

Diners (quick-service restaurants), **I**:309, **II**:87

Dion, Celine, **IV**:87

Dionne quintuplets, **II**:12

Dior, Christian, **II**:202–3, 330

DirecTV, **IV**:178–79

Dirigible travel, **II**:120–21

Dirty Dancing (1987), **III**:278–79

Disaster movies, **III**:175–76

Disc jockeys, **II**:99–100, 347

Disco movement, **III**:174, 185–86, 206–7

Discount shopping, **IV**:187–90

Discrimination. *See also* Racism: in homeownership, **II**:166; against Japanese Americans, **II**:148–50; legality of, **III**:135; in the military, **II**:148; reverse, **III**:135; against sexual orientation, **III**:139; against women, **III**:12–13

Dish Network, **IV**:178–79

Disney, Walt (Disney Brothers Studio), **I**:288, **II**:375. *See also* Walt Disney Company

Disney Cruise Line, **IV**:106–7

Disneyland, **II**:375–76

Disposable diapers, **III**:73, 254

Dix, Dorothy, **II**:43

Dixie Chicks (singing group), **IV**:86

Dmytryk, Edward, **II**:146

Doctorow, E. L., **III**:266

Do-it-yourself craze, **II**:365–66

Dole, Bob, **IV**:9

Domestic servants, **I**:303

Domestic terrorism, **IV**:10–12

Domino, Fats, **II**:353

Donadio, Rachel, **IV**:167–68

Donny and Marie (TV show), **III**:184

Doom (computer game), **IV**:98

The Doors (singing group), **III**:92

Dors, Diana, **II**:233

Dorsey, Tommy, **II**:218

Dos Passos, John, **II**:34

Dot.com bubble, **IV**:125–26

Double features, movies, **II**:49

Douglas, Aaron, **I**:355

Douglas DC-3 (airplane), **II**:122–23

Douglas Edwards with the News (TV show), **II**:323

Dove "Real Beauty" campaign, **IV**:149

Dow Chemical Company, **II**:342, **III**:152

Dow Jones Industrial average, **III**:242

Downs, Hugh, **IV**:113

Downloading music, **IV**:211–13

Downsizing corporations, **III**:244–45, **IV**:141

Doyle Dane Bernbach (advertising firm), **III**:22–23

Dr. Dre (rapper), **IV**:83–84

Dr Pepper (soft drink), **II**:90–91, **IV**:20–21

Dracula (Browning), **II**:58

Dragnet (TV show), **II**:323

Dramatic entertainment, **I**:150–51, **II**:65, 319, 327, **IV**:57–58

Dreiser, Theodore, **I**:36–37, 141

Dreyer's Grand Ice Cream, **IV**:74

Dreyfuss, Henry ("Democracity"), **II**:30, 31–32

Drive-in banks, **II**:374

Drive-in restaurants, **II**:152, 299

Drive-in theaters, **II**:232–33, 299, 374–75

Drug use: 1900s, **I**:42, 61, 64; 1910s, **I**:111, 125; 1930s, **II**:78; 1950s, **II**:300; 1960s, **III**:49–50; 1970s, **III**:130, 186, 201, 204–5; 1980s, **III**:261, 308; 1990s, **IV**:6, 10, 13, 21; 2000s, **IV**:228–29, 236

Duany, Andres, **III**:259

Dubin, Brian, **IV**:195

Du Bois, W.E.B.: as magazine founder, **I**:122; racism response by, **I**:41, 81, 110–11, 155

Duchamp, Marcel, **I**:219–20

Duke University (North Carolina), **I**:256

Dumont, Margaret, **II**:56

DuMont Network (television), **II**:188

Dunbar, Paul Laurence, **I**:41

Duncan, Isadora, **I**:52

Duncan Hines foods, **II**:88

Dungeons and Dragons (game), **III**:215–16

DuPont Corporation, **II**:204, 273, 329, **IV**:64

Duran Duran (singing group), **III**:302, 309

Duryea, Frank J., **I**:89

The Dust Bowl, **II**:8–9, 114, 129

Dust Bowl ballads, **II**:97–98

Dylan, Bob, **III**:84–85, 86, 199, **IV**:216–17

Dynasty (TV show), **III**:276–77, 291

E. Coli bacteria, **IV**:207

Eades, Michael R. and Mary Dan, **IV**:77

The Eagles (singing group), **III**:204

Eakins, Thomas, **I**:93

Earhart, Amelia, **II**:12–13, 122

Earl, Harley J., **II**:372

Earth Day, **III**:144–45, **IV**:244

East Building of the National Gallery of Art, **III**:159

Eastern Air Lines, **I**:351

The Eastland (steamship), **I**:116–17, 208–9

Eastman, George, **I**:50, 93, 204

Eastwood, Clint, **IV**:56

Easy Rider (1969), **III**:50, 53

eBay (online auction site), **IV**:99, 249–50

Ebony (magazine), **II**:176, **III**:20, 44–45

Echo Boomer generation, **IV**:157

Eclectic architectural style, **I**:129–31

Eco, Umberto, **III:**265

Eco-friendly design, **IV:**163

École des Beaux-Arts, **I:**131–32

Economic Opportunity Act, **III:**10

Economy/economic influences (1900s): big business and, **I:**7–10; global nature of, **I:**32; in labor/workplace, **I:**11–12, 24, 29, 51, 55; modern corporations and, **I:**8–9; poverty as, **I:**11, 34; the Wobblies and, **I:**11–12

Economy/economic influences (1910s): on advertising, **I:**120; on entertainment, **I:**153; in labor/workplace, **I:**109, 195; poverty as, **I:**109, 112, 193; during WWI, **I:**114–15

Economy/economic influences (1920s): on architecture, **I:**254; on automobiles, **I:**341–42; in labor/workplace, **I:**231, 236, 326; overview of, **I:**228; poverty as, **I:**234, 312; recession in, **I:**230; stock market crash and, **I:**239–40; unemployment, **I:**229, 230

Economy/economic influences (1930s). *See also* Great Depression: in business environment, **II:**14–16; on cab companies, **II:**119; in clothing industry, **II:**72; employment and, **II:**9–11, 106; in labor/workplace, **II:**7–8, 9–11, 33, 106; literature reflections of, **II:**129; on magazines, **II:**36; on movies, **II:**49; poverty as, **II:**8, 9, 114; streamlining as, **II:**29; unemployment, **II:**7–8, 33, 80

Economy/economic influences (1940s): for African Americans, **II:**148; agricultural, **II:**206; airplanes and, **II:**240; in labor/workplace, **II:**148, 149–50; on movies, **II:**96; post-WWII, **II:**153, 181, 188, 194; poverty as, **II:**142, 153, 166, 241; unemployment, **II:**147

Economy/economic influences (1950s): advertising and, **II:**268; on GNP, **II:**256; in labor/workplace, **II:**259–60; on magazines, **II:**289; on newspapers, **II:**292–93; poverty as, **II:**256

Economy/economic influences (1960s): on art, **III:**118; healthcare and, **III:**6–8; inner city issues and, **III:**115; in labor/workplace, **III:**66; post-WWII, **III:**118; poverty as, **III:**81–82; unemployment, **III:**7, 15–16

Economy/economic influences (1970s): architectural difficulties with, **III:**156; healthcare and, **III:**130–32; in labor/workplace, **III:**131; overview of, **III:**130–31; poverty as, **III:**244; with space program, **III:**218; on travel, **III:**217; unemployment, **III:**130

Economy/economic influences (1980s): business and, **III:**241–44; on fashion, **III:**288; on homeowners, **III:**261; in labor/workplace, **III:**244–45; on newspapers, **III:**271; poverty as, **III:**244, 261; on travel, **III:**325

Economy/economic influences (1990s): in labor/workplace, **IV:**140–41; poverty as, **IV:**5–6, 29; recession as, **IV:**6–7, 24

Economy/economic influences (2000s): **IV:**190–91, 193, corporate collapses, **IV:**139–40; dot.com bubble and, **IV:**126–27; downsizing as, **IV:**141; entertainment cutbacks, **IV:**178; financial markets, **IV:**138–39; healthcare and, **IV:**137; in labor/workplace, **IV:**192; "New Economy," **IV:**126, 241; poverty as, **IV:**136; real estate problems, **IV:**155, 157; recession as, **IV:**138; rescuing of, **IV:**190–91, 192; sports franchises and, **IV:**223; on travel, **IV:**238; unemployment, **IV:**141, 192, 225; *vs.* innovation, **IV:**137–38; on workplace, **IV:**140–41

Ecotourism, **IV:**103

Ecotourism: The Potentials and Pitfalls (Boo), **IV:**103

Ederle, Gertrude, **I:**332

Edison, Thomas, **I:**50–51

Edison phonograph company, **I:**315

Edsel (Ford Motor), **II:**369

The Ed Sullivan Show (TV show), **II:**316–17, 352–53, **III:**68–69, 89

Edward, Douglas, **II:**323

Edward VIII (King), **II:**12

The Eight (artists), **I:**95–96, 217

Eiseley, Loren, **III:**42

Eisenhower, Dwight D., **II:**158, 263, 273–74, **III:**114

Electric cars, **I:**211–12

Electricity: 1900s, **I:**88; 1910s, **I:**124, 176; 1920s, **I:**238, 303–4, 311

Eliot, T.S., **I:**146, 189

Ellington, Edward ("Duke"), **I:**319, **II:**92, 95–96, 213, **III:**95

Elliot and Dominic (Mapplethorpe), **III:**331

Ellis, Bret Easton, **III:**269

Ellsberg, Daniel, **III:**132

Elway, John, **IV:**18

E-mail (electronic mail), **IV:**15, 140, 142–43

Eminem (rapper), **IV:**85

Empey, Arthur Guy, **I:**145

The Empire State Building (New York), **I:**254, **II:**23

Endangered Species Act, **III:**144

Endurance contests, **II:**106–7

Energy crisis era, **III:**131

Energy drinks, **IV:**204–5

Enron Corporation, **IV:**139–40

Entertainment and Sports Programming Network (ESPN), **III:**314–15

Entertainment (1900s): Broadway, **I:**46–48; burlesque, **I:**48–50; comedy, **I:**48–50; dance, **I:**51–52; movies, **I:**50–51; vaudeville, **I:**45, 48–50

Entertainment (1910s): Broadway, **I:**153–54; comedy, **I:**152–53, 154; commercial theater, **I:**152–53; dance, **I:**156–57; European roots in, **I:**150–51; Little Theater movement, **I:**151–52; movies, **I:**157–65; people's theater, **I:**154–56; vaudeville, **I:**155–56

Entertainment (1920s): animated cartoons, **I:**288; Broadway, **I:**277–78, 315–16; comedy, **I:**250, 284–85, 332; cooking shows, **I:**306; dance, **I:**279–81, 316, 335–36; movies, **I:**281–88, 316; musical theater/revues, **I:**278–79; radio, **I:**288–91; vaudeville, **I:**277, 315

Entertainment (1930s): Broadway, **II:**67–68, 99; comedy, **II:**56–58, 63–64; dance, **II:**70, 97, 107; movies, **II:**49–62; musicals, **II:**53; radio,

II:62–66; television, II:66–67; theater, II:67–70; vaudeville, II:56, 63, 67

Entertainment (1940s): Broadway, II:180–84; comedy, II:184, 190, 216; dance, II:179–80; movies, II:190–96; musicals, II:183–84; radio, II:184–87; television, II:187–90; vaudeville, II:184–85

Entertainment (1950s): Broadway, II:326–27; comedy, II:316–17; dance, II:327–28; movies, II:298–310; musicals, II:305, 327; radio, II:310–13; television, II:313–26; vaudeville, II:313, 316

Entertainment (1960s): Broadway, III:64–65; comedy, III:54, 57–59, 62; dance, III:59–61; movies, III:48–53; musicals, III:62; radio, III:59; television, III:53–59

Entertainment (1970s): Broadway, III:186–87; comedy, III:184, III:172, 176, 200; dance, III:174, 185–86; disco movement, III:174, 185–86; movies, III:174–80; musicals, III:174, 186; on radio, III:186; television, III:180–85

Entertainment (1980s): Broadway, III:285–87; comedy, III:280; dance, III:278; movies, III:278–85; musicals, III:278–79, 287; television, III:273–78

Entertainment (1990s): Broadway, IV:56–58; comedy, IV:49–51; dance, IV:57; movies, IV:51–56; musicals, IV:56–57; radio, IV:51; television, IV:44–51

Entertainment (2000s): Broadway, IV:186; comedy, IV:182; dance, IV:214; movies, IV:182–86; musicals, IV:186; online, IV:181–82; radio, IV:175; television, IV:174–81

Entertainment Weekly (magazine), IV:41

Environmental architects, IV:27

Environmental concerns, IV:103–4

Environment Protection Agency (EPA), III:144

Epic Records, IV:210–11

Equal Employment Opportunity Commission (EEOC), III:12–13

Equal Pay Act, III:13

Equal Rights Amendment (ERA), I:236, III:136–37

Equitable Life Assurance Building (Portland), II:168

Erector set (toy), I:334

ER (TV show), IV:48

Escape (radio show), II:312

Esquire (magazine), II:199, IV:40

E.T.: The Extra-Terrestrial (1982), III:279–80

Ethnic fashion influences, III:191

Ethnic food/restaurants, I:309, III:78

Ethnic Heritage Studies Program, III:216

ETV waveband, television, II:313

Europe, James Reese, I:185, 186

European influences (1900s): architectural, I:25, 27; clothing choices, I:53, 59; dance, I:51; immigrants, I:11, 16, 62–63; literature, I:32; musical, I:68, 72; visual arts, I:93–94

European influences (1910s): entertainment, I:150–51, 278; immigrants, I:112; musical, I:182–83, 324–25

European influences (1920s): architectural, I:253, 258; immigrants, I:230–31; literature, I:266; musical, I:323

European influences (1930s): on architecture, II:24; on visual arts, II:126, 131

European influences (1940s): on Broadway, II:184; clothing styles, II:200; dance, II:179; immigrants, II:146; musical, II:222; quonset huts from, II:164; visual arts, II:242, 243, 247

European influences (1950s): clothing styles, II:329, 330; entertainment, II:309–10

European influences (1960s): clothing styles, III:66; entertainment, III:53; musical, III:86; visual arts, III:120–21

European influences (1970s): clothing styles, III:190; culinary, III:194; visual arts, III:227

European influences (1980s): clothing styles, III:292, 295; entertainment, III:302; musical, III:309

European influences (2000s): musical, IV:218, 219

Evans, Walker, II:246

The Eveready Hour (radio show), I:250

Everly Brothers, II:349

Evert, Chris, III:209

Evita (1979), III:187

Evolutionary science *vs.* religion, I:238

Executive Suite (1954), II:303

Expedia (online travel site), IV:238, 240–41, 242, 244

Extreme Makeover (TV show), IV:196–97

Extreme sports, IV:17, 88–89

Fabric rationing, II:197

Facebook (website), IV:145, 230–32, 233

Facelifts, IV:67

Fads/crazes: 1900s, I:51, 72–73; 1910s, I:204–5; 1920s, I:335–39; 1930s, II:106–7; 1940s, II:201–2, 232–34; 1950s, II:361–63; 1960s, III:104; 1970s, III:213–14; 1980s, III:317–18; 1990s, IV:68, 88, 95; 2000s, IV:198, 201, 203

Fail-Safe (Burdick), III:40

Fairbanks, Douglas, I:247, 286

Fair Employment Practices Commission (FEPC), II:148

Fairfax, Beatrice, II:43

Fair Housing Act (1968), II:166

Fair Packaging and Labeling Act, III:79

Fallout shelters, II:260, 281

Falwell, Jerry, III:148

The Family of Man (photography show), II:382

Family Ties (TV show), III:274

Fansler, P. E., I:208

Fantasy books, IV:35–36

Fantasy/horror movies, II:58

Farmer, Fannie Merritt, I:306

Farms/farming: 1900s, I:61, 63; 1910s, I:109–10; 1920s, I:230, 305; 1930s, II:8–9; 1940s, II:147, 206; 1950s, II:256; 1960s, III:80; 1970s, III:194; 1980s, III:244; 1990s, IV:77–78; 2000s, IV:199

Farrar, Geraldine, I:70

Farrell, Frank, **I:**196

Farrell, James T., **II:**34

Farrow, Mia, **III:**51, 171

Farwell, Arthur, **I:**69, 184

Fashion Institute of Technology, **IV:**65

Fashion (1900s): accessories, **I:**53, 59; cosmetics, **I:**57; Gibson Girl, **I:**54–55; hairstyles, **I:**59–60; hats, **I:**56–57; menswear, **I:**56–59; shoes/hosiery, **I:**53, 56; trends, **I:**54; for women, **I:**55–57

Fashion (1910s): accessories, **I:**169; clothing, **I:**167–68; cosmetics, **I:**169–70; Gibson Girl, **I:**166, 169; hairstyles, **I:**169–70; hats, **I:**169; influences in, **I:**171–73; menswear, **I:**167, 168, 170–71; shoes/hosiery, **I:**167, 169, 170, 171; in stores/print, **I:**171; trends, **I:**166–70; undergarments, **I:**168–69

Fashion (1920s): accessories, **I:**298–99; for children, **I:**302; collegiate styles, **I:**301; cosmetics, **I:**298; dresses, **I:**294; hairstyles, **I:**297–98; hats, **I:**298–301; menswear, **I:**299–302; and popular culture, **I:**292–93; retail clothing, **I:**293–94; shoes/hosiery, **I:**296–97; sportswear, **I:**294–95; swimwear, **I:**295–96; undergarments, **I:**296, 302; for women, **I:**293

Fashion (1930s): accessories, **II:**75–76; for children, **II:**78–79; cosmetics, **II:**75–76; hairstyles, **II:**76; hats, **II:**74, 78; menswear, **II:**76–77; personal grooming, **II:**78; sew-at-home, **II:**72; shoes/hosiery, **II:**77; sportswear, **II:**74–75; trends, **II:**74; undergarments, **II:**72–73, 77; for women, **II:**71–74

Fashion (1940s): accessories, **II:**198–99; Dior couture, **II:**202–3; fabric rationing, **II:**197; hairstyles, **II:**199; hats, **II:**198; menswear, **II:**199–200; ready-to-wear, **II:**200–202; shoes/hosiery, **II:**199, 200, 204–5; synthetic fabrics, **II:**204–5; for teenagers, **II:**200; trends, **II:**198; undergarments, **II:**199; for women, **II:**197–98; zoot suits, **II:**203–4

Fashion (1950s): accessories, **II:**330–31; for children, **II:**336; cosmetics, **II:**332; hairstyles, **II:**331–32; hats, **II:**330, 332; menswear, **II:**332–33; shoes/hosiery, **II:**330–31; synthetic fibers, **II:**329; for teenagers, **II:**333–36; trends, **II:**332; undergarments, **II:**331; for women, **II:**329–32

Fashion (1960s): accessories, **III:**67, 71; British trends, **III:**68–70; French influence, **III:**66–67; hairstyles, **III:**67–69, 72–**III:**73; hats, **III:**67, 68; for Hippies, **III:**71–74; informality, **III:**68; menswear, **III:**67–68; shoes/hosiery, **III:**69–70, 71; sports influence on, **III:**68; for teenagers, **III:**70–71; trends, **III:**67; undergarments, **III:**71

Fashion (1970s): accessories, **III:**193; as antiestablishment, **III:**192–93; blue jeans, **III:**189; cosmetics, **III:**192; extremes in, **III:**191–92; foreign influence, **III:**190–91; hairstyles, **III:**192; informality in, **III:**188–89; jewelry, **III:**189–90; leisure suits, **III:**190; menswear, **III:**190; shoes/hosiery, **III:**188, 191–92

Fashion (1980s): accessories, **III:**253–54; cosmetics, **III:**288; from films, **III:**289–90; hairstyles, **III:**294; leading designers in, **III:**295; menswear, **III:**253; from music, **III:**289–90; retail brand building, **III:**292–94; shoes/hosiery, **III:**251–53; from television, **III:**290–92; undergarments, **III:**292

Fashion (1990s): accessories, **IV:**65; body image, **IV:**68; breast enhancement, **IV:**67; business attire, **IV:**60; casual wear, **IV:**60–62; cosmetics, **IV:**65; formal wear, **IV:**59; gothic, **IV:**63–64; grunge, **IV:**63–64; hair, **IV:**66; hats, **IV:**62; haute couture, **IV:**60; hip hop, **IV:**62–63; jewelry, **IV:**65; menswear, **IV:**60, 62; plastic surgery, **IV:**67; rave, **IV:**63–64; school uniforms, **IV:**64; shoes/hosiery, **IV:**61–62; skate, **IV:**63–64; tattoos/piercings, **IV:**66–67; technology in, **IV:**64–65; undergarments, **IV:**67

Fashion (2000s): Botox use in, **IV:**197; for celebrities, **IV:**194–95; clothing styles, **IV:**193–95; cosmetics, **IV:**197; discount shopping, **IV:**187–90; economic boom and, **IV:**193; economic decline and, **IV:**190–91; hats, **IV:**194; hip hop, **IV:**194; menswear, **IV:**194; plastic surgery, **IV:**195–96; shoes/hosiery, **IV:**148, 194, 226; trends, **IV:**194; undergarments, **IV:**194; WalMart effect, **IV:**191–93

Fast Casual (magazine), **IV:**206

Fast food: 1930s, **II:**87; 1940s, **II:**210–11; 1950s, **II:**342–43; 1960s, **III:**78–79; 1970s, **III:**197–98; 1980s, **III:**298–99; 1990s, **IV:**72; 2000s, **IV:**199–201

Fast Food Nation: The Dark Side of the All-American Meal (Schlosser), **IV:**72

Fatal Attraction (1987), **III:**285

Father Knows Best (TV show), **II:**318

Faulkner, William, **I:**266, **II:**172, 283, **III:**35

Feature films, **I:**159–60, 162–63

Federal Aid Highway Act, **II:**241, 368, **III:**114

Federal Art Project (FAP), **II:**127–28

Federal Aviation Administration (FAA), **II:**377, **III:**221, 323–24

Federal Baseball League, **I:**196

Federal Bureau of Investigation (FBI), **I:**114, 230

Federal Communications Commission (FCC), **II:**66, 187, **III:**54, 247–48

Federal Emergency Management Agency (FEMA), **IV:**134

Federal Housing Administration (FHA), **II:**164, 279

Federal Music Project (FMP), **II:**99

Federal Reserve System, **I:**10, 110, **IV:**141

Federal Rural Electrification Program, **II:**103

Federal Theater Project (FTP), **II:**68–70

Federal Trade Commission, **I:**110

Federal Water Pollution Control Act, **III:**144

Federal Writers Project (FWP), **II:**35–36

Federline, Kevin, **IV:**236

Feirstein, Bruce, **III:**301

Felix the Cat (Messmer, Sullivan), **I:**288

Fellig, Arthur ("Weegee"), **II:**246

The Feminine Mystique (Friedan), **III:**12, 137

Feminism/feminist movement, **III**:12–13, 136–38, 167

"Fen-Phen" (diet drug), **IV**:77

Ferber, Edna, **I**:264–65

Ferdinand, Franz (Archduke), **I**:113

Ferlinghetti, Lawrence, **III**:43

Ferraro, Geraldine, **III**:238

Fiction. *See also* Creative nonfiction; Literary fiction; Science fiction: 1900s, **I**:33; 1910s, **I**:138, 141–42; 1920s, **I**:263–64, 266–67; 1930s, **II**:35, 37; 1940s, **II**:169, 172–74; 1950s, **II**:284; 1960s, **III**:35, 37–38; 1970s, **III**:163–65; 1980s, **III**:267–68; 1990s, **IV**:36–38, 39–40; 2000s, **IV**:166–67

Fields, W. C., **II**:55

Fierstein, Harvey, **III**:286

Fight Club (Palahniuk), **IV**:165

Film fashion, **III**:289–90

Film noir, **II**:195, 304

Fireside Chats (radio show), **II**:42, 65, 144

Firpo, Luis, **I**:353

First Blood (1982), **III**:282–83

First Nighter (radio drama), **II**:65

Fischer, Bobby, **III**:104–5

Fischl, Eric, **III**:327

Fisher, Bud, **I**:148, 149

Fitness fad/craze, **I**:193, 326, 338, **II**:357, **III**:318, **IV**:18, 88, 221

Fitzgerald, F. Scott, **I**:234, 266–67

Fitzsimmons, Bob, **I**:80

Flagg, Ernest, **I**:132

Flagg, James Montgomery, **I**:128, 215, 216

Flagler, Henry Morrison, **I**:87

Flagpole sitting (craze), **I**:248, 336

Flanagan, Hallie, **II**:69

Flapper style, **I**:287, 292, 293, 297, 307

Flashdance (1983), **III**:278, 290

The Flatiron Building (New York), **I**:26–27

Fleer, Frank (Fleer Chewing Gum Company), **I**:311

Fleming, Alexander, **I**:238

Fleming, Peggy, **III**:103

Fleming, Victor, **II**:60

The Flintstones (TV show), **III**:55

Flip Wilson Show (TV show), **III**:182

Flores, Pedro, **I**:338

Florida land boom scheme, **I**:251

Florida State Democratic Convention (1901), **I**:7

Flying Down to Rio (RKO), **II**:123

Flying saucer reports, **II**:361–62

FM radio broadcasting, **II**:311–12, 355, **III**:59

Folk music: 1900s, **I**:68; 1910s, **I**:182; 1920s, **I**:319–20, 321; 1930s, **II**:93, 99; 1940s, **II**:221–22; 1950s, **II**:349; 1960s, **III**:83–86; 1970s, **III**:199–200; 1980s, **III**:310; 1990s, **IV**:82

Fonda, Henry, **II**:301

Fonda, Jane, **III**:318

Fondue parties, **III**:76

Food and Drug Administration (FDA), **II**:273

Food and Nutrition Board (FNB), **II**:206

Food/eating habits (1900s): alcoholic beverages, **I**:42; coffee/tea, **I**:29; corporate farming, **I**:63; dietary habits, **I**:62–63, 66–67; drugs in, **I**:61, 64; favorites, **I**:65, 67; income influence on, **I**:62–63; innovations, **I**:67; restaurant trends, **I**:18; safety standards, **I**:61, 63–66; soft drinks, **I**:20

Food/eating habits (1910s): alcoholic beverages, **I**:112, 233–34; coffee/tea, **I**:167, 177, 181; culture of, **I**:175–78; dietary habits, **I**:174–75; dining out, **I**:180–81; favorites, **I**:175; grocery stores, **I**:177; restaurant trends in, **I**:180–81; soft drinks, **I**:124–25; sweets/candy, **I**:178–79

Food/eating habits (1920s): alcoholic beverages, **I**:233–35, 308, 312; beverages, **I**:312–13; candy/ice cream, **I**:310–12; coffee/tea, **I**:312; cookbook sales, **I**:265, 306; dietary habits, **I**:307; dining in, **I**:303–4; dining out, **I**:308–10; grocery stores, **I**:249, 307–8; meals preparation, **I**:305–6; new products, **I**:304–5; processing of, **I**:304–5; radio cooking shows, **I**:306; restaurant trends in, **I**:257, 308–10; soft drinks, **I**:312–13

Food/eating habits (1930s): alcoholic beverages, **II**:89–90; candy, **II**:84; coffee/tea, **II**:91; dietary habits, **II**:80–82; eating out, **II**:87–89; fast food, **II**:87; grocery stores, **II**:15, 82–83; preparation of, **II**:84–85; product types, **II**:83–84; refrigeration in, **II**:85–87; restaurant trends in, **II**:88–89; self-service shopping, **II**:83; soft drinks, **II**:90–91

Food/eating habits (1940s): alcoholic beverages, **II**:221; changes in, **II**:212; coffee/tea, **II**:208, 209, 227; dietary habits, **II**:206, 208, 212; fast food, **II**:210–11; frozen foods, **II**:209; grocery stores, **II**:209; malnutrition, **II**:206; modernized kitchens and, **II**:209–10; processed foods, **II**:209; recommended daily allowances, **II**:206–7; restaurant trends in, **II**:152, 210–11; soft drinks, **II**:158; victory gardens, **II**:208–9; wartime rationing, **II**:207–8

Food/eating habits (1950s): alcoholic beverages, **II**:343–45; barbecues, **II**:338; coffee/tea, **II**:343, 345; cookbooks, **II**:337–38; dietary habits, **II**:339–41; fast foods, **II**:342–43; frozen, **II**:340–41; grocery stores, **II**:338, 345; haute cuisine, **II**:343; pizza, **II**:340; restaurant trends in, **II**:276–77, 299, 342–43; snack foods, **II**:339; soft drinks, **II**:345; sugar cereals, **II**:339–40; supermarkets, **II**:338

Food/eating habits (1960s): agricultural upheavals, **III**:80–81; alcoholic beverages, **III**:76; coffee/tea, **III**:80; cookbooks, **III**:76–78; dietary habits, **III**:79, 80; dining in, **III**:75–76; ethnic types, **III**:78; fast food, **III**:78–79; grocery stores, **III**:76; health food, **III**:78; obesity from, **III**:79–80; pollution effects on, **III**:82; poverty and, **III**:81–82; restaurant trends in, **III**:27, 28, **III**:75, 78–79, 114; soft drinks, **III**:80

Food/eating habits (1970s): alcoholic beverages, **III**:151–52; cookbooks, **III**:197; dietary habits, **III**:197; dining out, **III**:197; fast food, **III**:197–98; grocery stores, **III**:196; health food, **III**:194;

restaurant trends in, **III:**197–98; soft drinks, **III:**195–96; trends in, **III:**194–96

Food/eating habits (1980s): alcoholic beverages, **III:**254–55; dietary habits, **III:**298; fast food, **III:**298–99; health food, **III:**297–98, 299, 301; Nouvelle Cuisine, **III:**300–301; restaurant trends in, **III:**298–99; soft drinks, **III:**299–300

Food/eating habits (1990s): alcoholic beverages, **IV:**75–76; bioengineering of, **IV:**77–78; celebrity chefs, **IV:**73–74; coffee culture, **IV:**74–75; coffee/tea, **IV:**74–75; craft brew market, **IV:**75–76; dietary habits, **IV:**69, 76–77; fast food, **IV:**72; health food, **IV:**69; ready-made, **IV:**70–71; restaurant trends in, **IV:**69–70, 72–73, 74–75; soft drinks, **IV:**76

Food/eating habits (2000s): alcoholic beverages, **IV:**236; casual dining, **IV:**206; coffee culture, **IV:**203–4; coffee/tea, **IV:**203–4; dietary habits, **IV:**202–3; energy drinks, **IV:**204–5; fast food, **IV:**199–201; health food, **IV:**198–99, 200; restaurant trends in, **IV:**199–201, 204, 206; safety concerns, **IV:**206–7; soft drinks, **IV:**202; on TV, **IV:**207–9; Food Stamp Act, **III:**9

Food stamp program, **III:**82

Food stand restaurants, **I:**310

Football: 1900s, **I:**75, 79; 1910s, **I:**199–201; 1920s, **I:**329–30; 1930s, **II:**103–4; 1940s, **II:**228–29; 1950s, **II:**360; 1960s, **III:**96–98; 1970s, **III:**211–12; 1980s, **III:**315; 1990s, **IV:**91; 2000s, **IV:**223–24

Footlight Parade (1933), **II:**53

Footloose (1984), **III:**278

Forbidden Planet (1956), **II:**307, 365

Ford, Gerald, **III:**133–34, 208

Ford, Henry, **I:**8, 90–91, 124, 126, 210–13, 281, 340–41

Ford, John, **II:**53, 195

"Fordism," **I:**212–13

Ford Motor Company, **I:**126, 256–57, 261, 341, **II:**368–69, 372, **III:**20, 113

Foreign films, **II:**309–10

Foreign influences on culture, **I:**338–39, **II:**80–82

Foreman, George, **III:**210

Formal wear, **IV:**59

Form *vs.* meaning, architecture (1910s), **I:**129–31

Forrest Gump (1994), **IV:**51–52

45-rpm records, **II:**347

42nd Street (1933), **II:**53

For Whom the Bell Tolls (Hemingway), **II:**172

Four Freedoms (Rockwell), **II:**244–45

Foursquare Gospel, **I:**237

Fowles, Jib, **IV:**150

Fox, William, **I:**160

Fox Cable Networks, **IV:**179

Fox Film Corporation, **I:**282, 316

The Fox Theatre (San Francisco), **I:**258

The fox trot (dance), **I:**281

Fractal art, **IV:**112

Frampton, Peter, **III:**203

Frank, Robert, **III:**121, 228–29

Frankenstein (Shelley), **II:**58

Franklin, Aretha, **III:**93

Franzen, Jonathan, **IV:**68

Frasier (TV show), **IV:**50

Frazier, Joe, **III:**210

Freak acts, vaudeville, **I:**49

Freed, Alan, **II:**349–50

Freedom Tower, **IV:**157–58

Free jazz, **III:**95

Freer, Charles, **I:**94

The Fremont Canning Company, **II:**85

French fashion trends, **III:**66–67

Freud, Sigmund, **I:**151, 338

Frey, James, **IV:**170

Friedan, Betty, **III:**12, 137

Friedlander, Lee, **III:**121–22

Friedman, Thomas L., **IV:**138–39

Friends (TV show), **IV:**50

Frisbee fad, **II:**363

Fromme, Lynette ("Squeaky"), **III:**140

Frost, Robert, **I:**146–47, 267, **III:**43

Frozen foods, **II:**209, 340–41, **IV:**70

Fubu (clothing label), **IV:**62

Fuller Brush Company, **II:**9

Fundamentalist movement (Christianity), **I:**237

Funk, Casimir, **I:**174

Funny Face (1957), **II:**331

Furey, Jim, **I:**199, 332

Furey, Tom, **I:**199

Furness, Betty, **II:**268

Futurism in advertising, **II:**158–59

Futurist art movement, **III:**226

G. I. Bill, **II:**151, 164

G. I. Joe doll (toy), **III:**105

Gabaldon, Diana, **IV:**37

Gable, Clark, **II:**56–57, 77, 116, 124

Gaiman, Neil, **IV:**43

Gaines, Ernest J., **III:**164

Gaines, William M., **II:**296

Gallant Fox (race horse), **II:**104

Gambling industry, **IV:**104

Game Boy (computer game toy), **IV:**97

Gandil, Chick, **I:**198

Gangs, **I:**192, **IV:**64

Gangsta rap, **IV:**84

Gangster films, **II:**51–52, 89

Gannett Co., **IV:**127

Gap Inc. (retail store), **IV:**62

Garbo, Greta, **I:**283–84, 299, **II:**89

Garcia, Jerry, **III:**91

Gard, Alex, **I:**275

Gardening activities, **IV:**221

Gardner, Ava, **II:**233

Gardner, Erle Stanley, **II:**33

Garfunkel, Art, **III:**85

Garland, Judy, **II:**59

Garros, Roland, **I:**208

Garvey, Marcus, **I:**232

Gasoline Alley (comic strip), **I:**149, 275, **II:**116

Gas rationing/prices, **II:**237, **III:**324

Gas stations, I:259, II:27

Gates, Bill, III:215, 245, IV:14

Gatorade (flavored drink), III:80

Gautier, Jean Paul, III:289

Gay and Lesbian Activists Alliance, III:138

Gaye, Marvin, III:93

Gayle, Crystal, III:202

Gay & Lesbian Alliance Against Defamation, IV:147

Gay Liberation Front (GLF), III:138

Gaynor, Gloria, III:207

Gay rights/community, III:138–40, 248–50, IV:8

Geddes, Anne, IV:110

Gehrig, Lou, IV:92

Gehry, Frank, IV:25–26, 156, 158–59

Gehry House (Santa Monica), III:160

Geldof, Bob, III:313

Gender issues, III:138–40

Genealogy searches, III:216

General Agreement on Tariffs and Trade (GATT), IV:6

General audience magazines, I:269

General Electric Company (GE), II:85–86, 273, 314

General Film Company, I:158

General Mills Company, II:18–19, 340

General Motors (GM), I:341, II:235, 267, 368, III:113–14, 220

Generation gaps, IV:142

Generation X, IV:17, 103, 125

Genetically modified foods, IV:77

Genovese, Kitty, III:13

Gentlemen Prefer Blondes (1953), II:305, 331

Gerber Baby Food, I:307

German Americans, II:146

Germany: depiction of, II:143; dirigible use by, II:121; Poland invasion by, II:142; during WWI, I:114

Gershwin, George, I:323–24, II:43, 68, 98

Gershwin, Ira, II:43, 68, 98

Gestural abstraction in art, II:243

Getty Center (Los Angeles), IV:27–28

Getty Museum (Los Angeles), III:159

Ghettos, III:261

Ghostbusters (1984), III:280

Ghost World (Clowes), IV:43

Gibbons, Cedric, II:31

Gibson, Althea, II:360

Gibson, D. Parke, III:20

Gibson Girl, I:54–55, 122, 166, 169, 215, 293, 307

Gilbert, A. C., I:203–4

Gilbert, Cass, I:133

Gilbert, Henry F. B., I:69–70

Gillespie, Dizzy, II:222–23, III:95

Gillette Cavalcade of Sports (TV show), II:360

Gillette Safety Razor Company, II:360

Gillin, Paul, IV:149–50

Gilmer, M., II:43

Gilmore, Gary, III:140

Ginger Ale (soft drink), I:313

Gingrich, Newt, IV:34

Ginsberg, Allen, II:287–88, III:43

Gip, George, I:329

Gish, Dorothy, I:160

Gish, Lillian, I:160

Giuliani, Rudolph, IV:113, 131

Glam rock style, III:306–8

Glass architecture, IV:26–27

"Glass house" design, II:167

The Glass Menagerie (1945), II:182

Glengarry Glen Ross (Mamet), III:286

Glenn, John, III:109, 217

Glenn Miller Orchestra, II:94, 213

Global Climate Change conference, IV:106

Globalization, IV:6, 138–39, 247

Global Positioning System (GPS), IV:105–6

GNP. *See* Gross national product

The Godfather movies, III:176–77

The Godfather (Puzo), III:40

Godzilla: King of the Monsters! (1956), II:310

Go-go boots, III:70

Goldberger, Paul, IV:158

Gold Diggers (1933), II:53

Gold Dust twins (advertising figures), I:247

Golden Boy (Odets), II:68

Golden Gate bridge (San Francisco), II:29

Goldman, Ronald, IV:11

The Gold Rush (Chaplin), I:285

Goldwater, Barry, III:23

Golf: 1900s, I:81–82; 1910s, I:194–95; 1920s, I:330–31; 1930s, II:104–5; 1940s, II:231; 1950s, II:360; 1960s, III:101–2; 1990s, IV:95; 2000s, IV:220, 227–28

Gone with the Wind (1939), II:60–62

Gone with the Wind (Mitchell), II:34

Good Housekeeping (magazine), I:306

Good Humor Bar/Man, I:311–12

Goodman, Benny, II:95, 213

Goodman, Tim, IV:179

Goodrich, Benjamin Franklin, I:89–90

Google (internet search engine), IV:14, 124–25, 126, 148, 232

Goosebumps series (Stine), IV:39

Gorbachev, Mikhail, III:241

Gordon, Duff ("Lucille"), I:172

Gordon, Jeff, IV:222

Gordy, Berry, Jr., III:93

Gore, Al, IV:128, 151

Gore-Tex (synthetic fabric), IV:64

Gorgas, William Crawford, I:92

Gosden, Freeman, I:290, II:63–64

"Goth" fashion, IV:63–64

Gothic architectural style, I:130, 133

"Got milk" advertising, IV:17–18

Goudge, Eileen, IV:37

Gourmet cooking trends, III:194

Gourmet (magazine), II:212, 343

Government. *See* Politics

Grable, Betty, II:205, 233

The Graduate (1967), III:50–51

Graffiti art/artists, **III:**225, 327–28, **IV:**112

Grafton, Sue, **IV:**36–37

Graf Zeppelin (dirigible), **II:**121

Graham, Billy, **II:**284–85, **III:**148

Graham, Martha, **II:**180

The Grand Canyon Suite (Copeland), **II:**99

Grand Central Terminal (New York), **III:**34

Grand Ole Opry (radio show), **I:**322, **II:**220, **III:**86, 201

Grange, Harold ("Red"), **I:**245, 329–30

Granola trends, **III:**194–95

Grant, Cary, **II:**55

Grapes of Wrath (Steinbeck), **II:**35, 114, 170, 171, 195

Grateful Dead (singing group), **III:**91

Grau, Maurice, **I:**70

Graves, Michael, **III:**258–59

Gray, John, **IV:**38–39

Gray, Judd, **I:**239

Gray, Macy, **IV:**85

Gray, Spalding, **IV:**58

Grease (1978), **III:**278

"Greaser" fashions, **II:**334–35

The Great Books of the Western World (Hutchins), **II:**288–89

Great Britain. *See* United Kingdom

The Great Depression: advertising during, **II:**14–16; music during, **II:**96–97; rural hardships, **II:**8–9; sheet music sales, **II:**94; unemployment during, **II:**7–8, 33; urban hardships, **II:**9

The Great Gatsby (Fitzgerald), **I:**234, 267

The Great Train Robbery (Porter), **I:**51

Green architecture, **IV:**27

Green Bay Packers, **II:**360, **III:**96

The Green Berets (1968), **III:**52

Greene, Henry & Charles, **I:**136

Green Lodging companies, **IV:**245

The Green Mile (King), **IV:**34

Greenpeace (environmental group), **III:**146–47

Greenspan, Alan, **IV:**190

The Gremlin (AMC Motors), **III:**220

Grenada invasion, **III:**240–41

Gretzky, Wayne, **IV:**92

Grey, Zane, **I:**141–42, 264, **II:**53

Grey Advertising (advertising firm), **III:**23

Greyhound Bus Lines, **II:**119, **III:**21, **IV:**106

Griffith, D. W., **I:**51, 158, 163–65

Griggs v. Duke Power Company, **III:**135

Grisham, John, **IV:**36

Groban, Josh, **IV:**213

Grocery stores: 1910s, **I:**177; 1920s, **I:**249, 307–8; 1930s, **II:**15, 82–83; 1940s, **II:**209; 1950s, **II:**338, 345; 1960s, **III:**76; 1970s, **III:**196

Grofé, Ferde, **II:**99

Gropius, Walter, **III:**25

Gross national product (GNP), **II:**256

Gruelle, Johnny, **I:**203

Gruen, Victor, **II:**276, **III:**28

Grunge fashion/music, **IV:**63–64, 80–81

Guerilla marketing, **IV:**145

Guess Who's Coming to Dinner (1967), **III:**49

Guild House (Philadelphia), **III:**27

Guitar Hero (video game), **IV:**211, 213, 232

The Gulf War, **IV:**13, 101–2

Gunsmoke (TV show), **II:**320, **III:**55–56

Guns N' Roses (singing group), **III:**308

Guskey, Audrey, **IV:**160

Guterson, David, **IV:**37

Guthrie, Arlo, **III:**84

Guthrie, Woody, **II:**96–97, 221, **III:**78, 83, 115, 199

Hadden, Britton, **II:**176

Hagen, Walter, **I:**331

Haggard, Merle, **III:**87, 201

Hailey, Arthur, **III:**40

Hair: The American Tribal Love-Rock Musical (1967), **III:**63–64

Hair metal music wave, **III:**306–9

Hairstyles: 1900s, **I:**59–60; 1910s, **I:**169–70; 1920s, **I:**297–98; 1930s, **II:**76; 1940s, **II:**198–99, 200; 1950s, **II:**331–32, 333; 1960s, **III:**67–69, 72–73; 1970s, **III:**192; 1980s, **III:**294; 1990s, **IV:**66

Halas, George, **II:**228

Haley, Alex, **III:**166, 184, 216

Halloween franchise, **III:**280

Hallström, Lasse, **IV:**56

Hamburger chain restaurants, **I:**310

Hamill, Dorothy, **III:**317

The Hamlet (Faulkner), **II:**172

Hammerstein, Oscar, **I:**153, 278, **II:**216–17

Hammond, John, **II:**95

Hampton Hotels, **IV:**246

Hamsher, Chuck, **IV:**250

Hancock Center (Chicago), **III:**156

Handbags, **I:**299

Handy, William Christopher (W.C.), **I:**189–90, 319–20

Hanks, Tom, **III:**249

Hansberry, Lorraine, **II:**279, **III:**62–63

The Happiness Boys (radio show), **I:**250

Hard Candy (makeup company), **IV:**65

Hard Copy (TV show), **IV:**13

Harding, Tonya, **IV:**93

Harding, Warren G., **I:**228

Hardy, Oliver, **I:**285

Hare Krishnas, **III:**149

Haring, Keith, **III:**327–28

Harlem Globetrotters, **I:**332, **II:**359

Harlem nightclubs, **I:**319

Harlem Renaissance. *See* New Negro movement

Harlequin Enterprises (publishing house), **III:**165

Harlow, Jean, **II:**72, 76, 89, 131

Harmon, William Elmer (Harmon Foundation), **I:**355

Harper's Bazaar (magazine), **I:**33, **II:**202

Harriman, George, **I:**275

Harrington, Michael, **III:**81

Harris, Eric, **IV:**12–13

Harris, Joel Chandler, **I:**39

Harrison, George, **III:**89–90, 199, **III:**57, 68–69

Harry Potter franchise, **IV:**166

Harry Potter series (Rowling), **IV:**40

Hasbro Toys, **II:**363

Hassam, Childe, **I:**94–95

Hasselhoff, David, **IV:**44

Hat fashions: 1900s, **I:**56–57; 1910s, **I:**169; 1920s, **I:**298–99, 300–301; 1930s, **II:**74, 78; 1940s, **II:**198; 1950s, **II:**330, 332; 1960s, **III:**67, 68; 1990s, **IV:**62; 2000s, **IV:**194

Hauptmann, Bruno, **II:**11–12

Haute couture, **III:**66–67, **IV:**60

Haute cuisine, **II:**343

Hawaiian music (1920s), **I:**323, 339

Hawk, Tony, **IV:**89

Hawks, Frank ("Meteor Man"), **II:**122

Hay, John, **I:**7

Hayes, Johnny, **I:**83

Hayworth, Rita, **II:**233

Healthcare issues, **III:**6–8, 130–32, **IV:**137

Health foods: 1960s, **III:**78; 1970s, **III:**194; 1980s, **III:**297–98, 299, 301; 1990s, **IV:**69; 2000s, **IV:**198–99, 200

Hearst, Patricia Campbell, **III:**141

Hearst, William Randolph, **I:**13–14, 147, 239, 274, 277, **IV:**127

The Heart is a Lonely Hunter (McCullers), **II:**172–73

Heavy metal music, **IV:**82–83

Hee Haw (TV show), **III:**87, 200–201

Hefner, Hugh, **II:**289–90

Heiden, Eric, **III:**316

The Heidi Chronicles (Wasserstein), **III:**287

Heinz, Henry J. (Heinz Food), **I:**23–24, 67

Held, John, Jr., **I:**274

Helicopter technology, **II:**238

Heller, Joseph, **III:**38–39

Heller, Rachael F. and Richard F., **IV:**77

Hellman, Richard, **I:**178

Hell's Angels: A Strange and Terrible Saga (Thompson), **III:**42

Hemingway, Ernest, **I:**266, **II:**172, 283, 285, **III:**35

Henderson, Fletcher, **I:**318–19, **II:**93

Hendrix, Jimi, **III:**91, 204

Henley, Beth, **III:**285

Henri, Robert, **I:**95, 217, 353

Henry and June (1990), **IV:**52

Hepburn, Audrey, **II:**331

Hepburn, Katharine, **II:**72

Hepburn Act (1906), **I:**6

Hercules: The Legendary Journeys (TV show), **IV:**45–46

The "heroin chic" look, **IV:**68

Herriman, George, **I:**148

Hersey, John, **II:**176

Hershey, Milton S. (Hershey's Chocolate), **I:**67, 178–79, 310–11

Herzog (Bellow), **III:**36

Heston, Charlton, **II:**306

Hicks, Taylor, **IV:**213

The Hidden Persuaders (Packard), **II:**268–69, 288

High-definition television (HDTV), **IV:**124, 174, 220

Hillbilly music, **I:**321–23

Hillerman, Tony, **III:**165

Hill Street Blues (TV show), **III:**275, **IV:**47

Hilton, Paris, **IV:**236

Hilton Hotels, **IV:**242–43

Hindenburg (dirigible), **II:**121

Hinckley, John W., **III:**238

Hip hop fashion, **IV:**62–63, 194

Hip hop music, **IV:**83–85, 213–16

Hippie fashion, **III:**71–74

Hiroshima, Japan, **II:**145

Hirsch, E. D., **III:**263

Hirshfeld, Al, **I:**275

Hirst, Damien, **IV:**113

Hirtzler, Victor, **I:**175

Hispanics. *See* Latin Americans

Historical American Buildings Survey (HABS), **III:**33

History News Network (HNN), **IV:**128

Hitchcock, Alfred, **II:**268, **III:**52

Hitchcock, Henry-Russell, **II:**24, 167

Hitler, Adolf, **II:**105–6, 142, 143, 230

Hobbies: 1930s, **II:**112–13; 1950s, **II:**365–66; 1960s, **III:**106–7; 1970s, **III:**214–16

Hobbies (magazine), **II:**112

The Hobbit (Tolkien), **III:**40

Hobby Lobby (radio show), **II:**112

Hockey: 1940s, **II:**231; 1960s, **III:**101; 1980s, **III:**316; 1990s, **IV:**91–92

Hoffman, Dustin, **III:**50

Hogan, Ben, **II:**360

Holiday Inns of America, **II:**276–77, 374

Holiday travel, **III:**321–22

Holistic health care, **III:**131–32

Hollywood movies. *See* Movies

Hollywood Star System, **I:**286–87

Hollywood war effort, **II:**159–60

Holyfield, Evander, **IV:**93

Home Box Office (HBO), **IV:**179

Homer, Winslow, **I:**94

Homicide: Life on the Streets (TV show), **IV:**47

Hood, Raymond M., **I:**254, 261–62

Hooper, Edward, **I:**353–54

"Hootenanny" folk music, **II:**221, **III:**85

Hoover, Herbert, **I:**228–29, 239–40, **II:**6, 108

Hoover, J. Edgar, **II:**117, 146

Hooverette dresses, **II:**72

Hooverisms, **II:**108

Hoover Suction Sweeper Company, **I:**124

Hopalong Cassidy (TV show), **II:**364

Hopper, Dennis, **III:**50

Hopper, Edward, **II:**127, 378

Hopper, Hedda, **II:**43

Horizons (Geddes), **II:**30

Horror movies, **III:**280

Hors d'Oeuvres and Canapés (Beard), **II:**212

"Horse cars," **I:**209

Horse racing: 1900s, **I:**75, 85; 1920s, **I:**332–33; 1930s, **II:**104; 1950s, **II:**360; 1960s, **III:**104

Hosiery. *See* Shoes/hosiery

Hostess Foods, **II**:84

Hotel lodging, **II**:373–74

Hot jazz, **I**:318–19

The Hot Mikado (FTP), **II**:69

The Housekeeper's Half-Hour (radio show), **I**:251

Housekeeping (Robinson), **III**:267

House Made of Dawn (Momaday), **III**:36

The House of Mirth (Wharton), **I**:40

House of the Future (Monsanto), **II**:277

House Oversight and Government Reform Committee, **IV**:139

House Un-American Activities Committee (HUAC), **II**:146, 195–96, 222, 262, 293, **III**:83

Housing. *See* Residential architecture

Housing Act (1949), **II**:241

Houston Majestic (Houston), **I**:259

Hovick, June, **II**:107

The Howdy Doody Show (TV show), **II**:189, 325–26

Howells, John Mead, **I**:254

Howells, William Dean, **I**:34–35

Howl (Ginsberg), **II**:287–88

"How Much Is That Doggie in the Window?" (1953), **II**:346

How to Win Friends and Influence People (Carnegie), **II**:35

Hudson, Rock, **II**:308, **III**:249

Huggies diapers, **III**:254

Hughes, Howard, **II**:122, 123

Hughes, John, **III**:284

Hughes, Langston, **III**:44

Hula hoop (toy), **II**:362–63, **IV**:95

Hull, Anne, **IV**:133

Humane Society of America, **IV**:206–7

Human Immunodeficiency Virus (HIV), **III**:317, **IV**:13–14, 93. *See also* Acquired Immune Deficiency Syndrome

Human Rights Campaign, **IV**:147

Hunger in America (CBS documentary), **III**:82

Huntley-Brinkley Report (TV show), **II**:323

Hurricane Katrina, **IV**:133–35, 214

Hurston, Zora Neale, **I**:268, 269

Hussein, Saddam, **IV**:7, 129

Hustler (magazine), **III**:170–71

Hutchins, Maynard, **II**:288–89

Hybrid Electric Vehicles, **III**:221

Hydrogen bomb, **II**:260

I. M. Pei architects, **III**:158, 159, 258

IAC Building (New York), **IV**:158–59

Iacocca, Lee, **III**:113, 269

I Am a Fugitive from a Chain Gang (LeRoy), **II**:51–52

Ianniciello, Pennie Clark, **IV**:167

IBM computers, **III**:245–46

Ice cream industry, **I**:310–12, **II**:84

Ice Cube (rapper), **IV**:83

Ice T (rapper), **IV**:84

Identity Theft Resource Center, **IV**:125

Idiot's Delight (Sherwood), **II**:68

Ile de France (ocean liner), **I**:348, **II**:123

Illinois Institute of Technology (IIT), **II**:167

Illustration art, **II**:130–32

Illustrations in literature, **I**:274–75

I Love Lucy (TV show), **II**:257, 263, 317

"Image" advertising, **II**:273

Image Comics, **IV**:43

Immigrants/immigration, 1900s, **I**:11, 16, 62–63; 1910s, **I**:112; 1920s, **I**:230–31; 1930s, **II**:128; 1940s, **II**:146; 1950s, **II**:340; 1960s, **III**:80; 1990s, **IV**:5

I'm Not There (2007), **IV**:217

Imported cars, **III**:221

Impressionistic art (1900s), **I**:94

Improvised explosive devices (IEDs), **IV**:132

Imus, Don, **IV**:215

In Cold Blood (Capote), **III**:41–42

Income tax, **II**:153

The Incredible Shrinking Man (1957), **II**:307

Independent films, **IV**:52

Independent Grocers Alliance (IGA), **I**:307

Independent Motion Picture (IMP), **I**:158

Indiana, Robert, **III**:120

Indiana Jones trilogy, **III**:280–82

Indian Gaming Regulatory Act, **IV**:104

Industrialism, **I**:16, 53, 63, 114–15, 120–21, **II**:24

Industrial Workers of the World (IWW), **I**:11–12, 112, 140

Infomercial advertising, **IV**:18

Initial public offerings (IPOs), **III**:243, **IV**:125

In-line skating, **IV**:88

Insider trading, **III**:242

Institutional advertising, **II**:156

Insurance companies, **I**:342

Intel Corporation, **III**:215, **IV**:14

Interactive rock video games, **IV**:211

Interior design: 1900s, **I**:28–29; 1910s, **I**:129–30; 1920s, **I**:261–62; 1930s, **II**:26–27, 30; 1940s, **II**:165; 1950s, **II**:281–82; 1960s, **III**:30; 1970s, **III**:160; 2000s, **IV**:162–64

Internal combustion engine, **I**:212

International Apple Shippers' Association, **II**:9

International Association of Outsourcing Professionals, **IV**:139

International cuisine, **III**:76, 78

International Lawn Tennis Challenge Cup tournament (Davis Cup), **I**:81

International modernism, **III**:156

International Olympic Committee (IOC), **I**:82, **II**:231

International Style, **I**:133, 253, **II**:23–25, 167, 275

International Style: Architecture Since 1922 (Johnson, Hitchcock), **II**:24

The Internet, **IV**:14–15, 124–27

Interstate Highway Act, **II**:368

Interstate highway system, **II**:240, 368

In the Heat of the Night (1967), **III**:49

Intolerance (Griffith), **I**:164–65

Invasion of the Body Snatchers (1956), **II**:263, 301

Investigative journalism, **I**:38

iPod (Apple), **IV**:211, 217–18

Iran, **III**:134

Iraqi films, **IV:**185–86

Iraq War, **IV:**7, 131–33, 170. *See also* War on Terror

Ironweed (Kennedy), **III:**268

Irwin, Will, **I:**147

Italian Americans, **II:**146

Italian cuisine, **I:**309

It Can't Happen Here (Lewis), **II:**69

It Happened One Night (Capra), **II:**56–57, 77, 116, 119

iTunes (Apple), **IV:**217

Ives, Charles, **I:**184–85

J. C. Penney's (department store), **I:**19

The Jack Benny Show (radio show), **II:**64, 184

The Jackie Robinson Story (1950), **II:**358

Jackson, Janet, **IV:**85

Jackson, Jesse, **III:**136

Jackson, Joe ("Shoeless"), **I:**197–99, 327

Jackson, Michael, **III:**255, 303–5, **IV:**19

Jackson, Randy, **IV:**175

The Jackson 5 (singing group), **III:**303

Jacob, Mary Phelps, **I:**169

Jacobs, Jane, **III:**33

Jagger, Mick, **III:**89–90, 204

James, LeBron, **IV:**224–27

James Bond films, **III:**52–53

Jantzen, Carl, **I:**295

Japan: atomic bomb on, **II:**145; food from, **III:**78; musicians from, **II:**349; Pearl Harbor attack by, **II:**142, 143; WWII depiction of, **II:**191

Japanese Americans, **II:**148–50, 203, 259

Jarvis, Al, **II:**100

Jaws (1970), **III:**176

Jay-Z (rapper), **IV:**245

Jazz Age, **I:**266, 274, 283, 292

Jazz music: 1900s, **I:**73–74; 1910s, **I:**189–91; 1920s, **I:**318–19, 323; 1930s, **II:**90, 92, 93; 1940s, **II:**222–24; 1950s, **II:**348; 1960s, **III:**94–95; 1970s, **III:**207; 1980s, **III:**305; 1990s, **IV:**82, 84

The Jazz Singer (Raphaelson, Cohn), **I:**287–88, 316

Jeep automobiles, **II:**236

Jefferson Airplane (singing group), **III:**91

Jeffries, James J., **I:**80–81, 199

Jell-O gelatin, **I:**67, 313

Jelly Roll Blues, **I:**191, 318

Jemima, Aunt (advertising figure), **I:**247

Jenga (toy), **III:**318

Jenner, Bruce, **III:**210

Jennings, Waylon, **III:**201

Jesus Christ Superstar (1970), **III:**187

Jet engine technology, **II:**238

Jethro Tull (singing group), **IV:**82

Jewelry styles, **III:**189–90, **IV:**65

Jewel (singer), **IV:**82

Jewett, Sarah Orne, **I:**32

Jewish Americans, **III:**16, 36

Jigsaw puzzle (toy), **II:**112–13

The Jitterbug (dance), **II:**97, 179

Jobs, Steve, **III:**215, 245, **IV:**211

Joe Camel (advertising icon), **IV:**20

Joel, Billy, **III:**204

The Joe Louis Story (1953), **II:**359–60

John, Elton, **III:**192, 203, **IV:**57

John Hancock Center (Chicago), **III:**20, 28

"Johnny B. Goode" (1958), **II:**350–51

Johns, Jasper, **III:**118

Johnson, Byron Bancroft ("Ban"), **I:**77

Johnson, Jack, **I:**80, 199

Johnson, Jimmie, **IV:**222

Johnson, John H., **II:**176

Johnson, Lyndon B., **III:**9–10, 15, 23, 114

Johnson, Magic, **III:**315, **IV:**13–14, 91, 93

Johnson, Philip, **II:**24, 167, **III:**25, 158–59

Johnson, Walter, **I:**197

Johnson Wax offices (Wisconsin), **II:**25–26

Johnston, France Benjamin, **I:**97–98

Jolie, Angelina, **IV:**184–85

Jolson, Al, **I:**156, 316–17

Jones, Bobby, **I:**331, **II:**104–5

Jones, George, **III:**201–2

Jones, Jim, **III:**149

Jones, Paula, **IV:**9

Jones, Quincy, **III:**303–4

Joplin, Janis, **III:**91–92, 204

Joplin, Scott, **I:**72–73, 188–89

Jordan, Michael, **III:**252–53, **IV:**18–19, 91, 94, 225–26

The Jordan Automobile Company, **I:**127

The Joshua Tree (1987), **IV:**218

Journey (singing group), **III:**204

Joyner, Florence Griffith, **III:**317

The Joy of Cooking (Rombauer), **III:**197

Juiced (Canseco), **IV:**228

Jukeboxes, **II:**99–100, 281

Jung, Carl, **I:**151

The Jungle (Sinclair), **I:**32, 39, 61, 63–64

Jupiter Communications, **IV:**238

Jurassic Park (1990), **IV:**51, 55

Jurassic Park (Crichton), **IV:**36

Kaczynski, Ted ("Unabomber"), **IV:**10–12

Kahn, Albert, **I:**261

Kahn, Louis, **III:**26

Kane, Helen, **I:**317

Karloff, Boris, **II:**58

Karr, Mary, **IV:**38

Katz, Jeffrey G., **IV:**242

Kaufmann House ("Fallingwater"), **II:**25

Kazan, Elia, **II:**181, 262

Keaton, Buster, **I:**48, 284–85

Keck, George Fred, **II:**26

Keeler, Ruby, **II:**70

Keller, Helen, **I:**49

Kelley, Florence, **I:**108–9

Kellogg, John Harvey, **I:**66

Kellogg, William K., **I:**66–67

Kellogg Foods, **II:**339, 364, **IV:**70–71

Kelly, Alvin ("Shipwreck"), **I:**337

Kelly, Gene, **II:**217, 305, 328

Kelly, Walt, **II:**294–95

Keneally, Thomas, **III:**268

Kennedy, Jacqueline, **III:**8–9, 66–67, 158, 171

Kennedy, John F.: assassination of, **III:**8–9; Cuban
    Missile Crisis, **III:**16; fashion trends of, **III:**68;
    space travel and, **III:**108; sports & leisure
    activities of, **III:**106

Kennedy, William, **III:**268

Kent State riots, **III:**142–43

Kentucky Fried Chicken (fast food restaurant),
    III:78–79, 198, 299

Keppard, Freddie, **I:**74

Kern, Jerome, **I:**153, 187

Kerouac, Jack, **II:**263, 286–87, **III:**35

Kerrigan, Nancy, **IV:**93

Kerry, John, **IV:**128, 150

Kesey, Ken, **III:**36

Ketcham, Hank, **II:**294

Khomeini, Ayatollah, **III:**134

Khrushchev, Nikita, **III:**16

Kidman, Nicole, **IV:**152, 153

Kilcher, Jewel, **IV:**38

Kimberly-Clark Company, **III:**254

King, Billie Jean, **III:**101, 208–9

King, Carole, **III:**199–200

King, Frank, **I:**149, **II:**116

King, Martin Luther, Jr., **II:**258, **III:**10–12, 136

King, Rodney, **IV:**6

King, Stephen, **III:**165–66, 263–65, **IV:**34

King Kong (RKO), **II:**58

King Kullen Market (supermarket), **II:**82

The Kingston Trio (singing group), **II:**349, **III:**83

Kinsey, Albert, **II:**152–53, 288

Kirby, Jack, **III:**46

KISS (singing group), **III:**205–6

Kitchen design, **II:**282, 341–42, **IV:**161–62

Klebold, Dylan, **IV:**12–13

Klein, Calvin, **III:**253, 318, **IV:**68

Klein, Charles, **I:**47

Klein, William, **III:**228–29

Kline, Franz, **III:**117

Knight, Marion "Sugar Beat" (rapper), **IV:**83

Knight, Phil, **III:**252

Knudsen, William S., **II:**235

Kodak Company, **I:**17–18, 50, 204, 356, **II:**129

The Kodak Girl, **I:**17

Kool-Aid beverage, **I:**313

De Kooning, Willem, **II:**243, **III:**117–18

Koons, Jeff, **III:**327

Koontz, Dean, **III:**166

Korean War, **II:**261, 293, 302

Korn (singing group), **IV:**80

Kostelanetz, André, **II:**99

Kramer, Larry, **III:**286

Krantz, Judith, **III:**166

Kraus, Carolyn Wells, **III:**168

Krazy Kat (comic strip), **I:**148, 275

Kristofferson, Kris, **III:**201

Kroc, Ray, **II:**342

Kroger (supermarket), **II:**83

Kuczynski, Alex, **IV:**194

Ku Klux Klan, **I:**112, 231–32, **III:**10–11

Kuwait, **IV:**7

La Bohème (Puccini), **IV:**57

Labor/workplace: 1900s, **I:**11–12, 24, 29, 51, 55;
    1910s, **I:**109, 195; 1920s, **I:**231, 236, 326; 1930s,
    II:7–8, 9–11, 33, 106; 1940s, **II:**148, 149–50; 1950s,
    II:259–60; 1960s, **III:**66; 1970s, **III:**131; 1980s,
    III:244–45; 1990s, **IV:**140–41; 2000s, **IV:**192

Lacayo, Richard, **IV:**169

LaChapelle, David, **IV:**109–10

Ladies' Home Journal (magazine), **I:**20–21, 23, 33,
    42, 122, 123, 270, **II:**176

Laemmle, Carl, **I:**158, 159

La Follette, Robert, **I:**110

Lagasse, Emeril, **IV:**69, 73–74, 207

Lajoie, Napoleon, **I:**77

Lake Shore Apartments (Chicago), **II:**167

Lamb, Thomas W., **I:**258

Lambert, Eleanor, **II:**201

Landis, Kenesaw Mountain, **I:**198

Landmarks Preservation Commission, **III:**34

The Language of Life with Bill Moyers
    (PBS broadcast), **IV:**38

L-A-N-G-U-A-G-E poetry, **III:**169

Lapine, James, **III:**287

Lasch, Christopher, **IV:**145–46

Lasker, Albert, **I:**23

Las Vegas, Nevada, **IV:**245–46

Latin Americans, **II:**146, 242, **III:**58, **IV:**5, 146, 172,
    214, 215, 232

Latino pop music, **IV:**85

Lauper, Cindy, **III:**311–12

Laurel, Stan, **I:**285

Lauren, Ralph, **III:**295

Lava Lites lamps, **III:**104

Lawn care obsessions, **II:**233, 280

Law & Order (TV show), **IV:**47–48

Lawrence, Florence, **I:**159

The Lawrence Welk Show (TV show), **II:**318–19,
    III:57

Layoffs in business, **III:**244–45

Lear, Norman, **III:**180

Leave It to Beaver (TV show), **II:**318

Le Corbusier, Charles–Édouard, **III:**25

Leddy, Chuck, **IV:**167

Led Zeppelin (singing group), **III:**206

Lee, Ang, **IV:**56

Lee, Harper, **III:**39–40

Lee, Jim, **IV:**42

Lee, Spike, **III:**252, **IV:**51, 137

Lee, Stan, **III:**46

Lego Company, **IV:**95–96

Leguizamo, John, **IV:**57–58

Leibovitz, Annie, **III:**229

Leisure suits, **III:**190

Lend-Lease program, **II:**208

Lenin, V. I., **I:**115

Lennon, John, **III:**57, 68–69, 89–90, 203, 313

Le Nouveau Guide (magazine), **III:**300–301

Leonard, Ray ("Sugar"), **III**:210
De Leon, Millie, **I**:49–50
Leopold, Nathan, **I**:239
LeRoy, Mervyn, **II**:51–52
Lesbian feminists, **III**:139–40
Less Than Zero (Ellis), **III**:269
Leveraged buyouts (LBOs), **III**:242
Levin, Ira, **III**:40
Levitt, William J., **II**:165, 280
Levittown, New York, **II**:164–66, 279–80
Lewinsky, Monica, **IV**:9–10
Lewis, Carl, **III**:316
Lewis, Jerry Lee, **II**:351
Lewis, Sinclair, **I**:264, **II**:69
Lewis and Clark Exposition (1905), **I**:85
Leyvas, Henry, **II**:204
Libby, Lewis "Scooter," **IV**:128–29
Liberace, Wladziu Valentino, **II**:318
Liberty (magazine), **II**:39–40
Lichtenstein, Roy, **III**:119, 227
Liefeld, Rob, **IV**:42
The Life and Times of the Shmoo (Capp), **II**:234
Life (magazine), **I**:269–70, **II**:38–39, 129, 200,
 246–47, **II**:281, 381, **III**:44
Li'l Abner (comics), **II**:46, 234
Lilith Fair (music festival), **IV**:82
The Limbo (dance), **III**:61
The Limited (retail store), **III**:292–93
Lin, Maya Ying, **III**:260–61, 326
Lincoln Logs (toy), **I**:204, 334
Lincoln Memorial, **I**:133–34, 257, 356
Lindbergh, Charles, **I**:247–48, 290, 301, 349–50,
 II:121
Lindbergh kidnapping, **II**:11–12
The Lindy Hop (dance), **I**:281, **II**:97
The Lion and the Mouse (Klein), **I**:47
Lionel Corporation, **II**:111–12
The Lion King (1994), **IV**:57
Liston, Sonny, **III**:98
Literary fiction, **III**:163–65, 267–68, **IV**:38, 167–70
Little magazines (1920s), **I**:271
Little Orphan Annie (comic strip), **I**:276, **II**:44, 45
Little Richard, **II**:353
Little Theater movement, **I**:151–52
The Living Newspaper (newspaper), **II**:69
Locke, Alain, **I**:232, 268
Loeb, Richard, **I**:239
Loesser, Frank, **II**:215
Lohan, Lindsay, **IV**:236–37
Lolita (Nabokov), **II**:286–87
Lollapalooza (music festival), **IV**:82
Lombardi, Vince, **II**:360, **III**:96
London, Jack, **I**:15, 33, 35, 80
The Lonely Crowd (Riesman), **II**:288
The Lone Ranger (radio show), **II**:64, 184
"Look-alike" fashions, **III**:70
Look (magazine), **II**:38, 246, 381, **III**:44
Lopez, Jennifer, **IV**:195
Lord Weary's Castle (Lowell), **II**:175
Lorimer, George Horace, **II**:37

Los Angeles County Museum of Art (LACMA),
 IV:250–51
Los Angeles Dodgers, **III**:100
Los Angeles Lakers, **III**:212
Louganis, Greg, **III**:316–17
Louis, Joe, **II**:105, 230–31, 359
Louisiana Purchase Exposition (1904), **I**:85
Louis Vuitton Moet Hennessy (LVMH), **IV**:65
Love Canal, New York, **III**:145–46
Love Story (Segal), **III**:167
Lowell, Robert, **II**:175, 287, **III**:43–44
Luce, Henry R., **II**:38, 176, 290
Luciano, Salvatore ("Lucky"), **I**:234
Lucky Strike cigarettes, **II**:21, 213
Ludlum, Robert, **III**:166
Lugosi, Bela, **II**:58
Luisetti, Hank, **II**:104
"Lunchables" portable meals, **IV**:70
Lunchrooms (quick-service restaurants), **I**:18, 309
Lusitania (ocean liner), **I**:114, 117, 118–19, 209
Lustron House, **II**:277
Lux Radio Theatre (radio drama), **II**:65
Lynch, David, **IV**:44
Lynn, Loretta, **III**:87, 202
Lysergsaure-diathylamid (LSD), **III**:90–91, 104

MacArthur, Douglas, **II**:293
MacDonald, J. Fred, **II**:186
MacDowell, Edward, **I**:69
Macfadden, Bernarr, **II**:39–40
Macon (dirigible), **II**:121
Macy's Holiday Parade, **I**:248, **II**:67
Mad About You (TV show), **IV**:50
Madame C. J. Walker Manufacturing Company,
 I:298
Mad (comic book), **II**:296
Mad cow disease, **IV**:207
Madison Avenue advertising (1910s), **I**:122–23
Madonna (singer), **III**:289–90, 305–6, **IV**:19, 87, 195
Mafia (organized crime family), **III**:14
Magazines: 1900s, **I**:38, 42–43; 1910s, **I**:121, 132,
 139–40, 171, 214–16; 1920s, **I**:249–50, 269–73;
 1930s, **II**:36–37, 40–41; 1940s, **II**:175–76; 1950s,
 II:289, 290–92, 366; 1960s, **III**:44–46; 1970s,
 III:170–72; 1980s, **III**:271; 1990s, **IV**:40–41;
 2000s, **IV**:171–72
Magic: the Gathering (card game), **IV**:98–99
Magic Eye pictures, **IV**:111
Magnificent Obsession (1954), **II**:308
Magnum, P. I. (TV show), **III**:275
Mahjong (Chinese game), **I**:335
Maiden Form Brassiere Company, **I**:296
Mailer, Norman, **II**:174, **III**:42, 167, **IV**:169
Mail-order business/catalogs, **I**:19, 29, **III**:66
Main Street (Lewis), **I**:264
Major League Baseball (MLB), **I**:327, **III**:315
Malcolm X, **III**:11–12
Mallon, Mary (Typhoid Mary), **I**:12–13
Mamas and the Papas (singing group), **III**:92
Mamet, David, **III**:286

Mancini, Henry, **III:**88

Mandrell, Barbara, **III:**202

The Man in the Gray Flannel Suit (1955), **II:**303–4

The Man in the Gray Flannel Suit (Wilson), **II:**269

Mankiewicz, Herman J., **II:**190–91

Mann, Sally, **IV:**110

The Mann Act, **I:**111

The Man Nobody Knows (Barton), **I:**265

Man o' War (race horse), **I:**332–33

Manship, Paul, **II:**130

Manson, Charles, **III:**13, 140, 168

Manson, Marilyn, **IV:**81

Mantle, Mickey, **II:**357

Manufacturing/industrial architecture, **I:**256–57

Manzanar War Relocation Center, **II:**149

Mao jackets, **III:**67

Mapplethorpe, Robert, **III:**326, 330–31

Marcel waves (hairstyle), **I:**297

The March of Time (newsreel), **II:**60

Marciano, Rocky, **II:**359

Maris, Roger, **III:**99

Marlboro cigarettes, **II:**20–21

Marley, Bob, **III:**206

Marriage rates, **II:**151, **IV:**142

Mars, Frank, **I:**179

Mars, Inc. (candy company), **I:**311, **II:**84

Mars exploration, **III:**218

Marsh, Reginald, **II:**127

Marshall Field's (department store), **I:**18

Marshall Plan, **II:**145, 153

Martha Stewart Living Omnimedia, **IV:**209

Martha Stewart Living (magazine), **IV:**41

Martial arts, **IV:**229

Martin, Ricky, **IV:**85

Martini fads, **II:**343–44

Marty (1955), **II:**304, 319

Marvel Comics, **III:**172, **IV:**41–43

The Marx Brothers (comedy team), **I:**285, **II:**55–56

Mary Tyler Moore Show (TV show), **III:**182

*M*A*S*H* (TV show), **III:**183

Masked & Anonymous (2003), **IV:**217

Mason, William E., **I:**63–64

Masses (magazine), **I:**140, 220

Mass transportation. *See* Travel/mass transportation

Masterpiece Theatre (TV show), **III:**154

Masters, Edgar Lee, **I:**146

Mathias, Bob, **II:**361

The Matrix (1999), **IV:**52

Matthau, Walter, **III:**62

Matthewson, Christy, **I:**197

Maude (TV show), **III:**182

Maus: A Survivor's Tale (Spiegelman), **IV:**41

Max Factor cosmetics, **II:**332

Maxim (magazine), **IV:**40–41

Maxwell House coffee, **II:**91

Mays, Willie, **II:**357

McAuliffe, Christa, **III:**239

McCain, John, **IV:**150, 229

McCall's (magazine), **II:**257

McCardell, Claire, **II:**201–2

McCarthy, Joseph (McCarthyism), **II:**261–62, 302

McCartney, Paul, **III:**57, 68–69, 89–90, 202

McClure's (magazine), **I:**38–39

McConnell, John, **III:**144–45

McCormick, Robert, **I:**149

McCorvey, Norma, **III:**137–38

McCourt, Frank, **IV:**38

McCoy, Van, **III:**207

McCullers, Carson, **II:**172–73

McCullough, J. F. & H. A., **II:**210

McDonald's (fast food restaurant), **II:**211, 277, 342, **III:**78, 151, 197, 299, **IV:**28, 30, 70, 72, 199–201

McDowell, Edward, **I:**184

McEnroe, John, **III:**211

McEwan, Ian, **IV:**167

McFarlane, Todd (McFarlane Toys), **IV:**42, 96

McGrady, Tracy, **IV:**225

McGwire, Mark, **IV:**92–93, 229

McInerney, Jay, **III:**268–69

McIntyre, O. O., **II:**43

McKim, Mead, and White (architectural firm), **I:**28, 96, 133

McKinley, William, **I:**4, **II:**6

McKuen, Rod, **III:**44, 170

McLachlan, Sarah, **IV:**82

McLain, Denny, **III:**100

McMansion home style, **III:**262, **IV:**28

McMurtry, Larry, **III:**166–67

McNicholas, Steve, **IV:**57

McPherson, Aimee Semple, **I:**237

McQueen, Steve, **II:**307

McVeigh, Timothy, **IV:**11

Meat Inspection Act (1906), **I:**6

Meat Loaf (singer), **III:**204

Meat recalls, **IV:**206

Media events, **II:**268–69, **IV:**148–50

Medicaid/Medicare, **IV:**5

Medical advances, **I:**238–39, **III:**7

Medical drama television, **IV:**47–48

Medicare/Medicaid, **III:**6, 7

Meet the Press (TV show), **II:**324

Meijer, Irene Costera, **IV:**146

Melamine plastic, **II:**282

Mellett, Lowell, **II:**159

Memoir writing, **IV:**38

Memorial Quilt for AIDS, **IV:**108

Men Are From Mars, Women Are From Venus (Gray), **IV:**38–39

Mencken, Henry Louis, **I:**140–41, 273

Menendez killings, **IV:**12

Menotti, Gian-Carlo, **II:**355

Men's fashion: 1900s, **I:**56, 57–59; 1910s, **I:**167, 168, 170–71; 1920s, **I:**299–302; 1930s, **II:**76–77; 1940s, **II:**199–200; 1950s, **II:**332–33; 1960s, **III:**67–68; 1970s, **III:**190; 1980s, **III:**253, 288; 1990s, **IV:**60, 62; 2000s, **IV:**194

Mercury Theatre on the Air (radio drama), **II:**65

Merman, Ethel, **II:**96

The Merry Widow (Lehár), **I:**47

De Mestral, George, **II:**329

Metafiction, **III:**35, 37–38

"Metalhead" fashion style, **III:**294

Metalious, Grace, **II:**286, 308–9

Metallica (singing group), **IV:**82–83

Method acting techniques, **II:**180–81

Metro-Goldwyn-Mayer (MGM), **I:**282, 316, **II:**190, 305

Metropolitan Insurance, **I:**24

Mexican Americans, **II:**146–47, 203–4, **III:**80, 153

Miami Vice (TV show), **III:**290–91

Michael, George, **III:**309–10

Michael Clayton (2007), **IV:**184

Michael Jackson and Bubbles (Koons), **III:**327

Micheaux, Oscar, **I:**286

Michener, James, **III:**166

Mickey Mouse (cartoon character), **I:**288, **II:**111, **IV:**101

The Mickey Mouse Club (TV show), **II:**326

Microbreweries, **IV:**75–76

Microsoft Corporation, **III:**215, 245, **IV:**14, 162, 240

Microwave ovens, **III:**296, 298

Middle class: 1900s, **I:**75, 86, 93; 1910s, **I:**180, 194; 1920s, **I:**260–61, 292–94, 305–6; 1930s, **II:**26, 84; 1940s, **II:**153, 214; 1950s, **II:**279, 367; 1960s, **III:**72, 82; 1980s, **III:**273, 278, 292; 1990s, **IV:**5–6; 2000s, **IV:**189;

Middle Eastern exoticism, **I:**339

Mies van der Rohe, Ludwig, **II:**167–68

Military. *See* United States military

Milken, Michael, **III:**242

De Mille, Agnes, **II:**179–80

Miller, Arthur, **II:**181, **III:**62, **IV:**57

Miller, Glenn, **II:**94, 213

Miller, J. Howard, **II:**155

Miller, Marvin, **III:**100

Miller Lite ads, **III:**151–52

A Million Little Pieces (Frey), **IV:**170

Milton Berle's Texaco Star Theater (TV show), **II:**189–90

Mimetic architecture, **I:**259–60

Miniature golf, **I:**338, **II:**376

Miniskirt fashions, **III:**69–70, 190

The Miracle Worker (1959), **II:**327

Miranda, Carmen, **II:**201–2

Miranda, Ernesto, **III:**13–14

Miró, Joan, **II:**242

Misery (King), **III:**263–65

The Misfits (Miller), **III:**62

Miss America Pageant, **I:**292

Mitchard, Jacquelyn, **IV:**32

Mitchell, George (The Mitchell Report), **IV:**228–29

Mitchell, John, **III:**132

Mitchell, Joni, **III:**200

Mitchell, Margaret, **II:**34, 61

Mix, Tom, **II:**53

Mobile homes, **II:**279

Model-making hobby, **II:**366

Model T car, **I:**125–27, 204, 212, 340–41

Modern dance, **II:**180

Modernism: 1900s, **I:**8–9; 1910s, **I:**120–21, 139–40; 1920s, **I:**266–67, 352; 1930s, **II:**24, 125;

1940s, **II:**242; 1950s, **II:**275; 1960s, **III:**27; 1970s, **III:**156; 1980s, **III:**259

Modified atmosphere packaging, **IV:**70

Momaday, N. Scott, **III:**36

Mondale, Walter, **III:**238

Mondino, Jean-Baptiste, **IV:**109–10

The Monkees (singing group), **III:**90

Monopoly (board game), **II:**110

Monroe, Marilyn, **II:**305, 331, **III:**227

Monsanto Chemical Company, **IV:**77–78

Monster.com (online job site), **IV:**241

Monster Energy drinks, **IV:**205

Monterey Pop Festival, **III:**92

Montgomery Ward (department store), **I:**19

Monthly book clubs, **II:**35, 169, 232

Mood rings (jewelry), **III:**213

Moody, Rick, **IV:**38

Moon exploration, **III:**218

The Moon Is Blue (1953), **II:**310

Moon's Unification Church, **III:**149

Moore, Charles, **III:**158, 159

Moral Majority (religious group), **III:**140, 148

Moran, Gussie, **II:**360

Morgan, J. P., **I:**6, 8, 9–10, 93

Morissette, Alanis, **IV:**82

Mormons (Church of Jesus Christ of Latter-Day Saints), **III:**216

Morrison, Herb, **II:**121

Morrison, Jim, **III:**92, 204

Morrison, Tommy, **IV:**93

Morrison, Toni, **III:**164, 268, **IV:**33, 169

Morrow, Vic, **II:**300

Mortal Kombat (video game), **IV:**97–98

Mortgage fiasco, **IV:**137–38, 191

Morton, Ferdinand ("Jelly Roll"), **I:**74, 188, 191, 318

Morton Salt Company, **I:**178

Mosaic art, **IV:**112–13

Moses, Anna Mary Robertson ("Grandma"), **II:**379–80

Motel lodging, **I:**346, **II:**117, 373–74

Motherwell, Robert, **II:**242

Motion Picture Association of America (MPAA), **III:**48

Motion Picture Patents Company (MPPC), **I:**157–58, 159–60

Motion Picture Producers and Distributors of America (MPPDA), **III:**48

Mötley Crüe (singing group), **III:**308

Motown Records, **III:**93

Mount Rushmore (sculpture), **I:**357, **II:**130

Movie palace architecture, **I:**258–59

Movies (1900s): early styles in, **I:**50–51; silent, **I:**72; *vs.* vaudeville, **I:**45–46

Movies (1910s): **I:**108; business of, **I:**157–58; early styles in, **I:**158–59; feature films, **I:**159–60, 162–63; notable actors in, **I:**160–62, 164

Movies (1920s): Academy Awards, **I:**286; music for, **I:**316; notable actors in, **I:**283; science fiction, **I:**284; silent films, **I:**283–86; small town theaters, **I:**281; studio system and, **I:**282–83

Movies (1930s): Academy Award winners, **II:**51; censorship in, **II:**52; child actors in, **II:**59–60; double features, **II:**49; fantasy/horror, **II:**58; gangster films, **II:**51–52; newsreels, **II:**60; notable actors in, **II:**50; police/G-men, **II:**52; screwball comedies, **II:**56–58; technical challenges, **II:**50–51; for teenagers, **II:**58; trains in, **II:**120; westerns, **II:**52–53

Movies (1940s): **II:**190–96, Academy Award winners, **II:**193; from book adaptations, **II:**170; combat films, **II:**192; Paramount decree, **II:**195; top actors, **II:**193; union strike, **II:**194–95; war effort and, **II:**159–60, 191–92; "weepies," **II:**192

Movies (1950s): Academy Award winners, **II:**303; automobiles in, **II:**372; censorship, **II:**310; Cold War and, **II:**301–2; drive-in theaters, **II:**299; film noir, **II:**304; foreign films, **II:**309–10; innovations in, **II:**298–99; notable actors in, **II:**299; nuclear fears in, **II:**261; religious epics, **II:**305–6; science fiction, **II:**306–7, 312; serious films, **II:**302–4; for teenagers, **II:**299–300; themes of, **II:**300; westerns, **II:**307–8

Movies (1960s): about space travel, **III:**112; Academy Award winners, **III:**64; drug themes in, **III:**50; notable actors in, **III:**63; racism in, **III:**49; rating system for, **III:**48–49; science fiction, **III:**57; sexual themes in, **III:**50–51

Movies (1970s): Academy Award winners, **III:**179; made for TV, **III:**185; overview of, **III:**174–80; science fiction, **III:**177–78

Movies (1980s): about marriage, **III:**283–84; Academy Award winners, **III:**282; action adventure, **III:**280–82; AIDS in, **III:**249–50; business films, **III:**283; horror, **III:**280; musicals, **III:**278–79; notable actors in, **III:**281; science fiction/fantasy, **III:**279–80; war films, **III:**282–83

Movies (1990s): Academy Award winners, **IV:**54; from books, **IV:**34–35; computer generation in, **IV:**51–52; filmmakers, **IV:**54–56; independent films, **IV:**52; notable actors, **IV:**53

Movies (2000s): about Iraq, **IV:**185–86; Academy Award winners, **IV:**180; notable actors, **IV:**180

Moxie (soft drink), **II:**90–91

Mozilo, Angelo, **IV:**140

Mr. Potato Head (toy), **II:**363

Ms. (magazine), **III:**137, 153, 170

Muck, Karl, **I:**70

Muckrakers, **I:**37–39, 109, 122–23, 139

Muir, John, **I:**87

Muller, Marcia, **III:**165

Munich Olympics (1972), **III:**141–42

Muntz, Earle, **II:**189

Murder, She Wrote (TV show), **III:**275–76

Murdoch, Elizabeth, **IV:**175

Murdoch, Rupert, **IV:**127, 231

Murray, Arthur, **I:**280

Murrow, Edward R., **II:**66, 143, 261, 324

Museum architecture, **IV:**27–28

Museum influence on art, **IV:**250–52

Museum of Science and Industry (MOSI), **IV:**250

Musicals, 1910s: **I:**153; 1920s, **I:**316; 1930s, **II:**53; 1940s, **II:**183–84; 1950s, **II:**305, 327; 1960s, **III:**62; 1970s, **III:**174, 186; 1980s, **III:**278–79, 287; 1990s, **IV:**56–57; 2000s, **IV:**186

Music (1900s): classical, **I:**68, 70, folk, **I:**68; hit songs, **I:**74; jazz, **I:**73–74; orchestral, **I:**68–70; ragtime, **I:**72–73; singers, **I:**70; Tin Pan Alley, **I:**45, 52, 70–71

Music (1910s): academic artists, **I:**184–85; African influence on, **I:**183–84; blues (R&B), **I:**189–91; classical, **I:**182, 184; European influence on, **I:**182–83, 324–25; folk, **I:**182; jazz/blues, **I:**189–91; orchestral, **I:**185–86; Ragtime, **I:**188–89; Tin Pan Alley, **I:**186–88

Music (1920s): blues, **I:**319–21; blues (R&B), **I:**319–21; on Broadway, **I:**315–16; classical, **I:**323–25; dance bands, **I:**316; distribution of, **I:**314–15; folk, **I:**319–20, 321; Hawaiian, **I:**323, 339; hillbilly, **I:**321–23; hit songs, **I:**317; in Hollywood, **I:**316; jazz, **I:**318–19, 323; orchestral, **I:**316, 318–19, 323–25; on phonograph records, **I:**315; on radio, **I:**315; singers, **I:**316–18; theater/revues, **I:**278–79; Tin Pan Alley, **I:**314, 323

Music (1930s): in advertising, **II:**99; African Americans in, **II:**92–94; audience fragmentation and, **II:**98; blues (R&B), **II:**92, 93, 97, 98; classical, **II:**98–99; dancing to, **II:**97; disc jockeys, **II:**99–100; Federal Music Project, **II:**99; folk, **II:**93, 99; during Great Depression, **II:**96–97; hit songs, **II:**97; jazz, **II:**90, 92, 93; jukeboxes, **II:**99–100; orchestral, **II:**93–94; sheet music, **II:**94–95; songwriting, **II:**97–98; swing dancing, **II:**90, 95–96, 97

Music (1940s): blues, **II:**219–20; blues (R&B), **II:**219–20; business of, **II:**213–15; classical, **II:**220; folk, **II:**221–22; hit songs, **II:**214–15; jazz, **II:**222–24; orchestral, **II:**215, 216, 220, 222–23; songwriters, **II:**215–19; styles of, **II:**219–22; technology of, **II:**213–15; for teenagers, **II:**217–19; war songs, **II:**214

Music (1950s): blues (R&B), **II:**350–51, 352; classical, **II:**355–56; country, **II:**348–49; folk, **II:**349; hit songs, **II:**346–47, 353; innovations in, **II:**347; jazz, **II:**348; orchestral, **II:**348, 354, 355–256; rock 'n' roll, **II:**349–53; singers, **II:**347–48; for teenagers, **II:**351; in television, **II:**318–19, 354–55; top 40's, **II:**346–47

Music (1960s): blues (R&B), **III:**86, 90, 91, 92–93; classical, **III:**94–95; country, **III:**86–87; folk, **III:**83–86; hit songs, **III:**89; jazz, **III:**94–95; orchestral, **III:**89, 94; pop, **III:**87–89; rock 'n' roll, **III:**89–92; soul, **III:**92–94

Music (1970s): blues (R&B), **III:**206–7; country, **III:**200–202; disco, **III:**185–86, 206–7; folk, **III:**199–200; hit songs, **III:**204; jazz, **III:**207; pop, **III:**202–4; progressive rock, **III:**204–6; reggae, **III:**206; rock 'n' roll, **III:**202–4

Music (1980s): blues (R&B), **III:**312; breakdancing to, **III:**305; British invasion in, **III:**309–10; CDs, development of, **III:**302; fashion from, **III:**289–90; folk, **III:**310; hair metal wave, **III:**306–9; jazz, **III:**305; Lennon's death and, **III:**313; male performers, **III:**310–11; pop, **III:**303; rock 'n' roll, **III:**308, 312

Music (1990s): alternative rock, **IV:**80–82; blues (R&B), **IV:**82, 85; country, **IV:**85–86; folk, **IV:**82; grunge, **IV:**80–81; heavy metal, **IV:**82–83; hip hop, **IV:**83–85; hit songs, **IV:**86; jazz, **IV:**82, 84; Latino pop, **IV:**85; pop music, **IV:**86–87; rap, **IV:**83–85; rock 'n' roll, **IV:**81–82; women in, **IV:**82

Music (2000s): American Idol and, **IV:**213–14; benefit shows with, **IV:**214; country, **IV:**216; downloading of, **IV:**211–13; hip hop, **IV:**213–16; iPods and, **IV:**211, 217; performers of, **IV:**216–18; pop, **IV:**210, 213, 215, 216; producers of, **IV:**218–19; rap, **IV:**213–16; rock 'n' roll, **IV:**216

Music Television (MTV), **III:**289, 302, 305

"Mutt and Jeff" (comic strip), **I:**147–48, 149

Mutual assured destruction (MAD), policy, **II:**306

Mutual Broadcasting System (MBS), **II:**62

Muzak (music style), **II:**100

My Àntonia (Cather), **I:**143

My Lai incident, **III:**15

MySpace (website), **IV:**145, 148, 173, 230–31

Myst (computer game), **IV:**98

Mystery books, **IV:**36–37

Mythmakers, art movement, **II:**242

N. W. Ayer and Son (advertising firm), **II:**157–58

Nabokov, Vladimir, **II:**286–87

Nader, Ralph, **III:**113–14, 150, 219

Nagasaki, Japan, **II:**145

The Naked and the Dead (Mailer), **II:**174

The Naked Lunch (Burroughs), **III:**36

The Name of the Rose (Eco), **III:**265

NAMES Project Foundation, **IV:**108

Napster (online music site), **IV:**212

National Academy of Design (NAD), **I:**214, 217

National Advertising Review Board (NARB), **III:**153

National Aeronautics and Space Administration (NASA), **II:**260, **III:**108, 218

National Air Races, **II:**122

National Air Traffic Controllers Association (NATCA), **III:**324

National American Women's Suffrage Association, **I:**111

National Association for Stock Car Auto Racing (NASCAR), **IV:**90–91, 221–23

National Association for the Advancement of Colored People (NAACP): court battles of, **I:**232; creation of, **I:**35, 41, 111–12; against death penalty, **III:**140; on entertainment racism, **I:**154–55; stereotype criticism by, **II:**64; violence against, **III:**10–11

National Association of Evangelicals (NAE), **III:**140

National Association of State Drug and Food Departments, **I:**64

National Baseball Agreement (1903), **I:**77

National Basketball Association (NBA), **II:**104, 229, 358

National Basketball League (NBL), **II:**104, **III:**100

The National Biscuit Company (Nabisco), **I:**21

National Board of Review of Motion Pictures (NBR), **I:**46

National Broadcasting Company (NBC), **I:**289, 315, **II:**62, 67, 187–88, 314, **III:**53, **IV:**230

National Broadcasting Company Symphony Orchestra (radio show), **II:**220

National Collegiate Athletic Association (NCAA), **III:**101, 208

National Commission on Terrorist Attacks, **IV:**131

National Education Television (NET), **II:**313–14

National Endowment for the Arts (NEA), **III:**225, 328, 330, **IV:**108

National Environmental Policy Act (NEPA), **III:**144

National Football League (NFL), **I:**330, **II:**228, **III:**96, 98, **IV:**91, 223

National Gallery of Art, East Building, **III:**159

National Historic Preservation Act (NHPA), **III:**160

National Hockey League (NHL), **III:**101, **IV:**92

National Invitational Tournament (NIT), **II:**104

National Lampoon (magazine), **III:**172

National League (NL), **I:**77–78

National Negro Baseball League (NNBL), **I:**328

National Organization for Women (NOW), **III:**12, 136–37

National Park Service (NPS), **II:**237, 373, **III:**324–25

National park system, **I:**87, 347

National Railroad Passenger Corporation (NRPC), **III:**223

National Recovery Administration (NRA), **II:**9, 106

National Research Council (NRC), **II:**206

National Television System Committee (NTSC), **II:**187–88

National Trust for Historic Preservation, **III:**33, 162

National Women's Party (NWP), **I:**111, 236

National Youth Administration (NYA), **II:**103

Native Americans: as activists, **IV:**80; in advertising, **III:**152; in armed forces, **II:**147; as art influence, **II:**242; as authors, **III:**35–36; civil rights of, **III:**12; as fashion influence, **III:**74, 191; film depiction of, **III:**55; gambling and, **IV:**104; malnutrition of, **III:**82; music influences, **I:**69; in sports, **III:**96

Native Dancer (race horse), **II:**360

Native Son (Wright), **II:**173

Native Tongues collective, **IV:**84

Naturalism in literature, **I:**34–37

Navajo "code talkers," **II:**147

Nazi Party, **II:**106, 231

Negro Digest (Magazine), **II:**176

"Negro spirituals," **I:**321

Nehru jackets, **III:**67

Nelson, Gaylord, **III:**145

Nelson, Willie, **III:**201

Neo-dadaist art style, **III:**118

Neo-Eclectic architectural styles, **III:**160

Neurasthenia (America's nervous condition), **I:**86–87

Nevermind (1991), **IV**:79–80

New Age followers, **III**:149

"New Coke" ad fiasco, **III**:256

"New Criticism" in literature, **I**:140–41

New Deal policies, **II**:26

New Diet Revolution (Atkins), **IV**:77

New Jersey Turnpike, **II**:368

New journalism, **III**:163, 167

"New Look" fashions (Dior), **II**:202–3

Newman, Paul, **II**:302, 360

New Museum of Contemporary Art, **IV**:109

The New Negro (Locke), **I**:232, 268

New Negro movement (Harlem Renaissance), **I**:183–84, 232, 268–69, 354–55, **II**:175

New Orleans, Louisiana, **IV**:133–35, 214

New Orleans jazz, **I**:190–91

Newport, Rhode Island resort, **I**:87

Newport Folk Festival, **III**:85

New Republic (opinion journal), **I**:140

Newspapers: 1910s, **I**:121, 147–49; 1920s, **I**:239, 249, 273–74; 1930s, **II**:41–44, 102; 1940s, **II**:176–77; 1950s, **II**:267, 292–97; 1960s, **III**:44–46; 1970s, **III**:172–73; 1980s, **III**:271–72; 1990s, **IV**:40–41; 2000s, **IV**:172, 199

Newsreels, **II**:60, 159

Newton John, Olivia, **III**:318

New York Central Park, **I**:194

New York City Ballet (NYCB), **II**:180, **III**:61

New York Giants, **II**:357, 360

New York Knicks, **III**:212

New York (magazine), **III**:170

New York Mets, **III**:100

New York Pennsylvania Station, **III**:33–34

New York Philharmonic, **II**:217, 356

New York Public Library, **I**:133

New York Stock Exchange (NYSE), **I**:9–10

New York Table Tennis Association, **II**:109

New York Times (newspaper), **IV**:11

New York World's Fair (1939–1940), **II**:27–29

New York Yankees, **I**:327, **II**:357, **III**:99

Niche marketing, **IV**:22

Nichols, Anne, **I**:277

Nicholson, Jack, **III**:50

Nickelodeons (storefront theaters), **I**:72

Nicklaus, Jack, **III**:101

Nielsen Television Index, **II**:315

Niggas With Attitude (rap group), **IV**:83

A Night at the Opera (Marx Brothers), **II**:56

The Nightmare on Elm Street series, **III**:280

'Night, Mother (Norman), **III**:285–86

Nike shoes, **III**:188, 251–53, **IV**:61–62, 148, 226

9/11 attack. *See* September 11, 2001

1980 Olympic Games, **III**:315–16

1988 Olympic Games, **III**:316–17

Nintendo Company, **IV**:97, 234

Nirvana (singing group), **IV**:79–80

Nixon: Richard M., accusations against, **II**:263; Brezhnev gifts from, **III**:221; détente attempts by, **III**:143; gender-based discrimination policy of, **III**:208; presidential campaign of, **III**:10; Vietnamization plan of, **III**:10; wage control program of, **III**:130; in Watergate scandal, **III**:132–33

No, No, Nanette (Harbach, Mandel), **I**:278

"No Child Left Behind" education plan, **IV**:129

Nonfiction: 1900s, **I**:32; 1910s, **I**:139–40; 1920s, **I**:265–66; 1930s, **II**:35; 1940s, **II**:169–71; 1950s, **II**:288; 1960s, **III**:35, 41–43; 1970s, **III**:163, 167–69; 1980s, **III**:269–71; 1990s, **IV**:32, 38; 2000s, **IV**:170–71

Noonan, Peggy, **III**:239–40

Nordstrom (department store), **III**:293–94

Noriega, Manuel, **IV**:7

The Normal Heart (Kramer), **III**:286

Norman, Marsha, **III**:285

Normandie (ocean liner), **II**:123

Norris, Frank, **I**:35–36

North, Oliver, **III**:241

The North American Free Trade Agreement (NAFTA), **IV**:6

Northern Exposure (TV show), **IV**:49

Northgate Regional Shopping Center (Seattle), **II**:166

The Northwest Methodist Temple in Minneapolis, **I**:255

Nouvelle Cuisine, **III**:75, 76, 197, 300–301

Novels. *See* Dime novels; Fiction

The Now Generation, **III**:19

Nuclear anxiety, **II**:260–61, **III**:40

Nuclear bomb, **II**:144–45

Nureyev, Rudolf, **III**:61

Nutra-Sweet sweetener, **III**:296

Nutritionists, **II**:80

Nylon fabric, **II**:204–5

NYPD Blue (TV show), **IV**:47

Oakland A's, **III**:210

Oates, Joyce Carol, **III**:39–40, 163–64

Obama, Barack, **IV**:135, 136, 150

Obata, Gyo, **III**:159–60

Obesity, **III**:79–80, **IV**:76, 201–2

O Brother, Where Art Thou? (2000), **IV**:184

Ocean travel: 1900s, **I**:92; 1910s, **I**:208; 1920s, **I**:348; 1930s, **II**:123–24; 1950s, **II**:377; 1960s, **III**:115; 1990s, **IV**:106–7

O'Connor, Flannery, **II**:173, **III**:39

Odets, Clifford, **II**:68

Odyssey (video game system), **III**:214–15

Off Broadway theater, **IV**:57

Office of War Information (OWI), **II**:154, 191, 215

Off-Off-Broadway theater, **III**:65

Ofili, Chris, **IV**:113

Ogilvy, David, **III**:21–22

Oil crisis/embargo, **III**:131, 221

O'Keefe, Georgia, **I**:220, 354, **II**:378

Oklahoma! (1943), **II**:183–84, 216–17, 305

Oklahoma City bombing, **IV**:11–12

Oland, Warner, **II**:52

Oldenburg, Claes, **III**:120, 227

Old Navy (retail store), **IV:**62

Olds, Ransom Eli, **I:**89

Oldsmobile Company, **III:**113

Olive Garden (restaurant chain), **IV:**73

Oliver, Joseph ("King"), **I:**191

Oliver, King, **I:**318

Olmstead, Frederick Law, **I:**194

Olympic Games: 1900s, **I:**82–83; 1910s, **I:**201; 1920s, **I:**333–34; 1930s, **II:**105–6; 1940s, **II:**231; 1950s, **II:**361; 1960s, **III:**103–4; 1970s, **III:**141–42, 209–10; 1980s, **III:**315–17; 1990s, **IV:**89, 90, 93, 94; 2000s, **IV:**153, 230

Omnibus (TV show), **II:**316

Omnicom (advertising agency), **IV:**151–52

O'Neal, Shaquille, **IV:**94–95

One Flew Over the Cuckoo's Nest (Kesey), **III:**36

O'Neill, Eugene, **I:**152, 155, 268, 278

Online culture: advertising, **IV:**22–23; auction sites, **IV:**249–50; blogs, **IV:**172; buying, **IV:**31–32; collecting, **IV:**99; distractions, **IV:**140–41; gambling, **IV:**104; gaming, **IV:**221; music downloads, **IV:**211–12; publishing, **IV:**32; shopping, **IV:**234–35; surfing, **IV:**99; travel sites, **IV:**239–44; TV watching, **IV:**181–82; videos, **IV:**232

On the Road (Kerouac), **II:**287, **III:**35–36

On the Town (1949), **II:**180, 217

On the Waterfront (1954), **II:**262

Op art, **III:**120–21

Open Door policy (U.S.), **I:**7

O Pioneers! (Cather), **I:**143

Opportunity (magazine), **I:**355

The Oprah Winfrey Show (TV show), **IV:**32

Orbitz (online travel site), **IV:**241–42

Orchestral music: 1900s, **I:**68–70; 1910s, **I:**185–86; 1920s, **I:**316, 318–19, 323–25; 1930s, **II:**93–94; 1940s, **II:**215, 216, 220, 222–23; 1950s, **II:**348, 354, 355–256; 1960s, **III:**89, 94

Ordinary People (1980), **III:**283–84

Organic architectural styles, **I:**134

Organic food trend, **III:**78, **IV:**199

The Organizational Man (Whyte), **II:**288

Organization of Petroleum Exporting Countries (OPEC), **III:**115, 130–31

Organized crime, **III:**14

Original Celtics (New York), **I:**332

Oscar Mayer "Lunchables," **IV:**70

Oswald, Lee Harvey, **III:**9, 122

Otay Ranch Town Center (San Diego), **IV:**160

The Other America: Poverty in the United States (Harrington), **III:**81

Ouija Board (game), **I:**203, **III:**105

Ouimet, Francis, **I:**194–95

Outcault, Richard Felton, **I:**43–44

Outerbridge, Mary Ewing, **I:**81

Outlaw country music, **III:**201

Ovaltine (chocolate drink), **II:**270

Owens, Jesse, **II:**106, **III:**316

Ozone concerns, **III:**147

Paar, Jack, **III:**58

Packard, Vance, **II:**268–69, 288

Pac-Man (video game), **III:**320

Paine, John Knowles, **I:**68–69

Paint-by-number techniques, **II:**380–81

Painting, visual arts: 1900s, **I:**93–96; 1910s, **I:**214, 217; 1920s, **I:**352–55; 1930s, **II:**125–28; 1940s, **II:**242–45; 1950s, **II:**378–81; 1960s, **III:**117–18; 1970s, **III:**226–27; 1980s, **III:**327; 1990s, **IV:**112, 113; 2000s, **IV:**254–55

Palahniuk, Chuck, **IV:**165

Paley, William S., **II:**188

Palmeiro, Rafael, **IV:**229

Palmer, Arnold, **II:**360, **III:**101–2

Palmer, Mitchell, **I:**230

Palmer Paint Company, **II:**380

Palmer Raids, **I:**230

Panama Canal, **I:**7, 92

Panama–Pacific International Exposition, **I:**323

Pan American Exposition (1901), **I:**4, 85

Pan American World Airways, **I:**351, **II:**377, **III:**321

Panasonic Corporation, **IV:**97

Panavision lenses, **II:**299

Papanicolaou, George (Pap smear discoverer), **I:**238

Paperback books, **II:**169, 232, 283–84

Paramount decree, **II:**195

Paramount Pictures, **I:**282

Paretsky, Sara, **IV:**36

Parker, Charlie, **II:**223–24

Parker, Tom ("Colonel"), **II:**352

Park-O-Meter (parking meter), **II:**116

Parks, Rosa, **III:**21

Parsons, Louella, **II:**43

Parsons School of Design, **IV:**65

Partnership for a Drug-Free America, **IV:**21

Parton, Dolly, **III:**202

Patchett, Ann, **IV:**167

Patterson, Floyd, **III:**98

Patterson, Joseph Medill, **I:**274

Pay-per-view television, **IV:**94

PC Travel (online travel site), **IV:**239–40

Peace Corps, **III:**21

The peace symbol, **III:**15

Peale, Norman Vincent, **II:**284

Peanuts (comic strip), **II:**294, **III:**173, **IV:**42

Pearl Harbor attack, **II:**142, 143, 215

Pearl Jam (singing group), **IV:**80

Pearlman, Lou, **IV:**87

Peck, Gregory, **II:**302

Peer-to-peer (P2P) networking, **IV:**212

Pei, I. M., **III:**158, 159, 258, **IV:**26–27

Pelton, Robert Young, **IV:**102

Penn Central Railroad system, **III:**223

Penn Central Transportation Co. v. New York City, **III:**162

Pennsylvania Turnpike opening, **II:**240

Pennzoil Plaza (Houston), **III:**159

Pentacostal religion, **I:**237

The Pentagon (Arlington), **II:**168

Pentagon Papers, **III:**132, 172

Penthouse (magazine), **IV:**40

People (magazine), **III:**171

Peoples Temple cult, **III:**149

People's theater, **I:**154–56

People United to Save Humanity (PUSH), **III:**136

Pepsi-Cola Company, **I:**67, 313, **II:**90–91, 345, **III:**21, 79, 300, 306, **IV:**19, 204–5

Pepsodent toothpaste, **II:**18

Pereira, William L., **III:**156–58

Period revivals, **II:**26–27

Perot, Ross, **IV:**7–8

Perry, Anne, **III:**165

The Perry Como Show (TV show), **II:**318

Perry Mason (TV show), **II:**33–34, 284, 323

Personal computers (PCs), **III:**245–47, **IV:**14

Peter, Paul, and Mary (singing group), **III:**85

Peter Gunn (TV show), **II:**347

Peters, Lulu Hunt, **I:**307

Petrini, Carlo, **III:**299

Pet rock fad, **III:**212, 213–14

Peyton Place (Metalious), **II:**286, 308–9

Pharmacia & Upjohn Drugs, **IV:**78

Phat Farm (clothing label), **IV:**62

Phelps, Michael, **IV:**230

Philadelphia (1993), **III:**249

Philadelphia Orchestra Association, **I:**70, **II:**356

The Philadelphia Savings Fund Society Building (New York), **I:**254

Philadelphia Savings Fund Society (PSFS) building, **II:**24–25

Phillips, Sam, **II:**352

Phonographs, **I:**186–87, 315

Photography: 1900s, **I:**96–98; 1910s, **I:**217; 1920s, **I:**355–56; 1930s, **II:**17, 128–29; 1940s, **II:**245–47; 1950s, **II:**381–82; 1960s, **III:**18, 107, 121–22; 1970s, **III:**228–29; 1980s, **III:**328–31; 1990s, **IV:**109–11; 2000s, **IV:**252–54

Photojournalism, **I:**356, **II:**128, 246–47, **III:**122

Photorealism school, **III:**28

Physical fitness fad, **III:**318

Picasso, Pablo, **III:**226

Pickford, Mary, **I:**157, 159, 160–61, 247, 286

Pick-Up Sticks (game), **II:**109–10

"Picto-Fiction" comics, **III:**172

Pictorialism, photography school, **I:**96

Piercings, fashion, **IV:**66–67

Piggly Wiggly grocery store, **I:**307–8, **II:**82, 83

Pilgrim's Progress (Bunyan), **I:**38

Pillsbury Flour "bake-offs," **II:**337

Pinball games, **II:**108–9

Ping-Pong (table tennis), **II:**109

The Pinto (Ford Motors), **III:**220

Pin-up girls, **II:**233

Pitt, Brad, **IV:**184–85

Pittsburgh Pirates, **I:**77–78

Pittsburgh Steelers, **III:**211

Pizza Hut (fast food restaurant), **III:**299

Pizza trends, **II:**340

Plame, Valerie, **IV:**128–29

Planet of the Apes (1968), **III:**112

"Planned obsolescence," **II:**31, 268

Plasman, Dick, **II:**228

Plastic/cosmetic surgery, **IV:**67, 195–96

Plater-Zyberk, Elizabeth, **III:**259

Platform shoes, **III:**191–92

Plath, Sylvia, **III:**44

Playboy bunny outfit, **III:**71

Playboy (magazine), **II:**289–90, **III:**45, 71, 170–71, **IV:**40

Playground Association of America (PAA), **I:**194

PlayStation console (computer game toy), **IV:**97, 233

Plessy v. Ferguson (1896), **I:**39

The Plot Against America (Roth), **IV:**168

"Pluggers" (music performers), **I:**71–72

Pocket Books (publishers), **II:**283

Poetry: 1900s, **I:**37, 41; 1910s, **I:**146–47; 1920s, **I:**267; 1930s, **II:**43; 1940s, **II:**174–75; 1950s, **II:**287–88; 1960s, **III:**43–44; 1970s, **III:**169–70; 1990s, **IV:**38; 2000s, **IV:**169

Pogo (comic strip), **II:**294–95

Pogo stick (toy), **I:**337

Poindexter, John, **III:**241

Poiret, Paul, **I:**172

Poitier, Sidney, **II:**300, **III:**49, 63

Pokémon (card game), **IV:**39, 99

Poland, **II:**142

Polanski, Roman, **III:**13, 51

Police/G-men movies, **II:**52

Police procedural television, **IV:**47–48

Politics: 1900s, **I:**5–6; 1910s, **I:**110; 1920s, **I:**229, 232, 236; 1930s, **II:**96, 106; 1940s, **II:**142–44; 1950s, **II:**273–74; 1960s, **III:**8–10; 1970s, **III:**132–35; 1980s, **III:**238, 273, 310–11, 315–16; 1990s, **IV:**7–8, 21–22, 108–9; 2000s, **IV:**150–51

Pollock, Jackson, **II:**242, 243–44, 263, 380

Pollution, **III:**82, 143–44

Polyethylene plastic, **II:**282

PONG (video game system), **III:**215

Ponzi, Carlo ("Charles"), **I:**251

Poodle skirt fashions, **II:**335

Pop art, **III:**118–20, 227–28

Popcorn snack food, **II:**339

Pope, John Russell, **II:**23–24

Pop music: 1960s, **III:**87–89; 1970s, **III:**202–4; 1980s, **III:**303; 1990s, **IV:**86–87; 2000s, **IV:**210, 213, 215–16

Pop Rocks (candy), **III:**194

Popular fiction, **I:**141, **III:**165–67

Popular Mechanics (magazine), **II:**116

Popular Photography (magazine), **II:**245

Porgy and Bess (Gershwin), **II:**68

Pork Chop Hill (1959), **II:**302

Porter, Edwin S., **I:**51

"Portion creep" in foods, **IV:**201

Portland Public Services Building, **III:**259

Portnoy's Complaint (Roth), **III:**36

Poseidon Adventure (1970), **III:**175

Post, Charles W., **I:**66

Post, Emily, **II:**43

Post, Wiley, **II:**121–22

Post Cereal Company, **II**:339
Postimpressionistic art, **I**:220
Postmodernism, **III**:156
Post-traumatic stress disorder (PTSD), **III**:143
Pound, Ezra, **I**:146
Poverty: 1900s, **I**:11, 34; 1910s, **I**:109, 112, 193;
	1920s, **I**:234, 312; 1930s, **II**:8, 9, 114; 1940s,
	II:142, 153, 166, 241; 1950s, **II**:256; 1960s,
	III:81–82; 1970s, **III**:244; 1980s, **III**:261; 1990s,
	IV:5–6, 6, 29; 2000s, **IV**:136
The Power of Positive Thinking (Peale), **II**:284
Prairie-style houses (Prairie School), **I**:29–30,
	135, **II**:278
Precisionism (Cubist Realism), **I**:354
Prefab housing, **II**:163–64
"Preppy" Ivy League fashions, **II**:333–34, 335,
	III:293
Presidential scandals, **IV**:9–10
Presley, Elvis, **II**:332, 333, 335, 351–52, **III**:52, 57,
	88, 202–3
Presumed Innocent (Turow), **III**:265
Priceline.com (online travel site), **IV**:238, 241
Pride, Charlie, **III**:86
Priest, Dana, **IV**:133
Prince (singer), **III**:311
Princip, Gavrilo, **I**:113
Private building architecture, **I**:134
Probst, Jeff, **IV**:178
"Process art," **III**:331
Processed foods, **II**:209, **IV**:69
Pro-choice *vs.* pro-life, **III**:137–38
Procter & Gamble company, **I**:248, **II**:267–68, 273,
	III:73, 79
The Producing Managers' Association, **I**:154
Production Code Administration (PCA),
	II:191, **III**:48
Product placement, advertising, **IV**:19–20
Professional Air Traffic Controller's Organization
	(PATCO), **III**:323–24
Professional Golfers' Association (PGA), **I**:331, **II**:360
Professional wrestling, **IV**:89–90, 220
Progressive Era: commercialization during, **I**:108;
	crime during, **I**:111–12; interest groups of,
	I:110–11; muckrakers and, **I**:37–39; politics
	during, **I**:5–6, 110; rural life during, **I**:109–10;
	ship tragedies and, **I**:115–19; urban life during,
	I:109–10; violence during, **I**:11–12; visual art
	during, **I**:93; WWI and, **I**:113–15
Progressive rock music, **III**:204–6
Prohibition, **I**:232–35, 308, 312, **II**:89–90, 100
Prostitution, **I**:111–12
Protein Power (Eades, Eades), **IV**:77
Protestant issues, **III**:16
Protest poetry, **III**:169
Prudhomme, Paul, **IV**:74
Psycho (1960), **III**:52
PT Cruiser (Chrysler Motors), **IV**:105
Public Broadcasting Service (PBS), **III**:53–54,
	153, 185
Public monument architecture, **I**:133–34

Public relations advertising, **II**:273–73
Public service announcement (PSA), **III**:152
Public transportation, **I**:343–45, **II**:118–19, 238
Public Works of Art Project, **II**:127
Puck, Wolfgang, **IV**:69, 74
Puka bead necklaces, **III**:189
Pulitzer, Joseph, **I**:147
Pulitzer Prize, **I**:264
Pulp Fiction (1994), **IV**:53, 56
Pulp magazines, **I**:271–73, **II**:40–41
Punk fashion trends, **III**:192–93
Pure Food and Drug Act (1906), **I**:6, 32, 39,
	63–66, 124–25
Purple Rain (1984), **III**:311
Puzo, Mario, **III**:40
Pyle, Ernie, **II**:171
Pynchon, Thomas, **III**:164

Quake (computer game), **IV**:98
Quant, Mary, **III**:69–70
Quayle, Dan, **IV**:84
Queen, Ellery, **II**:33
Queen Latifah (singer), **IV**:84
Queen Mary (ocean liner), **II**:123
Queen (singing group), **III**:206
Quiche, food fad, **III**:301
Quiz shows, television, **II**:321–23
Quonset huts, **II**:163–64
Quonset Point Naval Station (Rhode Island), **II**:164

Rabbit trilogy (Updike), **III**:164, 267
Racism: 1900s, **I**:42; 1910s, **I**:110–11, 154–55,
	183–84; 1920s, **I**:231–32, 268–69, 290–91; 1930s,
	II:19–20, 63–64, 92–93; 1940s, **II**:195, 226, 229;
	1950s, **II**:271–72, 280, 350–51, 355; 1960s,
	III:10–13, 49; 1970s, **III**:135–36, 168; 1980s,
	III:269, 274, 293; 1990s, **IV**:46, 73, 80; 2000s,
	IV:134–37
The Rack (1956), **II**:302
Radar Ranges, **II**:342
Radio: 1920s, **I**:250–51, 288–91, 306, 315, 322;
	1930s, **II**:12, 18–19, 42, 62–66, 92–93, 102–3;
	1940s, **II**:156, 184–87, 186; 1950s, **II**:266,
	310–13, 350; 1960s, **III**:59; 1970s, **II**:65, 186,
	III:215; 1990s, **IV**:51; 2000s, **IV**:175
Radio Corporation of America (RCA), **I**:289,
	II:66–67, 187
Radio Flyer wagon (toy), **I**:334, **II**:110
Rage Against The Machine (singing group), **IV**:80
Raggedy Ann dolls, **I**:203, 334
Ragtime music, **I**:72–73, 188–89, 318
Railroad travel: 1900s, **I**:86, 88; 1910s, **I**:209–10;
	1920s, **I**:347; 1930s, **II**:119–20; 1940s, **II**:238;
	1950s, **II**:376–77; 1960s, **III**:115–16; 1970s,
	III:223–24; 1990s, **IV**:106
Rainey, Gertrude ("Ma"), **I**:321
A Raisin in the Sun (1959), **II**:279, **III**:62–63, 186
Ramsey, JonBenet, **IV**:68
Ranch houses, **II**:277–79, **III**:30
Randolph, A. Philip, **II**:148

Rapid Shave commercial, **III:**22

Rap music, **IV:**83–85, 213–16

Rastafari movement, **III:**206

Rastus (advertising figure), **I:**247, **II:**20

Rating systems: for movies, **III:**48–49, **IV:**52; for television, **II:**314–15, **III:**53–54

Rationing: cars/car parts, **II:**237; fabric, **II:**197; food, **II:**207–8

Rauschenberg, Robert, **III:**118

Rave fashion, **IV:**63–64

Ravelo, Mars, **II:**178

Ray, James Earl, **III:**10

Ray, Rachael, **IV:**207–9

Raymond, Eleanor, **II:**167

RCA Victor, **II:**347, 352

Reader's Digest (magazine), **I:**269, **II:**37–38, 176

Ready-made food, **IV:**70–71

Ready-to-wear fashions, **II:**200–202

Reagan, Ronald: AIDS crisis neglect, **IV:**13; air traffic controller strike and, **III:**323–24; *Challenger* disaster and, **III:**239–40; economic policy of, **III:**241; era of prosperity and, **III:**237–39; foreign policy of, **III:**240–41; public relations broadcasting by, **II:**103

"Reaganomics," **III:**244, 286

Realism: artistic, **I:**214; in literature, **I:**34–37, 138–40

Reality TV shows, **IV:**175–78

Real Men Don't Eat Quiche (Feirstein), **III:**301

Reason-why advertising, **I:**123–24

Recession debate, **IV:**138

Recommended daily allowances (RDAs), **II:**206–7

Record technology, music, **II:**213–14, 347

"Red Baron." *See* Richthofen, Manfred Von

Red Bull energy drinks, **IV:**205

Redding, Otis, **III:**93

Redenbacher, Orville, **II:**339

Redford, Robert, **III:**283, 285

Red Lobster (restaurant chain), **III:**79, **IV:**73

The Red Scare, **I:**112, 115, 154, 230, **II:**262

Reebok shoes, **III:**253

Reed, Jack, **I:**140

Reform and Terrorism Prevention Act, **IV:**131

Refrigeration technology, **II:**85–87, 209, 342

Reggae music, **III:**206

Regionalism (art style), **II:**125–27

Regional Planning Association of America (RPAA), **II:**162

Regulation L-85 (fabric rationing), **II:**197, 201

Rehnquist, William H., **III:**138

Reimers, Ed, **II:**271

Reinhardt, Django, **II:**222

Religion: 1910s, **I:**192; 1920s, **I:**237–38; 1930s, **II:**20; 1950s, **II:**257, 284–85, 305–6; 1960s, **III:**16–17; 1970s, **III:**139, 147–49; 1980s, **III:**248; 1990s, **IV:**46–47; 2000s, **IV:**143

Remington, Frederick, **I:**99

Remodeling boom, **IV:**160–61, 163–64

Remus, George, **I:**234

Renaissance architectural style, **I:**130

Rent (Larson), **IV:**57

Reservoir Dogs (1992), **IV:**53

Residential architecture: 1900s, **I:**27–28, 29–30; 1910s, **I:**134–37; 1920s, **I:**260; 1930s, **II:**26; 1940s, **II:**163–64; 1950s, **II:**277–79; 1960s, **III:**30–31; 1970s, **III:**160; 1980s, **III:**261–62; 1990s, **IV:**28–29; 2000s, **IV:**160–62

Restaurant trends: 1900s, **I:**18; 1910s, **I:**180–81; 1920s, **I:**257, 308–10; 1930s, **II:**88–89; 1940s, **II:**152, 210–11; 1950s, **II:**276–77, 299, 342–43; 1960s, **III:**27–28, 75, 78–79, 114; 1970s, **III:**197–98; 1980s, **III:**298–99; 1990s, **IV:**69–70, 72–75; 2000s, **IV:**199–201, 204, 206

Retton, Mary Lou, **III:**316

Reverse discrimination, **III:**135

Revival styles, **I:**27–29, 260

Reynolds, R. J., **I:**180

Rhapsody in Blue (Gershwin), **I:**323, **II:**68, 98

Rhodes, James, **III:**142

The Rhumba (dance), **II:**179

Rhythm and blues (R&B) music: 1910s, **I:**189–91; 1920s, **I:**319–21; 1930s, **II:**92, 93, 97, 98; 1940s, **II:**219–20; 1950s, **II:**350–51, 352; 1960s, **III:**86, 90–93; 1970s, **III:**206–7; 1980s, **III:**312; 1990s, **IV:**82, 85

Rice, Elmer, **II:**69

Rice, Tim, **III:**187, **IV:**57

Richthofen, Manfred Von ("Red Baron"), **I:**208

Riders of the Purple Sage (Grey), **I:**264

Riesman, David, **II:**288

Riggs, Bobby, **III:**208–9

Rimes, LeAnn, **IV:**86

Rinehart, Mary Roberts, **I:**265

Ring, D. H., **III:**247

Rin Tin Tin (dog actor), **I:**286

Ripken, Carl, **IV:**92

Ripley, Alexandra, **IV:**37

Risky Business (1980), **III:**290

Riverdance (Celtic dance show), **IV:**57

RKO Pictures, **I:**282

Roadsides/roadways, architecture: **II:**276; construction of, **II:**240–41, **IV:**106; restaurants along, **I:**310

Robbins, Harold, **III:**166

Robbins, Jerome, **II:**179–80

Robbins, Tom, **III:**164

Roberts, Xavier, **III:**317

Robeson, Paul, **I:**321

Robie House (1909), **I:**30

Robinson, Earl, **II:**98

Robinson, Edward Arlington, **I:**267

Robinson, Jackie, **II:**226, **III:**100

Robinson, Marilynne, **III:**267

Rockabilly music style, **II:**352

"Rock Around the Clock" (1954), **II:**349–50

Rock Band (video game), **IV:**211

Rockefeller, John D., **I:**6, 8–9

Rocker, John, **IV:**93

"Rocket 88" (1951), **II:**372

Rockne, Knute, **I:**200

Rock 'n' roll music: 1950s, **II:**349–53; 1960s,
  III:89–92; 1970s, **III:**202–4; 1980s, **III:**308, 312;
  1990s, **IV:**81–82; 2000s, **IV:**216
Rockwell, Norman, **I:**20, 215–16, 274–75, **II:**131,
  132, 155–56, 244–45, 379
The Rocky Horror Picture Show (1975), **III:**176, 192
Rodeo fads, **II:**108
Rodgers, Jimmie, **I:**322–23
Rodgers, Richard, **II:**216–17
Rodman, Dennis, **IV:**95
Roe v. Wade, **III:**137–38, 183
Rogers, Ginger, **II:**54–55, 70, 123–24
Rogers, Kenny, **III:**202
Rogers, Rosemary, **III:**165
Rogers, Roy, **II:**53
Rollerblading, **IV:**88
Roller Derby (fad), **II:**107
Rolling Stone (magazine), **IV:**128
The Rolling Stones (singing group), **III:**204–5,
  III:89–90, **IV:**216
Rolodex rotary card file, **II:**281
Romance books, **IV:**37–38
Romanesque architectural style (1910s), **I:**130
Roosevelt, Alice, **I:**54–55
Roosevelt, Eleanor, **II:**43
Roosevelt, Franklin D.: assassination attempt
  on, **II:**7; baseball during WWII, **II:**225; "brain
  trust" of, **II:**6–7; prohibition repeal by, **I:**235;
  radio use by, **II:**65, 186; re-election of, **II:**144;
  on television, **II:**67; Thanksgiving date move
  of, **II:**11; WWII involvement by, **II:**143
Roosevelt, Theodore: as art critic, **I:**219; as athletic
  outdoorsman, **I:**75; diplomacy of, **I:**6–7; film
  entertainment and, **I:**45; food safety standards
  of, **I:**61, 64–65; football commission and, **I:**79;
  military expansion by, **I:**7; morality concepts
  of, **I:**4–5; national park system and, **I:**87;
  Panama Canal and, **I:**92; politics of, **I:**5–6
Root, Elihu, **I:**7
Roots (Haley), **III:**216
Roots (TV miniseries), **III:**184
Rose, Pete, **II:**226
Rose Bowl (1902), **I:**79
Rosemary's Baby (Levin), **III:**40, 51
Rosenberg, Bruce, **IV:**242–43
Rosenquist, James, **III:**120
"Rosie the Riveter," **II:**155–56
Ross, Diana, **III:**94
Rossner, Judith, **III:**166
Roth, David Lee, **III:**307–8
Roth, Philip, **III:**36, 164, **IV:**168
Rothko, Mark, **II:**243
Rove, Karl, **IV:**129
Rowan and Martin's Laugh-In (TV show), **III:**58
Rowling, J. K., **IV:**40, 166
The Roxy Theatre (New York), **I:**258
Rubber industry, **I:**89–90, **II:**237
Rubik's Cube (toy), **III:**319–20
Rubin, Rick, **IV:**218–19
Ruby, Jack, **III:**9, 122

Rudolph, Wilma, **III:**103
Rumsfeld, Donald, **IV:**129
Ruppert, Jacob, **I:**196
Rushdie, Salman, **III:**266–67
Russell, Jane, **II:**198, 331
Russia. *See* United Soviet Socialist Republic
Ruth, Herman George ("Babe"), **I:**77, 196–97,
  327–28, **II:**101–2
Ryan, Leo, **III:**149

Saarinen, Eliel, **I:**254
Sacco, Nicola (Sacco/Vanzetti case), **I:**231
Sack suits for men, **I:**58–59
Safeway (supermarket), **II:**82
Saint-Gaudens, Augustus, **I:**98–99
Saint Louis Olympics (1904), **I:**82, 193
St. Valentine's Day Massacre, **I:**234–35
St. Vincent Millay, Edna, **I:**267
Salinger, J. D., **II:**285, 344
Salk, Jonas, **III:**27
Saloon growth, **I:**75–76
Sam's Club stores, **IV:**167
Samuel Adams Lager, **IV:**75
Sandberg, Carl, **I:**146
Sanders, Harland ("Colonel"), **III:**78–79
Sanford and Son (TV show), **III:**181
San Francisco Chronicle (newspaper), **I:**148
San Francisco earthquake, **I:**15
Sanger, Margaret, **I:**111
Sanka (decaffeinated coffee), **II:**91
Sarazen, Gene, **I:**331
Sargent, John Singer, **I:**93–94
Sarnoff, David, **II:**187, 188
Sassoon, Vidal, **III:**70
The Satanic Verses (Rushdie), **III:**266–67
The Saturday Evening Post (magazine), **I:**33, 122,
  215, 249, 269, **II:**37, 119, 131, 176, 240, 244, 292,
  379, **III:**44
Saturday Night Fever (1977), **III:**174–75, 186,
  190, 278
Saturday Night Live (TV show), **III:**184
Saunders, Clarence, **I:**307
Savage, Augusta, **I:**355
Saving Private Ryan (1998), **IV:**55
Scheel, Fritz, **I:**70
The Schick Corporation, **II:**78
Schindler's List (1993), **IV:**55
Schindler's List (Keneally), **III:**268
Schlafly, Phyllis, **III:**137
Schlosser, Eric, **IV:**72
Schmeling, Max, **II:**105, 230
Scholastic Publishing, **IV:**40
School shootings, **IV:**12–13
School uniforms, **IV:**64
Schulz, Charles, **II:**294, **III:**173, **IV:**42
Science fiction: 1920s, **I:**272, 275–76, 284;
  1930s, **II:**46; 1950s, **II:**290–91, 306–7, 312;
  1960s, **III:**46, 57; 1970s, **III:**177–78; 1980s,
  III:279–80; 1990s, **IV:**35–36, 44–46
Science (magazine), **III:**217

Scientology cult, **III:**149

Scopes, John T., **I:**237

Scopes Trial, **I:**238–39, 290

Scorsese, Martin, **IV:**55

Scott, George C., **III:**51

Scott Paper Towels, **I:**8, 24

Scrabble (board game), **II:**363

Scrabulous (electronic game), **IV:**234

Screwball comedy movies, **II:**56–58

Scripps, E.W., **I:**147

Sculpture: 1900s, **I:**98–99; 1920s, **I:**356–57; 1930s, **II:**129–30; 1950s, **II:**381; 1960s, **III:**118, 120; 1970s, **III:**225; 1980s, **III:**331; 1990s, **IV:**109

Seabiscuit (race horse), **II:**104

Seacrest, Ryan, **IV:**175

Sears, Barry, **IV:**77

Sears, Roebuck and Company catalog (mail-order), **I:**19, 53, 61, 292, **II:**72, 86, 338

Sears Tower (Chicago), **III:**156

Seat of the Soul (Zukov), **IV:**39

Seattle Art Museum (Seattle), **IV:**28

The Secret (Byrne), **IV:**170

Securities and Exchange Commission (SEC), **III:**242–43

Seeger, Alan, **I:**145

Seeger, Pete, **II:**221–22, **III:**83, 85, 115

See It Now (TV broadcast), **II:**261

Sega Corporation, **IV:**97

Segal, Erich, **III:**167

Seger, Bob, **III:**203

Seinfeld (TV show), **IV:**18, 50

Sekula, Allan, **III:**228

Self-help books, **I:**265, **III:**269, **IV:**38–39

Self-improvement fads, **I:**338

Self Portrait (Mapplethorpe), **III:**330

Self-service shopping, **II:**83, 266

Sellers, Peter, **III:**51

Selznick, David O., **II:**61

Sephora (makeup company), **IV:**65

September 11, 2001: home safety concerns since, **IV:**161; movies about, **IV:**185; national unity from, **IV:**133; overview of, **IV:**129–31; rebuilding WTC after, **IV:**157, 158; recession from, **IV:**126–27, 190; travel impact from, **IV:**101–2, 244

Serial dramas, **III:**276–78

Serra, Richard, **III:**331

Serrano, Andres, **III:**328–30

Sesame Street (TV show), **III:**58–59

Settlement houses, **I:**6, 109

Seventeen (magazine), **II:**291, 335

7th Heaven (TV show), **IV:**46–47

7-up (soft drink), **I:**313, **II:**91, **III:**19

78-rpm records, **II:**347

Sewing machines, **II:**197

Sex and the City (TV show), **IV:**49

Sex pulp magazines, **I:**273

Sexual Behavior in the Human Female (Kinsey), **II:**288

Sexual Behavior in the Human Male (Kinsey), **II:**152–53, 171, 288

The Shag (dance), **II:**97

Shahn, Ben, **II:**378

Shakur, Tupac "2Pac" (rapper), **IV:**83–84

Sharkey, Jack, **II:**105

Sharkey's Saloon paintings, **I:**96

Shaughnessey, Clark, **II:**229

Shaving trends, **II:**78

Shaw, George Bernard, **I:**150

Sheeler, Charles, **I:**354, **II:**127, 378

Sheen, Fulton J., **II:**285

Sheet music publishing, **I:**68, 71, 186–88, 314–15, **II:**94–95

Shepard, Alan, **III:**218

Sheppard-Towner Act (1921), **I:**236

Sherman, Arthur, **II:**117

Sherman Anti-Trust Act, **I:**9

Sherwood, Robert E., **II:**68

S&H Green Stamps, **II:**273, **III:**20

Shilts, Randy, **III:**270–71

Shirtwaist fashion, **I:**56

Shmoos craze, **II:**234

Shoes/hosiery: 1900s, **I:**53, 56; 1910s, **I:**167, 169–71; 1920s, **I:**296–97; 1930s, **II:**77; 1940s, **II:**199, 200, 204–5; 1950s, **II:**330–31; 1960s, **III:**69–71; 1970s, **III:**188, 191–92; 1980s, **III:**251–53; 1990s, **IV:**61–62; 2000s, **IV:**148, 194, 226

Shopping centers: 1930s, **II:**116; 1940s, **II:**166; 1950s, **II:**275–76; 1960s, **III:**27–28; 1980s, **III:**292; 1990s, **IV:**24; 2000s, **IV:**159–60, 188, 193

Shore, Dinah, **II:**216

Show Boat (Ferber), **I:**264–65, 278

Shuffle Along (Miller, Lyles), **I:**278–79

Siciliano, Angelo, **I:**299, 338

Siegel, Don, **II:**263

Sierra Nevada Brewing Company, **IV:**75

Signage, architecture/design, **II:**276–77

Sikorsky Helicopter Company, **II:**240

Silent Spring (Carson), **III:**82

Silly Putty (toy), **II:**364

Simmons, Richard, **III:**318

Simon, Carly, **III:**200

Simon, Neil, **III:**62, **IV:**57

Simon, Paul, **III:**85, 199

SIMON (game toy), **III:**214

Simpson, Jessica, **IV:**210–11

Simpson, Nicole Brown, **IV:**11

Simpson, O. J., **III:**98, **IV:**12–13, 93

Simpson, Wallis Warfield, **II:**12

The Simpsons (TV show), **IV:**49

Sinatra, Frank, **II:**216, 217–18, 344, 347, **III:**87

Sinatra, Nancy, **III:**70

Sinclair, Upton, **I:**32, 39, 63–64

Singer Sewing Machine Company, **I:**203

The Singer Tower (New York), **I:**132

Single-product ad campaigns, **II:**160–61

Sissle, Noble, **I:**186

Sister Carrie (Dreiser), **I:**36–37

Sitcoms, **II:**317–18, **III:**180–83, 273–74

Six-day bike races (fad), **II**:107

60 Minutes (TV show), **III**:184

The $64,000 Question (TV show), **II**:321–22

Skateboarding, **IV**:63–64, 221

Skylab, **III**:218–19

Skyscrapers: 1900s, **I**:25–27; 1910s, **I**:129, 132; 1920s, **I**:253–55; 1930s, **II**:23; 1940s, **II**:167; 1960s, **III**:28, 30; 1970s, **III**:161, 162; 1980s, **III**:258, 259; 2000s, **IV**:158–59

Slapstick comedy genre (movies), **I**:284–85

Slaughterhouse-Five (Vonnegut), **III**:37

Sleepwalker (Fischl), **III**:327

Slick, Grace, **III**:91

Slinky (toy), **II**:232, 364

Slogans advertising, 1900s, **I**:17, 20; 1910s, **I**:121; 1920s, **I**:242; 1930s, **II**:18; 1940s, **II**:158; 1950s, **II**:266, 269; 1960s, **III**:19; 1970s, **III**:151; 1980s, **III**:252; 1990s, **IV**:17; 2000s, **IV**:145

"Slumming," **I**:96, 268

Smashing Pumpkin's (singing group), **IV**:80

Smith, Anna Nicole, **IV**:236

Smith, Bessie, **I**:320–21

Smith, Bob ("Buffalo"), **II**:189

Smith, Deavere, **IV**:58

Smith, Tommie, **III**:103

Smith, Mamie, **I**:320

The Smothers Brothers Comedy Hour (TV show), **III**:58

Snack foods, **II**:339

Snack Wrap Era, **IV**:201

Snickers Candy commercial, **IV**:147

Snoop Doggy Dogg (rapper), **IV**:83–84

Snowboarding, **IV**:88–89

Snow Falling on Cedars (Guterson), **IV**:37

Snyder, Ruth, **I**:239

Soap operas, **II**:64–65, 319–20, **III**:183

So Big (Ferber), **I**:264–65

Social media activities, **IV**:220, 230–32

Social Security Act, **III**:82

Society for the Suppression of Vice, **I**:277

Softball, **II**:103

Soft drinks: 1900s, **I**:20; 1910s, **I**:124–25; 1920s, **I**:312–13; 1930s, **II**:90–91; 1940s, **II**:158; 1950s, **II**:345; 1960s, **III**:80; 1970s, **III**:195–96; 1980s, **III**:299–300; 1990s, **IV**:76; 2000s, **IV**:202

Soft-sell (impressionistic) advertising, **I**:124

Sokoloff, Nikolai, **II**:99

Somebody Up There Likes Me (1956), **II**:360

Sondheim, Stephen, **III**:287

Song of Solomon (Morrison), **III**:164, **IV**:33

Sonny and Cher (TV show), **III**:183–84

Sontag, Susan, **III**:42

The Sopranos (TV show), **IV**:49

Sopwith, Tom (Sopwith's "Camel"), **I**:208

Sosa, Sammy, **IV**:92–93

Soul food, **III**:78

Soul music, **III**:92–94

The Sound of Music (1960), **III**:62

Sourlock, Murdoch, **IV**:199–200

Sousa, John Philip, **I**:185

South Beach Diet, **IV**:203

Southern Christian Leadership Conference (SCLC), **III**:136

South Park (TV show), **IV**:50

Soviet Union. *See* United Soviet Socialist Republic

Space travel, **II**:260, 276, 287, 365, **III**:108–12, 217–19

Spam (Hormel Company), **II**:85

Spandex fabric, **III**:68

Spanish-American War (1898), **I**:7

Spanish Colonial Revival style, **I**:260

Speakeasies, **I**:234

Spears, Brittney, **IV**:86–87, 194, 235–36

Spector, Phil, **III**:94

"Speed metal" music, **IV**:82–83

Spice Girls' (singing group), **IV**:86

Spider-Man (2002), **IV**:183

Spider-Man (comic book), **III**:272

Spider-Man (McFarlane), **IV**:42

Spiegelman, Art, **IV**:41

Spielberg, Steven, **IV**:55

Spillane, Mickey, **II**:169, 286

Spitz, Mark, **III**:142, 209

Split-level homes, **II**:277–79

Spock, Benjamin, **II**:151, 289, **III**:8

Spoon River Anthology (Masters), **I**:146

Spoor, George, **I**:159

Sport of Kings (race horse), **III**:104

Sports drinks, **IV**:71

Sports Illustrated (magazine), **II**:290, **III**:188

Sports/leisure activities (1900s): baseball, **I**:77–79; boxing, **I**:79–81; fads/crazes, **I**:51, 72–73; fairs/expositions/carnivals, **I**:83–85; football, **I**:75, 79; golf, **I**:81–82; horse racing, **I**:75, 85; Olympic games, **I**:82–83; saloon growth and, **I**:75–76; spectator, **I**:75–76; tennis, **I**:81–82; World Series, **I**:78

Sports/leisure activities (1910s): baseball, **I**:195–99; basketball, **I**:199; boxing, **I**:199; fads/crazes, **I**:204–5; football, **I**:199–201; golf, **I**:194–95; Olympic games, **I**:201; parks/playgrounds, **I**:193–94; recreation, **I**:192–93; spectator, **I**:194–95; tennis, **I**:194; toys/games, **I**:201–4; World Series, **I**:198

Sports/leisure activities (1920s): auto racing, **I**:333; baseball, **I**:327–28; basketball, **I**:331–32; boxing, **I**:328–29; fads/crazes, **I**:335–39; fashions for, **I**:294–95; football, **I**:329–30; golf, **I**:330–31; horse racing, **I**:332–33; Olympic games, **I**:333–34; swimming, **I**:332; tennis, **I**:331; toys/games, **I**:334; World Series, **I**:329

Sports/leisure activities (1930s): baseball, **II**:101–3; basketball, **II**:104; board games, **II**:108–10; boxing, **II**:105; chain letters/jokes, **II**:107–8; endurance contests, **II**:106–7; fads/crazes, **II**:106–7; football, **II**:103–4; golf, **II**:104–5; hobbies, **II**:112–13; horse racing, **II**:104; Olympic Games, **II**:105–6; softball, **II**:103; tennis, **II**:104; toys/games, **II**:110–12; World Series, **II**:103

Sports/leisure activities (1940s): baseball, **II:**225–28; basketball, **II:**229–30; boxing, **II:**230–31; fads/crazes, **II:**201–2, 232–34; football, **II:**228–29; golf, **II:**231; hockey, **II:**231; Olympic Games, **II:**231; tennis, **II:**231; toys/games, **II:**232; World Series, **II:**228

Sports/leisure activities (1950s): baseball, **II:**357–58; basketball, **II:**358–59; board games, **II:**363; bowling, **II:**359; boxing, **II:**359–60; fads/crazes, **II:**361–63; football, **II:**360; golf, **II:**360; hobbies, **II:**365–66; horse racing, **II:**360; Olympic games, **II:**361; swimming, **II:**361; tennis, **II:**360; toys/games, **II:**363–65; track and field, **II:**360–61; TV broadcasting of, **II:**324–25; World Series, **II:**359

Sports/leisure activities (1960s): baseball, **III:**99–100; basketball, **III:**100–101; board games, **III:**104–6; boxing, **III:**98–99; fads/crazes, **III:**104; football, **III:**96–98; golf, **III:**101–2; hobbies, **III:**106–7; hockey, **III:**101; horse racing, **III:**104; influence on fashion, **III:**68; Olympic Games, **III:**103–4; tennis, **III:**102; toys/games, **III:**104–6; World Series, **III:**100

Sports/leisure activities (1970s): baseball, **III:**210–11; basketball, **III:**212; board games, **III:**214; boxing, **III:**210; fads/crazes, **III:**213–14; football, **III:**211–12; genealogy searches, **III:**216; hobbies, **III:**214–16; Olympic Games, **III:**141–42, 209–10; tennis, **III:**211; toys/games, **III:**213–16; trends, **III:**212–13; women in, **III:**208–9; World Series, **III:**211

Sports/leisure activities (1980s): advertising and, **III:**315; baseball, **III:**315; board games, **III:**318–20; fads/crazes, **III:**317–18; football, **III:**315; Olympic Games, **III:**315–17; toys/games, **III:**317–20; video games, **III:**320; World Series, **III:**315

Sports/leisure activities (1990s): auto racing, **IV:**90–91; baseball, **IV:**92–93; basketball, **IV:**91; boxing, **IV:**93, 94; celebrity athletes, **IV:**94–95; collectible card games, **IV:**98–99; computer games, **IV:**96–98; decline in, **IV:**94; extreme sports, **IV:**88–89; fads/crazes, **IV:**68, 88, 95; football, **IV:**91; golf, **IV:**95; hockey, **IV:**91–92; Olympic Games, **IV:**89, 90, 93, 94; online activities, **IV:**99; scandals in, **IV:**93–94; toys/games, **IV:**95–96; women in, **IV:**90; World Series, **IV:**92; wrestling, **IV:**89–90

Sports/leisure activities (2000s): baseball, **IV:**228–29; basketball, **IV:**224–27; boxing, **IV:**220, 229; celebrity obsessions, **IV:**235–37; fads/crazes, **IV:**198, 201, 203; football, **IV:**223–24; golf, **IV:**220, 227–28; martial arts, **IV:**229; NASCAR, **IV:**221–23; Olympic Games, **IV:**230; online shopping, **IV:**234–35; technology impact, **IV:**230–32; toys/games, **IV:**232–34; video games, **IV:**220, 232–33; World Series, **IV:**228

Sports stadium architecture, **III:**29

Sportswear fashions, **I:**294–95, **II:**74–75

Sport utility vehicles (SUVs), **IV:**104

Springer, Jerry, **IV:**45

Springsteen, Bruce, **III:**203, 310–11, **IV:**216

Sputnik (Russian spacecraft), **II:**260, 276, 287, 365, **III:**108

The St. Francis Cookbook (Hirtzler), **I:**175

Stagecoach (1939), **II:**53

"Stagflation" in economy, **III:**131

Stamp collecting hobby, **II:**113

Standard Oil Company, **I:**9–10

Stanislavsky, Konstantin, **I:**150, **II:**180–81

Stanley Steamer, **I:**211

Starbucks Coffee, **III:**198, **IV:**30, 74–75, 204

Starr, Kenneth, **IV:**9

Starr, Ringo, **III:**57, 68–69, 89–90

Star Trek franchise, **IV:**44–45, 96

Star Trek (TV show), **III:**56–57, 112

Star Wars franchise, **III:**177–78, 214, 279, **IV:**35, 51, 96

Station wagons (automobiles), **II:**373

Steamboat Willie (cartoon film), **I:**288

Steam cars, **I:**210–11

Steel, Danielle, **IV:**37

Steichen, Edward, **II:**382

Stein, Gertrude, **I:**138, 141

Steinbeck, John, **II:**34–35, 114, **III:**35, **IV:**169

Steinem, Gloria, **III:**137, 153, 170

Stereogram art, **IV:**111–12

Stereophonic records, **II:**347

Stereo radio broadcasting, **II:**312

Stevens, Cat, **III:**200

Stevens, Ray, **III:**214

Stevenson, Adlai, **II:**273–74

Stewart, Jon, **IV:**183

Stewart, Martha, **IV:**41, 207, 209

Stewart, Rod, **III:**203–4

Stickley, Gustav, **I:**29, 135

Stieglitz, Alfred, **I:**96–97, 217, 354

Stine, R. L., **IV:**39–40

Stock market crash (1929), **I:**239–40

Stomp (Cresswell, McNicholas), **IV:**57

Stonehenge (Great Britain), **IV:**103

Stonewall Riots, **III:**138–39

Strategic Arms Limitation Talks (SALT), **III:**133

Strategic Defense Initiative ("Star Wars"), **III:**239

Streaking fad, **III:**214

Streamline Moderne style, **II:**22–23, 282

"Streamlining" trend, **II:**115, 120

A Streetcar Named Desire (1947), **II:**182–83

Streetcars, **I:**209–10, 344–45

Street Fighter II (video game), **IV:**97

A Street in Bronzeville (Brooks), **II:**175

Street photography, **III:**227, 228

Streisand, Barbra, **III:**88

Stringbands (hillbilly music), **I:**322

Studs Lonigan trilogy (Farrell), **II:**34

Sturges, Jock, **IV:**110

Styron, William, **III:**39

Sub prime loans, **IV:**137

Suburbs/suburban developments: 1900s, **I:**27, 86, 88; 1910s, **I:**109–10, 134; 1920s, **I:**260, 342;

1930s, **II:**18, 82, 87; 1940s, **II:**164–66; 1950s,
  II:277, 367–68; 1960s, **III:**30–31; 1970s,
  III:172; 1980s, **III:**292; 1990s, **IV:**28–29; 2000s,
  IV:159–60;
Suffrage movement, **I:**111
Sugar cereals, **II:**339–40, **III:**154
Sula (Morrison), **III:**164
Sullivan, Ed, **II:**348, **III:**57
Sullivan, Louis, **I:**25–26, 29
Summer, Donna, **III:**207
The Sun Also Rises (Hemingway), **I:**266
Sunbeam Corporation, **II:**86–87
Sunday, Billy, **I:**237
Sunday drive trend, **II:**114–15
Sundblom, Haddon, **II:**132
"Sunheated house" design, **II:**167
Sun Records, **II:**352
Super ball (toy), **III:**105
Super bookstores, **IV:**31
Super Bowl games, **III:**96–98, **IV:**91, 147, 173
Superhero comics, **II:**177
Superhighways, **II:**276, 368
Superman (comic book), **II:**48
Supermarkets, **II:**209–10, 338
Supermodel fashions, **IV:**68
Super Size Me (2003), **IV:**199–202
The Supremes (singing group), **III:**94
Surrealist movement (Surrealism), **I:**352, **II:**242
Survivor (TV show), **IV:**146, 176–78
Sutton, Mary, **I:**82
The Suzie-Q (dance), **II:**97
Swanson, Dick, **III:**229
Swanson Company, **II:**340–41
Swatch (watch company), **III:**253–54
Swayze, John Cameron, **II:**271, 323
Sweet jazz, **I:**319
Sweet Sweetback's Baadasssss Song (1971), **III:**177–78
Swimming/swimwear, **I:**295–96, 332, **II:**361
Swing dancing, **I:**281, **II:**70, 90, 95–96, 97, 179
The Swing Mikado (1938), **II:**69
Symbionese Liberation Army (SLA), **III:**141
Symphonic jazz, **I:**323
The Syndicate (theater group), **I:**153
Synthetic fabrics, **II:**204–5, 329, **III:**67, 68, **IV:**64
Syriana (2005), **IV:**184
Szarkowski. John, **III:**121

Tabloid journalism, **I:**274
Taco Bell (fast food restaurant), **III:**79, 198,
  IV:72, 74
Tae-Bo exercise program, **IV:**88
Taft, William Howard, **I:**110
Talese, Gay, **III:**167
Taliesin (Wright's home studio), **I:**135
"Talkies" (movies), **I:**281–82, 287–88
The Tammany Hall machine, **I:**6
Tang (flavored drink), **III:**80
The Tango (dance), **I:**280
Tap dancing, **I:**157, 280
Tarantino, Quentin, **IV:**53

Target (department store), **IV:**62, 162–63, 187,
  188–89
Tarnower, Herbert, **III:**197
Tartt, Donna, **IV:**38
Tarzan (comic strip), **I:**276
Tarzan of the Apes (Burroughs), **I:**272
Tate, Sharon, **III:**13, 140, 168
Tattoo fashions, **IV:**66–67
Taxicab transportation (1920s), **I:**344
Tax Reform Act (1976), **III:**162
Taylor, Elizabeth, **III:**51
Taylor, James, **III:**200
Tea (beverage). *See* Coffee/tea
Tearooms (mid-range restaurants), **I:**309, **II:**88–89
Technicolor movies, **II:**51–52, 60
Teddy bear toy, **I:**202–3
Teenagers: 1900s, **I:**51; 1910s, **I:**149, 192; 1920s,
  I:275, 338; 1930s, **II:**58–59; 1940s, **II:**200,
  217–19; 1950s, **II:**299–300, 333–36, 351; 1960s,
  III:59–61, 70–71; 1970s, **III:**183–84, 189, 191,
  199, 215; 1980s, **III:**253–54, 278, 284, 294, 306;
  1990s, **IV:**143
Teflon-coated cookware, **II:**342
Telemarketing, advertising, **IV:**18
Telephones, **I:**238, **II:**281
Television: 1930s, **II:**66–67, 101; 1940s, **II:**156, 161,
  187–90; 1950s, **II:**266–68, 313–26, 354–55,
  378–79; 1960s, **III:**9, 53–54; 1970s, **III:**180–85;
  1980s, **III:**250, 273–78, 290–92; 1990s, **IV:**34–35,
  44–49, 94, 109; 2000s, **IV:**174–81, 207–9, 221
Temple, Shirley, **II:**16, 59–60, 72
The Ten (American painter group), **I:**94
Ten cent socials, **I:**76
Tenement-style housing, **I:**134
Tennessee Valley Authority (TVA), **III:**14
Tennis: 1900s, **I:**81–82; 1910s, **I:**194; 1920s, **I:**331;
  1930s, **II:**104; 1940s, **II:**231; 1950s, **II:**360; 1960s,
  III:102; 1970s, **III:**211
The Terminator films, **III:**279
Terrorism, **IV:**10–12, 101–2, 244. *See also* War on
  Terror
Terry, Megan, **III:**63
Tet Offensive, **III:**15, 74, 103
Texaco Star Theater (TV show), **II:**316
T.G.I. Friday's (restaurant chain), **IV:**73
Theatre Guild on the Air (radio show), **II:**156–57
Theatrical Syndicate, Broadway, **I:**46
The Breakfast Club (1985), **III:**284
Thimble Theatre Starring Popeye (comic strip),
  I:276
The Thing (1951), **II:**306
The Third Jesus (Chopra), **IV:**170
30 Minute Meals (Ray), **IV:**207
33-rpm records, **II:**347
Thompson, Hunter S., **III:**42, 167–68
Thorpe, Jim, **I:**200–201
3Com Midwest Headquarters (Illinois), **IV:**28
3-D movies, **II:**298
Three Mile Island, Pennsylvania, **III:**146
Thriller (1982), **III:**303, 304–5

Thunderbird (Ford Motor), **II**:369

Tickle-Me Elmo (toy), **IV**:96

Tie-dyeing craze, **III**:73

Tilden, William ("Big Bill"), **I**:331, **II**:104

Tilzer, Harry von, **I**:71, 187

Time (magazine), **I**:269, **II**:365, **III**:239, 297, 300, **IV**:185

Time Warner Cable, **IV**:178

Tinkertoys (toy), **I**:204

"Tin Lizzie" cars, **I**:212

Tin Pan Alley (music publishers), **I**:45, 52, 70–**I**:71, **I**:187–88, 280, 314, 323

Tin plate toys, **I**:202

Titanic (1997), **IV**:52

The Titanic (ocean liner), **I**:115–17, 119, 208

Toaster designs, **II**:86

Toast of the Town (TV show), **II**:316

Today (TV show), **II**:326

Toe sock fad, **III**:212–13

To Kill a Mockingbird (Lee), **III**:39–40

Tokyo Imperial Hotel, **I**:136

Tolkien, J.R.R., **III**:40

Tom Corbett, Space Cadet (radio show), **II**:312, 364

Tomlinson, Charles, **I**:184

Tommy Hilfiger (clothing label), **IV**:63

The Tonight Show (TV show), **II**:326, **III**:57–58, 182

Tonkin Gulf Resolution, **III**:15

Top Gun (1986), **III**:283

Top 40 radio, **II**:312–13, 346–47, **III**:59

Torch songs, **I**:317–18

Torch Song Trilogy (Fierstein), **III**:286

Toscanini, Arturo, **II**:220, 355

Touched by an Angel (TV show), **IV**:46

Tourism industry, **II**:373, **IV**:102–3, 245–46

Towering Inferno (1970), **III**:176

Toys/games: 1910s, **I**:201–4; 1920s, **I**:334; 1930s, **II**:110–12; 1940s, **II**:232; 1950s, **II**:363–65; 1960s, **III**:104–6; 1970s, **III**:213–16; 1980s, **III**:317–20; 1990s, **IV**:95–96; 2000s, **IV**:232–34

Toy Story (1995), **IV**:51

Track and field sports, **II**:360–61

Trading stamp advertising, **II**:273

Trailers/campers, **II**:117–18, 279

Train travel. *See* Railroad travel

Transamerica Pyramid building (San Francisco), **III**:156–57

Transcendental Meditation (TM), **III**:149

Transcontinental and Western Air (TWA), **I**:351, **II**:377

Trans fats in food, **IV**:203

Travel Industry Association of America, **IV**:239

Travel/mass transportation (1900s), airlines, **I**:91–92; automobiles, **I**:89–91; city transport, **I**:88; electricity for, **I**:88; overseas, **I**:92; Panama Canal, **I**:92; by railroad, **I**:86, 88; vacations, **I**:86–87

Travel/mass transportation (1910s): airlines, **I**:207–8; automobiles, **I**:210–13; destinations of, **I**:206–7; overseas, **I**:208–9; by railroad, **I**:209–10; streetcars, **I**:209–10; vacations, **I**:206

Travel/mass transportation (1920s): airlines, **I**:348–51; automobiles, **I**:340–43; destinations of, **I**:346–47; overseas, **I**:348; public transportation, **I**:343–45; by railroad, **I**:347; vacations, **I**:345–46

Travel/mass transportation (1930s): airlines, **II**:120–23; automobiles, **II**:114–16; to fairs/expositions, **II**:28; lodging for, **II**:116–17; overseas, **II**:123–24; public transportation, **II**:118–19; by railroad, **II**:119–20; trailers/campers, **II**:117–18; vacations, **II**:75, 117

Travel/mass transportation (1940s): airlines, **II**:238–40; automobiles, **II**:235–37; to national parks, **II**:237–38; public transportation, **II**:238; by railroad, **II**:238; rationing, **II**:237; by roadways, **II**:240–41; vacations, **II**:235

Travel/mass transportation (1950s): airlines, **II**:377; amusement parks, **II**:375–76; automobiles, **II**:367–73; drive-in theaters, **II**:374; lodging/accommodations, **II**:373–74; miniature golf, **II**:376; overseas, **II**:377; by railroad, **II**:376–77; tourism growth, **II**:373; vacations, **II**:373, 375

Travel/mass transportation (1960s): airlines, **III**:115; automobiles, **III**:112–15; by diesel trucks, **III**:116; overseas, **III**:115; by railroad, **III**:115–16; in space, **III**:108–12; vacations, **III**:108, 114

Travel/mass transportation (1970s): airlines, **III**:221–23; automobiles, **III**:219–21; by diesel truck, **III**:224; by railroad, **III**:223–24; Skylab, **III**:218–19; in space, **III**:217–19; vacations, **III**:160

Travel/mass transportation (1980s): airlines, **III**:322–24; by foreigners, **III**:325; during holidays, **III**:321–22; vacations, **III**:324–25

Travel/mass transportation (1990s): for adventure, **IV**:102–3; airlines, **IV**:100, 101–2; automobiles, **IV**:104–6; by bus, **IV**:104–6; dangers of, **IV**:101–2; environmental concerns during, **IV**:103–4; gambling destinations, **IV**:104; global, **IV**:101; overseas, **IV**:106–7; by railroad, **IV**:106; vacations, **IV**:102–3, 106

Travel/mass transportation (2000s): airlines, **IV**:238–39; eco-friendly, **IV**:244–45; to Las Vegas, **IV**:245–46; luxury travel, **IV**:246; online sites for, **IV**:239–44; post 9/11, **IV**:244; vacations, **IV**:240, 242

Travelocity (online travel site), **IV**:238, 240, 241, 244

Travis, Walter J., **I**:81

Travolta, John, **III**:174, 190

Treaty of Portsmouth, **I**:7

Triangle Shirtwaist Company, **I**:108

Trivial Pursuit (board game), **III**:318–19

Troll Doll (toy), **III**:105

Trout Fishing in America (Brautigan), **III**:38

True Confessions (magazine), **I**:273

True-crime novels, **III**:169, **IV**:36–37

True Story Magazine, **I**:273

Truman, Harry S., **II**:144–45, 260

Trump, Donald, **III**:257

Trump Taj Mahal, **III**:257, 258

"Truth-in-Advertising" movement, **I:**251
Truth or Consequences (TV show), **IV:**177
T-shirt advertising, **III:**155
Tucker, Sophie, **I:**317
Tudor style, **I:**28
Tupperware Home Parties, **II:**341–42
Turner, Lana, **II:**198, 233
Turner, Ted, **III:**242, 314
Turner, Tina, **III:**312
Turow, Scott, **III:**265, **IV:**36
Turtleneck fashions, **III:**68
"Tutti-frutti" fashion fad, **II:**201–2
Tuxedo fashions, **I:**300
TV Guide (magazine), **II:**290, **III:**54, 271
Twain, Mark, **I:**34–35
12 Angry Men (1957), **II:**301–2, 319
Twiggy (Leslie Hornby), **III:**70
Twin Peaks (TV show), **IV:**44, 49
"Twin Towers." *See* World Trade Center
The Twist (dance), **III:**60–61
291 Gallery, **I:**97, 218
2 Live Crew (rap group), **IV:**83
2001: A Space Odyssey (1968), **III:**112
2000 presidential campaign, **IV:**151
Tyson, Mike, **IV:**19, 93, 229

UHF waveband, television, **II:**313–14
Ultimate Fighting Championship (UFC), **IV:**229
"Unabomber" (Ted Kaczynski), **IV:**10–12
Undergarments: 1910s, **I:**168–69; 1920s, **I:**296, 302;
    1930s, **II:**72–73, 77; 1940s, **II:**199; 1950s, **II:**331;
    1960s, **III:**71; 1980s, **III:**292; 1990s, **IV:**67;
    2000s, **IV:**194
Underhill, Paco, **IV:**190
Underwood, Carrie, **IV:**213
Unemployment, 1920s, **I:**229, 230; 1930s, **II:**7–8,
    33, 80; 1940s, **II:**147; 1960s, **III:**7, 15–16; 1970s,
    III:130; 2000s, **IV:**141, 192, 225
Ungaro, Emanuel, **III:**67
Unidentified flying objects (UFOs), **II:**361–62
Union organizations, **I:**11, 230
Union Party (1936), **II:**66
Union Station (Washington, D.C.), **III:**258
Union suit, men's undergarment, **I:**302
United Airlines, **I:**351, **III:**321
United Auto Workers-Congress of Industrial
    Organizations (UAW-CIO), **II:**156
United Church of Christ (UCC), **III:**139
United Farm Workers (UFW), **III:**81
United Fruit Company (Chiquita bananas), **II:**161
The United Graffiti Artists, **III:**225
United Kingdom (U.K.): fashion trends from,
    III:68–70, 191; folk music from, **III:**86; Nazi
    Party and, **II:**143; new music from, **III:**309–10
The United Press (UP), **II:**42
United Soviet Socialist Republic (USSR), **II:**145, 260,
    III:240, 290, 316
United States Football League (USFL), **III:**315
United States Golf Association (USGA), **I:**81
United States Information Agency (USIA), **III:**240

United States Lawn Tennis Association (USLTA),
    I:81
United States military: in art, **I:**98–99; in books/
    literature, **I:**34; discrimination in, **II:**148; militia
    movement, **IV:**10–12;
S.S. *United States* (ocean liner), **II:**377
United States Steel Corporation, **I:**8
Universal Pictures, **II:**190
University architecture, **I:**255–56
University of California at Los Angeles (UCLA),
    III:101
Unsafe at Any Speed (Nader), **III:**219
The Untouchables (TV show), **II:**323, **III:**54
Unwerth, Ellen von, **IV:**110
Updike, John, **III:**39, 164, 267, **IV:**169
Up from Slavery (Washington), **I:**40–41
Urban centers, development, **IV:**159–60
Urban Decay (makeup company), **IV:**65
Urban living, **I:**109–10, **II:**9, 82
Urban realism (art style), **II:**127
Urban renewal, **IV:**29–30
"Urchin look" fashions, **III:**70
U.S. Golf Association Open, **I:**194
USA (Passos), **II:**34
USA Patriot Act (2001), **IV:**130
USA Today (newspaper), **III:**271
U2 (singing group), **IV:**217–18
Usonian houses (Wright), **II:**26

Vacations: 1900s, **I:**86–87; 1910s, **I:**206; 1920s,
    I:345–46; 1930s, **II:**75, 117; 1940s, **II:**235; 1950s,
    II:373, 375; 1960s, **III:**108, 114; 1970s, **III:**160;
    1980s, **III:**324–25; 1990s, **IV:**102–3, 106; 2000s,
    IV:240, 242
Valachi, Joe, **III:**14
Valenti, Jack, **III:**48
Valentino, Rudolph, **I:**280, 287, 301, 356
Valiant Comics, **IV:**43
Vallee, Rudy, **II:**63
Van Alen, William, **I:**262
Vanderbilt, Cornelius, **I:**87
Vanderbilt, William K., **I:**87
Van der Rohe, Mies, **III:**25, 28
Van Halen (singing group), **III:**206, 307–8
Vanity Fair (magazine), **I:**275
Van Peebles, Melvyn, **III:**177–78
Van Vechten, Carl, **I:**268
Vanzetti, Bartolomeo (Sacco/Vanzetti case), **I:**231
Vargas, Alberto (Vargas Girls), **II:**234
Variety (magazine), **I:**315
Variety shows, **III:**183–84
Vatican II (Second Vatican Council), **III:**31–32
Vaudeville blues style, **I:**320–21
Vaudeville entertainment: 1900s, **I:**45, 48–50; 1910s,
    I:155–56; 1920s, **I:**277, 315; 1930s, **II:**56, 63, 67;
    1940s, **II:**184–85; 1950s, **II:**313, 316
Vedder, Eddie, **IV:**80
Vegetarian foods, **IV:**70
Velcro fastener, **II:**329
Venturi, Robert, **III:**26–27, 259

Verducci, Tom, **IV:**228–29

Versace, Gianni, **IV:**60

Veterans Administration, **II:**279

VHF waveband, television, **II:**313

VHS tapes, **IV:**183

Vick, Michael, **IV:**223

The Victim (Bellow), **II:**174

Victorianism, **I:**150

Victorian revival, **III:**261

Victor Talking Machine Company, **I:**70, 315, 324, **II:**95

Victory gardens, **II:**208–9

Vidal, Gore, **III:**164

Video games, **III:**320, **IV:**220, 232–33

The Viet Cong, **III:**15

Vietnam War, **III:**14–16, 43, 74, 83, 98, 143, 176

Vietnam War Memorial, **III:**260–61

Viet Rock: A Folk War Movie (1966), **III:**63

View-master (toy), **II:**111

Village People (singing group), **III:**207

Vinton, Will, **III:**255

Vionnet, Madeleine, **I:**294

Visa (credit card), **II:**257

Visual arts (1900s): painting, **I:**93–96; photography, **I:**96–98; sculpture, **I:**98–99

Visual arts (1910s): Armory Show, **I:**216–19; critics of, **I:**219; elitism in, **I:**219–20; fine arts, **I:**216–17; magazine illustrations, **I:**214–16; origin of, **I:**217–18; painting, **I:**214, 217; photography, **I:**217; post-Armory years, **I:**220

Visual arts (1920s): in books/literature, **I:**274–75; caricatures, **I:**275; "composographs," **I:**274; Harlem Renaissance, **I:**354–55; modernist movement in, **I:**352; painting, **I:**352–55; photography, **I:**355–56; schools/styles, **I:**352–54; sculpture, **I:**356–57

Visual arts (1930s): in advertising, **II:**16–17; illustration, **II:**130–32; immigrants and, **II:**128; painting, **II:**17, 125–28; photography, **II:**128–29; sculpture, **II:**129–30

Visual arts (1940s): painting, **II:**242–45; photography, **II:**245–47

Visual arts (1950s): painting, **II:**378–81; photography, **II:**381–82; sculpture, **II:**381; on television, **II:**378–79

Visual arts (1960s): op art, **III:**120–21; painting, **III:**117–18; photography, **III:**17, 107, 121–22; pop art, **III:**118–20; sculpture, **III:**118, 120

Visual arts (1970s): painting, **III:**226–27; photography, **III:**228–29; pop art, **III:**227–28; sculpture, **III:**225

Visual arts (1980s): graffiti movement, **III:**327–28; painting, **III:**327; photography, **III:**328–31; sculpture, **III:**331

Visual arts (1990s): computers and, **IV:**111–13; controversy in, **IV:**108, 113; painting, **IV:**112, 113; photography, **IV:**109–11; politics of, **IV:**108–9; public projects, **IV:**109; television and, **IV:**109

Visual arts (2000s): museums, **IV:**250–52; online auctions, **IV:**249–50; painting, **IV:**254–55; photography, **IV:**252–54

Vitamins, **I:**174, 307, **II:**206, 207

Vocal groups, **II:**348

Vogue (magazine), **II:**335

Voight, Jon, **III:**50

Volkswagen "Beetle," **II:**369, 371–72

Volstead Act, **I:**112, 233, **II:**89

Volvo Cars, **III:**220

Vonnegut, Kurt, Jr., **III:**36–37, 164

"Voodoo" economics, **IV:**193

Voyeur television (VTV), **IV:**178

"Vulgarian" fashions, **III:**70–71

Wagner, Honus, **I:**179–80, 196

Wagner, Richard, **I:**182

Wales Padlock Law, **I:**278

Walker, Mort, **II:**294

Wallace, David Foster, **IV:**38

Wallace, DeWitt & Lila, **II:**37

Waller, Robert James, **IV:**37–38

Wall Street (1987), **III:**283, 288

Wall Street (stock trading center), **III:**242–43, 326, **IV:**125

Wal-Mart Stores, **IV:**30, 70, 162, 191–93

Walsch, Neale Donald, **IV:**39

Walt Disney Company, **III:**324, **IV:**72, 106–7. *See also* Disney, Walt

War Admiral (race horse), **II:**104

War Advertising Council (Ad Council), **II:**154–55

Warhol, Andy, **III:**53, 119–20, 227, 326

Waring "Blendor," **II:**87

Warner Brothers Corset Company, **I:**169

Warner Brothers Entertainment, **I:**282, **II:**190

War of the Worlds (1953), **II:**66, 306

War on Terror, **IV:**131–33. *See also* Iraq War; Terrorism

War Relocation Authority (WRA), **II:**149

Warren, Robert Penn, **II:**174, 175

Washington, Booker T., **I:**32, 40–41, 81, 110

Washington Post (newspaper), **III:**172

Wasserstein, Wendy, **III:**287

Water beds, **III:**104

Watergate scandal, **III:**132–33, 169, 172, 184

Wa-Wan (music) Press, **I:**69

Wayne, John, **II:**301, 320, **III:**152

Wayne, Ronald, **III:**215, 245

The Web. *See* Online culture

Webber, Andrew Lloyd, **III:**187, **IV:**56–57

Weber, Bruce, **III:**253

Weedington, Sarah, **III:**137–38

"Weepies" (women's movies), **II:**192

Wegman, William, **IV:**110

Weight loss centers/programs, **I:**307, **III:**298

Weird Tales (magazine), **I:**272

Weissmuller, Johnny, **I:**332, **II:**77

Welles, Orson, **II:**66, 190–91

Wells, H. G., **I:**145, **II:**66, 190

Wells, Mary, **III:**23–24

Wells, Rich, Greene, Inc. (advertising firm), **III:**24

Welty, Eudora, **II:**173–74

Wendy's Old Fashioned Hamburgers, **III:**198, 255–56

Wertham, Frederic, **II:**296

West, Mae, **II:**55

Western Federation of Miners, **I:**11–12

Western genre (movies), **I:**284

Western movies/TV shows, **II:**52–53, 307–8, 320–21

Wham-O Toys, **II:**363

Wharton, Edith, **I:**40, 144

What Ever Happened to Baby Jane? (1962), **III:**52

What's My Line? (TV show), **II:**322

Wheeler, Harvey, **III:**40

"Where's the Beef" ad, **III:**255–56

Whistler, James McNeill, **I:**94

White, Byron R., **III:**138

White, Dana, **IV:**229

White, Pearl, **I:**159

White, Ryan, **IV:**13

White Anglo-Saxon Protestant (WASP), **II:**171

White Castle hamburger chain, **I:**257, 310, 311

Whiteman, Paul, **I:**316, 319, 323

White Slave Traffic Act, **I:**111

White Sox (Chicago), **I:**327

White supremacy, **I:**232

Whitewater Scandal, **IV:**9

Whitman, Charles, **III:**13

Whitman, Walt, **II:**175

Whitney, Phillis A., **III:**165

Whitney Museum of American Art, **IV:**248

Who's Afraid of Virginia Woolf? (1966), **III:**51

The Who (singing group), **III:**205

Who Wants to Be a Millionaire (TV show), **IV:**177–78

Whyte, William, **II:**288

Wickman, Eric, **I:**343

Wide-screen movies, **II:**298–99

Wii console (computer game toy), **IV:**233

The Wild One (1954), **II:**299–300

Wiley, Harvey W., **I:**63–64, 125

Wilkins Freeman, Mary E., **I:**32

Will and Grace (TV show), **IV:**50

Williams, Esther, **II:**361

Williams, Hank, **II:**348

Williams, Hiram ("Hank"), **II:**221

Williams, Paul Revere, **I:**262

Williams, Ted, **II:**227–28

Williams, Tennessee, **II:**182, **III:**62

Williamsburg, Virginia, **II:**27

Willis, Edwin B., **II:**61

Wills, Helen, **I:**331

Wills, Maury, **III:**99

Wilson, Kemmons, **II:**374

Wilson, Sloan, **II:**269, 303

Wilson, Woodrow, **I:**110, 113–14, 127, 346

The Wilsonian doctrine, **I:**115

Winchell, Walter, **II:**43

Winesburg, Ohio (Anderson), **I:**144

Winfrey, Oprah, **III:**298, **IV:**32–34, 169–70, 208–9

Winnie Winkle the Breadwinner (comic strip), **I:**275

Winogrand, Garry, **III:**121

Winterset (Anderson), **II:**68

The Wizard of Oz (1939), **II:**60–61

The Wobblies. *See* Industrial Workers of the World

Wolf, Naomi, **IV:**68

Wolfe, Tom, **III:**42, 167, 265–66, 267, **IV:**169

Wolfenstein 3D (computer game), **IV:**98

Women Accepted for Volunteer Emergency Services (WAVES), **II:**150

Women (1900s): on Broadway, **I:**47–48; dance entertainment for, **I:**51; fashion for, **I:**55–57; of literature, **I:**39–40; magazines for, **I:**42; in workplace, **I:**24, 29

Women (1910s): in dance, **I:**156–57; fashion for, **I:**166–70; sports and, **I:**195, 201; suffrage for, **I:**111

Women (1920s): fashion for, **I:**293–99; in labor force, **I:**236; magazines for, **I:**270; novelists, **I:**263–64; in politics, **I:**236; as primary buyers, **I:**242; as radio listeners, **I:**250–51; roles of, **I:**235

Women (1930s): advertising for, **II:**18; alcohol consumption by, **II:**90; fashion for, **II:**71–74

Women (1940s): in baseball, **II:**225; fashion for, **II:**197–98; movies for, **II:**192; WWII roles, **II:**150–51

Women (1950s): advertising to, **II:**269–70; fashion for, **II:**329–32; in movies, **II:**303; roles of, **II:**259–60

Women (1960s): advertising to, **III:**20–21; birth control by, **III:**17; fashion for, **III:**19, 66–67; in golf, **III:**102; NOW creation, **III:**12–13; stereotypes, **III:**53

Women (1970s): advertising to, **III:**150–53; feminism and, **III:**182; in literature, **III:**170; NOW creation, **III:**136–37; in religion, **III:**148; *Roe v. Wade,* **III:**137–38; in sports, **III:**208–9

Women (1980s): advertising to, **III:**253; dieting, **III:**298; fashion for, **III:**288–90, 292–94; in music, **III:**311–13; in newspaper jobs, **III:**271; on TV, **III:**275

Women (1990s): fashion for, **IV:**59; magazines for, **IV:**18; in rock 'n' roll, **IV:**82; in sports, **IV:**90; as writers, **IV:**36–37

Women (2000s): advertising for, **IV:**154; dieting, **IV:**202; fashion for, **IV:**194–97; in rap/hip hop, **IV:**214

Women's National Basketball Association (WNBA), **IV:**90

Wonder, Stevie, **III:**94

The Wonderbra, **IV:**67

Woo, John, **IV:**56

Wood, Grant, **II:**125–26

Woods, Tiger, **IV:**18, 94, 95, 152, 220, 227

Woodstock Music and Art Fair, **III:**92, **IV:**82

Woodward, Bob, **III:**172

The Woolworth Building, **I:**132–33

Woolworth's (department store), **I:**19

Working Girl (1988), **III:**283

Works Progress Administration (WPA), **II:**10, 68, 115, 127

World Championship Wrestling (WCW), **IV:**89–90

WorldCom Corporation, **IV:**139

World Cup tournaments, **IV:**90

The World Is Flat: A Brief History of the Twenty-First Century (Friedman), **IV:**138

World's Columbian Exposition (1893), **I:**72–73

World Series championships: 1900s, **I:**78; 1910s, **I:**198; 1920s, **I:**329; 1930s, **II:**103; 1940s, **II:**228; 1950s, **II:**359; 1960s, **III:**100; 1970s, **III:**211; 1980s, **III:**315; 1990s, **IV:**92; 2000s, **IV:**228

The World's Most Dangerous Places (Pelton), **IV:**102

World Trade Center (WTC), New York, **III:**161, **IV:**129–30, 131, 157–58. *See also* September 11, 2001

World War I (WWI): advertising for, **I:**127–28; African Americans in, **I:**113; candy sales during, **I:**179, 310; cigarettes during, **I:**180; commemoration in magazines, **I:**272; dietary changes from, **I:**175; magazine illustration of, **I:**216; military aircraft in, **I:**208, 348; overview of, **I:**113–15; post-war industry, **I:**229; soldiers' leisure activities, **I:**193; theater about, **I:**278; women recruits, **I:**236

World War II (WWII): advertising war effort, **II:**154–55; African Americans during, **II:**146, 147–48, 230; fabric rationing during, **II:**197; food rationing during, **II:**207–8; Japanese depiction during, **II:**191; movie industry and, **II:**159–60, 191–92; photojournalism during, **II:**247; politics during, **II:**142–44; racial influences in, **II:**146–50; radio reporting of, **II:**184, 185–86; "Rosie the Riveter," **II:**155–56; television launch disruption, **II:**67; *vs.* cold war, **II:**144–46; women's roles in, **II:**150–51

World Wide Web (WWW), **IV:**14

World Wrestling Foundation (WWF), **IV:**89–90

Wozniak, Steve, **III:**215, 245

Wrestling, professional, **IV:**89–90, 220

Wright, Frank Lloyd, **I:**25, 29–31, 134–36, 262, **II:**25–26, 278, **III:**25

Wright, Richard, **II:**172–73

Wright, Russell, **II:**31

Wright, Wilbur and Orville, **I:**91–92

Wrigley, William, Jr., **I:**21–23

Wrigley Chewing Gum, **I:**22–23

Wristwatch fashions, **I:**172, 302

Writers Guild of America, **IV:**174

Wurster, William, **II:**163

WWI. *See* World War I

WWII. *See* World War II

Wyeth, Andrew, **III:**225

Wyeth, N. C., **I:**275, **II:**130–31, 132

Wynette, Tammy, **III:**87, 201–2

Xena, Warrior Princess (TV show), **IV:**46

Xerox Corporation, **III:**150–51

The X-Files (TV show), **IV:**45

X-Large (clothing label), **IV:**63

X-Men (comic book), **III:**272

X-Minus One (radio show), **II:**312

Yahoo! web site, **IV:**124–25

Yamamoto, Yohji, **IV:**60

Yamin, Elliott, **IV:**213–14

Yankee Stadium (New York), **I:**196

Year 2000 (Y2K) problem, **IV:**126

Yellow Cab Company, **I:**344

Yellowstone Park, **II:**119

Yerkes, Charles Y., **I:**141

You Bet Your Life (TV show), **II:**322–23

Young, Cy, **I:**77–78, 197, **III:**100

Young, Lester, **II:**224

Your Hit Parade (radio show), **II:**213, 214, 354

Your Lucky Strike Hit Parade (radio show), **II:**100

Youth drama, television, **IV:**48–49

YouTube (website), **IV:**145, 148–49, 173, 211, 232–33

Yo-yo (toy), **I:**337, **II:**111

"Yuppies," **III:**243

Zahn, Timothy, **IV:**35

Zangara, Giuseppe, **II:**7

Zemeckis, Robert, **III:**279

Zeppelin travel, **II:**120–21

Ziegfeld, Florenz, **I:**47–48, 154, 156, 279

Ziegfeld's Follies, **I:**48, 156, 279, 337

Zimmermann, Arthur, **I:**114

The Zone (Sears), **IV:**77

Zoot suit riots, **II:**203–4

Zucker, Jeff, **IV:**180–81

Zuckerberg, Mark, **IV:**231

Zukov, Gary, **IV:**39

About the Editor and Contributors

SET EDITOR

Bob Batchelor teaches in the School of Mass Communications at the University of South Florida. A noted expert on American popular culture, Bob is the author of: *The 1900s* (Greenwood, 2002); coauthor of *Kotex, Kleenex, and Huggies: Kimberly-Clark and the Consumer Revolution in American Business* (2004); editor of *Basketball in Amoerica: From the Playgrounds to Jordan's Game and Beyond* (2005); editor of *Literary Cash: Unauthorized Writings Inspired by the Legendary Johnny Cash* (2006); and coauthor of *The 1980s* (Greenwood, 2007). He serves on the editorial board of *The Journal of Popular Culture*. Visit him on the Internet at his blog (pr-bridge.com) or homepage (www.bob batchelor.com).

CONSULTING EDITOR

Ray B. Browne is a Distinguished University Professor in Popular Culture, Emeritus, at Bowling Green State University. He cofounded the Popular Culture Association (1970) and the American Culture Association (1975) and served as Secretary-Treasurer of both until 2002. In 1967 he began publishing the *Journal of Popular Culture,* and in 1975 the *Journal of American Culture.* He edited both until 2002. He has written or edited more than 70 books and written numerous articles on all fields in literature and popular culture. He currently serves as Book Review Editor of the *Journal of American Culture.*

CONTRIBUTORS

David Blanke, author of *The 1910s* (Greenwood, 2002), is currently Associate Professor of History at Texas A&M University, Corpus Christi. He is the author of *Hell on Wheels: The Promise and Peril of America's Car Culture, 1900–1940* (2007) and *Sowing the American Dream: How Consumer Culture Took Root in the Rural Midwest* (2000).

Kathleen Drowne, coauthor of *The 1920s* (Greenwood, 2004), is Assistant Professor of English at the University of Missouri, Rolla.

Patrick Huber, coauthor of *The 1920s* (Greenwood, 2004), is Assistant Professor of History at the University of Missouri, Rolla.

Marc Oxoby, PhD, teaches English and Humanities classes for the English Department at the University of Nevada, Reno. He has worked as a disc jockey and as the editor of the small-press literary journal *CRiME CLUb.* A regular contributor to the scholarly journal *Film and History* and *The Journal of Popular Culture,* he has also written for several other periodicals as well as for *The St. James Encyclopedia of Popular Culture, The International Dictionary of Films and Filmmakers,* and *New Paths to Raymond Carver.*

Edward J. Rielly, Professor of English at St. Joseph's College in Maine, has taught on Western film and the history of the west for many years. He is author of several nonfiction books, including *F. Scott Fitzgerald: A Biography* (Greenwood 2005) and *The 1960s* (Greenwood, 2003). He has also published 10 books of poetry.

Kelly Boyer Sagert is a freelance writer who has published biographical material with Gale, Scribner, Oxford, and Harvard University, focusing on athletes and historical figures. She is the author of *Joe Jackson: A Biography* (Greenwood, 2004), *The 1970s* (Greenwood, 2007), and the *Encyclopedia of Extreme Sports* (Greenwood, 2008).

Robert Sickels, author of *The 1940s* (Greenwood Press, 2004), is Assistant Professor at Whitman College, Walla Walla, Washington.

Scott F. Stoddart, coauthor of *The 1980s* (Greenwood, 2006), is the Dean of Academic Affairs at Manhattanville College, New York, where he currently teaches courses in cinema and musical theatre history.

Nancy K. Young, is a researcher and independent scholar. She retired in 2005 after 26 years of a career in management consulting. With her husband, William H. Young, she has cowritten three recent Greenwood titles, *The 1930s* (2002), *The 1950s* (2004), and *Music of the Great Depression* (2005).

William H. Young, author of *The 1930s* (Greenwood, 2002) and coauthor of *The 1950s* (Greenwood, 2004), is a freelance writer and independent scholar. He retired in 2000 after 36 years of teaching American Studies and popular culture at Lynchburg College in Lynchburg, Virginia. Young has published books and articles on various aspects of popular culture, including three Greenwood volumes cowritten with his wife, Nancy K. Young.

ADDITIONAL CONTRIBUTORS

Cindy Williams, independent scholar.

Mary Kay Linge, independent scholar.

Martha Whitt, independent scholar.

Micah L. Issitt, independent scholar.

Josef Benson, University of South Florida.

Ken Zachmann, independent scholar.